A MASTERPIECE IN DISARRAY

DAVID LYNCH'S DUNE
AN ORAL HISTORY

MAX EVRY

A MASTERPIECE IN DISARRAY

COVER DESIGN: Chris Thornley
LAYOUT: Arkadii Pankevich

Image credits appear in the back of the book.

LIBRARY OF CONGRESS CONTROL NUMBER: 2023937699

LC record available at https://lccn.loc.gov/2023937699

ISBNs: 9781948221290 (hardbound), 9781948221306 (ebook)

1984 Publishing logo is © and ™ of 1984 Publishing, LLC.

Printed and bound in PRC.

1984 PUBLISHING
Cleveland, Ohio / USA
1984Publishing.com
info@1984publishing.com

Contact the author at evrymax@gmail.com.

FIRST EDITION
9 8 7 6 5 4 3 2 1

For Nicole, Eleanor & Noa...
LONG LIVE THE FIGHTERS!

CHAPTERHOUSES

PROLOGUE

"I can see clearly now, the rain is gone."

—*Johnny Nash*

Years ago, while attending a press event for a hit film, I met its A-list director at an arranged dinner. This filmmaker had been briefly attached to a big-budget remake of *Dune*, so during a casual moment I waltzed up with my drink and asked him if he had seen the recent documentary *Jodorowsky's Dune*, a semi-hot item in the geek community. He had neither seen nor heard of it. Nor did he seem to be aware that Alejandro Jodorowsky had ever planned on making *Dune* . . . and potentially didn't know who Jodorowsky was. He mentioned how challenging *Dune* would be to execute in a commercial way and particularly noted that he never wanted his (now-scrapped) *Dune* to be "campy like the David Lynch version."

"Campy." The Fremen warrior deep within me declared a kind of passive-aggressive holy war on this man, no matter how many billions his movies had made. Of course, not every successful filmmaker is a cineaste, and a few might barely enjoy movies at all. But still, this dismissive word bothered me: "CAMPY."

Not that I couldn't see his point. Lynch's 1984 adaptation of Frank Herbert's vaunted novel is flawed. Very flawed. Some of the effects are sub-Asylum level by today's standards, and the performances range from bizarre to laughably broad. That's not even taking into account how fatally compressed much of the 412-page narrative is when filtered into a 2-hour-17-minute movie. Despite all this, I continue to take exception to blithely writing off Lynch's vision as "camp."

One element that director was right about is how challenging Herbert's book is to adapt. Boy, oh boy, is it ever. Before Lynch came on board to make the picture for producer Dino De Laurentiis, it vexed both Jodorowsky and Ridley Scott. Tackling this film took three years of Lynch's life and a crew of 1,700 building 80 sets on 8 sound stages. Upon release it bemused critics and befuddled audiences, resulting in a box office dud that even Lynch has worked to distance himself from.

Nevertheless, I firmly believe 1984's *Dune* to be a landmark of science-fiction cinema. It's the byproduct of a supremely avant-garde artist (Lynch) working in conjunction with Hollywood machinery (Universal Pictures) for huge financial stakes (a reported $40 million budget, over $100 million adjusted for inflation) to produce a deeply eccentric blockbuster. When seen through the lens of today's tentpole films, whose four-quadrant aspirations render them hopelessly homogenous, Lynch's *Dune* is a unique oddity, equal parts baroque and philistine.

There are incredible moments in the film adaptation of *Dune* that have stuck with me since I first saw it as a tween in pan-and-scan form on TV: the mutated Guild Navigator confronting the Emperor while floating in a murky terrarium, Paul with his hand in "the box," Baron Harkonnen flying through the air while laughing maniacally, and Sting with a blade in his hand, wildly boasting "I will kill him!" Oh, and let's not forget those sandworms, which through a blizzard of miniature sand particles manage to evoke a phallus and vagina dentata simultaneously. One could easily blow up, frame, and hang at least three dozen shots from this film in a museum, and have them mistaken for anything from a Rococo-era genre painting to a Francis Bacon nightmare.

Luckily, this book has allowed me to do a deep dive into a film that has obsessed me since childhood. Hopefully, it will give *Dune* the same thorough examination that more praised films from the same era like *Blade Runner* or *Brazil* have received in the past. While I'm equally in love with those films, they are complete and successful works that have stood the test of time (provided you watch the director cuts). *Dune*, on the other hand, draws me in more because it's so blatantly imperfect. Missed cinematic opportunities are a dime a dozen, but rarely do they hew as close to pure brilliance as Lynch's epic. So how did it come to be so botched? Was Lynch too inexperienced? Too unfamiliar with sci-fi terrain? Or was it studio meddling? Penny-pinching producers? Is *Dune* simply, to pull an old chestnut, "unfilmable?"

The word "unfilmable" is often a euphemism for "challenging," "uncommercial," or simply not viable within a two- to three-hour feature length. Over a decade after Lynch's take, a 265-minute TV miniseries version, *Frank Herbert's Dune,* was mounted for the Sci-Fi Channel to mixed results. As I write, we are in the midst of Denis Villeneuve's mega-budget remake of *Dune* that will span two films, with the first already on home video earning Oscars and the second in post-production.

Until that new set of films proves it can stick the landing, we will always have the Lynch version to consider, or reconsider if you have already seen and dismissed it. This book will attempt to cast new light on a movie that has been misunderstood in almost every conceivable way, whether by audiences unfamiliar with the source material, or literature fans upset at the many changes and deletions. It will delve into some of the earlier attempted versions, the epic struggles 'Lynch and Co.' faced mounting such a large-scale project in Mexico, the aftermath for all involved, the versions that came after, and finally some modern critical takes looking at the nearly four-decade-old *Dune* with fresh eyes.

Hopefully, you'll come to see it with a new perspective as well, and the sleeper *Dune* fan within shall awaken. Even if you still can't bring yourself to call *Dune* a great film, perhaps I can convert some of you from red-faced haters to faint-praising it as a "bold swing-and-a-miss" or "fascinating failure." You might even start referring to it as a "secret masterpiece" awaiting discovery . . . just don't call it "campy."

—Max Evry

AUTHOR'S NOTE

Look, I get it . . . this is a long book. Too long? Not if you're a fanatical *Dune*-ologist. An epic film by an important filmmaker deserves an epic book. The volumes written on *Star Wars* and *Star Trek* over the years would—if you stacked them all on top of each other—kill a person if they fell over on top of them. The number of books devoted solely to Lynch's *Dune* would fit into a moderately sized woman's purse with room left over for mace, a Taser gun, and the latest Ipsy bag. In other words, I'm making up for lost time here.

Alas, your devotion to the Duniverse may vary, which is why I designed this book for many different kinds of readers. Find yourself and your respective reading instructions below:

Professor-Level: *"Belief can be manipulated. Only knowledge is dangerous." You have to know everything there is to know about Lynch's* Dune, *so start at page 1 and just keep going until there are no more words.*

Attention Deficit *Dune*-order: *This book is broken up into four major units (Pre-Production, Production, Post-production, and Legacy), each with general information and oral histories from brand-new interviews I've conducted. You'll also find subsections on specific points of interest (Casting, Music, Marketing, Fan Tributes, etc.), so you can jump around to what interests you the most. Follow your bliss!*

Straight from the Sources: *If you'd like to see the newest and (in my opinion) best information in this book first, jump to the Oral History sections. For two years I spoke to as many people as I could from the* Dune *team who are still around and willing to share their memories. Those who did were all kind and lucid, and often said things that blew my mind. Their stories will help you see the truth of it.*

A person needs new experiences. They jar something deep inside. I sincerely hope the experience of reading this book will be a jarring (and fun) one.

—I—

PRE-PRODUCTION

> "It's a strange world, isn't it?"
>
> —*Jeffrey Beaumont,* **Blue Velvet**

Dune Origins

F ranklin Patrick Herbert Jr. was born on October 8, 1920 in Tacoma, Washington, the state where he would live and work throughout his life. He grew up poor, though with an aptitude for reading and photography. Frank Herbert got his first newspaper jobs while still in his late teens, working at the *Glendale Star* and the *Oregon Statesman*. He married his first wife Flora in 1941, had his first child Penelope in 1942, and then served as a photographer for the United States Naval Construction Battalions (better known as the Seabees) for six months during World War II until he was discharged after an injury.

When the war was over, he enrolled at the University of Washington. Herbert was something of an autodidact, ravenous for knowledge but only on certain subjects, and never completed his degree. He left college with a new wife named Beverly, a fellow published writer whom he married in 1946. She later gave birth to their sons Brian and Bruce. Over the ensuing years, Herbert wrote for several different newspapers and also began dabbling in fiction, publishing his first pulp adventure story in *Esquire*.

An avid science-fiction fan since the '40s, Herbert published his first such tale, "Looking for Something," in the April 1952 issue of *Startling Stories*. His first stab at a long-form novel was serialized in *Astounding Science Fiction* beginning in late 1955, originally called *Under Pressure* but eventually released as a book by Doubleday under the title *The Dragon in the Sea*. It concerned a near future where covert submarines float into enemy territory to steal oil underwater. That theme of a futuristic battle over natural resources would reappear a decade later in his most famous work.

Around this time, Herbert and family joined up with fantasy author Jack Vance (*Dying Earth, Bad Ronald*)—then writing scripts for TV's *Captain Video*—and his wife, Norma, on an extended trip to Mexico, the same country where the 1984 *Dune* movie would be filmed. At first, they lived in a stucco rental house near Lake Chapala before moving to the lower-cost area of Ciudad Guzmán, both south of Guadalajara. There, Herbert was invited to the home of a retired Mexican Army general, where he accidentally consumed two cookies laced with North African hashish and began hallucinating. This experience may have inspired the mind-altering spice drug of *Dune*. "Paul Atreides' experiences with that drug mirror the author's personal experiences," Brian Herbert wrote in *Dreamer of Dune: The Biography of Frank Herbert*.

Alternately, mycologist Paul Stamets claims to have been told a different story by Herbert himself in the '80s, when the sci-fi author was often collecting mushrooms on his property in Port Townsend, Washington.

According to Stamets in his 2005 book *Mycelium Running: How Mushrooms Can Help Save the World*:

> Frank went on to tell me that much of the premise of *Dune*—the magic spice (spores) that allowed the bending of space (tripping), the giant worms (maggots digesting mushrooms), the eyes of the Fremen (the cerulean blue of Psilocybe mushrooms), the mysticism of the female spiritual warriors, the Bene Gesserits (influenced by tales of Maria Sabina and the sacred mushroom cults of Mexico)— came from his perception of the fungal life cycle, and his imagination was stimulated through his experiences with the use of magic mushrooms.

In 1959, while researching a magazine article about sand dunes in Oregon, Herbert first conceived of his masterwork *Dune*. It took him six years to write the book, which the sci-fi magazine *Analog* published in eight installments starting in 1963, the first half titled "Dune World" and the second "Prophet of Dune." The rights to publish the rewritten and expanded version of what ultimately became the first *Dune* novel were turned down by nearly two dozen publishers before editor Sterling E. Lanier offered Herbert a $7,500 advance. This first hardcover edition was put out by Chilton, a book company mainly known for auto-repair manuals.

Herbert said later of his process during a talk at UCLA in April 1985

> I spent six years preparing. In the middle of all of that, I went down to a place on the coast of Oregon called Florence, Oregon, because I was supporting a very expensive writing habit by being a journalist. I was going to do an article about the US Department of Agriculture's project at Florence, Oregon, to control sand dunes. Now, sand dunes are like slow-motion waves. They'll move across roads, across highways, they'll inundate whole plantations of forests, but they do it slowly. I was flying an airplane over this experimental project, this test station on the coast of Oregon, leaning out the window taking pictures. The desert of course is the wilderness of

the Bible, and the desert wilderness is where a great many religions have originated. I started researching ecology, how we inflict ourselves upon the planet. Well, after six years of this marvelously interesting research, I had the system loaded, and I sat down to do a book. The book, as I conceived of it, was the first three books. They were one book in my head. I told my agent this, and after he recovered from his heart attack he said, "Do you think you could split it into three at least? Maybe four?"

When it was released in 1965 at a whopping 412 pages—lengthy for a sci-fi novel at that time—it was a critical hit, winning both the Nebula and Hugo Awards. However, it took some time for *Dune* to catch on as a commercial success. It wasn't until 1972 that Herbert was able to retire as a newspaperman and take up fiction full-time. The first *Dune* book has now sold around 20 million copies and has been translated into dozens of languages, making it the bestselling science-fiction novel of all time.

What eventually became known as the *"Dune* Saga" branched out into five more books during the author's lifetime: *Dune Messiah* (1969), *Children of Dune* (1976), *God Emperor of Dune* (1981), *Heretics of Dune* (1984), and *Chapterhouse: Dune* (1985). Other works in the series, based on notes Herbert left behind, were penned posthumously by his son Brian Herbert alongside novelist Kevin J. Anderson, consisting of twenty more books so far, including both prequels and sequels.

Set thousands of years in the future, the original *Dune* novel takes place in a universe still reeling from a time known as the Butlerian Jihad, when artificial intelligence nearly overwhelmed humanity but was ultimately defeated and outlawed. Thus, the many inhabited worlds of the known universe now rely on several different groups, including the Spacing Guild (which facilitates space travel), the Bene Gesserit order (which deals in religion and politics), and the Mentats (living computers with immense strategic and calculative abilities).

The story opens with two great houses, the noble House Atreides and the amoral House Harkonnen, feuding with each other. The Padishah Emperor Shaddam IV has assigned House Atreides to take over the rights to spice mining on the planet Arrakis, also known as Dune. An inhospitable desert world, Arrakis is the only known source of the spice melange, a substance that not only extends life but enables the Spacing Guild Navigators to fold space itself, thus allowing different houses to travel to the far reaches of the universe.

Duke Leto Atreides has become a popular figure among the other Great Houses of the Landsraad, which could threaten the power of the Emperor. Thus, Shaddam IV secretly conspires with the Harkonnens (led by the degenerate flying fat man Baron Vladimir Harkonnen) to eliminate the Atreides once they are on Arrakis, away from the prying eyes of the Landsraad. Although Duke Leto is the main threat, the conspirators are unaware that his bound concubine Lady Jessica has used her Bene Gesserit skills to give birth to a son named Paul and train him in their psychic gifts. Paul has also been tutored by some of the Duke's elite advisors, including warriors Duncan Idaho and Gurney Halleck as well as Mentat Thufir Hawat.

Once the Atreides family arrives on Arrakis, the Duke seeks to forge an alliance with the mysterious indigenous population known as the Fremen. Before he can secure this alliance, the Duke is betrayed by trusted doctor Wellington Yueh, who allows the Harkonnens to destroy the Atreides army and take over spice production on the planet once again. Duke Leto is killed in a failed assassination attempt against the Baron, but Yueh arranges for Paul and Jessica to be delivered safely to the desert. While there, Paul's exposure to spice awakens his latent powers, including prophetic visions. He also realizes that his mother is Baron Harkonnen's daughter, and he the Baron's grandson. Paul and his mother eventually encounter the Fremen, solidifying an alliance with their leader Stilgar by agreeing to train them in the weirding way, a Bene Gesserit form of martial arts. Taking the tribal name of Muad'Dib, Paul falls in love with a Fremen warrior woman named Chani, with whom he eventually conceives a son who is killed in the final battle.

Unbeknownst to the Fremen, the Bene Gesserit order has foreseen these events, paving Paul's way by planting a messiah legend among the natives. Once elements of this myth become reality, Paul is perceived as a kind of god, prophesied to lead the Fremen on a jihad to reclaim Arrakis. He is able to fulfill the legend by riding one of the giant sandworms that inhabit the planet and drinking the sacred Water of Life. The latter gives him a level of clairvoyance that proves he is the Kwisatz Haderach, the genetic super-being Bene Gesserits have been working to breed for generations.

With his newfound power, Paul leads legions of Fremen against the forces of the Harkonnens and the Emperor, ultimately killing the former with the help of his young sister Alia (whose preternatural powers are equal to her mother) and subduing the latter. After a final knife fight between Paul and the Baron's nephew Feyd-Rautha in which the latter is killed, the Emperor abdicates the throne to Paul, who agrees to marry his daughter Princess Irulan while still pledging his true love to Chani. In the end, Paul is triumphant, but now realizes he will be unable to stop the bloodshed he has unleashed by empowering the Fremen.

Herbert's novel is full of Shakespearian intrigue as well as nods to Islamic culture, Russian terminology, Jungian analysis, environmental themes, and Buddhist spiritualism. This potent blend tapped directly into the zeitgeist of the '60s, as did themes of consciousness expansion and political revolution. The Spacing Guild and Bene Gesserit's dependency on spice are the author's obvious metaphor for the small group of OPEC nations that controlled oil production, and still do to this day. It's no coincidence that "Arrakis" sounds a lot like "Iraq."

"My Arab friends wonder why it's called science fiction," Herbert said in a 1984 interview with PBS. "*Dune*, they say, is religious commentary."

Herbert used *Dune* and its sequels to create a parable on the danger of giving power to charismatic leaders. He came to grips with this as a speechwriter for several politicians, as well as from 20th-century figures like Adolf Hitler (who oversaw the Holocaust) and John F. Kennedy (who got the US embroiled in the Vietnam conflict).

Herbert restated this theme in a 1984 interview with Bryant Gumbel:

> Don't trust leaders to always be right. I worked to create a leader in this book who would be an attractive, charismatic person for all the good reasons, not for any bad reasons. Then power comes to him. He makes decisions. Some of his decisions made for millions upon millions of people don't work out too well. I think that our society was formed on a distrust for government, and we seem to have lost that distrust in government. I kid around when I say that my favorite president in recent years has been Richard Nixon because he taught us to distrust government.

While this central conceit of *Dune*, unfortunately, did not make its way into the 1984 film, that movie kept most of the essential plot threads intact. The one thing the '84 film can absolutely boast of is that it was the only version to have the author himself involved and providing input on the set. Herbert passed away at age 65 on February 11, 1986, a little over a year after the movie was released. Lynch's fidelity to the material was not shared by some of the attempts that preceded his, however.

Previous *Dune* Attempts

Herbert's novel had a tortured history of high-profile failed adaptations before it finally landed in Lynch's lap. The challenges in mounting a movie of *Dune* are so great that many considered it to be "unfilmable"—both before and after Lynch's version was made. Here's a summary of three versions that never came to be.

Arthur P. Jacobs/Haskell Wexler Version (1971–74)

In a November 1971 edition of *Daily Variety*, iconic B-movie king Roger Corman was announced as having purchased the rights to *Dune* to begin shooting in Czechoslovakia during the summer of 1972. Corman was famous for directing classic B-movies like *Little Shop of Horrors* and a string of Edgar Allan Poe adaptations starring Vincent Price, among many others. As a producer, he helped launch the careers of directors like Francis Ford Coppola, Martin Scorsese, Peter Bogdanovich, and Ron Howard. Although he never got *Dune* off the ground, his New World Pictures did wind up distributing the Czechoslovakian/French animated coproduction of René Laloux's *Fantastic Planet* (*La Planète sauvage*) in America.

Also in 1971, producer Arthur P. Jacobs (*Doctor Dolittle*, the *Planet of the Apes* franchise) tried to option the *Dune* rights through his APJAC Productions. He wanted to hire screenwriter Robert Bolt and director David Lean, known for the 1962 desert epic *Lawrence of Arabia*, which had won Best Picture and Best Director Oscars. Although the desert setting of *Dune* seemed ideal for the pair, Bolt and Lean passed on the project early on. Still, Jacobs' vision for *Dune* was said to be a combination of *Lawrence of Arabia* and *2001: A Space Odyssey*.

Rights were not solidified until after Jacobs had commissioned a 38-page story treatment from Joe Ford and Robert Greenhut in March 1972 as proof of concept that the story could translate to the big screen. By August, the full rights were secured, and in November, screenwriter Rospo Pallenberg was hired to pen a new story treatment and potentially a first-draft script. Pallenberg had been an architect in New York before being plucked out of obscurity by filmmaker John Boorman (*Deliverance*) to write a screenplay for United Artists' planned adaptation of J. R. R. Tolkien's *Lord of the Rings*. Although that ambitious fantasy film never came to be due to the challenges of the source material, much of Boorman's vision was eventually funneled into 1981's Arthurian adventure *Excalibur*, which became Pallenberg's first produced screenplay.

In January 1973, Pallenberg turned in his *Dune* treatment, but by February, Jacobs had decided to end Pallenberg's contract. Then on March 6, 1973, a writer's strike began, and all work on *Dune* was put on hold. Jacobs was still eyeing different writers, having sent the novel to Dalton Trumbo (*Spartacus*) in Jamaica, where he was working on *Papillon* for director Franklin J. Schaffner. In addition to Trumbo, Jacobs also courted *Papillon* cowriter Lorenzo Semple Jr. of the *Batman* TV show and attempted to recruit Schaffner to direct *Dune* after their collaboration on the original 1968 *Planet of the Apes*. Jacobs clearly had an inkling *Papillon* was going to be a smash. . . it grossed $53 million upon its late 1973 release.

Although some sources, including Brian Herbert's *Dreamer of Dune*, list the preliminary budget as $15 million (roughly the same price as 1977's *Star Wars*), the actual budget for the planned 1973 shoot in Göreme, Turkey, was listed as $6 million. By December 1972, Jacobs' *Dune* had locked in the full cooperation of the Turkish government and was on track for an early 1974 release.

During the writer's strike, Jacobs attempted to rebuild his passion project by going after UK directors like Terence Young (*Dr. No*) and Charles Jarrott (*Anne of the Thousand Days*). On May 15, 1973, Jacobs stated that he was excited to have a writer lined up for *Dune*, although it's unclear whether that writer was Semple or Trumbo because deals were hindered by the strike. For director, Jacobs was pursuing respected cinematographer and director Haskell Wexler, who had made the era-defining 1969 political drama *Medium Cool*. On June 24, the strike finally ended, but just three days later, Jacobs died of a heart attack.

Michel Seydoux/Alejandro Jodorowsky Version (1974–76)

With the *Dune* project tied up in Jacobs' estate, APJAC International had until the end of 1974 to decide what to do with the rights. In December 1974, executive producer Jean-Paul Gibon and producer Michel Seydoux of the production company Camera-One led a French consortium to purchase the movie rights from the Jacobs estate for Chilean director Alejandro Jodorowsky.

A flamboyant figure, Jodorowsky had made his name with mystical surrealist cult films *El Topo* (1970) and *The Holy Mountain* (1973). After The

Beatles' John Lennon encouraged his manager Allen Klein to distribute the acid western *El Topo* in America, it successfully kicked off the "midnight movie" circuit. Klein then gave Jodorowsky $1 million for *Holy Mountain*. Now presented with an offer from Seydoux to make whatever project he wanted, Jodorowsky chose to adapt *Dune*.

The intended cast for Jodorowsky's *Dune* included his son Brontis, who had co-starred with his father in *El Topo*, as Paul Atreides. The 12-year-old Brontis began preparing with stuntman Jean-Pierre Vignau (*L'Amour braque*), who trained him in karate, jujitsu, judo, aikido, and other forms of martial arts, including knife and sword work. This physical training lasted for six hours a day, seven days a week for two years—the entire pre-production period.

David Carradine, hot off the success of his TV series *Kung Fu*, met with Jodorowsky about the role of Duke Leto, and upon entering the hotel room, proceeded to gobble up the director's entire $60 bottle of vitamin E. He was cast immediately.

Surrealist master Salvador Dalí was wooed by Jodorowsky to play Emperor Shaddam IV at a rate of $100,000 per hour, making him the "highest-paid actor in Hollywood." The filmmaker's workaround for this demand was to shoot Dalí for only one hour and then use a mechanical mannequin for the remaining shots, the sculpture of which was promised to Dalí's museum. The artist also recommended dark Swiss visionary H. R. Giger to do production art, specifically for the Harkonnens and their planet Giedi Prime. Giger stated that Dalí was later dropped from production after making statements in support of Spanish dictator Francisco Franco. Dalí's muse, the model-singer Amanda Lear, was also sought to play Princess Irulan.

Another get for Jodorowsky was his idol Orson Welles as Baron Vladimir Harkonnen. Welles was convinced to play the floating fat man when Jodorowsky cornered him at a Paris restaurant, where the *Citizen Kane* actor-director was enjoying an indulgent meal with six bottles of wine. Jodorowsky bought Welles another bottle and then promised to not only pay his fee as an actor but to hire the chef of that restaurant so that he could enjoy its culinary delights every day on set. Welles agreed on the spot.

Either Geraldine Chaplin or Charlotte Rampling was mooted to play Lady Jessica, but the latter (who eventually played Gaius Helen Mohiam in 2021's *Dune*) turned the part down after reading one particular scene in the script.

As Frank Pavich, director of the 2013 documentary *Jodorowsky's Dune*, tells the story [*IndieWire*]:

> The Algerian army was going to play extras. Jodorowsky was looking for who was going to play Jessica . . . He saw a movie with Charlotte Rampling and thought she would be perfect. In the script, there is a scene where . . . to insult Duke Leto (David Carradine), Rabban the Beast gets his army, the Algerian army, to pull down their pants in front of the palace and shit. There's going to be a scene of 2,000 extras defecating at once. Here's Charlotte Rampling, she agrees to meet with Jodo, she gets the script, she reads the script, and she says, "I can't be in a movie where there's 2,000 extras defecating on screen! I need to be in a movie that people are actually going to see! Who the hell is going to see this movie?"

Other intended casting included Gloria Swanson (*Sunset Boulevard*) as Gaius Helen Mohiam, Alain Delon (*Le Samouraï*) as Duncan Idaho, Hervé Villechaize (*The Man with the Golden Gun*) as Gurney Halleck, Udo Kier (*Andy Warhol's Frankenstein*) as Piter De Vries (called "Peter" in the script), and Rolling Stones frontman Mick Jagger (*Performance*) as a cross-dressing Feyd-Rautha. The rock groups Pink Floyd, Henry Cow, and Magma were hired to do the music for the film (each providing the musical voice of a different planet) along with German composer Karlheinz Stockhausen.

After an unsuccessful meeting with Douglas Trumbull of *2001: A Space Odyssey*, the production recruited a young Dan O'Bannon to take charge of the special effects department on the strength of his work on John Carpenter's 1974 directorial debut *Dark Star*, which had begun life as a student project at USC film school. The art direction of the movie would be entrusted to Giger, English sci-fi illustrator Chris Foss, and French cartoonist Jean Giraud (a.k.a. Mœbius). It was the latter who designed costumes and illustrated 3000 storyboards for a massive book created as a showpiece to sell Jodorowsky's vision for the film to Hollywood investors. Some costumes were physically created from these drawings.

Herbert flew to Paris in 1976, where he reported that $2 million out of the $9.5 million budget on the film had been spent in pre-production. He was shown the artwork the *Dune* team had produced and witnessed the many liberties that had been taken with his masterwork, but Jodorowsky actively discouraged the author's input. Nevertheless, the two remained amicable.

Jodorowsky wrote in a 1985 issue of *Métal hurlant*:

> I felt an enthusiastic admiration toward Herbert and at the same time in conflict. I think that the same thing occurred to him . . . He obstructed me . . . I did not want him as a technical adviser . . . I did everything to move him away from the project . . . I had received a version of *Dune,* and I wanted to transmit it: the Myth was to give up the literary form and to become Image.

After conceiving the scenario, Jodorowsky even employed Herbert's French translator, Michel Demuth, to provide dialogue for the script.

"I interpret and continue the book," Jodorowsky told *Rock & Folk*. "I don't believe that one should take a novel and fail to put it at one's service. As the anarchists say, 'Neither God nor Master!' I take the torch and continue further on. If not, it's not really worth it."

Even though the French consortium was providing $9.5 million to *Dune*, an additional $5 million and change was required from America to round out the $15 million total needed. The filmmakers flew to Hollywood and distributed their presentation book of artwork and story to the major studios, all of whom passed. Despite all the pre-production work and casting coups, this ultimately spelled the end for Jodorowsky's *Dune*.

After working in Paris for six months with special effects company Eurocitel, Dan O'Bannon returned to America in December 1975 to search for VistaVision equipment when he was informed of *Dune*'s collapse. A destitute O'Bannon spent time at a psychiatric hospital before crashing on his friend Ronald Shusett's couch. After a dozen failed scripts, the two of them wrote the screenplay for what became 1979's *Alien*, with O'Bannon convincing director Ridley Scott to hire his core group of *Dune* visualists: H. R. Giger, Chris Foss, and Mœbius.

Jodorowsky wrote:

> Me, I liked to fight for *Dune*. Almost all the battles were won, but the war was lost. The project was sabotaged in Hollywood. It was French and not American. Its message was not "enough Hollywood." There were intrigues, plundering. The storyboard circulated among all the large studios. Later, the visual aspect of *Star Wars* resembled our style. The project announced to America the possibility of carrying out science-fiction films to large spectacle and out of the scientific rigor of *2001: A Space Odyssey*.

Not all was lost, however. After his film fell apart, Jodorowsky and Mœbius would later channel many of their visual ideas and story concepts for *Dune* into their epic comic book series *The Incal*, which ran from 1980 to 1988 in the French magazine *Métal hurlant* (*Heavy Metal* in North America). It follows the P.I. John Difool on his quest to stop several factions vying for the title MacGuffin, a crystal with enormous powers. The series not only kicked off a "Jodoverse" of comic book titles that later included *The Metabarons, The Technopriests,* and *Megalex,* and also influenced the look of Luc Besson's 1997 film *The Fifth Element,* which featured some designs from Mœbius. In 2021, Taika Waititi (*Jojo Rabbit, Thor: Ragnarok*) announced he would direct a movie version of *The Incal*—with the full blessing of the 92-year-old Jodorowsky—for Humanoids and Primer Entertainment, cowritten by Jemaine Clement and Peter Warren.

The documentary *Jodorowsky's Dune* was released by Sony Pictures Classics in 2013, discussing the abandoned film while also highlighting its influence on such classics as *Star Wars, Raiders of the Lost Ark, Flash Gordon, The Terminator,* and *Contact.* It garnered nearly universal critical acclaim and collected dozens of awards, including Best Documentary from the Australian Film Critics Association, Fantastic Fest, the National Board of Review, and the Sitges Film Festival.

Dino De Laurentiis/Ridley Scott Version (1976–80)

Born in Torre Annunziata in 1919, legendary Italian producer Dino De Laurentiis was the son of a pasta manufacturer and later studied film at the Centro Sperimentale di Cinematografia school in Rome from 1937 to 1938. He began producing his own films in 1941, including neorealist classics such as *Bitter Rice* and early efforts by Federico Fellini like *Nights of Cabiria* and *La Strada,* the latter of which won him and Carlo Ponti the 1957 Oscar for Best Foreign Language Film.

From the late '50s on, De Laurentiis' career would be prodigious, marked by big bets like King Vidor's *War and Peace* (1956) and the Napoleon biopic *Waterloo* (1970) as well as cult schlock like Sergio Corbucci's *Navajo Joe* (1966) or Mario Bava's *Danger: Diabolik* (1968). For every commercial hit like *Serpico* (1973) or *Death Wish* (1974), there were embarrassments like *Mandingo* (1975) or *Buffalo Bill and the Indians, or Sitting Bull's History Lesson* (1976). By the time he set his sights on *Dune* (only midway through a seven-decade career of nearly 500 credits), his only previous foray into big-budget sci-fi had been Roger Vadim's 1968 camp classic *Barbarella*, in which a scantily clad Jane Fonda pranced her way across the universe with the aid of a hunky angel-winged John Phillip Law.

In 1976, De Laurentiis, riding high on his soon-to-be-released *King Kong* remake, purchased the rights to *Dune* from the French consortium for $2 million, roughly what had been invested in Jodorowsky's aborted version. The Italian producer initially hired Herbert himself to pen the screenplay and also had the author do an uncredited rewrite of Lorenzo Semple Jr.'s script for 1980's *Flash Gordon* to correct what Herbert recalled as "certain mistakes of verisimilitude."

Herbert said in 1979 [*Future Life* #14]:

> I have no idea who's going to play what, except that Dino De Laurentiis agrees with me that Paul should be an unknown, somebody who hasn't been on the screen before. We're looking for an important director, somebody with a superb track record. The problem is to find somebody who isn't previously committed. They are talking about a budget of up to $40 million. It turns my head. I can't even think in those terms. I will be doing the screenplay. The film treatments, the rough outlines, have already been done.

At the time, De Laurentiis had a reputation as a boisterous showman with incredible ambition but his reach often exceeded his grasp. For instance, at one point he planned to produce *The Bible* in 26 parts, but only wound up with a single film after the first 1966 John Huston picture lost money for 20th Century Fox. His planned *Dune* trilogy would ultimately echo this pattern.

"I happen to be an admirer of his," Herbert said of De Laurentiis. "I don't admire everything that he's done, and he knows that well! But he's a man who, when he puts his mind to it, has superb ability. He takes shortcuts, sometimes, but he's promised me no shortcuts with *Dune*. He wants to do a classic, quality movie, I quote, 'to rank with *Gone with the Wind* and the equivalent.'"

How this script was written is also interesting, since in 1979 Herbert already possessed a home computer with ten-and-a-half million bytes in its "very sophisticated typewriter and notes filing system," making him likely one of the first popular novelists to write on a computer.

One prescient suggestion De Laurentiis made was to break the novel into two films, a tactic Denis Villeneuve would later use for his own *Dune* epic. "Paul's story falls neatly into two packages," Herbert said in *Starlog* #27 in 1979, explaining that the first film would end with Paul's acceptance as leader of the Fremen, with the second dealing with Paul's battle against the Emperor. "I have no objection to breaking it up if that's the way we have to do it to tell the story . . . Obviously, we have to make a high-density film. How long a film can you make and still get the investment out of it? That's the real question."

However, that question was answered rather harshly when Herbert finally turned in his draft, which was too unwieldy at a reported 176 pages. De Laurentiis decided to take the author out of that particular loop.

"I did a screenplay, and it was awful," Herbert admitted in a 1983 Waldentapes interview. "It was too long. It lacked the proper visual metaphors. I was too close to the book to be able to see it as a film."

De Laurentiis personally read the *Dune* book at least three times before deciding the best course of action would be to hire a director first, then a screenwriter to help bring their vision to life. He found a director in Ridley Scott, a prolific British helmer of commercials before making his film debut with 1977's period drama *The Duellists*. But it was Scott's breakthrough success with *Alien,* lauded for its lived-in, claustrophobic visuals, that brought him to the forefront. Scott came on board *Dune* in January 1980, setting up shop at London's Pinewood Studios, where he oversaw drawings, storyboards, and special effects models. Italian cinematographer Vittorio Storaro (*Apocalypse Now*) was being eyed to lens the picture.

"I was attracted to *Dune* because it was beyond what I'd done on *Alien,* which was kind of a hardcore horror film," Scott said in Charles de Lauzirika's 2007 documentary *Dangerous Days: Making Blade Runner.* "*Dune* would be a step strongly . . . very, very strongly . . . in the direction of *Star Wars.*"

H. R. Giger would be the production designer, having won an Oscar for his work on *Alien* and having previously worked on the Jodorowsky version.

Giger wrote in his 1996 book *H. R. Giger's Film Design*:

> After my prior cooperation on the film in 1975 with Jodorowsky, I had started working together with Conny de Fries on the prototype of a bed I had designed, as part of a furniture project I always hoped to realize. The bed was never completed, but my involvement with the renewed *Dune* project provided the opportunity to construct my designs as the Harkonnen furniture pieces and to also have them fea-

tured in the film. It was agreed that my contract would allow the copyright of my designs to remain with me and that, later on, I would have the models at my free disposal.

Scott said of *Dune* in 2021 [*Total Film*]:

> It's always been filmable. I had a writer called Rudy Wurlitzer, of the Wurlitzer family, you know the Jukebox? He'd written two films: *Two-Lane Blacktop* with James Taylor, and *Pat Garrett and Billy the Kid*, which had Bob Dylan and Kris Kristofferson . . . We did a very good take on *Dune*, because in early days I'd work very, very closely with the writer. I was always glomming the look of the film onto what he or she was writing.

While Scott told Herbert he liked eight scenes from the author's script attempt, Scott and Wurlitzer wanted to root their *Dune* in more modern political commentary, with the desert-dwelling Fremen resembling third-world urban ghetto communities and the American Indian. Scott and his production team studied Gillo Pontecorvo's 1966 film *The Battle of Algiers* for reference. The script had a darker tone than the novel, with Paul frequently chastising the Fremen and thus willing his destiny to fruition. Paul's sister Alia became his incestuous child with Jessica in this version. Wurlitzer spent some eight months generating three drafts before it was complete.

Wurlitzer recalled [*Prevue* #54]:

> The *Dune* adaptation was one of the most difficult jobs I've ever done. It took more time to break it down into a working outline than to write the final script. I did two or three drafts before I was at all satisfied with the structure. I believe we kept to the spirit of the book but, in a sense, we rarefied it. We interjected a somewhat different sensibility. In one draft I introduced some erotic scenes between Paul and his mother, Jessica. I felt there was always a latent, but very strong, Oedipal attraction between them, and I took it one note further. It went right in the middle of the film, as a supreme defiance of certain boundaries, perhaps making Paul even more heroic for having broken a forbidden code. A true leader is never a clear model of Christian goodness. Many times, he is ruthless, very determined, and willing to make sacrifices to serve certain ends. That doesn't mean he has to be a consummate Machiavellian, only that

certain shadings in his character make him a little dangerous, a bit abrupt. Even Christ drove the merchants out of the temple. We wanted the Baron Harkonnen, for instance, to be less a caricature of evil. It was refined as it progressed. When adapting a book, one can get locked into a kind of weird internal dialogue with the author, which can be a strange process. One hopes not to commit sacrilege to the book, but still have enough courage to make changes which are redeemingly cinematic. I never met Herbert, who was probably at his home in Washington State while I was in London, but I was curious to know what he thought of my efforts.

Herbert was, understandably, not pleased with many of Scott and Wurlitzer's changes. After reading the initial draft, he found the script "juvenile," upset by the many omitted scenes and particularly incensed by the omission of Gurney's baliset, the playing of which would be shot for but sadly omitted from the theatrical cuts of both the 1984 and 2021 versions. According to his son Brian, Herbert was downright apoplectic when he read the third draft, which included the incest theme. He raged to De Laurentiis, who agreed this new dimension should not be added. The author was more sanguine when discussing it after Lynch's version (sans mother/son tomfoolery) was already in production.

"At one point, there was going to be an incest version made," Herbert said in Ed Naha's *The Making of Dune*. "I won't mention the filmmaker's name, but someone actually wanted to have a romance between Paul and his mother. That would have outraged every *Dune* fan in the world! I was rather bemused by it all. I'm a calm man. I found it all grist for the mill."

Ultimately, Scott's version was stalled by a Universal Pictures brass divided not over incest, but rather the ballooning budget of $50 million ($169 million today, almost exactly the budget of the 2021 *Dune*). Company president Ned Tanen approved it while another executive did not, with De Laurentiis caught in the middle. September 1980 thus saw the end of Scott's involvement as he went off to make the landmark Philip K. Dick adaptation *Blade Runner* instead. However, other factors helped put the kibosh on this production, including the death of Scott's older brother Frank.

Scott told Paul Sammon in the book *Ridley Scott: The Making of his Movies*:

After seven months, I dropped out of *Dune*. By then, Rudy Wurlitzer had come up with a first-draft script which I felt was a decent distillation of Frank Herbert's book, but I also realized *Dune* was going to take a lot more work—at least two and a half years' worth—and I didn't have the heart to attack that because my brother Frank unexpectedly died of cancer while I was prepping the De Laurentiis picture. Frankly, that freaked me out. So, I went to Dino and told him the *Dune* script was his.

Giger recalled:

Prior to signing the contract, I had already completed two new *Dune* paintings when I received the news from Ridley Scott that Dino had handed the film over to his daughter. What remained from the project was my own interest in the furniture, which I had financed myself. With the aid of Conny de Fries, the perfect partner for the realization of my design, over the next few years, we completed the project which evolved to include a table, mirror frame, and armoire, a complete environment.

Interestingly, Scott also later revealed another reason he bailed on *Dune*, which would later be a major source of stress for Lynch's version: shooting in Mexico.

According to Scott:

Dino had got me into it, and we said, "We did a script, and the script is pretty fucking good." Then Dino said, "It's expensive, we're going to have to make it in Mexico." I said, "What!" He said, "Mexico." I said, "Really?" So, he sent me to Mexico City. And with the greatest respect to Mexico City, in those days it was pretty pongy. I didn't love it. I went to the studio in Mexico City where the floors were earth floors in the studio. I said, "Nah, Dino, I don't want to make this a hardship." And so, I actually backed out.

The Man from Another Place: David Lynch

"What is the work I'm most proud of?
Well, I'm sort of proud of everything . . . except *Dune*."

—*David Lynch, June 2020*

Born in Missoula, Montana, on January 20, 1946, David Keith Lynch was the son of a Department of Agriculture scientist father and an English tutor mother. The eldest of three children, he led a transitory childhood due to his father's work, moving everywhere from Idaho to Washington State to North Carolina before eventually settling in Alexandria, Virginia. A happy child who made friends easily and loved playing outside, Lynch was an Eagle Scout, and his troop was present at the inauguration of President John F. Kennedy. He also displayed an early aptitude for art, and Lynch's friend Toby Keeler introduced him to his father, Bushnell Keeler. A fine artist, the elder Keeler took a liking to Lynch, allowing him and his friend Jack Fisk to rent space in his studio to do their own work.

Intrigued by the possibilities inherent in living "the art life," Lynch attended a series of schools, including the Corcoran School of the Arts and Design in Washington, D.C.; the School of the Museum of Fine Arts in Boston; and the Pennsylvania Academy of Fine Arts. It was at the latter school in 1967 that he met and married his first wife Peggy (who gave birth to their daughter Jennifer the following year) and made his first experimental short film, *Six Men Getting Sick (Six Times)*.

Produced on a budget of $150, *Six Men Getting Sick* led to a commission from a wealthy classmate to create a new film installation. This one, *The Alphabet* (1968), starred Peggy as a girl who speaks the ABCs over images of horses before dying in a dramatic spray of blood. On the strength of this, he convinced the American Film Institute to fund his next, *The Grandmother*, about a boy who grows a grandmother to care for him out of a seed. That film, made in 1970 for $7,200, led to Lynch and Peggy moving to Los Angeles in 1971, where he joined one of the earliest classes at the newly founded Center for Advanced Film Studies (later AFI Conservatory).

Lynch there began developing a project called *Gardenback*, but interference from faculty who encouraged him to add more dialogue ultimately led to him scrapping that film and nearly quitting. Encouraged by dean Frank Daniel to return for a second year, Lynch got a $10,000 grant to write and direct *Eraserhead*, a surreal story of an odd, anxious man who lives in an industrial city with a girlfriend who gives birth to their deformed child. Originally intended to run 42 minutes, Lynch's 21-page script began growing into a far more ambitious feature that eventually clocked in at 89 minutes.

Filming on *Eraserhead* began in May 1972 on sets built in several large stables on the AFI campus. His production team included several figures he would work with many times over his career, including childhood friend Jack Fisk (*The Straight Story*, *Mulholland Drive*) as production designer, Frederick Elmes (*Blue Velvet*, *Wild at Heart*) as director of photography, and Alan Splet (*The Elephant Man*, *Dune*, *Blue Velvet*) as sound designer. Fisk's wife, actress Sissy Spacek (who would later appear in Lynch's *Straight Story*), also helped out, often slating scenes before she eventually shot to stardom in Brian De Palma's *Carrie* (which Fisk art directed).

When the grant ran out after a year of shooting, Lynch funded the film in fits and starts over several years by getting a loan from his father as well as a paper route delivering *The Wall Street Journal* door-to-door. His leading man, actor Jack Nance (*Barfly*, *The Blob*), eventually joined him on this route. Regarding one 18-month gap in shooting, Nance remarked, "I got up and went through the door in one scene, and it was a year and a half before I walked out the other side." Also appearing in the movie are Charlotte Stewart (*Tremors*, *Twin Peaks*), Judith Roberts (*Orange Is the New Black*), Darwin Joston (*Assault on Precinct 13*), and Hal Landon Jr. (*Bill & Ted's Excellent Adventure*).

Jennifer Lynch, who was born with club feet requiring surgery, was a major inspiration for The Baby, the deformed creature at the center of the protagonist's neuroses. Lynch refuses to discuss how he created this alien-like being, but the imagery also inspired powerful visuals in *Dune*, including the giant third-stage Guild Navigator and the unborn Alia. The bleak industrial environment of *Eraserhead* came from Lynch's time living with Peggy and Jennifer in Fairmount, which in the late '60s was one of Philadelphia's more dangerous low-income neighborhoods.

Not long into the production, David and Peggy separated, and Lynch began living in the stables on his own sets, literally inhabiting his dream world. At one point Lynch's father and younger brother staged something of an intervention, trying to convince David to give up on his film and get a regular job to support his wife and daughter. In the middle of this ordeal in July 1973, Lynch began practicing Transcendental Meditation, which would have a profound impact on his life and outlook. He credits his practice with helping to free him from a lot of the anxiety he felt during this time, and also for partially inspiring the "Lady in the Radiator," a chipmunk-like girl with giant cheeks who appears to Henry in a vision where she sings the song "In Heaven" (written by Lynch and Splet) while stepping on sperm-like leech creatures.

The resulting film is filled with bizarre, surreal imagery shot in striking black and white, including a little boy carrying Henry's severed head to a pencil factory and a geyser of blood that comes out of the baby when Henry stabs it. The original cut proved to have too many of these surreal moments for its own good, and after a disastrous test screening for critics, Lynch excised 20 minutes to reduce it to under 90 minutes. Lynch and Splet then spent a solid year cobbling together the complex sonic tapestry of the movie's droning, nightmarish soundscapes. In all, *Eraserhead* consumed five years of Lynch's life.

After premiering at LA's Filmex festival in March 1977, it caught the eye of Libra Films impresario Ben Barenholtz, the originator of the midnight movie, who had previously championed such bizarre fare as Jodorowsky's *El Topo* and John Waters' *Pink Flamingos*. Barenholtz arranged for *Eraserhead* to play midnights at LA's Cinema Village, where it ran for a year. This trend of extended bookings continued at theaters in New York and San Francisco, and eventually, the movie became a cult sensation, grossing $7 million between 1977 and 1981. Critics were bewitched by its charms, with some comparing it to Luis Buñuel's surrealistic 1929 classic *Un Chien Andalou* or the writings of Franz Kafka. (The latter is a major influence on Lynch, who has long dreamed of adapting *The Metamorphosis* to the screen.)

One filmmaker who championed *Eraserhead* was Stanley Kubrick, who screened it for the cast and crew of his 1980 masterpiece *The Shining* to impart the sense of otherworldly dread he wished to evoke. He also showed it to other filmmakers, including George Lucas.

"That was a great moment," Lynch told Mario Orsatti in 2020. "It wasn't one of his favorites, it was his favorite. The producer and several people that were working with George Lucas would come to Elstree Studios to check it out for George to come and shoot there. They met Kubrick, who invited them up to his house that night and said, 'I want to show you my favorite film,' and he showed them *Eraserhead*."

Another industry figure who fell in love with *Eraserhead* was producer Stuart Cornfeld, then with Mel Brooks' Brooksfilms. When they met, Lynch pitched Cornfeld a new project, the surreal rock-and-roll fantasy *Ronnie Rocket*. After Cornfeld tried unsuccessfully to get funding for *Ronnie*, he convinced Lynch that he needed to direct a film from someone else's script before he could attract attention to his own project. Lynch met Cornfeld at Nibblers Restaurant in Beverly Hills to discuss four potential projects.

"I went there, and before we even ordered, I said, 'Stuart, now tell me,'" Lynch said in the 2001 documentary *The Terrible Elephant Man Revealed*. "And he said, 'Okay, David, the first script is a story entitled *The Elephant Man*.' And a small bomb went off in my head. Instantly I knew. I said, 'That's it, that's what I want to do.' I never heard the other three ideas."

Having nothing to do with the popular 1977 stage play of the same name by Bernard Pomerance (later adapted into a TV movie in 1982), the screenplay for *The Elephant Man* was written by Christopher De Vore and Eric Bergren. The two fledgling screenwriters went straight to the source, basing their work on a chapter from *The Elephant Man and Other Reminiscences,* a book by Sir Frederick Treves. Treves was the British surgeon who had become famous for taking in and caring for Joseph Merrick, better known as the Elephant Man.

Although he was born in 1862 a normal healthy child, Joseph (often mistakenly referred to as "John," including in Lynch's film) began developing extreme physical abnormalities by age 5. He may have suffered from the rare genetic disorder Proteus syndrome, though that has never been verified. Enlarged growths on his face and hands and his twisted gait made him prime fodder for traveling freak shows of the time, hauled around London music halls or carnivals as an exhibited curiosity.

In 1884, Treves discovered Merrick and brought him to the Royal London Hospital, where he was examined and studied. He eventually became a full-time resident. During his stay, he was treated with dignity and care for the first time in his life, and eventually revealed a latent intelligence that astonished many. Far from a monster, Merrick was a sensitive young man who had intense emotional reactions to his new experiences, which included meeting the Princess of Wales and actress Madge Kendal, the latter of whom became his major benefactor. Unfortunately, his condition worsened as the years went on, and Merrick died in 1890 at the age of 27.

Lynch's movie follows this story closely and, except for some abstract dream sequences that bookend the film, is a fairly straightforward biopic.

While the filmmaker wanted to make a more commercial film than *Eraserhead*, he still only had that film as a calling card. Although executive producer Cornfeld (who became Ben Stiller's main producer) and producer Jonathan Sanger (*Fatso, Vanilla Sky*) were fully behind Lynch making *The Elephant Man*, they still had one bigwig to convince: Mel Brooks, whose Brooksfilms would make the movie and get it financed.

Brooks was already a comedy legend, having started on *Your Show of Shows* in the 1950s before beginning a prolific directing career with 1967's classic *The Producers*. His many farcical hits thereafter (*Blazing Saddles, Young Frankenstein, High Anxiety*) belie the thoughtful and literate man who made them, so by the early '80s, Brooks wanted to use his clout to branch out into serious film work. Although he and his company Brooksfilms would be uncredited for it, *The Elephant Man* would be his first non-comedic production.

The script came to Brooks circuitously, as it was given to Sanger (assistant director on *High Anxiety*) by his babysitter at the time. Sanger passed the script on to Brooks' wife, the Oscar-winning actress Anne Bancroft (*The Miracle Worker, The Graduate*). She loved the material and gave it to her husband, who agreed to make the film. Brooks originally wanted to get a director like Alan J. Pakula (*All the President's Men*), so when it was time to meet Sanger's left-field choice Lynch, Brooks screened *Eraserhead* on the 20th Century Fox lot.

"I was waiting outside the theater," Lynch said. "As the story goes, the doors flew open after the film was over, and Mel ran toward me, embraced me, and said, 'You're a madman, I love you, you're in.'"

"I expected to meet a young Max Reinhardt," Brooks said, referring to the intense Austrian director. "I expected the guy to look like a Picasso, two eyes on one side of his nose, and here is a young Charles Lindbergh."

From then on, Lynch's experience making the $5 million *Elephant Man* was buoyed by having Brooks' full support. He was given free rein to work with De Vore and Bergren on restructuring the script, to shoot the film in black and white to match period photography, and to bring in Alan Splet to create the movie's moody soundscape. One aspect that didn't work out was Lynch's attempt to create the Merrick makeup himself, a disaster that shook the director's confidence and almost caused him to quit the film in frustration. Brooks convinced him that his job was to make the movie, not the makeup, and they brought in prosthetics expert Christopher Tucker (*Star Wars, The Boys from Brazil*) to work from the Royal London Hospital's original life casts of Merrick's body.

Lynch assembled a formidable cast, including Anthony Hopkins, Anne Bancroft, John Gielgud, and Freddie Jones. He had originally wanted to cast his *Eraserhead* lead Jack Nance as Merrick, but it was not to be. Instead, they landed English film and stage actor John Hurt, who had recently appeared in *Alien* and been nominated for an Oscar for *Midnight Express*.

Hurt stated in the 2001 documentary *The Making of The Elephant Man*:

> It was only later from David Lynch that I understood why, because I did ask, "Why, for instance, did you ask me to do this?" He said, "Well, I'd seen *The Naked Civil Servant*, and I'd seen Caligula in *I, Claudius*," and on both occasions, he paid me the highest compliment that anybody could ever play an actor: "I didn't recognize the actor, and that's what I wanted for *The Elephant Man*."

Lynch's admiration for *I, Claudius* may have played a role in the casting of two actors for *Dune*: Siân Phillips and Patrick Stewart, who portrayed Livia and Sejanus, respectively, in that 1976 BBC TV miniseries.

Hurt shot the entirety of *Elephant Man* while waiting to be needed on the set of Michael Cimino's runaway production of *Heaven's Gate*, where he said his absence wasn't noticed. Hurt would take on a grueling transformation under Tucker, with whom he had already worked on *I, Claudius*, arriving at 5 a.m. on any given day to spend seven to eight hours in the makeup chair before filming from noon until 10 p.m., followed by two hours to carefully remove the appliances. Due to the draining process, Hurt was only scheduled for every other day (despite being the film's lead) so he could take a breather between shooting. "I think they finally managed to make me hate acting," Hurt said at the time.

One of Lynch's key collaborators on his sophomore effort was Director of Photography Freddie Francis. Born in 1917, he was a veteran cinematographer who worked under Oswald Morris on several John Huston productions, including *Moby Dick,* before branching out as a solo DP on classics like *The Innocents*, winning his first Oscar in 1960 for Jack Cardiff's *Sons and Lovers*. Francis branched out as a director, helming low-budget gothic horror flicks for Hammer Studios and Amicus Productions, including genre favorites like *Dracula Has Risen from the Grave, Dr. Terror's House of Horrors*, and the 1972 *Tales from the Crypt*. His most personal project was the quirky 1970 horror comedy *Mumsy, Nanny, Sonny, and Girly*, which retains a cult following. His stark black & white work on *The Elephant Man* would mark his triumphant return to cinematography, although he would later direct *The Doctor and the Devils* for producers Sanger and Brooks in 1985.

Filming ran from October 1979 to May 1980. Because of Lynch's initial inability to create the Merrick makeup, the film began shooting at Shepperton Studios in Surrey, England, without John Hurt. Initially, Lynch and Hopkins did not mesh well, with the director asking Hopkins to shave a beard he grew for the role (he refused) and Hopkins talking the inexperienced director down to producers.

"Why doesn't he get that fucking hat off and stop playing at being a director and damn well direct?" Hopkins fumed at producer Sanger, according to Greg Olsen's book *Beautiful Dark*, specifically referring to Lynch's penchant for wearing a big brown trilby hat on set. "This guy's not going to help me in any way."

When it came time to shoot the scene where Hopkins' Treves first lays sympathetic eyes on Merrick during a street carnival where he is on display, only a stand-in for Hurt was available. Under these less-than-ideal circumstances, Lynch managed to capture Hopkins' haunted visage and a single unscripted tear in one take. Eventually, the actor and filmmaker came to an understanding, and Hopkins would later refer to Lynch as "one of the most pleasant directors I've worked with."

Lynch also got along splendidly with both Hurt and Gielgud, despite being intimidated by their experience. Gielgud in particular was a master Shakespearian who had been acting since the 1920s and later became one of a handful of actors to win the EGOT.

Lynch enthused in 2015 [via a master's student Q&A]:

> One morning I get up, and I'm putting on my underwear, thinking "Here I am putting on my underwear, and I'm off to direct Sir John Gielgud." He was solid gold, and I loved working with him, and after we finished, he wrote me a letter—I hope I still have it somewhere—and he asked me, he said, "David, you never told me how I did, were you happy with what I did?"

Although Lynch did not technically have the final cut on the film, it was effectively given to him by Brooks, who screened the cut with Sanger upon their return from England. Although Brooks suggested several tweaks, he ultimately agreed to release it as is. When *The Elephant Man* was delivered to theaters by Paramount Pictures on October 3, 1980, it received a rapturous critical response.

"Mr. Hurt is truly remarkable," Vincent Canby wrote in *The New York Times*. "It can't be easy to act under such a heavy mask . . . the physical production is beautiful, especially Freddie Francis' black-and-white photography."

Not only would the movie rake in $26 million in North America, making it a surprise hit, but it was also nominated for eight Academy Awards, including Best Picture (Sanger), Best Actor (Hurt), Best Adapted Screenplay (Lynch, De Vore, & Bergren), and Best Director (Lynch). Although it did not win any of those statues, it did win Best Film, Best Actor, and Best Production Design at the 1981 British Academy Film Awards (BAFTAs). It also took home a British Society of Cinematographers award for Francis and the César Award for Best Foreign Film for Lynch.

Lynch saw *Elephant Man* as the movie that would "take me from surreal obscurity into the mainstream, and at the same time not compromise. I was worried about that. I want to make art popular. I want to make good films that I can really get into and love doing, and yet that people will like. I just worry whether that is possible."

Detour to a Galaxy Far, Far Away

A beginning is a very delicate time. When David Lynch signed on to his third feature film in 1981, it was especially delicate, as it nearly wasn't *Dune*, but rather a little movie called *Return of the Jedi*.

To say that 1977's *Star Wars* had caused a Hollywood sea change is a drastic understatement. George Lucas' fast-paced space opera of laser sword–wielding wizards, hot rod–esque spaceships, and woo-woo mysticism had taken in $225 million (over a billion adjusted for inflation) during its blockbusting initial run in theaters, which lasted over a year. That success lit a fire under studios to greenlight a slew of sci-fi fantasies, some of which found a modicum of success, such as *Alien* and Robert Wise's snail-paced *Star Trek: The Motion Picture*. Many of the technicians who had helped bring *Star Wars* to life wound up working on these pictures.

Other efforts were not so lucky, with Disney's *The Black Hole* still reeking of Old Hollywood technique, Mike Hodges' *Flash Gordon* hopelessly mired in intentional camp, Stanley Donen's *Saturn 3* a nadir for all involved, and Peter Hyams' *High Noon*-in-space *Outland* a bit too cynical. Scraping the bottom of the barrel were the obvious rip-offs made for the exploitation market, including such lowbrow high adventure fare as *Message from Space*, *Starcrash*, *Battle Beyond the Stars*, *Galaxina*, and *Galaxy of Terror*.

The brooding, cerebral sci-fi of the previous decade such as *2001: A Space Odyssey*, *Solaris*, *Silent Running*, *Logan's Run,* and the *Planet of the Apes* franchise was out. B-movie pastiches with A-level budgets were in. If they could include a space dogfight or a laser gun battle, all the better.

Both *Alien* and *Star Trek* evolved into sustainable franchises, but *Star Wars* continued to be the gold standard. Lucas stepped out of the director's chair to take on a heavy-handed executive producer's role for 1980's sequel *The Empire Strikes Back*, helmed by Irvin Kershner. Despite a risky story gambit of going darker and more spiritual—not to mention a nail-biting cliffhanger ending—it still proved exceedingly popular, raking in $145 million in its initial summer run and then climbing to $200 million by the next year.

Despite all the critical and audience acclaim that *The Empire Strikes Back* reaped, it left Lucas in a creative and professional bind. A rift with producer Gary Kurtz over budget overruns on *Empire* shifted those duties on *Jedi* to Lucas' *Raiders of the Lost Ark* executive producer Howard Kazanjian, and likely left Lucas gun-shy about handing over the third film to another established filmmaker like Kershner. A dispute over credits had also forced Lucas to part ways with the Directors Guild of America, which would cause serious headaches in finding another director. Finally, they had to meet expectations for the wrap-up of what was turning into the most popular movie trilogy of all time. Would Lucas play it safe? Or would he follow his more esoteric, renegade instincts?

"By this time, these movies had gotten to be like television shows," Lucas stated in J.W. Rinzler's 2013 book *The Making of Star Wars: Return of the Jedi*. "In television, the executive producer is pretty much the creator or overseer . . . while the director fills the obligation of working with the actors and getting it on the screen."

Given Lucas' DGA issues, Kazanjian set about finding a filmmaker, preferably with a non-union affiliation. Thus, many candidates were English or Australian, although some Americans were also considered. The ideal candidate would be young and could bring a strong vision . . . while also willing to do things Lucas' way under the template established in the two films prior.

The list directors considered included Steven Spielberg, John Glen, Lewis Gilbert, Mike Newell, John Hough, Alan Parker, Peter Weir, Jack Smight, Bruce Beresford, Peter Yates, Jeremy Kagan, Robert Markowitz, Richard Donner, Desmond Davies, Hugh Hudson, Terry Gilliam, Stephen Frears, Graham Baker, Richard Lester, Richard Attenborough, Michael Anderson, John Boorman, John Carpenter, Roger Christian, David Cronenberg, Joe Dante, Richard Lester, Richard Fleischer, Jonathan Demme, John Guillermin, Tony Scott, William A. Fraker, and David Lynch, with the latter two personally recommended by Lucas. After these were considered, Welshman Richard Marquand was a late addition, throwing his hat into the ring after meeting with Lucas in England while fine-cutting his World War II–era thriller *Eye of the Needle*.

When Kazanjian first asked about Lynch, he was told the director was not considering any film offers until after he made his pet project, *Ronnie Rocket*. According to Rinzler's biography *Howard Kazanjian: A Producer's Life*, Lynch first met with the *Return of the Jedi* producer on November 23, 1980, a little over a month after *The Elephant Man* had been released to widespread praise: "David also now expresses concern over the possibility that a *Star Wars* film could swallow him up. Would he, for example, have input? He would want to do more with special sound (he felt that *Star Wars* and *Empire* were walls of music)."

The list was whittled down to around a dozen candidates after Kazan-jian interviewed A-list colleagues about those directors' ability to work with actors and crew and their tendency to come in on budget. Lucas then asked the remaining candidates if the two of them could honestly work together closely for two long years. From there, it came down to three to five filmmakers, with Lucas watching everything they had ever made and spending a day with each.

During a 2009 Q&A at New York's Hudson Union Society, Lynch de-scribed his experience during one of these George Lucas meet-and-greet courtship sessions:

> I was asked by George to come up to see him and talk to him about directing what would be the third *Star Wars*. I had next door to zero interest, but I always admired George. George is a guy that does what he loves, and I do what I love. The difference is what George loves makes hundreds of billions of dollars. I thought I should go up and at least visit with him, and it was incredible. I had to go to this building in L.A. first and get a special credit card, and I had to get special keys, and a letter came and a map. Then I went into the airport and I flew up, and then they had a rental car all ready for me and these keys and everything. I was to drive to this place. I came into an office and there was George, and he talked with me for a little bit, and then he said, "I want to show you something." Right about this time, I started to get a little bit of a headache. He took me up-stairs, and he showed me these things called Wookies. Now this headache is getting stronger. He showed me many animals and dif-ferent things. Then he took me for a ride in his Ferrari for a lunch, and George is kind of short, so his seat was way back and he was almost lying down in the car, and we were flying through this little town up in Northern California. We went to a restaurant . . . not that I don't like salad, but that's all they had was salad. Then I got almost a migraine headache, and I could hardly wait to get home. Even before I got home, I kind of crawled into a phone booth and called my agent and said there was no way, NO WAY I could do this. He said, "David, David, David . . . calm down, you don't have to do this." George, bless his heart, I told him on the phone the next day

that he should direct it. It's his film, he'd invented everything about it, but he doesn't really love directing and so someone else did direct that film. I did call my lawyer and told him I wasn't going to do it, and he said, "You just lost I don't know how many millions of dollars." But it's okay.

While an amusing anecdote, it doesn't quite line up with Kazanjian and Lucas' recollections. In fact, on February 5, 1981, Lynch's agent Rick Nicita of the powerful Creative Artists Agency (CAA) called Lucasfilm to inquire if they were still interested in hiring him. Lucas instructed Kazanjian to stall by calling Lynch and saying they would have a start date for the next *Star Wars* by April. On March 25, Lynch was added to their list of candidates, although Kazanjian noted, "I'm somewhat concerned because he wants to make a statement."

Furthermore, Kazanjian had recommended that Lucasfilm as an entity withdraw entirely from the Directors Guild. Because Lynch was a DGA member, his hiring would be heavily scrutinized by the Guild as well as Hollywood peers. It was even hypothesized in one memo that Lynch would be pressured to leave the picture or be blacklisted by the DGA, should he be hired.

In May 1981, Richard Marquand, tired of waiting, called Lucas for an impromptu meeting, once again pitching himself for the gig. Marquand was told that it was down to "One other guy and you." The next day Lucas called Kazanjian to say, "I want to go with David." When Lucas made this decision, he asked his producer to call Marquand and thank him as well, something Kazanjian did not do. Lucas' hesitancy to write Marquand off proved wise, because though Lynch was reportedly "thrilled" at first to be chosen, he declined the offer a day or two later.

Lynch confirmed to the Associated Press that he turned it down because he wouldn't have any creative leeway: "[Lucas] had already designed three-quarters of it."

Kazanjian says in his autobiography:

> The next day, David called and backed out. David told me he didn't want to do the picture because he didn't want John Williams. I was stunned. I'd work with Johnny on any and all movies. The second reason was David had his own sound effects guy [Alan Splet]. He didn't want Ben Burtt, who was George's man. George asked if I'd called Richard. I told him I had not. The next phone call was to Richard. Followed by one to his agent.

"Not long afterward, David announced that he was going to do *Dune*," Kazanjian remembers. "So obviously he was being simultaneously romanced by De Laurentiis. Richard doesn't even know this story . . . they were that close."

This raises the question of whether Lynch may have been using the *Star Wars* buzz as leverage for his *Dune* deal with De Laurentiis. We know which way he ultimately went, but it doesn't seem as cut and dry as being hosted by Lucas in his fortress one day and then bowing out the next.

"David obviously was a very out-of-left-field kind of idea," Lucas later admitted. "I like David a lot. I love his work. He's a very, very creative thinker. But I think I may have gone a bridge too far on that one. And I think he realized that when he started thinking about the actual reality of what was going to happen, and that was good."

In contrast, Marquand was ecstatic to direct *Jedi* and to let Lucas backseat drive. Far from the eccentric visualist that Lynch was, he was precisely the kind of journeyman that could adapt to working under Lucas' thumb (who was on set every day and directed the second unit), deferring to his executive producer on most creative aspects. Lucas' television analogy was no accident. Marquand was, to put it crudely, the round peg that fit into a round hole. In fact, Marquand's relationship with Lucas mirrored the "director as willing hired technician" practice that later formed the basis for Kevin Feige's stratospherically successful Marvel Studios.

This also proved to be a winning formula for Lucas, at least financially. By the end of its epic run in theaters in March 1984, *Return of the Jedi* had taken in $252 million. Adjusted for inflation, it remains the eighth highest-grossing movie of all time domestically, with $851 million in 2021 dollars. There was chatter of Marquand returning to helm one or more of the promised Star Wars prequels.

Nevertheless, *Jedi* is still seen by some critics and fans as a creative misfire. Where the first two films had taken big swings at reimagining Saturday matinee serials into rich, mythic storytelling, the final chapter in the original trilogy often feels like a rehash of what had come before. The sickeningly cute Ewoks are a transparent reach for the merchandising brass ring, and there is a menagerie of further action figure–ready creatures. Marquand seemed even more like Lucas' puppet when *Jedi* was re-released to theaters for a 1997 *Special Edition* loaded with alterations that couldn't have been approved by its "director," who had died 10 years before.

Lynch was not as strange a choice as he may seem now. Lucas himself had dabbled in experimental films while a student at the University of Southern California, and his debut feature *THX 1138* is fairly simpatico with Lynchian sensibilities. Lynch even used R2-D2 actor Kenny Baker as a carnival performer in *Elephant Man*.

It's not hard to imagine Lynch's bizarre gaze staging the deserts of Tatooine instead of the deserts of Arrakis. Or, for that matter, the grotesque giant slug creature that is Jabba the Hutt as opposed to the grotesque giant slug creature that is the Third-Stage Guild Navigator. The outsider pact between the rebels and the indigenous Ewoks is—teddy bear costumes on little people notwithstanding—not such a far cry from Paul joining forces with the Fremen. However, we must accept that a Lynch-helmed *Return of the Jedi* would hardly have been much different from the version we know. It was Lucas' show, all the way. It might have even been worse off, given Lynch's deep-rooted feelings of mismatch with the material.

"I've never even really liked science fiction," Lynch bluntly says in Chris Rodley's *Lynch on Lynch*. "I like elements of it, but it needs to be combined with other genres. And, obviously, Star Wars was totally George's thing."

Romancing De Laurentiis

In the afterglow of *The Elephant Man*'s success, David Lynch was suddenly a hot commodity. Because he was still a youthful 35 years old and had only directed two wildly divergent pictures that had been—by their own metrics—successes, the field for Lynch to play in was wide open. Besides turning down an upfront $3 million payday for *Jedi* (a little over $9 million today, not to mention untold profit participation and residuals), Lynch was courted for several other big studio projects.

The most logical would have been to re-team with his *Elephant Man* producers Sanger and Brooks along with screenwriters Bergren and De Vore for *Frances*, a biopic depicting the unconventional life of actress Frances Farmer and her harrowing battles with mental illness. Despite his early interest, Lynch ultimately decided not to take it on. The film instead served as the directorial debut of Graeme Clifford, an Australian assistant director and editor noted for his collaborations with Robert Altman and Nicolas Roeg. Although 1982's *Frances* received Academy Award nominations for Jessica Lange's title turn as Farmer as well as Kim Stanley as her mother Lillian, it only performed moderately well at the box office. Clifford himself would eventually work with Lynch, directing an episode of *Twin Peaks* in 1990.

Another script that came Lynch's way was *Tender Mercies* by playwright Horton Foote, which focused on a down-and-out alcoholic country singer who seeks redemption by sparking a relationship with a young widow and her son. The lead role was written expressly for Robert Duvall, who had played Boo Radley in the film version of *To Kill a Mockingbird,* also written by Foote. Many American directors declined offers to helm *Mercies*, including Lynch, who wrote in his 2018 autobiography *Room to Dream* that it "turned out to be a great film, but I didn't think it was right for me." The director's chair eventually went to Australian Bruce Beresford, and after positive reviews and a modest box office take, *Mercies* scored Oscar wins for both Duvall and Foote.

By this point, Lynch's career was something of a Rorschach inkblot, with executives seemingly able to read any number of things into *Eraserhead* and *Elephant Man*. For example, Thom Mount (president of worldwide motion picture production at Universal Pictures) recommended Lynch for a seminal teen sex comedy, *Fast Times at Ridgemont High*. With a screenplay by future *Almost Famous* Oscar-winner Cameron Crowe (based on his own "undercover high schooler" novel), the teenage slice of life is something we can hardly imagine being a viable Lynch vehicle today.

Although Lynch would explore the darker side of teenagerhood in *Twin Peaks*, *Fast Times* was a bubblier romp with a few melodramatic elements involving abortion and other teen concerns. Another AFI alum, Amy Heckerling, ultimately directed the project, which became a sleeper hit and kicked off the careers of Sean Penn, Jennifer Jason Leigh, Forest Whitaker, and future Lynch collaborator Nicolas Cage.

As wild as it may seem, Lynch did in fact go through the motions on *Fast Times*. "I had a meeting with David Lynch," Crowe recounted in a 2017 *Variety* retrospective. "He had a very wry smile on his face as I sat talking with him. He went and read it. We met again. He was very, very sweet about it, but slightly perplexed we thought of him. He said this was a nice story but 'it's not the kind of thing that I do, but good luck.' He got into the white VW bug and drove off."

The film Lynch had his heart set on—"the kind of thing that I do"—was *Ronnie Rocket*, a screenplay he had been working on since he finished *Eraserhead*. The story involves a detective straddling two alternate worlds by standing on one leg (while being pursued by "Donut Men"), as well as the oddball title character: a 3-foot teenage dwarf whose freakish need to be plugged into electricity turns him into a rock star. It was meant to be Lynch's first attempt at a color movie, visually inspired by French director Jacques Tati, and containing many surreal images amid industrial landscapes, including a 200-foot wall of fire. Although Mel Brooks and Stuart Cornfeld had acquired some financing for *Ronnie Rocket*, it wasn't enough, or as Lynch puts it, "way not enough." Francis Ford Coppola's American Zoetrope had planned to produce the film, with a young Dexter Fletcher of *Elephant Man* in the title role, but the failure of the 1982 Las Vegas musical *One from the Heart* put the company into bankruptcy.

Lynch presented the *Ronnie* script to producer Richard N. Roth, who passed but was intrigued by another idea the director pitched to him for a mystery story titled *Blue Velvet*. Roth helped set Lynch up at Warner Bros., where he generated two early drafts of *Velvet*, but the studio vehemently disliked both.

Roth had initially courted Lynch to adapt Thomas Harris' 1981 serial killer thriller novel *Red Dragon*, which instead was made by Michael Mann in 1986 as *Manhunter*. It served as the first film appearance of Harris' renowned cannibal character Hannibal Lecter (Brian Cox). It was a financial misfire for Roth and producer De Laurentiis, but now has a considerable cult following due to its style and being adjacent to Jonathan Demme's Best Picture–winner *Silence of the Lambs*.

"I was involved in that a little bit, until I got sick of it," Lynch said to *Rolling Stone*. "I was going into a world that was going to be, for me, real violent, and completely degenerate. One of those things: No Redeeming Qualities. The way I was thinking of it, I didn't want to let it into my country club."

Before *Elephant Man* even hit theaters, Lynch was reportedly offered the director's position for *Halloween II*. This was the sequel to John Carpenter's 1978 slasher *Halloween*, which had earned $70 million in its initial run to become the most successful independent film at that time.

From a 1980 *LA Times* by Laurie Warner: "*Halloween II*, which Carpenter will oversee, will be made with David Lynch, midnight-shocker *Eraserhead*'s creator, as its director." A January 1981 issue of *Boxoffice* magazine also "confirms" Lynch's involvement. However, it makes little sense that Lynch would take on a run-of-the-mill slasher sequel after having just completed a prestigious Oscar-caliber period piece starring Anthony Hopkins and John Gielgud, not to mention lucrative *Star Wars* overtures which could have personally netted him more money than the entire *Halloween II* budget. Although Lynch would later explore murder and horror in suburbia for projects like *Blue Velvet* and *Twin Peaks*, another AFI alum, Rick Rosenthal, made his feature directorial debut on *Halloween II*. Though Lynch never made the film, his loose association with it may have put him squarely in the orbit of Dino De Laurentiis, whose company co-financed the *Halloween* sequel.

This association may have directly influenced Lynch's work. In *David Lynch: The Man from Another Place*, Dennis Lim draws an interesting comparison with Lynch's 1992 suburban nightmare *Twin Peaks: Fire Walk with Me*: "The camera hovers along and behind the girls as they walk the tree-lined streets, in an echo of the stalking perspectives of John Carpenter's *Halloween* and other slasher movies."

Adding credence to this is a quote from Carpenter himself in an interview with *The Tampa Tribune* in December of 1984, shortly before his sci-fi movie *Starman* (which Lynch had also been offered) opened the same day as Lynch's *Dune*:

"We've seen technology a billion times," Carpenter says, "and you'll see that again this Christmas when you go to *2010* and *Dune*. We wanted to make it magic." Carpenter adds that he has seen director David Lynch's *Dune* already and, "There are parts of it that really, really impressed me. It's kind of daring stuff," he says. He also admits to liking Lynch, who Carpenter sees from time to time at their favorite Bob's Big Boy, in Los Angeles. "We discuss whether the Pappy Parker's Fried Chicken is better than the Bob's Combo Plate," Carpenter says. "We never talk about movies."

Whether or not Lynch was actually offered *Halloween II*, he had yet to gain proper representation. It wasn't until early 1981 that CAA's Rick Nicita began repping Lynch, and not long afterward dangled the carrot of *Dune* in front of him.

As Lynch told Rodley in *Lynch on Lynch*:

> I got onto Thomas Harris' *Red Dragon* with Richard Roth, who was going to be the producer of *Blue Velvet*. And then I got turned off that. About that time Dino De Laurentiis called the house. Dino says, "I want you to read this book, *Dune*." I thought he said "June."

By that time, Dino's daughter Raffaella De Laurentiis was running point on the *Dune* project. She had cut her teeth as a production assistant on *Hurricane* and then as a producer on the South Pacific romance *Beyond the Reef* (both 1979) and was hard at work shepherding the fantasy epic *Conan the Barbarian*. With Raffaella as the primary creative producer, Dino would take a less hands-on approach as executive producer, dealing more with the financial side—"less hands-on" being relative.

Like Lynch, Raffaella had begun her studies at art school, and she had intended to join her father's filmmaking dynasty as an art director or production designer before she switched to the producing side of the operation. Originally, her younger brother Federico had been intended to take the lead, helping their father produce *King Kong* and solo-producing a few other movies, including Frank Pierson's *King of the Gypsies*. It was, in fact, Federico who first took a shine to *Dune* and befriended Herbert and Lynch. However, Federico died in a plane crash on July 15, 1981, less than a month after Lynch signed on. The opening card of *Dune* is dedicated to his memory, and Raffaella told an interviewer in the *Sunday Sun* in 1984 that she found it "very hard to look at that dedication, but at the same time I'm very proud of it."

She recalled later [*The Guardian*, 1985]:

> My brother read the book in 1974. He came to me and said, "This is the greatest book I've ever read, and you must read it." I mean, he was a *Dune* fanatic. He gave the book to every member of the family, including my mother. We loved it, and we went to see Dino and said, "Dino, this could be a great, great movie," and to our amazement, Dino loved it. Dino said, "This is the Bible of the future" and 'This is the greatest book I ever read." My brother thought he was never going to understand this stuff, but he did and he bought the rights, but Federico died in a plane crash when David and I had just started working on the picture.

Raffaella's dedication to the project was never in doubt. When she went off to Tahiti for over two years (at age 23) to work on *Hurricane* and *Reef* and build a hotel, she left a note on her father's desk telling him he could not start *Dune* without her. During her time away making *Conan* with John Milius, her father roped in Universal on the venture, oversaw Ridley Scott's brief tenure, and renegotiated their option with Herbert on not only the first book but all its sequels, written and unwritten.

Both she and her father were unfamiliar with *Eraserhead*, which they didn't see until five or six months into working with Lynch (she laughed, he hated it). It was entirely on the strength of *Elephant Man* that Dino and Raffaella chose this oddball filmmaker. Normally a tough audience member, Raffaella had been moved to tears by the biopic, and she knew she had found her director.

Lynch was more unsure about Dino, who had a reputation for riding roughshod over directors and having a heavy hand in all his movies. Yet on first meeting at De Laurentiis' Beverly Hills office, where Dino served Lynch a great cappuccino, the director was instantly charmed by the producer's enthusiasm and warmth. That feeling was apparently mutual, as Lynch became a fixture at the De Laurentiis household, befriending not only Dino, Federico, and Raffaella, but also Dino's wife, actress Silvana Mangano, and their other daughters.

"I'd heard a lot of stories about Dino before I met him, and I didn't think it would go over well," Lynch said in the 2001 documentary *Dino De Laurentiis: The Last Movie Mogul*. "I didn't think I would like being around Dino. So, I went in with that in my mind, and as soon as I entered his office, even, as soon as I sat down, I felt like I was at home. It was strange, though."

Lynch was gravitating toward *Dune* far more than he had to *Star Wars*, especially after his friends began telling him, "Oh my God, that's the number one science-fiction book ever." This was a chance to design four different worlds out of whole cloth, branded with his unique aesthetic, through the guidance of Herbert's text.

"I read it and I had a meeting with Dino and I liked him right away," Lynch said in a 1985 publicity featurette. "I didn't know if I would like Dino, and I loved the book and so we started working together, but his daughter Raffaella was the producer and she was fantastic. She did a fantastic job of putting together a giant machine."

In the end, Lynch was lured not only by a handsome paycheck but also a three-picture deal which included—in principle—a promise from Dino to bankroll both *Ronnie Rocket* and *Dune II* upon the completion of the first *Dune* movie, with the intent of eventually making three *Dune* films altogether. Becoming "Mr. Dune" would not only give Lynch financial security but a real shot at finally making his *Ronnie* opus in true "one for them, one for me" fashion. Yet Lynch knew the De Laurentiis clan wanted the more straightforward director of *Elephant Man* and not the avant-garde artiste of *Eraserhead*. The problem with trying to muffle the artistic impulses of someone like Lynch is eventually the sleeper must awaken.

Building Four Worlds: Designing and Scripting *Dune*

O nce he signed on to what became a three-year odyssey, Lynch began assembling his core group of designers and writers for a "blue sky" period of inspiration.

In May 1981, Lynch took an office on the Universal lot. He and *Elephant Man* cowriters De Vore and Bergren (along with Federico) traveled to Washington State's Olympic Peninsula for a week-long consultation with Frank Herbert. The author's six-acre farm in Port Townsend—which included a solar collector, wind plant, and methane fuel generator—proved an ideal launch pad for the screenplay.

Bergren recalled [in *Prevue*]:

> It's an ecological haven, a very functional place. Our conversations centered on the topography and ethnography of *Dune*, but just as much to get into a general mode of orientation . . . One learns to combine elements, to fuse them, rearrange them, always keeping the intention where you can't keep the letter. Overall, we tried to maintain the attitude of the book, its feel, and its values. That was less of a challenge, though, than creating the structure.

As De Vore remembers it:

> We were given a free hand, but our biggest problem was length. We did four outlines before we started to flesh it out. Certain scenes in the novel were very hard to abbreviate or exclude because they were so wonderful and powerful. Additionally, there would be many touches that readers would remember and want to see again. For instance, the scene where Jessica undergoes the rite to become the reverend mother could never be eliminated. But that's a complex scene, with a myriad of elements that culminate and begin again. It must be cut down to an essence, or 20 to 30 pages could be used up right there.

The team wrote the first two drafts together in June, but their original script (meant to be broken into two movies) exceeded 200 pages when De Vore and Bergren had difficulty jettisoning what they felt to be key book scenes. That length, combined with Dino's insistence that the story not be split in two, led the pair to part ways with Lynch, who also wanted to add some of his own original scenes to the movie against their wishes. Now six months into the process, the director felt more in tune with Dino's expectations.

Lynch says in *Room to Dream*:

> Dino didn't understand that kind of abstraction or poem, no fucking way—he wants action. I felt bad when Chris and Eric left because they were banking on working on *Dune*, but I just continued working on the script on my own. I don't recall Dino ever saying anything about the script except that he liked it or "I no understand this." He'd never get ideas or anything; he would just react to things. Dino wanted to make money, and I didn't have a problem with that—that's just who Dino was.

The *Dune* production had another major hurdle to overcome: George Lucas' *Star Wars* movies had generously mined much material from Herbert's novel, including settings, themes, and terminology.

As Herbert told a reporter in *The Daily News* shortly after *Star Wars* opened:

> The editor of the *Village Voice* has been calling me and asking me if I have seen *Star Wars* and if I'm going to sue. I will try hard not to sue. I have no idea what book of mine it fits, but I suspect it may be *Dune* since in that I had a Princess Alia and the movie has a Princess Leia. And I hear there is a sandworm caucus and hooded dwellers in the desert, just like *Dune*.

In that same article, George Lucas is quoted as saying the only similarity between the book and the film "is that they both have deserts."

By December 1977, Herbert was quoted in the *Eugene Register Guard* saying he had seen the film (he was bored and his wife fell asleep) and had considered suing 20th Century Fox and Lucas over it.

Herbert opined of Lucas' possible plagiarism:

> I think there's reason to believe he did. Whether it's actionable, I'm not the one to judge. Larry Niven, Jerry Pournelle, Ted Sturgeon, Isaac Asimov, Barry Malzberg, and a few others of us who recognized elements of things we had done—or thought we did at least—in *Star Wars* are starting an organization that will be called, "We're Too Big to Sue George Lucas." This will only be viable if Lucas

agrees to become an honorary member and picks up all the dinner tabs whenever we get together.

"Through humor, Dad tried to mask the pain," Brian Herbert wrote in *Dreamer of Dune*, admitting his father was "livid" over the perceived theft.

Herbert later recalled in his book *Eye* that Lynch had trouble with all the material that had already been mined by *Star Wars*, which would have made the *Dune* movie a Johnny-come-lately in the eyes of the public. The 2012 Disney movie *John Carter* experienced this same effect when—despite Lucas having clearly been influenced by Edgar Rice Burroughs—the actual adaptation of *A Princess of Mars* (1912) was seen as too similar to *Star Wars* films, especially 2002's *Attack of the Clones*. Partly as a result, *John Carter* became one of the biggest box office bombs in history.

All in, Herbert found what he often referred to as "sixteen points of identity" between the *Dune* novels and *Star Wars* movies, including:

—**Desert Planet Setting:** Large parts of *Dune* and the first *Star Wars* take place on the desert planets of Arrakis and Tatooine, respectively.

—**Biblical Heroes:** In the New Testament, Paul was one of the 12 apostles, while Luke was a companion of Paul's among the 70 disciples appointed by Jesus.

—**Twins:** In *Dune,* Paul Atreides is the father of brother-sister twins Leto II and Ghanima. In *Star Wars*, Anakin Skywalker sired the twins Luke and Leia.

—**Villainous Family:** In *Dune*, a spice vision reveals that Lady Jessica is the daughter of Baron Harkonnen (with Paul being his grandson). In *The Empire Strikes Back,* it is shockingly revealed that Darth Vader is Anakin Skywalker, Luke's father.

—**Spice:** In *Dune*, the spice melange is the valuable resource used as both a life-extending drug and fuel for facilitating space travel. In the first *Star Wars*, the spice mines of Kessel are mentioned, later shown in 2018's *Solo: A Star Wars Story*. Running the illicit spice drug became a plot point in both 2019's *The Rise of Skywalker* and 2022's *The Book of Boba Fett* series.

—**Water Farming:** In *Dune,* moisture traps and dew collectors are used to harvest what little water there is to be had on Arrakis. In *Star Wars*, Luke's Uncle Owen runs a moisture farm on Tatooine using machines called vaporators.

—**Psychic Powers:** In *Dune*, the Bene Gesserit use a talent called the Voice to force others to do their bidding. In *Star Wars*, Obi-Wan Kenobi uses similar Jedi mind tricks which are later employed by other Force users in the series.

—**Training Robots:** In *Dune*, Paul Atreides fights an automated target dummy for blade training under Gurney Halleck. In *Star Wars*, Luke Skywalker fights a floating training remote with a lightsaber under the guidance of Obi-Wan Kenobi.

—**Empires:** In *Dune*, the Emperor of the Known Universe and central villain is the conniving Shaddam Corrino IV. In *Star Wars,* the main baddie is the Sith Lord Sheev Palpatine, also known simply as the Emperor. While the Emperor is only mentioned in the first film, he is introduced briefly in *The Empire Strikes Back* and becomes a central villain in *Return of the Jedi* as well as the prequels and sequels.

Raffaella De Laurentiis agreed [*Marquee* Vol. 9 #8]:

> A lot of things in *Star Wars* belong to *Dune*. I think George Lucas was real smart. It's difficult to turn *Dune* into what he did. With the idea of the Force, Lucas concentrated about 15 chapters, and that's smart . . . We turned to David Lynch out of fear of making a cold picture. Technology can look very cold in a sci-fi picture. We knew from David's earlier work that he could put heart in the characters, so that the audience would have more to hang onto than the special effects.

"What's great about the book is that so much of it is below the surface," Lynch said in the same interview. "A great film like *Star Wars* is, to my taste, too much on the surface. Also, in many science-fiction films, the human scale is missing. That's the reason I was asked to direct *Dune*."

It's not surprising that Lucas and others would continue mining Herbert's work for source material in the decades that followed. For example, the villainous Trade Federation in 1999's *The Phantom Menace* is quite similar to *Dune*'s CHOAM. The design of Jabba the Hutt in 1983's *Return of the Jedi* is strikingly similar to the description of Leto Atreides II in his God-Emperor form as a human-sandworm hybrid. The most recent major appropriation comes in J. J. Abrams' 2019 sequel *The Rise of Skywalker*, where Rey's strong connection to the Force allows her to commune with all the Jedi who ever lived. This is similar to how both Jessica and her unborn daughter Alia absorb all of Reverend Mother Ramallo's knowledge as well as that of all past reverend mothers during a Water of Life ceremony.

Despite having only previously penned abstract art films like *Eraserhead*, Lynch was no stranger to proper screenplay structure. During his studies at the AFI in the early '70s, he learned a surefire technique for crafting a screenplay, not dissimilar to Howard Hawks' famous mantra of "five good scenes, no bad ones."

Lynch in a video interview for *Frame Into Focus*:

> I met Frank Daniel at the American Film Institute, who was dean of the school, the Center for Advanced Film Studies. He taught a way to do it. You get yourself a pack of 3×5 cards, and you write a scene on each card. When you have 70 scenes, you have a feature film. So, on each card, you write the heading of a scene, then the next card the second scene, third scene, fourth scene, until you have 70 cards, each with the name of the scene. Then you flesh out each of the cards and walk away, you've got a script.

When Lynch turned in his initial 17 pages to Dino, the producer was suitably impressed, referring to them as the best *Dune* pages he had read from any writer. Six drafts in, Lynch's final version of the *Dune* script—which compresses the entire first book into one movie—crept up to 135 pages, with the intent of making a three-hour epic. The shooting draft was completed on December 9, 1982. "It took David to break the code for how to make this book into a film," Raffaella told *American Film*.

But as Lynch told that same magazine, he was hamstrung by many factors right from the start, including a contractual PG rating that would ensure maximum yield from a four-quadrant family audience.

"In some ways, I know I've had to hold back," Lynch said. "For one thing, this film has got to be PG. You can think of some strange things to do, but as soon as they throw in PG, a lot of them go out the window. I kind of like to go off the track, to go off in a strange direction, but I haven't been able to do that. But there are little things, a lot of them, that are strange and exciting."

Simultaneous to the writing was the initial design phase of *Dune*, spearheaded by production designer Anthony Masters, a veteran of over fifty films who had been Oscar-nominated for his game-changing art direction on Stanley Kubrick's 1968 *2001: A Space Odyssey*. Masters happened to have already read half of the *Dune* book only six months before Dino called him with an offer to design the film version. Masters later said in *Prevue* #56 that the offer was given with Dino's promise, "This-a film so good, you going to pay me to do it."

As Masters explained in *Cinefex* #21, "For *Dune*, David's first dictum was: 'If it's been done before, throw it out!' And although we were aware of, and had available, some of the design work done for the Jodorowsky and Scott versions of *Dune*, we immediately decided to throw that out and start totally fresh."

Masters and Lynch began the grueling process of designing what would eventually become 75 sets, an ordeal that would take close to a full year.

"I enjoy the organization and business side," Masters said in *Prevue* #56. "Knowing the details are arranged, that schedules and budgets have been ironed out, puts me at ease. I don't work well if I feel everything is in turmoil. There are no rules, no books to read when one starts a project of this magnitude. It must all come from my mind—and the director's."

"Dino was interested in me because of *The Elephant Man*," Lynch told *American Film* in 1984. "He wanted to make a science-fiction film that was about people and not about ray guns and spaceships. We wanted to make everything very real and believable. It's not high-tech sci-fi, like most of the outer space stuff you see. Everything looks old, like it's been around for a while."

While Lynch's script stayed fairly true to Herbert's book, including the many elements it shared with *Star Wars*, he and Masters were adamant that their movie not replicate the space fantasy aesthetic of *Star Wars* or the many other sci-fi films that had followed in the wake of *2001*. That meant the chunky, hyper-detailed, kitbashed surfaces of spacecraft were verboten.

"David didn't want the film to have a futuristic look," said Masters. "Instead, we went to the past, to a '50s style of overelaborated, functionless decoration."

The initial art department was led by Masters, who was in charge of budgeting, buying materials, and ultimately building everything. The group also included commercial illustrator Ron Miller as the main concept designer, alongside his wife, Judith Miller, who developed foamcore models of the various ships and sets. George Jensen (*Close Encounters of the Third Kind*) and Mentor Huebner served as storyboard artists. In addition to his boarding work on *Blade Runner*, Huebner was a veteran of a few other large-scale De Laurentiis productions, including *King Kong*, *The White Buffalo*, and *Flash Gordon*. This tight-knit group toiled in a small bungalow on the Universal lot. Marty Kline of John Dykstra's effects house Apogee, Inc., would also do some storyboarding during that company's brief tenure on the film.

One individual noticeably not invited back was H. R. Giger, and it may not have been simply because the filmmakers wanted to start from scratch. According to Giger, there was some animosity between him and Lynch over the iconic "Chestburster" creature from *Alien*, which Lynch felt too closely resembled the baby from *Eraserhead* (a film Giger admired).

As Giger told it in 2009 [*Vice*].

> *Dune* never happened with me. I was asked to do it two times. Once with Jodorowsky and then another time with Ridley Scott, but the daughter of Dino De Laurentiis had the rights for *Dune* and she gave them to David Lynch. Lynch was not very happy with me. He said that I had stolen his ideas, that I'd stolen his baby. I said I liked his baby from *Eraserhead*. I always said very nice things about him, but he was a little strange. And he was jealous because I exhibited in a New York gallery and he couldn't. He was sour. But I like him.

When Lynch visited the De Laurentiis family at their home in Abano Terme early in the process, Dino took him and Raffaella on an impromptu (and speedy) car trip to Venice, arriving directly in St. Mark's Square. Lynch took an instant shine to St. Mark's Basilica, specifically its intricate mosaics with elaborate geometric patterns. Lynch came back to the art department "raving" about the mosaic floor inlays.

"My favorite [set] is the Great Hall, influenced in its design by the cathedral in St. Mark's Square in Venice," said Masters in the January 1985 edition of *Film Review*. "The floor of the set has tile patterns based on the cathedral's paving."

Designing the Great Arrakeen Hall to Lynch's specifications proved to be a challenge, requiring at least fifty sketches. Besides the Byzantine and Venetian influences, *Dune*'s look would also take cues from Egyptian and early Victorian styles. The design team wanted each of the four planets portrayed to have a unique look so that the audience could instantly recognize where they were at any given time. This was laid out in a simple visual framework with different building blocks for each world:

Arrakis = Stone
Caladan = Wood
Giedi Prime = Steel
Kaitain = Gold

Masters explained [*Enterprise Incidents* #28]:

> David Lynch was totally convinced of the reality of each of these
> planets, and so he insisted that each appear to be a real place. I even
> drew an atlas of Arrakis so that the characters could find their way
> around. I think because we believed in these planets as real places, it
> helped the detail and the realism of the design of the sets. It helped
> make the sets seem as real a place as New York. You convince your-
> self it's real, and that makes the sets real . . .

The Emperor's planet of Kaitain was notable for its buildings of solid
gold and jade, with the throne room's baroque interior taking cues from the
Moorish architecture of Spain's Alhambra Fortress in Granada. The over-
industrialized Giedi Prime, a planet literally drowning in machinery and
seas of oil, is mostly built out of black metal and green porcelain, none of
which is meant to please the eye. Lynch's deep attraction to all things industrial dating back to *Eraserhead* is on full display here.

In Herbert's book, the ornithopter (a light aircraft) is described as having wings that flap like a bird's in steady beat: "Paul depressed the glowing
action-sequence switch on his panel. The wings snapped back and down,
hurling the 'thopter out of its nest. Power surged from the jetpods as the
wings locked into lift attitude."

While artist Ron Cobb had attempted to design a slick version of this
for Jodorowsky's *Dune*, the Lynch team could not conceptualize a way to
make the winged flight look anything less than laughable on screen. It took
over 150 revisions before the Atreides and Harkonnen versions of ornithopters were finalized. The Atreides' version had a diamond shape that
folded in to protect it from sandstorms, while the Harkonnens had 'thopters made from three interconnected steel tubes. Both ran on what Lynch
termed "ether benders," which were large magnetic pads with antigravita-
tional ability underneath each vehicle.

Ron Miller's contribution was also substantial, consisting of 15 large concept paintings as well as a few dozen illustrations. Drawing on his past work
with the Smithsonian Institution as a director of exhibits on futuristic and
astronomical art, Miller also provided the *Dune* production with much-need-
ed scientific guidance, at one point even bringing in astronomical consult-
ant William K. Hartman to make sure the fantastical concepts remained as
grounded as possible.

The North Star for the pre-production team remained Herbert's books. Although Herbert himself was consulting, even providing them with a pronunciation list for the many foreign terms, a relatively unsung contributor to the *Dune* literary legacy also had an impact: artist John Schoenherr. Posthumously inducted into the Science Fiction and Fantasy Hall of Fame in 2015, Schoenherr was the quintessential *Dune* artist, having illustrated the original serialization of Herbert's story in *Analog*, which earned him a Hugo Award. His painted cover graced the first edition of the *Dune* novel in 1967 followed by the serialization of *Children of Dune* in 1970, then *The Illustrated Dune* (1978), *Heretics of Dune* (1984), and *Chapterhouse Dune* (1985).

Herbert wrote in "Dune Genesis" [*Omni*, 1980]:

> You can imagine my surprise to learn that John Schoenherr, one of the world's most foremost wildlife artists and illustrators, had been living in my head with the same images. People find it difficult to believe that John and I had no consultations prior to his painting of the *Dune* illustrations. I assure you the paintings were a wonderful surprise to me. The Sardaukar appear like the weathered stones of Dune. The Baron's paunch could absorb a world. The ornithopters are insects preying on the land. The sandworms are Earth shipworms grown monstrous. Stilgar glares out at us with the menace of a warlock. What especially pleases me is the interwoven themes, the fuguelike relationships of images that exactly replay the way *Dune* took shape.

When it came time to tackle the film's keystone visual, the giant sandworms of Arrakis, Miller and the rest of the team struggled to land on a definitive design. Toward the beginning, Lynch grew fixated on a photograph of a red-and-black piebald elephant trunk, so that became the coloration that stuck, although in the final film, there is so much sand covering the worms that they mostly look gray. Masters tried a design using a three-lobed mouth but deemed it too close to Schoenherr's illustrations, only to eventually come back to that striking image.

As Miller said later [*Cinefex*]:

> The worms went through many changes, mostly having to do with varying their degree of obsceneness. After all, we were all more than well aware of the fact that we were dealing with the greatest phallic symbols in the universe, and that we would have to be very careful about our worm designs and the camera angles we would use to shoot

them. Eventually, though, the worms came around full circle, right back to the drawings Tony had done that looked like Schoenherr's. And I was happy. I liked that three-lobed mouth and argued for it for a long time.

"As for riding the worms, I'm going to show it three or four different ways," Lynch told *Marquee* Vol 9 #8. "These worms are 1,500 feet of pure raw power, and that's what will be on the screen."

After many months of toil—as well as an elaborate presentation of production art, props, and costumes—the *Dune* team finally got the green light from De Laurentiis and Universal Pictures to make the film in June 1982.

Casting a Galaxy of Stars

Casting director Jane Jenkins was tasked with the daunting job of assembling the film's massive international cast. Along with her partner Janet Hirshenson, Jenkins had formed The Casting Company and by this time had put together casts for films like *It's My Turn*, *The Escape Artist*, *Night Shift*, *Frances*, *Breathless*, and the De Laurentiis production of *The Dead Zone*.

Thanks to Jenkins and her original files stored at the Special Collections department of the Academy of Motion Picture Arts and Sciences, I was able to uncover a flurry of fascinating early casting ideas that have not previously been made public.

A tentative cast list from Jenkins' file dated November 24, 1982, shows just how much the players changed between then and the start of shooting in March 1983 Here are the roles that would either be swapped or completely recast:

PAUL: Val Kilmer *[no roles listed]* or Tom Cruise (*Taps*, *The Outsiders*)

JESSICA: Glenn Close (*The World According to Garp*)

DOCTOR YUEH: John Hurt (*The Elephant Man*)

PITER: Leonardo Cimino (*Amityville II*)

MAPES: Eileen Atkins (*Smiley's People*)

IRULAN: Anne-Louise Lambert (*Picnic at Hanging Rock*)

THE DOCTOR: Jack Nance (*Eraserhead*, *Hammett*)

SARDAUKAR GENERAL: Richard Lynch (*The Formula*)

Below is a listing of those who actually made it to the front lines of filming on David Lynch's *Dune* . . . and many of those who did not.

Kyle MacLachlan ("Paul Atreides") b. 1959

CONSIDERED: Val Kilmer (top of the list), Tom Cruise, Michael Biehn, Kevin Costner, Lewis Smith, Martin Hewitt, Rob Lowe, Dexter Fletcher, Timothy Hutton, John Dukakis, Kenneth Branagh, Griffin O'Neal, Steve Austin, Konrad Sheehan, John Stockwell, Matt Dillon, Vincent Spano, Michael O'Keefe, Timothy Patrick Murphy, Bradford Bancroft, Sean Penn, Zeljko Ivanek, Mark Patton, Zach Galligan

The lead of *Dune* would essentially have to play two parts: a strong but naïve royal heir named Paul Atreides and the powerful Fremen leader he becomes. The part needed someone who could project both boyishness and authority, and as Herbert had hoped from the beginning, the idea was to cast a virtual unknown.

Jane Jenkins used a 1923 photograph of the wedding of future King George VI and Queen Elizabeth as a helpful tool for auditioning actors to visualize the royal air of the Atreides family. There were up-and-comers seen in London like Kenneth Branagh or *Elephant Man* co-star Dexter Fletcher, although much of the main casting centered around New York and Los Angeles.

Others considered for the part ranged from Timothy Hutton, an Oscar winner for his feature debut in 1981's *Ordinary People*, to his *Taps* co-star Sean Penn, who was about to rocket to fame in *Fast Times at Ridgemont High*. Notable family connections included Ryan O'Neal's son Griffin O'Neal (who led *The Escape Artist* while Jenkins was at American Zoetrope), as well as John Dukakis (*Jaws 2*), whose father Michael would become the (unelected) 1988 Democratic Presidential nominee. Several rising stars who Jenkins helped cast in Coppola's *The Outsiders* were on deck, including Tom Cruise, Matt Dillon, and Rob Lowe, the latter of whom supposedly turned down the part because he heard (incorrectly) that his character would become a worm in later movies. That honor would go to Leto II, Paul's son.

Of this crop, two main contenders emerged: Tom Cruise and Val Kilmer, both of whom met Lynch on the same day in New York on September 20, 1982. Born Thomas Cruise Mapother IV, the 20-year-old Cruise had no formal training as an actor but signed with CAA shortly after arriving in Los Angeles. He quickly secured supporting roles in *Endless Love* and *Taps*. By 1982, he already shot his part as Steve Randle in *The Outsiders*, as well as toplining two teen sex comedies that would not be released until 1983: Curtis Hanson's forgettable *Losin' It* and Paul Brickman's zeitgeist-defining hit *Risky Business*. The latter would put Cruise on the road to becoming one of the biggest movie stars of all time, but when he was auditioning for the part of Paul, his ultimate trajectory was still a question mark.

Unlike Cruise, whose only acting experience prior to Hollywood was a New Jersey high school production of *Guys and Dolls*, 23-year-old Val Kilmer had more pedigree, though no actual cinematic visibility. He had been the youngest applicant ever accepted at Julliard's Drama Division (age 17) and played the servant to Mandy Patinkin's Hotspur in a Central Park performance of *Henry IV, Part* 1 opposite Kenneth McMillan and John Goodman (as well as Kilmer's former classmates Kevin Spacey and Linda Kozlowski). Jenkins was hot on Kilmer, having offered him the lead role of Ponyboy in *The Outsiders*, although he turned it down to make his Broadway debut in *The Slab Boys* opposite Sean Penn and Kevin Bacon.

While making inquiries in the Seattle Repertory Theatre scene, casting associate Elisabeth Leustig came across Kyle MacLachlan, just graduated from the University of Washington. Raised in a middle-class Republican household, the son of a stockbroker and a homemaker active in the arts community, MacLachlan began participating in a Yakima teen theater group at age 15, including as Henry Higgins in a production of *My Fair Lady*. Supposedly a descendant of Johann Sebastian Bach, the WASP-y MacLachlan was much loved by teachers, classmates, and co-stars. He eventually graduated cum laude from UW's Professional Actor Training Program, where he took his first lead role in a play by Welsh dramatist Emlyn Williams titled *The Corn is Green* about Wyoming coal miners, giving him the confidence to carry a show. Although *Dune* is often touted as his first time on camera, he earned a modicum of film experience while still a student, and on a horror classic, no less.

"I was an extra in a movie shot on campus called *The Changeling* starring George C. Scott," MacLachlan told *The University of Washington Alumni Magazine*. "I was paid $10 to walk up some stairs. It was my first movie experience and I had no clue what was going on, but I remember thinking it was kind of cool."

Upon meeting MacLachlan, Leustig put him on tape and recommended him to Lynch and De Laurentiis. He was then flown to L.A. to meet David, but the one-on-one "took a belligerent turn," according to Jenkins, with MacLachlan saying he only wanted to do the film if it was a pure adaptation of the book.

"That's my story," MacLachlan told *The News Tribune* in February 1984. "A silent rebel. Even in high school, I was the first one to be kind of punk before it was fashionable. I'm like Paul in the film. He's like a wolf, watchful and wary. I watch before I move."

This bold tactic worked in MacLachlan's favor, and after two different screen tests, Lynch decided to give him the part.

"In Kyle's first screen test, we could see that the kid could act," Raffaella told *The New York Times* in May 1984. "You have to act, or nobody will believe you're the new Messiah. The look was there too, but he had a punk haircut that didn't help."

"I didn't see the first screen test, but the second one made my stomach turn," MacLachlan told *Los Angeles Times* in 1990.

"We had so much trouble with Kyle's hair," Lynch recalled. "It was really straight, and it didn't look quite so dashing. But he didn't look like a potato, so we had him come down and test and he was fantastic. We just hit it off. We're both from the Northwest, and we had a lot to talk about, like we had both been to the same lake."

MacLachlan added:

> The first time we stepped in front of the camera together, it was a special moment. I had to do this big speech right to the lens, and it just blew my mind. I had never worked with a camera before, and I said to David, "I don't know if I can do this." But he said I would be fine. When I went back to my hotel room that night, there was a bottle of red wine on the bureau—we're both really into red wine—it was his way of saying "You're the guy."

"Like Paul Atreides, Kyle has gone from being a pretty together kid to being a together young man," Lynch stated in *Marquee* Vol. 9 #8. "Kyle has been solid gold. He's young, but he's already a great actor."

Kilmer was reportedly devastated to lose the *Dune* role, but would make his feature debut as the lead in Zucker–Abrams–Zucker's Cold War parody *Top Secret!* in 1984.

MacLachlan summed up his experience in December 1984 [*Enterprise Incidents*]:

> I say I've been given a tremendous start, because everything I believe in has been reinforced by this film. In the work and projects I'm involved in, it's very important to me to do things that say something or teach, be it good or indirectly bad toward a good end. I view acting as teaching, as healing, as helping, as enlightening, instructing, whatever. That's what I am as an actor right now, and with that goes a responsibility to the people who are seeing what I'm doing. With *Dune*, I feel it's all happened. I don't know if it happens very often, but I don't think it does.

Kenneth McMillan ("Baron Vladimir Harkonnen")
b. 1932, d. 1989

CONSIDERED: Paul Smith, Chuck Mitchell, Orson Welles, Divine

Ron Miller reported that production was at one point interested in casting singer-performer–drag queen Harris Glenn Milstead, better known by his stage name Divine. Considered the muse of director John Waters, Divine appeared in several early films of the Baltimore shock auteur, including *Pink Flamingos* and *Female Trouble*. Supposedly health concerns got in the way of casting Divine, although the idea of the actor behind such outrageous antics as eating dog feces in *Pink Flamingos* playing *Dune*'s literal heavy shows how big Lynch wanted the performance to be. Divine later branched out into non-Waters films like *Trouble in Mind*, though the two reunited one last time for the 1988 commercial hit *Hairspray*. Divine passed away from heart failure at age 42, a mere three weeks after *Hairspray* opened.

Another hefty thespian considered was veteran exploitation actor Chuck Mitchell, a singer and stand-up comedian who had his profile elevated when he played the title strip club owner in Bob Clark's smash hit 1981 sex comedy *Porky's*.

Born in Brooklyn in 1932, the Obie Award–winning character actor McMillan had been a salesman at Gimbels in Manhattan's Herald Square before deciding to make a serious go at acting around age 30. His first on-screen role didn't come until he was 41, when he appeared in Sidney Lumet's 1973 police drama *Serpico*, a Dino De Laurentiis production. He went on to have roles (often typecast as police officers) in several hit films, including *The Stepford Wives*, the TV version of *Salem's Lot*, Ulu Grosbard's crime film *True Confessions*, and as the bigoted fire chief Willie Conklin in Miloš Forman's *Ragtime*, another mammoth De Laurentiis production. At the time of his *Dune* casting, McMillan was familiar to TV audiences as Valerie Harper's grumpy boss Jack Doyle on the sitcom *Rhoda*.

"Whenever people recognize me and say, 'Who are you and why do I know you?', my mentioning *Rhoda* provides them with a total lock-in," McMillan told *The Pittsburgh Press* in February of 1983, shortly before filming with Lynch. "For *Dune*, which I'll do in Mexico starting in mid-April, I should be heavy. I play the Baron. I never walk. I float. It's science fiction with humor."

Right before *Dune*, McMillan reunited with Forman for eventual Best Picture winner *Amadeus* as the merchant Michael Schlumberg, a character not in the original play who only appears in the 2002 director's cut. He was under discussion to portray the father in Pittsburgh Public Theater's production of *Long Day's Journey into Night* when he landed roles in both films and had to pull out of the stage play. He also postponed playing the lead in San Diego's La Jolla Playhouse production of *Galileo* by a year due to his *Dune* commitments.

"I love to do plays—that's all I did until seven years ago when I did my first film, *Serpico*," McMillan told *Pittsburgh Post-Gazette* in November 1983. "The money's so good in film. You have to be prepared to take a loss when you do theater."

1984 would be a banner year for McMillan, with not only *Dune* and *Amadeus* but also the romance *Reckless*, the Goldie Hawn comedy *Protocol*, the crime drama *The Pope of Greenwich Village*, a pair of TV movies, and a lead role in the CBS series *Suzanne Pleshette is Maggie Briggs*, which only lasted six episodes.

Francesca Annis ("Lady Jessica") b. 1945

CONSIDERED: Glenn Close (top of the list), Joan Hackett, Kathryn Harrold, Rachel Ward, Lindsay Wagner, Olga Karlatos, Katharine Ross, JoBeth Williams, Bonnie Bedelia, Samantha Eggar, Gayle Hunnicutt, Carolyn Seymour, Bibi Besch, Meryl Streep, Jacqueline Bisset, Joanna Miles, Yvette Mimieux, Rebecca Stanley, Claudette Nevins, Shannon Wilcox, Vanessa Redgrave, Gena Rowlands, Ellen Burstyn, Fionnula Flanagan, Anouk Aimée, Louise Fletcher, Catherine Deneuve, Florinda Bolkan, Claudia Cardinale, Helen Mirren, Blair Brown, Christine Lahti, Nicola Pagett, Lisa Eichhorn, Kathleen Turner, Lee Remick, Ann Margaret, Lesley-Anne Down

Oscar-winning actress Glenn Close (*Fatal Attraction, The Big Chill*) was considered the top choice for the role of the regal concubine and Bene Gesserit Lady Jessica. A casting sheet from August 23, 1982, has Close's name with a rectangle drawn around it and a notation that says "YES," with Joan Hackett's name as "BACKUP."

"I was offered *Dune* right after *The World According to Garp*," Close told *Entertainment Weekly* in 2005. "I turned it down because there was this scene where they were running away from the big worm or whatever it was and the woman fell down, and everyone had to come back to get her. I said, 'What a cliché. I don't want to be the woman who falls down. I want to be the woman who's running just as fast as everyone else.'"

Instead, the filmmakers went with a name relatively unknown in the United States: Francesca Annis. Born to an English father and a Brazilian mother, Annis was trained as a Russian-style ballerina. She made her film debut as one of the youngsters in 1959's *The Cat Gang* (opposite future Boba Fett actor Jeremy Bulloch), but her appearance as Elizabeth Taylor's handmaiden Eiras in 1963's megabucks epic *Cleopatra* put her on the map. She earned the role after a chance meeting with director Joseph L. Mankiewicz, whom she came across as he was exiting a building.

"We had an informal chat, and the next thing I knew I had an acting career," Annis told *The Guardian* in 2013.

By 1964, she had roles in five major films, including the title part of a somnambulant young woman with ESP in *The Eyes of Annie Jones*. This aptly prepared her for a nude rendition of sleepwalking Lady Macbeth delivering her soliloquy in Roman Polanski's 1971 film version of *Macbeth*. Although many stage and TV roles followed (mainly in the UK), by the early '80s, she was still a little-known entity outside of Britain. When her agent first rang about *Dune*, Annis blew off two calls from Lynch, believing another actress had already signed for that part. Only when Raffaella and Lynch offered to fly to London to meet her was Annis' interest piqued.

"We wanted her, but she was very aloof about it," Raffaella admitted to *Sunday Sun*.

"I am not a science-fiction fan, but I loved the script and the role," Annis told *Evening Post* in December 1984. "It was then that I read the book—the first *Dune* book."

Just the year prior to making *Dune*, Annis had a major scene opposite Freddie Jones as the mystical Widow of The Web in Peter Yates' fantasy epic *Krull*, a big-budget flop blending sci-fi and high fantasy to dreary effect. Annis' showcase scene presented her in both full glamour mode as well as complex old-age makeup that took six hours to apply. She and Jones would be reunited on *Dune* when the filmmakers saw fit to hand her the plum role of Jessica (arguably the second lead of the movie), which Annis still considers a career high point.

"Getting the part in *Dune* was pretty amazing," she told *The Guardian*. "I couldn't believe David Lynch and his team wanted to meet me."

Interestingly, decades later, Rebecca Ferguson would take inspiration from Lady Macbeth for her own portrayal of Jessica in 2021's *Dune*.

"That is something that was offered up on the platter of possible resources of knowledge for me when we were doing the role," Ferguson told *The Gate*. "It's a recurring resemblance, right? Whether it's Nietzsche . . . Shakespeare, wherever we go. It's the women behind the men."

Jürgen Prochnow ("Duke Leto Atreides") b. 1941

CONSIDERED: Rutger Hauer (top of the list), Gregory Peck, Charles Dance, Robert Duvall, Christopher Plummer, Richard Chamberlain, Charlton Heston, Richard Jordan, Roy Scheider, Richard Kiley, Klaus Kinski, Martin Landau, Anthony Zerbe, Donald Sutherland, Sam Wanamaker, Jean-Pierre Aumont, Raul Julia, Patrick O'Neal, Scott Hylands, Nicol Williamson, Maximilian Schell, Richard Harris

A paper in Jane Jenkins' casting notebook indicates that Rutger Hauer planned to shoot *The Osterman Weekend* in late 1982/early 1983 (which would have caused headaches for scheduling) and that his fee for *Dune* would be $400,000.

Also in the notebook is a fascinating query letter to George Chasin, the powerful attorney and talent agent at the Chasin–Park–Citron agency who had famously represented such heavyweight talents as Marilyn Monroe, Clark Gable, Montgomery Clift . . . and Gregory Peck. It is Peck that the letter concerns:

Dear Mr. Chasin,

As I mentioned in our phone conversation yesterday, I'm casting a film called Dune to be produced for Universal Pictures by Raffaella and Dino De Laurentiis and to be directed by David Lynch. We are interested in exploring the possibility of Gregory Peck playing the role of Duke Leto Atreides. For now, there is no shooting schedule, but we plan to start shooting by February or early March 1983. The script is not available right now, so I'm sending along a copy of the book for your perusal. Briefly, the story is as follows: The Duke Leto Atreides, leader of one of the royal houses of the empire in the universe, is going to control the desert planet Dune. A youth drug known as "spice" is the only export and much sought after throughout the universe. Shortly after the Duke takes control of Dune, he's murdered. His son Paul and his wife Jessica escape to the desert where they are found by a band of elusive desert nomads for whom very little is known because of their contempt for the city dwellers. In time, Paul becomes the leader of these people and they take back that which is rightfully theirs by overthrowing the family who had taken the planet from them. Jessica, who has taken the spice, gives birth to the late Duke's daughter and becomes a Reverend Mother. At this point, all we need to know is Mr. Peck's availability and an approximation of price. I look forward to hearing from you.

Sincerely,
Jane Jenkins
Casting Director

According to my conversation with Raffaella De Laurentiis, the role of the noble Duke was at one point offered to English actor Charles Dance, who turned it down. A Royal Shakespeare Company alum, at the time Dance had limited film and TV appearances, with only a small part as a henchman named Claus in the James Bond film *For Your Eyes Only*. His eventual sci-fi/fantasy bona fides include *Alien 3*, *Last Action Hero*, *Your Highness*, and *Godzilla: King of the Monsters*. He also won fans as the ruthless Tywin Lannister in HBO's *Game of Thrones*.

Even though Robert Duvall (*Tender Mercies*, *The Godfather*) was in heavy contention, the role would go to Jürgen Prochnow, a German actor who studied acting at the Folkwang University of the Arts in Essen. He cut his teeth in film roles for German luminaries like Rainer Werner Fassbinder (*The Merchant of Four Seasons*), Ulli Lommel (*The Tenderness of Wolves*), and Wolfgang Petersen (*The Consequence, One or the Other of Us*). His breakthrough came as the lead in Petersen's 1981 World War II epic *Das Boot*, playing a sympathetic anti-Nazi sea captain leading the very young crew of a German U-boat. Two years in production, it was the most expensive German film ever at the time but became a huge critical and commercial success, grossing $84.9 million and nominated for six Academy Awards.

Das Boot sparked a successful Hollywood career for Petersen (*The NeverEnding Story, In the Line of Fire, Air Force One, Troy*) and served as a launching pad for Prochnow, who immediately moved to Los Angeles to capitalize on his newfound demand. At first, the actor seemed to have been typecast, portraying German military figures in 1982's *Love is Forever* and Michael Mann's 1983 WWII horror picture *The Keep*, although he also got to play a Jewish writer hidden from the Nazis by a loving countess (Jacqueline Bisset) in 1984's *Forbidden*. Interestingly, *The Keep* would suffer a similar fate to *Dune*'s: it was an ambitious genre project from an exciting young director that ultimately saw its runtime gutted to the point of incoherence by the studio. It maintains a cult following for its atmospheric visuals.

Lynch was initially concerned about Prochnow's thick accent but loved the authority the actor projected. Only in a sci-fi movie could a German father and English mother convincingly have a son with an American accent! Around this time Prochnow was also considered for the title role of the T-800 killer cyborg in James Cameron's *The Terminator*, which would open less than two months before *Dune*. Of course, that plum role went to Arnold "I'll be back" Schwarzenegger, whom Prochnow would portray in the 2005 TV movie *See Arnold Run*. In *Dune*, Prochnow does get to utter the line "I'll be back," although as the far less frightening "I'll be back, son."

"I loved David Lynch," Prochnow said during a Q&A at the 26th Brussels International Festival of Fantastic Film in 2008. "Every day I enjoyed working with him in Mexico when we did this movie, so that was a great experience. Great director, full of fantasy. As I said, every day was special."

Sean Young ("Chani") b. 1959

CONSIDERED: Elizabeth McGovern, Ora Rubinstein, Kate Charleson, Robin Sherwood, Rebecca De Mornay, Talia Balsam, Heather Locklear, Alexa Coblentz, Michelle Avonne, Caroline O'Neill, Meg Tilly, Diane Lane, Pamela Ludwig, Ingrid Anderson, Michelle Meyrink, Jennifer Jason Leigh, Kathleen Beller, Jodi Thelen, Emma Samms, Blanche Baker, Melinda Culea, Alexandra Paul, Doran Clark, Daryl Hannah

Mary Sean Young was born and raised in Louisville, Kentucky, where the shy girl eventually became obsessed with dance. After attending a performing arts high school in Michigan—the Interlochen Arts Academy—Young skipped college for the bright lights of New York City. While studying daily at the School of American Ballet and working nights at the Sloan–Kettering Cancer Institute, she took acting lessons and found work at a top modeling agency. By 1979, she acquired representation that started putting her up for film work, including a screen test opposite Tom Selleck to play Marion Ravenwood in Steven Spielberg's *Raiders of the Lost Ark*. She was up against stiff competition from Debra Winger, Stephanie Zimbalist, Amy Irving, Barbara Hershey, and Karen Allen, the latter of whom locked down the part. This would not be Young's last chance to work with Harrison Ford, though.

"I think I was really new to acting or kind of raw, and I think that was what my agent was told at the time . . . that I was a little bit raw," Young said of her Indiana Jones audition. "I don't know what that means, but I was a newcomer at the time. It was a great opportunity."

She bounced back by nabbing her debut film role as an aspiring New York actress in James Ivory and Ismail Merchant's low-budget art movie *Jane Austen in Manhattan* opposite Robert Powell. That British-produced film was never given a release in the United States, but it helped her land the lively love interest part of MP Louise Cooper alongside P.J. Soles in Ivan Reitman's military comedy *Stripes*, two parts that the director saw over 300 actresses for. With Bill Murray in the lead and co-star Harold Ramis penning the script, the film was a box office winner at $85 million.

"I hear people describe that character as a nerd, but he wasn't a nerd," Ramis told *GQ* of his role as Russell Ziskey. "He was a cool guy! I got Sean Young in that movie!"

At age 21, Young won her best-known role: the replicant Rachel in Ridley Scott's 1982 science-fiction masterpiece *Blade Runner*. She beat out Nina Axelrod (*Motel Hell*) after a vibrant screen test that enchanted Scott, who compared her to Vivian Leigh in her "acerbic toughness" as well as her beauty, quirkiness, and intelligence.

Young said in the documentary *Dangerous Days*:

> I think he recognized he could make a classic beauty–type picture with me in it. I remember being a little freaked out when I heard I got the part. I remember being almost depressed. I know that's kind of a strange reaction, but I think that it was because when I got the part, I realized I had to live up to the responsibility of playing the part, and I was pretty young. It was very unknown what would be expected of me, so I was probably a little scared.

Despite playing an android, she manages one of the most deeply sympathetic and human portrayals in the movie, especially during a moving scene where she describes an implanted childhood memory. There is also the blistering (and not-so-mildly problematic) love scene with leading man Harrison Ford where he violently pushes her against apartment blinds. Shortly before Philip K. Dick passed away four months prior to the *Blade Runner* release, the original author referred to Young (according to *Vanity Fair*) as the "super-destructive cruel beautiful dark-haired woman that I eternally write about and now I've seen a photograph of her and I know that she exists and I will seek her out and presumably she will destroy me."

Although it wound up bombing at the 1982 summer box office while up against *Star Trek II: The Wrath of Khan*, *E.T. the Extra-Terrestrial,* and the De Laurentiis production of *Conan the Barbarian*, *Blade Runner* (and its numerous alternate cuts) has managed to surpass all those films in reputation due to stunning multi-layered dystopian visuals and resonant themes. It has influenced innumerable films since, including some of the vistas of Lynch's *Dune*.

"One of my favorite films of all time is *Blade Runner*," *Dune* effects supervisor Barry Nolan told *Cinefex*. "I love the atmosphere in that movie, and we tried a bit to emulate that look in *Dune*."

Lynch had also seen *Blade Runner*, as he told *Starlog* #87: "When I heard about *Blade Runner*, I thought that I should be doing the film. I identified with it 100%. I know that people who worked on it had seen *Eraserhead*. But I was disappointed in the overall movie . . . not enough of a storyline. Most of the images, though, were totally beautiful."

Young was scheduled to meet with *Dune* casting on August 20, 1982, but her name is crossed out on the sheet. She was scheduled to meet again on August 24, 1982, but her name is again crossed out. The reason? Young never arrived for her audition. That story will be recounted in the oral history section.

Patrick Stewart ("Gurney Halleck") b. 1940

CONSIDERED: Aldo Ray, Warren Oates, Jack Kehoe, Donald Moffat, Rod Taylor, Kevin Conway, Harris Yulin, Tom Atkins, Paul Dooley, Max Gail, Robert Loggia, Charles Hallahan

When it came time to cast Paul's martial arts instructor and weapons master Gurney, Lynch turned to an unlikely choice: Aldo Ray. A high school football player who had served as a frogman for the Navy during WWII, Ray made his screen debut as a college footballer in the 1951 film *Saturday's Hero*. This earned him a contract with Columbia Pictures and a starring role in George Cukor's comedy *The Marrying Kind*. His macho 6-foot presence served him well in a string of successful pictures like *Battle Cry*, *We're No Angels*, and *The Naked and the Dead*, but his reputation as a heavy drinker was already casting a pall over his career. His unreliability eventually caught up to him, and by the 1960s, his star began to wane. He still booked tough guy roles in films like John Wayne's *The Green Berets*, but by the '70s, he could no longer land big parts and was frequently cast as a redneck in grindhouse fare like *Angel Unchained* or *The Centerfold Girls*. He even appeared in a nonsexual role for the 1979 pornographic film *Sweet Savage* alongside Carol Connors.

By the early '80s, Ray was getting small parts in cheap horror fare like *Mongrel* when his ex-wife Johanna Ray (who later became Lynch's go-to casting director from *Blue Velvet* on) helped him land the role of Gurney in *Dune*. Ray had been filming *To Kill a Stranger* at Churubusco Studios alongside Dean Stockwell, also eventually cast. Lynch, a huge fan of Ray's since childhood, spotted him in the studio cafeteria while prepping *Dune* and, despite Dino's warning that he was a "lush," was excited about having Ray in the movie. Such a high-profile gig would have been a comeback role for him, to be sure. One interesting fact: during a fashion show scene in Aldo Ray's 1956 noir *Nightfall*, it is mentioned that one of the characters (played by *Elephant Man* co-star Anne Bancroft) is wearing "blue velvet."

Ray's alcoholism again reared its ugly head, and general word is he showed up to set unable to function due to his drinking. Lynch found Ray accompanied by his and Johanna's seventeen-year-old son Eric DaRe (later cast in *Twin Peaks*) in the studio's green room at 8 a.m., hungover from drinking all night. Eric looked sullen, and Lynch asked Aldo if he could perform, to which the former leading man said, "No." Lynch suddenly recalled the name "Patrick Stewart," and the rest is sci-fi history.

Stewart was born in Yorkshire, where he became friends with noted actor Brian Blessed (*Flash Gordon*). Both men received grants to attend the Old Vic Theatre School in Bristol. Stewart became a longstanding member of the Royal Shakespeare Company from 1966 to 1982. He found steady work on stage and screen, and just before he took his iconic role as Captain Jean-Luc Picard in *Star Trek: The Next Generation* (1987–94), the actor admitted that he had only been out of work for three weeks over the course of his entire career to that point. In 1979, he won an Olivier Award for playing Domitius Enobarbus in the RSC's *Antony and Cleopatra*.

Before he joined *Dune*, Stewart made his film debut playing the role of Ejlert Løvborg in 1975's *Hedda*, an adaptation of Henrik Ibsen's play *Hedda Gabler* starring Glenda Jackson. That same year he also appeared in the British thriller *Hennessy*, led by Americans Rod Steiger and Lee Remick. His first entry into the fantasy genre (before the *Star Trek* and *X-Men* franchises) was playing King Leodegrance in 1981's *Excalibur*, John Boorman's soaring take on Arthurian legend which also featured costumes by Bob Ringwood.

While Lynch and Raffaella were in London in 1982 to speak with Dexter Fletcher about playing Paul Atreides, the teenager was part of Trevor Nunn's Royal Shakespeare Company production of *Henry IV* with Patrick Stewart as the title king. Lynch saw Stewart sitting in a corner learning his lines and asked Fletcher who he was. "Oh, that's Patrick Stewart," said Fletcher, and Lynch wrote the name down.

However, there may in fact have been a mix-up, as Stewart explained at Emerald City Comic-Con in 2013:

> *Dune* was an accident . . . The fact is David Lynch thought he had cast someone else, so all of that happened in a kind of daze. On Friday morning, I was filming in the Mosel Valley in Germany, and on Saturday night, I was having a costume fitting for a stillsuit in Mexico City—that's how quickly it happened. I was the wrong actor, but by then it was too late.

Dean Stockwell ("Doctor Wellington Yueh") b. 1936, d. 2021

CONSIDERED: John Hurt (top of the list), Norbert Weisser, David Warner, Jeffrey DeMunn, Tom Conti, Dennis Lipscomb, Peter Coyote, Donald Moffat, Scott Wilson, Richard Lynch, Ian McKellen

Born into a family of entertainers and a child actor since the age of eight, Dean Stockwell had appeared opposite Gregory Peck in the 1947 message movie *Gentleman's Agreement* and also played Nick Charles' son in *Song of the Thin Man*. His role as the title character in the 1948 cult classic *The Boy with Green Hair* made him something of a psychotronic film icon. Starting in the 1950s, Stockwell began intermittently dropping in and out of acting to pursue an education and explore the anonymity he had been bereft of as a child star. As he grew more mature his roles included 1959's *Compulsion* opposite Orson Welles, as well as the 1962 film version of *Long Day's Journey into Night*.

With the mid-'60s counterculture in full swing, he dropped out of the business completely for three years to be part of the Topanga Canyon hippie subculture alongside fellow child actor Russ Tamblyn and musician Neil Young. He continued to appear in episodic TV and B-movies to pay the bills, including a memorable lead role in AIP's "freaky" 1970 adaptation of *The Dunwich Horror*. By the early '80s, Stockwell grew despondent over his career and began selling real estate.

Lynch's *Elephant Man* star John Hurt was originally cast as the treacherous Doctor Yueh in *Dune*. A somewhat desperate Stockwell—who at this point had been doing dinner theater in New Mexico, and was south of the border filming straight-to-video thriller *To Kill a Stranger*—made it his business to meet David Lynch at a Churubusco commissary where *Dune* production was already ramping up. The director was surprised to see him for a very peculiar reason.

As Stockwell later told it [*Interview*, 1990]:

> It had been eight months or so since I finished *Alsino and the Condor* when I went down to Mexico to do another film. It was a three-week job. While down there, I heard David Lynch was at the same studio preparing *Dune*. I had read the *Dune* book and loved it, so I made an effort to go meet David and said, "I'd like to be in your movie." He said, "Sorry, it's all cast." And I said, "Nice to meet you. I'm a fan." Later he told me something funny about that meeting. He said, "If I looked a little strange when you walked into the commissary, it was because I thought you were dead." Anyway, I went back to Santa Fe. All of a sudden, there's a part in *Dune* 'cause the guy, John Hurt, had scheduling problems. And David had remembered me.

The backstory doesn't end there, however. It turns out that Stockwell's experiences in the '60s may have gotten the better of him, as he forgot he met Lynch years before at his own home [via the documentary *Pretty as a Picture: The Art of David Lynch*]:

> Back in the late '60s and during the '70s, I was living in Topanga Canyon. Every once in a while, I would have showings of 16-millimeter films at my house. David Lynch came through there and showed a film, one of his early films called *The Grandmother*. Speed the reel ahead, years go by . . . There I went down to Mexico and met David and during the first couple weeks of shooting *Dune,* he divulged to me that we've met before. "Don't you remember? I was over to your house, I showed *The Grandmother*." I said, "Oh? Oh yeah? Great. How was it? Did you have a good time?" There were some of us that were out of touch in the '60s and early '70s. We had a good time, we saw important movies, and then we forgot them!

For Stockwell, who was a longtime fan of Herbert's books, *Dune* served as something of a career turnaround, arriving in theaters the same year as his acclaimed turn in Wim Wenders' *Paris, Texas* opposite Harry Dean Stanton. This precipitated a full-blown resurgence via Jonathan Demme's *Married to the Mob* (1988), for which he received a Best Supporting Actor Oscar nomination, as well as the co-lead in the TV series *Quantum Leap*, for which he won an Emmy in 1990.

"*Dune* was the first major film I'd done in 12, 13, 14 years. I mean, a major, major film," Stockwell told *The San Francisco Examiner* in 1988. Even though the film was a flop, the actor considered it "a start. We were able to put a down payment on a house we call 'The House that *Dune* Built.'"

Freddie Jones ("Mentat Thufir Hawat") b. 1927, d. 2019

CONSIDERED: *Ralph Richardson (top of the list), Ian Wolfe, Jay Robinson, Ian Bannen, John Colicos, Richard Dysart, George Gaynes, Cornel Wilde, Dan O'Herlihy, Donald Pleasence, Jason Miller, Andre Gregory, Oliver Reed*

Distinctive English character actor Frederick Charles Jones made his Royal Shakespeare Company debut in 1962 for David Rudkin's *Afore Night Come*. His film debut came in Joseph Losey's 1967 kitchen sink drama *Accident*, followed by movies such as *Far from the Madding Crowd*, *Antony and Cleopatra*, and classic Hammer horror fare *Frankenstein Must Be Destroyed* and *The Satanic Rites of Dracula*.

Known for his chubby appearance and intensely vibrant presence, Jones' twitchy personality fit perfectly for the role of Merrick's brutal exploiter Bytes in Lynch's *Elephant Man*. He almost didn't take the role, though, comparing it as written to the cliché villain Bill Sykes from Charles Dickens' *Oliver Twist*. Lynch lured Jones to the part by giving him carte blanche to play the role as he saw fit, with the actor imbuing Bytes with a layer of pitiable humanity.

"I like highly theatrical roles and I can't bear playing nonentities . . . give me Charlie Laughton and Wilfrid Lawson any time," Jones told South Wales Echo in December 1983. "I always want to play Hamlet, in a sense, rather than his attendant lords."

In *Dune*, Jones' Thufir acts as a kind of benign Polonius to Kyle MacLachlan's Space Hamlet. Jones had just completed a part in another sci-fi fantasy bomb, *Krull*. In that movie, he shared a scene with Lady Jessica herself, Francesca Annis, not to mention performing his own stunt work (at age 56) by edging his way one-handed across a fiberglass spiderweb 30 feet above the ground.

Sting ("Feyd-Rautha") b. 1951

CONSIDERED: *Clinton Dean, Jeff Lester, Hart Bochner, Eric Boles, Dirk Benedict, Dennis Christopher, Scott Colomby, Clark Brandon, Bruce Abbott, Kevin Costner, Patrick Swayze*

Born Gordon Matthew Thomas Sumner, the recording artist and actor known as Sting started off as a school teacher while moonlighting as a jazz musician on evenings and weekends. He eventually formed a mainstream rock band, The Police, in 1977 with English guitarist Andy Summers and American drummer Stewart Copeland. Sting provided bass guitar, lead vocals, and much of the songwriting. The group's sound evolved from punk to "reggatta de blanc" (white reggae, also the title of their second album) to new wave pop. Their biggest hits include "Roxanne," "Message in a Bottle," and "Don't Stand So Close to Me."

Sting branched out into acting, beginning with the Mod named Ace Face in Franc Roddam's 1979 *Quadrophenia*, based on The Who's album of the same name. He then made an appearance in Christopher Petit's 1979 cult film *Radio On* before finally tackling a lead role in 1982 as an insidious young man asserting himself into the lives of a middle-class couple in Dennis Potter's *Brimstone and Treacle*.

Sting was offered the second lead of Fletcher Christian opposite Anthony Hopkins in 1984's De Laurentiis production of *The Bounty* after Christopher Reeve dropped out and before Mel Gibson was cast. He opted for the smaller role in *Dune*.

"Fletcher Christian would have taken too big a chunk out of my life and would have prevented me from touring," Sting told *Film Review* in January 1985.

Lynch and Sting felt a mutual reluctance about working together, though for different reasons: Lynch had reservations about Sting, while Sting had reservations about *Dune* itself. A meeting between the two at Claridge's Hotel in London's affluent Mayfair district (promptly followed by pub-hopping) cleared the air.

"When I first heard about Sting, I said, 'No way do I want a rock star to be in the picture,'" Lynch told MTV in 1984. "Then I saw *Brimstone and Treacle* and I saw Sting, but I saw Sting playing a character and he was fantastic."

"I'm doing *Dune* because of David Lynch and for no other reason," the musician confided in a September 1983 interview with *Rolling Stone*. "I didn't really want to do the movie, because I didn't think it was wise for me to be in an enormous movie. I'd rather keep a groundswell building up in my movie career. So, I sort of went along dragging my heels."

Paul L. Smith ("The Beast Rabban") b. 1936, d. 2012

CONSIDERED: John Milius, Erland van Lidth, Bruce M. Fischer, Brian Dennehy, George Dzundza, Hardy Krüger, Patrick Swayze

One interesting casting attempt made for the character of Rabban was filmmaker John Milius, whom Raffaella had just worked with when he directed *Conan the Barbarian*. A central member of the movie brat generation, Milius became known for making films loaded with machismo, including the scripts for John Huston's *The Life and Times of Judge Roy Bean*, Sydney Pollack's *Jeremiah Johnson*, and Francis Ford Coppola's *Apocalypse Now*. A self-proclaimed "Zen anarchist," Milius developed a right-wing wild man reputation in Hollywood, often stipulating in his contract that studios present him with a new gun as part of his payment. He had not amassed many acting credentials, only appearing in small parts like a marijuana dealer in his own film *Big Wednesday*, or a deleted cameo as a gun-toting Santa Claus in Steven Spielberg's *1941*, which he co-wrote. It's unknown how far he got in discussions for *Dune*, but Milius could have handily embodied Glossu Rabban's gleeful sadism.

In contrast to these stocky contenders for the "Beast" Rabban (including Milius, Brian Dennehy, and George Dzundza), Patrick Swayze was not only younger but incredibly fit, studying martial arts as well as being a trained Joffrey Ballet dancer. Swayze was also considered for the part of Feyd and would have paired quite well as Sting's brother in terms of resemblance. With his only other movie role to date being the roller disco dud *Skatetown, U.S.A.*, Swayze was likely pulled into the *Dune* casting by Jane Jenkins, who got him cast in Coppola's *The Outsiders*. That ensemble film completed shooting in May 1982, and as it happens, his next big lead role would be in 1984's *Red Dawn* for director John Milius. In another interesting coincidence, Swayze's final onscreen role was in the 2009 A&E series *The Beast*, which was canceled shortly before the actor's death from pancreatic cancer at age 57.

The imposing 6-foot, 4-inch American character actor Paul Smith was born in 1936. Before he went into acting, he found work as a bouncer and bodyguard. His first stage role was in a University of Florida production of Eugene O'Neill's *The Hairy Ape*, co-starring with a then-unknown Faye Dunaway.

"I liked the acclaim," Smith told *Esra* magazine. "The audience loved me. It was a good feeling. I decided to become an actor."

After beginning his acting studies in New York, he had his first on-screen role as a Jewish prisoner for Otto Preminger's 1960 Israeli epic

Exodus, where he fell in love with the country. He returned to Israel in 1966, working as a volunteer truck driver during the Six-Day War and eventually meeting his wife, Eve. It wasn't until the early '70s that Smith truly broke into films, initially in Israeli productions like the Richard Boone western *Madron*. Due to his striking resemblance to Italian funnyman Bud Spencer, Smith made a series of Italian Spencer-Hill-style buddy comedies alongside Michael Coby (real name Antonio Cantafora, a Terence Hill lookalike). Smith's breakout role came as the sadistic prison warden in Alan Parker's Oscar-winning 1978 drama *Midnight Express*. The next year he began appearing in more prominent Hollywood movies like *The In-Laws* and *Going in Style*. In an open-shut case of a part he was born to play, Smith took on the role of the title character's burly nemesis Bluto in Robert Altman's big-budget musical *Popeye*.

Before taking on the role of Rabban in *Dune*, Smith was initially approached to play the character's uncle, the Baron Harkonnen. As Smith recalled in the 2008 documentary *Paul Smith: The Reddest Herring*:

> When I went in for the meeting with David Lynch and Dino De Laurentiis and Raffaella sitting in the meeting, they wanted me to do the Baron. They said, "We'd like you to put on a hundred pounds." I said to myself, "I'm not going to do that," because as big as I am, another hundred pounds will put me in a box. I said, "I want to be in the movie but I'm not . . ." They didn't want to build a suit. In the end, they built a suit for the guy who did the Baron, but they didn't want to build the suit when they wanted me . . . and said I wouldn't. "It's going to kill me—I don't want to do that." So I did the nephew.

Smith proved to be quite effective as Rabban, being the perfect visual embodiment of the novel's description of him as a "muscle-minded tank-brain."

Brad Dourif ("Mentat Piter De Vries") b. 1950

CONSIDERED: Leonardo Cimino, Xander Berkeley, James Woods, Eugene Butler, Mandy Patinkin, Brad David, Barry Miller

Bradford Claude Dourif was born in West Virginia, the son of an art collector father and a community theater actress mother. After briefly studying film in Colorado, he quit college to move to New York City and study acting. After appearing in several off-Broadway plays, he was spotted by director Miloš Forman, who gave him his debut film role in the 1975 Best Picture–winner *One Flew Over the Cuckoo's Nest*. His sympathetic portrayal of mental patient Billy Bibbit earned him a Golden Globe and an Oscar nomination right out of the gate.

He continued on the big screen with a supporting role in the thriller *Eyes of Laura Mars* and the lead in John Huston's black comedy *Wise Blood*, and reunited with Forman for the Dino De Laurentiis production of turn-of-the-century epic *Ragtime*. At the time he landed *Dune*, Dourif was 34 years old and already teaching stage directing at Columbia University.

As Dourif remembered it in 2015 at Florida's Spooky Empire convention:

> I was teaching a course called "Directing Actors," and all my students were in love with David Lynch, who I had never even heard of. Apparently, they'd seen this movie *Eraserhead*, and were absolutely blown away by this guy. I got *Dune*, and they were all thrilled about it. Everyone was saying, "Tell David Lynch I love him." I went and Raffaella said, "Hi, I'm going to introduce you to David." I didn't know what to expect, but there was this preppy-looking guy with a blue sport coat, khaki pants, and a button-down blue shirt. He sounded a bit like Peter Lorre from Philadelphia . . . But I would say he is, visually one of the freest thinkers . . . he is a wild imagineer, there is no one else. He is a true surrealist, extraordinary, brilliant guy. He can write, he can paint, he can do anything.

Mirroring this image, Dourif told *The New York Times* in 1984 that Lynch "paints with actors." Wrote Greg Tozian in his *Tampa Tribune* review, "Brad Dourif is a perfect psycho, cast as a murdering rapist with eyebrows like twin muskrats."

"Brad Dourif plays Piter, sort of a crazy man," Lynch told *Prevue* #58. "But he's played so many loonies in films like *One Flew Over the Cuckoo's Nest* and *Ragtime* that he didn't want to do it again! He took some convincing."

Brad Dourif had worked with John Hurt previously in *Heaven's Gate*, although Hurt was replaced by Dean Stockwell before shooting began. In October 1984, Dourif also collaborated with *Dune*'s composers, the rock band *Toto*, appearing in the music video for "Stranger in Town" off their album *Isolation*. Directed by Steve Barron (*Electric Dreams*), the video was inspired by the British film *Whistle Down the Wind*.

José Ferrer ("Padishah Emperor Shaddam IV") b. 1912, d. 1992

CONSIDERED: John Gielgud, William Glover, Richard Aherne

While the role of villainous Padishah Emperor Shaddam IV may have been a perfect opportunity to reunite Lynch with his *Elephant Man* cohort John Gielgud (then fresh off his Best Supporting Actor Oscar win for *Arthur*), 'twas not to be. Gielgud's post-Oscar dance card was full, appearing in seven films and TV movies in 1984, including the mystery comedy *Scandalous* and romantic drama *The Shooting Party*.

Instead, the *Dune* production went with another veteran in Puerto Rican legend José Ferrer, widely known as the first Hispanic actor to win an Academy Award. He did so for his portrayal of the long-nosed poet Cyrano de Bergerac in the 1950 film of the same name, a role which also won him acclaim—and the first Tony Award for Best Actor—in a Broadway stage version that began performances in 1946. Two years after his *Cyrano* success, he was nominated for another Oscar for his portrayal of the diminutive artist Toulouse-Lautrec in John Huston's *Moulin Rouge*.

Born in San Juan, Ferrer moved to New York with his family in 1914, and later earned a degree in architecture from Princeton in 1933. In 1935, he made his first stage appearance for famed director (and Ferrer's college chum) Joshua Logan (*South Pacific*) and his first film appearance as French King Charles VII opposite Ingrid Bergman in the 1948 biopic *Joan of Arc*. Right from the start of his Hollywood career, he already had a royal air about him.

After a forced appearance before the House Un-American Activities Committee in 1951, politically leftist Ferrer refused to name names but was accused by progressives of groveling before the committee to save his career. The actor denounced communism and publicly spoke highly of the committee as "performing an important function," but was still effectively graylisted for a time, likely due to his Hispanic background and the racist nature of the HUAC movement.

It's probably no coincidence that José Ferrer was cast in *Dune* after his *Lawrence of Arabia* co-star Alec Guinness had made such a huge pop culture impression (and paycheck) playing Obi-Wan Kenobi in *Star Wars*. *Dune* had often been referred to as a sci-fi *Lawrence of Arabia*, and to get a recognizable face from David Lean's 1962 Best Picture winner was a real coup. Many other screen vets were vying for their own elder sage role in a fantasy franchise around this time, notably Ralph Richardson in *Dragonslayer* and Robert Preston in *The Last Starfighter.*

After a divorce from Rosemary Clooney and getting hit with a huge tax bill in the late '60s, Ferrer began making a series of unfortunate career decisions motivated by his financial predicament, appearing in a slew of mediocre TV movies and series. By the late '70s and early '80s, Ferrer was taking supporting roles in films that ranged from bloated (*Voyage of the Damned, The Swarm*) to pitiful (*The Big Bus, The Fifth Musketeer*) to embarrassing (*Dracula's Dog, Bloody Birthday, The Being*). Even a relative bright spot like 1982's *A Midsummer Night's Sex Comedy* is still considered second-tier Woody Allen and was a flop.

In the 2020 biography *José Ferrer: Success and Survival*, Ferrer is quoted as saying:

> I don't bear resentment. I was fifty when I made *Lawrence of Arabia*. In the years that followed, I should have been doing things that taxed my ability as an actor. I didn't get them. Instead, I played bankers and doctors and corrupt businessmen and did guest shots on TV. Actors in Europe are more fortunate. Richardson and Gielgud go on doing fine work. Pinter writes plays for them. Here, the older actor is refuse. If I could afford it, I'd never act again . . . I'm only doing things that pay the bills.

When Ferrer was announced for *Dune* in 1983, it was a lifeline: a key part in a big-budget blockbuster hopeful. Only a few months after *Dune* landed in theaters, he became the first actor honored with the National Medal of Arts, presented to him by President Ronald Reagan. His son Miguel Ferrer would later join the unofficial David Lynch repertory company by playing FBI Agent Albert Rosenfield in the TV show *Twin Peaks*, its movie prequel *Twin Peaks: Fire Walk with Me*, and posthumously in 2017's revival series *Twin Peaks: The Return*, as well as a TV network president named Bud Budwaller in Lynch's short-lived 1992 show *On the Air*.

Siân Phillips ("Reverend Mother Gaius Helen Mohiam") b. 1933

CONSIDERED: *Viveca Lindfors, Kim Stanley, Simone Signoret, Uta Hagen, Bette Davis, Sylvia Sidney, Mildred Dunnock, Mildred Natwick, Margaret Hamilton, Geraldine Page, Josephine Hutchinson, Frances Bay, Dolores del Rio, Marlene Dietrich*

One of these auditionees, Frances Bay, would later play Aunt Barbara in *Blue Velvet* and Mrs. Tremond in both the *Twin Peaks* series and in *Fire Walk with Me*. In 1983, the 64-year-old Canadian former radio actress was experiencing a career second wind after an appearance in 1978's *Foul Play*. However, the role of the Reverend Mother would ultimately go elsewhere.

Dame Jane Elizabeth Ailwên Phillips (stage name Siân Phillips) was born and raised in Wales and grew up speaking Welsh, only learning English by listening to the radio. At age 11, she did her first professional acting work for BBC Radio. She later entered the Royal Academy of Dramatic Art as a contemporary of both Diana Rigg and Glenda Jackson, rejecting several overtures to come to Hollywood while still a student there. She instead embarked upon a long and distinguished career in UK theater, including lauded roles in productions of Henrik Ibsen's *Hedda Gabler* and George Bernard Shaw's *Saint Joan*. She was married to legendary actor Peter O'Toole from 1959 to 1979.

Her work for film and television includes a Golden Globe–nominated performance in *Goodbye, Mr. Chips*; a BAFTA-winning role as Livia in the BBC series *I, Claudius*; Ann Smiley in *Smiley's People* (both of the latter co-starring Patrick Stewart); and Cassiopeia in the 1981 Ray Harryhausen fantasy *Clash of the Titans*.

When she got the offer for *Dune*, Phillips was apparently so enthusiastic that she waved off even reading the screenplay before officially signing on.

"I've known Raffaella since she was 13, and I admired David's work and wanted to do a picture with him," she told Sunday Sun in December 1984.

Catharine Rambeau of the *Detroit Free Press* stated in her review, "British actress Siân Phillips, as a Bene Gesserit high priestess, controls every scene she's in, drawing our attention as if she were using her order's secret command voice."

Everett McGill ("Stilgar") b. 1945

CONSIDERED: *Max von Sydow, Jack Palance, Fritz Weaver, Maximilian Schell, George Hearn, Helmut Berger, Christopher Plummer, Jürgen Prochnow, Stephen Macht, John Lithgow, Bryan Brown*

One potential Stilgar, Australian actor Bryan Brown (best known at the time for *Breaker Morant*), would later take the lead in Raffaella's 1986 Chinese epic *Tai-Pan*. According to Craig Campobasso, the decision to replace

Sean Connery with Brown in *Tai-Pan* came down to an office poll conducted by Raffaella where she asked her staff which of the two actors they would rather sleep with.

After graduating from the University of Missouri–Kansas City, Florida-born Everett McGill appeared in such Broadway productions as the Frank Langella–starring *Dracula,* as the romantic lead opposite Mary Tyler Moore in *Whose Life Is It Anyway,* and as the lead imaginary half-man/half-horse in *Equus.* He made his screen debut as Chad Richards during the 1975–76 season of the soap opera *Guiding Light.* By 1982, McGill estimated he had been out of work for 7 of his 12 years spent as an actor, mostly preparing for parts he never landed.

Before he auditioned for *Dune,* McGill was hot off of playing the lead caveman in Jean-Jacques Annaud's $12 million prehistoric fantasy *Quest for Fire,* which was shot in Scotland under arduous conditions. Despite having only a handful of big-screen appearances at the time (*Union City, Brubaker*), McGill won the lead over 2000 other performers. Ron Perlman and Rae Dawn Chong co-starred in early roles, and all the actors had to endure cold and exhaustion with only bear furs and layers of makeup to protect them from punishing Scottish highland winds. Over the course of the shoot, McGill contracted hypothermia and developed a bad skin reaction (swelling, discoloration) to the three hours of makeup he endured daily under Christopher Tucker, Lynch's *Elephant Man* maestro.

Ina Warren wrote in her February 1982 *Quest* review for *The Sun Times*: "As the central character Naoh, McGill gives the film its strength and sensibility. Under that modified simian brow, we read the eyes of a being with wisdom and intellect."

A preliminary *Dune* casting session on August 23, 1982, shows a rectangle around Everett McGill's name with the word "YES" next to it. His meeting with Lynch and De Laurentiis was scheduled for September 16, 1982, and he became one of the first people cast. In February, 1983, he told the Kansas City Star that he hoped the sci-fi movie would make him a household name.

"Stardom, as such, doesn't mean anything to me," McGill said. "I simply like to perform on stage. Unfortunately, most choice Broadway roles for men my age are going to film and TV personalities. That's why I'm making movies . . . in order to get the stage roles I want, I have to become a 'personality.'"

Alicia Roanne Witt ("Alia") b. 1975

CONSIDERED: Soleil Moon Frye, Maia Brewton, Schnootie Neff, Brandy Gold, Taliesin Jaffe, Morgan Webb, Maggie Dawson, Hayley Taylor, Alissa Haggis

No member of the *Dune* cast fit their character better than 7-year-old Alicia Witt, a child beyond her years playing a child beyond her years. The extent of her otherness goes back to her earliest childhood, when the red-headed Witt began talking as a 1 month old, telling her mother "the end" when a bedtime story was over. She was figuring out the alphabet, words, and numbers at seven months and reading Shakespeare by age 2 while scoring like a teenager on aptitude tests.

Her ability to type 140 words per minute led her parents to make a connection to the fingerwork required for piano playing. After only six months of piano lessons, she won a statewide competition for the instrument at age 7, playing pieces by Bach and Bartok. Along with her brother, Alicia Witt was homeschooled by her mother while their father headed a junior high school science department in their hometown of Worcester, Massachusetts.

Her prodigy leanings earned Alicia featured segments on programs like *Evening Magazine*, *The Today Show*, and *That's Incredible!* It was her appearance on the latter ABC reality show, reciting quotations from *Romeo & Juliet* with her brother, that caught the eye of Jane Jenkins, who invited the Witt family to meet with Lynch and Raffaella in New York on November 20, 1982.

"She not only articulated the complicated dialogue, she actually sounded as though she understood it," Jenkins wrote in *A Star is Found.*

Another interesting note about the casting process is on September 16, 1982, Lynch met with actress Jennifer Jason Leigh and made Jenkins note that she could be a possibility for a "grown-up Alia." Whether that means she would be part of a flash-forward in *Dune* or was being earmarked for sequels is unclear.

Max von Sydow ("Doctor Kynes") b. 1929, d. 2020

CONSIDERED: Jack Palance, Fritz Weaver, Maximilian Schell, George Hearn, Helmut Berger, Christopher Plummer, Jürgen Prochnow, Stephen Macht, John Lithgow, Bryan Brown

The imposing 6-foot, 4-inch Swedish thespian Max von Sydow had a legendary screen career spanning seven decades. His movie debut came in 1949's

Only a Mother, but it was the one-two punch of 1957 Ingmar Bergman films (*The Seventh Seal* and *Wild Strawberries*) that catapulted von Sydow to international stardom. *The Seventh Seal* and its surrealistic imagery of a knight named Antonius playing chess with Death on a beach became one of the lynchpin images of mid-century European art cinema. Like Mastroianni and Fellini, Mifune and Kurosawa, or De Niro and Scorsese, von Sydow and Bergman would become inextricably identified over the 11 films they made together, including *The Virgin Spring* and *Through a Glass Darkly*, both Best Foreign Language Film Oscar winners.

Von Sydow also had a fruitful working relationship with the De Laurentiis group, appearing in such varied output for the producer as *Three Days of the Condor, Hurricane, Flash Gordon,* and *Conan the Barbarian* before securing the part of Imperial Ecologist Doctor Liet-Kynes (the Judge of the Change) in *Dune*.

The top choice for the role, von Sydow was also considered for the part of Stilgar, since the casting sheets combined both Kynes and Stilgar into one call for actors, looking for similar stoic types. One of Stilgar's most memorable scenes from the book, where he spits on the floor in front of the Duke as a sign of respect, was given to Kynes in the film, although the scene would be deleted from the theatrical cut.

Besides his work in *Flash Gordon* and *Dune*, von Sydow would become a fantasy genre stalwart in pictures like *Judge Dredd, What Dreams May Come, Minority Report, Star Wars: The Force Awakens*, as the Three-Eyed Raven in the TV series *Game of Thrones* and, of course, his portrayal of elderly Father Merrin in William Friedkin's *The Exorcist* (and its less-than-stellar sequel, *Exorcist II: The Heretic*).

Virginia Madsen ("Princess Irulan") b. 1961

CONSIDERED: Anne-Louise Lambert (top of the list), Helena Bonham Carter, Dianne Kay, Cynthia Rhodes, Doran Clark, Darryl Hannah

In an interesting footnote, auditionee Cynthia Rhodes was the featured dancer in the music video for "Rosanna," the opening track and initial single from 1982's *Toto IV*. Fellow *Dune* auditionee Patrick Swayze also featured in the video by the band that would go on to score the film. Rhodes managed to parlay her fame from the video into roles in *Flashdance, Staying Alive,* and *Runaway*, the latter of which opened the same day as *Dune*. In a double coincidence, Virginia Madsen appeared in the music video for Kenny Loggins' track "I'm Free (Heaven Helps the Man)" from the *Footloose* soundtrack, which was originally supposed to feature songs by . . . Toto.

Virginia Gayle Madsen was born in Chicago to a firefighter father and an Emmy-winning documentary filmmaker mother. Virginia (nickname "Gina") studied acting at the Ted Liss Acting Studio in Chicago while her older brother Michael Madsen was working at the famed Steppenwolf Theatre Company. By 1982, she was making a living wearing skimpy outfits while delivering singing telegrams in restaurants and board meetings.

"In my worst moments, I could see myself doing that for the rest of my life," she told *International Features* in July 1984. "I used to go home and cry to mother and tell her I wanted to be a working actress now. In my better moments, I told myself it was good training, crashing in on a cold audience like that."

By age 22, she would get her chance to shine (albeit with some awkward nudity) via a bit role in Lewis John Carlino's 1983 prep school comedy *Class*. Unfortunately, her debut film—which lensed in Chicago around late 1982—lacked what the title promised despite a stacked cast of rising newcomers.

"Oh. Ew," Madsen recalled of her experience on *Class* during a 2013 *AV Club* interview. "I don't want to talk about that. Those guys were assholes. They were really shitty to me. It was bad. Bad memories."

Rob Lowe said later for the same publication:

> Her big part in that movie required her shirt to get ripped off, and looking back, it couldn't be a more egregious, vintage, lowbrow, 1980s *Porky's*-esque, shoehorned-in moment. You would never have that moment in a movie that aspired to be what that movie did today. So, my guess is a lot of it is predicated on that, and justifiably so . . . I can imagine it was not much fun to do that big sequence with a bunch of laughing, ogling frat-boy actors. I mean, can you imagine putting up with me, John Cusack, Alan Ruck, and Andrew McCarthy at 18?

Fortunately, that experience didn't sour her on filmmaking. Just as Michael Madsen was making headway with small parts in movies like *War-Games* and *The Natural*, she ventured to Los Angeles. Virginia almost immediately won the small but vital part of Princess Irulan in *Dune* after being cast based on one Polaroid photo.

In an amusing footnote, Madsen almost immediately decamped following the *Dune* production to be the lead in the computer-driven sci-fi comedy *Electric Dreams,* starring future *Twin Peaks* cast member Lenny von Dohlen. That film wound up getting released six months before *Dune*, with the *Los Angeles Times*' Kevin Thomas calling her "another discovery, as poised as she is beautiful."

Linda Hunt ("Shadout Mapes") b. 1945

CONSIDERED: Eileen Atkins (top of the list), Wendy Hiller, Marge Redmond, Gloria Swanson

Dame Eileen June Atkins was heavily considered to play Lady Jessica's loyal house servant, the Shadout Mapes, a small yet important role in establishing the link between House Atreides and the Fremen. Atkins had been a stalwart of the English, Irish, and Broadway stage since the 1950s as well as a British TV regular. She and fellow actress Jean Marsh helped create the influential ITV series *Upstairs, Downstairs*. Her film roles included 1975's cult horror film *Sharon's Baby* and Sidney Lumet's 1977 adaptation of Peter Shaffer's *Equus*. Her film prominence wouldn't come until the mid-'90s when she appeared in major movies like *Wolf, Cold Comfort Farm,* and *Gosford Park*, the latter heavily inspired by *Upstairs, Downstairs*.

Linda Hunt read with Val Kilmer at 12:30pm on September 16, 1982.

Born Lydia Susanna Hunt, the famously small-statured actress attended the same Interlochen Arts Academy that Sean Young did, later graduating from the Goodman School of Drama in Chicago. A notable theater performer who made her Broadway debut in 1975's *Ah, Wilderness*, Hunt entered the film world as part of the large ensemble of Robert Altman's musical comedy adaptation *Popeye* in 1980 alongside Paul Smith's Bluto. Her unlikely second movie role as a male Chinese-Australian photographer opposite Mel Gibson in 1982's *The Year of Living Dangerously* earned her an Academy Award for Best Supporting Actress. This made her the first actor in the history of the awards to win for portraying a member of the opposite sex.

"What I've found over the years is that by existing outside of the stereotypes, ultimately, the opportunities are so much greater," Hunt told *The Santa Fe New Mexican* in 1985. "I'm free to float around and do a wide diversity of roles."

Her role as Mapes in *Dune* was her first big screen outing after winning the Oscar, and shot almost immediately following New York productions of Lavonne Mueller's *Little Victories* and Caryl Churchill's *Top Girls*. She left her dual role in the latter from April 5 to April 15, 1983, to shoot her *Dune* scenes. Hunt's strong preference for theater around this time was made plain in an interview she did with *Bomb* in 1986:

> Actors mostly aren't directed in films; it's everything else that gets directed. The celluloid itself gets directed when it gets cut. Actors are coaxed into things in film . . . Film directors don't know how to direct, you see. They don't know how to rehearse. They don't understand what that process is. It's questionable whether that process, what we go through when we rehearse a play, is applicable to a film. But some process like it, some variation on that theme seems to me would be of great value.

As for her opinion on *Dune*? She stated her disappointment bluntly to the *New Mexican* in 1985: "There was no story."

Richard Jordan ("Duncan Idaho") b. 1937, d. 1993

CONSIDERED: Jordan Christopher, Leonard Mann, Everett McGill, Michael Nouri, Robert Viharo, Christopher Pennock, Daniel Pilon

Born Robert Anson Jordan Jr. to a family which included an Appeals Court judge grandfather and a New York City Council president stepfather, Richard Jordan (stage name) graduated from Harvard in 1958 before making his Broadway debut opposite Art Carney in a 1961 production of Henry and Phoebe Ephron's *Take Her, She's Mine*.

Over his career, the native New Yorker devoted eight seasons to the New York Shakespeare Festival but was also prolific on the big and small screens. Some of his most memorable roles include the manipulative ATF agent in *The Friends of Eddie Coyle*, a Golden Globe–winning turn as an Irish immigrant in the NBC miniseries *Captains and the Kings*, an abusive writer in Woody Allen's *Interiors*, a sly National Security Advisor in *The Hunt for Red October*, and his posthumous part as General Lewis Armistead in 1993's *Gettysburg*. Sci-fi fans probably best remember Jordan as the antagonist Francis in 1976's *Logan's Run*.

By the time Jordan was chosen to play the role of fan-favorite Duncan Idaho in *Dune*, he was fresh off an Obie Award–winning performance in the 1983 off-Broadway production of *Protest* by Vaclav Havel. Had *Dune* been a success, the relatively small amount of screen time he had as Idaho would have been expanded in sequels, in which the character is revived.

Silvana Mangano ("Reverend Mother Ramallo") b. 1930, d. 1989

Dino De Laurentiis' wife and Raffaella's mother, Silvana Mangano was an era-defining actress in the Italian neorealist pictures of the 1950s. Born to an Italian father and English mother, Mangano eventually supported herself as a model, winning the Miss Rome beauty pageant. She launched her film career in earnest playing the lead female role of a peasant named, yes, "Silvana" opposite Vittorio Gassman in Giuseppe De Santis' 1949 classic *Bitter Rice*. With a worldwide success under her belt, she married Dino that same year.

In 1951, she scored an even bigger hit as a sinner who becomes a saint (i.e., a nun) in Alberto Lattuada's melodrama *Anna*. Other career highlights included work for such titans as Pier Paolo Pasolini (*Teorama*) and Luchino Visconti (*Death in Venice*). Before she was lured back into the spotlight for *Dune*, Mangano had not made a picture since Visconti's 1974 film *Conversation Piece*. Sadly, it was tragedy that pushed her back before the cameras.

The death of their son Federico on July 15, 1981, threw Dino and Silvana into crisis. He considered leaving the movie business altogether, and she withdrew into a quiet grief, visiting her son's grave for hours at a time— "too often," as Raffaella said. Dino and Silvana were already distant, but Federico's death furthered the schism. As she sank further into a depression, he escalated a serious affair with one of his office workers named Martha Schumacher. Seeking to pull Mangano back from the brink, a concerned Dino and Raffaella made a play to cast her as Mother Ramallo in *Dune*.

As Dino recounted in his 2004 memoir *Dino*:

> When Raffaella was producing *Dune*, she thought of offering a part to her mother, in order to distract her, to pull her out of her depression. "You talk to her," I said. "If I ask her, the answer will be no. Maybe she'll do it for you." And in fact, Raffaella managed to convince her. And since Silvana always did a very professional job when she was working, she made the best of the opportunity: she was precise, punctual, never threw any tantrums, and never behaved like a diva.

Jack Nance ("Nefud") b. 1943, d. 1996

CONSIDERED: Allan Rich

Allan Rich was a recognizable character actor who had just given performances in *Eating Raoul*, *The Entity*, and *Frances*. His early New York theater career was cut short by the Blacklist, so he took up a second life on Wall Street, opening his own brokerage. Expertise in modern art led him to become a noted collector and publisher of lithographs by artists like Salvador Dalí. He re-launched his screen career with 1973's *Serpico* opposite Al Pacino. Lynch had originally intended for Nance to play the Baron's Doctor, but when Leonardo Cimino was replaced by Brad Dourif as Piter, Cimino shifted to the Doctor and Nance was given Nefud.

Marvin John Nance, an alumnus of San Francisco's American Conservatory Theater, had become an underground movie legend for his lead role as the anxiety-ridden Henry in *Eraserhead*. Lynch designed the actor's infamous hairdo, and Nance's then-wife Catherine E. Coulson would execute it, learning to do Jack's hair to save on barber bills throughout the years-long shoot.

"I wanted Jack's hair to be tall," Lynch mentioned in the 2002 documentary *I Don't Know Jack*. "His particular type of hair would just lock in. Everybody said, 'No, no, that's ridiculous, that's absurd, look at this!' But it was just so beautiful and perfect and because of fate became that look."

"David told me, 'You know, Jack, one of these days guys are going to be trying to get their hair to look like that,'" Nance said in a 1995 *Wrapped in Plastic* interview. "At which time I told him, 'Well, that's when I'm going to leave the country.'"

The part of Iakin Nefud is minor in Herbert's book, essentially a lackey who becomes the captain of the House Harkonnen guard. Nefud is also notable for his addiction to the drug semuta, whose effects are amplified by the playing of atonal semuta music, as seen but never discussed in the film. Lynch intentionally amplified the part for Nance to give his former star a nice job, especially after being unable to secure him the lead role in *Elephant Man*.

Leonardo Cimino ("Baron's Doctor") b. 1917, d. 2012

CONSIDERED: Jack Nance

A Juilliard-trained violinist, Leonardo Cimino decided to pursue a sideline in acting, making his professional stage debut at age 18 in 1936. After fighting in the second wave of the Normandy invasion during WWII, he returned to his passion by making his Broadway debut in *Cyrano de Bergerac*, directed by and starring his *Dune* cohort José Ferrer. The two would collaborate many times over their careers.

A Martha Graham-trained dancer, Cimino made his film debut in 1961's gangster biopic *Mad Dog Coll*, which also served as the first movie for Gene Hackman and Telly Savalas. His distinctive long face was featured in many memorable roles over the years in diverse films such as *Cotton Comes to Harlem*, *The Monster Squad*, *Moonstruck*, *The Freshman*, *Waterworld*, and 1999's *Cradle Will Rock* (he appeared in the original Marc Blitzstein musical play in 1937).

"He doesn't look like anybody else," Cimino's wife Sharon Powers told *The New York Times*. "If you want a Leo Cimino, you want a Leo Cimino."

Just prior to *Dune*, Cimino appeared as a church chancellor in 1982's De Laurentiis production *Amityville II: The Possession*, one of many Catholic authority figures he portrayed in his cinematic oeuvre. His role as the Baron's doctor does not appear in Frank Herbert's book and was created specifically for the film by David Lynch.

David Lynch ("Spice Worker") b. 1946

David Lynch purportedly took on this bit part as the dirty spice worker aboard the harvester—who communicates with the Duke's ornithopter—to see what it was like to be in front of the camera. He recalled in 1985 at a lecture:

> I don't know how it happened. I saw the dailies on that, and then I gave it to Tony Gibbs and said, "See what you can do." I'm surprised I'm in the picture as much as I am. I enjoyed it . . . I didn't enjoy the experience of doing it . . . I enjoyed it in a way because for the first time, I felt what it must be like to face those cameras. I'm glad I did it so I know what an actor goes through, but that's the only reason I'm glad I did it.

Lynch had several minor experiences as an actor prior to this, including as a mute nurse in his own 1974 AFI short *The Amputee* opposite Catherine E. Coulson. He also appeared as a painter in John Byrum's 1980 movie *Heart Beat* starring Sissy Spacek with production design by Jack Fisk. He made a brief appearance as "Man in Bowler Hat" during the scene where the mob chases Merrick in *The Elephant Man*.

The director would go on to flirt with acting over the ensuing four decades, including a major role opposite his then-girlfriend, Isabella Rossellini, in Tina Rathborne's *Zelly and Me* (1988). This led to his most iconic performance, the hard-of-hearing FBI bureau chief Gordon Cole on *Twin Peaks* as well as the later movie and revival series. He also voiced the role of Gus on *The Cleveland Show*, had two memorable appearances on the sitcom *Louie* playing a mentor to Louis C.K., and most recently portrayed famed western auteur John Ford in Steven Spielberg's Golden Globe–winning autobiographical film *The Fabelmans*. Even for a powerhouse like Spielberg, Lynch reportedly had to be persuaded by their mutual friend Laura Dern to reluctantly take on that single-scene role, which became easily the most celebrated in the picture.

Other actors the production met with for unspecified roles:

Michael Horse (Fremen), Frank McRae (Sardaukar), Stan Haze (Sardaukar), Kate Nelligan, Steven Seagal (martial arts), Mary Elizabeth Mastrantonio, Diane Franklin, Wilford Brimley, Kim Stanley, David Caruso, Corey Parker, Chris Makepeace, Frances McDormand, Cynthia Nixon, Stanley Tucci, Andrew McCarthy, Alan Ruck, Tyrone Power Jr., Kelle Kipp, Joseph Maher, Juliana Donald, I.M. Hobson, George Innes, Dawn Dunlap, Eva Le Gallienne, Kristian Alfonso, Shay Duffin, Jake Dengel, Susanne Ashley, Victor Campos, Anthony Shaw, Patricia Charbonneau, Arthur Wooten, Bill Nunnery, Tony Azito, Kim Delaney, Robert Bruce, Rose Gregorio, Captain Haggerty, Matthew Barry, Peter Maloney, Doug McKeon, Christopher Stryker, Paul Roebling, Michael E. Knight, Jack Eric Williams, Eugene Leonidovich, Eric Brown, David Heller, George Saunders, Michael J. Miller, Maia Danziger, Kate McNeil, Evan Handler, Patrick Hines, Peter Crook, Marco Barricelli, Roy Brocksmith, Timothy Owen Waldrip, Benjamin Rayson, Donald Moore, Patrick Taylor, Caris Corfman, Steven Langa, Joey Phipps, Stephen Mailer, John York.

Tom Hulce (*Amadeus*) was auditioned on September 16, 1982, specifically to play the character of Korba, who has a minor, nearly nonverbal role in the theatrical cut played by an unknown (possibly French–Uruguayan actor Martin LaSalle of Robert Bresson's *Pickpocket*), but was a part of Paul's Fedaykin in the novel and plays a significant role in the book of *Dune Messiah*.

Michael Horse would go on to play the role of Deputy (eventually Deputy Chief) Tommy "Hawk" Hill on Lynch's *Twin Peaks*, proving Lynch does not forget a face.

Oral History: Pre-Production

The following individuals were interviewed by the author for this section:

—Kyle MacLachlan (Actor, "Paul Atreides")

—Sean Young (Actor, "Chani")

—Everett McGill (Actor, "Stilgar")

—Alicia Witt (Actor, "Alia")

—Virginia Madsen (Actor, "Princess Irulan")

—Molly Wryn (Actor, "Harah")

—Danny Corkill (Actor, "Orlop")

—Raffaella De Laurentiis (Producer)

—Thom Mount (President of Universal Pictures, 1976–83)

—Jane Jenkins (Casting Director)

—Bob Ringwood (Costume Designer)

—Mary Vogt (Costume Assistant)

—Ron Miller (Concept Artist)

—Giles Masters (Art Department)

—David Paich (Composer, Toto)

—Steve Lukather (Composer, Toto)

—John Dykstra (Visual Effects Supervisor, Apogee, Inc.)

—Craig Campobasso (Production Office Assistant)

—Paul M. Sammon (Universal Pictures Publicity Executive)

—Terri Hardin (Stillsuit Fabrication, Stunt Double)

—Eric Swenson (Visual Effects, Motion Control)

—Penelope Shaw Sylvester (Assistant Editor)

—Richard Malzahn (Visual Effects Graphics, Storyboard Artist)

—John Pattyson (EPK Producer)

—Zach Galligan (Actor, *Gremlins*)

—Dexter Fletcher (Actor, *The Elephant Man*)

—Kenneth Branagh (Actor, *Henry V*)

—Stephen Scarlata (Producer, *Jodorowsky's Dune*)

Stephen Scarlata is the producer of the award-winning 2013 documentary Jodorowsky's Dune, *directed by Frank Pavich. Alongside screenwriter Josh Miller, Scarlata hosts the podcast* Best Movies Never Made, *which chronicles films that floundered in development hell, including a history of unmade* Dune *projects.*

After the Dune *property passed from the Arthur P. Jacobs estate to Michel Seydoux and Jean-Paul Gibon, it was placed in the hands of director Alejandro Jodorowsky of* El Topo *and* Holy Mountain *fame. In watching* Jodorowsky's Dune, *one might get the impression that Seydoux and Gibon did not necessarily have a solid grip as Jodorowsky's ideas became increasingly grandiose, perhaps too outlandish to be viable in the mid-'70s. Some have listed a possible length of 14 hours.*

STEPHEN SCARLATA: It was a different time back then. Seydoux was working with him the way you have to work with an artist like this, giving him the freedom to do what he wanted. It made sense. When you come to Hollywood, they're used to doing things their way, right? One of the things we cut from the documentary was they offered to give him a director to watch over him—John Guillermin, director of *The Towering Inferno*. You can't do that. You're insulting him. That's what Sam Raimi did with John Woo on *Hard Target*, but he didn't need to babysit him. He's fine. That was out of the question for Jodorowsky, so everything got stalled.

The length aspect is a challenge because everyone's going to give you a different answer. When you look at the storyboards, we don't know how long all of that was going to translate to. There are battle scenes, the Grand Ball sequences of parties . . . That banquet was Herbert's favorite part of the book, and it was in Jodorowsky's. He had multiple galas going on at the same time. One of the biggest ever was *The Deer Hunter* wedding scene, and this was going to insanely top all that. I don't know how long the battle scenes were, the hypnotic scenes . . . there's so much. But I don't believe the 14-hour rumor at all. I don't believe the 10-hour rumor. I can see four hours. Gary Kurtz said he heard they were making a really long film that might take three to four sittings. He hadn't heard of that kind of project since the Russian *War and Peace*, which was eight and a half hours in two-hour blocks. To this day, I doubt it would have been that long, because with all these special effects and the amount of money needed for a budget back then, it would have been way too outrageous. All that stuff just gets out of control. He exaggerates when he says something like that in the documentary.

As an expanded student film, Dark Star *was an exceptional low-budget feature film. However, the idea that the special effects work Dan O'Bannon did for that would translate to the massively ambitious sequences boarded for Jodorowsky's* Dune *is questionable at best. Oscar-winning* Star Wars *effects man John Dykstra did some initial work on David Lynch's* Dune, *but he was also at one point approached by O'Bannon to be part of Jodorowsky's production prior to* Star Wars.

JOHN DYKSTRA: I love *Dune*! I had read *Dune* and thought it was a great opportunity. I even was remotely involved with Dan O'Bannon and the guys who were doing Jodorowsky's *Dune*, which was great. It was smoke and mirrors, but it was great. The concepts were wonderful; there was just no way to execute them.

STEPHEN SCARLATA: I did find some clues of some of the effects people Dan was going to work with out there. What he did for no money on those sets at USC for *Dark Star* was pretty amazing. Once he puts his mind to something, what he could pull off is pretty remarkable. Don't forget this too: When you look at all the storyboards, it's not like there are dogfights in outer space for Jodorowsky's *Dune*, just ships traveling. The hardest thing would probably be a ship landing. George Lucas couldn't pull it off in the first *Star Wars*. There is a sequence where the Sardaukar are coming to Arrakis, and they're flying in a spiral pattern. Then when they land, they become towers themselves to other ships. It would have been interesting to see how you pull off a lot of those special effects. I'm curious to see who he would have worked with out there, what kind of aesthetic it would have had.

JOHN DYKSTRA: All of Jodorowsky's movies are efforts of passion, so you get used to that kind of concept. He's loose with his interpretation because he's often talking about stuff that's so ephemeral that it's incredibly subjective. Whether he has met a certain objective goal in terms of empathy or not is not the issue for him. He's always making the movie for himself and hoping that other people like it.

Besides all the beautiful artwork produced by Mœbius, Chris Foss, and H. R. Giger, there remains a question of where the $2 million that was sunk into Jodorowsky's film went? Some costumes were made. It wouldn't be out of left field to speculate that some drugs were purchased. What else was on that ledger?

STEPHEN SCARLATA: It would have been a lot of money because of all the different artists. They had an office, and he had to pay these people. Constantly producing art, flying all over the world. I'd be shocked if it was $2 million; that can be exaggerated.

Dino De Laurentiis became interested in purchasing the Dune *rights while it was still in Jodorowsky's hands. Whether he sabotaged the French team's attempts to sell their project to Hollywood is up for debate.*

STEPHEN SCARLATA: I don't know if he sabotaged it, but I bet at any time Dino could have stepped in. I think he wanted the project. Maybe he was like, "I think this is going to fail with him. I'm going to stand aside and wait for it to fail so I can come in and get it." He had the money to be like, "You know what? I see your storyboards. I see you. I'm going to support you; let's make this movie together." But does he see Jodorowsky as someone he can control? I don't think he could have worked with him.

If you look at the '84 movie, it's the classic story with David Lynch: "I didn't get my director's cut." Dino was the one in charge all along. Seydoux confirmed that De Laurentiis had Jodorowsky's *Dune* book. Dino bought the adaptation rights, but Seydoux never said for how much. Seydoux went to Los Angeles, and the lawyers prepared everything. He said, "We were going to sign it, the final document, one of those American documents. Huge, as usual. His daughter was there just behind him like some sort of bodyguard. There was Dino De Laurentiis, short behind his big desk opposite the Beverly Wilshire. All of a sudden, after signing all of that, he turns around without getting up and says, 'Raffaella, this is for you.' Then he gave it to her." I always liked that story. Maybe that's why he waited for it to fall apart. When I heard that story, it all comes together: This was a gift to her, you know?

RAFFAELLA DE LAURENTIIS: I was told I could never meet with Jodorowsky. Then I saw his documentary . . . Oh, my God, I felt so bad. I feel terrible. He put all that work in, but Universal told us, you can't look at anything. "It's done. You can't read the script. You can't do this. You can't do that." We had to respect that.

GILES MASTERS: I find it very interesting the Jodorowsky one has such a following. At the time we were doing ours, nobody had ever heard of him, really. I remember some talk of how they tried to do this a few years earlier in Yugoslavia. That was as much as was ever spoken about that version. We don't remember ever seeing any of those designs. It's not like today where you could go online and have a look.

In previous interviews, Raffaella had claimed that her late brother Federico had first introduced Dune *to the family in 1974, but for this book, she claims a different family member was actually responsible: her mother, Silvana*

RAFFAELLA DE LAURENTIIS: It was my mom who first gave me the book; she was the big sci-fi fan in the family, and I read the book and I loved the book. I had just finished doing *Conan* in Europe and I came back here, so I was not involved in the preliminary. I think Federico's great contribution was to recruit David, because he had done only that one film, and it was not the obvious choice. [Federico] passed away right when we were in the process, you know?

CRAIG CAMPOBASSO: After Federico's death, Raffaella kind of moved into that position, right? Because he was being groomed to be Dino. He passed away in a plane crash location scouting in Alaska, so she sort of became that.

THOM MOUNT: *Dune* had been kicking around for years, and leading up to '76 we—meaning people at Universal, myself included—had looked at Frank Herbert's book, read it, considered it, and passed on it multiple times. The reason we passed on it multiple times was we thought it was going to be prohibitively expensive to make it properly. It's a big, complex, rich, and robust environment. We also needed an attachment of a major-league filmmaker with a vision to undertake something like this. We just weren't up for the complexity of it. Prior to '76, Dino De Laurentiis made an 11-picture deal at Universal, including *Conan the Barbarian*. You will be delighted to know that Dino referred to Conan as "*Conana el barbario*," which—as I pointed out to him—was in no language known to man. It's not English. It's not Spanish. It's not Italian. "*Conana el barbario*." Who knows what that is? I really liked Dino, got along very well with him. Raffaella and I were friendly. Dino was a major producer in a long-term relationship with Universal.

Initially, Ridley Scott worked for seven or eight months on his version of Dune *for the De Laurentiis company, with a script by Rudy Wurlitzer. At this point, Raffaella was in Spain making the first* Conan *with John Milius.*

RAFFAELLA DE LAURENTIIS: I only had a meeting with Ridley for a long, long, long time, one meeting only.

THOM MOUNT: Two things impacted that. One is that Ridley was becoming a hotter and hotter director who was very much in demand, and he was getting multiple offers. Not just big offers, good offers. Another issue is Rudy's version of the script did not receive unanimous, glowing enthusiasm. That's another piece of the puzzle. The thing about a movie getting a go-ahead is that it's never a singular event. It's a confluence of intersecting indices which result in a moment when you just say, "You know what, let's do this." Without all of that, nobody ever gets a go-ahead.

When the budget for Scott's version came in north of $50 million, his version was abandoned. The terms of Universal's De Laurentiis Dune deal had to be firmed up.

THOM MOUNT: Dino said, "Well, let's divide the world up," because I said, "We're not going to pay for this damn thing entirely. You have to find some money." He did, and he took some international territories. We kept the rest of it, the US and a handful of other territories. Dino put in substantial money, and then the key to the deal for me—from a financial point of view—was that if there were overages in excess of 10% of the budgeted amount, Dino would have to eat the overages. This is not an uncommon thing when you're off making a big picture with a lot of potential for disaster. One wants to know that your exposure is limited. We needed to be in a place where Dino took responsibility for overage. He was, after all, producing the movie, and he had substantial investment in the movie, and we agreed.

The way we ran movies at Universal, generally, was extremely hands-on; we had some very good executives like Sean Daniel, Bruce Berman, various people. These executives had some experience by now, and we put them out in the field on movies all the time to kind of make sure our interests were protected, because we were fully financing the films. In this case, we were partially financing the film, and Dino wanted to be left alone. As a producer, I totally appreciate that. I've pushed long and hard on various movies to be left alone. It's been a good thing when people did leave me alone— studios are not always cooperative around that.

Then David Lynch joins the marching army, and that's really the turning point inside Universal for this because I was a huge Lynch fan. I pitched him for a lot of things because I loved David's idiosyncratic point of view. By the way, he would have been a great director for *Fast Times at Ridgemont High*, and when he turned it down, I was less than happy until one of my assistants brought in a short that Amy Heckerling directed at AFI called *Getting It Over With*, which was terrific. It had spirit and authenticity. I thought, "It's going to be less of a landmark film, but it'll be a good film, and it'll work." And it did.

RAFFAELLA DE LAURENTIIS: When I came back from working on *Conan* in Spain, David had already been approached and said he was interested if he could read the script and write the script. When I got back, I started immediately working with David. I had one meeting with Ridley, and I started with David and did the whole movie with David. I think we were simpatico to each other and liked each other and respected each other and had fun together. It was a nice journey. We got along well. It was a fun project. You know, it was an all-consuming four years of our lives.

As development on the script began, an art department was set up at Universal where production designer Anthony "Tony" Masters began working with David Lynch to create the four worlds of the film. Giles Masters, Tony's 19-year-old son, had just finished the first year of a four-year art school program and came out to work in his dad's art department to "help out and earn a little holiday money."

GILES MASTERS: My father, Tony, he sat down with David at the end of '81. They'd all read the books, and they were working on the scripts. One of the things David was very keen on was that he didn't want it to feel science fiction-y. Dino had recently done *Flash Gordon*, which is the ultimate kitsch science fiction. They'd done very well on that movie, and I'm not sure whether the producers felt that this was going to be another *Flash Gordon*, but certainly David didn't. He wanted the different planets to feel tangible to the audience and not too out of this world.

Right from the get-go, Tony went back to what would be the building blocks for each individual planet and how that would affect that architecture. You're going to another world, so all of the textbooks have gone out the window, everything we know from the orders of architecture, Greek and Roman, all of that never happened. You're starting again. He looked very carefully at the description of the planets, and Caladan is very much like Earth. It has water and oceans and forests, so they build out of wood.

There's no wood on Arrakis, it's a desert planet, so the building blocks are going to be sandstone. Then Giedi Prime, the oil planet, it was plastic, some iron and chrome and metal. The Emperor's planet was gold and jade. It was choosing very simple building blocks to begin with, and developing an architecture from that. Having each planet with a very specific building block helped give the audience geography so when they land in a place you want the audience to know immediately where they are. Jumping from Giedi Prime to Arrakis to Caladan is confusing enough, but if the architecture and design can help the audience within a moment, you're okay. Suddenly everything's made out of wood, you know you're in Caladan. The pencil sketches that went before the main team, he would crank them out very fast. For every painting that you've probably seen, there's a Pantone sketch or a pencil sketch that came before it. Ron Miller very often took those designs and illustrated them.

Lynch and Masters handpicked Ron Miller to work as a concept designer on Dune *based on his astronomical book about the solar system,* The Grand Tour.

RON MILLER: When Tony called me, he explicitly singled out my depictions of the Martian landscape. He said that he and David thought they looked like Arrakis. It took just over a year to design the film. When I joined the film, there were scarcely half a dozen people working on it. Aside from the office help, it was David, Raffaella, Tony, and Bob Ringwood.

BOB RINGWOOD: I was doing *The School for Scandal* in Brussels at the Théâtre Royal du Parc, and I didn't speak French. I was doing something on the set in the daytime when a message came over the loudspeaker and the only two words I understood were "Monsieur Ringwood" and "Hollywood." I went to the stage door and said, "I think there's a call for me," and it was Golda Offenheim. She was Raffaella's assistant all her life, a wonderful Jewish lady just steeped in film.

CRAIG CAMPOBASSO: Golda Offenheim was our production coordinator. She was our glue. Raffaella loved her, used her on every movie. I think Clark Gable or somebody asked her to marry them early on when she was young. She really held things together in the *Dune* office.

PENELOPE SHAW SYLVESTER: She was this little English lady, but she'd done all the Bond films. She was like the mother hen, just looked after all of us. If somebody would get upset, she'd say, "Don't worry, it'll all be different tomorrow." She just took it all in her stride. Nothing would faze her.

BOB RINGWOOD: She was saying they wanted to meet me in London to discuss designing *Dune*. I had no idea what *Dune* was and I didn't know who Raffaella De Laurentiis was, but I flew over. I read the book. It took two days to get the book in English, which wasn't easy in Brussels. When I walked up the stairs into their little office at Shepperton Studios, Golda said as I sat down, "You're going in to talk to them, and if you get the job, you're going back to the hotel in a limousine, but if you don't get the job, you're on your own." After the interview, they asked me to sit in their office while they discussed the meeting, then after half an hour she said, "I'm very pleased to say you're going home in a limousine." Interesting beginning to a film.

I got the film because Raffaella had started work on it with another costume designer. I'm not sure who it was because she never told me. He or she, the other costume designer, wasn't getting on with David Lynch, and so they agreed mutually not to continue. [Raffaella] was a bit depressed, went home late in the evening, got herself a glass of wine, switched on the television, and on the screen was a scene in *Excalibur* with Igrayne dancing where I'd designed a dress that was all made of camel hangings. She saw this dress and picked up the phone to England, woke up Golda at home and said, "There's a film on the television called *Excalibur*, find out who designed it, I want to meet him." If she hadn't gone home, got the bottle of wine out, and put the telly on, I would never have been offered *Dune*. I was lucky at the beginning. I was about 36 years old after I saw them in London when they asked me to fly to New York to meet Dino, who had an office on Central Park in a tower block.

I spent my life designing theater. I do sets and costumes a lot. I was a production designer on *The Draughtsman's Contract*, so I don't only do costumes, but I have done a lot, and that's why I wear jeans and sloppy jumpers. Hideous clothes, comfortable clothes.

I arrived at Dino's very smart office in New York and said to the secretary, "Oh, excuse me. My name is Bob Ringwood, I've come to meet Dino." She looked at me and said, "You can't possibly be a costume designer." I went through to Dino's office, an enormous room with a Napoleonic desk that was literally raised up on a dais and he was sitting on a throne behind it. He was a tiny little man of about 5-foot-4, with this deep, deep voice. Then I walked in and he just said, "No, no, no, no, no, no." Raffaella was there, and she said, "What do you mean 'No, no, no'?" He said, "He's a boy! Is a boy, you can't design this." I said, "Well, I think I'm four years older than your daughter and she's producing it. I don't see why I can't design it." And he just said, "Oh, he's okay. He's okay. He can design." Because I stood up. He liked being stood up to, Dino. He didn't like walkovers.

Around 1945, after serving in the army for six and a half years during WWII, Tony Masters ended up in Rome working for army newspapers as a cartoonist, which played into how incredibly fast he was as a draftsman.

GILES MASTERS: Everything had to be designed. Everything. Tony was prolific with the sketches. I have thousands of pencil sketches and Pantone pen sketches that were done in developing the look of each place, a lot of things that were never used. In the six months before I started on the show, which would have been summer '82, he and David just brainstormed the show. You start off with a sketch, and then David would look at it. He'd often look at it in the mirror because it changes things when you look at something in the mirror, and then would push it in a certain direction or another direction. Sketch after sketch after sketch.

BOB RINGWOOD: I caused absolute havoc on the production at first. Tony Masters had been on it for at least six months, and he'd designed it completely. It was almost complete, all the sets, the props. They lost the other costume designer, and then I came in quite late. I said to them, "I would be interested in coming to America and talking about designing the film if you're not going to do it like a space film with silver spaceships and spacesuits with glass balls on, the usual thing. I think it should be more extraordinary and sophisticated." They agreed on that. They said, "Oh, no, we haven't done anything like that." They flew me out to Hollywood for two or three weeks to see whether either of us wanted to continue. When I walked into Tony Masters' large art department, he had art all over the walls. I just looked at all these and looked at him—I'd never met him— I said, "This is just '2002'! Everything Raffaella and David told me you weren't doing, you're doing." He designed the stillsuit even, it was a silver spacesuit with a big glass helmet on the top.

GILES MASTERS: When I first started on the movie, my father and Bob Ringwood had been working on it already for some time. I don't think there was ever a time that it was *2001* or *Flash Gordon* or anything like that. They were always looking for something grounded elsewhere in a universe that had a reality to it. I think what Bob was saying is pretty much what everybody was saying: "We don't want to just churn out stuff that's been done before. We want to find a look to this."

RON MILLER: I think that Bob may be referring to the Jodorowsky attempt. Or perhaps some early concept drawings that Tony may have done, but those would have been just placeholders. I never saw a single serious costume design until Bob came on shortly after I started working.

Recently unearthed Dune *storyboards by Apogee do depict a wildly different look to the stillsuits, with plated armor and a see-through helmet with breathing/speaking apparatus. This look was later transferred over in simpler form to the Sardaukar.*

BOB RINGWOOD: I talked to Tony for about an hour, and then I went to Raffaella and David and said, "Look, I'm sorry, I don't want to do your film. I'm not going to do it. It's not at all how I see the film and the story. I wish you well, but I'm going back home." There was an emergency meeting that day, and they call me in the next morning from the very nice hotel and said, "We've just scrapped all the designs for the film, thrown them out." I felt like I behaved very badly, and Tony Masters was absolutely charming about it. He said he had worked on it so long with David not knowing what it should be and he felt that what he was doing was wrong. He had basically done *2001*, another version of what he'd done before, and in a way was relieved because I'd upset the applecart. I don't think anyone knows that story, but that did absolutely happen and they persuaded me not to leave the production.

RON MILLER: I think that Tony gets credit for eschewing the kitbashed look. He told me that every movie spaceship since *2001* looked alike, and he felt some responsibility for that. He very deliberately set out to create a look that was wholly different and original.

Some of the concepts tossed out included a massive space-age control room aboard the Heighliner, an Atreides ornithopter with insect wings (as described in the book), and an elaborate landing pad for the 'thopter. Many ships and buildings were honed to their most simplistic form. Ron Miller spoke of evolving the Guild ship from "a waffle iron and a 1950s Pontiac hood ornament to just a slab with a lump on one end."

RON MILLER: The sketch of the ornithopter with wings was a very, very early concept. It was done even before I began work on the film.

GILES MASTERS: The ornithopter started off very much like the one that I've seen in the trailers for the new *Dune*, very insect-like. It went through many different stages. David was keen on this as a ship that could just land, close up, and survive a sandstorm. That ship was probably the one David had the most influence on, the diamond shape that was left when it shut itself down.

RON MILLER: The Atreides control room I had not seen before. It looks like it may have been done very early on. I suspect that, like many similar sketches, it was abandoned because the scene was deemed unnecessary. The color sketch of the Atreides ornithopter landing pad was one of the first paintings I did when working on the film. As usual, the scene wasn't shot mainly because of its complexity. The largest paintings took about a day or maybe two days to do, the smaller ones just a few hours. I don't recall ever doing any over again. An idea might be abandoned, though, if something different seemed better.

GILES MASTERS: The wedge shapes you see in the movie came from that feeling David had that these ships could survive in a sandstorm. Basic shapes . . . like Bugatti in his cars: If it looks right, it probably is. A simple shape is often the purest form, and you can overdo design. On this movie, the design wasn't overdone. It wasn't convoluted. Sometimes movies have so many different concept artists that it all becomes crazy and overworked. This was two artists: David Lynch and Tony Masters. There was continuity in design at all times between the two of them.

Visualizing the many worlds of the novel involved taking inspiration from historical sources. The entire city of Arrakeen wound up taking on aspects of Tibetan architecture, while Giedi Prime was inspired by the same industrialized Victorian England that Lynch had been so fixated on recreating for The Elephant Man.

RON MILLER: I never much liked the book! I had started reading it two or three times before I ever heard about the film . . . and each time, I set the book down and simply forgot that I was reading it. It wasn't until I had to, that I finally sat down and read it clear through. I will probably earn the ire of a lot of *Dune* fans, but I think that *Dune* is actually science fantasy rather than science fiction. When I mention this, fans will say "But it is all about ecology!" That is kind of like saying *Moby-Dick* is science fiction because it's all about cetology.

BOB RINGWOOD: I have to confess, I think the books are not very good, and when you design a film, you design the script, not the books. I think the books are interesting, but I don't like his writing style very much, and when I met him, I didn't like him very much, but I did think they could make an extraordinary film.

RON MILLER: One of the things that most impresses me about *Dune* visually: all the effort made to make each planet distinctively different. All of the designs, from costumes to props, were done with the history, culture, and available native materials in mind. A goal was for someone to be able to walk into the prop shop, pick up anything at random and be able to tell which planet it came from. Even the history of a culture played a role in the design elements. For instance, a small panel in the back of Paul's bed on Arrakis featured the figure of a fish, reflecting a time when Arrakis had open seas. This attention to making every planet unique to convey distinct cultures and history is something I have rarely seen in science-fiction films.

BOB RINGWOOD: I argued that in the future—and they didn't take this up fully—things that would be cherished were things from what would then be seen as the ancient past. A million things would all be hugely collected and saved, and I thought we could revamp some of the past civilizations and incorporate them in the film as though they'd influenced the deep future. I was very keen on a lot of high decoration. I mentioned Venice, and so Raffaella organized a trip from Rome, and we flew up to Venice. David, who'd never really been anywhere, got very excited standing in front of Saint Mark's. He was only in Venice for 20 minutes, but he did see Saint Mark's and somehow absorbed something over it.

RON MILLER: The Emperor's throne room is based on Alhambra . . . turned upside down. The architecture of turn-of-the-last-century Vienna was also a big influence.

BOB RINGWOOD: I had several meetings with Tony, and he was lost . . . only temporarily, because he was a highly experienced production designer and a very clever one. I suggested two things to him: One was to look at the work of Otto Wagner. Otto Wagner is a Viennese Jugendstil architect, and nearly all the sets were based on Otto Wagner. He'd never heard of Wagner. I went down to Hennessey + Ingalls—a big art bookshop in Santa Monica—and bought him two books on Wagner because I felt so guilty they'd thrown his designs out. The other thing I said is to look at the swimming pool at San Simeon, the Randolph Hearst Castle. If you Google that swimming pool, you'll see some of the sets are quite like it. Tony leaped on this idea and started to redesign the production.

GILES MASTERS: There were lots of conversations and David went through lots of designs, and lots were thrown out in the early days, but it was never *2001* or *Star Wars* in design. Very early on there might have been [these types of designs], but I've never seen them. It was always a very large step to the left, always looking for a parallel universe that had history to it. Certainly, Bob and Tony were always looking for that. I wasn't aware of Bob not wanting to do the show, but he was on board when I first met him, so I don't know about that part of the story. I don't think Tony was ever trying to step on any toes, and he and Bob worked together fantastically well.

BOB RINGWOOD: We started all over again, and I started designing clothes. I've always felt slightly guilty about doing that. I was doing it because I was wanting to leave the film. I didn't think they'd throw his designs out. That wasn't my intent, but the sets that I saw were absolutely in that *2001*/*Star Wars* mode. You could have slotted them into those other two films.

One piece of forward-thinking design that mirrored Tony Masters' work on 2001 *that did make it into the final film was the iPad-like device that Paul uses to watch filmbooks. In addition to similar tablets shown in* 2001, *there were also tablet-style devices in* Event Horizon, *for which Giles Masters was the art director. These designs popularized by father and son would eventually come to fruition in real life.*

GILES MASTERS: It's funny, isn't it? The fact that they had those tablets in *2001* is the crazy part. In *Dune*, obviously, you are 15 years later—things have moved on a little bit. When we first started, the Walkman had just come out. The call sheet was still being typed—it was very early days for computers. It's always interesting with science fiction when you're looking ahead and trying to figure out what might come. You come up with ideas;

some of them might land in the future. In *2001*, they were looking 35 years in the future. I'm sure Apple looked at *2001* and said, "Well, that's cool. Maybe we'll make our iPads look a bit like that."

BOB RINGWOOD: My criticism of my own work is the Emperor's world, which I was trying to base on a stylized, late-17th-century look blended with the Habsburg Empire. Now, I would do it slightly more futuristic, just a little bit more spacey. I was pushing for that world to be copying an earlier period. As fashions go, the Regency era was very keen on Ancient Rome, and all the ladies wore muslin dresses. I was trying to get them to do that. All these things wouldn't have occurred to David. I think it made it very uncomfortable for him because I don't think he quite understood what I was saying or what Tony was saying. What was great about him is he went along with it, because he saw that it could make it much more interesting.

One area of Dune *worldbuilding that was completely in Lynch's dark wheelhouse was the Victorian-inspired Giedi Prime. Many S&M–themed books were kept in the art department specifically to inspire the look of the Harkonnens.*

BOB RINGWOOD: The world David was most comfortable in was the Baron's world. He loves that because you could have the dripping oil and all the filth. I was pushing for the industrialization of Giedi Prime and the sexualization of the Baron. That's an obscene place. David loves that. The more we pushed into that, the more he loved it. He indulged himself on that, and it worked out very well.

MARY VOGT: Bob had a huge collection of S&M books. I'm surprised we even got them into Mexico. That was kind of a no-brainer for him to do that. You can get away with that stuff with the Baron Harkonnen because it's all based in reality. He wasn't making it up, it's all real.

Continuing to hone the Dune *script over several drafts as the film struggled to get a green light, Lynch made a peculiar impression on Ned Tanen, then president of Universal's film division.*

THOM MOUNT: Ned's a complicated bundle of snakes, but a smart guy. He thought this was a good idea as long as Dino had responsibility for overages beyond a certain point. That was really the caveat for all of us.

Ned, at a certain moment, said, "You know, I've never met David Lynch." We hadn't started shooting yet. David was working in an office on the lot, so I called David and said, "Listen, Tanen's never met you, I'm going to bring him over there if it's cool with you to just say hello. Tell him he's a wonderful guy, and we'll get out of your hair, but at least that way he's met you." David said fine, and 30 minutes later, I drag Ned over to the Producers' Building up to the third floor, and we find an office that says "David Lynch" on the side of the door. We go in, and there's an empty office and no David Lynch. This doesn't make any sense. I walk through the office, and I see that Lynch is holed up underneath his desk, in the footwell of the desk, writing. He's got a bunch of yellow paper, and he's writing away underneath this thing. I guess he felt comfortable there, which is fine. This did not seem particularly insane to me, but I dragged Ned around and said, "Ned, David Lynch." David stuck his hand up out of the footwell and shook his hand and blah, blah, couple of sentences, nothing lengthy at all. Ned said, "You know, this is a difficult movie . . ." The standard speech. David said, "Yeah, I'm just doing some rewrites right now, I think everything's going to be fine and blah, blah." We left and David was still under the desk. This later came back to haunt me because I think Ned fixated on the idea that David was some kind of kook, as opposed to a guy who has a tremendous creative burden and needs to find his platform, his methodology, whatever that is.

BOB RINGWOOD: I myself am about a third of the way up the autistic scale, and I'm sure David's autistic or at least Asperger's. He does have these obsessions, which he uses wonderfully.

RICHARD MALZAHN: David's a scary dude. Not scary in a mean way, but he comes up with ideas that I don't ever want to live. He did the fish kit and the chicken kit, these little pictures where he took apart these animals and put them on a board, put little tags on it like a model kit. "Here's the heart. Here's the . . . It's all pieces that you need to make a chicken." It's like, "Really? This is who we're dealing with?"

JANE JENKINS: He would always have bizarre little art projects in his office. There would be rocks on the wall with strings coming down from the rocks. There were photographs of him dissecting a chicken and all these weird David Lynch things.

PENELOPE SHAW SYLVESTER: David gave me a print for my 30th birthday . . . it's a chicken kit! It says, "To Penny, Happy Birthday. Chicken Kit." He told me it was unique because he put his thumbprint on it. He would get dead chickens, or he would ask people to collect roadkill for him. Then he would spread it out. It says, "Warning: Do not set fire to your chicken or people will eat him. Please follow instructions carefully . . . Mexico City generally has a mild climate. However, the late nights and early mornings can become chilly and uncomfortable . . . You may wish to purchase feathers for your chicken. They can be attached as per instructions."

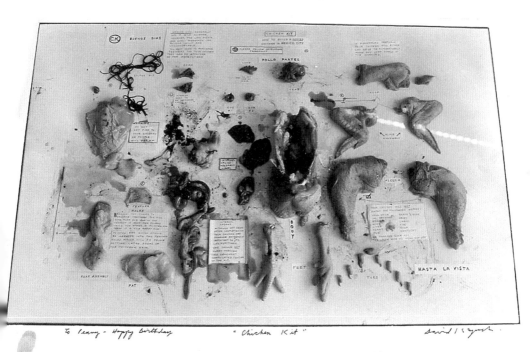

CRAIG CAMPOBASSO: He always talked like he was from the '50s: "Peachy keen. Neato keeno." He was extremely nice to work with. David's office was cool. He had a black couch, things on the wall, he had Woody Woodpeckers lined up.

JANE JENKINS: Woody Woodpecker. He was very much into Woody Woodpecker and Bob's Big Boy.

BOB RINGWOOD: David, when I first started to work with him, insisted we eat at Bob's Big Boy every single day at lunchtime, at the same time. He always had to have the same meal, some hamburger thing. He'd eaten there every day and always had the same meal at the same time, a strange artistic obsession.

CRAIG CAMPOBASSO: David loved Bob's Big Boy. He and Raffaella and I and some other girls from the office would go to Bob's Big Boy every day, right? Almost every day. The guys in the art department made him a Bob's Big Boy with a *Dune* suit on it. They made it out of plaster, and it had blue-within-blue eyes and the little nose thing. They signed it on the bottom.

BOB RINGWOOD: After a month, I rebelled, and Tony Masters said, "Thank God." I said, "I'm never going to eat at Bob's Big Boy ever again. I'm sorry." Tony had been going to Bob's Big Boy for months and was so sick of it. There was a French restaurant, and Tony and I insisted that David go there for lunch with us the next day. He'd never eaten anything. He'd never eaten garlic. He'd never eaten anything that was foreign food. He was hugely American, obsessed with cheese. I think he was a bit staggered by suddenly being introduced to European food and French food and garlic and all these extraordinary things. I don't think he liked it very much.

When he wasn't tooling away on the script, David Lynch became a fixture in the art department, where he was known to do abstract doodles that were then interpreted by the design team. Miller discovered the director's three favorite things were small triangles, black rubber, and little twisty wires. Lynch's habit of carrying multicolored markers in the front left pocket of his signature white shirt influenced Doctor Yueh's outfit, which has many pieces of apparatus embedded into the upper left.

BOB RINGWOOD: I think I might have done that as a sort of homage to David, now that you've reminded me. I do have some drawings that David did. There was a pig-like head, an early thing of the Guild Navigator. David did sometimes do lovely little scribbles. They were charming, beautiful little drawings.

RON MILLER: He can draw very well, but he once paid me the compliment of saying I was on his wavelength, perhaps because I could see what may have looked like an abstract drawing and recognize something in it.

GILES MASTERS: David often used sit in the art department and hang out. It was a quiet place. It can be quite a calm place when you're in the middle of a big movie and everybody's trying to find you and ask you questions. He used to sit down in the corner and just have a quiet time with the creative juices all flowing around him.

BOB RINGWOOD: This sounds rude and I don't mean it to sound rude, but he's an uneducated intellectual. He's got incredible intellect, an amazing ability to see the weird and strange. He's a real artist. I'm not sure film is necessarily his best outlet. He could have been a painter or a proper artist. Well, I think he is all those things put together. He's a sort of genius, in a way. Unlike most people.

RON MILLER: I had no part in creating the storyboards, though Mentor Huebner and George Jensen (who were the storyboard artists) worked in the same room with Judith and myself. Mentor had a very distinguished career, both as a fine artist and as a storyboard illustrator, having worked on many Hitchcock films. I was also impressed by the fact that he had designed Robby the Robot.

RICHARD MALZAHN: Mentor was . . . you aspire to certain things that you probably will never achieve, and he was one of them. He was like . . . whoa. I mean, it's crazy. Ultimately one of the great storyboard artists of the business.

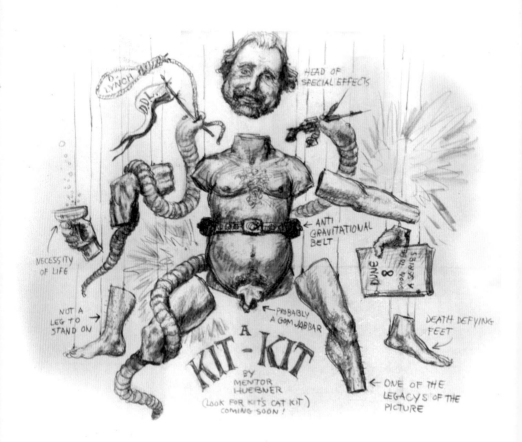

One small bit of controversy was how visually similar the sandworms in the film were to the cover paintings for Herbert's books done by artist John ("Jack") Schoenherr.

RON MILLER: That became a bone of contention later when I learned Jack bitterly resented (a) being left out of the film and (b) seeing the sandworms resemble his concept so closely. I was embarrassed to learn he blamed me for the latter, though I had argued for a long time for his involvement. Sadly, a quote in *Cinefantastique* came out sounding as though I had been arguing for usurping his design. That rankled with him, and I was never able to explain. I did come up with a number of alternate designs for the worms, as did Tony, but David really liked the three-lobed mouth. We tried to make it different from Jack's version by including inner lips that opened separately from the mouth. It wasn't ever different enough.

A key piece of costuming was the stillsuit worn by the native Fremen to survive in the deep desert. This wound up being Ringwood's most iconic design in the film.

BOB RINGWOOD: When I originally designed them, I wanted the suits to be like bodies, and I wanted them to be functional. I saw this sculpture in the Slade Gallery in London. There was a sculpture of the torso of a man made in leather, hanging on clips. A sort of crucifixion of a nude body in black leather, a bit fetishistic. I remembered that sculpture and used it as an influence for *Dune*. Being an honest person, I contacted the agent of the sculptress, and he was very unhelpful and wouldn't give me contact with the girl. I thought she inspired it; why don't I get her to help make the prototype for this costume? He suddenly started demanding huge amounts of money, so I didn't pursue that, but I did try. I thought it was the right thing to do, but I just did it myself. That's where that suit came from.

TERRI HARDIN: Bob Ringwood showed me the sculptor who did the muscle structures out of leather; it was an Austrian woman. He said, "This is an artist who gave me the spark to do the stillsuits." I saw the similarity right away.

After doing much of the design work himself, at a certain point Ringwood hired a young Mary Vogt—who had been an assistant costume designer on Diner—*to work as his assistant and wardrobe buyer.*

MARY VOGT: The main thing about *Dune* for me was the opportunity to work with Bob. I saw *Excalibur*, and I thought, "My God, these clothes are unbelievable. It's magical, just absolutely gorgeous." When I saw Bob's name on screen, I got chills. I thought, "Maybe someday I'll get to work with him." It just so happened he was at Universal doing *Dune*, and a friend of mine said he was looking for an illustrator. I met him, and Bob was like, "You know, this really isn't that hard. Anyone could do it." Bob is so brilliant that he doesn't think it's hard. He has no ego, which he never did. He hired me first as an illustrator, and then he needed an assistant to do fabric swatching and to basically take notes for him and just be his assistant. It was a great position because I could observe how he creates things.

BOB RINGWOOD: Mary was wonderful. I desperately needed somebody. She may have come on a bit before we went to Mexico, but not much. I think we did start making clothes in Hollywood, prototypes to get the approval.

Mary Vogt worked with Ringwood and Don Post Studio to fabricate the many stillsuits needed for production in Mexico. Post had just worked with the De Laurentiis company creating the iconic masks for 1982's Halloween III: Season of the Witch.

MARY VOGT: The stillsuit was like a spacesuit. It was a functional suit that had to recycle water in the body. That was very important to Bob. Sometimes you see costumes—they've got knobs on them, and it's just decoration. But for the stillsuit, it was very important to him that everything makes sense. Everything on the astronaut suit is for a purpose. He went to JPL [NASA Jet Propulsion Laboratory] because they recycle things in astronaut suits. It couldn't look like a costume with things on it that don't make any sense, like wires going to nowhere. They're not wearing this to make themselves look more muscular.

BOB RINGWOOD: I thought they had to be sexy—it was a sexy story. The story is good. It's a pseudo-religious book but [has] a sexual undertone in it. Max von Sydow one day was on the set in the desert with very hot sun, and the sweat was dripping out of his fingertips at the end of the stillsuit. I went up to him and apologized, and he says, "Don't worry. Wearing this stillsuit, I've now got the body I've always wanted, so I'm willing to put up with the sweat and the heat." It made the actors feel a bit confident—it gave them bodies that all of them had never really had.

MARY VOGT: Don Post was doing the stillsuits in Van Nuys. All of them were made here and then shipped to Mexico. Stan Winston would have been the obvious choice to go to for this. I think Stan was around, but would not have done what Bob wanted. Bob is like, "I have absolute power, I have absolute control." Don Post was more willing to let Bob run the show.

BOB RINGWOOD: I heard about Don Post Studios; they made these rubber masks. I went to Don Post and said, "I'm doing this film and I've got this idea of making these stillsuits," and showed him the drawings. Every single suit was handmade. We made them for men, women, and children.

MARY VOGT: At that time, they didn't have imaging. You had to do plaster bodycasts, which are not easy to do. A bodycast was done of all the actors.

A well-known young cosplayer named Terri Hardin—an expert in foam sculpting who had consulted with Don Post previously on a 7-foot-tall Wookie suit she wore to conventions—was hired by the studio to work with supervisor Mark Siegel on bodycasts of actors and fabricating the stillsuits for $10 an hour.

TERRI HARDIN: *Dune* was the first movie I had worked on. We were this ragtag group of sculptors, casters, artists, designers, puppeteers, etc.

A little ball of people that would float from one job to another. Bob Ringwood was an amazing, fun guy. I wish I'd taken a picture with him. When you're working on these sets, it's not fandom, it's your colleagues.

EVERETT MCGILL: I met Bob Ringwood, Mark Siegel, and the many assistants at their studios in L.A. where I began a full-body casting. I remember the gnawing deep cold of wet plaster and the opposing relief when the curing heat arrived. I was also surprised at how much the stiffening made it difficult to breathe. I was placed on a plank tilted at a slight angle and the back half of my body was quickly layered with plaster-soaked strips of gauze. Where the seams had been planned, there was inserted a separation membrane to allow for removing the sections of the mold one at a time. When the back half had taken a set, I was simply tilted the opposite way, and the front half was done. The process was several hours.

TERRI HARDIN: Max von Sydow did his bodycast, and while he was taking a coffee break, I told him my favorite character that he did was King Osric from *Conan*, and that I believed he was ancient in *The Exorcist* only to find that he was still very young. Max was a lot of fun to be around. We did his suit for when they open it up to show the water spewing out. It was all these tubes and wires.

MARY VOGT: For actors that weren't there—who were in England or something—there was a mannequin, a facsimile. For the extra costumes, it was going to be Mexico, and there are a lot of Mexican people in Los Angeles. We just picked certain body types that we could then fit in Mexico. The costumes were based on a four-way stretch leotard that was custom-made with the big, long zipper, with sculpted muscles made with foam, then it was sprayed in rubber. Don had these big walk-in ovens that you would cure them in.

BOB RINGWOOD: They did a wonderful job on them. They lasted, and when they were in the desert, they went through hell. They never fell apart. It wasn't meant to be fascistic or rubbery, but it did end up being black. I was originally going to do it the color of the sand. I thought the sand might be red with oxide and stuff. I mentioned that to David, and he did do a scene where they painted themselves with red paint on the shoulders. That did work quite well.

TERRI HARDIN: Theresa Burkett was making bodysuits with Mark at the helm. It was taking a lot of time and costing a lot of money, so Theresa took the suit home and created a version where you could put all the pieces on fabric. All you had to do for extras was sew up a seam. She made hundreds of those and saved them a lot of money. You couldn't tell the difference too much. They were so accurate that Bob Ringwood began to say, "I wonder if this would have worked for the principals?"

BOB RINGWOOD: I wanted to drape them in dark Arabic robes, but David wasn't very keen on that. I wanted layers of Arabic robing, black and dark. I never understood why Arabs or Bedouins in the desert wear dark clothes when that will absorb the heat. You'd think they'd wear pale clothes. But the overlay was cut—they didn't like the idea of that.

The process of waiting for production to ramp up began to get on Ringwood's nerves, leading to an amusing confrontation with Raffaella.

BOB RINGWOOD: We all got on very well, but there was a lot of tension. You felt the film could collapse any minute. There was a small crew, Tony and about six people in his department, and there was just me and a desk. The film was constantly delayed, had trouble getting money, trouble getting approvals. A million reasons.

I worked on it solidly for almost a year before we started to go into production at all. I designed the clothes over and over and over and over. After a few months, I went to Raffaella and said, "Look, I'm going back to England because you're not ready to go into production, and I just can't keep designing the same clothes. It's very boring. Clothes are being rejected that I designed a few months ago because you're bored with seeing them. It's not very productive." She was very naughty. She said, "Well, all right, then I'll arrange it. Bring in your passport." I gave her the passport, thinking she was going to arrange for me to fly home. She took out my immigration papers—the green slip that's stapled in—and just tore it up. [*laughs*] I was therefore in America illegally. Raffaella was like that. I mean, Dino's basically a gangster, Raffaella is sort of a daughter of a gangster, so they play by their own rules. By the way, I adored Dino. Absolutely adored him and I adored Raffaella, but they were very naughty. I had to be smuggled out of Mexico and then flown back in legitimately, applying for new immigration. I was horrified when she tore it up, because being in America without the paperwork is quite serious.

A series of concept art and costume displays were held for various Universal executives before the film was finally given a green light in June 1982. Miller's paintings in particular went a long way to selling the vast scope of the picture, as well as several paper models of sets and vehicles crafted by his wife, Judith.

RON MILLER: All modesty aside, I think they played a big role, but so did the drawings Tony did and Ringwood's designs. Even Judith's models. Some of the final models followed her details exactly. On the carryall, the model makers duplicated everything she conceived. She also contributed to the final design of the Guild Navigator. The most important model she did was the sietch set. It was far too complex to be translated into working drawings by the drafting team. Instead, carpenters built the full-scale set directly from her model. I recall there being a couple show-and-tell sessions where a room was set aside and filled with models, paintings, sketches, and preliminary costume designs just for the brass to file past and be impressed by. At one of these sessions, they even got Judith all made up.

BOB RINGWOOD: There are lots of photographs of his wife, who was extremely beautiful, wearing some of the prototype costumes.

MARY VOGT: There was always a presentation going on, permanent mannequins set up. Maybe they were always trying to get money. There was a big photoshoot for the toy people where everything had to be perfect because it was for toys.

PAUL M. SAMMON: Nothing was made more toyetic. David, in particular, never struck me as someone who'd intentionally go in that direction.

That isn't altogether true, though. In one case, literal LJN movie merchandise (the "Spice Scout" and "Sand Scout" vehicles) snuck its way into the actual movie during post-production.

ERIC SWENSON: Back in LA, we had two shots we did in the parking lot outside, and those were of the toys. They were all running away from the harvester and there were these little vehicles with two wheels. They're quick shots where you're looking down and this thing just zooms across the frame. We had two different racer versions of the spice harvesters. A lot of smoke and steam and sand flying, pulling it on a string just to get it to go through the frame at high speed . . . and what we were using was the prototypes of the toys. They were actually made out of wood because these are real prototypes with Bondo and stuff on them. Prototypes for the toys appeared in the film. It's a weird shot, one of those, "Why is that there?" It's because you had to have the toy in the film so you could sell the toy. There was never a model made for the movie, so we used the model of the toy in the movie. I wouldn't know if that's ever happened before.

BOB RINGWOOD: Merchandising in films isn't something that occurred to me. It probably did in Dino's mind, certainly in the studio's mind. It was only my second film. I designed about 300 theater productions by that point. I suddenly realized I was doing the same job I've done in theater but being paid 100 times more.

MARY VOGT: Bob would have never stood for toy people telling him what to do. He listened to David, being the director. If Dino De Laurentiis had a comment, he would have listened to Dino, or maybe Tony Masters, but certainly not a toy manufacturer. Oh my God, if the toy manufacturer had the nerve to even comment on a buckle, Bob would have throttled them to the ground.

BOB RINGWOOD: At that time there was a new clip, those little plastic clips with two little prongs that go in and click. We use them everywhere now, for skiing and everything else. They'd just been invented that year, and I used them on the stillsuit. We did a prototype stillsuit presentation to Dino, and he was outraged that the clips were plastic. He said, "They can't be plastic, they must be metal." Not wanting to waste his money, I had one set made in metal, put them on the same suit, took it to him, and said, "There, now we've made them metal. Are you happy?" He never knew that we never changed them on all the other suits. He was willing to have all those clips remade in metal at great cost. He never cut corners in the costume department at all. In fact, I never had to go and ask for more money. They never gave me a budget. We just started making the film and kept making the film.

From 1980 to her retirement in 2017, Jane Jenkins was one of the top casting agents in Hollywood. After forming The Casting Company with partner Janet Hirshenson, the pair would eventually find actors for over 100 movies, including Harry Potter and the Sorcerer's Stone, Jurassic Park, *and* Home Alone. *Interestingly, prior to* Dune, *Jenkins' origin story as a casting director was inextricably tied to Dino De Laurentiis.*

JANE JENKINS: I had worked with Frank Pierson on a film that Dino was producing called *King of the Gypsies*, working out of Dino's offices here in Los Angeles. I will never forget this as long as I live. Back then, there used to be a script-typing service and we had a new script typed up for *King of the Gypsies*. They asked me what color I would like the cover to be. I said, "I don't know, how about purple? That's a royal color. It's called *King of Gypsies*." So, they delivered these piles of scripts with the purple cover. Dino happened to be walking through the library, he saw the purple cover and said, "What is this? What is this? Somebody get those covers off. Purple is the color of death!" They had to rip all the purple covers off the script and change it to . . . I don't remember what we changed to. I went, "Oh my God, will I be in trouble?"

Now, I had done a lot of research for Frank on *Gypsies* to the point where I got myself invited to an actual gypsy wedding, which was a trip and a half. He had said he would take me to New York to continue working as his assistant, but then the day before Christmas, as everybody was partying, I was fired and told that I wasn't going to New York. It was very crushing as I was a single mother with a child to support going, "Okay! Now what am I going to do for my next trick?" I had watched the casting from the beginning, and because I had done all this research on gypsies, I kept on saying, "They're bringing in people that don't look like gypsies; they don't feel like gypsies." I went, "Casting . . . that could be a really good job." Ralph Waite, who played Pa Walton on *The Waltons*, was an old boyfriend of mine at that point. When I got fired from *King of the Gypsies*, I called up Ralph and said, "You know, this casting thing could be an interesting job. Can you help me meet any of the people at the casting office for *The Waltons*?" Ralph, in his inimitable fashion, said, "I'll do you one better. They just gave me a million dollars for a script that I wrote; I'm going to produce, direct, and star in it. You can cast it." I said, "Ralph, are you out of your mind? I don't know how to actually cast a movie. I just want to get a job as somebody's assistant so I can learn." He said, "No, no, no, you already know how to do it. Just go to the Screen Actors Guild and get the rulebook. You know the difference between a good actor and a bad actor." I said okay. Then he said, "Can you work for free?" I said, "Remember David, my son? I have him to feed." I said I could do it for $100 a week off the books so I could continue to collect my unemployment. I cast Ralph's movie [*On the Nickel*]. That's how I got into casting.

For Dune, *David Lynch's preference was to find potential actors primarily by looking at simple black-and-white headshots, as opposed to focusing on performances in films, readings, or more traditional auditions.*

JANE JENKINS: His concept of casting from a black-and-white photograph is very visionary. David did a lot of divining the casting. He would look at somebody's black-and-white picture and say yes or no. I would say, "Maybe we should meet them besides?" But he did not audition a lot of people. He sat and talked to people. I don't remember any kind of edict that we needed a specific type, just to find people who seemed like the right people. There were only a handful that I remember vividly auditioning. Most of them came in and either met David or were offers.

VIRGINIA MADSEN: David clearly has always been extremely good at casting. Whatever he does, his casting is spot on. The best directors are excellent when it comes to casting, and that's what David did as well. If you look at all of his films, he has a sense of people and a feeling about his actors. When I watched every film that he did after that, I'm like, "Yeah, that's right."

RAFFAELLA DE LAURENTIIS: We saw so many people in London. We saw Charles Dance, who's been in *Game of Thrones*. We wanted him to play the Duke. I think he turned us down, if I remember correctly.

JANE JENKINS: Jürgen Prochnow had just done *Das Boot*, and I thought it was incredible. Then I found out that he was in Los Angeles doing publicity for the film.

Whether Lynch saw Das Boot *or met the actor in person, Prochnow wound up being one of the first cast, along with Dino's wife and Raffaella's mother, Silvana Mangano. Dino generally would only have cursory final approval over the actors chosen.*

CRAIG CAMPOBASSO: I never brought actors in to read for Dino. He would say, "Craig, I just want to see them in person. I want nothing else. I just need to say the last 'yes.'" I would tell the actors, "You're not going to sit down. He just wants to see what you look like in person, that's it." Some actors would get angry. One actor broke stuff in the lobby afterward because he was so incensed. I said, "Okay, well, we're not ever going to hire that actor."

JANE JENKINS: David and Raffaella were the main arbiters of casting. Dino was in the background expressing his opinions to them, but he was not involved in the actual day-to-day casting, just with Silvana.

BOB RINGWOOD: They couldn't cast that Reverend Mother. I said to Dino, "You've got the perfect woman, you're married to her. Why on Earth are you searching the world for some old lady, when you've got a beautiful old lady?" She wasn't that old. I said, "Just ask your wife to do it." They took that suggestion and flew her in.

JANE JENKINS: Back then—back in the good old days—they hired a director, they hired a casting director, they put us in a room together, Raffaella was involved. "We want this person." There wasn't this whole chain of command we have now because there's video on everybody available. Everybody at every studio needs to see everything. Back then, "This is who we want to hire." I don't remember any involvement on my end from the studio. I'm sure Raffaella had those conversations.

Along with Prochnow and Mangano, Everett McGill was one of the first people cast, later participating in screen tests for Tom Cruise and Val Kilmer. David Lynch went on to collaborate with him many more times, affectionately calling him "Big E."

JANE JENKINS: He was one of those people at that time. He had the power. He had the chops. There was something powerful about him that was very right for this.

EVERETT MCGILL: I met David and Raffaella in the New York casting office of Jane Jenkins. David went straight into a big grin, praising my performance in *Quest for Fire* and praising Raffaella for insisting that he see the film the evening before. I remember Jane highlighting my Broadway roles that called for some significant training in the classics which, considering Herbert's resonant characters, was the word that likely went out with the first casting calls. In an effort to make a case for myself, I probably shared the first margin note from my copy of Herbert's *Dune* where I describe Stilgar as a "fierce yet supple leader with a sharp command of language and thought," but I had so little to go on since I had been told the film script was not ready and that there would be no readings.

I also recall a brief discussion of both David and me having worked with Tony Hopkins, which I'm sure I wanted to move away from since I knew Tony was not happy on *The Elephant Man*. I asked David about growing up in Montana, and before long, it was just two boys from the heartland, born a few months apart, talking about music and fast cars. Then I asked David about his Lynch heritage, and when he mentioned Lynchburg, Virginia, I suggested that we might be related since my mother's mother was a Lynch whose distant ancestors were stonemasons in that city.

JANE JENKINS: He had a terrific New York agent by the name of Jeff Hunter, who when we were starting to do his deal said, "You know, it's not a very big part, and Everett has done much bigger parts. Maybe we could credit him as 'E. McG'?" I went, "What? I don't think that will fly."

EVERETT MCGILL: I knew I wanted Stilgar badly and I thought the meeting went well, but my best hope was that I would be asked to read at some point. But, a week later my agent received the script, an offer, and word that only Jürgen and Silvana were set thus far.

The most sought-after role was the lead, Paul Atreides, for whom the production considered many rising young actors, including an 18-year-old Zach Galligan fresh off filming a lead role in the surreal comedy Nothing Lasts Forever. *Galligan came in for a New York City casting session on August 19, 1982 (coincidentally, exactly 40 years to the day I interviewed him) at 4:45pm, and then again on August 23 at 6pm.*

ZACH GALLIGAN: Standard operating procedure is I went in on the 19th and met with Jane or Janet for their casting pre-screen so she could take a look at me to be like, "Is he suitable? Does he look okay? Is he bad? Is he covered with tattoos?" Am I familiar with the books? Was I familiar with David Lynch's work? The 23rd is when I went in and met David.

The *Dune* project with Lynch attached to it had a lot of heat, so everybody who went up for it . . . it wasn't like you were just going up for another movie. You were going up for a BIGGIE. I was way more nervous for my *Dune* interview than I was for my *Gremlins* interview. *Gremlins* was Spielberg, but it was also not Spielberg, it was Joe Dante, but it's still Spielberg so it was exciting. Going up for *Dune*, you could feel it in the waiting room, you can feel the tension. The fact that you had no script to go over, which in some ways is your safety net, made it worse. I remember very vividly hanging in the waiting room with other actors, and people are getting up and pacing, doing practice questions in their heads. Some people would do the opposite; they'd sit and deep-breathe and close their eyes and try and calm themselves. It was a big deal going up for that, going up for the lead. That's when I felt like, "Okay, I did *Nothing Lasts Forever*—I'm in the big leagues now." I have very fond feelings for Jane. I always thought she was a very nice woman. She met me before for *The Outsiders*. Along with Juliet Taylor and a few other classic '80s casting directors, she was the epitome of nice, kind, and really interested in actors.

VIRGINIA MADSEN: Jane and Janet Hirshenson were THE casting directors at that time. There were only like four of them that were important, but you weren't going to go anywhere unless you had the support of those two women. Unlike today, that was a time when what they were doing was trying to make you look the best you could look. Not physically, they were more like acting coaches. They wanted all the actors to be really good before they appeared to the director and producers.

Although he was well-prepped by Jenkins, Galligan does not have fond memories of Lynch's "speed-dating" casting methodology.

ZACH GALLIGAN: What Lynch did that is weird—and accounts for some of his casting—is he doesn't read actors. You're literally just going in there and meeting the man and talking to him for 15 minutes. It may have been longer, but it feels like it was a 15- or 20-minute conversation with him. It was nerve wracking in a way because I'm 18 and thinking—probably stupidly—"I just want to be what this guy wants me to be." You want to please him and be the character somehow, but how do you do that? That's impossible. Like, "Okay, how are you doing today?" "Oh, I was thinking of, like, becoming an emperor and taking over the planet." How do you audition for Paul-Muad'Dib, you know? I knew there was no way to do that, so I just decided I was going to go in and be myself and hope that was good enough.

CRAIG CAMPOBASSO: Even Johanna Ray—who's my casting mentor and became David's casting director from *Blue Velvet* on—would just bring in actors for him to meet, and he would either say yes or no. That was it. We never really saw anybody read. The only reading was during the screen tests.

ZACH GALLIGAN: When I met him in 1982, David was chipper, upbeat, something very Midwestern-feeling about him with his pompadour hairstyle and genial demeanor. You walk in the door, and it's like, "How the heck are ya today?" Almost something out of *Fargo*. People have a hard time believing that's real, but he's exactly like that. He's like, "What have you been doing? What do you like to do? What are your hobbies? Have you lived in New York all your life? What's it like living in Manhattan? Wow, gee, so you just finished high school? What are your plans now? Shucks, it's great to meet you." To me, as an actor, that was very frustrating because I love the *Dune* books; I knew all of the dialogue. I would say to my friends, "fear is the mind-killer." It was frustrating because this is such a random and not merit-based procedure. I wanted to show him what I could do. I was on a roll. I had just worked with Bill Murray and Dan Aykroyd, and I was feeling good about myself. "Hey, I'm an 18-year-old up-and-comer! Let me show him what I can do!" And it was just like, "Well, he either likes me or he doesn't." If you look at the casting in some of his movies—I won't name names—it is kind of like, "Well, that person got lucky in the meeting." To me, it defeats the purpose because the whole point of acting is to not be yourself, to vanish into a character the way Sean Penn did in *Milk* or *I Am Sam* or Spicoli.

The feedback I got from Jane was, "David just didn't respond, and it's not going any further." I can remember saying to my agent, because I was 18 and a little whiny, "That's so unfair that I don't get a shot to read." There are other directors that do the same approach. Jon Amiel, who did *Copycat* with Sigourney Weaver, he did that approach. I met with Richard Lester who directed *A Hard Day's Night*. A lot of British people did not read actors; they just had the assumption that, "If a casting director is sending them to me, they can do anything. Let's just see how they are and if I can get along with them."

The search for Paul didn't stop in America, though. They also looked at English talent to possibly take the lead role.

JANE JENKINS: He was open to an international cast. A lot of those people we did not meet. He may have looked at footage of Francesca Annis and some of those people.

In an interview I personally conducted with Oscar-winner Kenneth Branagh (Belfast, Hamlet) in November 2017 for Coming Soon, he went into detail about auditioning for the role of Paul at the age of 21, along with his feelings toward Lynch's film.

KENNETH BRANAGH: He nailed it, in my view. It's so personal. I love the design, the look and feel of it. I have a soft spot because it's one of many films as a young actor I auditioned for and didn't get anywhere near. I was a 21-year-old meeting with the not-very-much-older Lynch. He was so nice and so kind, and I was nobody; there was no reason to be as gentlemanly and civil and interested as he was. He was looking for actors, I suppose, and had a vested interest to do so, but he was a good example on how you might comport yourself in this business. It was a memorable meeting because I was in awe of *Elephant Man*. He's a big hero of mine.

When I insinuated that Branagh probably didn't get the role because David Lynch was looking for someone who looked like David Lynch, Branagh laughed and complimented Kyle MacLachlan on his work in the movie and in general.
Another young British thespian looked at was Dexter Fletcher, who played the key role of "Byte's Boy" in Elephant Man *and had also been considered for the title part in Lynch's unmade passion project* Ronnie Rocket.

DEXTER FLETCHER: It was a great, great experience working on *Elephant Man*, I learned a lot from him. We were filming in London and there was an old man walking down the street with his arthritic dog, and David went, "Oh, my God." He got the guy and pulled them aside and put him in a costume and opens a shot of when Treves first finds the Elephant Man. There's the old cobblestone street, and it starts on the back of that old man and his arthritic dog walking up the street. I remember it very clearly, David saying that and the authenticity of that and making it part of the storytelling that he was doing. I try to live by what's around you— "What's there? What's helping you in the environment? In the world?"— to tell the story that you're telling and use what's there to your advantage. "What's cinematic? What's original and authentic?" I live by that. Even to myself, I'm very much somebody who turns up and tries to see what the world that we've created is offering.

While Fletcher nabbed roles in movies like Lock, Stock and Two Smoking Barrels *before transitioning into an A-list director of films* Eddie the Eagle *and* Rocketman, *he told me in a 2022 interview partly for* SlashFilm *about his experience on* Dune.

DEXTER FLETCHER: I was working at the Royal Shakespeare Company when I was 16, a couple years after *Elephant Man*. Raffaella and David came to see me on a break, and I was not particularly focused. I didn't know what it was about, so I was a bit cocky and wasn't in the right place. I saw David a few times over the years. I went and met him for *Mulholland Drive*, which I had an early draft of, and I read it and went and saw him. We talked about *Dune* then, and he said, "Yeah, you weren't ready." That's fair enough. That's a fair enough assessment. He was right. It didn't work out with *Mulholland*, but that's the thing: I've seen him from time to time over the years, and he's always very lovely to me.

JANE JENKINS: I think the biggest shake-up early on was that we were going to go with Val Kilmer for Paul. I had done a huge search around the country. I'd gone to Chicago, New York . . . There were a handful of actors that we talked about.

CRAIG CAMPOBASSO: We screen-tested Michael Biehn, Kevin Costner, Lewis Smith. There were a few others. Val Kilmer, of course, because Val was actually the number one choice up until Kyle did his screen test. That was a very hard screen test to do. Paul-Muad'Dib is not an easy character. Timothée Chalamet made it look easy. Kyle made it look easy, but if you saw all the other actors struggling . . . Michael Biehn did not live up to it. Kevin Costner did not. It's not that they're bad actors; they just didn't fit the criteria for Paul-Muad'Dib because you're looking for this inner strength. Kevin Costner wasn't known at that time, and I do remember him being nervous because I helped him get into the costume of Paul-Muad'Dib and I could feel his sense of nerves about it. I would be totally nervous if that were me.

SEAN YOUNG: I auditioned with Val Kilmer, and I auditioned with Tom Cruise. I was there in Mexico City when they were there, and they were auditioning people. When I got there, I went to this hotel and these people don't speak English. I'm thinking, "Oh my God, I don't fucking know how to even call out." So, I went upstairs to the lobby and Val was there wearing a baseball cap, and I thought, "Oh, an American crew member. I'll ask him." I walk up and I'm about crying, and then I realized it was Val, who I had met on auditions several times in New York. He says, "It's okay, all you have to do is dial this and this, get a front line out this and that. Let's go to lunch." We go to lunch, and the next day at the studio, we audition. We had three or four meals together during the audition, and then he's leaving and he goes, "Do you wanna switch numbers?" I'm like, "What for? You're dating Cher! Why would I need your number?" I saw him sometime after, and he said, "I really respected when you did that." I was like, "Oh dear . . ." [*laughs*]

JANE JENKINS: Certainly, Tom was in that group of boys. I met Rob Lowe when he was barely 18 years old, and he keeps talking on his podcast now about the fact that he's 56 years old. I keep on saying, "No!!! That's not possible!" Kevin was right in that group of kids. It would have made sense for him to come in. We gave him his SAG card. He was an extra in the movie *Frances* with Jessica Lange. I think the director asked him to say something to Frances and that upgraded him. Then I hired him for *Night Shift*, Ron Howard's movie where he's one of the frat boys. I hired him for *Table for Five* with Jon Voight where he was a permanent extra. Half the movie was shot on a cruise ship going down the Nile. Kevin had a nice trip to see the pyramids. Val came in early on and met with David. They were negotiating his deal.

RAFFAELLA DE LAURENTIIS: We did tests, so many tests, and I remember really liking Tom Cruise's. He came to Mexico and he was great. David liked him, too. I think the studio didn't like him, and Dino wasn't so sure. They were all concerned that his smile would light up the screen, which of course, it was proven that it did. I sometimes wonder what would have become of the movie if Tom had been in it.

SEAN YOUNG: Val was a little more courageous or heroic. Tom wasn't on his best game. I just remember him not really having a footing. I was a little bit taller than Tom, and I think that bothered him. He didn't want to audition opposite somebody that was looking down, and that's been a problem in a lot of instances for me.

CRAIG CAMPOBASSO: They just felt he was too young. He wasn't famous yet, but he looked like he was 16. He was baby faced, and I think they wanted somebody a little more mature. That was what they said afterward.

EVERETT MCGILL: I have a faint recollection that Tom Cruise had some difficulty with the language during his screen test.

SEAN YOUNG: Maybe they hadn't gotten him at the Scientology Celebrity Centre yet, helped him with his speech.

EVERETT MCGILL: My memories of Val are clearer in that he was represented by my agent, I knew him, and I was called to Mexico City just for his test. Val's classical training was at Juilliard, and he showed a smooth yet forceful poise and was very comfortable with the rhythm and texture of the dialogue. I would say his Paul, to use a metaphor, was more Daniel Craig than Pierce Brosnan. I thought he did very well, but later I heard Dino had misgivings over the shape of his lips.

JANE JENKINS: Something, yeah. That's the way Dino would express himself. It was never explained to me exactly why at the 11th hour we were having second thoughts. Just that Raffaella was not sure he was the right guy. I thought he was perfect. Val has always had that otherworldly look to him, which is part of what I thought was so perfect for this.

RAFFAELLA DE LAURENTIIS: I don't remember his deal being negotiated, and I don't even remember him being in Mexico. I remember very clearly doing a screen test on him here in the Valley, somewhere in Sherman Oaks or Burbank. That day we tested so many people. I remember him in particular, but I don't think he ever got further than the screen test. I think we saw a lot of people that read, and then the ones that we really liked we put in costume, we put them in makeup, we put them in wardrobe, just to see. I certainly remember that with him.

JANE JENKINS: They were already negotiating. They were testing his eyes to make his eyes blue, putting stuff in his eyes.

CRAIG CAMPOBASSO: Val was with us a lot. Raffaella said to me and Val one day, "We're going somewhere." We went in the car and didn't know where we were going. We ended up in this weird guy's strange laboratory at his home in Topanga Canyon, something out of *Frankenstein*. This little guy was moving around, "Okay, lie here, do this, do that." We were lying down. I didn't know what he was doing, and he just grabbed my eyeball and pours liquid into it. I'm like, "What are you doing?"

MOLLY WRYN: Raffaella asked me before the filming began to go see this guy who was making blue contacts to see if that would work. It was horrific. I don't know where Raffaella found him, but I let that man put all sorts of gunk in my eyes to take molds. Then I had these plastic things in my eyes that were blue. One time after, I was blinded. I couldn't see to get home. It took a day for my sight to come back. I would have done anything to not mess up my part in *Dune* and I was willing, but hindsight tells me that guy did not know what he was doing. It was scary.

CRAIG CAMPOBASSO: They were taking molds for contact lenses for the blue-within-blue eyes. Once you poured it in, you were blind, and you had to leave your eye open. You couldn't see until he pulled it out. Raffaella did it. Val did it. Of course, they realized they couldn't use them because the eyes had to breathe. They will be on hot sets, and they couldn't keep popping them in, taking them out, popping them in . . . That took them a lot to figure out, how to do the blue eyes.

MOLLY WRYN: I never got the final product. He'd already damaged my eyes so much, and he called trying to get me to come back. I said, "No, I will not come back. You hurt my eyes." I didn't know that other people did it. I thought I was the guinea pig. Raffaella did talk to me later about it, acknowledging I didn't have a good time.

BOB RINGWOOD: Val volunteered to come in for a screen test where they were trying blue dyes in the eyes. I think it nearly blinded him. I said to Raffaella, "Listen, it's fine to have blue dye in the eyes for one day, but you're shooting for 11 months. It would blind everybody."

Raffaella recalled in the May 1984 issue of Prevue, *"We were ready to give up and sign an actor who was the best compromise, after we tested him about seven times to convince ourselves. But Dino insisted we find someone who was Paul and . . . we did."*

JANE JENKINS: Then at the very last moment, just before Christmas, Raffaella called and said, "I don't know, there's something about Val, I just don't feel that he's right. I think you should do another fast search." I said, "A fast search? It's like two weeks before Christmas." I went, "Wait a second, are you pulling the plug on Val?" I mean, they were negotiating his deal. They were testing the blue stuff in his eyes. I said, "We're all the way, he's got this job. Everybody knows that. He's the guy." Raffaella said, "Well, we haven't finished his deal." She said, go to Chicago and New York. There was a young French woman who was my associate named Elisabeth Leustig—who very sadly was killed in a hit-and-run in Russia when she was working on *The Saint*—she went to San Francisco and Seattle.

KYLE MACLACHLAN: I knew the book well, so when the call came on my little answering machine in Seattle . . . I actually got calls from people in Seattle first. The junior casting agent, the late Elisabeth Leustig, had been sent to Seattle to sift through actors there. My name had come up a couple times because I'd worked at Ashland [doing *Romeo & Juliet* at the Oregon Shakespeare Festival] and I was working at The Empty Space theatre so people kind of knew of me. I'd graduated from the training program there at the U of Washington, which was a pretty sophisticated program. People knew the actors that were coming out of there, and they were like, "Oh, that sounds like Kyle because he's about the right age." She kept hearing this name, and so she finally reached out to me directly, but prior to that people would call me and I didn't understand. I was like, "They're doing what? They're doing *Dune*? How do you do *Dune*? They're making a movie? Okay." "They want to meet you for Paul." In my brain, that just didn't compute. I was trained in repertory theater; I was going to New York. Movies and TV were something I hadn't even thought about. It took me a minute to go, "And why are they coming here?" All these things kept going through my brain, and finally I said, "Oh, okay, okay, okay. It's an audition. All right. I get it." I thought someone was pranking me initially because people knew how much I enjoyed the book and they were telling me, "Oh, you're going to audition for Paul." "Ha ha. Don't be an idiot. Why would they come here for that?"

But it turned out to be true, and I met Elisabeth at the Four Seasons Olympic Hotel in downtown Seattle. She's so nice. She's this lovely little French lady, and so kind and so warm and so positive. I just said, "How does this work?" She saved me for last because she wanted to spend more time with me because enough people said, "You should seek out blah, blah, blah." I prepared the sides. I went in, and she had a little camera. She filmed me.

We did a few rehearsals, and she was very helpful. She said, "Do this, do this, do this, do this." I was like, "Okay." It was literally in her hotel room. There was a bed there and we sat and talked, and then I filmed it there. Then she said, "I'm going to San Francisco, and I'm going to see some people there, but you're high on the list." And I said, "Okay, that's nice to hear. So, like, where on the list?" Now I was starting to try to figure out what was going on here. She said, "Unless there's somebody really great there, I'll suggest you." She did tell me that she was going to bring me up.

JANE JENKINS: I remember Elisabeth calling me from San Francisco saying, "There's one guy who I think is really good, but he has kind of a funny jaw. I don't know." We wound up bringing him down.

KYLE MACLACHLAN: A few days later, I got a call and she said, "They like the tape, and they'd like to meet you. We'll fly you down." I'd been to Los Angeles but not like this before. There were some complications because I was working, doing *Tartuffe* at The Empty Space at that time playing Damis, and they needed to get the understudy ready because I was going to be staying over. That got sorted out. I flew down to meet David Lynch before I screen-tested, then I came back and went back into production. We did that all in one day so I could get back to the performance. Jane and Janet at The Casting Company must have said, "You'll be meeting David, and this is what he's like, and he directed this movie . . ." I'd seen *Eraserhead* when I was in college and was just like, "Wow, what is this?" There was a *Rocky Horror* and *Eraserhead* double bill in Seattle at the Neptune. Jane and Janet must have coached me a little bit, and then a PA picked me up at the airport.

CRAIG CAMPOBASSO: I went and picked him up at the airport. He was going to stay at the Universal Sheraton. I said, "Let's get you set up in your room, change, get freshened up, and then I'll take you to meet David." We did that and brought him in. He had a nice meeting for several hours with David in his office behind closed doors.

KYLE MACLACHLAN: David was at lunch at Bob's Big Boy. I was a little early, I sat in the office space, a very nondescript bungalow in the back. I didn't really know where I was, then David came in and was just as he's always been: "Aww shucks, great to see you. Great to meet you. Thanks for coming down." Very optimistic, positive, good vibe. We shared the Northwest connection; we talked for a bit.

JANE JENKINS: Kyle apparently was a *Dune* aficionado.

As it turns out, MacLachlan had his "Excalibur moment" at age 15 when a childhood friend named Jim Lundblad first handed him a copy of Frank Herbert's Dune.

KYLE MACLACHLAN: I was hanging out at Jim's place and either remarked on the book or he just pulled it off the shelf and said, "Oh, you should read this." Because he'd read it, and I was like, "Okay." It was just like that. I read a lot as a kid. I read all through The Hardy Boys, Tom Swift, The Three Investigators, *A Wrinkle in Time*. I remember reading all these books through grade school and junior high school, and this one was a little more complicated than those. I had to go back about three times. I'd get to about page 60 with a lot of thumbing back to the glossary of terms and then I'd say, "Huh, okay, I have to go back to the beginning . . ." About the third or fourth time through, I kept going and it was okay, but I remember really enjoying the book and identifying so strongly with Paul. Of course, I was the perfect age at 14 or 15 to read that. I read it a number of times, in high school primarily and a little bit in college. Paul became kind of my spiritual guide. His life and his sayings and his journey I sort of adopted as my own. It was pretty profound.

JANE JENKINS: I sat in the room, and he literally was asking David if his intentions in making this movie were honorable. What was he going to do with it? I went, "Wow, this kid has chutzpah." He's not going to do the movie unless . . . He's done nothing except a few theater things. He was very forthright about his commitment to making this the purest version of the book that could possibly be made.

KYLE MACLACHLAN: I certainly wasn't that fanatical. I didn't know anything. I hadn't read the script. I didn't know what I was going into. We didn't talk about the movie much. He just said, "Okay, here's the script, I want you to read the script and the five scenes are prepared. Come back in a few days; we'll set it up and we'll have the screen test." I remember reading the script on the plane on the way back and going, "Yes, it's kind of like *Dune*, but there's a lot of stuff missing." I didn't understand what screenplay structure was, how it was set up, but the scenes were there. I remembered the scenes from the book. It was beneficial because I knew the book so well, so I knew the context of scenes and what was happening. I prepared as best I could, got off book, and did all the things that I was trained to do in school. Instead of auditioning with a person, you're auditioning in front of a camera with another person. Then about four or five days later, they decided that I can't continue with the show, so the understudy became the permanent actor on *Tartuffe*.

JOHN PATTYSON: I sent Scott, my cameraman/partner up to Los Angeles, and he actually shot the screen test with Kyle MacLachlan. I remember that Kyle was great. He was doing theater in Seattle and just came out of nowhere, essentially.

KYLE MACLACHLAN: I came down to Los Angeles because I didn't know how long I was going to be there. I auditioned at John Dykstra's Apogee studio. There was an actress there that we worked with, very nice actress, wasn't Francesca.

CRAIG CAMPOBASSO: The screen test was full blown. We built a set, and they were put in the regal outfit that Paul had to wear with Gurney Halleck and Thufir. When Kyle got up there, he was just smooth and captivating. Now I have well over 30 years of casting movies and TV, but even back then, I was like, "That's the guy, right? That's the guy." Raffaella leaned over to me after he finished, and she said, "Should I change his last name?" And I said, "No, I think it's good."

MARY VOGT: Raffaella thought, "Well, let's show the tapes to the crew and see who likes who." There were 20 of us, maybe more, seeing an audition tape. It was Kyle and Val Kilmer, and he just jumped out. Kyle jumped off the screen. Val Kilmer was a really good actor, but there was something about Kyle that was just . . . he's so good looking, for one thing, and he was just mesmerizing on film. Val was a good actor, but he didn't have the presence. All the girls in the audience were like "ahhhhhh" when Kyle came on. Every one of these 25 people was attracted to Kyle, and I don't know how many other people Raffaella might have shown this to. There was something about Kyle, a sweetness about him and a sincerity, which was important for the character. And an innocence.

KYLE MACLACHLAN: I knew that Val was top running, and that Tom was being looked at because he was hot at that time, definitely in the pipeline as a young star. I don't know why David chose me over the other fellows, I really don't. I think he said, "You could play the innocence of Paul in the beginning as a prince, and then I also believe that he could be the leader at the end." He should have felt like I was capable of doing both of those things, but I don't know how that relates to Tom or Val. I never talked about it with them and obviously never saw their screen tests. Everett is the one that has all the inside scoop!

EVERETT MCGILL: Kyle was unique in so many ways. He was fresh from obscurity, guileless, very curious for a young man, and extremely bright. I think everyone saw Kyle as the son they would be most proud to have.

BOB RINGWOOD: They chose Kyle in the end. I don't know why they chose Kyle, but they did. I always thought he was too wholesome for the part. He wasn't very sexual, and I thought that boy should have a much more . . . I thought Val might have been a better casting for that. He was slightly stranger and slightly more off the wall. This is my theory: David felt very comfortable with Kyle because they're almost the same. They're very white-bread Americans. Kyle was the only person that was like him on the production. We're all foreigners, we're all different, and suddenly this boy walked in, a real upright American guy. David just went "wham" and grabbed him, and I don't think it served the casting.

JANE JENKINS: Val was much more on the horizon. He had gone to Juilliard; he was known in New York. We had auditioned him for *The Outsiders* and wanted to hire him, but he had a commitment to do a play in New York. He was a much more visible, known entity than MacLachlan from Seattle, who nobody ever saw. We did do a screen test, and then he got the part.

BOB RINGWOOD: It's like people that get married, especially with gay couples: They marry people that look exactly like themselves. A lot of people marry people that are very physically similar. It's a sense of security. Kyle and David were almost interchangeable. David was more sophisticated, but physically, they were like twins.

MOLLY WRYN: To me, they're like brothers with different mothers. I know how close they became and look at all the stuff Kyle's done with David. Jealous!

RAFFAELLA DE LAURENTIIS: They don't look alike at all. No. One is blonde, one is dark. They don't look alike at all, not in my mind.

KYLE MACLACHLAN: I've never really felt that David and I look alike. [*laughs*] People say it and I'm like, "I don't see it," but we are both from the Northwest and we do have a positive attitude on things. We do have a similar sense of humor, just a little off-kilter. I don't know. Certainly, when I did *Blue Velvet* and even more *Twin Peaks*, Cooper is modeled a little bit on David, some of David's mannerisms. They just kind of came—it wasn't intentional. He just happened to be appropriate for the character. But for Paul, I didn't think that.

SEAN YOUNG: I never saw that. I never saw that Kyle looked like David. I mean, people said that, but I never saw that. He looks like a lot of actors that have the chiseled face, dark hair, the Rock Hudson look. A leading man kind of look.

MARY VOGT: You hear people say, "Oh, well, they hired him because he looks like David Lynch." I never understood that. He doesn't look anything like David Lynch. Maybe the bone structure is not genetically unsimilar, but I never really understood why people would say that.

BOB RINGWOOD: I begged them to thin out Kyle's hair, because it was just this thatch of black hair, but they wouldn't. I thought that was a massive mistake, because he had far too much hair, although he was a very handsome man.

MOLLY WRYN: Kyle and I would talk about his hair. We both agreed it shouldn't be so damn neat. "Why is it so neat? David wants it that way?" I don't know. David had a vision, this perfect hair. We thought, "No, he wouldn't have perfect hair."

KYLE MACLACHLAN: They flew me to Mexico City to screen test again because my hair wasn't right. Dino said, "I no like hair." Went to Mexico City and screen-tested again, different hairstyle.

This final round of tests involved MacLachlan in an outdoor set in both his regal uniform and a shirtless fight scene to see where he fell on the beefcake meter.

GILES MASTERS: I was there when they were auditioning, getting a bottle of water or whatever. That was when Val Kilmer and Tom Cruise and various people came through, and Kyle was certainly our favorite. Not that I knew who Tom Cruise was. The guy from *Endless Love*, Martin Hewitt, was the only one I actually recognized, funny enough. Val was in a white t-shirt with a pack of Marlboros rolled up in the sleeve, aviator glasses . . . he was like Iceman. [*laughs*]

KYLE MACLACHLAN: I stayed down there and that's how I got the call, at the Hotel Royal where I was staying. I was hanging out with some of the guys from the art department, Kevin Phipps and Tony Masters' son Giles and another young woman, because we were all the same age pretty much, just hanging out, drinking a beer.

GILES MASTERS: We used to hang out a lot, especially early days in preparation. We were all 19, 20. I think he was about 22.

KYLE MACLACHLAN: Then someone else from somewhere said, "You got a phone call." I went to the phone booth and picked up, and they said, "You're the guy. You'll do Paul." I was like, "Great, thank you. Okay, good. This is great." I hung up the phone and then went back and said, "Looks like it's me. They cast me." Again, really no understanding of what that meant. I had just been plucked from—I won't even say relative obscurity, it was complete obscurity—and thrown into this new world. I stayed for a day or two, and then I did go back home and got ready. I think this was probably early January of '83. Then I went back down to stay and rehearse and do all that kind of stuff in Mexico.

CRAIG CAMPOBASSO: Dino signed him to an eight-picture deal . . . Jessica Lange had that same contract. She was in hell. She just wanted out after she signed on to do *King Kong*. Elisabeth Leustig's husband Jack got involved in Kyle's career and may have been managing him early on.

RAFFAELLA DE LAURENTIIS: I remember getting very upset with Jane over Kyle, because they found him and then when they found out we were interested in hiring him, they signed him up as managers. I thought that was inappropriate. I was trying to make a deal for somebody that I paid them to find for me. I remember being very upset over that.

JANE JENKINS: I did not make those deals. Those were all studio deals because it was the possibility of multi-pictures. Casting generally makes the smaller deals because we were shooting in Mexico. On a normal picture shooting in the United States, casting directors usually make deals, maybe up to but certainly not over $100,000. Anything over that is done by studio attorneys because then there's all the other stuff that goes with it. I would normally cast the day players, weekly players if they were not making a bajillion dollars, but I don't remember making deals on this movie at all. My attorneys did all of it.

Due to Bob Ringwood's now-iffy legal status in America thanks to Raffaella's previously mentioned passport maneuver, he had to find something to do on the stagnating production, and wound up aiding in the expansive casting process.

BOB RINGWOOD: I stayed on the film after Raffaella tore up my immigration papers. I was homeless and stuck in America, desperately terrified I might be arrested. [*laughs*] One day I said to Raffaella, "Look, I can't go home, but I can tell you right now I will not design another costume. Some of those costumes are redesigned 10 times, and they needn't be redesigned once. You've got to find me something else to do." They said, "Why don't you help us with the casting?" They hadn't got a casting director at that point, so I leaped into it. I thought this is a wonderful idea.

I started ringing around and making casting lists for people I thought could play the roles. I rang Marlene Dietrich's agent and said, "The Reverend Mother, would Miss Dietrich be interested in playing it?" He said, "If you saw her, you wouldn't want her, she drinks a bottle of whiskey a day!" I personally rang Gloria Swanson. Got her address from her agent, sent the script, and rang her about a week later. Gloria Swanson answered the phone. I said, "Miss Swanson, I sent you the script of *Dune*. Hope you've read it. I wonder if you'd be interested in playing the part?" She launched into how she would love to play the part, it was extraordinary and she saw herself as the Reverend Mother and it would be just wonderful. I said, "Excuse me, Miss Swanson. That isn't the part. The part they were interested in you playing was Shadout Mapes." There was a 30-second silence on the phone, and then she said, "Young man. You get into a spaceship. You fly 20,000 years into the future. You get off the spaceship. There's a hill and a castle. You go up to the castle. It's pouring rain. You bang on the door, and the door is opened by Gloria Swanson playing a maid? I don't think so. Goodbye." *Click.* I think Craig was there when we rang Orson Welles.

CRAIG CAMPOBASSO: Raffaella was always our fearless leader, and she called a few of us into her office and said, "Okay, I'm a little scared. I'm about to call Orson Welles. I'll put him on speaker." He answers the phone. She says, "Mr. Welles, this is Raffaella De Laurentiis. I'm producing *Dune*. I would like to talk to you about playing the Baron Harkonnen." There was dead silence, and he says, "You mean the floating fat man?" Then it went *click*. It was just like, "Okay, well, that's his answer."

BOB RINGWOOD: It was explained he would be hanging on wires the whole film. Welles said, "I weigh 600 pounds. Do you want to be known as the people that killed Orson Welles?"

CRAIG CAMPOBASSO: If he was already attached to it earlier [for Jodorowsky], why would he act that way? Or did he take it as a personal insult that, you know, he was heavy? And that's the only reason they were asking him? Who knows what was going through his mind, but what a brilliant performance that would have been if he had come on. It's like if Elvis Presley did Barbra Streisand's *A Star is Born*. That would have been the greatest performance of his life. He wouldn't do it for obvious reasons—it was too close to home.

The role of the royal concubine Lady Jessica proved to be another problem part in terms of casting. One person considered but passed on was Joan Hackett, who had recently received a Best Supporting Actress Oscar nomination and a Golden Globe win for her role in the successful Neil Simon adaptation Only When I Laugh. *The problem was that Hackett would not take no for an answer.*

BOB RINGWOOD: Joan Hackett was ringing David and Raffaella daily. They said to me, "This woman is driving us mad. You're helping on the casting—take her out for dinner and get rid of her." I thought, "Oh God." I went to the Hotel Bel-Air, booked a table, and took her to dinner. She was desperate for the role, and I said, "Look, I'm sorry, they've thought about it and they don't really want you to play the role." She burst into tears, had a huge hissy fit, just collapsed into tears. She was dying of cancer. She said, "I have only got nine months to live, and I thought I could play that role. It'd be my last role." I felt terrible. It was tricky. She did indeed die. But I said, "Well, it's no good. They won't let you play the role." She's a wonderful actress, and I loved having dinner, but at the end, she was just sobbing. It was the most horrible experience for both of us, and my heart went out to her.

Hackett (whose notable screen turns included Support Your Local Sheriff! *and* The Last of Sheila*) died of ovarian cancer on October 8, 1983, a month after* Dune *wrapped principal photography.*

RAFFAELLA DE LAURENTIIS: I think we tried too hard to find the perfect Jessica, and this girl that played her in the new one was great. We tested Glenn Close, but she never got the job, and I just did a movie with Glenn and we were talking about that screen test.

BOB RINGWOOD: I suggested Glenn Close. I went and saw *The World According to Garp*, one of her early films. I went back the next day to David and Raffaella and said, "I've just seen a film and it's got this actress called Glenn Close. She's not pretty, but she's a bloody good actress." They did see her, and after they saw her, I said, "Oh, how did it get on with Glenn Close?" They said, "She's plain, she's ugly, and she'll never be a star." I said, "I think you might be wrong about that." They didn't cast her, and of course, she went on to become an enormous star.

JANE JENKINS: Glenn Close, we seriously considered her. I do remember her coming in to meet David. I thought she would have been fabulous. I was a big fan of Glenn's. There was something else that I had just seen her in, could have been *Garp*. That was around that time. Francesca Annis had done some BBC something. I can't remember how we went from Glenn to Francesca, but we did!

BOB RINGWOOD: They were desperate because Jessica couldn't be cast. The year before I'd seen Francesca at Stratford-upon-Avon playing in *Measure for Measure*. I hadn't been aware of Francesca Annis up until that point, but she was so good in *Measure for Measure*. I said, "I have seen this actress last year, an English actress . . . well, she's half-Brazilian . . . and she's incredibly beautiful. She's an incredibly good actress and I think it's worth you seeing her." They rang her but she was busy doing something in England, so Raffaella and David agreed to fly over and see her. Raffaella called me too and said, "If you fucked up and this woman is no good, you're in big trouble! We're spending money flying all the way over to England to see her." Anyway, they did eventually offer her the role. If I hadn't gone to Stratford to see that production, no one would have known she existed. She was a bloody good actress. She still is very beautiful, even in old age, but she was incredibly beautiful then. She had a 22-inch waist, wore her clothes beautifully.

Sean Young, then hot off of back-to-back winners Stripes *and* Blade Runner, *almost missed her shot at playing Chani.*

CRAIG CAMPOBASSO: The Sean Young story is hysterical.

RAFFAELLA DE LAURENTIIS: Sean Young was the funniest one. We went to New York for casting, and we were supposed to meet Sean Young. She didn't show up at the interview, right?

SEAN YOUNG: I had an appointment with David Lynch in New York City that I couldn't make because I had a flight to LA. The appointment ended up being too late, and I didn't think I would make it, so I called my agents and canceled it.

CRAIG CAMPOBASSO: She doesn't show up for a lead role in a giant movie that's going at Universal?

RAFFAELLA DE LAURENTIIS: Then we were flying back from New York to LA, and she was on the plane with us.

SEAN YOUNG: David Lynch and Raffaella were on the plane, right? Pretty much a coincidence. That's how we ended up meeting, and then I ended up getting the part.

RAFFAELLA DE LAURENTIIS: David was upset, and so I went up there and said, "You know, you stood us up and David is upset?" We gave her a nice bollocking because she hadn't shown up at the meeting.

CRAIG CAMPOBASSO: They ended up talking and drinking. Sean and Raffaella were so drunk that Raffaella said, "Just come and stay at my condo." Sean did spend the night at her condo because they were a little wasted, you know?

RAFFAELLA DE LAURENTIIS: Then we became friends, and then she did the movie.

SEAN YOUNG: It was science fiction, and I was making a name for myself in science fiction because of *Blade Runner*. I don't feel the need to dramatize what was the appeal: The appeal was that I was hired! [*laughs*] I'm 23 years old, I've had two big hits, and I haven't worked in a year. I think the appeal was that they wanted me. David must have been a fan of *Blade Runner*. At the time, that was a pretty big deal in people's minds. It showed me off pretty well. It was a pretty intense movie, and I think people were impressed with it. I can't imagine he hadn't seen that.

The story of how '50s icon Aldo Ray earned and then subsequently lost the part of Warmaster Gurney Halleck also began on a plane.

RAFFAELLA DE LAURENTIIS: We met him on a plane, and David fell in love with him. Maybe it brought back memories of his childhood?

TERRI HARDIN: Kyle was the base for the stillsuits. From there, they were going to make all the other stillsuits for everybody else. They ran into this problem where they originally cast Aldo Ray as Gurney. I am so excited, a big Aldo Ray fan.

RAFFAELLA DE LAURENTIIS: Everybody told us not to hire him, that he had a history of . . .

TERRI HARDIN: They showed me a picture of Aldo Ray, and he was fat. He was seriously overweight. Someone who has a little more in the middle has no physique. They pulled out the body cast of him, which was two and a half times Kyle MacLachlan, and they said, "Look, can you make a suit for Aldo? Would you be so kind as to make him look good? We'd really like him to look good when he's walking around in this suit." I designed the pieces so that the shoulders were broad. Tucked in at the waist so he looked like he was more muscular than he was fat, right? Bob Ringwood flipped over the suit, so excited. "Oh my God, he'll love this suit."

RAFFAELLA DE LAURENTIIS: But his first day of shooting, he didn't come out of his dressing room. We couldn't get him out.

BOB RINGWOOD: Aldo Ray was there for two days, and then they had to send him home because he was so drunk.

TERRI HARDIN: Word came from Churubusco that Aldo had been flown down there early and he got in a brawl. He got drunk, got arrested, jailed, and Mexico didn't want him in their town. He was a big bull elephant. Somebody said something he didn't like, and he just started tearing up the town. Then the police came, and he started fighting them. It was a big mess. There was no recourse. He was done, and I was heartbroken. It would have been great to have him as that character. No more Aldo Ray in the role of Gurney. My suit never got screen time.

CRAIG CAMPOBASSO: Aldo Ray was Johanna Ray's ex-husband. She wasn't with *Dune*, but she was around because she was casting *Conan the Destroyer*. She was always in and out of the office and bringing actors in.

JANE JENKINS: She didn't work on *Dune* at all. I don't think Johanna had a relationship with David. They may have developed a relationship because of Aldo.

Johanna Ray went on to become Lynch's go-to casting director from Blue Velvet *on, while Johnna and Aldo's son Eric DaRe (who was on the* Dune *set with his father) went on to play Leo Johnson in* Twin Peaks. *With Aldo out of the picture, Lynch turned to another actor he had met in England.*

DEXTER FLETCHER: I was in "Henry IV, Part 1 and 2," and Patrick Stewart was in it. David looked over and Patrick was in the corner reading his lines. He said, "Who's that actor? Remind me of his name?" I said, "Oh, that's Patrick Stewart." Then the film came out — which I was compelled to see — and there was Patrick Stewart. I was like, "Ahh, right." Whenever I saw Patrick he said, "Oh, yeah. I got the job in *Dune* because of you, Dexter. Sure." Which we laugh about. He's very generous.

RAFFAELLA DE LAURENTIIS: We saw Patrick Stewart in London when we went there to see Siân Phillips. We were at the London theater, the big theater. We saw him there and she introduced us. David said, "How about that actor we met in London?" We made one phone call and got him on a plane from that. I just worked with him again on *Dragonheart*.

KYLE MACLACHLAN: I know he cast Patrick Stewart because he'd gone to see a play in London that Francesca was in, and she was great and he was like, "Oh yeah, she'd be great." Aldo was cast for Gurney, and then that didn't work, that fell through, and then he remembered, "Oh, what about that actor? Remember, he was that kind of brutish guy, big beard?" It must have been some production that was more feral. "What was his name? Patrick Stewart? Yeah, let's get him." Patrick shows up a few days before filming, and he's clean shaven. He's, you know, Patrick Stewart. I think in David's mind he had the image of the guy who was bearded and brutish that he was playing. Patrick tells that story that he didn't think David recognized him for the first few days he was there, which is just Patrick being funny.

TERRI HARDIN: We got the new Gurney, and he was fit and fine Patrick Stewart. He didn't need anyone to do a special suit for him.

CRAIG CAMPOBASSO: I can't see anybody but Patrick playing that part.

MARY VOGT: Patrick Stewart was such a dynamic personality. He was so fantastic. Completely different from Aldo Ray. Almost a *King and I* presence about him. You notice him, which is important because there are so many characters.

*Another London recruit was Sting, occasional actor as well as lead singer/bassist for popular rock band The Police. At the time, the group had released four studio albums, the most recent of which (*Ghost in the Machine*) had gone triple platinum and charted at #2 in the US. Their fifth and final album as a group,* Synchronicity, *would go to #1 in the US and virtually all other major territories, turning Sting into a certified global icon. His casting was a coup for the* Dune *team.*

JANE JENKINS: His role was very tiny. He was also with a manager that I was friendly with, Keith Addis, who said, "Well, what do you think about Sting for that?" I went, "Are you serious?" Good timing.

RAFFAELLA DE LAURENTIIS: We didn't luck out—we worked really hard at it! He was a very hard get. He didn't want to do it, and he turned us down. Finally, David got on a plane and flew to London.

CRAIG CAMPOBASSO: He was becoming extremely famous from The Police, a hot property. Or was he playing hard to get? Right? I know what agents do to make you want them more by saying, "Well, not sure . . . not sure . . . not sure." Of course, if they're saying that you know, in the end, you're going to make a deal because an actor really wants to do it. If you were actually talking to the actor, it would be, "Oh my God, my agent's working on that deal. I can't wait till it's done, I just want to be in that movie so bad." That's the reality of it, but when you have agents and managers involved, that is not the reality. They keep it like it's almost unattainable, but if you keep upping the game with money and things of that nature . . .

JANE JENKINS: It was also the idea of making the cast international. That was always something of interest so the movie could open in all these countries. There's a whole other psychology. A number of years later, when I was doing *The Da Vinci Code* for Ron Howard, we very purposely went for a very French person and a German person and an English for it. The book was enormous—as is this book—and it's a very international book, so it was of great value to have this very international cast.

MARY VOGT: I actually went up to Los Angeles to measure Sting. He was at A&M, recording something there. Bob had me take up a full-body leotard and a tape measure and go around his arms to write the inches. We took it back to Mexico and found someone who fit those measurements. It was made on that. He wasn't available at all. He wasn't even available to do a body cast because he was touring and recording. I got him for like 15 minutes. He thought it was just measurements, and I said, "Well, can you put this leotard on?" I measured that and then wrote on it. This is all Bob's idea, very clever. Then we found someone in Mexico to use as a good body double, and the costume fit great.

TERRI HARDIN: I did the body cast for Sting, and it was fast. He ran in, we did it, he was gone. We were told to get it done and get him out. I kept getting these phone messages where people were like, "Are you taking a body cast of Sting? Could you duplicate his crotch for us?" When I was doing the mold on him, I said, "You know Sting, you could make a lot of money." And he was like, "What?" I said, "I don't know what it is, but people are calling me and saying they'd like to have a cast of your crotch. Why is that?" He just started laughing and said, "Seriously?"

Despite production going through a range of possibilities for rock stars to provide music for the soundtrack, Jenkins, Raffaella, and members of Toto all expressed to me that there was never any discussion to have Sting record a song for Dune.

JANE JENKINS: Not that I was ever aware of.

RAFFAELLA DE LAURENTIIS: If there was, I don't remember? I don't think so.

DAVID PAICH: Now that I think back on that, that's really an obvious choice. That would have been a great idea. I wish I'd thought about that. I knew he was starring in it, but they should have included a Sting track on the record somehow.

STEVE LUKATHER: This is before all that, having a rock song in every film, which is not necessarily always the right thing. Product placement, song placement . . . all that shit is about the money. David Lynch being the consummate artist . . .

DAVID PAICH: That's some forward thinking, but I don't think people were that far along with movie soundtracks and getting people that star in them to do that. I think that was a little early on or just at the very beginning. That's a great idea, though.

John Hurt, Lynch's Elephant Man *lead, was originally signed to play the part of Dr. Wellington Yueh. The role eventually went to Dean Stockwell.*

KYLE MACLACHLAN: Aldo was there when I was there, but I didn't see him. I don't remember if I saw John on set. I don't know if I met John or not. An amazing actor.

BOB RINGWOOD: I went to do some measurements and talk to John Hurt. I could tell by the way he was talking to me he wasn't going to do it.

I went back to Raffaella and said, "This actor is not going to do it. I can tell you right now he won't do it." He was being so offhand, even rude and dismissive. He almost immediately after said he didn't want to do it. He was a strange man. A wonderful actor, but a strange man.

MARY VOGT: I remember meeting him. I later worked with him on *Recount*. I think he had a terrible riding accident. That's why he didn't do *Dune*.

John Hurt was involved in a horseback riding accident on January 15, 1983, where he was thrown from his horse while trying to get in shape to play a jockey in the film Champions. *His longtime girlfriend Marie-Lise Volpeliere-Pierrot, attempting to catch Hurt's runaway mount, fell off her own horse and onto her head, putting her into a coma. She died the same day. While it's uncertain if this event caused Hurt to exit* Dune, *he did begin filming* Champions *on March 15, 1983. This cleared the way for Dean Stockwell to take the part of Yueh, a comeback for him.*

JANE JENKINS: Dean was wonderful. Very sweet guy. I'm of an age where I actually remember crying hysterically at a movie theater when I was eight or nine years old over *The Boy with Green Hair*. He had such an erratic career. There was a period of time when he was living in New Mexico selling real estate. When his career started getting resurrected, it was out of nowhere. Harry Dean Stanton had a lot to do with Dean coming back into the film business. I cast Dean Stockwell in other movies, and when he died, I was thinking, "How did he wind up in *Dune?*" I don't remember him ever coming to LA. It's possible he was in Mexico and David saw him.

SEAN YOUNG: Dean was fun. I remember hanging on the set with Dean, asking him about *The Secret Garden* because he had been in show business for so long. He had my attitude, which is "hit your marks." He was very practical like me.

One of Jane Jenkins' biggest discoveries on Dune *was Alicia Witt, a 7-year-old she found from an episode of* That's Incredible! *where Witt recited Shakespeare at age 4. Despite her relatively young age, Witt still retains vivid memories of auditioning to play Paul's sister Alia in November 1982.*

ALICIA WITT: I thought Jane happened to be watching an episode of *That's Incredible!* and saw me, but that's not what happened. She was searching for Alia and not having any luck going the regular route, so she got in touch with *That's Incredible!* because they had kids on sometimes. She was specifically sent the tape of my episode and then got in touch with my family, because it said on the show what city we were from. I remember when my mom came out of her bedroom after the call with Jane and described it, and that feeling I had. Although I had been making up characters and reenacting scenes from shows or musicals that I'd loved for as long as I could remember, growing up in Worcester with teacher parents and not knowing anybody in the acting business . . . it certainly wasn't anything I ever thought of doing, right? I thought it sounded fantastic.

I was so excited to go to New York and have an audition for this movie. I remember the first meeting with Jane, what she looked like and how kind and matter of fact she was. I did each scene once, and then she instantly said, "The director David Lynch is coming in tomorrow, and I would love to put you all up for another night so that you could read for him." It happened very quickly, a "yes" from her. Unlike in years to come when I realized what the stakes were in a situation like that and butterflies would come in, I was seven and didn't have any expectation or fear whatsoever. I just thought, "This seems like fun, to pretend to be somebody else."

What I remember most vividly is the experience of David, because even if I hadn't ended up making the movie with him, I believe the time I spent with him that afternoon would have still been a formative memory. He just seemed like a family member to me immediately, and he obviously is fantastic with children. He had Jen and Austin by then. David spoke to me like I was an equal of his in that way that people who are great with kids can do. The first thing we did was just talk, and I don't remember how we got on the subject, but I gave him a briefing on all of the neighborhood dogs where I lived. David remembers the details of our first meeting as well, which is amazing to me because how many hundreds of people did he meet for that movie? And over the course of his life? But he still remembers the dogs I told him about, and every time I've seen him for a visit or for work, he asks me about my parents and about my brother. He takes a keen interest in knowing how I am. That's not a polite thing like with so many people who'll ask how you're doing, but their eyes are glazed over. He genuinely wants to know how I'm doing, and he won't forget what I share with him, whether it's about somebody I just broke up with or what my folks are up to. When he talks, those are the things that he'll share as well. That's one of the reasons why his work affects people so viscerally, because although it has a surreal element to it, it's grounded in human behavior and what makes us all tick.

Given the fact that she was a prodigy from a young age, her red hair, and even the closeness of their names, the similarities between Alia and Alicia were uncanny.

ALICIA WITT: That's for certain. I mean, for sure. I wouldn't have been able to verbalize that at the time, but being homeschooled and not having any friends, the strange experience of being the only person my age that I knew . . . I think that's very similar to Alia's experience relating more to adults as a result of not only the intelligence and the advanced-ness, but also Alia was not surrounded by other kids. It has a strange effect on a child regardless of whether you're "advanced." But yes, there were eerie similarities between me and Alia. Without question, that was a God working that I found my way into it.

While the roles of Harah's sons Kaleff and Orlop would require no dialogue whatsoever, playing one-half of the dynamic bro duo (the Orlop half) was 9-year-old Chicago native Danny Corkill. The part of his slightly older brother Kaleff (with an equally frizzy 'fro) was an unknown and uncredited child actor.

DANNY CORKILL: I felt bad because I was just going over the cast list, and I don't even see the guy they brought in to play my brother, Diego Gonzalez. He doesn't even show up on IMDb or anywhere else as a named part. *Dune* was the only movie I never had to audition for. David Lynch had seen *Without a Trace*, called my agent, and said, "I want this kid in my movie." It was fantastic. I don't believe I read a single time. It was a straight phone call. I'd done a movie in New York called *Without a Trace* with Kate Nelligan and Judd Hirsch, the first movie I ever auditioned for. That was an open casting call in Chicago, and my mom took me down just because I'd been bugging her for a while. They asked me to tell a joke. I blanked, remembered one dirty joke I heard my dad telling and it's what got me the job. That's what made me stand out from all those kids: I was the only one who walked in and told a dirty joke. I ended up getting the job, so that screwed up the next six years of our lives.

*For the significant part of Harah, who becomes Paul's wife by custom and Alia's caretaker, a total unknown was brought in by sheer providence. In her early 20s, Molly Wryn moved to L.A. after growing up in Oregon doing civic theater. Trained by the likes of acting coach Jeff Corey (*True Grit*), she had gotten a bit of work doing voiceovers, including dubbing the performance of Alana Hamilton for director Richard*

Compton's post-apocalyptic 1979 movie Ravagers. *At age 26, it seemed that Wryn had finally gotten the big break she was waiting for.*

MOLLY WRYN: Right before I found out *Dune* was in production, my dad had given me *Dune* to read. I stayed up however long it took, maybe three nights, to get through the book. I loved it so much. I used to get *Drama-Logue*, one of the industry papers, and shortly thereafter, it mentioned that *Dune* was being made. So, I just wrote David a letter, sent a couple of pictures, said that my dad gave me the book, and I'd love to be in the film. I got a call. I was so surprised.

Wryn's fateful meeting with Lynch happened at 4:45pm on September 16, 1982.

MOLLY WRYN: I had this long gauze dress I put in a pot of tea on the stove to dye it sand color. I wore desert boots, my hair was long, and I walked in there. David later told me that I got the part the minute I walked in the door. I probably at the time was interested in Chani, of course, but I imagine he saw strength and passion. I tried to walk in like a proud Fremen woman. Maybe that did it. I loved that book; it meant so much to me because dad gave it to me. It absorbed me into that world. I wanted to be in that world, so it really didn't matter what part. When I met Frank Herbert later, he signed my book "to the perfect Harah." Raffaella wanted me to play Princess Irulan, and David said, "No, I want her to play Harah." Gina was perfect for that.

*One of the last major players cast was relative newcomer Virginia Madsen (*Class*), filling the small but critical role of Princess Irulan, daughter of the Emperor. A young Helena Bonham Carter had purportedly been set at one point and then dashed.*

VIRGINIA MADSEN: There was a scheduling problem, it sucked that they did that. It wasn't the *Dune* people; it was the *Room with a View* people. As I understood it, it was only over a couple of overlapping days, but that was a drag.

JANE JENKINS: I don't remember that we ever had anybody that we actually cast. They had names that we talked about, but there was nobody for that part. It was elusive. We couldn't find somebody for the Princess. They were already in Mexico, and I was still casting and shipping three-quarter-inch tapes, calling Raffaella and telling her about somebody or other. Virginia Madsen literally just arrived in Los Angeles from Chicago. Her agent called me up, and I met her on a general meeting.

VIRGINIA MADSEN: You used to be able to have general meetings, where you would just go in and say, "Hi, I'm new, got anything for me?" Just a way to introduce yourself around town.

JANE JENKINS: Then I said, "You know, there's this part . . ."

VIRGINIA MADSEN: I was brand new and immediately got powerful representation. Jane and Janet had my back. They took a liking to me and got me in the door with a Polaroid. There were so many actresses in the mix because everybody wanted to be in the next *Star Wars*. A lot of people auditioned for it, but that was before I got to town, and then it was just David's choice. It was all very mysterious, a hard role to get. You couldn't really fight for it, just wait to be picked. The project was very important, a big deal. I was incredibly nervous, thought I was playing the princess of the universe. If you got it, they were going to make three of these movies. This was very '80s, and I wore a little white minidress with white lace leggings and little white scrunchie socks. It's absurd, but I thought that made me look like a princess. [*laughs*] They met and talked with me for a good long while, then took a Polaroid.

CRAIG CAMPOBASSO: I took Virginia's picture and resume directly to Dino at the Beverly Hills Hotel. She got cast right after that, because Jane had suggested her.

JANE JENKINS: When I called Raffaella, I said, "I think I found the perfect girl," and must have faxed pictures to her. We still had faxes back then. She said, "Well, let's put her on a plane to Mexico," because nobody was here anymore.

VIRGINIA MADSEN: That was it. I didn't audition beyond that. He just chose the picture, and I was on my way to Mexico. "Do I have a script?" "No. You're on a plane tomorrow morning, so get ready."

JANE JENKINS: We put her on a plane. I said to Virginia, "If I were you, I'd pack for the long haul. I don't think you'll be coming back so fast," which is what happened.

VIRGINIA MADSEN: I was like, "All right, I'm not even going to hope for it, I'll just wait and see if I get it. There's nothing I can do. I can't read on tape. I can't do anything. If they pick me, great. If they don't, I just got here. [*laughs*] I've got time."

JANE JENKINS: She was so brand new, so breathtakingly, interestingly beautiful. That doesn't happen anymore, just called the producer: "Here's her picture."

VIRGINIA MADSEN: That's what he chose. God knows how he saw Irulan in a little white minidress. I think he saw something in my face, something classic about the way I looked, and I think he just said he liked it.

MARY VOGT: Virginia was great. She just had that one golden, black, gorgeous, corseted dress. She was fabulous, but she was a little late. The costume was the kind of thing that you could adjust to her because it was laced up in the back.

DANNY CORKILL: I had done one legitimate theatrical movie [*Without a Trace*] and a little PBS *American Playhouse* production [*A Matter of Principle*] that Virginia Madsen ironically was in. [*laughs*] Both of our next projects after that was *Dune*, as random as that is. From a tiny PBS movie shot in the 'burbs of Illinois to *Dune* in Mexico. I think that's kind of funny just to show up one day, and there's Virginia on set. I had just worked with her three or four months prior. Only two movies under my belt, and I'm there with somebody else. She and I didn't interact very much on set—we had different parts and plot lines. She was very nice.

VIRGINIA MADSEN: I did a TV movie, I did *Class*, but to be in that group meant the world to me. That meant there was something to me, that this was an important film and I would be okay. I was going to be good. I was going to be more than okay . . . I was going to be excellent.

. . .

—II—

PRODUCTION

Location, Location, Location

When it comes to making Hollywood-style motion pictures, Mexico has never been a picnic for Americans. In Joseph Cotten's autobiography *Vanity Will Get You Somewhere*, the actor describes working with director Robert Aldrich on his 1961 Universal western *The Last Sunset*, a vehicle for Rock Hudson and Kirk Douglas. They shot in Aguascalientes, cattle country about 500 miles north of Mexico City.

Cotten wrote:

> Production seemed to take forever. We were held up because we lost most of the extras . . . Everything happened to delay us . . . Bottled water was as scarce as a tree-ripened orange in Florida. We boiled the water, we flavored it with tea, we sterilized it with alcohol, but some of us became weaker and weaker, and finally—when we were barely able to stand or pull socks over our feet, which had turned to sandpaper—a blessed Mexican Florence Nightingale arrived with glucose and needles. Within a few hours, our hydration meters were pointing upward toward normal again. We discovered—alas, too late—that one of the largest buildings in town was the Canada Dry bottling works.

As it happens, not much about shooting in Mexico had changed between 1961 and the start of principal photography on *Dune* at Estudios Churubusco Azteca in early 1983. This studio location was chosen after a worldwide search conducted by Raffaella De Laurentiis for a suitable spot to lens the Frank Herbert epic . . . at a cost. Destinations as varied as Australia, England, India, Italy, North Africa, Spain, and Tunisia (where *Star Wars* had shot)—even in combinations (Italy and Tunisia, etc.)—were considered before the De Laurentiis' gave Mexico City the green light, despite David Lynch and Tony Masters being initially opposed.

Part of the appeal of Churubusco was its proximity to a desert, as well as the studio's three spacious backlots and eight soundstages. One of the oldest movie studios in Mexico, it had produced many big pictures over the years, including *The Exterminating Angel*, *Butch Cassidy and the Sundance Kid*, and *Bring Me the Head of Alfredo Garcia*. In the years after *Dune*, it would host the productions of such hits as *Total Recall*, *Romeo + Juliet*, and *The*

Mask of Zorro. It was founded in 1945 and has been under government control since 1958. It most recently played host to Alejandro González Iñárritu's 2022 film *Bardo*.

Other Mexican locations used within proximity of Churubusco included the Samalayuca Desert outside Juárez, a warehouse at Iztapalapa where a 100'×300' reservoir was built (for the Fremen water reserves), a 65-foot-high lava rock that was constructed at Las Aguilas Rojas (not far from the Popocatépetl and Iztaccíhuatl volcanoes) and Latin America's largest football arena, Azteca Stadium, which became the Arrakis landing field. There was also a one-day shoot at Mexico City's Hospital Metropolitano, and one day in the Tlaxcala Desert doubling for the Samalayuca. Aguilas Rojas—whose actual name translates as "The Red Eagle"—was nicknamed "The Dead Dog Dump" after . . . well, the name says it all. A clean-up crew spent weeks clearing carcasses, trash, and broken glass, but even then, lava dust would puff up from people's footsteps as they shot there.

It was estimated that the movie would have cost around $75 million had it been shot on studio lots in Los Angeles, with at least $20 million going toward Hollywood stage rentals alone. Studio setups in Europe all lacked the stage space and proximity to a desert required by the production. In Mexico, the degradation of the peso meant that the exchange rate was 150 to 1 US dollar. Everything cost one-fifth what it would have in the States, with the budget initially set at $30 million and coming in at an estimated $42 million. At one point, it was even rumored that Dino De Laurentiis would buy Churubusco outright. Unfortunately, in the years prior, the studio had fallen into disrepair, mostly used for low-budget exploitation fare like *The Devil's Rain* or *Sorceress*. The Mexican government was ready to close the studio down until *Dune* came in. A great deal of simple infrastructure, like modern wiring, had to be installed during the six months of pre-production there.

Whatever the De Laurentiises saved by lensing in Mexico was surely offset by the myriad technical problems of shooting in a third-world country. Telephones would be cut off a minimum of once or twice every week. Frequent brownouts would occur in the middle of takes, with electricity out for hours at a time, necessitating generators. Hundreds of military personnel had to clear three square miles of desert terrain of rattlesnakes, scorpions, and other wildlife and vegetation. There was frequent union pressure, and customs delayed important shipments, sometimes for months on end, due to "petty corruption at all levels of government" (via *Philadelphia*

Inquirer, September 1983). Mexico City's high elevation—8000 feet above sea level—precipitated oxygen deprivation symptoms like dizziness, fatigue, hyperventilation, and sleeplessness. Between the worst air pollution in the world (the equivalent of breathing in 40 cigarettes a day), bad food, and a tainted local water supply, most of the cast and crew became ill at one time or another with "intestinal maladies." At least one key crew member suffered from internal bleeding. The producer herself got salmonella poisoning three times. Around 15% of the crew was hospitalized during the first month of production.

"It's fascinating because you see the country for what it's really like, not like a tourist," Francesca Annis told the *Richmond Times-Dispatch* in December 1984. "That's one of the perks. It also helps sort out your values about your own area."

This empathy extends to the many Mexican artisans who labored to construct the film's 70-plus sets, most of which were handmade since they had little access to power tools. There were 2 exterior and 23 interior sets initially, which were then struck after use to make way for more. The Emperor's palace alone had 24,000 decorative "stalactites" hanging from the ceiling. Only 105 of the 600-person crew on the film were not Mexican.

Tony Masters said at the time [*Philadelphia Inquirer*]:

> We couldn't have made this film anywhere but in Mexico. No place else could have found so many sound stages of such size. No place else could have found the number of remarkable craftsmen we needed to build our ornate sets. The carpenters, in particular, have been splendid; the wood carvings in this movie are spectacular.

The film company formally moved to Mexico to begin pre-production and set construction in July 1982. Altogether, Lynch and Raffaella De Laurentiis spent one and a half years in Mexico until model photography wrapped in February '84.

Raffaella told *Starburst* #78:

> In the building of the sets here, we have saved 50%, but that's the only area. Maybe if you come here to do a regular modern movie, the picture will be cheaper, but with *Dune*, we had to create a whole world and bring in entire crews, put them up in hotels, and send them home when their marriages were breaking up. This takes a lot away from the cost effectiveness of cheaper labor.

Start of Production

*D*une was a monster of a movie. Or, as Raffaella De Laurentiis described it, a "mastodon." The workforce this movie required was off the charts: 53 speaking parts, 900 crew members, and 20,000 extras working on roughly 70 sets (15–20 standing at any given time), built and torn down over six months of principal photography from March 30 to September 9, 1983. There were over 150 department heads and key personnel.

"It's different for the producers, but for me, it's exactly the same," Lynch told Knight-Ridder's Rick Lyman on set about the size of *Dune*. "I never know on any given day what I'm going to shoot the next day until they tell me."

"A lot of people said the biggest gamble was not the $40 million, but David Lynch. That's what I'm most proud of," Raffaella De Laurentiis told the AP in December '84.

Lynch, who sometimes stepped in to help paint the sets, had originally wanted to continue his trend of making exclusively black-and-white movies on *Dune*, but eventually was convinced otherwise.

Lynch said in April 1984 [*Chicago Tribune*]:

> I'm not really wild about color. Something like *Dune* shot in black and white would have a nice foreign feeling to it. However, you have to be practical. *Dune* is a commercial venture, something I'm constantly reminded of by the numbers of merchandising people passing through preparing to manufacture sandworm dolls and what-have-you. That doesn't bother me because it's their world, not mine. It does reinforce the fact that this is a moneymaking enterprise. It would have been difficult differentiating [the four planets] in black and white, and Freddie Francis is shooting *Dune* in a way that not only makes the colors richer than anything we've seen in years, he's also making the shadows soft and subtle to create an unusual beauty.

An ambitious exec at Universal's publicity department named Gordon Armstrong conjured the idea to have a behind-the-scenes video crew embedded with the *Dune* production from beginning to end. Lynch agreed on the condition that he pick this crew: a cameraman named Anatol Pacanowsky who worked with Lynch back in his AFI days, along with Canadian writer

Kenneth George Godwin, who had written a favorable article on *Eraserhead* for *Cinefantastique* with Lynch's participation. Using high-speed Panasonic VHS cameras, Pacanowsky served as DP while Godwin worked the boom mic and conducted most of the interviews with cast and crew.

In addition to this behind-the-scenes crew filming over 70 hours of footage, an EPK producer was also hired by Armstrong to gather more standard material, as Julie Salamon wrote in her book *The Devil's Candy*:

> John Pattyson of Pattyson Productions saw the future in behind-the-scenes coverage back in 1983 when he produced a feature on the making of *Dune*, a science-fiction film. That early experiment in the genre helped introduce the studios to the idea of creating news features to promote their movies. Rather than clutter their movie sets with independent producers whose footage couldn't be monitored, the studios preferred to oversee their own behind-the-scenes productions shot by someone they could trust.

Like many big effects films today, the need for secrecy was critical. Locals recruited to work on the film came to the studio with cameras around their necks, looking to make a buck by nabbing a shot of a sandworm or Sting. A memo to the production from Lynch (via *Twilight Zone*, December 1984) emphasized the need for secrecy by comparing the film to "steam in a giant boiler. It is already building up considerable pressure. Any leaks concerning what we are doing on this project will decrease the curiosity factor and cause us to lose power. I beg you to keep this in mind."

Common Threads: Costuming

After his exquisite work on John Boorman's *Excalibur*, 37-year-old Bob Ringwood was brought in to replace the previously hired costume designer at the last minute. Ringwood quit art school at age 18, apprenticed at the London Theatre, and was assistant costume designer on *Corn is Green* and *Quadrophenia* (with Sting!) before landing *Excalibur* in 1981. When he was initially approached for *Dune*, Ringwood suggested hiring four entirely different designers to make clothes for each of the different worlds, but eventually took it all on himself.

This was no simple task. Between 3000 and 4000 costumes were eventually handmade to meet demands. Ringwood wanted costumes with a revival look rather than a futuristic one, which matched Lynch's vision. The overarching style could best be described as "medieval futurism." Adding to the challenge, Dino De Laurentiis tended to wake up around 4 a.m. every day, and meetings with Ringwood and others on the *Dune* team were frequently held only two hours later.

The central costume of the movie was the stillsuits used to survive in the deep deserts of Arrakis. Lynch's original conception of baggy diving suits with a window helmet was later co-opted for the look of the Emperor's Sardaukar terror troops. The filmmaker specifically didn't want the stillsuits to look "spacey," so Ringwood based the rubber outfits on anatomical charts. Kaftan-like robes were worn over the stillsuits in the book, but Lynch argued against wide opposition from his team to have the suits on full display sans accouterment. Being the director, Lynch won out.

"David is not a visual person, but he has remarkable ideas," Ringwood told *Prevue*. "His concepts sound crazy, but once they start to blend, they're quite interesting. He may not be sure of what he wants, but he certainly knows what he doesn't want, once he sees it."

Despite going through many iterations, the final approved design resembled the first one Ringwood turned in . . . after roughly 20 attempts. The suits were made of Lycra body stockings covered with foam appliances and then rubberized. Once on set, the stillsuits proved both hot and uncomfortable for the actors. The Hall of Rites rally scenes (for which Lynch originally wanted 3000 extras) required Ringwood to clothe 800 extras in stillsuits, or at least what would look like stillsuits from a distance inside the dark, smoky cave.

Ringwood waited until most of the cast was in place before he created many of the costumes. He hired 45 people on three different units to output thousands of pieces, with 20 people consistently working day and night. Some of these were rented from costume houses all over Europe (Spain, Italy, and England) and then drastically altered, with as many as 500 made from scratch. The cloak worn by Jessica during the Water of Life ceremony (and again by Paul at the end of the film) was the most complex, handwoven by nine Mexican needlework experts over four months.

Aside from Mexican cotton, a majority of the fabrics were imported from New York and LA. Ringwood's assistant Mary Vogt (*Diner*) had trouble bringing materials such as silks and trims from New York through customs, where extortion was a regular occurrence. (A half-ton of spaghetti was delayed three months.) The costume department began smuggling cloth and accessories into Mexico via assistants with hand-carried suitcases, often enlisting Raffaella and Masters to take them off their hands at the airport upon arrival.

Kenneth McMillan's fat suit for the Baron alone cost $25,000. Due to the suit's colossal weight, McMillan had to be wheeled onto set until he got used to it. Even after he learned to walk in it, he couldn't go up or down stairs without two people supporting him. Feyd and Rabban's bulky, samurai-inspired costumes were made out of the same type of rubber that lines the inside of car doors.

"I spent a lot of time studying pictures from the '50s," Ringwood said in *Prevue*. "Cars, trains, styles—everything was streamlined. David is very much a '50s child, and many of our designs have that decade's technical appearance."

Actors' Experiences

Two weeks were set aside for rehearsal before cameras began to roll on the many thespians who populated the worlds of *Dune*. Memories of both their experience and their director tend to be positive, even when they were under incredible strain.

"Paul is difficult to play because every reader has a personal picture of the character," Kyle MacLachlan told *Prevue* #59. "In addition, he does many things that aren't very nice, yet he must remain a sympathetic character. He's really two people: Paul, the life affirmer, and Muad'Dib, the mystical angry god."

MacLachlan, who had studied karate (brown belt) and fencing since age 12 and kept in shape by weightlifting prior to the film, worked closely with fight choreographer Kiyoshi Yamasaki for his knife skirmishes with Jamis (Judd Omen) and Feyd (Sting). This included practice with a katana, a short crysknife and a dagger, with samurai and aikido techniques thrown in for good measure. Yamasaki had previously trained Arnold Schwarzenegger for *Conan the Barbarian*.

"He kept me busy constantly," MacLachlan told *Enterprise Incidents* #24. "Primarily sword work and a little bit of Tai Chi. We'd fight mock battles together with the little crysknives that the Fremen of Arrakis use."

"I had a fight trainer during the shooting, and had another good trainer when I was at the U," MacLachlan told the *Tacoma News Tribune* in February 1984, referring to his time at the University of Washington. "The stillsuit, that's the suit—like a diving suit—they had to wear on Dune to keep moisture from escaping. It wasn't designed as armor, but it turned out to be that. It was difficult to get bruised in it."

MacLachlan's meal of choice during the shoot? Peanut butter on whole wheat bread, with a big supply of both being regularly brought in from the States for him during his long time in Mexico. This was probably a smart choice, since the highly processed foods provided healthy carbs and protein without a risk of getting the leading man sick, which would delay production. He also consumed copious amounts of coffee and Mexican sugar cookies during the "hurry up and wait" tediousness of shooting, yet still managed to lose 15 pounds.

MacLachlan's Great Hall sparring partner Sting was so popular among cast and crew that on his wrap day, everyone formed a human trampoline and threw him in the air to celebrate his time on the film.

"I am Feyd. I honestly didn't have to do any preparation. He was Martin Taylor in a space suit," Sting told *Film Review*, referring to his *Brimstone & Treacle* character.

Sting was a charged presence on the *Dune* set since the June 1983 release of The Police album *Synchronicity*, which topped the UK charts for two weeks and the US charts for 17 weeks on the back of hit singles like "Every Breath You Take" and "Wrapped Around Your Finger." It eventually sold eight million albums stateside, with the BBC and *The Guardian* agreeing that The Police were—at that moment in time—"the biggest band in the world."

Fellow Englishman Patrick Stewart was seemingly the only one who was late to the party on this, as he recounted in 2013:

> Music—at least popular music—has never played a big part in my life until the last few years. I had never heard of Sting; that's how isolated I was from the music world. I'd been there a couple weeks before Sting arrived, and when he arrived, there was this kind of frisson everywhere. The whole of Mexico City was abuzz that Sting was coming. I heard he was a musician; that's all I knew. The second or third day we're just hanging out on set, him and me, and I say, "So you're a musician?" He said, "Yeah." I said, "What do you play?" I swear, I cross my heart, he said, "Bass," and I said, 'You know, I often wondered what is it like carrying that huge thing around everywhere you go?" God bless him, Sting said, "No, bass guitar, that's what I play," and I said, "Oh great, that's fantastic, beautiful instrument, and are you a solo artist?" and he said, "No, no, I'm in a band," and I said, "Oh, what kind of band?" He said, "The Police." Folks, I said, "You play in a police band?"

Sting, MacLachlan, and Everett McGill would pass the time with impromptu hotel jam sessions (with Kyle on guitar), although free time was fleeting for the movie's lead. A typical day for MacLachlan looked something like this, which presumably matched up to several other performers' routines:

7 a.m. – Wake up
8 a.m. – Studio arrival, protein shake, makeup, hair, costume

9 a.m. – Filming (4 hrs.)
1 p.m. – Lunch break
2:30 p.m. – Filming (4.5 hrs.)
7 p.m. – Wrap
9:30 p.m. – Dinner, then script meetings with Lynch or free time
Midnight – Bed

"People came and went," MacLachlan (who arrived on set a month before filming) told *Starlog* #89. "They would stay for one, three, or five weeks, depending on what they were needed to do. I was there the whole time, Francesca Annis was around for a long period of time, and so was Everett McGill."

"I didn't find the part particularly exhausting, though I was ill for a time, as we all were at one time or another when we were filming in Mexico," Francesca Annis told *Evening Post* in December 1984. "My son was very good. He didn't do anything unkind like trying to trip his mother up when we were running away from the giant sandworms across the desert."

Annis was apparently nothing like her stoic concubine character. She got along swimmingly with Sean Young, as seen in the latter's Super 8 YouTube footage.

"Francesca Annis was one of my favorite people," Young says in that video. "She had a great sense of humor, didn't take herself seriously at all, and was constantly laughing and having a good time."

"The Reverend Mother must combine the seductive wiles of a courtesan with the untouchable majesty of a virgin goddess, holding these attributes in tension so long as the powers of her youth endure," described Annis in *Prevue* #55. "For when youth and beauty have gone, she will find that the place between, once occupied by tension, has become a wellspring of cunning and resourcefulness."

Despite—or perhaps because of—the length and complexity of the shoot, Lynch didn't do a Kubrick-ian number of takes with his performers.

"I let the actors work out their ideas before shooting, then tell them what attitudes I want," Lynch told *Prevue* #58. "If a scene isn't honest, it stands out like a sore thumb. Often, we'd compromise. I need honesty on screen. I don't like shooting excessive footage, so we worked out the problems in rehearsal, and got most scenes in two or three takes. Still, there's over a million feet of film shot."

It's not surprising given his devotion to Transcendental Meditation, but Lynch was looked upon almost in guru-like terms by the cast, as Young stated in her video: "Every single actor who worked on that movie loved David and would have done anything for him. He was inspiring to the actors, everybody loved him, and he had a great sense of humor."

Siân Phillips recalled in 2015 [*Red Carpet News*]:

> Working for David was quite unlike working for anybody else. It is an experience in itself. He is meticulous, but you don't really know what's going on in his mind! When you're working for him, he asks you to do things that don't really make much sense to you at the time, but when you see the finished results, you absolutely see why he asked you to do it, so you have to trust him to a large extent. When he asks you to do something quite mad, there is a point to it. I've always felt very confident in his taste and judgment, so I would do anything he asked me to do.

"There's no phoniness about David," Kenneth McMillan told *Enterprise Incidents* #27. "You can be upfront with him and tell him exactly what you think. He was full of ideas of his own, but he was also open to other ideas as well. You could talk with him. Sometimes we fought about how the part should be played, but we always respected each other. In fact, he's considering me for a part in *Blue Velvet*."

In fact, there are many base similarities between Baron Harkonnen and *Blue Velvet* baddie Frank Booth and his defining phrase, "I'll fuck anything that moves!"

McMillan added:

> The Baron would have sexual contact with anything, which I think came out of the movie. I think they were a little perturbed by that. There's this scene where they bring me this little kid. The kid got scared. I pulled his heart plug and had contact with the blood and everything . . . I don't know if we should say things like this. People will get the idea that it's another kind of movie, even though this stuff is there, you know?

"David's a painter," Dourif told *The Sacramento Bee* in 1990. "When he talks about things, he talks about them as if they were a brush stroke. He talks about this little detail and that little detail of a performance. He'll say something like 'lighter!' Whatever you think he means, you just do it. If you're not doing what he wants, he'll say, 'That's not what I mean.' So, you just play, and eventually it gets there."

"There's a lot of acting in *Dune*," Dean Stockwell told the *Star-Phoenix* in December 1984. "It's not just a special effects movie, although it has the greatest sets I've ever seen. They did some big mockups of these worms for the actors to get close to. You know, I did both *Dune* and *Paris, Texas* in the same year. One worm in *Dune* cost \$2 million . . . more than the entire budget of *Paris, Texas.*"

Stockwell's character of the treacherous Yueh grew more complex and sympathetic with his portrayal.

"He's not completely villainous," Stockwell told *Enterprise Incidents* #28. "He wanted to be faithful to the Atreides, but he didn't know whether the Baron killed his wife or not. He betrays his family, but it's also because of him that Paul and Jessica are saved."

MacLachlan was quoted in *José Ferrer: Success and Survival* speaking fondly of the film's elder statesman and direct link to *Lawrence of Arabia*. "It was wonderful," MacLachlan said. "José was a lovely guy. Would always come to work wearing golf pants. And he would go off when we finished and play golf."

"*Dune* was very good for me, and Lynch was interesting to work with," Ferrer said in the same book. "He works very quietly and very privately. He's very explicit about what he wants; he could tell me in three words, and that was it."

"José Ferrer was complaining that he was overweight, but I thought he looked just right . . . he looked decadent," Frank Herbert told *Star Invaders* in Spring of '85.

Ferrer added in December 1984 of working with Lynch [*Miami Herald*]:

> I tried to make myself useful to him, so that my strips of film would fit in the scheme he had in his head, the vision he had carried around for years. My acting problems were so simple. All I had to do was look like a powerful older guy who was afraid that his power was being taken away from him. I had very little dialogue, I did a lot of looking, a lot of worrying, a lot of listening, a lot of thinking frightened thoughts. But there wasn't any deep character investigation. In a film like this, you hope to be an efficient piece of machinery, and that depends on something entirely other than fine acting. You want clean, clear efficient acting.

"Max von Sydow was perfect too," Herbert added. "He was in the part, always."

In May 1984, von Sydow said [*Starlog* #82]:

> I'm fascinated by *Dune*, the book and the story. The character of Kynes is extremely interesting and complex. I wish more of him were in the film. He's an enigmatic figure with many ideas and loyalties which he finds difficult to follow all the time . . . I wish to keep him an enigma. In a way, his task in the film is to introduce Paul to the Fremen and the dream of making Dune habitable again. It's a small part, but it's very rich in the book. There's no way they could put all that in the script.

It wasn't hard for the Bergman regular to stay in character given the immersive nature of Tony Masters' "live-in" sets. "On these sets, you don't have to put energy into ignoring the fake," von Sydow told *The New York Times* in September 1983.

During the filming of *Eraserhead*, Jack Nance had performed all sorts of on-set duties like moving scenery and even helped Lynch on the daily paper route he had to pay for shooting. Things were different on *Dune*.

Nance waxed rhapsodically in a segment from Jonathan Ross' *For One Week Only*:

> Just like a dream come true, beautiful, beautiful . . . I loved working on *Dune*. It was great. I didn't lift anything heavier than a beer bottle . . . 2,500 people in costumes on this thing. We walked in from rehearsal and it was the first time I'd ever seen this particular set, and these people and I just cracked up. Sometimes Lynch and I would look at each other and crack up laughing.

Alicia Witt turned nine while on set in August 1983, and she was presented with a birthday cake and breaded sandworm to eat, as well as a charcoal rendering by Carlo Rambaldi of Alia standing next to E.T.

"I never thought of *Dune* as being work, only fun," Witt told *Starlog* #91.

"I think she memorized the entire script," said Lynch in a January 1985 edition of *The Olympian*. "She's very natural and not afraid of the camera. All you have to do is tell her what to do, walk her through it, and she takes it from there. She's very, very proper. She's like a little lady. But she warms up to you. She really made close friends with people."

"It was so much fun," Witt said in the same article of her three months in Mexico City. "All the people who worked there were so extremely nice. I think Frank Herbert, when he wrote the book *Dune*, must have had a great imagination because none of these things ever actually existed."

"It's much darker and much more bizarre," said Francesca Annis, comparing *Dune* to *Star Wars* in December 1984 to the *Richmond Times-Dispatch*. "It's very weird. There was more acting when it was shot. Unfortunately, a lot of it had to be cut. It is amazing when you see it through. Everyone makes their mark very, very clearly. The individuals don't get lost in the special effects."

The experience was so positive that even actors whose characters had perished wanted in on *Dune II*.

"Jabba the Hutt was a rip-off from Frank Herbert, the author of *Dune*, and so were a lot of other *Star Wars* ingredients down the years," McMillan told *TV Week* in April 1984. "I've seen quite a bit of *Dune* and I like it . . . and I'm not saying that just because my character is guaranteed a major role in the sequel!"

"If they make a sequel to *Dune* I'll try to talk David into letting me come back in some weird makeup so no one will recognize me," Stockwell said in *Incidents* #28. "I enjoyed working on the film. I'd like to do more science-fiction films because I think it's an important genre. There's room for so much imagination—there's no limit!"

After taking over for Aldo Ray, Patrick Stewart was thrust headfirst from reading Herbert's book on the plane from London directly into the closed quarters of an ornithopter cockpit at Churubusco containing, as he described it to Kenneth George Godwin, "an American, a Scandinavian, a German, and myself, a truly international cast." Despite his supposed "miscasting," Stewart quite enjoyed himself on the film.

Stewart told Emerald City Comic Con in 2013:

> Some great, great actors in that movie, some of whom have left us and that's incredibly sad. Ken McMillan in particular, who was a wonderful guy. I got to go out to dinner once a week with Max von Sydow, who was one of my heroes, and I used to sit across the table from him and we would eat tacos. Kyle MacLachlan has become a lifelong friend and buddy, as has Everett McGill who is also in that movie. The three of us hung out together a lot.

Production Problems

The most universally known and frequently uttered Spanish phrase during the filming of *Dune* in Mexico was "*¿Qué pasa con la luz?*"

Translation: "What's gone wrong now?"

One problem straight away had to do with how Tony Masters' sets were constructed "live-in" style as opposed to modular sections that could be easily moved to accommodate the camera angles.

"When you build a set on a stage, there ought to be lots of room around it for moving equipment," DP Freddie Francis told *On Location* in December 1984. "You have to be able to float parts of the sets, and for some reason, the sets were built pretty solid—not like normal sets. I had to treat the sets as if we were on location at actual buildings because we had exactly the same problems."

Francis was also forced to use older cameras with antiquated Todd-AO lenses, whose poor definition required hundreds of lights. There was no access to Eastman high-speed 5294 film stock until close to the end of shooting, so Eastman 5247 was used for most of the shoot. The DP's original choice to use arc lamps was hobbled when local electricians were unable to keep them burning. Consequently, Francis had to rely on Dino lamps, specially designed bulbs made for Dino De Laurentiis by Lee Electric for *Flash Gordon*, used to light huge bluescreens. Each Dino burned 24 one-kilowatt bulbs, incandescent instead of the carbon lamps Francis wanted.

Francis kept the Dinos far away to make sure shadows blended in, or he burned out the shadows with other lamps. He suffered through daily electrical disruptions, with high odds of electricity being shut off in the middle of a take. As many as 13 generators at a time had to be brought in to power the sets since the studio didn't have any of its own. Rental fees for generators were enormous. Francis used mostly prime lenses, not caring for zoom lenses unless they were essential. A Chapman Zeus crane was employed, as well as an industrial crane for battle sequences, with Francis often suspending cameras on parachute elastic to free up the movement.

For the sandstorm sequences, a specially made glass box, not unlike an aquarium, was attached directly under the camera lens. Sand was inserted into one side of the box and blown out the other side to give depth to the storm.

There were also language barriers. Raffaella De Laurentiis speaks five languages and had to use four of them every day with a crew that came from seven countries.

"Oh, things can get a little more complicated, the language can be a barrier, but before too long you can adjust to it," Lynch told *The Philadelphia Inquirer*.

Small pests also plagued the sets like Biblical locusts. During night shoots, moths and mosquitos would frequently encircle Francis' lights, requiring a crew member with an insecticide sprayer on their back to kill thousands of moths between takes, with an additional helper handing out surgical masks to the crew so they didn't inhale the chemicals. Another good reason many of the crew kept those masks on was the tremendous amount of dust and fuller's earth (dyed yellow or red) frequently being blown by fans to simulate the desert.

Lynch joked to *Starburst* #73:

> If you look at the continuity editor's script, you can tell by which pages are yellow and which are red, what scenes we were shooting on which of those dusk-to-dawn shoots. As a matter of fact, you can hardly see the type anymore. Just yellow and red pages! When we all staggered back to our hotels in the mornings, as the sun was coming up, we always thought they were going to pitch us out, the way we looked. I mean, these filthy bums. We looked like a hundred or so Al Jolsons, every day!

As for the lavish sets, Masters only spent a reported two-thirds of his budget allotted for them, likely owing to cheap Mexican labor. This thriftiness led to problems, though. Masters saw one of the sets and realized something was wrong with the pillars, and couldn't pin it down until he realized that—although they were *exactly* as he had designed them—they were placed in the set upside down.

In June 1983, an emergency occurred during off-hours when the film's second lead, 38-year-old Francesca Annis, was at her rented villa in San Ángel. While she was making her children rice pudding, a gas stove blew up in her face.

As Annis recounted it in 1984 [*Calgary Herald*]:

> Suddenly there was an enormous explosion, and I was flung back against the wall. My face was completely black. I looked like the af-

termath of an atom bomb. I had no eyelashes or eyebrows. I was wearing my hair at the time with a long fringe that fell off into the basin when I bent over. I kept saying to everyone, "I'm perfectly all right, please don't fuss." But my arms and hands were all burned, and I couldn't keep still because of the pain.

After being rushed to the hospital, Annis was given a special ointment that had previously been used on plane crash survivors. Miraculously, five days later the bandages came off, and there were no scars. Cleverly, the production took a few days off at the insurance company's expense . . . even though Annis hadn't been scheduled to shoot those days.

Then there was the heat during the 11 days of desert shoots in Juárez. Filming under cloudless skies during July used both Mexican extras and Texans bussed in from over an hour away from Bassett Center in El Paso every day at 5 a.m. Four large dune buggies and 11 "pee-wee" motorcycles with trailers were used to transport equipment via special routes. Shots were rarely rehearsed so as not to destroy the ripples in the sand, so they were planned from a distance. Outfitted in stillsuits, many of the extras had to run in the sand for hours, often fainting from high temperatures and exertion.

"It was great, you could lift up your arm, and a stream of sweat would squirt out by your hand," recalled extra Michael Myers to the *El Paso Times* in December 1984.

The Texans were paid $20 a day plus lunch (a baloney sandwich) and all the salt pills they wanted. There was a distinct hierarchy on set, with the above-the-line filmmakers, stars, and crew at the top, Juárez and Texan extras in the middle, and a division of Mexican Army soldiers at the bottom. Lead actors reportedly never interacted with extras. Complaining about conditions was universal, and the simmering tensions escalated when the crew would bring out water containers.

"It was like the water riots in India. There were about 500 guys fighting for a few gallons of water," extra Tracy Levin said.

Many extras who dropped out before the 11 days finished were referred to fondly as "Dune Pansies." Those that remained sometimes had to inhale black smoke from tire fires during the battle scenes. Right before a take, the fires would be juiced with sulfur, making the smell even more unbearable. Even Kyle MacLachlan lost his voice at one point from taking in the fumes.

"They had no regard for our health at all," extra Jon Gore added.

At one point during the two-week Juárez shoot, Raffaella caught Lynch putting all his energies into grabbing a shot of one of his actors' eyes. The producer admonished him, saying he could easily grab the same shot in a studio when hundreds of extras weren't fainting as they waited in the heat to be filmed.

For a man at the helm of such a monster undertaking, the 37-year-old Lynch set up many artistic distractions for himself. He dissected animals for "Duck Kit" and "Chicken Kit" photographs, which he made prints of for the crew. He curated a showing of 50 of his drawings (watercolor, pen & ink, pencil) at Galeria Uno, a gallery in Mexico's Pacific Coast resort of Puerto Vallarta. This was his first such showing since his art school days in the '60s.

"I would still keep drawing and painting if no one ever saw it, but this adds to it," Lynch told the Associated Press of the show in January 1984. "I'm a film director mainly, but I've got an awful lot of urges for these sideline things."

Another sideline thing that allowed him to do very little drawing but still served as a creative outlet was a weekly comic strip for the *Los Angeles Reader* titled *The Angriest Dog in the World*. Consisting of four panels that never change (only the word balloons spoken by an unseen family are altered), it follows a crudely drawn black dog—shaped almost like a tadpole—chained in a picket-fenced yard close to a smoke-spewing factory in the distance. Lynch would generate new dialogue each week and phone it into the paper. This lasted from 1983 to 1992, adding to a list of Lynch's recurring rituals. These also included wearing the same clothes and eating the same meals every day, going to Bob's Big Boy at the same time daily, not driving anywhere until he saw a license plate with the number "9" . . . and eventually doing daily internet weather forecasts.

Many on the crew reportedly became homesick for Italy, Spain, or England, depending on where they were from. Some became a surrogate family, going on shopping trips and weekend flings together, while others despised the heat and dysentery so much, they left the production early.

Things That Make You Go Boom: Special Effects

Many of the film's big physical effects fell to Kit West, the British technician who had won an Oscar for his work on *Raiders of the Lost Ark*. As mechanical effects supervisor, West was responsible for overseeing construction on the full-size ornithopter, robot fighter, and many other bits of pyrotechnics.

Kit West's impressive (and strangely phallic) training robot was operated by six people via a combination of radio control, compressed-air vacuum control, and invisible wires. The original storyboarded choreography for Paul's fight with the golden, knife-decorated robot had to be jettisoned once it was built and difficulties during filming began. MacLachlan got a limp from a bruised ankle during a roll.

"It's the most difficult scene yet," MacLachlan told *Prevue* #59. "All my training goes out the window when that machine is operated. David told me, 'Don't get killed!' But he's not doing the tango with a killer robot!"

During the battle sequences shot in Juárez, West's team was in charge of planting numerous explosives in the desert sands. One problem: the extras who navigating these dangerous explosions were inexperienced . . . and spoke another language.

"The majority of the extras were the Mexican Army, and naturally these boys have never experienced anything similar to this," West said during the 1984 TV documentary *The Making of Dune*. "When you get two or three thousand people running, there's always somebody who might think it's quicker to go to the right instead of going where he's told he's to go, and then we're in trouble."

A large to-scale midsection of a worm was built and installed in the desert on specially manufactured railroad tracks, and would be pulled by a truck to create movement. It would frequently grind to a halt and stall in the middle of a take.

West and his team created flying rigs to make the Baron Harkonnen live up to his rep as "the floating fat man." McMillan later described the process [*Starlog* #91]:

> Kit rigged this harness up that went under my arms and around my chest and was attached to wires. Depending upon the scene, they

would either light around them—which is a credit to cinematographer Freddie Francis—or, in certain cases, they would paint the wires out of the shot, which is costly. In each scene, depending upon the soundstage and the way I flew, they had a different apparatus. Some allowed me to come directly at the camera, while if I wanted to land feet first, they would attach weights to my feet.

One serious accident happened under West's watch involving actor Jürgen Prochnow, which we will cover in the oral history section.

Oral History: Production

**The following individuals were interviewed
by the author for this section:**

—Kyle MacLachlan (Actor, "Paul Atreides")

—Sean Young (Actor, "Chani")

—Everett McGill (Actor, "Stilgar")

—Alicia Witt (Actor, "Alia")

—Virginia Madsen (Actor, "Princess Irulan")

—Molly Wryn (Actor, "Harah")

—Danny Corkill (Actor, "Orlop")

—Raffaella De Laurentiis (Producer)

—Thom Mount (President of Universal Pictures, 1976–83)

—Frederick Elmes (Additional Unit Cinematographer)

—Bob Ringwood (Costume Designer)

—Mary Vogt (Costume Assistant)

—Luigi Rocchetti (Makeup Artist)

—Barry Nolan (Special Photographic Effects)

—Eric Swenson (Visual Effects, Motion Control)

—Ron Miller (Concept Artist)

—Giles Masters (Art Department)

—Craig Campobasso (Production Office Assistant)

—Ian Woolf (DGA Trainee)

—Jane Jenkins (Casting Director)

—Penelope Shaw Sylvester (Assistant Editor)

—Kenneth George Godwin (Production Documentarian)

—John Pattyson (EPK Producer)

—Paul M. Sammon (Universal Pictures Publicity Executive)

—Terri Hardin (Stillsuit Fabrication, Stunt Double)

—David Paich (Composer, Toto)

—John Dykstra (Visual Effects Supervisor, Apogee, Inc.)

FREDERICK ELMES: David felt he had the support to go ahead and do what he wanted to do, certainly during pre-production and in the beginning of production as we got started shooting. Everybody was happy with what they were seeing, and we got a lot of support.

Arguably the most enlightening passage in production documentarian Kenneth George Godwin's diaries chronicling the Dune *shoot is an exchange between him and Lynch early on in production. Godwin asks, "How does it feel to have all this being done for you?" Lynch replies, "It isn't being done for me." On one hand, it's a very pragmatic answer, but on the other, it speaks volumes about the lack of ownership Lynch felt over the film even early on, telling others he felt like a sellout. The massive cast and crew weren't in Mexico City for Lynch, but for the multimedia enterprise that was* Dune.

KENNETH GEORGE GODWIN: It was clear from the start that it was so much bigger than him, and obviously so much different from what he had done before. Although *Elephant Man* was a job for hire as well, it was very much a David Lynch film. It allowed him to do the things that interested him, whereas *Dune*, as big as it was, didn't give him that kind of freedom. All those resources were there more for Universal and De Laurentiis. David was supposed to guide everything, but he definitely wasn't in complete control. He was very enthusiastic, but the whole machine was carrying him along rather than him guiding it in these directions.

BOB RINGWOOD: When we started shooting, he was totally lost. Tony rang me up at the end of the second week of shooting and said, "We're in really big trouble with this director. I just don't know what's going to happen." He predicted that the film wouldn't be very good, and he was right. David was doing one thing in his mind, and suddenly an express train hit him, which was this epic film. It was all very well talking about it in Hollywood, but when you actually got on the soundstage and there were thousands of people around you . . .

Frank Herbert came to inaugurate the first day of principal photography, slating the clapboard on a daylight courtyard scene on Caladan between Paul and Jessica which—as with many scenes to come—ultimately didn't make it into the movie.

CRAIG CAMPOBASSO: Frank was a great guy. He was only in the office a few times, and then he was there on the first day of shooting.

KYLE MACLACHLAN: I met him on the first day of filming. He came down to the set, and we have that great photo of us all sitting in that semicircle on Day 1, Scene 1.

KENNETH GEORGE GODWIN: That was very early. The Atreides family have been told they're going to Dune, and they're going to have to leave Caladan. There was a scene between Paul and his mother talking about having to leave their home world for this strange new world. That was probably ditched early in the editing. There's another scene later between Paul and his father where they talk about that, so it would have just been duplicating the same point. It's more dramatic with Paul and his father standing on that balcony overlooking the crashing seas.

PAUL M. SAMMON: Among my greatest joys on *Dune* was meeting Frank Herbert and his wife in Mexico. I very much enjoyed the conversations Frank and I had on-set and later over the telephone. We discussed everything from Arrakis to the science-fiction authors we both knew to the basic jungle survival training I'd been taught by SEALs when I was a Boy Scout living in the Philippines.

The decision to shoot at Estudios Churubusco had a bit of groundwork laid when the previous Dino De Laurentiis productions of Amityville II: The Possession *(1982) and* Amityville 3-D *(1983) had also shot at the studio.*

RAFFAELLA DE LAURENTIIS: I was not involved in *Amityville*, but I knew that Dino had shot it there. I did budgets for everywhere in the world where there was a desert, and we needed a lot of stages.

CRAIG CAMPOBASSO: It was the cheapest route to go because the movie was so expensive, so they decided to shoot down there. They had a lot of problems because of electricity, using all the generators. They had to overcome a lot of obstacles.

JOHN DYKSTRA: Oh, yeah. It was sketchy at best.

RAFFAELLA DE LAURENTIIS: We built those nine Churubusco stages twice over. There was a lot of set construction.

JOHN PATTYSON: The sets were just massive. The artisans in Mexico were incredible. They would build these sets you couldn't build back in Hollywood for anywhere near that price. They're all made out of wood.

FREDERICK ELMES: I'd spend off-hours wandering around the sets to see what they were building next, to learn what characters were shooting in this one or that one. I was like a kid in a carnival seeing this all happen on a very big scale.

JANE JENKINS: I do remember being in Mexico, and the sets were being built, that whole huge staircase. There was still a lot of stuff being done, even though they were in pre-production in Mexico for a long time. We were still casting a lot of those soldiers, and Ringwood was making all of those black rubber suits. Nightmare.

IAN WOOLF: Every prop, every stitch of clothing had to be designed and built from scratch because you couldn't go to a rental house and rent Fremen wetsuits. You couldn't go rent a Fremen spear. Everything had to be made. We had an entire prop shop that was just building all the armaments and the furniture.

RON MILLER: I really liked designing props! It made me feel like a junior production designer! What fascinated me was the unique experience of seeing something I had drawn turn into something I could hold in my hand. I designed a lot of the smaller items: props and weapons, for instance, and things like Paul's poison detector.

KYLE MACLACHLAN: The English guys that did all the special effects, Kit West and his crew, the hunter seeker . . . all these designs were all manufactured there.

IAN WOOLF: It was crazy. We had all eight stages. There were tunnels and caves. Over the course of eight months, we shot 74 different sets. In the Emperor's throne room, they had Mexican artisans laying actual gold leaf on the floor.

GILES MASTERS: Churubusco's got eight big stages, and we filled them two and a half times over with all the different sets that were called for. When you're doing this sort of show, it's challenging for everybody.

IAN WOOLF: We had the back lot, and a location we called the dead dog dump. It's this bad area of Mexico City [Las Aguilas Rojas] that was a dump, a lot of dead dogs. We spent weeks cleaning it out. It became one of our battleground sequences.

GILES MASTERS: The Mexicans obviously were great. A lot of British crew, American crew, Italian crew, Spanish crew. De Laurentiis had made *Conan the Barbarian* in Spain, so some of those people came. An eclectic bunch that gelled really well.

BOB RINGWOOD: It was the strangest experience. We're all in a foreign country—it was all very weird and exotic. Volatile. David was naive in many ways. We were all more sophisticated, more European. The production designer was English. The set dresser was Italian. Artists were Mexican. David was the only true American there.

RAFFAELLA DE LAURENTIIS: At the end of the day, it was the right place because of the desert that we found and the stages, and it was competitive prices. I made a lot of money on the exchange rate.

IAN WOOLF: Dino was a brilliant, brilliant producer because at the time if you put dollars in a Mexican bank and they changed it to pesos, they were paying 150% interest on your money. What Dino did is he put a ton of money into the bank in Mexico City to make *Dune*. Because we were there for over a year—construction started probably a year and a half before principal photography—the interest he made off the money in the bank he used to make *Conan the Destroyer*.

SEAN YOUNG: I asked Tony how much money is being spent. He was quiet for a bit, and then what he basically said—without saying it too much— was that "it's looking like it's more money than it really is." In other words, it could have been a Dino laundering operation. [*laughs*] Which I think made sense. Otherwise, why go to Mexico City? That's what we all felt, that it didn't cost as much as he was saying it cost. Which is fine, only because we knew how cheap things were there. He's a little bit of a gangster, y'know?

MARY VOGT: I think the accountants ended up going to jail on that film. I think there were some . . . problems.

RAFFAELLA DE LAURENTIIS: There was a lot of bribery going on. You had to pay the customs people. It was totally allowed back then. Today you could never get away with doing that; you'd end up in jail.

CRAIG CAMPOBASSO: Customs was horrible. We always had to send two shipments of the exact same thing, because one of the shipments would be stolen every time. Every time.

IAN WOOLF: There was a Mexican production company called Patsa Productions. There was a guy we called Airport Freddy or Customs Freddy who was able to facilitate and get things through with very little paperwork.

MARY VOGT: With a giant bag of money. We had a customs broker that would meet us at the airport with literally a giant paper bag of money. That bag of money was always in the cars, like if police stopped you when you were driving around. There was always a lot of cash around for bribing people. That's the only reason we got things in. Anyone who came into Mexico from Los Angeles or New York brought a suitcase of our stuff with them.

We always needed batteries, which you couldn't get in Mexico. We would have someone go to someone's house and ask, "Do you mind taking this extra suitcase to Mexico for the costume department?" Now nobody would do it, paying people off, but at that time it was okay.

ERIC SWENSON: I was there for about two months while we waited for Van der Veer's motion control equipment to come through customs. It got held up. They had a guy on staff who paid off the people at customs. He was the most important person on the shoot, to get everything through the gauntlet. That was part of the process.

BOB RINGWOOD: The interpreter was a very sweet little man, a bit of a gangster. He said, "You're not giving them the bribes." I said, "What do you mean?" He said, "Well, you know, they want things like VHS tapes and cameras and film stock and things like that. When you pack your suitcases and costume boxes, on the top layer put empty VHS tapes and batteries and that sort of thing. They'll just take those off the top—they won't even bother to look in the boxes." I did. Lots of other departments didn't do that, and they lost an awful lot. I bribed all the customs people with all my goodies and chocolate. Lots of chocolate, they liked that. I always used to litter the tops of the suitcases so when you open them, there was something to steal. We didn't lose much after that, and we didn't have to pay any import tax.

DANNY CORKILL: We almost caused an international incident at customs—I'm not even exaggerating. We went to pick up our dog who got shipped down on a Friday, and they weren't going to let her out to us until Monday. It was a non-air-conditioned warehouse and highly unlikely anyone was going to be regularly taking care of the dog, who was in a little crate. My mom and four American kids and our poor driver—who was so apologetic—basically staged a five-hour sit-in at the customs warehouse in Mexico until our dog was released to us.

JOHN PATTYSON: We went through customs, and they impounded all of our equipment. Just took it all. They wanted cash. I call Raffaella, woke her up in the middle of the night, and she was pissed off. She called Dino. Dino called the President of Mexico and basically said, "These are my boys, we're bringing you a lot of money. Get the camera equipment, because we need it, blah, blah." The next day, this military convoy comes flooding up to set just to hand us our equipment back.

Although the words "kidnapping" and "Mexico" have been known to appear in the same sentence, Raffaella insists that was never an issue production had to deal with.

RAFFAELLA DE LAURENTIIS: Back then, it was not as dangerous as it has become. It wasn't that bad. We used to live there.

LUIGI ROCCHETTI: Working and living for over a year in Mexico became my second home. In the '80s, it was a completely different situation than the current one.

PENELOPE SHAW SYLVESTER: In those days, Mexico was very safe. I bought a car when I was there and drove myself around Mexico City. I used to drive out into the countryside with friends on weekends, didn't think twice about it. I wouldn't be able to do that now. And, of course, we were all on American per diems.

MOLLY WRYN: We felt safe in Mexico City most of the time. One time I got in a cab and the guy didn't take me where I was going, and I thought, "Uh oh." He finally did, but I so young and naive. I trusted everybody. One night Linda Hunt, Gina [Virginia], Siân, and I all went out to dinner, and we got harassed as we're walking down the street. This drunk guy was following us and harassing us, but we were all together. At one point, I turned and yelled at him to get away from us and he wouldn't. Siân said, "Just ignore him. Let's just keep walking."

RAFFAELLA DE LAURENTIIS: Back then, it was more dangerous because of food poisoning and things like that.

KENNETH GEORGE GODWIN: There was quite a lot of sickness with the foreign crew that were brought in. Dino actually built a restaurant at the studio and brought in an Italian chef to provide "safe" food for the crew.

MARY VOGT: Every day there was a "sick list" of everyone who was sick, to the point where Dino decided to bring in food from Italy. At the time, he had a company called the DDL Foodshow, so we had our own restaurant. The only mistake they made was they served wine with lunch. After lunch everyone was useless, but it was great. The food was fabulous. It cut down people being sick.

CRAIG CAMPOBASSO: I remember Kyle telling me, "You know, there are a lot of stray dogs missing off the lot . . . Wonder if they're in the commissary?"

MOLLY WRYN: Virginia and I went out one time for dinner at a wonderful restaurant. I didn't eat meat—I'm a vegan—so it had to be vegetable something. We came home and got violently ill because we're Americans. We both thought we would die and called each other, "Are you dying yet?"

VIRGINIA MADSEN: I got terribly, terribly ill. I got the Montezuma's Revenge. I had to stand for hours on end for that big end sequence, sweating bullets. I was so sick, had a high fever: "Oh God, I don't want to fall over. I don't even have a big part in this movie, I can't afford to be sick." Some prop guy put a barstool under my gown, and you know what? I use that trick. Anytime I have a movie where I've gotten a hoop skirt, any period piece where you've got a corset, those costumes are so heavy. I can just sit there. It allowed me to stand upright without having to tell anybody I was sick. "Nobody else was having a problem except this newcomer, huh?" So embarrassing. Forever grateful for whoever gave that stool to me.

RAFFAELLA DE LAURENTIIS: I had just finished building a hotel and producing my first movie [*Beyond the Reef*] on a desert island. I was there for two and a half years where there was nothing to be brought in and no telephones and no way of communicating with the outside world. One big boat called the *Taparo* came in every Wednesday, and if you didn't have what you needed on that boat, you had to wait till next Wednesday. If you wanted to talk to the mainland, you could do it at 6:45 for 10 minutes every morning, and that's it. Mexico was easy compared to that.

The mechanics of this epic shoot involved a stable of technicians filming with three full units at once, with Lynch bicycling between each unit throughout the day.

IAN WOOLF: The DGA trainees were a little better paid than a PA. My duties were to get cast through makeup, hair, and wardrobe. It was such a huge production.

MARY VOGT: There were very often no call sheets, so nobody knew what anyone was doing. It was like a verbal call sheet, and everyone spoke a different language.

IAN WOOLF: The first assistant director was Kuki López. Still alive, lives in Madrid. Amazing first AD, did *Papillon* and *Lawrence of Arabia*. Kuki would always say, "Whatever you do, we're management. We don't wear shorts. As an AD, no matter how hot it is or how miserable you are, you're management. You got to wear long pants." I violated that rule a few times. His real name was Juan Carlos López Rodero. He had a brother, José López Rodero, who was also called "Pepe." Because Kuki wasn't in the DGA, he couldn't be listed as the first AD on *Dune*. They listed Pepe as first AD in the credits. You had to have a DGA-qualified first assistant director, and José was in the DGA. That's how they twisted the rules a little. Pepe was more like an associate producer working side by side with Raffaella. To get into the DGA, there's all sorts of stuff you have to document and forms you have to fill out, so I helped Kuki get all his paperwork to get him into the DGA. On *Dune*, he was only credited as "Assistant to David Lynch," but he was, in fact, the first AD.

MARY VOGT: There were these two brothers from Spain who were very good first ADs. They did a lot of the organizing.

MOLLY WRYN: Kuki wrangled all of us. One time, there were several of us actors in a row and he was telling us what to do. We spoke different languages. He stood in front of me and started speaking Spanish, and I just nodded and kind of laughed. He went, "Oh," and then told me in English.

IAN WOOLF: There was this Mexican key second named Miguel Lima. Then there was me—the DGA trainee—and one PA. If you go on a set today, there are a dozen PAs, a key second, a second second, an additional second . . . Back then, it was just the four of us. You basically run the whole thing. You're setting background, getting the cast to set, keeping track of the cast. Everything that assistant directors and production assistants do on set is what Miguel and myself and this guy Arturo did. We were on the first unit; Freddie Francis was the DP.

MARY VOGT: David was more about the actors. He trusted the people that were doing the visuals. David had this 1940s cast iron telephone on his desk, and he said to Bob, "This is what I want the movie to look like." Bob was like, "Okay, I get it." I think David could see that Bob was brilliant and trusted him. You're not going to get any better than Tony Masters, Freddie Francis, and Bob Ringwood. David trusted them with the visuals, then he went and did what he needed to do.

IAN WOOLF: There was a full second unit that a guy named Jimmy Devis was directing. Then there was an insert unit that Fred Elmes was in charge of.

Director of Photography Frederick Elmes had been part of the AFI while Lynch was also attending in the early '70s. Elmes was intent on getting to shoot a movie and was initially unable to pair with any directors in the program (which included Terrence Malick). An opening was created when cinematographer Herbert Cardwell left Lynch's thesis movie Eraserhead *after a month and a half due to lack of payment.*

FREDERICK ELMES: Herb photographed the beginning of *Eraserhead*, and then David needed somebody to step in and the teachers introduced me to him and we seemed to hit it off. I joined the crew, which by that time was down to about six people. All sorts of people came and went. On big production days where we had to actually push the dolly and have acting involved and make a lighting change or some effect, we just asked our friends to come and help us for a while. It was an adventure in that sense. I was at the AFI as a fellow, to take classes and work on other things if I could. David was a night owl, so we worked at night. We would start shooting on *Eraserhead* in the late afternoon or look at dailies, have a bite to eat, then shoot half the night, take a break, shoot a few more shots and go home. It would leave me a couple hours to sleep before I had to get up the next morning to go to classes. It was a real protracted shooting experience.

At the same time I met David, I met John Cassavetes, who was a filmmaker-in-residence at the AFI who used student labor, offices, and an edit room for *A Woman Under the Influence*. I loved that movie and watching John and Gena Rowlands work. John asked me to work on *Killing of a Chinese Bookie* and *Opening Night*, to basically be the cinematographer, although he disliked titles or anything that reeked of Hollywood structure, so I was a "camera operator." I got to do most of the lighting and work things out with him, which was totally the opposite of working with David. It was great being exposed to them simultaneously. In the midst of *Eraserhead*, I would tell David, "I need to take about two months off to work on this other movie. I'm taking the crew as well, because it's a paying job." But the few of us on the *Eraserhead* crew wanted to see it done, even though David said, "Look, I can't pay you anymore. There's no per diem or anything, and if you're lucky, you'll get lunch." We all said, "We just want to get it done. We've been working on it for so long. We know that you know that it's going to be a successful film, so we want to finish it." That's kind of why we hung in there.

Eraserhead was successful, but took years to complete, then more time to screen at festivals like LA's Filmex, then played the midnight circuit through Ben Barenholtz's Libra Films. It was difficult for Elmes to acquire work on the back of its success.

FREDERICK ELMES: David made a deal with him and sent him the only answer print, so we had no access to it. All we could do was talk about it. I couldn't really sell myself unless the next potential director could go to a New York screening. There was no way to show off the film for years and years. Finally, there were four or five prints made and it got into other cities, but it was really through word of mouth.

When we were filming, David would look at a shot and say, "I think I see detail in that shadow area there. I don't want to see any detail. I want it to be black." I would say, "Okay, we'll use less light and we'll turn it down." The joke on set was always, "Well, why not make it dark because we know what it'll look like in theaters and it's never going to be on video anyway!" Sure enough, three or four years later, we're trying to make a video master out of this very, very dark film we created. It didn't really want to look good on video in the beginning, it took a long time, but we did get it. We showed the video copies on a local cable network in Los Angeles, Z Channel. That was the first open, public way anyone could see it.

For The Elephant Man, *Lynch used cinematographer Freddie Francis, whose stark black-and-white work was nominated for a BAFTA. When it came time to do* Dune, *Lynch would continue with Francis in charge of principal photography but wanted to bring Elmes back into the fold.*

FREDERICK ELMES: He had changed a bit. He'd had the experience of doing *Elephant Man* in London with Freddie and a professional crew. A big film, lots of period art design, great costumes, and wonderful actors. He had a real professional experience, and it was something he liked. He liked the scale, he liked the ability to ask for things and they would get done, whereas on *Eraserhead*, we'd have to do it all ourselves. It was a great experience for him, and *Elephant Man* is a fabulous film. He was really gearing up to do a bigger film, and when *Dune* came along, it was right up his alley because it was science fiction, a very big, epic story with lots of interesting characters. This appealed to David, creating those places that you're not familiar with, like wherever *Eraserhead* took place. Creating that world with a consistency that's believable, and *Dune* was the perfect big-scale trial run of that.

In between Eraserhead *and* Dune, *Elmes had busied himself as a camera operator on several films, including two from Albert Brooks (*Real Life *and* Modern Romance*) as well as the Chuck Norris action flick* A Force of One. *He had just completed work as the director of photography on Martha Coolidge's influential 1983 comedy* Valley Girl *when he received his marching orders for Arrakis.*

FREDERICK ELMES: I was thrilled. I'd worked on small features in 16mm and 35mm, but not extensively and certainly not on this scale. To see David get this big job was really wonderful. David and I hadn't lost touch since the end of *Eraserhead*—we lived just a few blocks from each other and were in continuous touch. Even when he was in London doing *Elephant Man*, he came home a couple of times; we always talked. I knew the stresses and strains of that production. We talked about *Dune* when it came up as a possibility and he did want me to be involved somehow, and they figured out what I could do best.

IAN WOOLF: Fred did all the water drops and all that weird David Lynch stuff.

FREDERICK ELMES: That's completely true. That's what I did. It was not practical for me to become part of Francis' camera crew, because they'd all worked together and had an established relationship. David preferred that I'd be off to the side doing special effects or visual things that would help the main unit by taking a little load off. They could shoot the actors in a set, and then I could move in and do things afterward. Another part was to create these abstract images that David and I had talked about for quite a while, including fire and flames, smoke, elements in other sequences. He would be very specific about what the fire had to be doing, and we would figure out how to create that. Another big one was water drops, since there is no water on this planet. The magic and importance of it was integral to the story. I had a great—if small—crew of technicians that could help me create any visual effects in-camera that I could imagine. We did all those abstract things. To get the light right for those water drops, to get it to be perfectly smooth, required some hard work. We shot in a tank that was four meters across, it had to be quite big, and the lighting rig for it had to be big.

Elmes elaborated on some of the other side projects he was involved in, shots which helped to infuse the movie with more of Lynch's sensibility.

FREDERICK ELMES: I did some of the crowd scenes. One of our little projects was the kinds of levers in the smaller ships and the fact that when you work them, funny images are projected on your face. There's no explanation for it; it's just obviously the way you pilot the ship. Those were little movies that I made that were projected. All those funny little details in the background were things I got to do. Contraptions that were in the sets when the fortress is being invaded or the shield goes down or some things go wrong . . . David loved all that. That sense of the set and the mechanics of it and getting it to sync up and look very strange but somehow neat.

When he wasn't working on effects shots or small bits of business, Elmes was at dailies to make sure his work matched what was coming off Freddie Francis' first unit.

FREDERICK ELMES: I watched dailies, and that's the most important thing. I was there during the preparation when those sets were being built and painted, and oftentimes when they were being lit. Since we were all in the same studio complex, I could go by the first unit and watch some of the action. At the end of the day, we would sit in a theater and watch the dailies from the day before. That was really the most telling thing, because I could hear David and Freddie talking. I knew what they were up to and what was important to them and perhaps what shots they needed in this sequence and how I could go about doing it. After first unit dailies, David and I would sit for my second unit dailies. It was a great process.

JANE JENKINS: You know, David had a vision to do it in black and white. He didn't want to do it in color.

ERIC SWENSON: You know he wanted *Dune* to be in black and white, right? There was no way that was ever going to happen.

BARRY NOLAN: As I understand, David wanted to do the picture in black and white like *The Elephant Man*, and Dino said no.

FREDERICK ELMES: He does like black and white quite a bit. I can imagine David saying that. When you're in the production of a big movie like this where someone is putting up so much money, they kind of want to keep their options open and color seems to be one of them.

RAFFAELLA DE LAURENTIIS: I think because of Elephant Man being in black and white and Freddie Francis being the DOP, that assumption was made. In a strange way, I think the movie is in black and white, in its choice of color.

ERIC SWENSON: Look at the color palette of *Dune*—it's really subdued. There are no bright colors. The desert planet is all browns and darks and dark greens. You'd think the water planet would be a lot lusher, but it's still all muted. There's brown and black or gray in every color, so he's doing the best he can to make a black-and-white film out of a color one.

The key to bringing a black-and-white world to David Lynch's first color feature film was the Lightflex, a device designed by British DP Gerry Turpin (The Last of Sheila) that was affixed to each camera and contained a small generator, filter hood, and a rheostat to change the intensity of the light.

BARRY NOLAN: They reached somewhat of a compromise: Freddie Francis introduced them to the Lightflex, a light source that goes in front of the camera with a diagonal mirror and reflects a small amount into the camera. It desaturates the contrast and color. You can even change the color a little bit. With a potentiometer—like a volume control—you can adjust it to make it look like it did. The colors were very muted. He worked very hard to get that look, and it was pushing it a little bit more toward black and white by desaturating the colors.

KYLE MACLACHLAN: Freddie Francis was working with this apparatus on the front of the camera, a Lightflex, where you had a filter and he was always messing with it. I didn't really understand it. Light would come through the lens a little bit and enrich the film. You see it, and it's just so rich and beautiful.

FREDERICK ELMES: I used it some of the time. Much of what I did effects-wise, I couldn't do with the Lightflex, it was too cumbersome or it got in the way, but it wasn't necessary all the time.

ERIC SWENSON: The Lightflex was a device that would affect the film as it came into the camera, so you're messing with the negative. Back in the day, getting a perfect bluescreen was the main goal. You had to get from edge to edge, top to bottom, left to right a perfect bluescreen and an exposure within a tenth of a tenth of a stop from the entire bluescreen corner to corner, top to bottom. That's just nuts if you compare it to now, because you could be several stops off and have two different colors of green and digital can now work all that out. Back in the day, it had to be super, super perfect. If you were shooting a shot in front of a bluescreen with a Lightflex in it, it was contaminating the blue. It was a glowing box above the camera, and it would flash the film with whatever color you're using. Even if it was white, you're washing out the blues and you wanted a perfect blue. *Dune* was a warm movie. I couldn't tell you all the colors that he used. I think he even had a knob where he could dial up and down the amount of light or flashing that was happening, but it was antithetical to having a good bluescreen. I'm sure whenever Freddie wasn't there, Barry would have taken all that stuff off.

BARRY NOLAN: I wouldn't let them use it on any of the effects shots, and it caused nothing but fighting. Freddie was totally pissed off at me. He said I was going to ruin his picture, that I could never match what he was doing. I said, "I promise you all the effects will look exactly like the rest of the picture." When we did them, I did the same thing. We created the effects, put them together, and then we put our own Lightflex on the optical printer, which saturated the colors to match everything they did. When the picture came out, Freddie Francis sent me a letter apologizing and thanking me for everything I did to match what he did. I still have that letter. I thought that was very nice of him to do that.

November 1, 1984

Mr. Barry Nolan
VAN DER VEER PHOTO EFFECTS
724 S. Victory Blvd.
Burbank, CA 91502

Dear Barry,

As I told you in Mexico, big science-fiction movies such as DUNE are not the sort of projects I choose and, indeed, this one I did because of my relationship with my dear friend, David Lynch. The reason for my not being keen on this type of movie, and this I have constantly told the press, is that I like to know that what I see on the screen at dailies is what I will see at the cinema and the thought that my original work is to be tied up for many months while other people affix their own work and signatures to my original negative horrifies me. This is even more scary when one has tried to give the movie a style.

In the case of DUNE, these intervening months have passed and my original negative has been worked on and worked on and worked on by you and the gang at Van Der Veer. To my great delight, all these other signatures that have been added to my original have not only left it completely unharmed, but have enhanced the movie an enormous amount.

Should I do another movie of this type, I shall see to it that you are alongside from the word "go" to insure that I will not again have to go through all the "worrying" months.

Once again Barry, my heartfelt thanks for a really wonderful job.

Warmest regards,

Freddie

Freddie Francis

FF/hlh

PLEASE REPLY TO: 724 SO. VICTORY BLVD. 2ND FL. • BURBANK CA 91502 • 818-954-0120 • TELEX: 662511 • DUNE UVSL

DUNE PRODUCTIONS, LTD. • 1 GULF & WESTERN PLAZA • NEW YORK, NEW YORK 10023 • PHONE: 212-399-0101 • TELEX: INT'L 427683, DOMESTIC 645059

FREDERICK ELMES: On some of those matching scenes, I had to use the Lightflex, and I found it kind of a creative tool, a nice thing to play with, and have used it on other films. We used it on *Wild at Heart*, actually. Not through the entirety of the film, but in some of the lovemaking scenes between Sailor and Lulu. We introduced color in-camera so it didn't have to be an optical effect later—we could do it all right there. We could choose colors very specifically and look through the viewfinder. You could see how it worked, so it was the right tool for the job.

Another point of contention between Lynch and Dino was the decision to have sets and lighting be brighter (Dino's preference) vs darker (Lynch's preference). This was partly motivated by the burgeoning VHS market and the perception that darker films didn't translate to videotape well.

FREDERICK ELMES: Dino was the one who had to deal with Universal, and Universal had thoughts about it. It's kind of a traditional concern: if you make it too dark you can't see actors' faces clearly, which may hurt the picture financially. The other view is you can make a picture that has that certain mood to it, special or edgy or a little provocative. Or you can play it a little safer. You have to find where that line is. It's not an easy discussion ever. VHS was a pretty poor substitute for watching a movie, but a big concern for everybody involved. This other potential market for distribution was important, and these movies that had big scope were at risk because you weren't going to get any kind of magic out of VHS.

CRAIG CAMPOBASSO: David always said, "Light is for life, dark is for *Dune*." He made us all t-shirts that said that.

FREDERICK ELMES: That was a little disconcerting watching *Dune* on TV the other night, it was so bright. They really changed it in a way where much of the photography lost its mood and character completely. It becomes a whole different movie than David had intended.

GILES MASTERS: The lighting played into that as well so you'd get an emotional feel for each different location you're in. Tony Masters and Freddie Francis worked pretty well together.

LUIGI ROCCHETTI: The working relationship with Freddie Francis was good and always very cordial, his crew as well. As always, working with cordiality helps everyone, especially for the final result. I only remember once he asked me to opacify the bald cap for his reflection problems, but I replied that by opacifying it the visual result would have worsened and he remedied this with a light correction. With Freddie, there has always been a great respect on both sides.

GILES MASTERS: The sets were built as sets. Every set was challenging for Freddie because you're not just walking into somebody's front room. You're in caves. A lot of time went into designing these sets so you could shoot them. Freddie did a great job, but he did like to complain that they were difficult sets to light and film. You could still wild walls out and that sort of thing, but a lot of the sets had a lot of plaster on the walls because it was rock. When you need to wild out of all that it takes, perhaps, a little longer than if it was just a standard scenic flat. We had the glow globes with all the wiring that had to go up . . . not only for the glow globes but for the Baron and every shot having physical effects. Freddie complains a little bit about how difficult it was to light, but at the same time, that's why you have somebody like Freddie do it because it was never going to be easy.

MARY VOGT: There was a first unit, second unit, and third unit all shooting at the same time. Fred Elmes was the cinematographer on the third unit, and people from the second unit were always going to his third unit and saying, "Sorry, Fred, we need your camera." They'd take his camera away.

FREDERICK ELMES: Yes, it's absolutely true. It was crazy. We were not a priority, which is always the case, I must say. That is one thing I have learned in shooting over the years: there's never enough equipment to cover all the bases, and you're always sharing something with somebody. If it's not equipment, it's an actor. "We got her, you gave her to us, and we need her for three hours in order to do this sequence." They would say, "Well, we need her back." [*laughs*] All of a sudden that whole shot, that whole complicated affair that we'd set up with extras and crew and choreography and lighting, we didn't get to do that day because they wanted her back for whatever. That's always the way it is with the first unit and additional units. But yes, they stole our equipment and our Lightflex.

IAN WOOLF: Jimmy Devis had a terrible accident. He had fallen off the cliff in the backlot and got hurt really bad.

FREDERICK ELMES: I remember when it happened. Jimmy came in partway through the production because we were getting behind and they wanted to form another second unit. He inherited the bigger things that had more to do with battles and some tricky night exterior photography, the big stuff. Pretty near the beginning, he slipped. He was shooting something up on a rock. I don't know if it was a real ledge or set? He was up in a precarious spot working on a shot, and he slipped, fell down on rocks, and got hurt. Fortunately, not any worse than he was. He was back on with crutches, going slow for a while.

BARRY NOLAN: I got into fights with Jimmy Devis. We would set up shots that would be pieces for a final composite. They would set them up, and I'd say, "No, that's not the way it's supposed to be. This is an element that goes with five or six other elements. You're making it look pretty by itself, but we're not doing it that way." I would say to him, "You're fighting with me now, you don't want to do it my way, and in a month you'll be gone and in three months I'll still be working on this picture trying to fix the things that you wouldn't shoot the way I wanted." Right? Jimmy Devis and I finally sat down, had a couple of drinks, and resolved our differences, that I wasn't trying to take over the show.

The major makeup effects and appliances were created by Giannetto De Rossi and his main assistant Luigi Rocchetti. The heavy fat suit worn by Kenneth McMillan was a collaboration between De Rossi's team and Ringwood's, and even included a cup and catheter system developed by NASA so the actor could pee in-suit.

LUIGI ROCCHETTI: I loved all the actors on *Dune*; there is not a favorite. The main contact was with Kyle, Siân, and Sean Young, but all are a precious memory.

SEAN YOUNG: I love Luigi. He's so sweet. The main guy, the bigger guy, the older guy—Giannetto—did Kenneth McMillan with all the pustules on his face.

JANE JENKINS: Ken was huge, literally and figuratively. He was great. The performance was just under camp. I remember David saying he wants all these pustules on his face and I was like, "Okay . . ."

ERIC SWENSON: Nobody has matched his Baron, man. He was the best. The grossest, the most disgusting. So, so repulsive.

TERRI HARDIN: Ken McMillan, what a pain in the ass! We were like, "He's perfect!" We had to do his body cast, and he whined and moaned. I kept wanting to say, "If you stop whining, it'll be done and you can go home." Played opera really loud while we did the casting. He was perfect for the Baron—we could see why David Lynch cast him because he was this whiny, pissy guy. You see him as the Baron, and he's great, the same pissy, moany character, and you just giggled. He was so funny; it shows you what an actor brings to it, and he did a fantastic job.

BOB RINGWOOD: He was adorable, that man. He was the funniest man you've ever seen in the world, so charming and lovely. He used to go out into restaurants with the makeup on and the painted nails of the Baron. Everybody was wondering what the fuck he was doing in this restaurant!

SEAN YOUNG: Kenneth had to get all those pustules on his face. He used to fall asleep in this sort of barbershop chair that would lean back. He would lie down and fall asleep while they did all the stuff. It was amazing. There was a lot of contribution by the makeup people.

LUIGI ROCCHETTI: Even for the Baron, the ideas came from Giannetto and David, who wanted it as ugly as possible. Despite the antiquated materials, the result was excellent thanks to the great merit of Kenneth, who was able to give life to the character. The body was not made by us, but we made it up and added some hair with the punching system.

BOB RINGWOOD: When we designed the Baron, that was all rather sinister because it was made of colostomy bag rubber. It somehow informed the costume. That silicone fat body was made by Peyton Massey, a rather strange, eccentric man.

MARY VOGT: Bob found this guy who was a prosthetics man near Wilshire Boulevard who made prosthetic eyes, and for some reason, Bob thought he would be great to make the Baron Harkonnen outfit. He thought he would bring something interesting or real to it. He was one of the first people that did a lot of silicone implants and stuff, and Bob wanted that for the suit because he's supposed to be fat.

BOB RINGWOOD: It was basically made as an interior body that fitted Ken and an exterior body that was cut like the fat suit. Then it was put on the stand, and they injected silicone until it filled the body and then let it set.

JOHN PATTYSON: We were there the first day Kenneth had the fat suit on, and he freaked out. He just couldn't believe it because it really was a fat suit. He probably weighed 300-plus pounds with that thing on, but he was friggin' hilarious. He was walking around in the fat suit doing jokes and things.

LUIGI ROCCHETTI: Poor Kenneth was harnessed and supported by steel wires and hung for several hours. The silicone body weighed about 180 pounds, a huge effort for the actor.

BOB RINGWOOD: Ken insisted that if it was a 400-pound man, his suit must weigh 400 pounds, and it nearly killed him, poor Ken. When we put him in that suit, he couldn't walk because it was too heavy. Then we had to have an A-frame made because when he was on the set he never walked, even when he wasn't in shot. He was always on wires because he couldn't stand up in the suit. Those guys that did the flying rigs were bloody good. The one where he goes round and round Sting was an amazing rig because it was like a whirligig in the air.

MARY VOGT: That suit the Baron wore weighed a ton, miserably uncomfortable. I remember saying to Kenneth once, "I'm sorry this weighs 500 pounds." He goes, "No, I love it because it's so horrible, it really helps my character." He had this leather coat over it. When it came to the S&M stuff, Kenneth McMillan was there in a heartbeat. He jumped on that; he loved that. I don't remember discussions about it. It was just like, "This is what it is." Kenneth McMillan was right there: "I love this stuff! I love this stuff!" All the Harkonnen people were totally into that—there was no pushback from them. Sting was like, "Okay, this is what I wear." His was more of a sculpted costume, and then the flying jockstrap . . . Somehow Bob got him to wear that, because later he was like, "I can't believe I wore that." But he looked fabulous. He was in perfect shape. He looked like a sculpture coming out of the steam.

One of the most iconic images in Dune *is the winged jockstrap Sting wears with gusto. A rumor has persisted that Sting was meant to originally appear nude.*

MARY VOGT: He was always going to be covered up due to the rating. There was no frontal nudity in this Universal movie they were hoping to get a big audience for.

CRAIG CAMPOBASSO: Sting was a very nice man. I sent him a bunch of the press stuff back when we were still at Universal and asked him to sign the picture of him in the winged jockstrap. He mailed it back, and I was like, "Oh, he didn't sign it? Why didn't he sign it?" I was upset, just put the picture in my closet. Years later, I got it out, and I'm looking at it and right around his nipple he wrote "Sting" really small.

BOB RINGWOOD: I wanted Silvana to have a bald head, and she absolutely flatly refused. She insisted a gray wig be made. Her idea was she'd just have gray hair scraped back. They did a screen test, and I was sitting next to Silvana. She turned to me and said, "Well, Bob, what do you think?" I said, "You look like Granny Clampett." She didn't know who that was, so we showed her a picture of Granny Clampett—then she agreed to have the bald head.

LUIGI ROCCHETTI: The makeup I am most proud of is definitely the Reverend Mothers. The look of the Bene Gesserit was studied and designed in agreement with David by Giannetto, and the result is still enviable by many colleagues. I was lucky enough to prepare and follow Mrs. Siân Phillips, and she was also very helpful throughout. The first time she came on set, I heard some of the crew who thought we had shaved her head. For me as a young man of 26 years, this was an enormous satisfaction. I prepared the bald caps, something I had been doing for many years before in the family company. To apply and color them, I used an old but fantastic system that Giannetto taught me which still works wonderfully.

Spanish effects veteran Emilio Ruiz del Río was handling some remarkably complex forced perspective miniatures which integrated live actors—shot at a distance—with detailed models positioned close to the camera.

RON MILLER: I was free to wander around everywhere . . . and did! So long as I stayed out from underfoot, everyone was very generous in letting me look on and explaining what they did. I was especially fascinated with the work of Emilio del Río, who also worked on *Red Sonja* at the same studio I was at in Rome while on *Total Recall*, so I got to see a lot of his work for that, too. He was really nice about everything and incredible to watch at work.

ERIC SWENSON: By the time I'd come, they'd pretty much filmed all the live action. The forced perspective miniatures were done too.

BARRY NOLAN: Forced perspectives were shot before I arrived there. Carlo Rambaldi and Emilio Ruiz del Río were people that Dino wanted to bring in on these things, and they were very good at what they did.

ERIC SWENSON: Remnants of Emilio's work were there, this big tall tower that was 30 or 40 feet tall with this miniature landing field with a hole in it. The hole would look down and see the soldiers. This was all in one shot. So amazing to see those things. They were in decay, they'd been in the rain falling apart, but the two of them that were left were stunning.

FREDERICK ELMES: The film is filled with such wonderful photography on all fronts. The biggest, widest shots are often floating miniatures or matte paintings. In those cases, I was just watching because the masters had been brought in to do those very special shots. I absorbed it all and got to see how they made these tricks work.

Another effects whiz on hand to lend his specialized talents to the film was matte painter Albert Whitlock, a Disney veteran who won Academy Awards for his work on Earthquake *and* The Hindenburg.

BARRY NOLAN: The matte paintings were done all by Al Whitlock. He was working on his own. He came down, they shot the matte paintings of the big hall with the Fremen, one over Giedi Prime, one over Arrakeen, and stuff like that. Because they wanted to make pans and tilts on the big hall, they shot in VistaVision with a camera running up and down instead of sideways, and then composited that shot in there. I really didn't have much to do with them. They took care of all that stuff.

RON MILLER: I recognized a lot of things that were taken directly from my paintings. Some shots are almost like seeing animated versions of my artwork, and when Al Whitlock did the matte art, he followed my sketches very closely, even to including some random details. The most literal representation is the line of Atreides ships filing into the Heighliner: That was a literal translation of one of my paintings down to the minutest detail.

ERIC SWENSON: We had a matte department at Van der Veer with a matte camera. Van der Veer could have done the matte paintings, but I think it was just too much for the small company that it was—it would have been too stressful. It wouldn't have enough throughput, but the stuff Whitlock did was amazing, of course.

MARY VOGT: Bob struck up a friendship with Al Whitlock, and we would go into his office where he had a life-size maquette of the Creature from the Black Lagoon. He had all these glass paintings all over this small office.

RON MILLER: All of the filmbook images of the various planets were painted by me. The two moons are my artwork. My favorite planet to visualize was Arrakis. Caladan from space is very earthlike, Kaitain was kind of fun because of its rings, Giedi Prime was just a shiny black ball . . . but Arrakis had a very alien landscape and you could see it. I even created a large globe of the planet. I also came up with the idea of having the flood of sand pour through the breached shield wall.

Meanwhile, three-time Oscar-winner Carlo Rambaldi was responsible for the mechanical creature effects such as the sandworms, baby Alia, and the Guild Navigator. Rambaldi was a controversial figure since Dino had put his work on King Kong *up for the visual effects Oscar in 1977. The trouble was that Rick Baker had done 99% of the actual Kong work, while Rambaldi's life-sized Kong robot malfunctioned and was only featured in one shot. Rambaldi's Oscar-winning E.T. designs were also heavily inspired by Baker's work on an unmade Spielberg project,* Night Skies. *As it happens, De Rossi and Rocchetti wound up having to come to Rambaldi's rescue by touching up his "fake"-looking* Dune *work on several occasions.*

BARRY NOLAN: Rick Baker was *King Kong*, all the makeup and things. Dino put Carlo up for the Academy Award, and Rick came in and said, "Wait a minute, I did just as much stuff as Carlo did." The Academy got really upset. There was a lot of resentment about Dino in Hollywood, and they decided to give the award to *Logan's Run*, which I worked on also. Eventually, they decided to show they weren't kicking the Italians out and gave both *Logan's Run* and *King Kong* special effects awards. I think Rick was better and more successful than Carlo.

LUIGI ROCCHETTI: I met Carlo Rambaldi when I was a child. I have always admired his works starting with Luigi Comencini's *Pinocchio, King Kong, White Buffalo*, the legendary *Alien, E.T.* . . . . We are definitely talking about a great artist.

BOB RINGWOOD: I thought the Guild Navigator in the big tank was wonderful. The thing was, I didn't like the fact that it looked like a cunt. I thought that was a terrible, terrible mistake. This was Rambaldi, and I did say, "You know, come on." It hadn't occurred to them that's what it looked like, but they insisted it would stay the same.

BARRY NOLAN: Carlo was more into mechanical lever–type stuff. He didn't get into the new modern technologies, but it all worked. When the navigator came in the big fish tank, there were over a dozen people in the back. The whole back of it was a platform, because the platform was like a flatbed car.

JOHN PATTYSON: We were there the first day David saw the Navigator in its container. This giant tank rolls out with puppeteers off to the side, things blowing and moving. David was so excited. When he gets excited, he can't talk. He stutters.

BARRY NOLAN: The whole thing rolled in. The monster was on the front of it, all the controllers on the back of it. A lot of my crew were in there working the controls.

LUIGI ROCCHETTI: For the Guild Navigator, David asked us to complete the makeup because it lacked color and materiality. He asked us to step in and add more real shades to the creature.

JOHN PATTYSON: Then David looks at it, he goes, "It needs something. It needs something. We need some kind of gelatinous something all over the head of it so it's gooey, drippy . . . No, we need some afterbirth." The translator says it to Carlo Rambaldi, and his face just goes like, "What?" The translator says it again, and he goes "What?" I don't know what it was, but they found something. Carlo went away and came back with this gelatin-type stuff that he put all over the front of the Navigator. David goes, "Perfect! Just perfect!"

LUIGI ROCCHETTI: David's vision is incredible, and while I was at work, he asked me to take raw meat for hamburgers from the set catering and apply it in some places. It amused and amazed me. He is a man with a thousand ideas that surprise you continuously. It took a full day to complete what he wanted, and in the end, he was very happy with the result. We did final makeup interventions for Alia too.

PAUL M. SAMMON: I always felt the goriest shot in the film was the God's-eye view of the fetal Alia moving through Jessica's bloody womb. Rambaldi built that Alia puppet. I was fortunate enough to be on set the day David shot that. He kept smiling.

The fact that Loyxo—the bald-headed mouthpiece for The Spacing Guild who appears alongside the Navigator and throughout Dune *from the first scene to the last— doesn't have a credited actor is puzzling. Luckily, someone was able to shed light on this.*

KENNETH GEORGE GODWIN: That Navigator was Arturo García Rubio, who began as an assistant director and got drafted into the cast. He was also the technician who maintained our video equipment. He had a background in television news as a cameraman and technician.

MOLLY WRYN: Arturo! He was such a cool guy. They just pulled him in. He was one of the Mexican crew. I don't know why they didn't credit him—he was so wonderful. He used to bring me stuff to eat—he was so attentive to everybody, such a sweetheart. Then when he got that part, we were all like, "Yay!" He was so devoted to his job and quiet and serious, and then . . . voilà, he has his debut. It was so cool.

KENNETH GEORGE GODWIN: It's one of my big regrets that I didn't end up as an extra in a scene or two, as a number of crew members did.

CRAIG CAMPOBASSO: They were filming the scene with Kyle holding the weirding module, and the thing blows up. I was there during that. They wanted me to get in a stillsuit and be an extra, but I was like, "I really want to go see Mexico." I didn't do it. Now I wish I would have. Last chance for *Dune* immortality.

Bob Ringwood and Mary Vogt faced a formidable challenge fabricating the thousands upon thousands of costumes the movie required.

KYLE MACLACHLAN: I do remember the Reverend Mother outfits and pretty much everything that was done, the detail, the craftsmanship. Bob Ringwood did the wardrobe and the costumes, the Reverend Mother, the way those things float and every little bead was sewn on. I mean, it was ridiculous. It's crazy.

BOB RINGWOOD: Dino and Raffaella owed money all over Europe to costume houses because they're always doing films and late with the payments. I was obliged to ring the Cornejo in Madrid and Tirelli in Rome and all these costume houses at which money was owed. They'd done a deal, "We'll give you this huge film and make all these clothes, and we'll pay you the money in that way." I was flying around the world like a mad ass, going to every country doing clothes: in Rome and Mexico and Madrid and Los Angeles and Florence. When I was away, Giannetto put that terrible fucking white ribbon thing in Francesca's hair. I blasted him because she was meant to have this space-age head. I was so angry, I can't tell you. It reduced her impact. If you see the scenes where she doesn't have that ribbon in her hair, she looks so strong, and when he put that in, she just looks like she's going to a wedding.

Problems arose not only when Ringwood was unable to make it to set, but when the creatives were unable to come to him while he was overseas.

BOB RINGWOOD: The tailoring on all those Caladan uniforms was made in Cornejo, Spain. The Spanish costumers knew about military cutting. They're immaculate, those clothes, fit the bodies like there's no tomorrow. The desert uniforms that rolled up with string to cool you in the desert—they didn't show it in the film—we made all those in Madrid. Kyle and Raffaella and David were flying in to see some of the prototypes. That week was my birthday on the Friday. They were flying in on Wednesday but then couldn't come. They couldn't come on Thursday. I booked a whole restaurant and invited 40 people for a birthday party on Friday. They didn't come on Friday. Raffaella said, "You can't go back, you have to stay there." I didn't get to my own birthday party. I was furious. They had given me a suite in The Palace Hotel in Madrid, and so I ordered a meal. I ordered a Nebuchadnezzar of champagne, five pounds of caviar, twenty different things, the most expensive things on the menu. Eight o'clock came, and there were seven tables—on wheels—of food. The bottle of champagne was three feet tall. You couldn't lift it. It was on a cradle you had to turn to pour it. The manager asked, "How many waiters would you like when your guests arrive?" "There are no other guests. Just leave the food." I had some of the champagne and some of the caviar and some of the things. Then I rang them and said, "You can take it all away." I think it cost them something like $10,000. This is where Dino and Raffaella were really stylish: They never mentioned it. They knew they'd fucked up. Really classy not to say anything.

Less classy were the baggy black Guild member outfits, which were made out of old body bags . . . USED body bags. This fact was kept from the actors.

MARY VOGT: Most of them didn't speak English. I don't think they were told what they were; there would be no reason to tell them. We got on a little plane to someplace in California to this firehouse where these body bags were. They were period. This totally came from Bob—I don't know where he got this idea from. We bought all of them and shipped them to Mexico where they were quilted. It would have been easier just to make them from scratch. Bob just liked the history, the feeling of what they were. It gave it another level. By the time they were quilted, they had these big rings around the bottom, and they were super cool costumes.

You may marvel at the level of detail and embroidery in Ringwood's costumes, but there was another motivation for that fine detail beyond the visual.

MARY VOGT: We lived in this area called the Zona Rosa where the hotels were. There were a lot of people on the street selling things. There was a woman who was an indigenous Aztec sculptor weaving a basket out of pink straws. She even had a baby with her. Bob said, "Wow, if she can do that, she can do anything! She should work with us." We went back the next day with someone who spoke Spanish and asked her if she wanted a job. She came and worked on *Dune*, and it completely changed her life. Now she has her own shop just because Bob saw her and said, "This person's got talent."

BOB RINGWOOD: They could do anything with their hands. Why not use that talent? I designed that cloak he wears in the court at the end particularly to keep them employed. I have a great sense of conscience when it comes to exploiting people. If I hadn't invented very elaborate things to be made, they would have been fired. I kept inventing more and more elaborate clothes that were pleated and had endless things embroidered for them to be employed, because there wasn't much work down there then.

MARY VOGT: When Paul Atreides gets indoctrinated into the Bene Gesserit, he's got a robe on that is absolutely gorgeous that 25 women spent two months embroidering, took forever. The symbols on it were beautiful. Symbols are hard—you have to make sure that they don't represent anything.

BOB RINGWOOD: On the cloak, I embroidered my name down the front in Fremen language. One side says "Bob Ringwood" and the other side says "David Lynch," and the names of all the Mexican ladies that embroidered that cloak are around the hem. Ron Miller invented the Fremen alphabet for us. We had these amazing Mexican and Guatemalan seamstresses sewing, and they were so lovely, so clever.

MARY VOGT: We tried to give people a ride home sometimes. We didn't find out until later that they didn't want us to know they lived in a converted Maytag refrigerator box. Bob wanted to give people as much work as possible, and he did. He made sure everyone got paid. The crew adored him. If he said, "Hey, guys, we're going into hell to have a picnic," they'd say, "Yeah, let's go, Bob!"

Raffaella's job included constant problem solving not only on a production level, but also on a human level with her cast and crew.

RAFFAELLA DE LAURENTIIS: That's what producing is, right? That's the job.

GILES MASTERS: I think everybody on the crew would agree she was the mother figure. She looked after us. You felt she had your back. If there were any problems, you could go to her to get it sorted out. There was no challenge too big; you just had to figure it out and maybe look laterally at things.

CRAIG CAMPOBASSO: She had a great sense of humor. We would be in serious meetings, right? I would be eating a sandwich and would just go like [*makes gesture*], right? Then she would do something funny back and we would pretend like nothing happened. Some people were like, "What's going on?" We would do these silly, funny things. She would always go for the fun joke. When I wanted something, I always told her, "Okay, when we get you out to dinner next time, we'll get you drunk and make you sign a piece of paper. Because in the morning, you'll say no."

BOB RINGWOOD: David and Raffaella adored each other. I don't know if they ever had an affair, but it was a sort of love affair between them . . . certainly an intellectual one. There were terrible moments of massive tension, but there was never any falling out. It's all a bit like being in an Italian opera.

GILES MASTERS: I remember her always saying, "Okay, I've got that sorted out, bring on the next emergency."

And emergencies there were. One of the big problems on set, possibly due to language barriers or lack of experience, was miscommunication. Camera film would run out in the middle of takes, and in one case, a whole army showed up in a parking lot for a shoot that wasn't scheduled for another week.

KENNETH GEORGE GODWIN: A lot of those glitches were in part due to the scale of the project. The logistics were unbelievable. At the time, it was one of the most expensive films ever made, so things are bound to not go entirely smooth. The thing with the army showing up was entirely something to do with the Mexican military, because some officer had got the schedule wrong and he sent all these guys on the wrong day. That wasn't even a production office thing.

BARRY NOLAN: David wanted Fred Elmes on the picture, gave him a third unit that was hidden most of the time. The English didn't like it, so they gave him a Mexican crew to work with. There was supposed to be matching Mexican crew for all the English crew—that was part of their negotiations.

FREDERICK ELMES: Oh yeah, it was terrible. I was very slowly learning Spanish, not particularly well, and they were very patient with me. Their English was pretty good. We communicated with sign language and notes and so on. It was all part of the experience of moviemaking on another scale and being in another country.

In another case, complex setups involving wires that Elmes had created for the hunter-seeker sequence were being taken down before a shot was completed.

FREDERICK ELMES: There were complications like that. The hunter-seeker was the sequence that we did the model shots, but they were all real, in-camera. There are not any tricks to it. It's either a glass reflection or a wire. The mechanical effects crew was very good, really helpful with all sorts of neat rigs. It's really just the insert stuff. First Unit shot the actors pretty much completely. The other shots are time consuming to get things to look right and wires to disappear.

KENNETH GEORGE GODWIN: The studio had done some big films in the past, but this was the biggest thing that had ever happened at Churubusco. Infrastructure was stretched by the sheer scale. All soundstages were being used. Massive numbers of craftspeople. Sets were being built, torn down, new ones built continually on all the stages simply because there were so many. They might realize they needed to shoot something but the set was already gone, so they would have to put something together in a corner of a soundstage just to shoot small pieces to fill in the gaps.

"Where there's smoke, there's fire." That's a lesson learned the hard way by actor Jürgen Prochnow when a special makeup effect went awry on his last day of shooting. The scene where smoke from the poison gas tooth emerges out of Prochnow's cheek seemed destined for disaster from the outset.

KENNETH GEORGE GODWIN: David had bizarre, weird things he wanted to do, his personal little obsessions. Like the scene where Duke Leto is on the table and the Baron is there. They do the whole thing with the poison gas tooth. Lynch wanted to surgically open Jürgen Prochnow's cheek, so they could puff that stuff out of it. [*laughs*] You could tell how much he was in his own head when he's dealing with things like that. You can't do that stuff. Raffaella got a little angry about that: "You can't do these things; you have to do things by the rules, not by your personal, weird, obsessive non-rules." I think he would have liked to do it. He even said, "Let's do it to me, and I'll be the stand-in for the Duke." And again, Raffaella had to say, "I'm not going to let my director be surgically chopped up in the middle of this film." That wasn't a good idea. They would butt heads about odd things like that.

LUIGI ROCCHETTI: For the scene of Duke Leto's death, it had been decided to see smoke coming out of the cheek torn by the Baron. For the effect, a latex foam prosthesis was prepared with a pipe underneath for the release of smoke when it was opened. The smoke would have been opened by the VFX, and we were recommended to not send it before the tear was opened. Unfortunately, the times were not respected, and the smoke given in advance at the opening acted as a combustion chamber causing a superficial burn to Jürgen. Today it would have been done in CGI with zero risks.

MOLLY WRYN: I was there when his face got burnt. Oh, so horrible. Traumatic. He got burned bad on his face. Obviously, it wasn't safe, having something on your face that would burn. We were horrified that had happened. I know David felt awful. I saw Jürgen recovering from burns.

Because he refused to shoot it again, the scene where the actor was burned is the take used in the film. Prochnow wasn't the only one feeling the heat, as hundreds of extras and crew sweltered during the vast desert location filming where many of the film's epic battle scenes were staged.

JOHN PATTYSON: Juárez wasn't a perfect shot before they got there. There was actually vegetation popping out over things. Today, if they wanted to clean that out, they'd rotoscope every single frame. For *Dune*, the military sent guys out there to literally handpick every piece of vegetation as far as the camera needed to see.

MARY VOGT: The stillsuits were gorgeous, all black and shiny. Then— when we got down to Mexico—the first time 30 people had the stillsuits on, David said, "They don't look like they've been in the desert. They're too clean." So, we got these Japanese blowers where you put things in them and crank them and this dust comes out. It looked like the orange spice. They went down a line and powdered all these guys down. It was a great idea from David because it looks so much better when they were dusty and dirty than when they were super pristine and clean.

TERRI HARDIN: I stunt-doubled for Sean Young. She stayed in the trailer and I did a lot of the running scenes. Most of them were cut. David was a real advocate; he asked me to do this. He said, "I think I'll need someone, and nobody fits her outfits." That's how it happened. Not because I was a good actress, I was just small enough at the time. I don't remember if I got paid. All the below-the-liners were all together in a few hotels, then you're driven out to the desert, you're thrown in an outfit and you go to work. They stuck me out there with thousands of other extras, but when I had to do Sean Young stuff, it was from the back and in the distance.

IAN WOOLF: We did shoot south of Juárez for all the dune stuff, about an hour and a half away from Churubusco. The whole company moved up there. We were in a hotel. It got too hot, 125 degrees. We had extras that were wearing those Fremen stillsuits in 120-degree weather, dropping left and right. There wasn't bottled water in 1983 like there is now, so we had Mexican laborers that were walking around with five-gallon jugs of water to keep everybody watered down. It was really hot.

JOHN PATTYSON: Down inside the dunes was like 145. The extras are all Mexican Army guys they threw in rubber suits with no ventilation, nothing. They're falling over like flies. To get the guys all fired up for the big attack scene, there was a man at the very bottom of the dune holding up this huge jug of water, and that's their incentive to come down. They were just piling down there to get a drink of water.

TERRI HARDIN: The reason we did it in Churubusco was because the extras were paid in shoes. Mexican migrants were getting suited up as the characters. We were running all over these dunes, and all of a sudden you fall over because it was so flippin' hot. You weren't good for more than 20 minutes, but they said August was the only time they could shoot. They were moisture-retaining suits, but that was because you had a bodysuit of spandex. Then you had foam glued with a barge and balloon rubber over it. It got heavier and heavier the more you sweated. There's one scene in the film I remember specifically where they're all lined up in a row.

DANNY CORKILL: All the Fremen are standing in a line in the sand where Paul is about to call a worm for the first time. You see all these adult

Fremen, and then there are two shorter ones. There's another shot later . . . if you look closely, it's all the adult Fremen and there's one little kid. It's because the second shot was taken after I passed out standing in the sun on a sand dune in Chihuahua in a rubber suit all day long. I think by that point they had me under an umbrella frantically spritzing my face with water, trying to make sure they didn't kill a kid.

BOB RINGWOOD: I didn't go on desert shoots because I was busy making clothes. We were down in Mexico, and the one thing they didn't spend money on was paying extras. They got beggars. Literally street people that had no money, poor things, and of course, they came with lice. They weren't getting enough salt and water.

MARY VOGT: They were really horrible costumes to wear because it was hot in Mexico. They were made out of an organic foam, so they got bugs, they got lice. They had big zippers down the front, so people would take them off and they would break the zipper. People would get marks, really horrible things to wear, but the principal actors didn't have much of a problem with it because theirs were very carefully cleaned every night. They were taken better care of, weren't really outside in the blazing sun as much as the extras were. I don't remember actors complaining too much. They sucked it up and said, "Okay, this is what we signed up for."

SEAN YOUNG: It was a very physically uncomfortable situation for most of the actors, unless you were lucky enough to be Virginia, who never had to get in a suit. I think the nicest time we had in general was lunchtime. Most of the people who played Fremen all had to wash our hands thoroughly, wash our face a little bit because there was dirt all over it. Then we could sit, and by that time, you didn't even bother to take off your costume unless you just had to. Sometimes it could take half an hour to get that thing squeezed up on you. We would wear our costumes halfway off, but not bother to take it all off. Just let it hang back and have your t-shirt on under it and basically smell terrible, because you're sweating in this rubber suit.

TERRI HARDIN: Did any of my scenes where I stood in for Sean Young actually get used? I have no idea. It was group scenes, and I could not tell. I do remember she spent a lot of time in her trailer. She wasn't the only one. I always thought she was very nice, but I didn't see her a lot. The actors did as much as they could, because it was the desert and it was very rough and dusty.

MOLLY WRYN: Because of timing. I ended up using one of Lady Jessica's spare stillsuits that Francesca wore. They were tight, and we sweated. It was hot. Sometimes it took a couple people to get it on me. You wore a ballet catsuit thing under it so you could get in because it's rubber. One time my arm accidentally came loose, and I backhanded this nice wardrobe woman right in the chest! She was so good-humored about it.

EVERETT MCGILL: Bob and Mark had not anticipated the material shrinkage and stiffening that would take place as the foam rubber suits aged against weeks of sweat, body oils, and off-gassing. So, as there was universal diarrhea among the cast, there were endless hours of joy watching one another try to quickly remove a wickedly tight stillsuit.

TERRI HARDIN: A lot of the stuff that I did was second unit. There were some shots with David on a big crane directing us through the classic Cecil B. DeMille bullhorn style. There were some sequences where there were a lot, a lot, a lot of Mexican people. There were translators. I was probably only down there for about a week because they found there were plenty of people who would get paid in shoes. Why fly me and put me up when you have the villagers, right? Made sense to me.

DANNY CORKILL: In terms of things that affected a 9-year-old's perspective on life . . . Those scenes were big. As a named character, I was taken to the trailers and then hopped onto a pickup truck and driven way the hell out in the desert to where they were filming on these dunes. I had a bad experience that day where I literally passed out. Skin expands, rubber contracts, you have to take a deep breath, and you can't do it. It's hot! Summertime in Chihuahua, man. The thing that really hit me was coming back in the pickup truck after that happened because I got a ride and all those extras didn't. They walked. I was watching guys keel over. I watched another guy open his stillsuit, and sweat literally poured out of it. There was a different level of attention paid to named characters as opposed to extras out there. I've read some stuff, historically speaking, in terms of famous Mexican actors who had bit parts in it . . . From what I saw in Chihuahua, that must have been really, really tough. I know it was hard for me. I can't imagine having to walk back after a day like that. It wasn't a personal negative experience in that nothing bad happened to me. I was taken care of—it wasn't that big a deal—but you're watching other people going, "Yeah, those people aren't really getting taken care of very well out here."

JOHN PATTYSON: Juárez eventually became one of the biggest killing fields for the drug cartel, who would dump the bodies and leave. That was later on, on the border.

In many ways, the experiences of the actors were just as fraught with difficulties as the rest of the production was having. There was also much joy and laughter as well. Lynch began referring to MacLachlan affectionately as "Kale," based on Dino's fractured pronunciation of "Kyle."

KYLE MACLACHLAN: It was a process. I got more and more comfortable with the idea of filming. I was very obsessed with continuity, which was ridiculous, but our continuity gal Yvonne was very happy to have me be so particular.

SEAN YOUNG: We showed up at the beginning of 1983. I was a little bit shaky, like, "Oh, I haven't actually worked in a year." I remember feeling a little bit nervous.

MOLLY WRYN: I just have chills when I'm talking about it. It was such a visceral, emotional effect on me. I feel myself getting tears, because being there on set . . . the sets were so beautiful, and then the costumes.

CRAIG CAMPOBASSO: The Emperor's room . . . if you were to see that in person, it was absolutely breathtaking. Molly and I went in when nobody was on the sets, and we took pictures in the Emperor's chair.

MOLLY WRYN: I was Harah—there was no question. That's when I felt truly alive was as Harah. It was so easy to be in that world. It was a magical experience. It was so real to me, so easy to believe it while I was doing it.

DANNY CORKILL: I don't think my parents were officially divorced at this time, but they were certainly heading toward it. We're in a hotel in Mexico City for a short period of time, then they actually rented us a house in Cuernavaca. We were three months in a house with maids and an inground pool for a part that doesn't even make the final film, really, but what a great experience.

ALICIA WITT: I was there for about three months, which is an incredibly long amount of time given the fact that I'm not even born until wherever in the movie where Alia comes along. It speaks volumes to the kind of budget they had. There were many days my family and I were there that I didn't work, but it was such a wonderful adventure. We didn't have very much money growing up because my dad was the only one with an income, so going out to dinner wasn't something we ever did. At the time we went there, the peso was worth so much, I think it was 140 pesos to 1 dollar. We would go out to eat every single night. At the time, I was eating red meat, so steak dinners are the kind of dining that we never did before that.

SEAN YOUNG: Mexico City in 1983 was two years before the earthquake there. It was a tough place. We were at the Zona Rosa, and there was no such thing as a 12-hour turnaround on the show. Whether there should have been or not, or whether he was going against SAG policy, they woke us up whenever they wanted to! [*laughs*] That's good ol' Dino De Laurentiis. It was a grueling kind of shoot. Eventually, it did move into the hot months. It was just a grimy shoot at Churubusco Studios. I don't recall there being any air conditioning in there.

Mirroring their onscreen bonding, the trio of Kyle MacLachlan, Everett McGill, and Patrick Stewart formed a tight-knit group, frequently pranking each other.

EVERETT MCGILL: Our closeness was immediate and lasts to this day.

KYLE MACLACHLAN: I don't know why we bonded together. Sometimes location can be a lonely place. You need to make your family, especially in a foreign city.

EVERETT MCGILL: In my opinion, Kyle's Paul was exactly what Herbert envisioned, and he was enormous fun off-screen. Pet-naming him "young buck" had the regrettable outcome of me becoming sadly "old buck." I do know that our love for one another extended to Patrick as he came in to replace Aldo, and I think the shared affection can be seen in our work together.

KYLE MACLACHLAN: One time, we were doing the scene where we're watching the breach of the shield wall. We use atomics to blow a hole through the wall so we can get in and take over the city. Everett's quite tall and I'm sort of regular tall and Patrick, you know . . . he's not short but he's smaller. It goes Everett, me, and Patrick, right? We were lined up, and I remember looking at the frame on the monitor and I thought it looked kind of funny because Patrick's head was floating. I'm here and Everett's here, we're around him. My line was something like, "Take it out, Gurney!" or something like that, and then Gurney turns and says "Atomics!" in that great Patrick Stewart timbre. But this time I said, "Everett, when I say 'take it out, Gurney' we're both going to look down at Patrick's nether regions and look at each other and just go 'Whoa.'" We did that. It never made it into the final version, of course, but it exists somewhere. Definitely made for the blooper reel.

Another thing that MacLachlan and McGill shared was they both did secret voice cameos as other characters in Dune. *In MacLachlan's case, he provided the computerized voice at the beginning explaining the four planets.*

KYLE MACLACHLAN: That was me. Our on-set publicist Anne Strick was a female voice on it, the one who said, "See: storms." Everett was the voice of the Navigator.

EVERETT MCGILL: Regarding the Guild Navigator, I have only a distant memory. I was called from makeup to go to post at Churubusco where David was reviewing Navigator footage with Raffaella. He asked if I wouldn't mind having a go at it, and I think we did it in one or two passes.

KYLE MACLACHLAN: I remember Everett would be on set, and he built this contraption because he wanted to keep his Stilgar voice in the lower register so it would have that depth. He's got an amazing voice. We were on these crazy locations with all this dust in the air, and he had a small plastic Dr. Pepper bottle with one end cut off and a wet paper towel inside. He would breathe in through that, and it would moisturize his vocal cords and his lungs and act as a filter so he wouldn't breathe in the dust that was all around whenever we were shooting on those sandy areas. He did it to protect his voice and keep that low timbre. That's all Everett; there was no manipulation on that. He's got a good deep, round voice.

VIRGINIA MADSEN: It was such a huge, huge movie, so many movements. These extraordinary actors from the Royal Shakespeare Company, and my embarrassing crush on Patrick Stewart. It was ridiculous. [*laughs*] I'm serious. I'm really serious. When he was around, I just never spoke. "There's that man. There's that man with the voice." I told him many, many years later that I had a terrible girl crush.

KYLE MACLACHLAN: There were other moments that were inadvertently funny. When I met Patrick in the desert after it's been a couple of years and he's now working with smugglers and I say, "Gurney, you don't recognize . . ." and he says, "Paul?" and then we embrace. We had those weirding modules, those crazy things that would fit right over your larynx. They were Velcroed on, and they stuck out. They were part plastic, and when I went to hug him, my module just embedded right into whatever he was wearing and jabbed me right in my throat. If you look at the movie, you can kind of see me go like this [*makes noise*]; I couldn't speak or breathe. It was like you got hit right in the Adam's apple, and he was just like, "You young pup! You young pup!" And I collapsed. Never mind the tire fumes that also stopped your breath remarkably quickly. Breathe in a little bit of that, and it basically froze your breathing apparatus. Couldn't have been healthy.

Some actors had a better grasp on the material than others, with MacLachlan frequently coming to his fellow thespians' rescue.

JANE JENKINS: I was not a fan of the book. I could not make my way through it. It was hard enough to make my way through David's script. I attempted to read the book. I didn't know what the hell they were talking about. All those weird names, it was just overwhelming. When I finally got the script and started breaking it down, it was still very confusing, but at least they had a little more structure to try to envision a person to go in that part.

DAVID PAICH: I had heard about it, but I'd never read it. I read it on my way down there, and Frank Herbert happened to be on the same flight along with John Dykstra. I was impressed these guys were also flying down to meet with Lynch in Mexico.

SEAN YOUNG: I knew I had the part, and I went to see my grandma in Louisville, Kentucky, and read the whole book there. Then I read the second one and I found that I couldn't put those books down. The third one I didn't like as much. It was just important to read the first one, but I read the first two. I thought that Frank Herbert had done this great job.

DANNY CORKILL: I had not read *Dune* by this point. My first introduction to science fiction was through Michael McKean of all people. He gave me *Childhood's End* by Arthur C. Clarke on the set of *D.A.R.Y.L.* I was so unfamiliar with what was going on. Knew we were making a movie, but didn't know we were making *Dune*, right? I wish I'd had a little more awareness of that. I've read all the *Dune* books since, all of Frank's books up to five or six. I blew through those in high school.

ALICIA WITT: I did read the book ahead of it. I realize that sounds strange! There are many, many ways in which I am not and was not advanced, but reading and speaking and writing were always my superpowers. I was a very advanced reader, and I did read the whole book in between getting cast and making the movie. As David tells often, I also read the entire script and knew all the other actors' lines. I could understand all of it. [*laughs*] I'm sure there's depth to what was going on that I would pick up on better if I were to read it again today.

KYLE MACLACHLAN: "Oh, shouldn't we have headgear? You know, like a wrap? Shouldn't there be a cape, as described in the book? Shouldn't there be a mask filter for the open desert?" Any of those thoughts about the design of everything I just said, "Well, they know. This is how they did it, and they must know."

TERRI HARDIN: Frank Herbert walked around and scrutinized every single little thing that we did. He wanted the face mask thing, and production didn't want it. Frank was there saying he wanted it sculpted, this is how he wanted it to be, this is the way it was in the book. It was a battle back and forth. They finally just said, "Frank, we're not doing it." But it was sculpted. It was absolutely done. It got nixed because actors didn't want to wear it, and he was sad.

KYLE MACLACHLAN: I had to put aside my . . . the books were so important to me. I knew everything about them. I really appreciated what Frank Herbert created down to the description of the items that the Fremen had, the way the water rings were tied so that they wouldn't make sounds when you walk, do you know what I mean? Those are so beautiful, and I really wanted to capture all of that, but there were other people interpreting all of this. You just go along with it. You say, "Okay."

EVERETT MCGILL: Much of the research on tribe unity, leadership, and harsh environments was simply lifted from my preparation for *Quest for Fire*, and actually surviving that filming.

VIRGINIA MADSEN: My goal was to be a working actor, so that I could work until I was like Bette Davis in her 80s. I had to find a way to establish myself, which is very difficult to do in my business, but you hustle, you work your ass off. This was a great way for me to get in the door. I had a monologue, but I didn't understand any of the words because it was like speaking a different language.

KYLE MACLACHLAN: She had a tough assignment to talk right to the camera and tell the story to open things up. I was like, "That's not easy."

VIRGINIA MADSEN: I didn't know anything about the book until Kyle gave it to me. David explained a lot about the plot and Paul's journey and what was happening with the priestesses and what the spice was because—I'm sorry—I didn't have time to read the book. Even though I was way into sci-fi, this book was not on my radar at all. Kyle came up with this big thick paperback that was all dog-eared, which was his copy that he carried around. I don't know what I did with it, but he gave it to me and sat with me. I said, "I don't know how to say these names. I don't know what I'm saying." He goes, "Okay, I'll tell you." He had things underlined for me he told me how to pronounce and he was there. He was filming, but he tried to stay for most of what I was doing. I was terribly nervous, but really playing it cool, man. "Well, whatever, it's a job. I'm a working actor."

KYLE MACLACHLAN: I think a lot of people were in her same boat. I definitely had an advantage. Patrick was the same way—he didn't know this world, this book, and it's a hard thing to get through. I knew it backward and forward, so I was a reference point for people and happy to explain to them the arc of their character and where they come from and what they're about.

VIRGINIA MADSEN: He had a lot of work to do, so there wasn't time to really hang out, but maybe because he was new too is why he helped me the way he did. I have been able to thank him, to tell him how much he saved my ass and how much that meant to me . . . For the lead actor in the movie to come to my rescue.

KYLE MACLACHLAN: Virginia is so nice, so beautiful. Just lovely, a really nice person.

CRAIG CAMPOBASSO: That whole debacle in the beginning when they're trying to explain the film to you beforehand. Universal was saying, "Nobody's going to understand this movie, and you need to explain it." They had her do this explaining, which pissed a lot of people off.

VIRGINIA MADSEN: Having the giant closeup seems like it would be intimidating, but for a young actress you're like, "Oh my God, it's my closeup." Even though the camera's right in your face, it's easier than blocking something and moving around. All I had to do was sit there and concentrate on my speech. It was a great way to begin my career, because after the monologue was done—which was the first thing that I did—then I was familiar with everyone and was pretty much a glorified extra. All I had to do was stand there, and I got to watch all those amazing actors perform and listen to their voices. I'm very particular about that, and even now that means a great deal to me, an actor's vocal instrument. I had a very heavy Chicago accent when I started, which took me a really long time to get rid of. In some of my earlier work, I was stilted or I have a slight accent because I couldn't go on a set and sound like this "when I was talkin' about, ya know, the plan-it Dewn." It wasn't going to work. To hear them and see how cool everyone was . . . everyone was really cool.

BOB RINGWOOD: I admired Silvana a great deal. I knew her film career and couldn't believe I was going to meet her. We didn't have proper dressing rooms at Churubusco, so there was what had been a toilet. I had it all ripped out and completely decorated and lined with fabric. I had a sofa and a bottle of champagne, a huge display of lilies and everything. On the day she flew in, we took her to this dressing room where the prototype clothes were on stands. She walked in, then she turned around and said, "Some people know how to do it right, and some people don't. Look at this. This is right."

SEAN YOUNG: Silvana Mangano got there and she's in the movie for 30 seconds, and they've got her up on the top-floor dressing room because Dino was married to her. There's a lot of ego. This goes way back in acting, the "star dressing room," the bigger motor home, all that stuff. To me, that's the height of stupid. I just can't find any meaning in that whatsoever.

ALICIA WITT: I can't imagine my life without this having come my way, because it changed everything. I often share the fact that I set foot on the set in March 1983 when they were still building the sound stages. My mom and I came to do wardrobe fittings and just a few rehearsals ahead of the main shooting, which happened that summer. I had an absolute sense at that young age, walking onto the soundstage, that I was going to make movies for the rest of my life. That I had already found my vocation. That was long before we even started filming.

Witt wasn't the only child on set. Harah is mother to young boys Orlop and Kaleff, played by Danny Corkill and a strangely uncredited Diego Gonzalez. Although not yet a mom at the time, playing one gave Molly Wryn a glimpse into raising children.

MOLLY WRYN: I would have been better and more attentive had I already been a mother, but I adored them. They were just little boys. Sometimes they were rambunctious, and I'd have to settle them right before we shot.

DANNY CORKILL: That's probably a good way to describe it, like having a mom on set. She was definitely looking out for us, aware of what we were doing, but always positive and made a nice environment to work in. That was nice to have, because there was a lot going on. Molly was wonderful, extraordinarily kind.

MOLLY WRYN: I love them. I think about them. I looked up Danny and saw that he's not in the business anymore, and I don't know what happened to Diego. They're very sweet boys. Then I had a daughter. Motherhood is the best thing ever, even when they make you crazy. It's the best. Role of a lifetime, you know?

To hide the fact that Witt was several years older than her character of Alia, the production used tricks to hide her height, in some cases wheeling her around on a dolly so she could crouch down on her knees.

ALICIA WITT: There was nothing else to be done because Alia is supposed to be 4. It's easy enough to make somebody shorter when they're in the abaya and you can't see their legs. Any scene in the movie where you see me standing, I'm actually kneeling. Then I was on a little scooter that would be pulled, like the finale scene as I'm coming in was definitely a scooter. Any time that they could, if it was from behind, there was a 3-year-old double who was a Mexican girl named Paola.

VIRGINIA MADSEN: David was really calm and creative, so kind. I was only 19 or 20, and he helped me. I thought every director was going to be like that. I thought a director is there to help you be a good actor, and most of them aren't . . . but he was.

ALICIA WITT: One thing I remember very specifically was a direction he gave me in the audition as well as on set to help with the fear emotion, which was to lean up against a wall and just tremble against it. The physicality of trembling caused me to feel afraid. That was cool. When I think of him as a director, I think of the way he'll describe the world that he's seeing. He often looks to a place off in the distance, and then he comes back and focuses right on your eyeballs. You feel as though he's bringing you along into the dreamscape that he's visualizing. He made it all about the work and let the actors focus on that. That experience really set the tone for all the jobs I've had in my life, because he's the OG director to me and that is the gold standard. Directors I've worked with who are not pleasant and make you have acid reflux—that's just not acceptable. I wish they all had a course from David.

Lynch's ability to help actors bring their best to the table was often tested. During the filming of the knife fight with Jamis (Judd Omen), Kyle MacLachlan had difficulty in the scene directly after when he has to cry over Jamis' death. The whole sequence (including the fight) was shot but ultimately cut out of the picture, with MacLachlan admitting to Starlog *that he was "pleased to see it gone."*

KENNETH GEORGE GODWIN: That was a massive setup. It was an Aguilas Rojas location. They had a huge construction crane with a massive metal cable that the camera was hanging on. The camera operator was basically dragging it around on this cable. You're following the fight down in this gully. The follow-up to that fight—which narratively was really, really important—was after he kills the first man he's ever killed—Jamis— Paul cries, and the Fremen camp are like, "why are you leaking water for this guy?" It's like, "this guy is different from us." That's the beginning of him becoming their messiah. It was a big night.

KYLE MACLACHLAN: In the book, the structure was that I'm drawn into this fight and I don't want to fight. There's a delay, so it doesn't happen right then; we go back, and it's more a ceremonial thing. What I'm trying to get at is there's a period of time between the actual killing and the realization. It was challenging to go through the idea that you're killing and the adrenaline is running through you—the kind of energy that has—and then to stop that and suddenly have, "Oh, I just killed someone, and now I'm crying because I killed them." The book had set it up perfectly so you killed him, there's a period of time, and then as I am expressing my feelings—having thought about it for a while—and expressing my relationship to Jamis . . . It's one of the beautiful parts of the book where all of his things are scattered around, and people come forward and say, "I'm going to take this baliset he had because I remember he saved me in the valley of the birds when we were being . . ." or "he gave me water." Some connection that each of the tribe people had, and then I go forward and say, "Jamis taught me something," and that's when that emotion comes.

PAUL M. SAMMON: Kyle became upset because he was having trouble summoning up the proper tearful response to his killing of Jamis. It was more an actor's frustration at not being able to tap into the required emotion, especially when he had hundreds of people standing around watching during a major story sequence.

KYLE MACLACHLAN: All of a sudden, that's all been squeezed like this. I'm like, "All right, so I'm killing him and now I'm supposed to be crying." I was young, and when you're that age, that's one of the things that stops you dead in your tracks, because you know what's coming and you're like, "Ahhh, I don't know." But I wasn't really helped by the situation, to be honest, looking back.

PAUL M. SAMMON: David was very understanding and kind during that, by the way. He supported Kyle instead of criticizing him.

SEAN YOUNG: David really believed in him. He had to fight for Kyle. There were a lot of other people who had more credit. David won that fight, so he would take a lot of time with Kyle. He wanted to be vindicated for that choice.

KYLE MACLACHLAN: They said, "Okay, we're going to do this thing, we'll give you this menthol." And I was like, "What's that?" They said, "You breathe this and . . ." and I was like, "Ugh, that's a cop-out. That's not the way it should be done. It's got to be organic." I was all into that idea, but they gave me this menthol and it's still not working. I'm frustrated. I'm like, "Goddammit!" I rubbed my eyes like this, get the menthol IN my eyes, like, "Oh, my God!" Then I'm really crying. It didn't work. Didn't work the way it was supposed to. I look back and understand because it wasn't really an organic progression, it was squeezed, and that's just not going to work. I love the scene in the book, the fact that he had to fight, he was forced into this thing. That leaves you where you really don't know what you're thinking. Then you have this little passage of time, and there's the moment of mourning, you know what I mean? That's when the realization hit him. That progression makes sense to me as the actor, but it wasn't the way it was.

According to an interview with Francesca Annis, an unnamed actor was screaming at both her and MacLachlan during the scene, making the situation worse. Young supported a rattled Annis (not used to this type of on-set treatment) by telling her that actor's performance would likely wind up on the cutting room floor, which it did.

PAUL M. SAMMON: Francesca Annis was referring to Judd Omen, who played Jamis. Judd was doing a Method thing, shouting out—just before takes—the vilest profanities at Jessica and Paul—not Francesca and Kyle!—to steer himself into what Judd felt was the proper mindset for Jamis: homicidal rage. Actors do all kinds of things to find the moment. Whatever works, you know? Although that was one of the more memorable "methods" I've witnessed.

SEAN YOUNG: As an actor, when I'm working with other actors, we all know who's the deadwood. We all know who it is. We may not say it, but we'll avoid them. It's like you're in a dance class. You know the dancer that's bad; you can't fake it.

KENNETH GEORGE GODWIN: I wouldn't say it had anything to do with Judd Omen. He was very nervous, but they shot the entire fight scene. They cut all of that out in the theatrical, and even when they stuck most of the fight back into the extended TV cut, they still cut that ending with the crying off.

This sequence shot at Aguilas Rojas also serves as an introduction to Stilgar, something that went through an evolution in the scripting stage.

EVERETT MCGILL: I made an early attachment to the first time we see Herbert's Stilgar. The scene remains in Villeneuve's film, and although the image of Stilgar appearing to spit offensively during the sensitive first meeting works well on the page, I came to believe it didn't add to the mystique of the Fremen. In many ways, it makes the Duke's crew look overly delicate. David decided, rightly so, to first reveal the Fremen materializing, as a troupe, from the crags of Arrakis. I always prefer less over more, and my final hope is that *when* we see Stilgar, he packs a punch.

Chani was also introduced in this scene, quickly forming a bond with her love interest Paul as she gives him pointers on Jamis' fight patterns before the knife brawl.

SEAN YOUNG: We were outside in the rocks and the cold, shooting at night. My first scene in the movie was Chani's introduction. They sort of shot in order.

Despite the fact that Herbert was involved and even provided a pronunciation guide, Chani's name is pronounced "CHAH-nee" in Lynch's film as opposed to the more accepted pronunciation "CHAY-nee," as said in Villeneuve's version.

SEAN YOUNG: I remember there being a pronunciation person. Frank wasn't there the whole time. On my first night, I said, "Chah-nee." I think at that point, since it had been shot, that was it. I don't think that became a discussion because it was already done, and nobody had said anything to me. Oh well.

Although Wryn played Harah (the wife of Judd Omen's character Jamis), she and Omen never met on set due to different schedules. That is, not until years later . . .

MOLLY WRYN: This dog wandered into my yard and had a tag. I called the owner, and Judd shows up with his girlfriend. It was their dog. I had never met Judd. We were like, "Oh my gosh, it's you! It's you!" So that was fun. I saved his dog.

Another difficulty MacLachlan encountered had to do with his contract. On July 7, 1983—the 109th day of principal photography—first unit production was shut down entirely when Kyle walked off the set, something he said he would do if he didn't have a signed contract by the 6th. One can assume this must have taken a great deal of courage for a newcomer to pull such a power move, but MacLachlan did.

KYLE MACLACHLAN: It was a weird time because I love Raffaella De Laurentiis, and everyone was really happy, happy, happy . . . But while filming was going on, I didn't have a signed contract because they kept changing it, and they wouldn't sign it. Stephen Strick was the lawyer for Dino and, according to my lawyer, was just not getting it done. We were trying to get this thing signed, trying to get this thing signed . . . It went on over a long period of time, and so they said, "This is not going to be easy, this is going to be tough, blah, blah, blah. We recommend that you do this just so we can get this thing signed, and then we know that they know that we mean business." I said, "Okay," and I didn't go to work. That certainly got their attention, and I think the contract was signed, done, and dusted. We accomplished what we needed it to do. I remember the reaction was, "Why didn't you just tell us?" [*laughs*] It was almost a situation where the right hand didn't know what the left hand was doing, right? Everything was going great filming, but back in the offices—on the business side of things—it was not going great. My team was incredibly frustrated, and they said, "This is not a great idea, but this is what we advise you to do." We needed to get this signed because we were at the point where it was getting close to the finish and then we didn't have a contract. They were just worried about what could happen. Were they going to add more *Dune* pictures? Were they going to add other pictures? What were they going to do? I didn't have any real strength at all to stand on except there was no way they could get out of *that*. It forced their hand and it might have been a little bit scorched earth, but I said, "Okay, well, if you recommend this, let's just get it done." And I think it did help. It was a little bit of an antagonistic relationship between all the people that were negotiating, the contract lawyers, etc. It was scorched earth, and they got everything done quickly.

Sean Young got off on the wrong foot with veteran actor José Ferrer. They later became friendlier on the Hawaiian set of the 1986 TV movie Blood & Orchids.

SEAN YOUNG: He was prickly toward me, oh yes, he was. I know why. I asked him about the House Un-American Activities Committee. I just wanted to know about that. He said, "Well, I don't know why anyone got upset with me." And I said, "Well, did you name names? Because I think that would explain it." [*laughs*] He was friendly to me, though. He was nicer in Hawaii.

One detail from Ferrer's personal life was incorporated into the Emperor's appearance: a gold under-lobe earring on his left ear. The actor had gotten the piercing in the mid-'70s (to much tabloid interest) in solidarity with his wife, Stella Magee, who was afraid of getting her own ears pierced. That earring became one more token of the corrupt Emperor's golden greed.

BOB RINGWOOD: We were on the set and it was quite late, and we were about to shoot. He said something about wanting an earring, and I of course had never heard of it. I didn't have any earrings, and Raffaella took that earring off her ear and put it in his ear. It was just like that. It was her earring, a small gold stud with a diamond in it. He was a very clever, inventive, and rather courageous actor. He wanted to go for it. He was a wonderful man. I loved him. I felt very privileged to work with him.

DANNY CORKILL: I don't know how much time we spent in that Great Hall, shooting those end scenes with all those people who all get their own closeups, who all get their own reaction shots . . . you're there forever. There's a lot going on, and that could have been really overwhelming. I never really felt like it was, which is a credit to who I was working with. I don't believe we ever knew why Diego was holding the dog, but I also very much remember thinking, "My gosh, how awesome is it that I don't have to hold that dog for six hours a day?" [*laughs*]

MOLLY WRYN: When Sting and Kyle were fighting, Sean was off doing something else so I stood in off-camera for her. When Sting is saying that remark about Chani being his pet, he's looking at me. I only know that, now you do.

Cast and crew did various things to keep themselves amused over the six-month shoot.

ALICIA WITT: We went to the pyramids; we went to the zoo. We had a driver assigned to us named Jesús —he would take us on days off. Part of the arrangement was Jesús would come when we wanted to go on an adventure. We went to the marketplace, and we went to a manmade water system that you can take boats on throughout Mexico. We had an absolutely wonderful time.

DANNY CORKILL: We had a driver named Tino who was with us all the time. My brothers and sister eventually came down. I'm nine years old, so forgive me, but I was so excited to have a Pizza Hut in Mexico City that I could go get something familiar from. I was excited to watch a Cubs game because Fernando Valenzuela was pitching, so it was broadcast throughout all of Mexico.

Around 65 international distributors (along with their spouses) were treated to a set visit in Mexico City to observe filming. The press got similar red-carpet treatment.

PAUL M. SAMMON: I brought press junkets down to Mexico City so journalists could watch the filming and do interviews. I also acted as the junketeers' social director, taking them around to local restaurants, stores and—more than once—to the fantastic ruined metropolis of Teotihuacan, the amazing pre-Aztec archaeological site most famous for its Pyramid of the Sun and Pyramid of the Moon.

ALICIA WITT: We went to the set many times when I wasn't working just to watch. One of the perks of my dad's job as a public school teacher was he had summers off. My mother and brother and I were required about two or three weeks before my dad got off of teaching, and then he joined us for the rest of the summer.

MARY VOGT: From the midway to the end, people started keeping animals. A lot of people had dogs, cats . . . everyone had an animal they would be constantly petting.

MOLLY WRYN: While shopping in the outdoor markets in Mexico City, Virginia and I rescued a sweet chihuahua by buying the poor little guy. Coincidentally, Sean had rescued a gray kitten. The three of us decided to trade. Sean took the dog, who ended up with a loving family of one of the crew members before she left. I flew with the kitten back to L.A. and named her Harah.

MARY VOGT: Bob decided he wanted to get these two toucans and this blue macaw. The macaw ate wooden hangers, and the toucans ate fruit and mosquito balls that Bob custom-made. One day, Maria Shriver came to interview Bob, and it was feeding time for the toucans. They were out of their cage, and one was sitting on Bob's head. Maria didn't think it was even slightly strange.

IAN WOOLF: A bunch of us married Mexican women on the crew. My wife and I just celebrated our 37th wedding anniversary. I know the sound mixer, Nelson Stoll, married a Mexican woman. Carlo Rambaldi's assistant Bruno married somebody. The prop master who just passed away recently, Ron Downing, he married somebody. The still photographer married somebody. It was crazy. You're down there for a year, and it's life changing.

GILES MASTERS: Then there were divorces and all sorts of things. I was only 20 for most of it so it was a different time for me, but an extraordinary show with that kind of crew and that kind of budget and camaraderie. I don't know if they get done in that way anymore. I talk to friends of mine working on these huge science-fiction films that we all know and love, and they say it's miserable. We weren't miserable on *Dune*. We rented a lovely Mediterranean-style house and had an open day on Sunday. Everybody used to come up to the house and hang out.

SEAN YOUNG: They had this house that everybody would come over to during the weekends, because they had a pool. We worked six days a week, and there was a pool party at Tony's every weekend and every day off. It really was great.

CRAIG CAMPOBASSO: Tony Masters' house was this mini-mansion with a ton of butlers and maids. It cost like $900 a month. We had fun pool parties there.

GILES MASTERS: Raffaella used to cook a huge pasta, and people would just sit around the pool and play Scrabble. Raffaella made it feel like you were in a family. There were always parties. It was hard work, that movie, but we loved being in Mexico. I have very fond memories of that movie, and I think you'll find most of the crew would say the same thing . . . 90% might look back and say, "Okay, maybe the film didn't work out, but it was an extraordinary time."

RAFFAELLA DE LAURENTIIS: It's hard enough to do what we do, so if on top of it, everybody is miserable, it's really not worth it. I try to keep it as happy as possible. The few experiences of my life that I have unfortunately had with unhappy sets were miserable. If you're going to dedicate most of your life to making these films happen, then it's the biggest part of your life. You better enjoy it. We'll make sure everybody is taken care of. I see that also as part of the job.

While Dune *was winding down at Churubusco Studios, Raffaella De Laurentiis was simultaneously ramping up work on the blockbuster sequel* Conan the Destroyer, *with old-hand Hollywood director Richard Fleischer taking over where "movie brat" John Milius began with the 1982 original. Arnold Schwarzenegger would swing his sword once again, in many cases on "revamped" sets from* Dune.

KYLE MACLACHLAN: The building of the sets . . . these were not flats. This is plaster done on a frame, gold leafed. No wonder they used some of the sets for *Conan*. They were giant rooms. The Mexican craftsmen did amazing work.

RAFFAELLA DE LAURENTIIS: *Conan* came after *Dune*. Actually, it came at the end of *Dune* and simultaneously because I was producing *Conan* at the same time as we were shooting the models on *Dune*.

GILES MASTERS: I started on the show when I was 19 and was still in Mexico on my 21st birthday, but by that time, we had finished on *Dune* and were working on *Conan the Destroyer*. De Laurentiis did them back-to-back. A lot of the crew went from *Dune* onto *Conan*. The *Dune* crew was still doing a lot of the visual effects while we were prepping and even shooting *Conan*.

RAFFAELLA DE LAURENTIIS: I remember one day in the Juárez desert I had on the right of one big dune Arnold and the skeleton of a mammoth, and on the left side of the dune, we were doing reshoots for *Dune* and I had the Fremen and Paul. That was fun . . . I don't think I could do that again.

BARRY NOLAN: I was doing two movies at the same time: *Dune* and *Conan the Destroyer*. I was wearing out running from stage to stage, so they had a golf cart driver who sat out there and would drive me from one stage to the other.

LUIGI ROCCHETTI: We started *Conan* when we still had to finish some shots for *Dune* on location in a small desert in northern Mexico, the Samalayuca Desert. It happened that on the same day, the two sets were shooting a few hundred meters apart, separated only by a desert dune. It was a day of races from one set to another, but when you are young, that doesn't matter and indeed it was also fun.

IAN WOOLF: When we were done with principal photography on *Dune*, Raffaella moved the whole AD department—Kuki López, myself, Miguel—onto *Conan the Destroyer*. There's a big panorama photograph in her office of her standing on a dune somewhere south of Juárez, and on camera left, they were doing reshoots on *Dune*, and to the right of her—just on the other side of the dune—it was our first day of principal photography on *Conan the Destroyer*.

CRAIG CAMPBASSO: I remember that whenever they couldn't find Grace Jones, they would go on the *Dune* sets to grab her. The actors were going to the other sets to see what was going on.

LUIGI ROCCHETTI: Working on *Conan* was fun on one side and less on the other. The fun was getting to know Arnold and Grace Jones, both of them great people. The other side is that our director wasn't like John Milius had been in the first *Conan*. I hope you understand what I mean; I don't want to prolong myself in this.

RAFFAELLA DE LAURENTIIS: There was no rivalry from Richard, but definitely from David. I used to call David "Richard" and Richard "David," so I started doing the English thing and calling them both "governor" so I couldn't make a mistake.

PAUL M. SAMMON: I came away with a great respect for Raffaella's professional skills. She virtually produced *Dune* and *Conan the Destroyer* at the same time, on the same stages, with two different casts and crews. A remarkable achievement.

By December 1983 (as cameras still rolled on Conan's muscles and Dune *models), John Schlesinger's Soviet spy thriller* The Falcon and the Snowman *was also lensing in and around Mexico City. The stars were Timothy Hutton and Sean Penn, both of whom had been considered to play Paul Atreides. Studios started to catch on to Mexico as a viable shooting location, with* Under the Volcano, Romancing the Stone, *and* Rambo: First Blood Part II *all shooting in and around that area at this time.*

RAFFAELLA DE LAURENTIIS: After that, everybody started to go to Mexico.

In the final months, the wheels of Dune *began to wobble off as the movie went over budget. While there were many issues, some point to Dino as one cause of the chaos.*

BOB RINGWOOD: David always says that he had trouble with Dino, but from what I saw, Dino supported him. I think Dino didn't really understand where he was going, but he just kept finding more and more money and supported the project.

THOM MOUNT: I developed, supervised, financed, and released over 200 movies at Universal. I was there 13 years. In a certain way, *Dune* was one of the least troublesome movies ever because Dino took so much of the weight, and because they're in Churubusco and generally out of our hair and our radar range.

However, the picture started going aggressively over budget. That became clear to me, because not only am I seeing dailies all the time, but I'm also looking at cost-to-date reports, which in the beginning are coming in weekly. Then they stopped coming in weekly. I talked to Dino and said, "Let's get these reports going properly so we have some idea what's going on." Then I understood the numbers were climbing—we were clearly going to blow through the budget. The question was, "How bad?" I went to Ned [Tanen] and said, "We're going to blow through the budget; it'll just happen, and Dino is going to be on the hook." Ned said, "I know Dino; he's never going to let himself be on the hook. I don't care what it says in the contract—he's going to find a way to squeeze the money out of the studio." I said, "Ned, how is he going to do that? There are really only four people in the entire Universal context that could say yes to an increased budget. One is Lew Wasserman. He's not going to say yes; he's the chairman of the company. He won't even have the meeting. So that leaves three. That's you, me, and Sid Sheinberg." Those three guys all have—relatively speaking—the power. My power to say "yes," by the way, was limited to $20 million or something as the junior of the senior executives. I couldn't just say "yes" to an endless amount of money.

Tanen then said, "Whatever you do, don't let Dino get his hands on Sid, because a little flattery and he'll talk Sid into a commitment, and if Sid makes a commitment, we're on the hook. Keep Dino away from Sid." I'm thinking, "How the fuck am I going to do that?" Sid didn't have anything to do with the movie division. Sid ran the company MCA Inc. administratively. I start watching carefully what Dino's up to. In other words, if he's going to travel, I need to know it. I deputized one of the key crew members on the set to keep me posted about Dino's travel, someone who would know all the time. That guy was someone I had worked with in the past and was loyal, and he finally called one day and said, "In two days, Dino is going to be in Los Angeles." Then I called Wasserman's secretary, and the reason I called her is that she was good friends with Sid's secretary. I called her and said, "I need you to find out from Sid's secretary . . ." If I went and asked for a piece of information about what Sid was up to, it would be immediately politicized.

Wasserman's secretary got ahold of Sid's secretary, and we discovered that, indeed, Dino had asked for dinner with Sid and—worse than that—Dino had invited Sid to his house, which was then the big mansion above Greystone in Beverly Hills. Dino said to Sid that he was going to cook him "a wonderful Italian dinner." I said to Tanen, "This is what's going to happen. I don't know how to derail it, but it's going to happen." He said, "Oh, fuck, Dino gets his hands on Sid, and he'll talk him into anything." Sid was a hard-nosed businessman, but he was very, very susceptible to flattery. Ned said, "Maybe I can stop this." Ned went to Mr. Wasserman and said, "Here's the situation: If Sid says we're going to spend more money on this picture, we have a contract that binds Dino, and we want to enforce it. We don't want to spend X more . . ." Now tens of millions of dollars more, because it was clear that the budget was not going to be $5 million over budget, it was going to be some tens of millions over budget. The night comes, and then we all come in that next morning. I'm sitting in Ned's office when he comes in at about 8:30 a.m. I said, "So what do you know about last night?" He said, "I don't know anything yet, but give me a minute." He makes a couple of phone calls, then he puts the phone down and says, "We're fucked." I said, "Okay. Tell me why?" He said, "Because Dino says that Sid said that we should ignore that clause in the contract and Universal would eat the additional overage beyond 10%." So we did. At Universal, that was a key piece of politic that made everybody crazy, you know?

BOB RINGWOOD: I did see days where Raffaella was tearing pages out of the script. I mean literally. I've never seen that before. It's the first time I ever saw someone walk on the set, scream at the director, and then just take five pages and tear them out of the script and throw them on the floor.

THOM MOUNT: We didn't send any serious executives to Mexico. In other words, if we had been serious about really being the suits and doing something draconian, I would have shown up, Ned would have shown up, but neither of us did. What we did instead is we sent guys from physical production. Good guys, but guys who are all about the mechanics of making a movie. They would go down, and they'd say, "Well, we could save this by cutting this scene out, and you don't need it." We made a few small changes, but I have to say, from my point of view, this was really David's movie.

KENNETH GEORGE GODWIN: There were issues in terms of schedule. At some point, Universal sent people down to start chopping things out of the script, because they were going to fall behind schedule. While they were doing that, David was writing little new scenes to put in. It was almost a little passive-aggressive contest going on. "You can take these things away, but I'm going to put new things in." It's amazing that principal photography was completed in the allotted 25 weeks, but there were always issues about whether or not he was actually getting what he really needed.

For a scene where the Atreides family first passes through the Arrakeen streets, Ringwood designed and manufactured costumes and hats for 1000 extras. Production downsized the scene to 200 extras, and then it was completely cut from the theatrical version. When it finally showed up in the TV cut, only a few dozen extras were seen on a mountain, with one proclaiming, "The mother and the son!" No hats were worn.

BOB RINGWOOD: We made 1000, all vaguely medieval Arabic–influenced. They had huge hats on to screen them from the sun and the light, absolutely beautiful.

RON MILLER: All of the Arrakeen street clothes and hats were for that planned sequence, which was mainly just to establish Arrakeen as a real place. It was all intended solely as background.

BOB RINGWOOD: They fucked up and cut it and cut it, and in the end, we didn't even shoot on the 1000—he only shot 200. This poor milliner made these hats in his factory that we set up in Churubusco, and we took them all out and ceremoniously burnt them in the studio garden. That's when I started to hate David Lynch for a short time. I hated him because he lost control of his own film. Things were going awry very badly. "I'm busting a gut getting all this done and you're not using it!" He didn't realize how much work went into making all that, how many people were killing themselves.

THOM MOUNT: I didn't go to Mexico. I'm in the studio trying to manage this to the extent I can. The responsibility for management of the movie belonged entirely to Dino, even though we now became the majority financier of the film after Dino's seduction of Sid Sheinberg. I would talk to Dino on the phone with some frequency, maybe not every day but every couple of days, and those were not always happy conversations. They ran out of money, and we started pumping more money. We didn't let them stop, we didn't let them run off a cliff, but we're trying to keep as much pressure on the ever-growing size and scale of the movie as well as the failure of the system around the filmmaker to help him get what he wanted inside a reasonable budget. That's a tumultuous and often fractious balancing act. You want the best possible version of the movie, because that's why we're all here. We're not making this for our health; we're making it because we love it. We think it has potential. We think it can do something, we think it can touch people, and we think it can make money. It became harder and harder to believe that.

Raffaella was having arguments with Lynch, but she was also having persistent issues with her father.

CRAIG CAMPOBASSO: I saw them at it all the time. It was always in Italian. I don't speak Italian, but I know when they say the bad words. That's how Italians are—they get very excitable, but when it's over, they don't look at it as a fight. It was, "I got my point across about what I want."

RAFFAELLA DE LAURENTIIS: There was always friction, but it's all good. Yeah. It's tough to work with family; it makes it harder than anything else.

CRAIG CAMPOBASSO: Dino always trumps Raffaella, so I'm sure Dino would get his way most of the time, but might have relented in some cases. If she won, she won. Dino was always like that. He was very excitable but could be very sweet and kind. He was not in the trenches every day. Raffaella was in the trenches and knew what was going on and what needed to be done.

BOB RINGWOOD: The De Laurentiis empire is run like a family business: "You'll do the pasta, and you'll make the salad." It was like being part of a family, and that was a nice side of it, an extremely high-end amateur approach except it had some wonderful results. Dino had produced wonderful films. It wasn't like a regular production company at all. You're part of the family, or you weren't. A bit like Judy Garland, "let's go to the barn and make a film." They were highly professional, but the approach was sort of amateur. It was like *The Godfather*. Dino was absolutely like Corleone. One of the best experiences of my life, working with them.

While Lynch was well-respected by the cast and crew, he was still human and had his moments, especially as production wore on after months and months.

KENNETH GEORGE GODWIN: I don't think there was a noticeable turning point. Part of it was just sheer exhaustion. It was such a huge project. We were shooting five and a half days a week. Long days. There were a lot of on-set mechanics that had to be dealt with. You're not getting a lot of rest, and it was over 25 weeks. You can't sustain those energy levels for that length of time, nonstop.

CRAIG CAMPOBASSO: I don't remember him being exhausted. He was always very even kilter, but every day at three o'clock, he would go in his office and nobody was to disturb him. I never knew what he was doing, then at some point, somebody told me he was meditating. Years later, I learned he is a big part of the Transcendental Meditation group. He was focusing his energies every day at that time.

KENNETH GEORGE GODWIN: He knew early on that it's not really his film, but he was doing what he could to make it his film. A lot of that comes through in design rather than narrative content. It's all moods, moments, and weird little details. He kept doing that, but the machinery was grinding him down.

SEAN YOUNG: I made fun of him for saying, "We'll fix this in post." That's what one of his phrases was, "We'll fix it in post." [*laughs*] I said, "David, you can't fix everything in post." At some point, you can't fix it.

DANNY CORKILL: It felt like a couple people were getting a little frustrated with the process or decisions being made. One of the only people who was a little louder—she was never unpleasant to me—was Sean Young. I remember her voice louder. Maybe Sting once or twice questioning what was going on.

MOLLY WRYN: The ONLY time I ever heard David swear was at Sean Young!

SEAN YOUNG: I had my sister come to Mexico City, and she auditioned for the part that Virginia Madsen got. I really campaigned for her. While she was there, she was in one of the scenes with Silvana Mangano. They were doing this shot of Silvana where they were way pulled up to her and they had this long dolly back, and as they dollied back, there was a tunnel full of Fremen women on both sides. David was on the dolly looking forward at Silvana, and I turned to my sister and gave her a really dumb look, rolling my eyes, just silly. What sisters do. David saw it and he went "CUT!" Then he fucking yelled at me in front of everybody.

MOLLY WRYN: She was misbehaving on set. David said something to the effect of, "Knock it off or get the fuck off my set." He was going to throw her off set. David said "fuck"! The horror! We all froze in shock and, perhaps, fear. If DAVID—the sweetest man on the planet—lost his temper, what could be next? The set became deadly silent. Memorable.

SEAN YOUNG: I took it. We finished it. Then I called him outside where no one could hear us, and I said, "David, if you ever fucking yell at me in front of this crew again like that you will regret it, I promise you. Don't ever embarrass me in front of these people like you just did. Now, if you have a problem with me, you can tell me. You can walk me off the set and tell me your problem, and I'll apologize or do whatever. But don't you ever fucking yell at me like that again." And he never did. He never did. He was very nice to me after that, but I was really pissed that he did that.

As far as the crew was concerned, Lynch's behavior began to mirror Guido Anselmi (Marcello Mastroianni), the famous director who dances around and avoids the myriad production people questioning him as he makes his science-fiction movie in Federico Fellini's 1963 classic 8½.

BOB RINGWOOD: There were tensions; there were always tensions. David was a bit like the White Rabbit, always rushing down the corridor escaping. There was this sense that he didn't want to be questioned. We were always chasing him, visually and mentally. He was always slightly resistant or running away, because I think the scale of it was just overpowering for him.

KENNETH GEORGE GODWIN: Raffaella was very supportive. They hired him for very specific reasons: He was an extremely creative person. They were hoping that would have some impact on this huge thing they set in motion, but they also had their business attitudes. He couldn't be allowed to be completely free to do what he wanted. There were always tensions. Initially, it was moving in a particular direction, and they were all agreed on where they were heading.

BOB RINGWOOD: When he started on *Dune*, he was obsessed with the minutiae, the miniature, the atmospheres, all these tiny strangenesses. What the film required was an epic vision, and that was not easy for him. It needed David Lean or Visconti. Visconti wouldn't have touched it with a bargepole because it wasn't sophisticated enough. David's not interested in epic storytelling; he's interested in minutiae. He suffered a lot on that film. I don't think he was at all happy shooting *Dune*.

KENNETH GEORGE GODWIN: More and more tensions developed during production simply because of the size, the pressure to get this done in a certain time. Lynch was very much interested in the little details of what he was doing, and that could slow things down. There was always pressure for him to just keep moving, "get it done, get it done, get it done." You can tell from all his later films that he's not the kind of filmmaker that's brought in to be a traffic cop and just get things done.

DANNY CORKILL: Every production has its own vibe. *Dune* felt a little stressful. Even at nine and even as an ornament, you could tell the people around you were definitely hustling and stressed all the time, which effects how they deal with each other. Everyone felt like they were rushed. You can feel it.

MARY VOGT: It was always an absolute free for all, but you had great people on it. Freddie Francis could have done the whole movie by himself. The actors were right there all the time. They could move really fast, and they were flexible. A lot of them were theater actors, so they were used to having to move fast. It was one of my first films, so I thought, "That's why people say filmmaking is hard." Then I started doing normal pictures—call sheets came out the night before. "Wow, what a great idea: a call sheet that tells you everything you're doing."

ALICIA WITT: One way in which David was so formative for me is that as a director he is so even-keeled. When times are really tough, as I realized in retrospect they were on the set of *Dune*, you wouldn't have known it from his demeanor. He never carried that energy over to the actors, and that's not the case with many directors.

MARY VOGT: There was so much chaos going on, and he was always very centered. He had a real innocence about him, like he wandered in from another planet.

LUIGI ROCCHETTI: The relationship with Lynch was always friendly and full of great esteem toward us. This certainly leads you to work better and with more peace of mind. A relaxed air on set helps everyone, cast and technicians, even if at that time, we did not yet have the technological means. We all worked hard to always do the best, and this only happens if the director believes in his collaborators.

ALICIA WITT: I know I was only a child, and certainly there were energies I might not have been aware of on the set, but I'm certainly very acutely aware of what the environment was on the other three sets I've worked with him on, and it's always been the same. I do not have a memory of him blowing up on the set of *Dune*. If that ever happened, it certainly didn't happen when I was on set.

VIRGINIA MADSEN: I was never aware of him having trouble. I wasn't there that much. That was a different time. Now that there are these giant sci-fi Marvel Universe movies, directors are automatically in a position to have more power. I don't know if they did that back then. You were in danger of being under the yoke.

SEAN YOUNG: At a certain point, he was getting much more tense, not so friendly. Kyle and I used to say that David was a wolf in sheep's clothing. He was always so nice on the outside, but then when he snapped, it was kind of like, "What?"

CRAIG CAMPOBASSO: If you ever saw him get mad, it wasn't like he was mad, right? He would say, "Oh, that just really makes me mad!" It wasn't horrific, angry, big blowouts like most people in the film business.

SEAN YOUNG: It was past the middle of the shoot. The endurance it took to be there, just with the grime and the sweat and the heat and all the decisions he had to make. He was a pretty big drinker, let's be honest, and so was Raffaella. They both drank a lot. I think the whole shoot drank a lot—I don't think it was just them. We were all getting more and more drunk by the end of the show because we wanted to leave.

MARY VOGT: The drinking was not toward the end; it was from Day 1. People were drinking. It stayed steady—it didn't go up and down. The excuse was, "We have to brush our teeth with vodka because of the parasites." Well, you don't have to drink vodka like water because of parasites. You didn't even notice that after a while.

MOLLY WRYN: I was not a big drinker at all, but some of the guys on set used oxygen, saying that cured hangovers. Guys had oxygen masks on.

TERRI HARDIN: I was young and a teetotaler, so if there was a lot of drinking, I went back to my hotel room. They knew I was a kid compared to a lot of other people. If they went to go drinking or get high, they didn't invite me. On *Ghostbusters*, they used to "go bowling," and I thought they meant bowling, but they meant "bowling." They never invited me. A lot of that went on during *Dune*, and I remember the next day people were moving slower.

Despite the fact that Jack Nance arrived in Mexico City sober, he quickly fell back into his old habits. Lynch doing Nance the "favor" of bringing him on board this massive production was turning out to be a detriment. Kenneth George Godwin, who befriended Nance and even tried to get a feature film with him off the ground, bore witness to this rapid deterioration.

KENNETH GEORGE GODWIN: David is very loyal to everybody he's ever done things with. Jack was a wonderful guy, but he was an alcoholic. He had these problems, ups and downs. Lynch wrote the part of Nefud specifically for Jack. It's not really in the book—it's just this little side character. He did it to give him some financial security, but at the same time, it's a very small part. Jack had an awful lot of time in Mexico City because his scenes were spread throughout. He'd have weeks between doing scenes, so he did begin drinking again. It was a generous act in one way, but not necessarily the best thing for Jack.

As the budget climbed and resources dwindled, Lynch & Co. ended principal photography on September 9, 1983, with months of model shoots and visual FX work still to be executed as the final film took misshapen form.

MOLLY WRYN: I was there for the wrap party; it was held at a bullfighting ring. They had a baby bull, which are not like cute little calves . . . they're formidable. A group of us women jumped into the ring to do it, and they didn't have enough of those cape thingies so I took off my jacket to use that. "Toro!" The women—Raffaella was down in there with us—were the best actually, but when the bull charged me, I forgot to move my coat to the side, I was just mesmerized, and he knocked me up in the air! I landed on my feet, but I was out of breath. David jumped over and came to see if we were all right. It was very gallant. When the guys did it, they got thrown left and right. They had been drinking, and they got battered quite a bit by the baby bull.

FREDERICK ELMES: It's a painful process to see it come apart. I do think that David understood what position he was in and that he had very good support from the company. They really had come through and delivered these actors and this giant palette to build the story on and these sets which were phenomenal. They were committed to seeing it through. It was all very genuine.

THOM MOUNT: We gave Dino more money, but it was a much more parsimonious enterprise at that point. Our physical production guys were going down to Mexico to try to help speed the process up or whittle down scenes or find alternatives. That was very marginally successful. I didn't want to savage the movie, hobble it; there was no reason.

BOB RINGWOOD: There were always dramas going on all the time on that film. People were criticizing David quite a bit, but strangely none of us—including David—lost their sense of friendship. That was what was so strange. It was like an amazing family. There were about four or five hundred crew, and there was a very intense sense of family. Everyone felt very protective toward the film.

FREDERICK ELMES: It's a stressful time coming to a close. There are never enough days to finish the photography, and parts of the script didn't get done. They were the less important parts in some people's minds, not in David's necessarily, stuff he thought they might be able to do without or try to get later. All those conversations happen around that time. At some point, with six months of photography, the producers really like to say, "Okay, just stop. You have to stop shooting. We probably got 99% of it, so why don't you stop? If we need something, we'll edit it or we'll go get that one little thing and not all these other things." [*laughs*] It's like stopping water running down the river.

THOM MOUNT: It cost an insane amount of money relative to our deal. It was the most expensive movie Universal had produced at that point. At the end of the day, it doesn't matter whether it cost $35 million or $45 million or $55 million . . . if it's a great movie. If it lives up to the promise of David's singular vision, it's all worth it. That's the horse we're betting on. A lot of us bet on David because David was clearly deeply talented, really creative, and fresh. That's very hard to find in the pantheon of acceptable directors in the world.

BOB RINGWOOD: It was like you're on a rollercoaster: Nobody knew quite where it was going. There was no sense of direction. A lot of departments retreated into their own little worlds and intensely did what they thought was right for the thing they were doing. Carlo and all these other people, everyone was doing their bit and quite a lot of the time it did come together . . . and then sometimes things didn't.

SEAN YOUNG: Everybody making the picture started out with the highest of hopes because at that point David had all these good outcomes like *Elephant Man* and *Eraserhead*, so he was a bit of a golden boy. At some point, he realized that he had so much footage, and he'd bit off a lot. It was going to be very hard to put it all together cohesively. It's hard when you start in the business at the top because you can only work your way down. It's like, "Oh, no!" It's easier to start at the bottom and then work your way up and have a steady climb. It's very hard to do the reverse.

. . .

—III—
POST-PRODUCTION
AND RELEASE

"Do you think that if you were falling in space . . . that you would slow down after a while, or go faster and faster?

Faster and faster. And for a long time, you wouldn't feel anything. And then you'd burst into fire. Forever . . . And the angels wouldn't help you. Because they've all gone away."

—Donna Hayward and Laura Palmer,
Twin Peaks: Fire Walk with Me

Band-Aids and Chewing Gum: Visual Effects

After principal photography wrapped in September 1983, four of the eight stages at Churubusco not being used by *Conan the Destroyer* were occupied by the visual effects crew in charge of miniature photography. Alarmingly, it was not the effects crew originally hired to do the job.

When George Lucas' Industrial Light and Magic proved too busy with *Return of the Jedi*, the initial VFX responsibilities fell entirely under the umbrella of Apogee, Inc., led by Oscar winner John Dykstra (*Star Wars*, *Star Trek: The Motion Picture*). They had been brought on after a year-long bidding process involving multiple effects houses. The appeal of Apogee was their ability to handle every aspect of the effects: miniatures, opticals, motion control photography, bluescreen, etc.

The reasons Apogee ultimately walked off the production varied wildly in the press. One story said Apogee wanted to photograph the models at their offices in LA—even shooting test footage of the worms there—but Raffaella De Laurentiis wanted to save on costs by shooting in Mexico. Dykstra was wary of the faulty electricity at Churubusco ruining complex motion control setups. Other reasons cited by the producer were that the prices of everything were skyrocketing under Dykstra.

Raffaella told *Starlog* #88:

> It didn't work out because of the way his operation works. I had no control over costs. I can't work unless I know where I'm putting my money . . . to know that if you spend those $10 on this, you'll get an effect on the screen worth $20 . . . I just saw this money disappearing, not knowing where. I couldn't cope with it. Dykstra didn't want to work my way, and I didn't want to work his way, so it was just better to terminate it.

Whatever the case, after three months of work in Mexico—including constructing models, building two massive bluescreens, and creating detailed VFX storyboards with Lynch—Apogee was out.

In their place, Raffaella recruited her B-squad, led by Barry Nolan of Van der Veer Photo Effects, a go-to for her and Dino on pictures like *King*

Kong and *Flash Gordon*. Nolan's team would supply motion control, opticals, and revamped storyboards.

"Barry was the cheapest," Lynch said in *Room to Dream*. "Dino also probably put the fuckin' screws on Barry to make him even cheaper to get the job. Barry probably hardly made any money. Dino would knuckle people down to the bare bone."

Model construction was overseen by English technician Brian Smithies, whose work had graced hits like *Superman* and *The Dark Crystal*. He led a crew in building many of the settings and vehicles needed, including a slew of spaceships.

Models ranged from 9 to 75 feet in length and had to be shot at 10 times normal speed. The worm sequences consisted of over 100 shots that took around three months to lens against a bluescreen on the large 70'×100' desert backlot set. Background plates, bluescreen footage, and shots of miniatures were frequently combined. Smithies created an additional 100 spaceship models and directed two effects units, with Nolan helming the other. Each unit had 35 personnel, with 400 effects shots scheduled in Mexico, but by the time production completed in October, the number of opticals had more than doubled to 1000. Background plates, bluescreen footage, and shots of miniatures were frequently combined.

"For the live action on the harvester, we actually built three scales, the smallest one being about three inches," Smithies said in a "Models" featurette from the 2006 *Extended Edition* DVD. "Then we had the large one, only about seven or eight feet long, and that was the one which we did establishing shots on. The one that was swallowed by the worm was probably about a foot long, maybe 14 inches."

Matte photography was handled by Albert Whitlock, a skilled Disney veteran whose painted backdrops on glass appeared in productions like *Diamonds Are Forever* and *The Thing*. He worked on sequences like the Atreides fleet arriving on Arrakis, Piter's trip through the bowels of Giedi Prime, and the massive Hall of Rites rallies.

Whitlock recalled [*Enterprise Incidents* #26]:

> We had all sorts of ideas for things we were going to do. They gradually got whittled down by degrees to just a few scenes, but those scenes are very important. I worked on the big scenes like the Arrakeen valley. Then there's the big interior where the spice is allegedly made. There's an aerial sort of tramway in it and people moving

down. It's supposed to be a very big interior. There's another scene with a great wall in it. Some of those are successful, others aren't. When you read a story where it says that the cliffs are three miles high and they're black, allegedly they are supposed to be against the black stratosphere. In fact, they're not because it would blend together. It's very hard imagery to carry through. The written word can set the imagination going with anything, but actually putting it down in pictorial fashion is something else. Even on a clear day when looking out at sea, you don't really see beyond five miles. When you have to see 25 miles and make it work, that's not possible.

Two additional artists familiar to the De Laurentiis organization were brought in: creature designer Carlo Rambaldi (*Alien, E.T.*) and foreground miniaturist Emilio Ruiz del Río (*Spartacus, Conan the Barbarian*).

The work of del Río involved nine miniature dioramas—often elevated—placed directly in front of the camera with a hole strategically placed so that live actors far away from the model would be photographed through the hole. If lit and photographed just right, the line between model and real actors was seamless. Because these shots were accomplished entirely in-camera with no post-production optical processing, they remain some of the most jaw-dropping and impressive in *Dune*. They include the Guild's arrival on Kaitain (the Guild ship model was 36 feet long), the Atreides' arrival on Arrakis, troops ascending the stairs of the Arrakeen fortress, legions of soldiers pouring out of mountains and boarding Atreides ships, Sardaukar emerging from the Harkonnen drop ship, and thousands of Fremen warriors running across sand dunes. Small soldier doll movement was done using pulleys and bicycle pedals. Some floating miniatures were as wide as 40 to 50 feet.

"Working with Emilio was not cheap," Raffaella revealed in the 2008 documentary *El último truco*. "He knew how to work cheaply for low-budget films, but with us, he worked at the highest level."

When John Dykstra saw del Río at work, he referred to him as "Emilio the Wizard," a nickname that stuck. "David Lynch said that my system could not be forgotten," del Río said in the documentary. "That it was old-fashioned, but that nobody should forget it because my work was still very interesting."

Rambaldi was in charge of puppets for the Third-Stage Guild Navigator, Baby Alia, and—most crucial of all—the many varieties and scales of sandworms, from the infant ones that puke the blue Water of Life to the big mommas whose in-world measurements are meant to be a quarter of a mile long. Rambaldi's sandworms alone cost the production $2 million. The skin of the to-scale sandworm cross-sections was reportedly made from thousands of slime-covered prophylactics. Barry Nolan called the worm sequences the most challenging in the film.

"When the producers changed horses [optical houses] mid-stream, the bone of contention was how to shoot the worms, and I said they could be shot in the studio," Freddie Francis told On Location. "Everyone disagreed except Dino and Raffaella. I went back and shot the start of the worm sequence myself so that from then on everything Barry did had to match my conception."

Rambaldi designed 30 worms of differing sizes, ranging from 9 to 75 feet. Every worm was made of polyurethane rubber, divided into three sections at his North Hollywood studio, and shipped to Mexico in a "very long truck" for later reassembly. After three weeks of practice supervised by Rambaldi, it took 12 people to remote control the mechanisms for simultaneous movement inside each worm, which was supposed to appear to be 120 feet in diameter onscreen. He brought five of his own operators with him to Mexico, with an additional 20 hired on-site.

"The movement the worms required had never been tried before," Rambaldi told Film Review in February '85. "Because worms have no bones or joints, you have almost endless fluidity. Realistic movement was our problem. The worms were seven months in preparation. We had 16 of them with a minimum of six people operating each one."

Microballoons, typically used as filler material, were used to simulate miniature sand and manufactured by 3M. These hollow glass spheres two-and-a-half thousandths of an inch in diameter (60 microns) mixed with sand-colored tempera would move like water when they came into contact with miniatures. Real grains of sand would be disproportionate and appear the size of golf balls compared to the model, while a powder like flour would clump. Shot at 15 times normal speed, the microballoons flowed like real sand. This material was first used by ILM for a snow sequence in The Empire Strikes Back.

"These are no toy dragons rising out of the ocean to eat Kyoto . . . these things look real!" Herbert joked about the worms to Prevue #57.

The Third-Stage Guild Navigator built by Rambaldi (then sweetened by makeup man Giannetto De Rossi) measured 18 feet long, with the head itself being 6 feet high. It took 15 people three months to build, and 22 remote control operators to manipulate its 40 points of movement.

"He's very ominous, with totally mobile features . . . the head is 30 times the size of a human's," Herbert added. "With a flattened nose, tiny mouth, and articulated eyes. He's uglier and more repulsive than I ever expected him to be."

Lynch requested the Guild Navigator—whom he initially sketched and described as a "fleshy grasshopper"—have more articulation in the jowls. The helmer's daughter, Jennifer Lynch, operated the left hand and lower jaw of the creature.

"He would create things, like an infant child, and I had to work on it—otherwise it would look like a plastic doll," De Rossi explained in a 2020 interview on Arrow's 4K release. "The huge Navigator needed makeup because it was made of plastic."

One talented crew member went uncredited for his work: makeup effects artist Christopher Tucker. Lynch's old *Elephant Man* cohort was hired to build the Second-Stage Guild Navigator, whose look was not far from Joseph Merrick but more pig-like. As the missing link between the oozing-skull First-Stage Navigator and the grasshopper-like Third, it was an effective mutation, but ultimately scrapped.

Tucker recalled in 2020 [Arrow 4K *Dune* release]:

> We may have been using radio control for the Guild Navigators—some of which were mechanized and therefore quite complex—to control the mouth movements, eye movements. I made a phone call to Rambaldi when he was actually on location . . . eventually, they were able to produce him, and he announced himself as 'The Great Rambaldi'! That conversation didn't proceed terribly well after that. I think I had a similar experience to Rick Baker. He was telling me his experiences of Carlo Rambaldi!

Tucker also created silver dentures for Siân Phillips' Reverend Mother. Meanwhile, Lynch's yen for the grotesque lived on in the pustules applied to the Baron's face by Giannetto De Rossi.

"Sores on skin . . . are really, incredibly beautiful," Lynch told *Rolling Stone* in December '84. "If I start seeing people suffering with sores on their skin, then it gets to me. But if you took a photograph of it and looked at it as texture, it's fantastic."

After supervising effects in Mexico, Nolan shot additional effects footage at Van der Veer's studio in L.A. until October 1984. The shields were animated over the span of a year by Nolan's technical crew. Every pass on the 38 shots in this fight sequence was animated over the live-action footage, with various distortions achieved on an optical printer rather than through computer means. There were 48,000 frames of blue eye rotoscope animation spread over 30 minutes of film, also taking nearly a year to complete.

"It's a nifty film . . . it's different," Lynch told the *L.A. Times'* Dale Pollack in Dec 1984. "*Dune* is a special effects picture, but we always thought of it as an organic film, in which the effects would be integrated. There are 900 optical shots and tons of different processes, but most of the effects don't really have to be understood. It's like open heart surgery—a really neat process."

As you'll discover in the oral history section, though, things were not as "nifty" as the filmmaker imagined. A look at some of Apogee's original VFX storyboards showcases cut scenes from the far more ambitious and visually dazzling film Lynch was trying to pull off:

—Paul's hand in a different version of "the box" made out of energy shields.

—A much more elaborate sequence of a Third-Stage Guild Navigator folding space. A script draft from June 1982 featured an ambitious sequence in the Heighliner's 2000-foot-high control room where 20 Third-Stage Navigators—along with an unseen Fourth-Stage Navigator—swim through spice over a six-dimensional, miniature replica of the whole universe. The navigators emit electrical currents, controlling the mini-universe, until a huge roar signals the universe beginning to bend into a "U" shape. The navigators and all human passengers aboard the ship glow with blue light. The Fourth-Stage Navigator would later be revealed as a 500-foot-long pale worm with a human face as in *God Emperor of Dune*.

—A whole fleet of Atreides 'thopters on a massive landing field; Duke Leto's flyover inspection of spice factories; a dozen spotters flying over the spice harvester; the Duke overlooking the airfield at sunset.

—Harkonnen 'thopters leaving the mothership to attack the Atreides fortress.

—Rabban in a 'thopter flying over the wreckage of spice harvesters, saying he will "falsify the reports."

—A fleet of conical flying bombs (referred to in the movie as "atomics"); worms swallowing up whole squadrons of Sardaukar; worms smashing the Emperor's golden tent by throwing themselves against it. One cut effect from this sequence reportedly involved 5000 'thopters flying in formation above 300 sandworms while 20 nuclear bombs went off.

—A horrifying vision of the Reverend Mother with blood pouring from her eyes emerging as a blob out of Paul's mouth (breaking his teeth), followed by fire spewing out of his mouth.

—An elaborate alternate ending where Paul moves through a tunnel with visions of other Reverend Mothers and energy rings as his face gets wildly distorted. Dozens of tiny Navigators emerge from the light, swarming Paul's face and burrowing into his skin and eyes as streams of blood flow from the eye cracks. Paul vomits glowing stars, and the Navigators fly away as the stars turn into angels and Paul's face transforms into a golden mask, which Paul sees as a reflection in water. An insect flies out of the mouth of a glowing Alia fetus, light pours out of Jessica's mouth, and a golden lotus is formed out of a drop of water.

Brad Dourif said later in the 2003 documentary *The Films of David Lynch*:

> Some of the special effects and so forth got very cheap. They ran out of money, and no, in a lot of those cases he didn't get what he wanted. They just didn't have the money for it. I mean, there are descriptions in the screenplay of folding space which are just gorgeous, and I know he would have loved to have done. Had the film been done a few years later, he could have, and they would have been gorgeous.

When Lynch was not at Churubusco—either in his office (where an early poster for his unmade *Ronnie Rocket* hung) or overseeing miniature photography—he was back in his hotel room, working on scripts for a second and third *Dune* film, which the company planned to lens back to back from 1985 to 1986.

"I wrote half a script for the second *Dune*," the director says in *Lynch on Lynch*. "I really got into it because it wasn't a big story . . . more like a neighborhood story. It had some really cool things in it."

By the time he left in February 1984, Lynch had spent a year and a half in Mexico.

Slice and Dice: Editing

After completing photography in September 1983, Lynch told *The New York Times*, "My real problem is still squeezing *Dune* into the length of an ordinary movie."

Two weeks after the September wrap (but before model shots were executed) a four-hour-plus assembly cut was screened in Mexico for the crew, with many "Scene Missing" slugs inserted where VFX were incomplete.

Although they had been editing material since the shoot began, the fine cutting with Antony Gibbs and his assistant Penelope Shaw in Burbank after the entire Mexico shoot was complete went on from March to November 1984. At one point, Lynch showed a 3.5-hour work print version to Herbert, which met with the author's approval: "You feel that all the things that aren't on screen are happening at the periphery. Making a movie of a book is like translating English to Swahili, but David's translation is close enough."

Raffaella found the rough cut "boring," and both she and the studio knew that a four- to five-hour film does not break down into a releasable length with ease, so major cuts as well as reshoots to bridge those cuts were in order.

The first big subplot removed was the Jamis–Harah plotline, including the big fight sequence between Paul and Jamis (Judd Omen) in the desert as well as all major scenes of Molly Wryn as Harah, including a dramatic confrontation between her and Alia. The reasoning behind this was the filmmakers felt it was "boring" and a "sideline" that stopped the movie cold. Also excised was the original scene of Paul taking the Water of Life in the sietch along with several other connected scenes, which were condensed down into one new reshot scene in the desert.

Lynch stated in December 1984 [*Film*]:

> The old lesson is "never fall in love with a scene." Yet it's a real wrench to take out one that really matters. That's when you need other people. If you watch a film by yourself, you'll pretend everything's fine, but if you're there with people you respect, you'll become crazy as things don't work. You're always trying to be true to the material, and you're listening to all the signals. You just hope you're reading things right . . . *Dune* isn't a miniseries like some books are. You can take away a lot from the book and still have *Dune*.

Despite cuts already made, Lynch still felt the best version would be around three hours long, but exhibitor pressure for a shorter film won out. Ultimately the studio and Dino De Laurentiis agreed to a length of 2 hours and 17 minutes, which was catastrophic for Lynch, considering all the footage discarded. This decision came down during model photography, so few of the VFX for the three-hour director's cut were completed—which is why the film technically never had an official director's cut. Lynch could do little since Dino held final-cut privilege. The director has referred to having the film reduced like this as "a nightmare."

"You work real hard on a painting, then somebody comes in and cuts it up and throws a bunch of it away, it's not your painting anymore," he said in *Room to Dream*. "And *Dune* wasn't my movie."

"David wanted a three-hour movie and Dino wanted a two-hour movie, and Dino won," Gibbs said in *Impressions of Dune*. "It was a fight to get it down. David was very reluctant to give stuff up, and I could understand why. But I think we found a good way out of it and I think the picture stands up in the way it was finally worked out, but I know it was heartbreaking for David for it to come down to that length."

"With *Dune*, the pressures were magnified so many times," Lynch told the *Democrat and Chronicle* in 1986. "When you're spending so much money, people get upset when they feel they aren't going to get it back. You're working under strange pressure, so you make decisions that are safer. That's a bad thing."

One major late-in-the-game change involved replacing the original opening monologue by Silvana Mangano's Mother Ramallo (explaining CHOAM and the messiah prophecy) with an even longer, broader expository monologue by Virginia Madsen's Irulan. Rumor had it that Dino may have demanded Mangano's role be reduced after the couple had separated. This Irulan exposition also extended to a newly written voiceover to clarify points thought to be confusing, as well as to smooth over material that had been excised. In some cases, whole scenes and plot points were replaced with a single V.O. line. Although hearing certain characters' thoughts in voiceover was baked into the original script, 40% more of these inner thoughts were added in post as additional, often extraneous exposition.

"It can be a beautiful thing, to hear thinking," the director said in *Lynch on Lynch*. "But when it's just for information, you smell a rat."

Reports dating January 1983 still pegged *Dune* as a 1984 summer release, but by October, reports stated that the film's original mid-year launch date was not looking likely. A Knight-Ridder piece from January 1984 titled "Movie Moguls Hold Off On Films" indicates the movie was pushed back, possibly due to visual effects delays and reshoots involved in bringing the movie down to a suitable length.

By late 1984, rumors of the film's budget ranged everywhere from $40 million to $60 million, with *Film Review* reporting that the movie had gone at least $7 million over budget. Lynch told Matt Wolf of Associated Press, "Every part of *Dune* was complicated and expensive, because there were so many people involved doing so many things. Material dictates cost. If I fell in love with something else that cost this much, I would do it."

"Forty-two million! You want to be accurate, right?" Dino boasted to *The Guardian* in May 1984. "It's a lot of money, but sometimes you take a bigger risk with a five-million-dollar movie which you can't pre-sell. *Dune* is an easy movie to sell . . . I'm sure it will be a hit, but how big I don't know."

Close to release in December 1984, a Knight-Ridder article called the movie "the biggest potential disaster" of the holiday season: "*Dune* received wonderful press while still in production . . . more recent reports have turned sour. Although Universal marketing president Marvin Antonowsky fumed to the Los Angeles Times that the press has done a hatchet job on *Dune*, the film reportedly was not well-liked by audiences at research screenings."

Unfortunately, this price tag put the film in a position in which making anything less than $100 million at the box office would brand it a failure.

"I was rewriting during shooting, and then in the editing I was recutting it, trying to keep it comprehensible for people while still keeping it moving and remaining faithful to the spirit of the book," Lynch told *Space Voyager* #14. "It's the trickiest, hardest thing I've ever done and maybe ever will do. But I think it's right. It's true to the book, and that's what we set out to do."

By the release date, Lynch seemed resigned to a compromised picture even in the press, telling *The Guardian*, "The trouble with making a film like *Dune* is that you never see the whole of what you've done until way beyond the eleventh hour. Then, of course, it is virtually too late to change more than a little detail here or there."

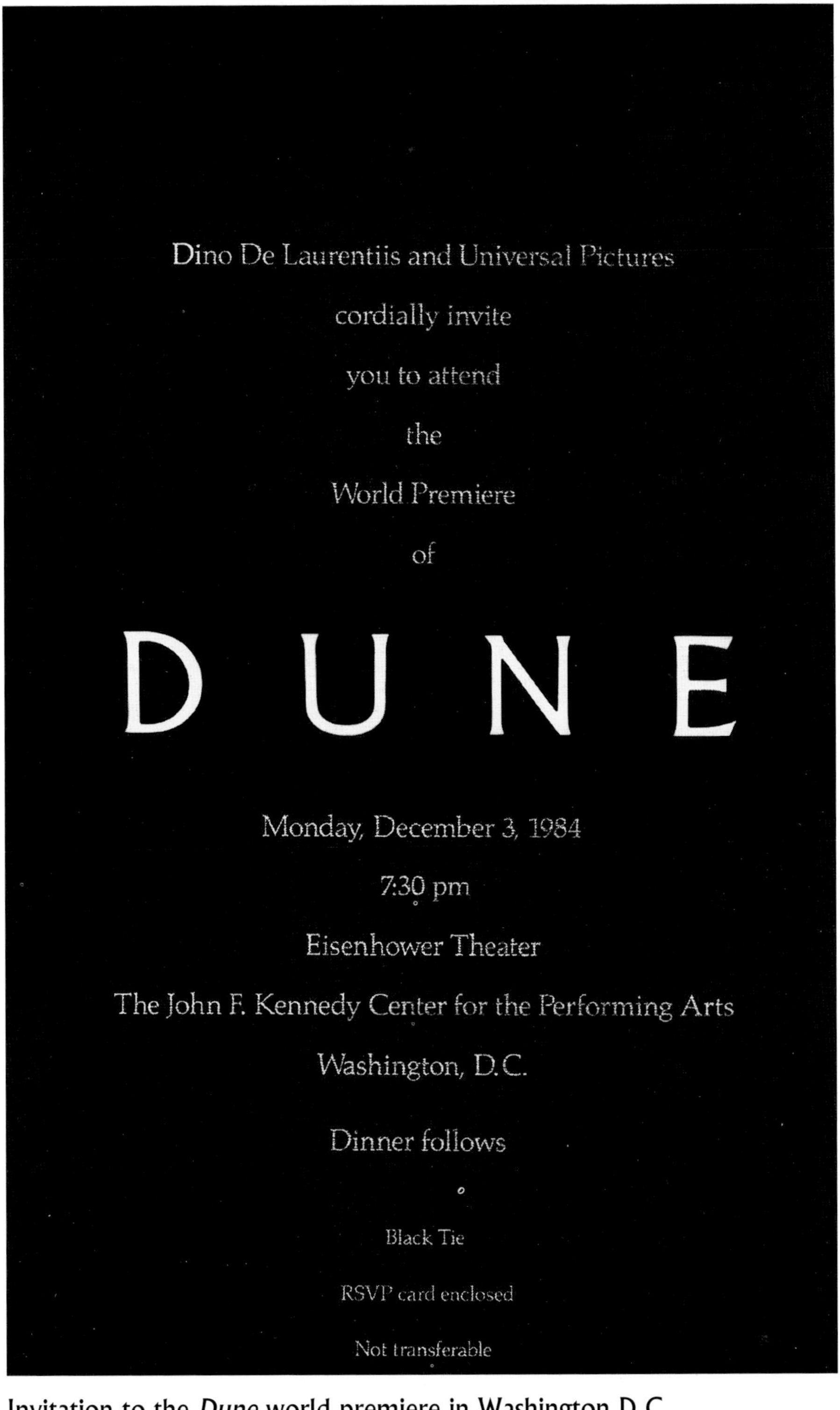

Dino De Laurentiis and Universal Pictures

cordially invite

you to attend

the

World Premiere

of

DUNE

Monday, December 3, 1984

7:30 pm

Eisenhower Theater

The John F. Kennedy Center for the Performing Arts

Washington, D.C.

Dinner follows

Black Tie

RSVP card enclosed

Not transferable

Invitation to the *Dune* world premiere in Washington D.C.

Two views of the art department.

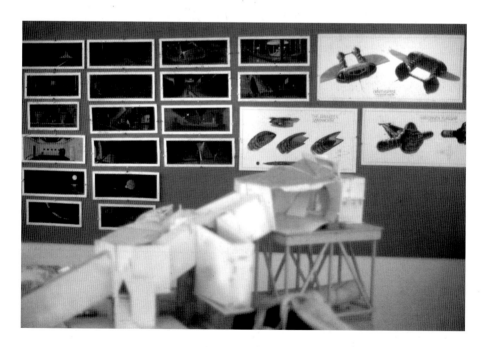

Mentor Heubner, Anthony Masters, and David Lynch in the art department.

Heubner painting a Atreides family portrait to be burned for one of Paul's (deleted) vision sequences.

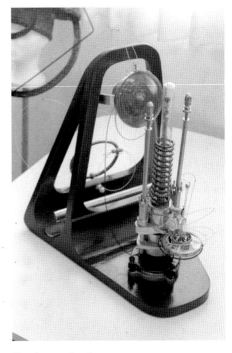

Desktop device prop.

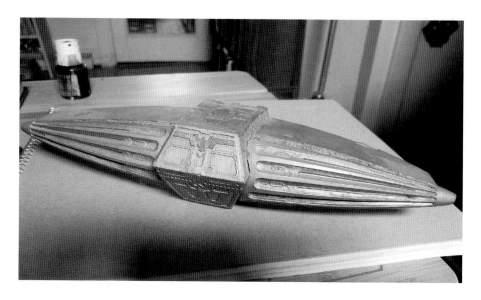

Atreides ship model by Judith Miller, and full-scale bigature.

Judith Miller sculpting the Third Stage Navigator.

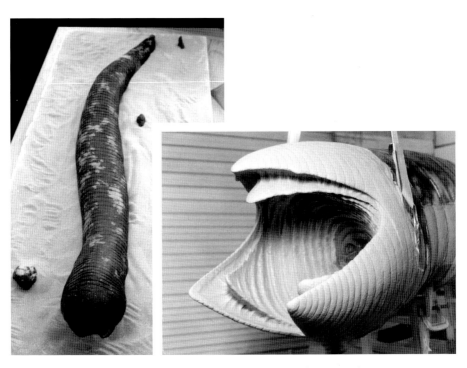

Prototype worm models by Judith Miller, and a large-scale worm sculpture by Carlo Rambaldi.

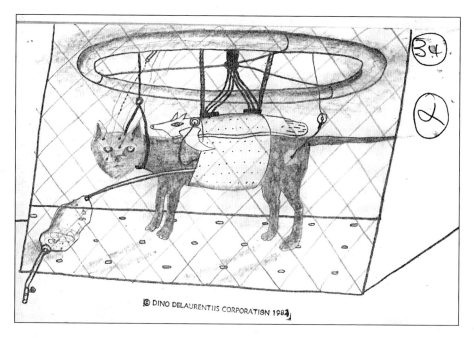

Cat/rat antidote box design and random sketches by David Lynch.

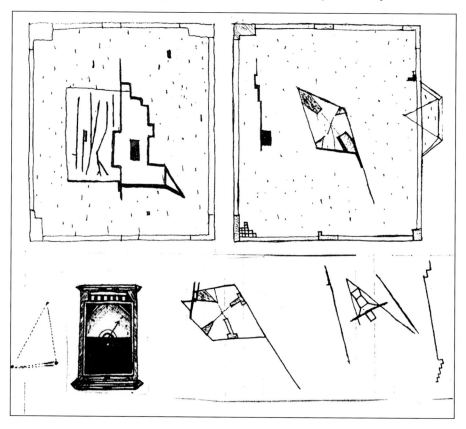

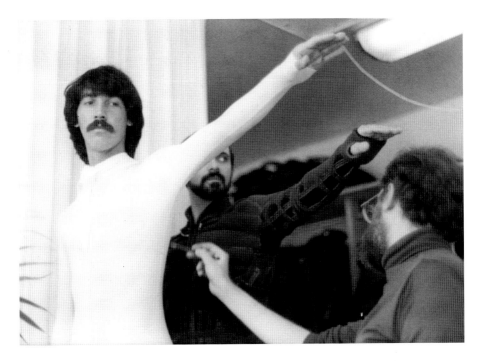

Costumers making
background stillsuits.

Stillsuit and a guard costume tests.

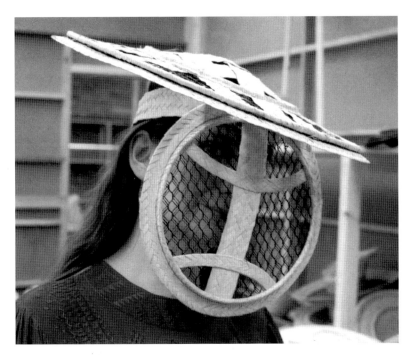

Judith Miller wearing two of the thousand hats made for the cut Arrakeen arrival sequence.

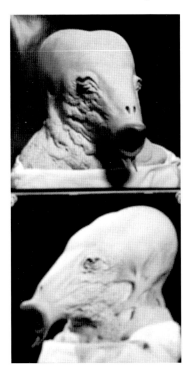

Prototypes for the Second-Stage Guild Navigator by Christopher Tucker.

Rock wall with hinged center section for the initial Fremen sequence.

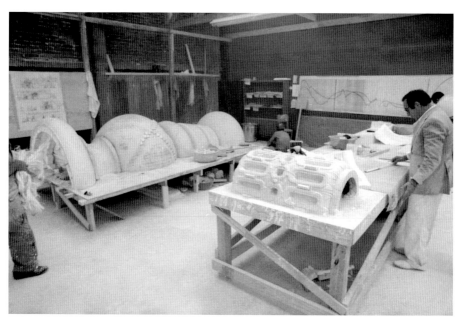

Plaster shop making materials for Caladan fortress and the Great Hall.

The plaster shop's work implemented into Great Hall (*top*) and Caladan fortress (*bottom*) sets.

Entrance to the Atreides family shuttle ship.

Paul's bedroom on Arrakis.

Paul's bedroom on Caladan.

Interior sand Dune set being prepped.

Paul's training robot.

Two views of the ornithopter hanger set under construction.

The rose garden courtyard on Caladan set, barely seen in the movie.

Las Aguilas Rojas (a.k.a. the "Dead Dog Dump") being prepared for shooting April 22-27, 1983.

A second view of the rose garden on Caladan set for the first scene shot, later discarded.

Francesca Annis, Kyle MacLachlan, and Frank Herbert slating the first shot of production.

Lynch at his office in Los Angeles.

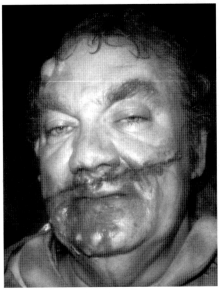

Closeup of Kenneth McMillan
in makeup for his death scene.

Kyle MacLachlan looking chipper
on set.

Emilio Ruiz del Río orchestrating hundreds of miniature soldiers
on pulleys.

Soldiers rehearse in the streets of Mexico.

Lynch having sunscreen applied by Raffaella De Laurentiis while filming in the desert.

Silvana Mangano and Raffaella confer with Lynch.

Sting, Lynch and MacLachlan shooting the final knife fight.

Sting in his iconic
Feyd-Rautha costume.

Polaroids of Antony Masters and Penny Shaw in the editing room
(*top l & r*) and Craig Campobasso and Lynch in the production office
(*bottom l & r*).

Frank Herbert, Barry Nolan and Lynch in front of effects storyboards.

Bob Ringwood sick with Montazuma's Revenge, with Craig Campobasso cheering him up. Mexico City, 1983.

The Masters Mansion.

Lynch snapping a photo of a hotel parrot.

Pool party
at the Masters
Mansion.
Molly Wryn,
Craig
Campobasso,
Everett McGill
& his wife
(*l to r*).

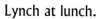
Lynch at lunch.

Cutting room
at Churubusco
Studios, 1983.

International poster by
Renato Casaro, and final
North American one-sheet
by Tom Jung.

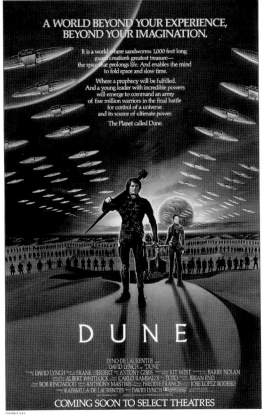

Two Spanish lobby cards for the film featuring the two moons artwork.

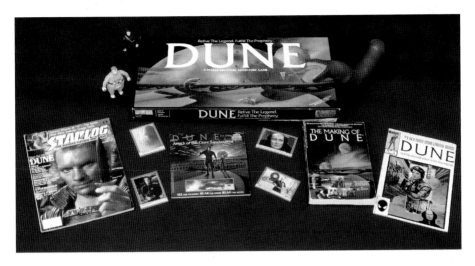

Various pieces of merchandise circa 1984.

LJN action figure production samples from superfan Frank Turner's collection.

Original Bill Sienkiewicz art pages from Marvel's Dune comic book adaptation.

Two pages from the comic book by Ralph Macchio and Bill Sienkiewicz.

Duran Duran's Nick Rhodes and Grace Jones at the Royal premiere after party at Blondies. December 13, 1984.

Lynch (*r*) and more at the London Royal premiere after party.

Raffaella De Laurentiis, Antony Gibbs, Craig Campobasso, David Lynch.

Production designer Anthony Masters at the Royal premiere.

Denis Villeneuve introducing his *Dune* film on October 8, 2021 at the New York Film Festival.

Illana Becker parodying Princess Irulan in Sean Crespo's pilot *Alternate Side Parking.*

Super7's line of ReAction figures
based on the original LJN toys.

Andre Du Bouchet flexing his tattoo
of the Desert mouse known
as "Muad'Dib."

Jerry Belich and friends in garbage bag stillsuits for "*Dune* Sweded."

Not in Kansas Anymore: Toto's Music

An extensive search for a music group to score *Dune* in the same manner Queen had on *Flash Gordon* led David Lynch to Toto, whose recent fourth studio album, *Toto IV*, had triumphed. It spawned hits like "Rosanna" and chart-topper "Africa," winning three Grammy Awards, all while the group aided the making of Chicago's *Chicago 16* and Michael Jackson's *Thriller*.

This peak moment for Toto was undercut by the original lineup falling apart, with bassist David Hungate departing to spend time with his family and singer Bobby Kimball fired due to voice-damaging drug use. While literally regrouping as their fifth album came together, the band decided to use their clout to detour from pop.

Drummer Jeff Porcaro said in November 1984 [*Billboard*]:

> We wanted to do a movie score, so we grabbed the heaviest one that could be thrown at us. It's no rock'n'roll or pop music. It's serious composition. So, we decided to take a few months off and dive head-first into the heaviest mess we could get ourselves into, movie-wise. It's probably one of the greatest things we ever did, because we were able to write a lot of Toto music that nobody would accept from Toto, the six-piece rock'n'roll band. It let us get a lot of musical frustration out of our bodies.

Over the six-month job, the group as a whole would perform the music, but most of the composing duties were relegated to the group's lead singer-songwriter David Paich along with his father Marty Paich (*Model Shop*), an experienced film composer. Jeff Porcaro—whose father Joe Porcaro had worked on many films from *Bullitt* to *Outland*—contributed heavily to the percussive music for the training scene at the beginning. The Paiches created a mystical, quasi-religious mood piece integrating everything from choirs to electric guitars. Some friends of the group helped out as well, including TV composer Allyn Ferguson (*Barney Miller*, *Charlie's Angels*) doing additional orchestration, while future nine-time Oscar-nominee James Newton Howard (*The Fugitive*, *The Dark Knight*) did his first movie work cowriting the cue "Trip to Arrakis" with Paich.

The group ran into several issues along the way, with Lynch bringing in ambient pioneer Brian Eno to do one track after falling in love with the temp music he'd implemented from Eno's 1983 album *Apollo: Atmospheres and Soundtracks*. Toto keyboardist Steve Porcaro attempted to ape the droning Eno track to the best of his ability, but to no avail. The eventual piece, titled "Prophecy Theme," by Brian Eno, Roger Eno, and Daniel Lanois—which used synthesizers that mimicked the human voice—was submitted as is and excerpted throughout the movie. Eno himself was credited prominently in the movie's opening credits and poster, which created tension with Toto. Although he was one of the musicians Lynch was originally considering to score the film, the pervasive rumor that Eno had ghostwritten music for the entire film is bogus.

As he told *The New York Times* in 2020:

> I didn't ghostwrite anything. The only thing I wrote was that piece. This was in the days when people used to fly you everywhere—ugh, I'm glad those days are finished—but David flew me to Los Angeles to see *Dune*, as it was at that point. It wasn't finished then. And I don't know whether his intention or his hope was that I would do the whole soundtrack, but I didn't want to, anyway. It was a huge project, and I just didn't feel like doing it. But I did feel like making one piece for it, so that's what I did.

There was also difficulty during recording as the Paiches worked with the 90-piece Vienna Symphony Orchestra and Vienna Volksoper Choir, who were tuned to the wrong frequency from the pre-recorded music done by the band or on synthesizers. The decision to record in Vienna over London was a budgetary one to reportedly save $150,000 in reuse fees.

"I saw that amount go by once a week in ridiculous waste," Paich told *Billboard*. "If I ever do a movie again, I'll have the word 'London' written in my contract."

Sadly, the band never did compose another soundtrack. While David Paich and Steve Lukather would work on other films in a support capacity, neither man ever took the full reins again. The group was generally unhappy with the experience for numerous reasons, including the way their music was edited as well as the soundtrack being released by Polydor almost in tandem with their studio album *Isolation*, something the band felt was done deliberately to confuse their fans.

Knife Fights on Lunchboxes: Marketing

Though myriad and bountiful, the marketing of *Dune* had one major flaw: No one seemed to like the film, even its director. As Lynch & Co. were hawking the movie on a press tour throughout America, Europe, Japan, and even China, the writing must have already been on the wall. The movie was neither the heir apparent to *Star Wars* that Universal and its merchandise partners wanted it to be, nor was it quite the avant-garde think piece Lynch's fans had come to expect from him.

Gordon Armstrong, vice president of advertising, publicity, and promotion at Universal, initially forged licensing deals with LJN Toys, General Mills' Parker Brothers, Coleco Industries, and Marvel Comics.

"We've set ourselves up to merchandise this picture in every possible way," he told *Advertising Age*. "It's a well-known commodity in science-fiction circles, but we want to introduce *Dune* to younger people as well. We're looking for an audience of six years and up."

Merchandising for a wannabe blockbuster is a big gamble. Vendors and promotional partners are making that bet before the film has even lensed, due to the long lead times required to produce merchandise. Universal sensed it was a troubled film by late 1984, but it was too late for stores stocking *Dune* items aplenty.

"Although the film hasn't opened, *Dune* artifacts are already available in stores," Michael Blowen wrote on December 6 in *The Boston Globe*. "There's a *Dune* calendar, a *Dune* storybook, a book called *The Making of Dune*, *Dune* toys, and a *Dune* soundtrack by Toto. When *Dune* day finally arrives, producer Dino De Laurentiis is praying it doesn't become doomsday."

Other items included a set of 132 trading cards from Fleer (with stickers and bubble gum), a View-Master gift set, a board game by Parker Brothers, a two-part Kid Stuff children's storybook and read-along 45 rpm record or cassette (*Battle for the Known Universe* and *Attack of the Giant Sandworms*), Revell model kits (Sand Crawler, Harkonnen Ornithopter, Sandworm), t-shirts, puffy stickers, pencil cases, jigsaw puzzles, bed sheets, lunchbox and thermos set, brass belt buckle and—perhaps most perplexing—children's party favors featuring cups, napkins, paper plates, blowouts, and "You're Invited" cards with menacing Sardaukar and a phallic sandworm on them. There was even a set of three manga-style Chirashi flyers made for Japanese cinemas to promote the film.

A primitive *Dune* video game by Atari (modeled after a previous game, *Adventure*) was also in development, with representatives of the company even visiting the set. Programming by Bruce Poehlman and Gary Stark ceased along with most Atari 2600 game development when the company was taken over by Jack Tramiel in mid-1984 due to a crash in the video game market.

One thing is clear: The studio's eyes were bigger than the public's stomach.

LJN Toys

Businessman Jack Friedman founded LJN Toys in 1970, which had an emphasis on licensing beginning with a line based on the hit Universal Television show *Emergency!* By 1982, LJN was on a hot streak after having successfully licensed *E.T. the Extraterrestrial* as well as a line of dolls based on the actress Brooke Shields. It was LJN's intention to hop on the *Dune* bandwagon in hopes of repeating Kenner's unprecedented success with 3.75" *Star Wars* figures.

Toys that LJN released to stores in 1984 included 5.5" action figures (retailing for up to $6.95 each) with "Battle-Matic Action" ("Secret Lever makes arms movie!"): Paul Atreides (in Atreides uniform), Stilgar the Fremen, Sardaukar Warrior, Baron Harkonnen, Rabban, and Feyd (with milking cat box accessory). There were also larger toys like the Fremen Tarpel Gun (with electronic sounds and flashing lights, $10.95), Spice Scout (holds an action figure in the front compartment, $29.95), three different Rough Riders Motorized Sand Scouts ($10.95 each for the Sand Crawler, Sand Tracker, and Sand Roller, all with "4x4 Power for Climbing Tough Terrain"), and, of course, the mighty Sandworm ("Large Posable Monster from Beneath the Desert Surface," $8.95).

According to Joel Spivak—owner of Philadelphia's '80s "geek headquarters" toy store Rocketships & Accessories—in a December 10, 1984 edition of *Philadelphia Daily News*, the hype was real for all this *Dune* merch.

"It will help if the movie is a hit, but we've been getting orders from collectors all over the country for the last three months," Spivak said. "They've got to have an ornithopter or a sandworm. You know what I think will be the biggest toy of all? The doll of the villain that's played by Sting. He's a rock star with fans of his own."

Frank Turner's History of LJN's Dune *Line*

Dune superfan Frank Turner offered me this history of the toy line:

> Prototypes for the LJN toys exist from multiple stages of the production process. Concept boards were used in pitch meetings to give an idea of the line showing "cartoon" style drawings of the eight proposed characters—including the unproduced Gurney and Lady Jessica—in action poses. A concept sketch for the unproduced 'thopter vehicle showed how the flapping wings play feature might work.

> The Baron Harkonnen was sculpted in acetate by Bert Brooks, creating a highly detailed figure whose features are far clearer and sharper, as some details were lost during the production process, most noticeably in the cheek boils. Early clay sculpts with supporting rods for Rabban and Feyd also exist by Ric Hughes. A wax master head for Stilgar exists from the toy designer Rich Roland, showing that a number of toy sculptors and designers worked on the line in a variety of materials.

> Urethane hardcopies exist in both unpainted and more coveted hand-painted forms. Created from silicone molds of the original sculpts,

hardcopies are used for paint masters, sales, catalog photography, and tooling masters to create the steel molds for production figures. Hardcopies are held together by metal pins or dowels and hand-finished. Unpainted hardcopies are now relatively common *Dune* prototypes with collectors. Hand-painted hardcopies are much rarer and command larger aftermarket sums. Finally, there are test shots for *Dune* figures in plastic created to test the molds. These are the hardest *Dune* prototypes to find. The sandworm test shots are notable as their heads differ from the production version—their maw is ridged, lacking the "teeth." A stillsuit Paul-Muad'Dib figure could have been added later if it continued, reusing the Stilgar body as a cost saving measure.

The forthcoming *Dune* license and its potential are mentioned in the 1983 LJN annual report. An internal confidential line list from February 1984 for distribution contains item names, item numbers, pricing, and case size for the full planned line, including the unproduced 'thopter and 22-inch sandworm. Planning for the line was well before its intended Christmas '84 launch; then the line was sold to dealers and retailers.

The 1984 LJN dealer catalog photography uses hardcopy prototypes with noticeable paint variations between them and the production figures. For example, Paul has his blue dress uniform rather than production green. The catalog features images of the full line, including the unproduced Gurney Halleck and Lady Jessica figures, the Harkonnen 'thopter vehicle, and weapons gift set. Also mentioned is the 22-inch stuffed sandworm, but no further information on this item has turned up.

The New York Toy Fair was held in July 1984, where LJN had extensive display walls showcasing the film sets and characters: Paul in stillsuit, the Emperor's throne room, table dioramas with hardcopy prototypes, and mock-up box art posed on "desert" sand. There was even a sales model wearing a stillsuit with rope, holding a maker hook and crysknife akin to Paul Muad'Dib. The sandworm was not shown and kept "top secret." Public relations were done by Gerald Freeman, Inc., who sent out a press release that mentions the 22-inch sandworm, but the 'thopter and weapons gift set are not included, suggesting they were dropped first and the Sandworm later. Due to the popularity of Sting, the Feyd figure was emphasized.

Internationally, the line was hyped in Matchbox's 1985 dealer catalog: 'Their *Dune* product range will rapidly take over from *Star Wars* toys." The line was distributed internationally in late November/early December 1984.

A December 24, 1984, issue of *Newsweek* mentions one of the earliest items related to the film: the *Dune* promotional kit sent out to schools, which contained a copy of the novel and teaching resources. The article also uses a unique image of a child playing with the figures, with Feyd fighting a sandworm against a backdrop of shelves of *Dune* toys. The March 1985 issue of *16* magazine includes a *Dune*-related competition, the grand prize being a phone call from Kyle MacLachlan and runner-up prizes being *Dune* toys. The line was featured in various toy store newspaper adverts in late 1985 when the toys were discounted and closed out.

Trailer

Universal's jumbo-sized, 3-minute theatrical trailer was narrated by the late Hal Douglas, whose voice graced literally thousands of movie previews. Many of those Douglas-voiced trailers were kicked off with the immortal catchphrase "in a world . . ." The *Dune* trailer only has a slight variation, and then extrapolates on the phrase to another level entirely:

> You are about to enter a world where the unexpected . . . the unknown . . . and the unbelievable meet. Where kingdoms are built on earth that moves, and skies are filled with fire. Where a young warrior is called upon to free his people. A world that holds creation's greatest treasure . . . and greatest terrors. A world where the mighty, the mad, and the magical will have their final battle. *Dune*, a spectacular journey through the wonders of space and the mysteries of time. From the boundaries of the incredible to the borders of the impossible. Now, Frank Herbert's widely read, talked about, and cherished masterpiece comes to the screen. Dino De Laurentiis presents *Dune*, a world beyond your experience, beyond your imagination.

The trailer was initially attached to Universal's *The Last Starfighter*, running before that underperforming sci-fi film in July 1984.

Dune Fan Club

Paul Sammon told me:

> I became the president and guiding light of the in-house *Dune* Fan
> Club. I arranged to have little write-on address forms delivered to
> theater concession stands around the country. If you wanted to join
> the club, you filled in your information and dropped the form into

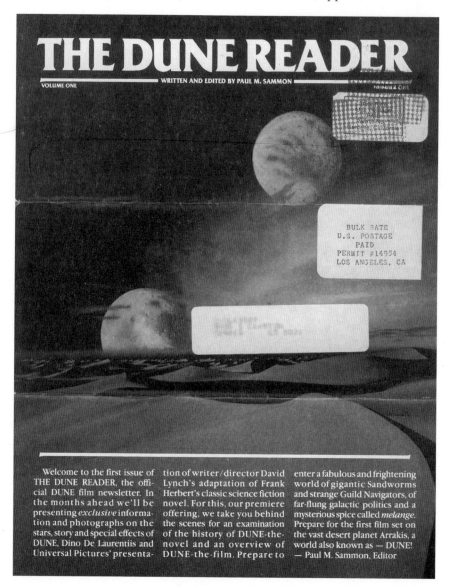

THE DUNE READER

VOLUME ONE — WRITTEN AND EDITED BY PAUL M. SAMMON — NUMBER ONE

BULK RATE
U.S. POSTAGE
PAID
PERMIT #14954
LOS ANGELES, CA

Welcome to the first issue of THE DUNE READER, the official DUNE film newsletter. In the months ahead we'll be presenting *exclusive* information and photographs on the stars, story and special effects of DUNE, Dino De Laurentiis and Universal Pictures' presentation of writer/director David Lynch's adaptation of Frank Herbert's classic science fiction novel. For this, our premiere offering, we take you behind the scenes for an examination of the history of DUNE-the-novel and an overview of DUNE-the-film. Prepare to enter a fabulous and frightening world of gigantic Sandworms and strange Guild Navigators, of far-flung galactic politics and a mysterious spice called *melange*. Prepare for the first film set on the vast desert planet Arrakis, a world also known as — DUNE!
— Paul M. Sammon, Editor

a special box, which was then sent back to the studio. That way we had a mailing list. I also wrote, pulled the photos for, and did the layout for everything in *The Dune Reader*, the first of what was going to be a series of Fan Club text and photo updates on the film. A number of *Dune Readers* were mailed out. A second issue never got off the ground due to the studio's increasingly cold feet about the film.

Books

As reported by Knight Ridder on December 15, 1984:

> Bookstores began stocking up on *Dune* items more than a month ago, and representatives for a half-dozen stores in Philadelphia and New York say business has been fairly brisk. Among the items for sale are reissues of all five *Dune* books, including a 1.4-million-copy special edition of the original book with a redesigned cover tied in to the movie's poster art. For those who feel lost in the desert, Willis E. McNelly has published a *Dune Encyclopedia*, purporting to contain biographies of all of the book's characters and various tidbits of *Dune* lore. Younger readers who may not be able to slosh through Herbert's voluminous tomes can satisfy themselves with *The Dune Storybook*, which capsulizes the story and includes dozens of color stills from the film. A *Dune Activity Book* also has been released for very young fans, as have *The Dune Cut Out Activity Book*, *The Dune Pop-Up Panorama Book*, *The Dune Coloring Book*, *The Dune Coloring & Activity Book*, and *Dune Puzzles, Games, Mazes and Activities*. Marvel Comics is releasing *Dune: The Official Comic Book*. Masters' production design drawings also have been collected and published as *The Art of Dune*, a volume that contains Lynch's complete screenplay. Los Angeles–based writer Ed Naha has published a series of on-set interviews with the film's principals under the title *The Making of Dune*. If the movie flops, it'll make quite a bonfire.

Sadly, *The Art of Dune* was canceled before publication, although Giles Masters has told me that he still has thousands of his father's drawings in storage and hopes to collect them in a volume someday.

On the plus side, Herbert's original book got a big boost, selling roughly 250,000 copies during the first two weeks of the film's US release.

Marvel Comic Book

Originally published by Marvel Comics on December 4, 1984, as a magazine-format Marvel Super Special, the 68-page comic book adaptation of David Lynch's *Dune* hailed from writer Ralph Macchio (no relation to the *Karate Kid* actor of the same name) and artist Bill Sienkiewicz (whose distinctive artistic style feels like the bastard child of Gustav Klimt and Ralph Steadman).

There are many differences between the theatrical cut of the film and the comic book, such as the way shields are depicted. In the film, they are blocky, whereas in the book, it's more of a sparkly forcefield not dissimilar to the ones in Villeneuve's film. There are also deleted sequences like Rabban in the bath or Thufir's death scene. In many cases, scenes are reimagined whole cloth simply because Sienkiewicz had no reference stills to base the panels on.

Years earlier, the Marvel comic book adaptation of *Star Wars* written by Roy Thomas and drawn by Howard Chaykin had played a role in building up buzz for that film, with the first issue being released on April 12, 1977, over a month before 20th Century Fox's May 25 movie release date. Contrary to this, Marvel's *Dune* didn't release its three-issue serialization for comic book shops and grocery store shelves until April–June 1985, long after the film had vanished from American theaters. Berkley Publishing also issued a reformatted 164-page pocket book version.

Editor Bob Budiansky told *The Comics Journal* in 2021

> The people who worked on the book, including myself, went to the preview of the movie before it had been released to the public. We all came out thinking, "Well, our adaptation works a lot better than the movie did . . ." Bill did a good job of capturing not only their likeness, but he turned them into Sienkiewicz characters. It's this really amazing alchemy he pulls off. He made them very dramatic. There's a gravity attached to them.

Interview: Bill Sienkiewicz (Artist, Dune: The Official Comic Book)

A star creative from the '80s comics boom, Bill Sienkiewicz emerged alongside Alan Moore, Frank Miller, Art Spiegelman, Charles Burns, and others who redefined the medium. Entering the field at age 19, Sienkiewicz broke out on the Marvel title *Moon Knight* before establishing his abstract, painterly style of illustration during a classic run on *New Mutants*, including the "Demon Bear" storyline later adapted to film. Around this time, he and editor Ralph Macchio (also of *Moon Knight*) got the assignment for Marvel's *Dune* movie adaptation. Rumor had it that Lynch handpicked Sienkiewicz.

Sienkiewicz told me:

> I'd love to say anecdotally that I was handpicked by David Lynch, but I can't. I pitched it. I told the editor I wanted to do this adaptation. I'm a huge David Lynch fan because *Eraserhead* was one of my favorite movies, influenced a lot of what I did. It got under your skin and into your skin and messed with your comfort. Plus, I'm a *Dune* book fan. Working on it was a labor of love. There was a whole design aesthetic because I realized everything on Caladan was very ornate. There was a congestion and a patterning and a beauty to observe, baroque. I wanted to contrast that with Arrakis, which felt austere.

After landing the gig, Sienkiewicz set out to put his own spin on the material, despite restrictions imposed by Universal's marketing department. This is particularly noticeable in his depiction of Baron Harkonnen as a hyperexaggerated, balloon-like figure not dissimilar to his famous rendering of Daredevil villain Kingpin. He also used innovative techniques like having the panels themselves fold in on each other.

He recalled:

> Working on movie adaptations is a thankless gig. Say, for the Michael Keaton *Batman*, you end up having to do The Joker looking like Jack Nicholson, as opposed to looking like The Joker. I felt like Vladimir Harkonnen is huge and monstrous. I wanted to show his decrepitude and didn't want him exactly like Kenneth McMillan. Lynch even said he viewed the Harkonnens as Larry, Moe, and Curly. I wanted to make my own commentary, to be able to do what comics did. I felt a constant back-and-forth with Universal. Ralph and I went to California. Coming from New York/Marvel out to Los Angeles and dealing with whatever executive we dealt with was classic Hollywood central casting. He made it seem like we were really fortunate to be on this, but he was going to crack the whip, make sure we nail the likenesses. Some execs are impediments and some are facilitators. They insisted that McMillan only has pustules on one

side of his face: "You've given him pustules on both sides, plus you've made him way too heavy. He looks more cartoony." I'm negotiating with him about pustules. I said, "Look, if you give me a couple hundred pounds, I'll reduce his pustule count by about 40." It felt like a conversation out of a David Lynch movie.

Photo references were scarce, putting the artist between a rock and a hard place trying to be true to Lynch's vision with few actual shots to work from.

Sienkiewicz said:

> It was not quite what Howard Chaykin went through with the *Star Wars* adaptation where he had to make everything up. They did send me a couple sheets of color Xeroxes and a bunch of slides of the sandworms and stuff. They had their money shots they would get me the reference for, but other stuff that was secondary in terms of importance . . . The whole sequence where he takes the Water of Life and he's hallucinating and sees Alia, I had no reference for any of that. I had to fall back on abstract comic book things I was doing and try to make sense of the narrative. They would send me an image of the weirding module, but it was a drawing. There was one photograph which showed all the Guild Navigators where their ship landed from the beginning, before they brought in the huge tank. I had images like the spice harvester, the lifting device, the contraptions and vehicles, stillsuits, or whatever. All the battle scenes, it's not like I actually had any stills to lift one-for-one. I had to make it all up. It became a patchwork, a quilt. I'm doing an illustrated version of the CliffsNotes, but it became more like a tone poem. There's no way you're going to get every beat into it. For me, the thing about *Dune*—and it didn't really come across in the adaptation with the rain at the end—is Herbert's whole point is to be wary of idols. That movie ending felt a little pat and anti-climactic because the book had a whole different take on it. They were trying to make him into the Kwisatz Haderach, the idea of giving him a superheroic ending where he's almost a god who's going to save them.

While some of these new thematic elements from the film bothered Sienkiewicz, he was also juggling Universal's demands while trying to satisfy his own artistic impulses. At one point, execs realized that Macchio and Sienkiewicz were working from an old shooting script instead of the revised version of the movie being rewritten in the editing room.

It started to feel more and more like the production was in trouble. They didn't know quite what they wanted to do. The scene with the headshot of Irulan came in at the last minute, so we had to rejigger the pages. I was with Bob Budiansky in his office on the phone going through pages one by one. "Page 3, Panel 4," you know? We were on his small sofa talking to them and I kept gesturing for another page, and at one point Bob leaned into me because he had completely fallen asleep. He was so bored. I ended up drawing more pages than made it into the book simply because of how crazy things were, at least seven or eight pages. When I was doing the cover painting, that was a real headache. I was having a very hard time finding the right image because, again, back and forth with them about, "We need to see the sandworms, we need to see . . ." It was art direction to death.

Because the comics adaptation of *Dune* was done ahead of the filmmakers, some deleted sequences remain in Sienkiewicz's book while others are closer to Lynch's original intentions, such as the Guild Navigator folding space.

That Victorian bowels of the ship where he folds it is interesting, but the whole thing where he's vomiting out space-time is definitely not what Lynch intended. It was going to be literally folding space, from what I remember. His hands grabbing the fabric of space, which I thought was really very cool. Lynch ran into budgetary issues toward the end, which you can really see with the special effects stuff.

Seeing the final film proved to be a sobering—but not unexpected—disappointment:

I remember going with Chris Claremont and my girlfriend to the theater—it might have been a premiere—on Third Avenue or Lexington or something. We were lowly comic book people who weren't usually invited to those things. I remember my heart sinking within the first 30 seconds, when Irulan started fading in and out. "Oh yes, I forgot to tell you . . ." People started snickering. The movie really didn't go over well. I don't know if people were expecting *Star Wars*. I saw some of the toy ads coming out like, "Hey kids, get your sandworm!" An action figure of the Baron? As I was working on it, I'm going, "I don't know if this is the right thing for kids or for the movie."

It certainly didn't feel like the book or the movie I read. I was depressed that people responded so negatively to it, almost took it personally.

While the reaction to the movie was lackluster, over the years, fans have enjoyed the Marvel adaptation almost as an alternative illustrated cut of the film.

"The comic is the perfect aperitif to get someone into Lynch's film," says superfan Frank Turner, who owns some original art from the Marvel book. "What Sienkiewicz did with the comic book is take Lynch and then hype it up even more while getting it done in three issues. It's one of the best, if not THE best, film adaptations."

Sienkiewicz has heard the same:

People feel like it actually is better than what was on the screen. It works. Somehow, as a comic, it seemed to work. It broke my heart because there was a magazine format, roughly 8.5 by 11, that had to be resized for the comic book, which meant a whole sliver of pages would have to be excised to fit the different proportions. They handed my paper original pages off to production, and they used this white tape, non-removable. This is all pre-digital, so when I got the pages back, I tried to remove the tape. It was a lost cause, and I was furious.

"It's interesting to see the changes that were made between the original art and the production version," adds Turner. "There's a page with the Baron floating over Jessica. On the original, there are two panels at the bottom with the Baron spitting on Jessica that got cut out. They just extended the Baron floating to a splash page."

"I'm still glad I did it," Sienkiewicz admits. "If we had not put our foot down and said, 'We want this to be about comics, to do what comics do best . . .' To their credit, they actually worked with us and said, 'Okay, you can make him look a certain way.'"

Not long after *Dune*, Sienkiewicz would team up with Frank Miller for an '86–'87 limited series titled *Elektra: Assassin*, now considered a masterpiece of the superhero form. Over the years his brand of painted photorealism would be applied to titles like *The Shadow, Batman, Wolverine,* and *The Sandman,* as well as personal works like *Stray Toasters* or an illustrated biography of Jimi Hendrix called *Voodoo Child.* As a commercial artist, he would receive two Emmy nominations for work on *Where on Earth Is Carmen Sandiego?,* and do album covers for Kid Cudi and RZA.

Bill Sienkiewicz still believes that "comics are an art form that are worthy. They're not just simply a Happy Meal. They're comics and they deserve respect." His work on *Moon Knight* and *Daredevil* has been acknowledged in the TV series of the former and the Sienkiewicz-style appearance of Kingpin in the Oscar-winning *Spider-Man: Into the Spider-Verse*. In 2018 I was lucky enough to visit the Boston set of Fox's *The New Mutants* movie where I spotted Sienkiewicz seated in video village alongside director Josh Boone, giving advice on an outdoor scene featuring Demon Bear. It was amazing to witness a comics creator given his due by Hollywood.

"Josh made me feel incredibly welcome," Sienkiewicz said of *New Mutants*.

Sienkiewicz would return to *Dune* in 2021 when Abrams Books released a three-part comics adaptation of Frank Herbert's original book, penned by son Brian Herbert and Kevin J. Anderson. Sienkiewicz provided covers for these with a far more abstract style than his '80s work.

Sienkiewicz said of reuniting with the property:

> I love that. Even Legendary brought me over to do the cover for the comic adaptation of Villeneuve's version. I did all the cast portraits. I'm doing stuff with the second as well. The fact that I'm part of the *Dune* family is special. Working with Brian and everybody at Abrams . . . I got the third cover, and that's due shortly. Not that I'm considering myself a link to the past, but I do feel like it's nice to be part of that whole continuity.

Rating

David Lynch wrote and directed *Dune* with a deliberate eye toward a studio-mandated PG (Parental Guidance Suggested) rating, foregoing many of his more far-out or dark ideas as a concession for the film to reach as wide an audience as possible. However, due to the backlash to a pair of particularly intense PG-rated Steven Spielberg productions in the summer of 1984—*Indiana Jones and the Temple of Doom* and *Gremlins*—a new rating system was born. At Spielberg's behest, the Motion Picture Association of America (MPAA) and its president Jack Valenti created a new intermediate rating of "PG-13" (Parents Strongly Cautioned) for films deemed to potentially be inappropriate for children under the age of 13. John Milius' conservative fever dream *Red Dawn* was the first to receive this rating when it was released by United Artists on August 10, 1984.

Thus, the MPAA granted *Dune* a PG-13 rating (certificate #27507). While this was before the board released their official reasoning for ratings, the Parents Guide on IMDb does list the litany of the movie's violent imagery, including lasers, explosions, corpses, gas inhalation, a burning hand, thumbs in eyes, bleeding heart plugs, bloody noses, bloody tears, a bloody severed head, a stabbed throat, and "several scenes of people making faces of agony during telepathic rituals and attacks." To paraphrase Cat Stevens, Arrakis is a wild world.

Premieres

After six months of shooting, six months in post-production, and nine months of concentrated editing, *Dune* was ready to be unleashed onto 1,700 screens worldwide simultaneously, a rarity then. There were four gala premieres scheduled for the film: Washington, DC; Los Angeles; Miami; and London.

The D.C. premiere at the Kennedy Center took place on December 4 and included Herbert, MacLachlan, Francesca Annis, Dean Stockwell, Martha Schumacher, Raffaella, and, of course, Dino. The latter was even able to wrangle Lynch and his wife, Mary Fisk, invites to a White House state dinner to meet President Ronald Reagan, whom Lynch admired. One has to wonder what Reagan would have made of *Dune* had he seen it.

"It is an important town for an important movie," Dino told *The Washington Post*. "The Kennedy Center is the most important in the United States. That is why we have the premiere of *Dune* here."

MacLachlan, smiling between book signings at the premiere, told a reporter:

> I don't feel like a God Emperor, just an actor. Actually, the process of filming it was boring and tedious. The fun came in seeing it in its final form. This is the second time for me, I saw it once before in New York. Yes, I do hope there's a sequel. I'd like to be in lots more. I'd read all the *Dune* books years before the movie, but once I was cast in it, I began to read them voraciously.

"I think the movie captures the book," Herbert opined. "Of course, it leaves out scenes, but it would have to, otherwise we'd be here 14 hours."

"When I first went to see the film at the premiere—and I've only seen it once—as soon as Princess Irulan started to talk in voiceover at the beginning, explaining the story, I thought 'Uh oh, this film is in trouble,'" Annis told *Deadline* in 2021. "Any Hollywood film that has to explain itself in detail at the beginning is in trouble."

Lynch tried to quell the bad buzz (*Variety* had already dubbed it a "Dune-boggle") to the *Los Angeles Times* shortly after this premiere, saying:

> I don't know how the rumors got started, but they aren't based on truth . . . that the picture was in trouble, it wasn't going over well and that we had a bad preview. Well, I was at the Los Angeles preview, and the feeling I got was that we had a successful preview. The feeling I got at the premiere was an awful lot better. *Dune* is a film built for a big screen with big sound, and they had that at the Kennedy Center.

Herbert was also banging the drum for the movie and its planned follow-up, bragging to *Philadelphia Daily News*, "The principals of the cast and the director, David Lynch, have all been optioned for two more films. We have enough outtakes from this one to make a four-hour TV miniseries. We're already plotting the screenplay of the sequel."

"It's really the characters, the people, that you concentrate on in this film," Herbert told the *Minneapolis Star Tribune*. "There isn't as strong an emphasis on the ecological theme as there is in the book, but that will come in *Dune Messiah*."

A copy of the script for *Dune II* was even seen in Herbert's office when he was interviewed for *Prevue* magazine in December 1984: "That's David's rough draft of *Dune Messiah*. Now that we speak the same 'language,' it's much easier for both of us to make progress, especially with the screenplays."

Some reports from the time even claim that Lynch had written scripts or treatments for both *Dune Messiah* and *Children of Dune*. The director told one reporter that *Messiah* was his favorite of the books and the one he was the most excited to put on screen. He elaborated even further on his plans to shoot *Dune II* and *Dune III* back-to-back in *Starburst* #78:

> Raffaella will be the producer again, and hopefully a lot of the same team will come back. Right now, I'm writing the script for *Dune II*. *Dune II* is totally *Dune Messiah*, with variations on the theme. *Dune III* is the one that's going to be trouble for me. I'm not wild about *Children of Dune*, and I want to read it again and see what kind of ideas I get. I want to get to the point where I'm really dying to do it. *Dune Messiah* is a very short book, and a lot of people don't like it, but in there are some really nifty ideas. I'm real excited about that, and I think

it could make a really good film. It starts 12 years later, and this creates a whole new set of problems. It's a kind of thing unto itself. The whole place where the characters live is now different. It's the same location, but everything has changed. And it should have a different mood . . . it should be 12 strange years later.

"As those who have read the books will know, there is no possibility of simple reruns," MacLachlan said of a sequel in December '84 to *Evening Post*. "At the end of the first book, Paul has defeated his enemies, avenged his father, and become a kind of Messiah. The second book starts 12 years later. Paul changes . . ."

At the Royal London Charity Premiere benefiting the National Association for Mental Health on December 13 were Lynch, MacLachlan, Annis, Sting, Patrick Stewart, Siân Phillips, and Raffaella partying at the Empire Theatre in Leicester Square alongside special celebrity guests like Prince Andrew (Duke of York), The Police (Andy Summers, Stewart Copeland), Andrew Ridgeley and George Michael (Wham!), Gary Kemp (Spandau Ballet), Nick Rhodes (Duran Duran), Roger Taylor (Queen), Grace Jones (*Conan the Destroyer*), Julie Walters (*Educating Rita*), Danny Huston (*Wonder Woman*), Billy Connolly (*The Hobbit*) and the American artist Jean-Michel Basquiat.

There is even a photograph of Annis and Sting smiling as they cut a large (truthfully, disgusting-looking) *Dune* cake with a chocolate sandworm suggestively placed between fondant representations of Arrakis' two moons.

One last premiere was held concurrently the night of the London event at the Dadeland Triple Theater in South Miami, Florida, to benefit the Coconut Grove Playhouse, where José Ferrer was artistic director. Ferrer attended the public event alongside actor Brad Dourif, with tickets available for $20 for the film (with pre-show champagne reception) or $50 for the film and a gala party with the stars. Patrick Macnee and Jordan Christopher were also in attendance. A critics' screening and press conference with Ferrer and Dourif were also arranged, attended by John Sayles and Maggie Renzi, who had intended to screen *The Brother from Another Planet* in Cuba but were denied visas, so they settled for watching *Dune*. The reception by the press at the conference was reportedly icy.

During a London press conference in January 1985 (once writing was on the wall regarding *Dune* failing), Raffaella made a bold and not inaccurate prediction (via *Space Voyager* #14): "No, it won't flop. It's too original. It doesn't look like anything that's been on the screen before. I think it's going to become a big cult movie."

Dune and Gloom:
Classic Reviews from 1984

Dune faced many obstacles during its tortuous two-decade trip to the silver screen. As it turned out, the critical reaction would be an epic ordeal of its own.

In a chapter from his 1989 book *Harlan Ellison's Watching* titled "In Which The Fabled Black Tower Meets Dune With As Much Affection As Godzilla Met Ghidrah," famously abrasive sci-fi author Ellison called the executive group at Universal's Black Tower "deranged" for the way they mishandled *Dune*. This goes particularly for the film's presentation—or lack thereof—to the press (Ellison was writing for *USA Today* at the time). He details supposed behind-the-scenes intrigue of Universal chairman Frank Price claiming to those under his charge that the film was "a dog" that no one would understand, and that exhibitors were furious at the film's lack of commercial potential.

Things came to a head when Herbert, a longtime pal of Ellison's, called to inform him of a secret screening at Universal on November 30 (three days from the premiere in D.C., and two weeks from the general release) intended for just two reviewers from *Variety* and *The Hollywood Reporter*. Ellison arrived on the lot to visit a friend and then wandered over to Projection Room #1, where he was greeted by Booker McClay, a longtime publicist for Universal. Ellison showed McClay his letter of assignment from *USA Today* to review the film and explained he did not intend to do a "hatchet job," but was denied entrance.

Ellison then asked McClay to phone Frank Wright, National Publicity Director for MCA, who was incensed that Ellison had known of the screening and denied him entry once again, stating that the writer needed stronger accreditation. Ellison then got on the screening room phone and called Wright directly, who said that if he got word from Ellison's editor Jack Matthews, then they could allow him in. Ellison got Matthews to call Wright, and 10 minutes later, Wright called back and told Ellison for the third time that he could not screen *Dune*, after which he gave up and left.

When Ellison and other L.A. critics finally got to screen *Dune* at 8:30pm on December 12 (two days before its opening) at the Universal lot's famed Alfred Hitchcock theater, he became one of two major critics—the other being David Ansen of *Newsweek*—to give the film a glowing review. Here are excerpts from the man who popularized the term "bugfuck":

> *Dune* is an epic adventure as far ahead in this cinematic genre as *2001: A Space Odyssey* was in 1968 . . . In its way as compellingly surreal as something Buñuel or Fellini might conjure up, this faithful translation of the enormously popular Frank Herbert novel offers the wonder of secrets within secrets . . . The very strengths of *Dune* contain the seeds of its possible failure in 1984, and is a casebook study of why most science-fiction films of recent memory have been so sophomoric . . . an sf film with a brain . . . a film that deals with the concepts of home and courage, loyalty and love of family, nationalism and the wonders of the universe.

In the end, Wright ironically wound up using quotes from Ellison's review in the *Dune* advertising campaign along with Ansen's. Both men later appeared on the 2006 DVD release to sing its praises as a misunderstood epic. It is Ellison's assertion that by cutting so much filmed material from the finished product, and subsequently hiding the movie from critics until the last possible minute, Universal manufactured a "created disaster," with most film writers (and likely audiences as well) smelling blood before it ever played a single multiplex.

To read the rest of the reviews as they unfurled in papers across the country is to see a pattern of criticism not only for the film itself but the budget, its discordance with Lynch's previous art house films, and its qualities in relation to George Lucas' *Star Wars* trilogy. Did Universal's withholding the film from critics until the 11th hour engender misgivings, putting a target on *Dune*'s back? Or was it simply an inherently flawed film? Read these sometimes insightful—though often scathing—review excerpts from critics of the time and decide for yourself:

David Ansen, *Newsweek*:

> It is a dark, spellbinding dream, full of murmurs and whispers, byzantine plots and messianic fevers. It finds its iconography of the future deep in the past. It's not always easy to follow, but it's even harder to get out of your system. For better and for worse, it takes more artistic chances than any major American movie around.

Pauline Kael, The New Yorker (in a piece titled "David and Goliath"):

> It doesn't take long to realize that basically this isn't a David Lynch movie, it's *Dune*. Lynch doesn't bring a fresh conception to the ma-

terial; he doesn't make the story his own. Rather, he tries to apply his talents to Herbert's conception. He doesn't conquer this Goliath, he submits to it, as if he thought there was something to be learned from it. He's being a good boy, a diligent director. And though Herbert's prose can prostrate a reader—it's dry, with gusts of stale poetry—Lynch treats the book so respectfully that he comes out with a solemn big-budget version of *Up in Smoke* ... Despite the care that has gone into the staging, the editing rhythms are limp and choppy, and the narrative loiters on dull scenes and then rushes past the climactic ones.

Roger Ebert, *Chicago Sun-Times*:

> It took *Dune* about nine minutes to completely strip me of my anticipation. This movie is a real mess, an incomprehensible, ugly, unstructured, pointless excursion into the murkier realms of one of the most confusing screenplays of all time . . . *Dune* looks like a project that was seriously out of control from the start. Sets were constructed, actors were hired; no usable screenplay was ever written; everybody faked it as long as they could. Some shabby special effects were thrown into the pot, and the producers crossed their fingers and hoped that everybody who has read the books will want to see the movie. Not if the word gets out, they won't.

In "Ebert's 15th Annual Movie Disaster Awards," Ebert asserts (in a year that included *Slapstick of Another Kind*) that *Dune* may have been the worst of 1984:

> All kidding aside, was the year's worst movie really *Dune*? Well, yes and no: Yes, if you didn't see *Windy City* . . . Some people don't know how lucky they are: Sting refused to give interviews about *Dune* because he was upset by how little time his character was on the screen.

Gene Siskel, *Chicago Tribune*:

> Even on the level of pure spectacle, *Dune* is disappointing, including a number of 10-cent special effects every time we get an outer space shot. One scene of its young hero waterskiing on the back of a giant worm is particularly laughable . . . *Dune* contains some of the grossest material ever included in a mainstream film, including people having their nipples ripped open so that fluid can be drained, McMillan having boils lanced on his face, and the birth of a premature

fetus amid buckets of blood. Oh, how I wish I could have left this movie early. I really didn't need to stick around for the predictable conclusion that tastelessly mixes imagery from Christianity and the Third Reich.

Michael Wilmington, *Chicago Tribune*:

> *Dune*, with its evocative and densely detailed vision of a desert planet where mammoth worms capable of swallowing whole express trains burrow through the sand, is one of the year's most peculiar films. It's cold, strange, and remote. It's lit in such dark tones that, watching it, we often seem to be wandering through some vast, echoing mausoleum. It unfolds at a measured, lugubrious, almost maddening pace. And Herbert's byzantine plot is ruthlessly condensed and shoehorned into a 140-minute running time that seems barely adequate. Yet the movie is also packed with sometimes spellbinding, sometimes splendiferous, always bizarre imagery. If it fails—and certainly it fails as the *Star Wars*-style comic-book extravaganza those only vaguely familiar with the novel may expect—it's at least one of those memorable, spectacular failures that stick in your mind obsessively.

Janet Maslin, *The New York Times*:

> Several of the characters in *Dune* are psychic, which puts them in the unique position of being able to understand what goes on in the movie. The plot of *Dune* is perilously overloaded, as is virtually everything else about it. As the first king-sized, Italian-produced science-fiction epic, *Dune* is an ornate affair, awash in the kind of marble, mosaics, wood paneling, leather tufting, and gilt trim more suitable to moguls' offices than to far-flung planets in the year 10191. Not all of the overkill is narrative or decorative. Even the villain, a flying, pustule-covered creature, has more facial sores than he absolutely needs . . . There are no traces of Mr. Lynch's *Elephant Man* in *Dune*, but the ghoulishness of his *Eraserhead* shows up in the ooze and gore distinguishing many of the story's heavies.

Kirk Ellis, *The Hollywood Reporter*:

> This lofty $40 million allegory of interplanetary insurrection, long thought unfilmable, is at once a work of almost visionary beauty and surprisingly conventional adventure. Fans shouldn't mind the ex-

cessive length and too deliberate pacing, and while those elements could well render the picture's infinite intelligence inaccessible to certain other audiences, it is nonetheless a hotter property than the inexplicably cold feet of its distributor, Universal, would seem to indicate . . .

Richard Corliss, *Time* (in a review titled "The Fantasy Film as Final Exam"):

Most sci-fi movies offer escape, a holiday from homework, but *Dune* is as difficult as a final exam. You must cram for it . . . One can admire the world Herbert and Lynch have created even as one feels like an illegal alien visiting it . . . The actors seem hypnotized by the spell Lynch has woven around them—especially the lustrous Francesca Annis, as Paul's mother, who whispers her lines with the urgency of erotic revelation. In those moments when Annis is onscreen, *Dune* finds the emotional center that has eluded it in its parade of rococo decor and austere special effects. She reminds us of what movies can achieve when they have a heart as well as a mind.

Leonard Maltin, *Entertainment Tonight*:

Elephantine adaptation of Frank Herbert's popular sci-fi novel set in the year 10,191. You know you're in trouble when a film's opening narration (setting up the story) is completely incomprehensible! Visually imaginative, well cast, but joyless and oppressive—not to mention long.

Paul Attanasio, *The Washington Post*:

How maddening *Dune* is! As you would expect from visionary director David Lynch, it is a movie of often staggering visual power, the most ambitious science-fiction film since *2001*; it's also stupefyingly dull and disorderly. *Dune* doesn't get going till fully two hours have elapsed, so only the most patient will wait for the images to build to their crescendo. Lax in its storytelling, *Dune* gives us sublimity unmoored.

Rita Kempley, *The Washington Post*:

Dune the book is to *Dune* the movie what the Sahara is to the sandbox . . . David Lynch's disastrous film adaptation of Frank Herbert's science-fiction classic turns epic to myopic.

Kathryn Buxton, *The Washington Post*:

> Although much of *Dune* is too much to take in during a two hour–
> plus sitting, several good performances come out of the movie.
> Sting's much anticipated acting debut is a failure. With parts meatier
> than this as the bad baron's sadistic henchman, he could make the
> transition from rock music to film quite smoothly. Dourif, as anoth-
> er of the baron's goons, and Ferrer, as the double-crossing emperor,
> also play their parts well. Lynch, director of the cult films *Eraserhead*
> and *The Elephant Man*, coordinates the movie's special effects and
> elaborate sets well. Combined with Bob Ringwood's excellent cos-
> tumes, the sets do justice to Herbert's sweeping tale, giving it a life
> that the movie's script does not have.

Desmond Ryan, *The Philadelphia Inquirer*:

> It is the unique gift of the navigators in *Dune* to "fold space," an act
> of compression that allows men to traverse otherwise insuperable
> distances across galaxies. Against equally insuperable odds, David
> Lynch has tried his own version of this feat and run out of room.
> Of his attempt to fold Frank Herbert's sprawling and richly im-
> agined novel into a manageable space, it can at least be said that he
> has not mutilated it. *Dune* is not a great film and only occasionally
> a good one. Its interest lies not so much in the prolix story that un-
> folds as in the approach Lynch brings to his herculean task. Visually
> imposing, ponderously and sometimes pretentiously written, and
> crushed under the weight of mysticism that often is simply mystify-
> ing, Lynch's lavish effort remains fascinating.

Rick Lyman, *The Philadelphia Inquirer*:

> In the early days of autumn, we published our annual fall preview
> of the arts. I scanned the vast array of movies scheduled to open
> between the advent of autumn and the end of the year, considered
> the artists involved, read the capsule summaries, and came up with
> the movies I most longed to see . . . *Dune*, which I really had looked
> forward to most of all, turned out to be a stale, uninvolving botch,
> a heartbreaking disappointment, mercilessly faithful to Frank Her-
> bert's overrated book with only a few smatterings of the kind of
> devious fun the project needed. In the second half of the story,
> when Herbert cranks up his desert Holy War, I-am-the-messiah
> stuff, the movie becomes downright ridiculous.

Michael Blowen, *The Boston Globe*:

> Like Howard Hughes' famous Spruce Goose, David Lynch's *Dune* flops. Hughes' bulky, 190-ton wooden plane, bathed in preflight fanfare, crashed after traveling less than one mile in less than a minute, and Lynch's ballyhooed adaptation of Frank Herbert's cult novel follows the same inauspicious route. It would be nice to single out at least two elements in this mega-flop that succeed. But, except for Kenneth McMillan's evilish, slurping performance as the Baron, *Dune* will probably even disappoint the Dunatics . . .

Linda Deutsch, Associated Press:

> The only real heroes in this lumbering, overinflated epic are the army of special effects coordinators and technicians who create a fantastic, otherworldly environment peopled by creatures weirder and threatening than Jabba the Hutt. Freddie Francis' photography is constantly impressive. But technical wizardry alone cannot save *Dune* from a crash landing.

Bill Cosford, *The Miami Herald*:

> One has the sense before *Dune* is well underway that it is the kind of film that may reveal itself over several viewings—and certainly, there seems to be $47 million worth of things to look at. But fidelity to the source can be a trap, and Lynch fell into it; his movie is big and splashy and nearly nonsensical.

Tim Hewitt, *The Sun News*:

> Don't get the impression that I dislike *Dune*. It's a marvelous film, awesome and majestic in its scope. It is the sort of film that will no doubt yield more on subsequent viewings than on the first. It is a remarkable piece of work, the first truly epic science-fiction film. It's just not a "movie" movie. *Dune* is more akin to artwork than it is to the Saturday matinee. That may cost it some of its audience, but that doesn't make it any less impressive. There are some that will say David Lynch's *Dune* is a failure, and in some respects, they will be right, but what a failure! Would that all films failed so well!

The Infamous Glossary

Due to the internal perception that *Dune* was a virtually impenetrable, galaxy-brained disaster, Universal's marketing department went to unorthodox lengths to ensure audiences would understand the movie. With over 45 minutes of material excised from Lynch's preferred cut, the brass felt the best way for audiences to comprehend the film's odd terms was to hand out a printed glossary to ticket buyers. It was adding insult to injury.

Dubbed "*Dune* Terminology," the two-sided page covered every term under the Arrakis sun—from Gom Jabbar to Shai-Hulud—in front of a faded black & white image of Ron Miller's art of two moons above the desert (also the film's teaser one-sheet). It literally looks like a "*Dune* 101" study sheet. Oddly, most of the terms, such as "kanly" (vendetta) or "Muad'Dib" (mouse shadow on Arrakis' second moon), are explicitly defined through spoken dialogue in the film, rendering the glossary mostly redundant.

Even Frank Price, then head of Universal Pictures, admitted to me during our interview that the glossary was not a good look: "If you have to do that, you're in trouble. There were people always trying to figure various ways of patching things up. When it's dead on arrival, most of those things are decorating the corpse."

This desperate gambit did not go unnoticed by the press. Critic David Elliott of the Copley News Service mocked the handout in his review:

> If you can follow the film's jargon—a glossary of 37 terms was handed out at the screening I attended—you may pick up on the feverish schemes of the blood-feuding House Atreides and House Harkonnen to mine the spiced sands of Arrakis, and the ordained rise of young Paul Atreides to be the Kwisatz Haderach (savior), utilizing blue-eyed "Fremen" and the huge worms to overthrow the Padishah Emperor Shaddam IV (played as if sleepily reaching for a check by José Ferrer).

Paul M. Sammon, who was part of the marketing team on the film, has a more positive perception of the handout. "I'm amused by how history has rewritten the reception of that glossary," he told me. "Yes, there was some confusion and derision when people received this list of bizarre nomenclature. On the other hand, some major mainstream critics I knew at the time were *thankful* for that list, if for no other reason than they now had a handy spell-check sheet."

Comedy writer Andrés du Bouchet (*Late Night with Conan O'Brien*) saw the film in theaters at age 13:

> I remember very clearly being handed a glossary sheet on my way into the theater, which had all the terminology that you were going to have to know: Shai-Hulud, Muad'Dib, Kwisatz Haderach . . . on and on and on. It was a full sheet of 8.5×11 paper covered in terms . . . and I thought that was weird. Even then my cynical showbiz brain was like, "I don't know if this movie will do so well if you feel like you need to give people a glossary." Like you're going into *The Fast and the Furious* and they hand you a booklet with every kind of car you're going to see.

Another teenage ticket buyer who received the handout was Michael Gingold, now a movie journalist beloved in the horror community for his work with the genre magazine *Fangoria* since 1988. He is also a screenwriter (*Leeches, Halloween Night*) and author of three books from 1984 Publishing: *Ad Nauseam: Newsprint Nightmares from the 1980s* (2018), *Ad Nauseam II: Newsprint Nightmares from the 1990s and 2000s* (2019) and *Ad Astra: 20 Years of Newspaper Ads for Sci-Fi & Fantasy Films* (2019). Gingold shared not only the original "*Dune* Terminology" handout he received (see below), but also his memories of acquiring it.

D U N E
TERMINOLOGY

ARRAKEEN (Ar-ra-keen): the capitol of the planet Arrakis, known as DUNE.

ARRAKIS (Ar-rak-is): the desert planet known as DUNE.

ATREIDES (A-tray-i-deez): ruling House of the planet Caladan. The Atreides family currently comprises Duke Leto, his formal concubine the Lady Jessica, and their son Paul.

BENE GESSERIT (Be-na Jess-er-it): the ancient school of mental and physical training established primarily for female students. The program had as its object the breeding, over generations, of a person they called the "Kwisatz Haderach," a term signifying "one who can be in many places at once." Specifically, their selective breeding program aimed at producing a human with mental powers permitting him to understand and use higher order dimensions, including that of prescience.

CALADAN (Ca-la-dan): the lush green home planet of House Atreides.

CARRYALL (Car-ry-all): the aerial transport of Arrakis, used to carry, place and pick up large spice mining and refining equipment.

CRYSKNIFE (Kris-knife): the sacred knife of the Fremen on Arrakis. It is made from the teeth of dead sandworms.

"*Dune* Terminology" Reminiscences by Michael Gingold

The biggest sci-fi hit that fall was *The Terminator*, which came out of nowhere. Nobody had heard of that before the week it came out. Anticipation for *Dune* was huge, as big as any sci-fi film at that time. This was going to be a serious adult science-fiction film based on this classic novel . . . as opposed to all the "children of Star Wars." I knew makeup effects artists Giannetto De Rossi and Carlo Rambaldi were working on it, they were huge for those of us into horror effects. With those two, we were going to see some weird stuff.

I saw *Dune* at the Triangle Theatre in Yorktown Heights, New York . . . also where I saw *The Evil Dead* for the first time. We didn't know the glossary handouts were coming until we were in line. They gave it to us with our tickets. The ad didn't say, " . . . and you'll get a free glossary with each ticket!" We all got handed this thing, and I was like, "Oh, boy, this can't be good. This must mean the studio doesn't expect us to understand what's going on here." I was kind of familiar with a few of the terms. I knew what Arrakis was, some of the characters, but I did look over it because, you know, what are you supposed to do? You can't look at this in the dark while the movie's on, right? It was two sides full of text, so I looked at as much of it as I could before the movie started, like cramming for a test.

That's the thing—you're making this movie feel like homework. What's going on here? I realized, even then, why we were getting the glossary. It was not a favor: They were afraid nobody was going to understand what was going on. I don't think any of my friends who were with me at the screening had an especially negative or intense reaction to it. They were just like, "Oh, what is this?" We kind of laughed at it, like, "Oh, now we have to study before we go see the movie." It definitely took me aback when I saw that. Even back then I was collecting memorabilia, so I was like, "Oh, this is a nice little souvenir of the movie I can save, at least."

You didn't have the internet, so not as many people read reviews at my age. I was the sort of nerd who would follow reviews, but I'd also learned critics weren't as respectful to science fiction as they are now. Not all the reviews for *Dune* were awful, but a lot of them were. Rex Reed totally trashed it. Then it had the unfortunate timing to come out a week after *2010* and the same weekend as John Carpenter's *Starman* and Michael Crichton's *Runaway*. Universal must have thought, "Well, we've got the real goods and these other ones are just pretenders." *2010* did okay, but none of the other three. Even *Starman*, which is a great film, did not do huge business at the time. They cannibalized each other.

Box Office and Awards

According to *The Numbers*, *Dune* was given its nationwide rollout in the United States and Canada on December 14, 1984 (simultaneously with international rollouts in the UK, Ireland, Australia, and West Germany), opening in 915 theaters to take the #2 spot at the American box office that weekend with $6,025,091.

It was beaten by Eddie Murphy's action-comedy *Beverly Hills Cop*, which took in $11.5 million in its second week of release in 1,532 theaters. *Dune* managed to jump ahead of heavy competition also opening around the Christmas holiday, including Francis Coppola's gangster musical *The Cotton Club* at #5, John Carpenter's sci-fi romance *Starman* at #6, and Michael Crichton's sci-fi action thriller *Runaway* at #7. It also opened against the platform debut of David Lean's swan song *A Passage to India*, playing in only three theaters—a minor coincidence considering Lean was once offered the chance to direct *Dune* in the early '70s.

On its second weekend, *Dune* barely expanded to 944 theaters and again held the #2 spot with $4,769,713. By its third weekend, it inched up to 975 theaters but dropped to #8 with $4,942,030, which was actually a 4% uptick despite heavy competition from films like *Protocol*, *Micki + Maude*, and Disney's re-release of *Pinocchio*. Coming into January 1985, *Dune* dropped by over 50% to the #10 spot with $2,390,736 despite no new competition, proving definitively that word-of-mouth was not helping in its fourth weekend. The theater count dropped to 967.

In its fifth weekend, it dropped 38% for a $1,477,945 take at #14 in 717 theaters. As *Dune* passed the one-month mark January 18 weekend, it went up to #13 but fell 42% to take $852,765 in 645 theaters. This sixth weekend is the final one on record, ending with a sum total of $27,447,471. However, IMDb lists its US & Canadian total as $30,925,690 after limping a few more weeks in second-run houses.

The film carried a reported $40 million-plus price tag as well as $7–10 million for prints and advertising. With roughly half its earnings going to exhibitors, $30 million was not even close to putting Universal or De Laurentiis in the black, and put the kibosh on sequels or a merchandising bonanza. The *L.A. Times* estimated all-in costs as high as $55 million, including P&A. Even the $43 million in pre-sales to ancillary markets that De Laurentiis rounded up would not protect him with a P&A spend reported as high as $15.6 million. *Dune* was the *Heaven's Gate* of sci-fi.

It also appeared to be a final straw for studios burned one too many times by Dino's packaging process, wherein a Hollywood major like Universal, Paramount, or MGM fronted as much as 60% of a film's budget (and frequently all P&A) in return for North American distribution rights, as well as a $1 million producer's fee for De Laurentiis. The Italian mogul would then pre-sell foreign distribution to cover the remaining budget. Since the genres he produced (horror, crime, sci-fi) were well-received abroad, his exposure was minimal. Not so for the major studios.

"Our record of joint involvement [with De Laurentiis] is quite bad," Universal's Sid Sheinberg told a 1986 *Wall Street Journal*. "Bottom line is it's just not profitable."

Although very little data tracking the film's international box office exists, IMDb does list initial theatrical admissions for France (2,322,911), West Germany (1,594,087), and Spain (675,715). These numbers match Harlan Ellison's assessment in August 1985's issue of *The Magazine of Fantasy & Science Fiction*, where he reported *Dune* was breaking box office records in countries like West Germany, Italy, Austria, South Africa, and France. "In England, in its third week, *Dune*'s take was up by 39%, the sort of increase in attendance generally credited to word-of-mouth promotion," Ellison wrote.

In May 1985, England's *The Guardian* likewise said that the film "is attracting big audiences everywhere despite poor to moderate reviews."

Frank Herbert echoed these statements in *Eye*: "overseas there were none of these negative signals, and *Dune* set box office records. It was up 29 percent the third week in Great Britain. There were some 40,000 viewers each day the first three days in Paris alone, and to quote a French commentator: 'Visually magnificent, rich enough for many repeat viewings.'"

Sadly, *Dune* only received one Academy Award Nomination in 1985 for Best Sound (Steve Maslow, Bill Varney, Kevin O'Connell, Nelson Stoll); it lost to Miloš Forman's *Amadeus*. The obvious merit of Tony Masters' production design and Bob Ringwood's magnificent costumes were roundly snubbed.

In the genre world, the Academy of Science Fiction, Fantasy, & Horror Films' Saturn Awards were more generous, granting Ringwood a Best Costumes award, while also nominating *Dune* for Best Science Fiction Film (it lost to *The Terminator*), Giannetto De Rossi for Best Make-Up, and Barry Nolan for Best Special Effects.

Sci-fi's other big ceremony, the Hugo Awards, granted *Dune* a nomination for Best Dramatic Presentation to Lynch and Herbert. It lost to Peter Hyams' now mostly forgotten *2010*.

Dune and Raffaella De Laurentiis also had the ignominious honor of receiving the Worst Picture Award at the 7th annual Stinkers Bad Movie Awards. *Dune* beat out such distinguished competition as Bo Derek's erotic romance *Bolero* (Worst Picture Razzie winner), the ill-conceived Dudley Moore–Eddie Murphy comedy *Best Defense*, the notorious "Sylvester Stallone sings!" comedy *Rhinestone*, and the South African ethnic laugher *The Gods Must Be Crazy*.

Filmbooks: Home Video Releases

D*une* has had many iterations in the American home video market:
—In May 1985, MCA Home Video released the film on VHS, Betamax, and LaserDisc (the latter split onto three sides), as well as a two-disc set via RCA's short-lived CED "videodisc" SelectaVision format. A VHS promo touted Ansen's *Newsweek* review ("Rich . . . spellbinding") and Ellison's from *USA Today* ("Compelling . . . brilliant . . . an oasis for the imagination"). Its cable debut on HBO was in November '85.

—In 1997, a new widescreen LaserDisc version was released by MCA/Universal.

—On March 31, 1998, Universal Home Entertainment released the first DVD edition of *Dune*. In 2006, a new DVD (and HD DVD) set featured both the theatrical and extended "Alan Smithee" cuts. Bonus material included eleven deleted scenes with an intro by Raffaella and four mini-docs. This DVD set proved so popular that the following year (2007), USHE re-released it in a new *Extended Edition* steelbook.

—In 2010, the theatrical made its way to a USHE Blu-ray edition.

—In 2021, Arrow Video released the film in a special 4K UHD box set containing the theatrical cut and all previous extras. The image on this new 2160p 4K restoration from the original camera negative appears to have been graded darker, falling in line with Freddie Francis' statement that he shot it so it could be printed darker.

One feature notably missing from the 2021 Arrow 4K was the 82-minute documentary *The Sleeper Must Awaken*. Directed by Daniel Griffith, it tells the story of the *Dune* production with some of the talent interviewed for this book (Giles Masters, Ron Miller, Paul Sammon, Jane Jenkins). Due to an unforeseen delay, the doc was taken off the Region 1 4K bonus disc with only the new music and merchandizing docs remaining. The film was made available for the Koch Films 4K edition released in Germany two months after the Region 1 version. It was eventually released to Arrow's streaming service in 2022.

"I have always championed Lynch's *Dune* as being the best example of worldbuilding from any film produced in the 1980s," Griffith told me. "Working on the documentary provided me with the opportunity to be a sounding board for all the wonderful artisans, storytellers, and historians who either worked on the film or continued to preserve its legacy for future audiences to discover."

"When Daniel was putting all the components together and Arrow started doing all the packaging, the documentary wasn't ready," confirmed Craig Campobasso, an interviewee for both the documentary and this book. "He was so busy with everything else, and so he said it was just going to be released on its own. After seeing it, he did such a great job. I thought it was really fantastic."

Plans Within Plans: Alternate Cuts

Dune: Extended Edition

After several years of critics and fans vocally requesting a more complete version of *Dune*, in 1988, MCA Universal finally decided to put together a longer three-hour version of the film to broadcast over two nights on syndicated TV in June of that year and later for cable television (2 hours per night, including commercials). The project was hotly anticipated by fans, and was mooted just as MCA Home Video was getting into the restoration business in a big way, releasing new cuts of classics like *Lost Horizon*, *Spartacus*, and *Frankenstein*.

"The additional *Dune* footage is there, but it had to be scored and conformed," MCA's Mike Fitzgerald told Gannett News Service's Mike Cidoni in 1987. "Sound effects, mixing, and dubbing were needed. Basically, the only thing that was done was the shoot. If it had been economically feasible, I'd have loved to put it out."

Lynch was initially enthusiastic about taking a mulligan on the film, confirming as such to both *Variety* and the *Chicago Tribune* in late 1986, explaining to the latter that the original 2-hour and 17-minute version was "too short."

Commenting on a proposed four-hour version for the VHS market, he said in 1988 [*Twilight Zone Magazine*]:

> It's in the works, but whether or not it'll happen has yet to be seen. As Raffaella De Laurentiis and I used to say, *Dune* was our baby, but it didn't turn out so good. So now we're going to give it an operation. It's like *Eraserhead* in that respect . . . It was a nightmare, but the film's reputation has gotten better and better since then, so there's a lot of interest in a larger version. But you really "die the death" at the time, I'll tell you...

However, Lynch was ultimately unwilling to participate in a new version, either because the studio refused to pony up the right amount of dough or because he was no longer interested in revisiting a painful experience.

Raffaella told Faisal A. Qureshi in 1997:

> Universal asked David and me to work on a "long" version of *Dune* to be prepared for television. David was busy and not prepared to

go back to work on *Dune* without further compensation . . . I don't think Frank Herbert lived to see that long version. DDLC was not involved as they had sold the TV rights to Universal. I worked closely with Universal to help them with the long version, and I thought the final version was pretty good. I always wanted David involved, but unfortunately, it never worked out with him. I think a re-release could be possible only with David's involvement, and I don't see that happening.

The TV cut was 50 minutes longer than the theatrical version with nearly 70 alterations and extensions, but included only roughly 35 to 40 minutes of actual restored material assembled by Harry Tatelman, vice president of MCA Television's special projects division. This is the same division of the Universal Pictures Debut Network that later released the highly compromised version of Terry Gilliam's *Brazil* known as the "Love Conquers All" cut. Since the ultimate "Extended Cut" was made without his participation, Lynch had his name removed from the final product, taking the DGA-mandated pseudonym "Alan Smithee" for the director credit as well as the moniker "Judas Booth" (a sly portmanteau of the Biblical traitor Judas and Lincoln assassin John Wilkes Booth) for his screenwriting credit. As such, this version is colloquially referred to as the "Alan Smithee cut" by derisive fans.

"I was given permission to remove my name from the TV version," Lynch told the *Los Angeles Times* in June of 1988.

"The guy did a monumental job, no question," Tatelman said for the same article. "He's a visionary. I thought it was an honor to work on his film."

The most distinctive feature of the 189-minute Smithee cut is a new narrator (William Phipps), who lets loose torrents of exposition throughout the proceedings in place of Princess Irulan. Phipps is perhaps best known as the voice of Prince Charming in Walt Disney's *Cinderella*, and he also made his mark in sci-fi classics like *Invaders from Mars* and *The War of the Worlds*.

At the start, the viewer is shown the cover of Herbert's book *Dune* as if it were the Bible, an old-fashioned opening straight out of classic Hollywood. A new, 7-minute introduction traces the prehistory of man starting with the human revolt against machines, through the founding of the Bene Gesserit and the Spacing Guild, and right up to the Emperor's plot against the Atreides. This ponderous new opening was scripted by Francesca Turner, who along with Gene Palmer had presided over many butchered TV versions of Universal films including *Earthquake*, John Carpenter's

The Thing, and the infamous TV-safe cut of *Scarface* where Tony Montana quipped, "this town is like a great big chicken, just waiting to be plucked."

The intro is accompanied by hastily produced concept illustrations that don't quite match the film's aesthetics. These paintings were done by Jaroslav Gebr, who had done the distinctive *Saturday Evening Post*-esque drawings interspersed throughout 1973's Best Picture winner *The Sting*.

From there, the movie contains numerous whole scenes and scene extensions not in the theatrical cut. Unfortunately, since visual effects (and in some cases live-action footage) were not executed for these scenes, many sequences are fabricated either from outtakes, rough test footage, or even repeated from other parts of the film. For instance, shots of the Harkonnen flagship arriving in the dusty winds of Arrakis are used throughout, even for ships arriving on other planets. A new scene of Reverend Mother Mohiam landing on Caladan contains this effects shot, as well as a shot of the cockpit view of the Duke's shuttle leaving Caladan, a shot of the Harkonnen pilots who take Paul and Jessica to the Arrakis desert (gagged Paul and Jessica are in frame), and a shot of the Reverend Mother in her chair inside the Duke's palace. The effect is sloppy and takes an already hobbled film and reduces it to B-movie schlock. It's no mystery why Lynch had his name removed from it.

The version of the Smithee cut released for the first time in anamorphic widescreen on the 2006 DVD is only 177 minutes long and excludes several scenes (some of which remain intact for the theatrical cut), including the Baron removing the servant's heart plug, Thufir discovering the burning weirding modules, and Thufir's death scene. It is easy to tell which scenes were reconstituted from cut footage, since the Fremen lack their signature "blue within blue eyes" in all the new scenes; Universal did not deem it worth paying for new effects.

Remarkably, Lynch now seems to feel more open to the idea of doing his own *Dune* re-edit, at least more than in the past. He said in 2022 [*The AV Club*]:

> People have said, "Don't you want to go back and fiddle with *Dune*?" I was so depressed and sickened by it, you know? The thing was a horrible sadness and failure to me, and if I could go back in, I've thought, well, maybe I would on that one go back in. But I mean, nobody's . . . it's not going to happen . . . It's not like there's a bunch of gold in the vaults waiting to be cut and put back together. Early on, I knew what

Dino wanted and what I could get away with and what I couldn't. I started selling out, and it's a sad, sad, pathetic, ridiculous story, but I would like to see what is there. I can't remember, that's the weird thing. I can't remember. It might be interesting. There could be something there, but I don't think it's a silk purse. I know it's a sow's ear.

Channel 2 Edit

In 1992, an enterprising Fox affiliate in San Francisco called KTVU managed to splice together a new hybrid version of both the theatrical and Alan Smithee cuts. Coming in at 180 minutes, it reinstated much of the violence of the theatrical cut edited for television, while removing much of the "cobbled together" hodgepodge footage haphazardly inserted throughout the Alan Smithee cut. An *Extended Edition* DVD released in Europe in 2005 features a 177-minute version of this cut.

Dune: The Alternative Edition Redux (Spicediver Fan Edit)

In a similar spirit to the Channel 2 edit, a fan using the pseudonym "Spicediver" patched together an edit in the 2010s using all known footage, including deleted scenes from the 2006 DVD release as well as the Extended Cut. Despite being the same three-hour length as the Extended Cut, this version eliminates all of the sloppily reused "stock footage" of the TV version, rearranges the order of certain scenes, introduces a few new effects, and—most boldly—a repurposed and truncated ending that remains truer to the spirit of Herbert's book by eliminating the "make it rain" finale.

This version was made without the participation or permission of Universal Pictures and has been disseminated online in a grassroots fashion. It's the most comprehensive cut currently in existence, and many die-hard admirers of Lynch's film prefer this cut. Its only major snag (besides being unauthorized) is that it uses about 35 minutes of low-resolution footage unavailable in 1080p or higher. Because deleted footage from the 2006 disc has only been released in the 720p DVD format, Spicediver has refused to release a version in higher resolution (1080p or 4K) because the mix of high-definition footage and low-resolution DVD footage would be too jarring. However, around the same time as the release of the 2021 *Dune*, an intrepid fan released a 4K version to YouTube that had been scaled up using artificial intelligence software. The Spicediver edit was also released as part of Koch Films' *Der Wüsterplanet* (Ultimate Edition) German Blu-ray set in 2022.

Interview: Spicediver (Fan Edit Creator)

Spicediver (who we'll refer to as "he/him" to preserve his anonymity) first saw *Dune* when it opened at the cinema. While his school friends hated the film, Spicediver had more mixed feelings.

"I loved the way it looked and its otherworldly atmosphere," he remembered. "I loved its strangeness. My appreciation grew from there."

The spark for his fan reconstruction came in 1990 when he bought a VHS tape of the *Extended Edition* dubbed by another fan from a rare Japanese LaserDisc release:

> It had all this extra footage, and I was fascinated. I had these two versions of *Dune* on tape and tried to make a video composite that added all the good stuff from the *Extended Edition*, but never got past first base because of the Macrovision copy protection on VHS machines. It colors and distorts the picture, so that was the end of that little adventure, but I never stopped thinking about doing it.

Years later, Spicediver began work in earnest, releasing two earlier versions to the fan community before unveiling a final version in 2012 titled *Dune: The Alternative Edition Redux*. It used footage from the theatrical cut, deleted scenes on the special edition DVD, and extra footage from the Alan Smithee TV version, along with quotes from Herbert's book to bridge the four sections of the film. He also drew on "never-heard-before" music from the extended version of the soundtrack album, including a haunting piece titled "Secrets of the Fremen." Since the Smithee version was cobbled together haphazardly without Lynch's input, it features sloppy transitions and repeated shots, which Spicediver tried to correct.

He explained:

> Just fixing all those errors gave me plenty to do, including correcting the wrong order of some scenes, like where the baby maker is drowned to produce the Water of Life. I also changed music cues more in line with how music is used in the theatrical version, because in the Extended Version, it's really repetitive and sometimes very inappropriately used. The male narrator in the Extended Version I quite liked in parts, despite my choosing Princess Irulan as the narrator in *Redux*. I particularly liked parts of the narrated prologue where you learn what the mental training schools are and why they came into existence: because of a religious crusade against artificial intelligence after humanity

became enslaved by cyborgs and robots. Lynch didn't script that prologue, and it contains some howling errors, but this history of humanity is absolutely fundamental to Herbert's worldbuilding. I hit on the idea of reinventing parts of the narrated prologue from the *Extended Edition*, turning them into additional filmbooks you see Paul watching. With that element restored to the story, the architecture and technologies you see in *Dune* make a lot more sense. More importantly, it reveals the reasons behind the characters' obsessions with mental abilities.

His new edit also eliminates many of the extraneous inner monologues that were tacked on in the final phases of Antony Gibbs' editing in 1984.

Spicediver explains:

The inner dialogue device adapted from the novel is completely redundant about 50% of the time and hurts the film. The Litany against Fear translates well to screen, but that's because it's a Bene Gesserit mantra, not inner dialogue about some person or item. This is not a book, it's a film. You have visuals, actors, and body language, so let the actors and the camera do their work instead of spoon-feeding the audience.

In addition to re-editing sequences and audio, Spicediver also meticulously added new special effects tweaks, such as completing the Fremen blue eyes that were missing in added footage from the *Extended Edition* as well as some deleted scenes:

I did the eyes in Adobe After Effects..I had to match the color and luminosity and do it frame-by-frame because the actors were usually moving in some way. That took me absolutely ages; there were lots of late nights. I also fixed or removed some of the dodgier special effects shots, and created the custom titles and credits by sampling existing letters or bits of letters from words on screen and rebuilding them into words.

Before preparing his cut, Spicediver read all seven published drafts of Lynch's script, although the script changed during filming. There are scenes in existence that were not in any of those drafts. He also absorbed a plethora of *Dune* articles, interviews, and documentary material over the years, all of which gave him a wide knowledge of the material that is missing from both the original and *Extended Edition*.

As he explains:

> According to Raffaella, the assembly edit with the best takes of all the actors' scenes was about 4 hours and 20 minutes. If you calculate how many pure effects or wide scenery shots might be added to that, the total footage comes to something around five hours. Who wanted a five-hour movie in 1984? Nobody. That's when they realized they wouldn't be able to tell the story as scripted. Nobody can blame them when they removed the six or seven scenes around Paul taking the Water of Life and shot a single replacement scene, the one where all the worms come and gather around Paul on the sand. That decision was made on the journey toward Lynch's preferred three-hour fine cut. It's an extraordinary scene, my favorite in the movie, and it's not even in Herbert's book. Hats off to David Lynch. I wouldn't want to restore those cut Water of Life scenes because I'd have to lose what replaced them, but I would love to restore other key plot strands that were mostly removed from the film's second half: Alia's development and the Fremen's fear of her, Paul and Chani, Paul and Jamis' widow Harah, more of Jessica and Paul's interactions, and—most crucial of all—Paul's ambivalence about his "terrible purpose."

Arguably the most significant change Spicediver made was removing the final scene of Paul literally making it rain on Arrakis. Herbert famously objected to that ending, since he never intended Paul to be a true "God" in that sense. Using his powers to make it rain would also have (as Paul hints at earlier in the film) ended spice mining forever, as all worms would die. Spicediver replaced it with a reprise of the Guild Navigator being destroyed by Paul and some abstract imagery of folding space.

"All that swirling blue light is much closer to the ending that Lynch scripted in the first two or three drafts," said Spicediver. "That ridiculous rain ending was conceived closer to the start of production, but I only changed the ending after a lot of experimenting, until I finally worked out how I could make it work cinematically. The end of the movie still hits a kind of emotional crescendo."

Spicediver plans to continue tweaking his cut if some of the deleted footage eventually becomes available in higher resolution, or if further footage is uncovered:

> The negative of the *Extended Edition* and other cut footage may have been destroyed in the Universal Studios fire in Los Angeles in 2008. That's still unconfirmed rumor, but where there's smoke . . .

A fan who saw the Spicediver edit once wrote an online review quoting Liet-Kynes: "You see through to the truth of a thing." In this author's opinion, it is the closest we may ever get to seeing Lynch's true vision onscreen.

Spicediver told me:

> I hope *Redux* captures the spirit of the *Dune* movie that was actually shot. But it's not the director's cut, and Lynch is well and truly done with the movie, so we'll never know exactly what his cut would have looked like.

"There are bits of the Spicediver edit I prefer," said Mark Bennett of *DuneInfo*. "I think the final battle is more understandable. It seems clearer somehow."

Terri Hardin, who worked on the original *Dune*, enthused:

> I didn't appreciate the movie until my husband showed me something made by Spicediver. It was what I think the movie really wanted to be. It's a Swiss cheese movie if it wasn't for Spicediver. I really love it—it's really beautiful. I'm grateful to him for doing all that painstaking work. We got to see what we were all working toward. This is what we wanted, exactly what we wanted.

"It was really fun, even better than I anticipated . . . more of me is always fun," joked Molly Wryn, who was happy to see Harah reinstated into this cut. "He did a good job. It always brings back memories. I was pleased some of my stuff was there. If David did it again it would be perfection, but I really appreciated what Spicediver did."

No one involved in the original film had ever reached out to Spicediver about *Dune: The Alternative Edition Redux*, so I asked him a simple question: "If you could have one minute alone with David Lynch, what would you say to him about his film?"

He replied:

> I'd say: "I know *Dune* is a great sadness in your life because you didn't have final cut and it bombed in theaters, but you should be proud of the art direction and design, areas in which you had a lot of input as a graphic artist. The film looks and feels extraordinary. It's a unique work of art. Thank you for making it." Then I'd ask him if he wants to go out for cherry pie.

The Book vs. The Film
(with Mark Bennett)

Major and minor differences between Herbert's text and Lynch's film are bountiful. I was able to get noted *Dune*-ophile and founder of the *DuneInfo* website Mark Bennett to expand upon some of the most important additions and exclusions below, starting with one that almost seems perverse not to have been included by noted caffeine junkie David "Damn Fine Coffee" Lynch.

Not in the Movie: Coffee!

MARK BENNET: There should be a scene with Fremen smoking spice cigarettes and drinking spice coffee. I've never really thought about that, to be honest. There's not an awful lot of eating or drinking in Lynch's *Dune*. There's a bit where Paul is testing his food with the poison sniffer. We see a bit in the Villeneuve *Dune* where they're spitting into the machine to make the coffee, and maybe we'll see the coffee service in Part Two. There's a certain amount of ceremony with coffee in the novel, but Lynch has ditched that one completely.

Not in the Book: Telepathy

MB: There's this bit where Paul knows that Alia has killed the Baron, and there's a scene right at the beginning where Reverend Mother Mohiam is listening in. Yeah. The Bene Gesserit skills in the novel are . . . I'm not going to say realistic, but they have a physicality to them. They control their body to a minute level. Even the Voice, Frank Herbert has said in one of the books that if he knows a little bit about you, he can say something that will make you angry based on politics or religion or something like that. He's extrapolated that a little bit beyond the bounds of realism, but there's still a basis for that in reality. With telepathy, we're into the realm of ESP where I don't think there's any hard science to back any of that up. It pushes the Bene Gesserit skills into a more mystical realm, a bit more Jedi-ish. Likewise, at the end, Paul effectively becomes a god and makes it rain, which is not a power that Paul or the Bene Gesserit has [in the novel]. They might be able to predict or see the future, to see all possible possibilities to choose the right path. We do know Paul was trained as a Mentat as well, so he's between that and the Bene Gesserit training, with the spice pushing his ability to superhuman level.

(Practically) Not in the Movie: Salusan Bull

MB: That does appear in Lynch's *Dune*. We do see them pack the bull up when Duncan is going off to Arrakis. Then in the Great Hall, Rabban has taken the black-and-green Atreides flag and stuffed it into the bull's mouth, although we never actually see that. When Paul walks into the Great Hall at the end, if you watch, he does look up and he's looking at the bull, processing the flag stuffed in the mouth. A great touch, but it's never explicitly mentioned. In the novel, there's an argument between Leto and Jessica about where the bull's head should be because she hates it, but he wants it in the dining room. It's something that's consistent throughout Paul Atreides' journey from Caladan right to the very end of the film. We've got that in the new *Dune* as well: "Grandfather liked to fight bulls, look where that got him!"

Not in the Book: Heart Plugs

MB: The infamous heart plugs are very iconic. They're in the video intro scenes to the Westwood games as well. Heart plugs are a pure Lynch invention. Lynch very much likes the texture of organic material, and the heart plugs seem to fit into that fascination or obsession. There's a bit of a misconception that Alia kills the Baron at the end by pulling his heart plug out. The Baron and Feyd don't have heart plugs; she pulls his suspensors out, the things that are keeping him afloat. The part where he pulls the servant boy's heart plug, that's almost a sexual assault. I'm almost surprised that they got away with as much as they did, considering it was a PG-13 rating.

Not in the Movie: Banquet Scene

MB: That was Herbert's favorite scene, and he was upset that it wasn't in the film. It's in the miniseries, but it's a bunch of people sitting around the table talking. It's not very cinematic. There's a lot of information that comes out in that, and it shows how Paul can read people. He's aware of what's going on. He's assuming authority when Leto asks to leave. There are all the politics and the infighting and allegiances and spies and traitors.

It's a great scene, but how do you make that cinematic? Also part of the banquet is the subplot in the original novel where the Harkonnens effectively framed Jessica as the traitor in the Atreides' midst. Leto lets everyone else in the Atreides household believe that he believes that Jessica is the traitor to force the Harkonnens' hand, believing he's fallen for their trick. In the banquet scene, that's why Leto is called away when they found a message. In Lynch's second draft, the fact that Jessica was a suspected traitor remains, and then there's a confrontation with Gurney later on when he's reunited with them. That whole plotline was simplified and then just removed completely in the later drafts and never filmed. Technically Thufir thinks that Jessica is a traitor as well, and that might be in the second draft as well, when he apologizes to Jessica at the end. In the novel, that's part of the reason why Thufir agrees to work for the Harkonnens—he wants his revenge on Jessica, and the Baron lets him believe that Jessica was the traitor.

Not in the Book: Pugs

MB: Ahh, pugs! Not a part of the *Dune* universe at all. The only dogs that we get in *Dune* are chair dogs later on in the series, which are organic furniture. We didn't get to see those, yet Lynch has introduced a number of dogs into the film. We see dogs in the first scene when the Emperor is clearing his throne room. Leto is constantly carrying around a dog, and that dog goes charging into battle with Patrick Stewart in an infamous scene that keeps appearing online. The *Dune* battle pug finally makes it to the end of the film as well when we see the pug being held by Harah's children as Paul enters the throne room. Happy end for the pug. Why Lynch decided to introduce pugs into *Dune* . . . we'd have to ask David Lynch on that one.

Not in the Movie: Jessica's Harkonnen Lineage

MB: In the novel, Paul realizes after his exposure to spice that he is the grandson of Baron Harkonnen, and his mother Jessica is the daughter of the Baron. Jessica, being raised as Bene Gesserit, doesn't know who her true parents are. That's a bit of a shock to everyone at that point. When Alia kills the Baron in the novel, she refers to him as "grandfather," which is accurate, but probably confuses the Baron even more. Paul also refers to Feyd as his cousin. That lineage is quite interesting because it's like in *Star Wars* where Luke and Vader are part of the same family. Paul realizes one of his future paths is to join forces with the Baron, to effectively become a Harkonnen. All of that is removed or only hinted at in the Lynch movie, and all we've got is the fact that Jessica and Alia have got the red hair of the Harkonnens.

Not in the Book: Water of Life Desert Ceremony

MB: The Water of Life scene plays out differently in the film, because originally it was filmed very much like the book where Paul takes the Water of Life inside the sietch after drowning a baby worm. There's the deleted scene of that when Jessica is about to take the Water of Life, but after it was filmed, it was decided that they could condense several pages of dialogue into a single scene. Paul runs into the desert with the Fedaykin and Chani and takes the Water of Life in the desert, then all the sandworms surround Paul but don't attack him. Not in the novel, not how sandworms react. They're very territorial, and the idea of a sandworm not attacking humans doesn't come up until much later in the *Dune* series when there's a character who can control the sandworms. They ride the worms in the novel, but [there isn't] the idea that a sandworm won't attack a particular person because that person has some control over them. That is one of my favorite scenes in the Lynch movie, because it just looks so great. It condenses quite a static scene inside a room where not much is happening into this epic moment.

Not in the Movie: Count and Lady Fenring

MB: The Fenrings! Who we've never seen completely in any adaptation. Jodorowsky's version would have had Count and Lady Fenring. The miniseries has The Count, but no Lady Fenring. Villeneuve's *Dune* had a casting announcement for Lady Fenring, but it isn't clear if we're going to get The Count. In Lynch's film, neither The Count nor Lady Fenring make an appearance. In trying to get the film in 2 hours and 17 minutes, that was a sensible decision to remove that entire subplot. In the book, the Count is the close friend of the Emperor, and his wife is a Bene Gesserit. Count Fenring was a failed Kwisatz Haderach himself, and so they are trying to also bring about a Kwisatz Haderach. Lady Fenring seduces Feyd to conceive a child who they hope will then be a Kwisatz Haderach that they will control, not the Bene Gesserit. Plans within plans within plans, and even Frank Herbert drops that plot point in *Dune Messiah*. It is picked up in the Brian Herbert and Kevin J. Anderson prequel books. In Jodorowsky's *Dune*, it was going to be addressed, where Paul tells Lady Fenring that the child will be a vegetable.

Not in the Book: Weirding Modules

MB: There's the rain at the end, and there are the weirding modules . . . there's a lot of hate for both of those in the community. Personally, I don't mind weirding modules too much because Lynch said he didn't want to have kung-fu in the desert. Rather than having the Atreides pass on a fighting technique to the Fremen, they pass on a physical object to the Fremen—the weirding module—to improve their fighting technique. The problem with that is we never see the Fremen as great fighters. It's almost like anybody with this weirding module could have overthrown the Sardaukar. As opposed to enhancing their abilities, it almost seems to be a substitute for them. We never see the Fremen fight, apart from the Jamis fight, which was cut. There is no combat other than Fremen firing weirding modules at smugglers or Sardaukar. It's disappointing from the Fremen point of view that we don't get the sense that these are hardened warriors that could take out Sardaukar on their own. Instead, we get a magic box that allows you to scream at people. I understand the change from being a fighting technique to a weapon; I just don't think it was implemented as clearly or as well as it could have been.

In the novel, Yueh's plan to save Paul and Jessica seems wafer thin. He's betting on the fact that the Harkonnens will listen to him that they should dispose of Paul and Jessica in the desert, rather than just killing them outright. That they should take them in a specific 'thopter, in which he's stowed the bags with the stillsuits and the Fremkit. That Paul and Jessica will be able to escape from the Harkonnens, find the Fremkit, and somehow survive the desert. I was never that impressed with Yueh's plan! It seems like it could have gone wrong in so many different ways. In the Jodorowsky script, Yueh's plan is a little bit more direct in that he smuggles Paul and Jessica out once Leto has agreed to try and kill the Baron. He gives Paul and Jessica to some spice smugglers to escape with; however, they get drunk and the scene continues pretty much as in the novel, but at least he's got an active role in that. In the Lynch movie, he does go one step beyond that and provides Paul the plans to the weirding module for an eventual revenge against the Harkonnens and ultimately against the Emperor himself. He tries to redeem himself a little bit more in the Lynch version, but we never really get too much of an idea of why Yueh's betrayed them. We understand it's his wife, but that isn't really explored very much, why he felt that was the only course of action he had to try and save his wife.

Not in the Movie: Feyd the Gladiator

MB: In Lynch's *Dune*, Sting's Feyd gets something like three lines. Considering he's a big pop star, he's on all the posters and promotion material, he's in it very little. Some of the filmed scenes were cut, as when he tortures Dr. Yueh. That's in the deleted scenes but not in the theatrical cut. The actual gladiator scene, we don't see at all. The end is a confrontation between Paul and Feyd. We've seen Feyd coming out of the shower, but is he any good in a knife fight? That isn't established at all. We're not clear on how much of a threat Feyd is to Paul. The amount of danger isn't clear. It's an odd way to structure a film, climaxing with a fight with someone that we've barely seen that we don't know is any good? The film would have benefited if we did see Feyd as more of a mirror image of Paul. If the Bene Gesserit plan had come to fruition, Feyd would have been the father of the Kwisatz Haderach. Paul should have been a girl, Feyd would have married . . . Paula, let's say, and their son would have been the Kwisatz Haderach. He is, in some sense, the equal of Paul. He's been trained, certainly not by Bene Gesserits or Mentats, but he's got the lineage and the fighting prowess in the book. In the film, [he's] just some random guy who shouts a lot. From Feyd's point of view, Paul has betrayed the Emperor, he's threatening spice production, and he's killed his grandfather. Why shouldn't he fight this upstart who's trying to disrupt the universe's economy? *Dune* is feuding houses who only meet when they're about to kill each other.

Not in the Book: The Baron's Doctor

MB: The Baron's Doctor, who gets first credit at the end because it's in alphabetical order. Yes, a bit of a strange addition who seems to speak in rhyme as well. "Stick the pick in there, Pete. Turn it 'round real neat." Again, a wonderful Lynch invention for the Baron, again loving the textures of organic decay. The Baron's pus and boils are not explicitly from the book. We do know that the Baron is diseased; that's part of why he's so obese. In some of the prequel novels, it's said that the Bene Gesserit effectively infected the Baron at some point. All of the instruments the doctor has, the glass sphere with the blood oozing into it . . . Giedi Prime in particular is very Lynch. I think he said that he was most at home on the Giedi Prime sets. We never see what happens to the Baron's Doctor; maybe he survives?

Not in the Movie: Leto II (The First)

MB: Paul and Chani have a son in the first novel who is named Leto II. However, that child is killed in the Harkonnen raid on the Fremen, which leads Paul down a dark path. Not only is he fighting to take revenge for his father and his house, but also now for his own son. That's in the miniseries, but isn't in the Lynch film at all. It simplifies that plot point, because otherwise you're introducing a character who is killed very quickly. The problem with that is Paul and Chani's relationship in Lynch's *Dune* is effectively a footnote, so you'd have to strengthen their relationships in order for them to have a child in order for that to have any impact. He's briefly mentioned in the Jodorowsky version and in one of the Jacobs versions as well.

Not in the (First) Book: Third-Stage Guild Navigators

MB: Apparently, Herbert wasn't too happy about that and at one point threatened to sue because apparently the film only had rights to characters from the first novel, and the Third-Stage Guild Navigator isn't discussed until *Dune Messiah*. He decided that once the movie bombed it wasn't worth trying to sue. Avalon Hill's 1979 *Dune* board game had a similar problem where they had the Guild Navigator as one of the characters, but they didn't have the rights. That almost caused the game to be canceled at the last minute. In the book, we understand that the Guild takes Spice, and that mutates them, turns them into a kind of fish person. It's described a little bit more like in the miniseries. In the Lynch film, we have these three stages: The First Stage, which we see, where their head is oozing spice and they've got tubes; the Second Stage Navigators, which wear hoods . . . Originally, they were going to be actual heads, and most of those heads still exist, sold on auction years ago. There's a picture in Ed Naha's book and some color ones from the auction site. Those didn't look right or were going to be too expensive so they replaced it with hoods. Simple solution. Then we've got the giant Third-Stage Guild Navigator, created by Carlo Rambaldi. Lynch described him as a giant grasshopper. It's a marvelous creation. Very strange that the mouth movement is . . . some people have likened it to a part of the female body. Very Lynchian, all the textures and the organic nature of it. Not how it was described in later books, but a fantastic depiction of a mutated human.

In the novel, the Guild is very much a passive observer. They don't want spice production to be disrupted, but they don't try and control it. They just want the spice to flow, which isn't in the novel either. That phrase—"The spice must flow"—is a Lynch creation, which does a great job of distilling the point of the novel down into four words. It appears on merchandise for the new film, but it's not from the novel. It's a Lynch creation. "The sleeper must awaken" is not Herbert either. There's a phrase in the book of Leto telling his son that "you must awaken to whatever's going on." That concept of a sleeper awakened is in there, but it's distilled very nicely into "the spice must flow" and "the sleeper must awaken," some great quotable dialogue.

Not in the Movie: Fremen Polygamy and Harah's Relationship to Alia

MB: The whole Fremen marriage/partnership ritual is not touched upon at all in the Lynch movie. In a deleted scene, we see Paul kill Jamis and then as part of that, Harah—Jamis' wife—effectively offers herself to Paul as in, "You've defeated my husband, so you can take me as your wife or I can be a maid." Any sexual awakening in Paul is reserved for Chani in the Lynch movie, as much as there's any relationship between Paul and Chani. Stilgar offers to take Jessica as a wife, more for political reasons to strengthen Jessica's position in the tribe and secure his own as well.

Marriage in the Duniverse is, particularly for the great houses, arranged marriages or multiple wives. The Emperor is trying to conceive a son and the Bene Gesserit [is] having their own way and not conceiving sons for the Emperor. It's more Middle Ages; there is very little love. That's partly why Jessica's betrayal of the Bene Gesserit has such an impact, because she does actually love Duke Leto.

In the novel, Harah's first husband Jeff—great space name, Jeff—was killed by Jamis, who we learn is a bit of a hothead. He challenges Paul, and Paul defeats him, so Harah now has a potential third husband. She's got two children, one from Jeff and one from Jamis, who Paul effectively treats as his sons although he never actually married Harah. She becomes a companion to Paul and Jessica and a nanny to Alia, who is pre-born, so she's got all the ancestral memories of the Reverend Mothers. Alia is not like the other children, which frightens the heck out of the Fremen. Harah is almost like a bodyguard to Alia, trying to act as that buffer between the Fremen culture and this abomination. There's a deleted scene between Jessica and Harah where Alia comes in. That ended up on the Koch special edition as well.

(Practically) Not in the Movie: Duncan Idaho

MB: Duncan's death is massively simplified in the Lynch film. One of the adaptations Lynch did was to simplify Paul and Jessica's escape, because in the novel they're in a 'thopter, they defeat the Harkonnens, they escape and meet up with Duncan and Kynes, they get into another 'thopter, escape into a sandstorm, and it crashes. There's a double 'thopter ride, and Lynch condensed that into a single 'thopter ride, which makes a lot of sense. That does mean we don't get Duncan's last stand against the Sardaukar in the same way. We see his last stand as Paul and Jessica are being taken out of the Arrakeen palace. Duncan's character is almost unnecessary in the Lynch film. If it wasn't for the fact that he wanted to do *Dune Messiah*, you could eliminate Duncan from the Lynch film, without it making any difference. He's played by Richard Jordan, who was in *Logan's Run*.

Although he's killed off in the first book, Duncan returns in all of the five subsequent novels written by Frank Herbert, and is a core character, particularly in *Dune Messiah* when he's reunited with Paul. Practically all of *Dune Messiah* is about what Duncan Idaho is going to do. In Lynch's [film], he's got three scenes, none of those particularly important. Anyone could have told Paul to go see his dad. Anyone could have told Leto about the Fremen. When he's killed, he could just be another random friend for the impact it has on the story. It's disappointing that he was one of the casualties of trying to reduce the 600-page novel into a 2-hour-17-minute film. That's part of the problem of the Lynch film: they're trying to be too faithful. It's like, "We've got to have Piter, we've got to have Duncan, we've got to have Thufir, we've got to have all of these characters." If you knew you were just going to do one film, you could strip out a lot of those characters because you could tell a simpler story. Trying to be true to the novel, you need all those characters, particularly Duncan, and you then can't tell their story effectively.

The following individuals were interviewed
by the author for this section:

—Kyle MacLachlan (Actor, "Paul Atreides")

—Sean Young (Actor, "Chani")

—Alicia Witt (Actor, "Alia")

—Virginia Madsen (Actor, "Princess Irulan")

—Molly Wryn (Actor, "Harah")

—Danny Corkill (Actor, "Orlop")

—Raffaella De Laurentiis (Producer)

—Thom Mount (President of Universal Pictures, 1976–83)

—Frank Price (President of Universal Pictures, 1983–86)

—David Paich (Composer, Toto)

—Steve Lukather (Composer, Toto)

—Penelope Shaw Sylvester (Assistant Editor)

—Barry Nolan (Special Photographic Effects)

—John Dykstra (Visual Effects Supervisor, Apogee, Inc.)

—Eric Swenson (Visual Effects, Motion Control)

—Richard Malzahn (Visual Effects Graphics, Storyboard Artist)

—Bob Ringwood (Costume Designer)

—Mary Vogt (Costume Assistant)

—Steve Maslow (Sound Mixer)

—Frederick Elmes (Additional Unit Cinematographer)

—Craig Campobasso (Production Office Assistant)

—Ian Woolf (DGA Trainee)

—Kenneth George Godwin (Production Documentarian)

—Paul M. Sammon (Universal Pictures Publicity Executive)

—Terri Hardin (Stillsuit Fabrication, Stunt Double)

—Renato Casaro (Poster Artist)

—John Pattyson (EPK Producer)

—Alex Cox (Director, *Repo Man*)

Upon completing his lead performance in the biggest science-fiction movie ever made, Kyle MacLachlan found himself strangely adrift. In the months after wrapping Dune *in September 1983, he was in New York auditioning unsuccessfully for several plays, including Neil Simon's* Biloxi Blues. *Eventually, he found himself sleeping on a friend's couch in Seattle as he refocused on stage work.*

KYLE MACLACHLAN: After I was cast and after we filmed the movie, I couldn't work in film or television in a production until *Dune* came out. Kind of restrictive, but I was like, "Oh, that's fine. I'll find something else to do." But I didn't realize how critical that was because it meant all my eggs were in the *Dune* basket. A lot of times people hedge on you, they bet on you. "He's going to be in *Dune*? Okay, I'll cast him for this and I'll cast him for this . . ." If one movie doesn't work, maybe the other one does. You have a few options if the movie you're in doesn't work, and I didn't have that option . . . So, I went back and did a play at the Tacoma Actors Guild, just went back to theater, and then that play transferred.

The transfer of that show—playing seminarian Mark in Bill C. Davis' Mass Appeal*—allowed MacLachlan the chance to spend some downtime with Frank Herbert at his ecological haven in Port Townsend.*

KYLE MACLACHLAN: He showed me his place. It was really fun to see. Really. I mean, he was such a lovely guy. The play went up to Port Townsend for a couple of weeks in the summer, I did a fun thing up there near Frank, and we hung out. We went up on the boat. It was like meeting a hero.

MacLachlan and Eric Dunham founded the wine company Pursued by Bear in 2005, which is based in Walla Walla, Washington. Some of Herbert's ecological concerns have crept their way into the actor's own Pacific Northwest business cultivation.

KYLE MACLACHLAN: I'm certainly aware of it. In the process of winemaking, you want to have as little impact as possible on the quality of what you're doing. I guess in some ways that's similar to Frank's outlook. He dabbled in so many different things and had so many different interests. He had an insatiable curiosity about that stuff. The thing that always struck me about him was that he was able to take all these varied interests and research arenas and use them to form a book and a structure and a story that's pretty airtight. My mind doesn't work like that. I was so impressed by that. Everything relates to something else. Everything has a position and a reason to be there. It's very balanced. This happens, and then this happens, and this is how the planet got to be like this. Everything is connected.

Even before the film wrapped, a rift developed between John Dykstra's Apogee, Inc. and the De Laurentiis organization. It was a business relationship that had begun promisingly, with Apogee beating out the Van der Veer Photo Effects company that had previously done visual effects for King Kong *and* Flash Gordon.

JOHN DYKSTRA: The bidding process was the way a bidding process always is: We went and met with the director and the producers and read the script and broke it down into an evaluation of what shots were and what those shots cost. The component that is always the differentiating issue beyond cost is whether or not the creatives agree with the assessment you've made of the written page. I got along really well with David Lynch, and we seemed to hit it off. The numbers were appropriate for what they wanted to do.

BARRY NOLAN: Eventually *Dune* came along. They approached us. We didn't bid; we wrote up techniques as to how we might do the effects.

RICHARD MALZAHN: I think Dykstra came to the table with a much more extensive pitch. Apogee at that time had a lot of clout, a lot of people; they had big departments that had done big things. They were an impressive group, they really were. Barry went in and pitched it, but we were all assuming we were going to get it because of the history with the De Laurentiis Group. Then we saw in the trades that Apogee got the gig. It was really disappointing because everybody wants to work on a big sci-fi blockbuster.

BARRY NOLAN: They decided to go with Dykstra. He pulled in Carlo Rambaldi from *King Kong* to do the mechanical worms.

JOHN DYKSTRA: The sandworms were the big deal. We were pursuing the environments primarily with matte paintings. The 'thopters and Harkonnen ships and a lot of the hardware were going to be miniatures. The sandworms were going to be animatronic. It was a weird combination of miniatures with an animatronic worm, and we were going to build scalar deserts with scalar sand, which we'd already explored on *Battlestar Galactica*. We were going to move the sandworms through that environment while photographing it at high frame rates, which gives you scale. The microballoons were these five-micron-diameter glass beads that we used for snow, and it was very effective in a scalar sense for replicating sand. We made avalanches with it [for *Avalanche Express*]. We wanted to figure out a way to color it and make that become our desert, to build a big miniature. The stuff is permeable, so we were going to move a real animatronic model that would not be motor-driven. It would be puppeteered, but with all manner of articulation in terms of the worm being able to move and the opening of the mouth or maw and what the interior of the maw looked like.

Apogee had been in Mexico preparing various bluescreen stages, models, and storyboards for many months. In his Dune *production diary, Kenneth George Godwin wrote on June 18, 1983 (Day 90 of filming), that "The Apogee people are all gloomy because David doesn't have a practical idea of what's involved in the effects work and Raffaella doesn't want to pay for what they're asking Apogee to deliver." By June 26 (Day 98)—with some screentests for the sandworms already in the can—Dykstra had officially vacated the movie and—like MacLachlan—had no signed contract at the time. Barry Nolan had just returned from Tahiti after completing work on the De Laurentiis production of* The Bounty.

BARRY NOLAN: About 90% into production, Raffaella called me. They had a shot with the dirty dude, the Baron. Alia zaps the Baron with her powers, and he spins off. The building rips apart, and he flies out into the air and gets swallowed by a worm. He spins. Dykstra wanted $30,000 to build a special device to make the camera spin. She said, "Can you help me?" I said I have such a device I built for *Flash Gordon* to make the spaceships rotate. She said, "How much do you want to rent it?" I said, "Well, I built it for you guys, so you can have it for free." We sent it to her, and then a couple of days after that, she called me and said, "I have a ticket for you to get on a plane tomorrow morning. Will you come here and visit me?" I went to Mexico City. They were almost finished shooting, and I sat down to have lunch with her and Sting. We talked about the things I could do. She never asked for a price or a bid. She asked if I could do all these things. I said yes, and I was hired. Apparently, every time they made a slight move for something different, Dykstra wanted a lot of money for it. They were getting tired of dishing out money for him.

JOHN DYKSTRA: De Laurentiis didn't want to pay taxes. All right? It's that simple. The profit margin on the work would have been wiped out if we had been taxed for it. We're a California corporation. At that time, there was a big court case going on as to whether services were taxable events. In other words, if you bought an object, you paid California sales tax on it. If you did a service, you didn't pay tax on it. The state was suing for the idea that there'd be a California sales tax on services. Since the work was being produced in California—the finished work and the corporation were there—we would have been taxed. I don't know what it was, 7.25% or whatever. I went to Dino and I said, "Here's the deal: pay the taxes, put it into an escrow account so if the lawsuit is found for the state and those taxes become due, then that escrow account goes to the state. If the state loses, then you can have the money back." He said, "No, I don't pay taxes." And that was it.

RICHARD MALZAHN: Apogee were a very talented group. They had seven owners or whatever they had. That's a tough thing to have seven captains pulling you in different directions. Dykstra was famous when I started. You hear stories about no budget ceilings, spending money. If you're going to pick the biggest, gnarliest project to do, *Dune* is right up there.

ERIC SWENSON: The way I heard it—and I'm a young, impressionable 23-year-old back then—was that Apogee were spending all of Raffaella's money. She didn't like the way the money was being spent, like for the Blue Max.

JOHN DYKSTRA: There was equipment, we had all our motion control equipment down there, we had model makers making various things, the 'thopter being one of the most important parts.

ERIC SWENSON: Wow, I remember that really super-incredibly complicated ornithopter, the gold one with a whole control panel that ran it and a whole series of relays with all the legs and stuff could come out in a certain way. I think Raffaella was more along the lines of puppeteering it with a couple of sticks and wires and things like that. Apogee went way heavy on the electronics.

RICHARD MALZAHN: That 'thopter they built was crazy. I mean, it was really cool. It did all this stuff, but when you look at the number of shots it's in, it's got 6 seconds of screen time and you've spent I don't know how many hundreds of thousands of dollars. The talent is crazy, but at some point, you've got to do this on a budget.

JOHN DYKSTRA: There was a lot of R&D that went into the worm. Then there are the design and execution of things like the shields and how those work. We were in the process of breaking all of that down, working with David to come up with what the concept images were going to be. Before we got into the real production of much beyond the 'thopter, the issue came up with the money, and we had to back out.

BARRY NOLAN: Raffaella said he constantly kept jacking the prices on things. The ornithopter was one of the most expensive models in it. For the fact that it was just a model that opened up and closed, it was a very expensive model.

At one point, Raffaella told Ed Naha that it seemed as if it was going to cost her $30,000 every time Apogee turned on a camera in Los Angeles, as opposed to her supervising her own (more frugal) team in Mexico.

RAFFAELLA DE LAURENTIIS: If I said that, it's probably true, but I just think that it was going to put the budget at a place where it would have really, really been a disaster. It's a leap of faith looking at it from the outside, but when you were in it, I really saw what was going on. It was going to be a disaster.

RICHARD MALZAHN: I hate to say it, but Raffaella works on a budget. She's a producer's producer. "Come in on budget"—that's her deal. Ultimately, the problem was budgetary. It wasn't creative; Apogee was always ahead of the curve on that.

JOHN DYKSTRA: Raffaella was in on it. I like Raffaella; we got along fine, met up from time to time later on in subsequent environments, but there was no problem with it. There weren't creative problems. There weren't political problems. It came down to money. Dino didn't pay taxes. That's why he was exiled. He couldn't return to Italy because they wanted him for tax evasion. He couldn't go home for a long time.

CRAIG CAMPOBASSO: That was not pretty. John and Raffaella got into a big fight, and he was no longer on the movie.

KENNETH GEORGE GODWIN: The thing with Apogee was they had done some really big productions up to that point. They were one of the top companies, so I'm sure their prices were pretty high at that time. They were hired because the company wanted good quality and these were the guys. As production goes on, you're doing budget meetings, you're crunching this, you're cutting that; they just started trimming what was available for the effects work.

DAVID PAICH: They had been working on it so long that you could see the car was eventually going to run out of gas, which in the movie people's cases is budget. You only have so much budget, and I think David was afraid he would get shortchanged on special effects, which always are the last things to be put in place on movies.

RICHARD MARZAHN: We get the call from Raffaella, and all of a sudden, we're just scrambling around to deal with it.

BARRY NOLAN: We came on, and 95% of the Dykstra crew went home. We went back to Los Angeles and picked up all the materials they had, all the VistaVision negatives/prints at Apogee. They shot some bluescreen stuff, some miniature stuff.

JOHN DYKSTRA: I said, "I'm done. I can't do this deal." That was it. I was hugely invested with it, and then when it was no longer something I was going to participate in, I lost interest. Not because I lost interest in the story, or the creative concepts, or David Lynch, but because I went, "Well, there's no point in aggravating over this. There's nothing I can do about it." I talked to David before I left. He goes, "I get it." He worked with Dino; he understood. The thing that was so easy about it is it was too big a gamble. It was fiscally irresponsible for me on behalf of my partners in the company to agree to that kind of a deal. I couldn't do it.

BARRY NOLAN: Dykstra was going to do bluescreens, and they had developed a system called the Blue Max with the 3M material. We shot all that with the Dykstra people. They had a special camera and everything set up. They stayed on. We had two stages with the giant 3M screens on them. One was a big back of the worm that everybody was riding on. All of that stuff was shot in VistaVision. That was all the Dykstra people did.

ERIC SWENSON: A couple of Apogee guys were there because they were the only ones that knew how to operate the ornithopter—they were there to run it.

JOHN DYKSTRA: They had motion control systems because that was part of the close of the deal. There was a potential lawsuit involved because of contractual shit. All it is was a way to make us burn money to try to force the issue, so we agreed to rent them the equipment we had in Mexico, because it had already been transported down there. That remained on site, and was used by whoever ended up using it.

ERIC SWENSON: There was no Apogee motion control there at all when I arrived. I would've loved to work with their motion control. Ours was so crude. It was just a series of switches that I would have to switch on all at the same time.

KENNETH GEORGE GODWIN: From what I heard, it was pretty much unequivocally that Dykstra reached a point where he said, "I can't deliver work I would be happy with on the money that you're now providing." I suppose that might sound like a slight to whoever came after who said, "Yeah, we can do it cheap."

PAUL M. SAMMON: There was no plan to cheap out on the special effects. Apogee did the FX for everything from *Star Trek: The Motion Picture* to Tom Hanks' *Big*, and was on *Dune* from prep through some of production, but contractual disputes caused Apogee to pull out during the shoot. That left *Dune* without a specific special effects company at the worst possible moment.

ERIC SWENSON: Barry was a scientist. On *Flash Gordon*, he created the EOB, the first electronic printer. That was basically the start of laser scanning and CG getting film into a computer. I didn't consider him to have a lot of art in it, but there were art directors around and a lot of people who had the creativity that kept it going. Barry had Richard Malzahn, my mate at school. Very talented artist.

RICHARD MALZAHN: I was the resident art guy. We had matte painters, but I was the only one who had art training.

BARRY NOLAN: Richard Malzahn and Eric Swenson came from the University of Long Beach. We were on the movie for a year. The Dykstra people didn't put anything together. They gave us completion dates for different pieces of it. We really had to work long, long hours to meet those completion dates.

CRAIG CAMPOBASSO: Then they brought in Van der Veer Photo Effects which, umm . . . if you look at some of the visual effects, it's like high school. The ornithopter is a block of wood spray-painted gold, and it's moving across the screen. I remember seeing that and going, "That is just horrible." A lot of times they didn't have things, so they'd use Ron Miller's actual airbrush paintings as the background. I understand producers and budget and what they have left, but I think *Dune* would have been so much more spectacular with John Dykstra doing the effects.

KENNETH GEORGE GODWIN: There are some effects in the film which are—even by 1984 standards—a little bit dodgy, but there had been very few films done on this scale. Everybody's still figuring out a lot of stuff. This was pre-CGI, so it was all done optically with miniatures, composites, and so on.

PAUL M. SAMMON: Raffaella quickly sent out a worldwide distress call and pulled together—in an admirably short time—a substitute international VFX crew. This inadvertently became another bruise on the production. Apogee was obviously one of the world's top-tier effects companies. If they'd completed the picture, I'm sure the overall VFX quality of *Dune* would have, at the very least, been more of a piece.

JOHN DYKSTRA: It was all about money. We could have done the movie. Working with what they had, they did a fine job on that movie. There's some stuff that's cheesy, but you've got to remember there were no computers then, right? You had to physically put subjects in front of the camera and photograph them and deal with real world physics, including optics and depth of field. You couldn't cut and paste, you couldn't do a Photoshop job on anything. You had to do photochemical composites, which for multiple-element compositing was a real nightmare. We were set up to do that and ILM North was set up to do that, but nobody else was. They were trying to assemble the aircraft while they were flying.

Once the Van der Veer team was in place, they quickly began fashioning plans to work within the budget and time limitations they had.

BARRY NOLAN: One of my business associates, Richard Malzahn, came with me. Richard sat down with Mr. Lynch and redid all of Apogee's storyboards. David had a second chance to redo things the way he wanted. David changed his mind a lot. He said, "If it's been done before, I don't want to do it again. I don't want any of this high technology showing up in the picture. I want something that looks different."

ERIC SWENSON: He was an experimenter. He wanted to see what he could do that nobody's seen before but also fit his vision for the film. Make it as "weird" as he could. I can't say he would use that word—that's just me summarizing it in one word. Every director wants it done like it's never been done before. They want to break new ground, and effects people want to do that, too.

RICHARD MALZAHN: Well, they all do, and they want to see it on your reel. "I want something I've never seen before . . . can you show me something like that on your reel?"

ERIC SWENSON: *Star Wars* and *2001* would be the last thing you would want to do. It's kind of funny because the Guild Heighliner has a *Star Wars*-ian look: The long tube with the plates and panels and greebles and nurnies all over it.

RICHARD MALZAHN: When we started, I was put on as a storyboard artist to work with David. They gave me an office and a bunch of art supplies. I'd meet with David for an hour every day, sit with all his Woody Woodpecker dolls, and we'd talk about *Dune*. When Apogee was doing it, it was a one-stop-shop; they could talk in shorthand. Now it was an international crew doing the visual effects, and David felt he had to be very specific on this stuff because he was dealing with a bunch of people that didn't know each other. The ball was rolling, and we came in to get the rest of it done. I don't think there was a lot of fat left on the bone by the time we got there. They revisited it a few times and said, "Look, this is what we can do."

*After principal photography wrapped in September of '83, the remaining shoot at Churubusco revolved around miniature photography, with English model builder Brian Smithies (*Superman, The Dark Crystal*) now in charge of fabricating a virtual armada of ships and vehicles as well as settings like Giedi Prime city. They managed to accomplish six months of work in roughly two months.*

BARRY NOLAN: Most of the miniatures were shot in Mexico City. Brian wasn't under me; he worked for Raffaella, brought in at the same time I was. He went to Los Angeles and hired model people, including Danielle Versè. I worked with Danielle afterward doing models for me. I designed and built a snorkel system that they used to shoot some of the miniatures, with the lenses on a long tube that hangs down at a diagonal line so you can get right up close on things and move through things. I leased our motion control system to them, and they brought it down and set it up on a stage.

RICHARD MALZAHN: The motion control system we used on *Dune* was embarrassing . . . okay? Embarrassing.

BARRY NOLAN: We had been working on the computer interface to run the motion control. That requires a lot of redesigning the circuit boards. Each motor was run by an indexer that we could set up to plot out the moves. Eric Swenson did that.

ERIC SWENSON: There was no computer involved; it was just steppers on switches. We figured out how to link all the motors to turn on with one switch—that's about as good as it got. There's one shot when you're going into Giedi Prime, and the camera's moving forward and it goes up. You can see it go "bwwweeerp" because it's all the machine can do. It couldn't ramp any slower. No curves of any kind, just a ramp that would go up, across, and then back down. Trying to get something interesting looking and smooth out of that was difficult. We were mostly limited to very simple flyby shots. Luckily, most of the stuff in the show was pondering. The Harkonnen ships and Giedi Prime stuff were very David Lynch, plodding along.

Lynch describes the motion control apparatus in his autobiography as looking akin to "a child's wagon" on rails, held together by Band-Aids, lamp cords, and bare wires.

BARRY NOLAN: Dykstra wanted to shoot everything, including the worms, in Los Angeles. They were going to shoot them outdoors because they were shooting four or five times normal speed. They felt it was best shooting in sunlight—they would have an awful lot of light. Raffaella didn't want to shoot them in Los Angeles; she wanted to stay there in Mexico. I saw the tests that they did. I'd previously worked with Carlo Rambaldi on *King Kong*—we were somewhat good friends. They had it all set up there in L.A. Dykstra said there's so much smog in Mexico City, it's going to cut down on the light level, which I thought was kind of iffy.

RICHARD MALZAHN: Barry's a smart man, good at taking the idea and distilling it down to get the essence of that idea and not lose a lot visually. Very good at problem solving. His agenda was different than Apogee's. His agenda was, "How can we make this work on the money you have?" Apogee's was, "Well, this will be fun. Let's go for it, see what happens." Apogee worked on big, huge budgets, and this probably had a big, huge budget, but not big enough. This one needed an unlimited budget. [*laughs*]

BARRY NOLAN: Everything Apogee was doing—except for the Blue Max stuff—was pretty much the same way I would do it. The microballoons, the 3M stuff that gives you cancer, were mixed with paint powder to give them color because microballoons are what's on 3M Scotchlite. It pours/flows like miniature sand, because they're round balls. It'll flow just like sand will when sand gets up to a certain point in height and starts to slide down. We used microballoons in the foreground sets of all the miniatures where the worms were. We had some shots that we had to do extreme closeups, so they built fake dunes out of plaster and smoothed them down because when we get close to them, you would see the texture. Sand doesn't behave naturally if you over-crank it, but microballoons did. I didn't know that was Dykstra's decision, but it was a good one.

RICHARD MALZAHN: David watched dailies, and if he didn't like something or wanted to move something around, they did go back and shoot it again. David's strength is he doesn't micromanage. He allows people to do their work. He's not necessarily a technical director; he's an emotional director. There are technical directors that say, "Okay, we have to do XYZ to get here." David felt it.

BARRY NOLAN: I was not there during the shooting, but my technicians were running all the equipment. When we did *Flash Gordon*, we had such large bluescreens that the lighting people developed what they called a "Dino light": They took aircraft landing lights—which are run off DC and are 24 volt or maybe 1000 watt—and they put 24 of them on a panel and called them Dino lights. They made lots of them. Lee Electric in England started producing them. We had a dozen or so of these Dino lights to light the desert. The sequence where the worm comes up to swallow the harvester was done outside, but the other worm stuff was done inside.

One Dykstra choice that fell by the wayside was the decision to shoot effects shots in the VistaVision format. Only 10% of VFX shots had already been done in Vista, so Nolan switched over to his preferred format of 4-perf.

ERIC SWENSON: Van der Veer was one of the few houses in the world that had VistaVision optical printing capabilities. They had a VistaVision rotoscope camera as well because they had worked on *Tron*. The difference between VistaVision and 4-perf is horizontal and vertical. Film goes through a camera vertically, with four perforations on the side of a film frame. As it gets moved, it goes down. VistaVision goes sideways through the camera, and it's 8-perf, twice as big. Basically, the size of a 35-millimeter film frame. With twice the image area, you have less degradation every time they go through an optical process making mattes, dupes, inner negatives, and inner positives. Every time you go through that, you were degrading the image, so the bigger the image you start with makes it better in the end. That's why they used VistaVision during *Star Wars* and all those effects films. I can't think of any good technical reason to switch to 4-perf. I can think of a money reason to do it, because of the amount of film. I could see a resources problem, because they had four optical printers and three of them were 4-perf and only one of them was VistaVision and it'd be working all the time.

Freddie Francis had originally intended to leave Dune *at the end of principal photography, but stayed on at the beginning of post to supervise the miniature worm photography to make sure it was in sync with his first unit work.*

BARRY NOLAN: Once Freddie thought it was in good hands, he left. David wanted black smoke on stages in the background with the worms, and the only way they could get black smoke was to burn rubber tires. We would set the shot up, get ready to shoot, start burning the rubber tires . . . we all have masks on . . . shoot the shot, and then everybody would run off the stage until it was vented and cleaned. I had to duplicate it afterward, I can put black smoke over things, but he wanted the depth of interaction. He likes stuff flying through the air and dirt and cruddy stuff and things like that. At one point, I was getting ready to do a picture called *Total Recall* for Dino with David Cronenberg. I met Cronenberg in Italy at the airport to talk about *Total Recall*, and he said one thing he noticed about *Dune* was it was so dirty. [*laughs*] I said, "That's the way David wanted it!" He wanted us to make things to clutter the air up, debris and little specks of dirt flying through.

ERIC SWENSON: Working with an artist, creating an artist's vision was exciting and inspirational. I'm pretty young then, and to be put into that role at that level was eye opening. It was a phenomenal experience to work with somebody who had that kind of take on the world. I know that was the thing, "Why are you giving this guy this big, major effects film?" Everybody's got to do their first one.

BARRY NOLAN: David didn't always understand the effects process, but he knew what he wanted. I did *Bill & Ted's Excellent Adventure*, and at three o'clock in the morning on the last night of shooting, the director wanted me to explain how this whole thing went together. All I wanted to do was go to bed. "It'll go together, just believe me." I didn't get questions like that from David. I would tell him the pieces that needed to be made. He left how we put them together to us.

Since Lynch specifically did not wish to use stop-motion for the sandworms, mechanical puppeteering was employed on the microballoon desert miniatures, shot at high frame rates. Often these shots would be unusable because the worms would look too . . . phallic.

BARRY NOLAN: My famous quote: "There goes our PG rating." In one shot, Paul has control over the worms, and in the background, there are three worms standing up. They looked like three big penises standing up in the air. We changed that so they were down on the ground. He wanted the worms live. It had been mentioned several times when they were looking for people. I talked about miniature worms, and I talked about stop motion and various things. David pooh-poohed stop motion as a technique he didn't want to use.

Bluescreen technology was still in relative infancy at this point, but Nolan considered himself to be the best in the business at it. Still, the $50,000 Blue Max system proved formidable at 33'×108', the largest bluescreen ever made at the time.

ERIC SWENSON: Barry was one of the best in the world at pulling a bluescreen matte. There were a lot of companies, including ILM, that would go to him for pulling out the tricky stuff, but even the bluescreen technology wasn't all that great. Sometimes you would be trying to eliminate blurs because you couldn't pull a good matte off of it. The ornithopters were flybys that, in the end, I think we probably should have shot on wires to get a little more motion blur to them.

BARRY NOLAN: The whole sequence with everybody on top of the worm was shot with the Blue Max. We did have one problem: We got an internal ghost reflection of the people in it. We had to work hard to eliminate that. I told the Dykstra people about it. The three or four people he left on had built the 3M screen. We were friends with them, we worked with them. There was no animosity.

ERIC SWENSON: Barry had to take over the whole Blue Max thing. That was a pretty expensive process with a giant reflective screen made out of little 4-inch squares of Scotchlite, all sewn together by Mexican craftsmen. It was a pretty elaborate thing, and then after the shoot, it all just got thrown away and we all walked away with little souvenir pieces.

One major incident in October 1983 involved a fire that destroyed a soundstage (Stage 8) housing a Blue Max bluescreen built by John Dykstra's Apogee team.

JOHN DYKSTRA: What else is new?

BARRY NOLAN: Somewhere in the middle of shooting, Raffaella and I were talking, and she got a phone call that one of the stages had caught fire. She was really freaked out, I'll tell you, when she heard that.

IAN WOOLF: We had a fire on one of the stages, a bluescreen we used. I don't know how it started, but they were able to put it out before it got to any of our sets.

FREDERICK ELMES: That was not a pleasant thing. It was an accident that probably could have been avoided. Somebody got a little sloppy and lit the thing on fire.

GILES MASTERS: That was funny. To protect the 3M screen—it was fragile—they put a curtain over it. In those days, everybody was smoking, but not on that stage, to make sure it was as safe as possible.

JOHN DYKSTRA: The sets were built wall-to-wall. The temperature on the sets was incredibly high, especially on that stage because the Blue Max didn't produce any heat, it just put out blue light, but in order to light the subject matter that was in front of the screen and carry the stop, you had to have a lot of lights.

FREDERICK ELMES: Part of the trick of that Blue Max, in particular the worm shots, was because it's a miniature, you had to shoot at a very high frame rate. It requires multiple times lighter to get the exposure up there. The scale of that sand dune set the worms worked in was gigantic, the better part of the stage. It required an enormous amount of light, hence heat.

JOHN DYKSTRA: The overheads where the lights were could be as high as 130 or 140 degrees. They were old, all wooden stages. It was an accident waiting to happen.

GILES MASTERS: It was a lamp or something that sparked. The curtain covering the screen caught fire. As this whole thing went up in flames, the still photographer turned to David Lynch and said, "Uh, is it all right if I smoke now, guvnor?"

BARRY NOLAN: I turned to Raffaella and said, "I'll show you how to do it real cheap and just as good." We went outside into the backlot and built a bluescreen about 10 to 15 feet high and about 30 or 40 feet long, then built a desert in front of it. I said, "These people are all in black, the desert is white. We've got a bluescreen on there. We've got so many easy ways to pull mattes off of it." They built a scaffolding up 40 feet into the air to shoot it all, and that's the way we shot it. I've done lots of exterior bluescreens where we just lit them with sunlight. I said, "You can collect the insurance, and we'll do it cheaper. You can make some money on the deal!"

Shooting on the new, old-fashioned, hand-painted, sunlit bluescreen erected on the backlot wound up saving time as well, as all the shots intended for the Blue Max were shot in three days as opposed to the allotted three weeks.

RICHARD MALZAHN: The Achilles heel of *Dune* was money. I think David suffered on *Dune* because he had big ideas, and budget limited his big ideas. You hire David when you have some money and you're willing to let him do his thing.

BARRY NOLAN: At one point in Mexico City, Dino said, "Stop." Both David and I got really upset because we weren't quite finished yet. Dino didn't want to spend any more money. That's what Pepe told me: "Dino says you guys have got to stop. You're spending too much money."

ERIC SWENSON: Not that there was any threat to our jobs or anything, because we were staff. I remember Dino just being done. Done with it. You had to finish.

BARRY NOLAN: We kept right on working. Nobody pulled the plug on me. I worked just as hard. We didn't stop. We kept on going until we got it. Once we got back, I was off the payroll for them; they were just paying for effects they wanted. Usually, I'd sit and break down every effect and lay a price on them. I was never asked to do that because I had worked with them before. We had a good relationship on other movies. Prices were fair—we were not a real expensive optical facility.

RICHARD MALZAHN: Part of you says, "Oh, wow, the opportunity is crazy!" But it's all money. You're almost better off with a little show where you have a reasonably good budget and you can expand it, as opposed to a huge show that you have to figure out what you're going to cut out because you can't afford to do it all. "Pick 10 things you're going to get rid of." That's hard because it's such an elaborate story.

After model photography ended in January/February 1984, the Van der Veer crew regrouped once again in L.A. for months of optical work and insert shots, working right up to the film's completion in November '84.

CRAIG CAMPOBASSO: When they returned from Mexico, we left the Universal lot and moved into Van der Veer. They wanted to take the film away from prying eyes that might slip into our offices in the middle of the night. People want to see stuff as it's going on, and filmmakers don't want to show anything until something's ready.

BARRY NOLAN: We had a two-story building in Burbank where Van der Veer was, and the top floor was empty. We leased it to Raffaella, and David's office was up there. I thought, "This is kind of a stupid idea bringing her into the building." I told her that afterward. "What will this be like when I've got you over me all the time?" But it worked out beautifully! I could go up and talk to David anytime, or bring him down to show something. David was at our beck and call, total communication with each other. He told us what he wanted. He wasn't a nitpicker.

ERIC SWENSON: Shooting all these little intimate scenes with David and Barry . . . it was just the three of us a lot of the time. Didn't even have a camera assistant, that was it. I would light it, then Barry would come in and put his meter up.

BARRY NOLAN: The big spaceships were shot in Mexico, but all the fog elements and clouds they fly through, we shot with cloud tanks in Burbank.

ERIC SWENSON: I remember that more fondly and with more ownership than when we're going through the Guild Heighliner or shooting ornithopters or any of the stuff we did over five months in Mexico. That stuff doesn't stick with me nearly as much as the stuff later, like the giant vagina for the birthing sequence. The model shop made a giant tube, almost three feet across, all made out of foam. On the inside, it had all the inner walls of a birthing canal, probably 15 feet long. I strung it on wires from the ceiling. We had a camera—with that long snorkel lens on it—on a big pole that went through this tunnel. We put lights on it and lights through it. Everybody was squeezing/hugging it to get it to undulate, and we just rammed the camera through it. That was the giant vagina, another one of these fun pickup shots!

BARRY NOLAN: One of the big problems that they kept putting aside was the blue eyes. They tried dyeing people's eyes, they tried contact lenses. They had Digital Productions—one of the big CGI graphics companies in Los Angeles with a Cray computer—do them, but it didn't look very good. David wasn't happy with it, and they wanted more than double what I wanted for it.

RICHARD MALZAHN: At that point, Raffaella was a little bit gun-shy of big ideas because the Apogee experience wasn't as good as it could have been for her. She felt a more traditional approach was in her best interest. A movie that size has a lot of unknowns. All these people are saying, "Oh, this'll work, that'll work." Then you get in there, and it may or may not work. It gets financially/budgetarily a little bit terrifying. When somebody comes to you at that point in time and says, "Hey, I got this computer, and it'll do all this stuff for you without a problem . . ."

BARRY NOLAN: I said, "Well, give me a piece that you shot, and I'll run the test on it." I developed a technique that could do the blue eyes quite easily. It didn't turn them blue; it just turned the white of the eyes blue. They look like normal eyes but the white was blue, and it worked. They're all rotoscoped. I developed a special optical technique in order to put them together to not make it look like they glowed. I produced something really quick for them, and they said, "That's it." I had no budget. The only thing I ever gave them a price on was to do the eyes, which was $250,000.

RICHARD MALZAHN: It's the Egyptian approach: Throw a lot of people at it.

BARRY NOLAN: The other thing that they were holding off on was the shields.

RICHARD MALZAHN: That was David's design, the translucent box around them.

BARRY NOLAN: David told me how he wanted the shield to look. I gave one of my animators back in L.A. a piece of material, and he did it. On the first go, David said, "That's it. That's the way I want it." That was the next problem that we resolved.

RICHARD MALZAHN: He was a good communicator—he said, "This is what I want," we did it, and he'd go, "Yep, that's what I want." Then it was just a matter of a bunch of rotoscope, optical camera testing, and a bunch of labor to make this thing work.

BARRY NOLAN: It was all rotoscoped and animated. I would have liked to have gone to something more nebulous, but David liked it that way.

RICHARD MALZAHN: We essentially roto a scene with an outline of the people. Jeff Burks and I split the animation part between the two of us. We'd animate the shape as a whole, then we'd break out the individual facets. The mattes for those would go into optical, and each facet would get a different distortion on the background plate, then composited into the scene. It was a simple idea. Implementation was difficult, only because there were so many passes. Sometimes we would combine the same distortion on two facets just to make it a little easier to build in the camera. The girls—I say "girls" because the whole ink and paint department were women—had the brunt of it. They would get stacks and stacks of paper.

ERIC SWENSON: For each one of the facets of the shield, a matte is created. It's a white piece of paper either painted in black or cut out with an X-Acto knife on the white paper and laid on a piece of black, so you get a black matte.

RICHARD MALZAHN: The facets were polygons that we would draw, and then you'd cut them out, so you'd have a piece of paper with a hole in it. You'd have a stack of paper for one facet for however many frames it is. Then you put it down on the roto stand, shoot it on a piece of black paper, and slate it to death to make sure nothing got mixed up. Take that film out of the camera, process it, then give it to the lineup guys. They'd line up the elements, and then the camera would shoot it. They had a bunch of ripple wheels . . .

ERIC SWENSON: In order to create the distortion, I built a little motorized wheel for the optical printer. You've got your camera and your projector . . . that's what an optical printer is, you're re-photographing the film. When you re-photographed that single facet on one pass, there was a little wheel that went through with a little motor. Some of them had epoxy on them, and some I melted. We tried a whole bunch of different wheels shapes, and every time the film ran through the projector, another part of the wheel was being used or going in different directions. Every one of the facets was doing something different to distort the shield.

RICHARD MALZAHN: We wanted a lot of distortion, trying to make it as smooth as possible, sort of a wave. We animated the glints and highlights trying to make it look like they're in a glass box.

Close viewers may notice several shots of both Paul and Gurney during this scene that are obvious stunt doubles, even with all the heavy distortion.

RICHARD MALZAHN: There was probably a discussion along the way: "We need to distort this one more." They did it as much as they thought they needed to in order to get away with what they were doing. From my perspective, the cut was what the cut was. It could have been something as simple as they just didn't have the footage. They were trying to make something else work.

BARRY NOLAN: There was a big optical house in New York doing *Predator*, and they wanted to know how I did the shields. I explained that to them, and possibly they used a similar technique to create the invisibility shield around the monster.

RICHARD MALZAHN: If I got any recognition on the movie at all, it's for that. It was extensive and unique enough that at the time it was like, "Whoa, that's kind of cool."

If the shield-fighting scene in Dune *reminds you of the lightsaber duels in* Star Wars, *there may be a reason for that.*

BARRY NOLAN: I did the lightsabers in *Star Wars*. I did all the rotoscoping and set up the whole process.

ERIC SWENSON: I built a model for the shield corner, these things that floated up above the shield wall model. I got to shoot some of that stuff by myself. Also, the little bullet that could go through Duncan's shield as long as it was in slow motion . . . I made that. Put it on a handrail and shot it.

One scene that was nearly eliminated due to being unworkable was the folding space sequence, which Lynch insisted be included in some form.

ERIC SWENSON: We were really pushing for folding space. "What could it be? How would that look? What did folding space mean?"

RICHARD MALZAHN: All you have to say is "folding space." "Huh. How are you going to do that one?" There aren't words. It's like describing red to a blind man.

ERIC SWENSON: David likes to push the limits. He's like, "Can we do space in reverse?" Like white space with black stars.

BARRY NOLAN: Herbert's folding space was not the same. His was the Navigators looking into the future with the spice. They would try different experiments and see what happened until they found one where everybody wasn't killed. They would pick that one and navigate.

ERIC SWENSON: We were playing with goo and rubber. I made a big fish tank full of Jell-O, then put flakes of plastic in it to be stars, then we'd shake it and the stars would do weird wiggling. We tried a lot of different things to create vibrations, and loud speakers was one of them. I was doing whatever I could to get harmonic moves, 'cause the goo was basically a starfield. I had to look around for something that we could shoot through that was still clear and then something that would hold its space in the goo—which was Methasil—that wouldn't sink to the bottom or float to the top. I end up using a certain size of plastic chips from cutting Plexiglass. Some of that stuff ended up in the film! What a wild fun time! Try the craziest things you can think of to get something super-weird and different.

FREDERICK ELMES: During post-production, Universal decided it was going to be a shorter film. Suddenly some of the visual effects that were part of the story that they promised David weren't going to happen, not on that scale or complexity because it was not such an easy thing to make sophisticated visual effects back then. It's a very complicated process to do that stuff on an optical printer and with animation combined. It was going to be costly and take longer. These were things that the studio wasn't going to spend money on at this point.

ERIC SWENSON: The stress never affected me at all. At that age, it's a lot of energy and sleepless nights and living on, you know, "What's for pizza?" Happy doing it. Never felt the stress of "How are we going to get this done?" Opticals took a long time. I think it was a year after they wrapped in Mexico. Raffaella had this big Apogee crew spending a lot of money. Then she brings in Van der Veer with, like, four guys and a bunch of kids that are getting it done. For no money. Folding space, as an example, could have been a lot more time and a lot more budget, but it wasn't. It was what could be done with whatever was available: Me and Barry. That's what you got.

RICHARD MALZAHN: There was a budget, and then that budget got eaten up a bit by the Apogee thing. Then they said, "Okay, we have to re-group." You come up with a smaller number, then it all comes down to, "What can you afford to do?" It needed more money than it had, and then the way they implemented the front end and the budgetary decisions made early on had an effect down the road. As you get closer and closer to the end, the reality starts crashing. "Well, you still haven't done this, you still haven't done that. This is going to cost more money. You're running out over here, running out over there."

PAUL M. SAMMON: I wouldn't say that the film's eventual uneven VFX were simply a matter of poor workmanship, more the result of time and money. Some of the effects departments on *Dune* did excellent work. On the other hand, some didn't, but having to course-correct in the middle of a huge production and then play unending catch-up definitely had something to do with the uneven shape of the final product.

STEVE LUKATHER: Some of the special effects in the film were temp pieces. Like where Kyle's in the box and it looks totally cheese because it was a temp effect that was never turned into the high-end effect where they were going to make that look like a real cool thing. "Sorry, we don't have any money! Put it in there anyway." Lynch is going, "Fuck! This is not my film!" I can imagine the guy losing his shit.

PENELOPE SHAW SYLVESTER: Another thing that was disappointing to David was some of the special effects, which we looked at and went, "Oh, dear." But that was the top of the art at that point. We're talking about 40 years ago.

ERIC SWENSON: I think what you're describing is part of the charm. *Dune* has the charm of its day like Ray Harryhausen's stuff had the charm of its day. You have that suspension of disbelief to buy into it.

DAVID PAICH: I was not impressed with the special effects. I think he ran out of money; the whole budget was spent. This is just my opinion, that the whole budget had been used to shoot the thing and get the cast together. When it came down to putting the cherried-out Lucas-type of effects that are supposed to be in a film like that, they missed out on a lot of what the special effects could have been. I don't think it was up in that John Dykstra level.

David Lynch looked at numerous musicians and bands to do the film's music (including Giorgio Moroder, the "Father of Disco") before he went with Toto, the rock group led by keyboardist-vocalist David Paich. Also consisting of Steve Lukather on guitars and vocals alongside Steve Porcaro (keyboards), Mike Porcaro (bass guitar, percussion), and Jeff Porcaro (drums, percussion), the group had just released a triple platinum album, Toto IV. *Singles like "Rosanna" and "Africa" catapulted them to mega-stardom. Then their lead vocalist Bobby Kimball left the band, which helped push them in a new direction. It was a somewhat natural progression, as the band leader's father Marty Paich also did music for film and television.*

STEVE LUKATHER: We'd just won Album of the Year. We won every accolade we could get! Really wonderful time. Then our singer kind of went south, and we had to make a change. It was very unfortunate timing, but we found ourselves writing a record that we didn't have a singer for. We took a break and had to regroup. We were looking for something to do to buy us some time before we got back to our own thing. Another project to be creative, make a few bucks, and have a laugh until we found somebody to replace our singer, and these opportunities came up.

DAVID PAICH: I had been interested in film composing since I was 18 or 19. My dad had been scoring the popular TV series *Ironside* with Raymond Burr, a cop thriller. The producer hired me to write a song every week tailor-made to the script, so I started cowriting with my father. He would weave those themes into the music, and I thought that was very clever. Around that time, I met Jerry Goldsmith, who was a colleague of my father's, and he really inspired me. Let me watch a couple of sessions he did. I got bitten by the bug at a very early age. Later, after I'd done certain things, I told myself I'd like to try my hand at film composing.

STEVE LUKATHER: David Paich and his father Marty Paich were really the team leaders on this thing in terms of having the experience of doing this sort of stuff before. It was a big undertaking.

Ultimately, Toto had to choose between two plum projects: Dune *and* Footloose.

DAVID PAICH: *Footloose* was definitely in our wheelhouse.

STEVE LUKATHER: *Footloose* wasn't a score; they just wanted some songs from us because we were the big band at the time. Who knew that was going to sell 12 million albums? You never know with this shit. You hear actors all the time, "I turned down the part that won the Academy Award!" We could have done a track for *Footloose* because I sang lead on a bunch of stuff. David Paich sang lead on fucking "Africa," one of our biggest songs.

DAVID PAICH: *Dune* was just a stroke of luck. Ridley Scott was originally directing it when we found out about it. I was a very big Ridley Scott fan. I knew of David Lynch because he had done *Elephant Man*, which was a great movie.

STEVE LUKATHER: When I heard the name "David Lynch," I had to stop, because I had been a fan since *Eraserhead*. I used to take everybody to see this thing at the Nuart Theatre in Santa Monica. Every couple of weeks, I'd go grab a handful of people and go see it. One of the times we went, Jack Nance was sitting two rows behind us. I turned to one of my buddies and said, "Look, it's Eraserhead!"

DAVID PAICH: When it passed hands from Ridley to David, the band got together and said, "Should we still pursue this?" Jeff Porcaro said that was a definite positive "Yes." It would be a very cool thing to do.

STEVE LUKATHER: When I heard we could possibly work with David Lynch . . . And we were sold on, "It's going to be the new *Star Wars*." Dave was sold the same thing.

Paich was invited to fly to Mexico City during production to meet with David Lynch and play the chords that eventually became the movie's signature theme.

DAVID PAICH: We pursued it, and I flew down. I was able to play my main theme for David Lynch. They loved it and hired us on the spot. He had a Walkman, put this set of phones on me, and said, "Tell me if you can make this kind of music for my movie?" He put on two Shostakovich symphonies: Shostakovich's 5th Symphony and I think it was the 11th or the 13th. He made me listen to these symphonies, and here's my quote from David Lynch: "I want this music LOW, and I want it SLOW." I thought, "Well, I can handle that." This isn't *Star Wars*. He's making the anti-*Star Wars* movie. He wanted me to avoid anything that's uplifting, that's happy, that's joyous, that's compelling. He hates popular movies that make people come and eat popcorn and stuff. Super-nice guy, though. He wanted things low and slow.

STEVE LUKATHER: Always. Always. Sometimes you want to rowdy it up a little bit. We thought, "It's too much. It's too much." It wasn't about us. That's the thing about scoring film—it wasn't about, "Oh, let's dig the Toto music." A lot of people were like, "Who's scoring the film? Those guys?" Like we're going to write "Africa" for the film or something. They didn't realize that we can do all kinds of shit. We worked with Miles Davis, Quincy Jones, Michael Jackson, Steely Dan. We were all over the map.

DAVID PAICH: Everybody was getting a little anxiety, a little stressed by the time we got involved in it. It was the end of the movie, and they wanted the music to be put in there. Lord knows people have differences of opinion about music all the time, but I got along with Lynch great and I think he got along with Steve Lukather and the rest of the band. We had no problem with David.

STEVE LUKATHER: He's such a unique filmmaker and a unique human being. We were working on stuff on and off for about three months together. The weirder it was, the more David liked it. He didn't like real busy stuff, he liked more ominous. We did it all in LA. We worked at Jeff Porcaro's studio, The Villa. David would come a lot when he was still starting to cut the film. We weren't around when they were actually filming anything; it was all afterward in post. Some of the actors would come, like Kyle MacLachlan would hang. Kenny McMillan, who I fucking loved in the film, he was a great cat. It was a positive experience in terms of the hang.

Around this time, a lot of pop musicians like Danny Elfman, Stewart Copeland, Thomas Dolby, Mark Mothersbaugh, and Joe Jackson were getting into film composing. Something was in the air that made movies seem like a viable next step for Paich and his contemporaries. Toto wrote no lyrical songs for Dune, *instead conjuring a big, sweeping orchestral sound with only a few guitar chords here and there.*

DAVID PAICH: That's where my head was at because I grew up with orchestras. My father was an orchestral arranger, an orchestrator for Jerry Goldsmith. He did some movies and a lot of TV and constantly conducted orchestras all his life. I come from the old-school orchestra scoring of a movie. When Queen did *Flash Gordon*, I thought, "Wow, that's interesting to have a band score a movie." We took it that way and did our own thing. Kind of Toto-ized it trying to follow David Lynch's instructions, which put limitations on what we're trying to do.

STEVE LUKATHER: David Paich gets to scratch his itch to write an orchestral score with all of us contributing compositional ideas, but—in all fairness—Paich was really running the show on this one. I got to give credit where credit's due.

DAVID PAICH: Then I wrote the theme. What people don't know is that the desert theme was a second theme that was written for the main title because [Lynch] wanted something that had more Toto in it. Steve Lukather and I wrote that theme, and that was a potential for the main title as well. We took thematic material from that in the movie, so you probably are hearing shades of that.

STEVE LUKATHER: We were still in our 20s. I was 25 years old. I'd never done anything like that before. It was a new experience for me, and I learned a lot.

While Paich and Lukather were always the main composers for the film, another artist Lynch considered bringing in from the get-go was British ambient pioneer Brian Eno. After experiencing a bout of "temp fever," the filmmaker ultimately decided to supplement the score with a single 12-minute synth track by Eno (alongside Daniel Lanois and Roger Eno) known as the "Prophecy Theme," which caused a bit of tension with the members of Toto.

STEVE LUKATHER: He temped a scene with Brian Eno's music, and we tried to fucking satisfy him and nothing would do it until he finally said, "I'll pay Brian to do this."

DAVID PAICH: It was a little touchy at first, because we thought that he wanted to go in a different direction, that he wasn't satisfied with Toto. We read that wrong. All they wanted was to be more inclusive with the music and bring in some other elements to it. I totally understand now what I didn't understand then, which is why the additional music had to be brought in. Now that I look back on it, it was the perfect call. I was lucky to be part of all that.

STEVE LUKATHER: The shitty part of it was the way it read on the poster: "Music by Toto and Brian Eno." I've never met Brian. Love his work, but he wrote a 30-second theme and got the same credit as us. They used him because of his name value, so people attributed our work to him and his work to us and it was confusing. It was much hipper to say Brian Eno wrote the score than Toto at the time. If they didn't like the movie, they'd go after us. If they liked it, they'd give Eno all the credit. I have no beef with Brian Eno, I have no beef with David. That's what he wanted so he should have it, but it shouldn't have been on the poster. It should have been at the end: "Additional Cue by Brian Eno." Whoever decided they needed Brian Eno on the poster got their wish. Why didn't he ask Brian to do the whole fucking thing if that's what he wanted? Right? By the way, Brian had nothing to do with that. I love Brian Eno. David Paich just worked with him recently.

DAVID PAICH: When I look back on it, the sound design aspect was Brian Eno. He brought in those luscious and compelling and haunting voices that were in some of the scenes. It was a great mixture to have both elements between Eno and Toto. He pre-recorded stuff he just thought would be good for the movie and sent it to David Lynch and that was the music. Toto did all the percussion in L.A. here, and Steve Lukather did some of the guitar backward sounds.

PENELOPE SHAW SYLVESTER: David had a strong audio vision too. The sound. He had one of his sound designers, Alan Splet, who unfortunately isn't with us anymore. He came on the film, and he was on David's wavelength for that.

DAVID PAICH: There was a lot of sound design going on with Lynch at the same time this orchestral stuff was being conceived. Lynch is very into the combination of those things. I remember when I went to his house, he had this haunting, low, whistling sound. I said, "What is that?" He said he went to Scotland up into the hills where there was supposedly a haunted castle. This was the wind whistling through the castle, and he recorded that. He puts it on all of his movies. This low wisp of a sound. It's kind of haunting and almost like a foghorn. David Lynch was one of the champions of sound design and movie music going together.

Paich's father Marty was brought in to lend his years of expertise in composing and conducting honed on films as varied as Model Shop *and* Hey There, It's Yogi Bear. *The elder Paich also spent years as a jazz musician and producer-arranger–music director for artists like Peggy Lee, Ray Charles, Mel Tormé, Barbra Streisand, and Elton John. Recording for* Dune *was conducted by Marty Paich and Allyn Ferguson with the Vienna Symphony Orchestra and the Vienna Volksoper Choir.*

DAVID PAICH: His contribution was definitely in the orchestration, and it spilled over into compositions. I would give him some two-part harmony themes I had written out, and he would put 90 pieces to it. He would orchestrate it, and when my father orchestrates, it's really like a classical composer. I was very lucky to have him be my personal orchestrator for this. I think you hear him a lot in this movie.

STEVE LUKATHER: His father Marty had experience doing this because he had scored on television and films. He'd done a few things. I studied orchestration and stuff, but I didn't do the orchestrations. Marty Paich did because he was the best in the fucking world. You get the best guy for the gig.

VIRGINIA MADSEN: I was there one time when the orchestra was playing to the big screen, and David was directing them. I was just like, "Oh my God, this is what I've dreamed of. This is how it used to be done." I learned at the very beginning of this experience to just keep quiet and watch. I had this quality to stand there without anyone knowing I was standing there.

DAVID PAICH: I didn't know there were two philharmonic orchestras in Vienna. There's a Vienna Symphony Orchestra, and there's a Vienna Philharmonic. I'd seen one of them work with Leonard Bernstein, and I thought that was the orchestra. I made a mistake. It was a different orchestra, and they were very inexperienced with headphones and click tracks.

STEVE LUKATHER: Raffaella didn't want to pay anyone. We wanted to do it in London. She said, "London? Grrr. Here's $20 bucks, go do it in fuckin' Vienna." That's not far off, bro. We had no control, we had to do what we were told. We can't go, "No, we're not going to do it." We didn't have that power. Vienna was a whole story because they tuned to 442 [Hz] and we recorded everything to 440.

DAVID PAICH: I gave them a tuning note to tune to from our 24 track, and they said, "We don't tune up to you, you have to tune up to us." That involves VSO-ing—variable speed oscillating—and slowing the machine down to where you have to tune up to them. That's exactly not the way to do that, and so it was very rigorous and challenging. A lot of challenges with trying to work with them.

Paul M. Sammon told me during our discussions that Paich's main theme for Dune *has a startling similarity to the bombastic main theme from Roger Corman's 1963 horror film* The Haunted Palace. *That composition was made by Ronald Stein, who worked with Sammy Davis Jr. on "Katherine's Love Theme" for the 1963 movie* Of Love and Desire . . . *around the same time Davis was recording* The Marty Paich Sessions *for Reprise Records. Whether or not the tune was swiped from Stein, its repetition in the film rubbed Raffaella the wrong way.*

DAVID PAICH: Oh really? I have not seen it. What's it called again? Were there similarities? [*laughs*] I'll have to check that out.

RAFFAELLA DE LAURENTIIS: I love the music. I just think that in the mix David's dad—who is a composer—had done a lot of the bridging of the scenes more traditionally, but somehow in the final mix in Europe, we ended up taking all that out. I thought it was just a little repetitive because we fell in love with those bars and kept using those a little too much.

DAVID PAICH: I didn't have much to do or say in the editing room. That was all David Lynch with Raffaella De Laurentiis. The music that we recorded got edited a whole lot, just chopped up and put in different places. They moved all of our music cues around to different places. Not only that— speaking of low and slow—he took some of the music that was already low and slow and half-sped the machine so it was twice as low and twice as slow. That came as a real shocker to notice that was going on with the editing. Very creative. Again, that comes under the heading of sound design, and I applaud it, you know?

STEVE LUKATHER: I was the representative during the final mix, and at that point, David was getting pretty frustrated because I think they yanked the funds on him. The film started to get away from him.

The final music mix was handled by Steve Maslow, a two-time Oscar winner for The Empire Strikes Back *and* Raiders of the Lost Ark.

STEVE MASLOW: A re-recording mixer is like Betty Crocker: I get the ingredients and mix them. I don't do any editing, per se. In 1984, there were three men on a console: dialogue, music, and effects mixers. During that period, I was just a music mixer. The reel-to-reel stuff the editors handled, and they transferred all that stuff to 35-millimeter mag and then cut the mag accordingly to sync the film.

STEVE LUKATHER: Steve Maslow was a great old friend of ours from when he worked in a recording studio.

STEVE MASLOW: Yes, this was for Toto at the Sound Factory on Selma Avenue in Hollywood in the early '80s, some sessions for overdubs on an existing track.

STEVE LUKATHER: He was back there in the day with us, so when I found out he was there . . . because there was all this union shit. "Nobody who's not union can touch the console." Maslow was great because he was a record guy, he wasn't just one of those film union guys, and I got to stick with him.

STEVE MASLOW: The system we used was called a Quad Eight, which was also for mixing records. There were three sections. One section on the left—facing the screen—was dialogue. The center was music, so you can hear the left and right stereo equally. The right side was effects. I worked at a studio, which was Goldwyn at the time. When the film came on the stage, it was the final cut. The sound designer would show up and make sure that the sound that he supplied was handled the way he thought it should be. Steve Lukather was the guitarist for Toto, and he showed up on the final mix. He came in and sat next to me.

STEVE LUKATHER: I'd tell him, *[whispering]* "I know I'm not supposed to tell you, but if you could . . ." He was very great.

STEVE MASLOW: He was concerned about how his music was presented so that it didn't embarrass him. On this film, the Toto music I got was already completely mixed, so it wasn't like I could push the guitar. I had no discretion other than maybe making it brighter or pulling the bass up.

STEVE LUKATHER: I was fighting with the sound effects guy. The dog was panting louder than the music and shit like that. We had these little petty arguments. I was sitting representing the music side with Maslow, and there was a little battle with the sound effects guy. "Come on, man! There's this beautiful string piece, but the dog's going *[makes panting sound]*. Are you serious, dude?" Lynch is like, "Stop." In the end, it was Dave's call, but there were silly moments like that.

STEVE MASLOW: There were so many people on the stage . . . the sound effects guy would say something, the director would say something, the music guy would say something . . . just for one sequence. We were an extension of what they wanted, so it was always a compromise and trying to please everybody. That was difficult.

DAVID PAICH: I believe that. I know it must have been a real tug-of-war. It always is between sound effects and music—there's always a little battle that goes on there about who gets to have volume in what areas. Who gets to have presence.

STEVE MASLOW: The console was about 30 feet long, and in front of it were theater seats, and David Lynch would sit in front of the console. Here's what we'd see: [*holds up two hands, palms up*] It would be . . . [*brings right hand higher*] That would be louder music . . . [*brings left hand higher*] That would be louder effects. So, he'd direct with his hands. He had certain dictates specific to sound effects, but music was either louder or lower. If they wanted to hear more of that worm . . . I was really confused watching that movie. How David wanted to present a particular scene was always up to David. It was pretty much loud on everything. [*laughs*] Obviously you have to hear the dialogue, but when there was no dialogue, the music and effects were driving the scene, and he liked everything as loud as he could get it without destroying anything.

STEVE LUKATHER: When you're working on the scene, all you do is listen to your music going, "Oh, look how great!" It's loud. You spend all this time, and at the end of the day, it's dialogue-based. The music is supposed to help set the mood for the dialogue and the dramatic things that are going on. That was our job . . . But when you spend fucking two weeks on a cue and then [*makes dog panting sound*]. We're sitting at the premiere in our chairs going like this [*covers face*], slowly going, "Oh man, what's going on here? What happened?"

STEVE MASLOW: We would rehearse all day, I would take notes, and then we'd say, "Okay, let's go to lunch." David always invited me to lunch. He owned a 1957 Studebaker Silver Hawk. We would drive by, and people gave us the thumbs up and . . . there's a restaurant called Bob's Big Boy. He liked to go to Bob's Big Boy.

STEVE LUKATHER: I used to love to go to Bob's with David Lynch. He'd eat the same thing every day. I'm like, "Yeah, I like burgers. I'm in my 20s. I can eat anything." Now I don't really eat that kind of food, and he's a vegetarian.

STEVE MASLOW: He'd order apple pie and vanilla ice cream up front, eat his dessert first, and then have his meal. We did that with him maybe half a dozen times during the mix. He also wore the same outfit every day.

I don't know if it's the same clothes, but it was always a black blazer jacket, khaki pants. It never changed for the six weeks he was on the stage. I thought, "Wow, that's interesting. He never has to think about getting dressed." When he liked something, he used to say, "Oh, that's cool enough." I never got the impression he didn't know what he was doing. He was always there every day on the final. He was instrumental in instructing us on how he wanted to present each scene.

STEVE LUKATHER: There was a race to the finish. "You have to hurry up and finish because David's not going to be involved in the very, very end of it. We need to finish this and put it out because there's a deadline." Lynch bailed on the last part, he wanted his name off the film, and it just got weird. Like, "What the fuck happened?" I was told they defunded him, he just ran out of money, and they pulled the film from him. I don't know what the truth is. Basically, the whole thing went pear-shaped. I don't know whose fault it was. Dave was unhappy and never really got to finish his film. That's how I see it. There was no negativity toward us. David felt kind of bad. He was worried about how we felt, which is probably why we've been able to retain a friendship. We spent time in the trenches together.

RAFFAELLA DE LAURENTIIS: It's almost 40 years since *Dune* came out, and I've never seen it again except once I was asleep in a hotel room on location somewhere and music woke me up. The TV was on, and I said, "What is this music? I know this music!" It was *Dune*. That was the last time I've ever seen it.

STEVE MASLOW: Like I said, I didn't quite understand the film. Because it was confusing. My coworkers . . . my dialogue guy and the sound effects guy . . . we didn't quite get it. The dialogue mixer read the book so he could figure out what was going on. [*laughs*] I thought we presented the film in a way that represented a good mix.

STEVE LUKATHER: We like to take musical challenges, and that was a big one. How many rock bands go in and actually score a film? Guys come in and do their stuff, then they take the vocal out and use the instrumental part, but actually sitting down and going, "Look, we're writing an orchestral score. It's not going to sound like a Toto record." I snuck a little electric guitar in here and there, you can hear it once in a while in some of the thematic stuff with the strings. It wasn't about turning this into a rock-and-roll epic. This was David Lynch's film, and we wanted to facilitate whatever he asked of us and try to give him our very best.

DAVID PAICH: I had mixed feelings about it. I liked it because I'd worked on it. It was my first film, and I was proud of it. I was a little confused at some of the editing choices when they were chopping the music up and going to scenes and not letting it play like we scored it originally. But that's the film business. You have to have a rough skin and not let it get to you.

THOM MOUNT: In any event, they get the movie finished. They stagger out of Mexico, they go into post-production.

Soon after finishing principal photography, a new challenge was presented to the Dune *production in November 1983: Frank Price became president of Universal Pictures. Price started in the TV story department at CBS. In 1959, he joined Universal TV, where he helped develop the concepts of the "made-for-TV movie" and the miniseries. In 1978, he was named president of Columbia Pictures, where his string of hits included* Kramer vs. Kramer, Tootsie, Gandhi, The Karate Kid, *and* Ghostbusters.

FRANK PRICE: I was at Columbia, and Coca-Cola had bought Columbia and gradually we were in conflict. For instance, they tried very hard to persuade me not to make *Ghostbusters*. They could have stopped me from doing it by firing me, but they weren't prepared to do that. I went ahead with *Ghostbusters*, but I felt it was time for me to move on. I got an offer from Lew Wasserman and Sid Sheinberg to take over Universal Pictures. I'd been at Universal for 20 years, so it was familiar ground. I'd been on the board at MCA. I agreed and made the deal. I had to leave behind at Columbia a couple of very important projects. One was *Out of Africa* and the other was *Back to the Future*, which were in development.

ALEX COX: I don't know anything about the circumstances of *Dune*, but the change of regime—Bob Rehme out, Frank Price in—was an unpleasant one. The surviving Universal execs set about sabotaging Rehme's projects, correctly assuming that Price would not want them to succeed. *Repo Man* and *Rumble Fish* were among the films which suffered from this tomfoolery.

FRANK PRICE: The first thing I did was meet with everybody. I don't think Bob Rehme was very happy having somebody come in over him. I had to review everything to see what I thought of it. I realized fairly soon, as pictures started coming in, why Wasserman really wanted me because there were a number of big commitments on pictures that weren't very good, or were problematic. There was a Burt Reynolds film called *Stick*, which was an expensive, no-good picture. *Legend* was made by a good filmmaker, Ridley Scott, but it just didn't work with Tom Cruise as this forest elf. There wasn't much you could do about it. It is what it is, right? If you're a surgeon, sometimes you examine the patient and realize you can't really do anything. Just sew them up and let them proceed. Then there was *Brazil*, the Terry Gilliam picture. *Brazil* was well done for what it was. The problem was it was a limited audience-interest picture, much too expensive. It's the kind of picture you make for $3 or $4 million, and then you're fine. This was made for $15 million.

PAUL M. SAMMON: *Dune* was an expensive, top-line production with a hot young director adapting a best-selling book, all of which looked good on paper. But this being the dawn of blockbuster science-fiction films, it was my feeling that the studio didn't fully understand who and what they had going in, much less what science fiction was in general. Universal's reaction reminded me of what I'd seen during the making of *Blade Runner*, where certain power brokers involved with that film had unrealistic expectations. When they didn't get a *Star Wars*, they went ballistic.

RAFFAELLA DE LAURENTIIS: The team at Universal that was making the movie when we started was Ned Tanen and Bob Rehme was head of marketing. Then Tanen left and Frank Price came in. Had he come in earlier, I think Frank Price would have stopped the movie from happening. I think he never liked the movie, he never believed in it, and he didn't want to have anything to do with it.

CRAIG CAMPOBASSO: Frank Price was coming in when *Dune* was being done, and there was a rumor that he and Dino did not like each other. I remember Universal was not liking the film, and I don't think they were supporting it under Frank.

FRANK PRICE: *Dune* I'd been aware of for a long time. It wasn't something I would have made. It was complex and difficult to get a good storyline through there that makes a motion picture. Dino I always met with, but I think in regards to the specifics on *Dune*, it was Raffaella and David Lynch. There was *Firestarter* . . . I liked Dino, but never found the pictures he came up with ones I wanted to make. I got along with him. I had a meeting with Dino, and his accent was such that I had to listen extremely carefully and kind of interpret the words that he was using, make them into English words that I recognize. After half an hour, this was exhausting.

PAUL M. SAMMON: *Dune* already lost a great deal of in-house support by the time Price came in. Price acted as any other incoming production head does: Distanced himself from the previous regime's projects to concentrate on his own slate.

RAFFAELLA DE LAURENTIIS: He had just finished a big sci-fi movie in London that didn't work, *Krull*. I think he really didn't want to have much to do with *Dune*.

FRANK PRICE: With *Krull*, I was trying to basically move a medieval story into a science-fiction story, and it didn't work. Some things don't work.

PAUL M. SAMMON: Universal's gradual disenchantment with *Dune* was a slow detachment. Little by little, studio enthusiasm waned, resources were diverted elsewhere. By the time Frank Price came in, memos had already been flying fast to make the film "more exciting," "more accessible," and "more comprehensible"!

FRANK PRICE: If I could contribute something, great, but I thought the patient had whatever the patient had. I couldn't figure out how to fix it. There are two important stages in a picture, from my standpoint. The first is when you're getting the script in place. You can control everything, you can rewrite everything, blank slate. Once you pass that stage, the next stage you can rewrite the picture is when you have that first cut. You see what has worked, what hasn't worked.

*On the film since the beginning of shooting from March '83 were Antony Gibbs and his assistant editor Penny Shaw, the daughter of actor Robert Shaw (*The Sting, Jaws*).*

PENELOPE SHAW SYLVESTER: My credit read "Penelope" because my father always said, "Use Penelope, it'll take up more screen space." [*laughs*] I was on *Dune* from the beginning until the end. I hadn't worked with Tony Gibbs before, but I had worked with Tony Masters, who was the production designer on *The Deep* with my dad, the first film I ever worked on. When I moved to LA, Tony took me under his wing, and all the English crowd used to meet in Westwood every Saturday for lunch. He said to me one day, "Ooh, I've got this project coming up in Mexico. They're using an all-British crew, but they're posting in LA. Tony Gibbs is the editor, and

I don't think he has an LA-based assistant. I would like to introduce you."
We started in Mexico. Tony never cut on the KEM—he cut everything on
the Moviola. He was an experienced editor, very relaxed. Always played
music in the cutting room, would blare it really loud. He used to say, "It
gets my rhythm going." He loved showtunes, would play *Fiddler on the Roof.*
He never got flustered. If stuff wasn't coming in then we'd shut down the
cutting room, take a long weekend, and come back when it was there. Tony
was right behind: As everything came in, it was assembled. When you're
cutting a film like that, the first goal is to assemble everything. You want to
put everything in there, the whole lot. Once you've got it all assembled and
you've seen everything, that's when you start to think, "Well, this is a bit long."
I have to tell you, I worked on *Heaven's Gate*, too, and our first assembly
was REALLY long! [*laughs*]

THOM MOUNT: It's a company, and you hear things all the time—there's
a constant jungle telegraph of information coming to my office, and the
word was that it was getting to be very difficult to cut it together in anything like an acceptable length. For us, for the studio, the next threshold of
conflict is all about the length of the picture. Internally, Sid had stepped up
now and inserted himself in this movie, gone way out on a limb and poured
more money in, and everybody in the company was going, "This is the
most expensive picture we've ever made." We knew there was a four-hour-
plus cut in Mexico; there are no secrets. We also knew a four-hour-plus cut
doesn't easily come down to a two-hour cut.

MARY VOGT: I remember this four-hour version that we saw in Mexico
where everything made it into the film. It was just me and Bob and the editor, because Bob became friends with the editor. He said, "I want you to
see this thing that I put together." That's the version I remember, one of the
most genius films I've ever seen! If Dino had bought the film, taken it away
from Universal, brought it to Europe, and released it as a four-hour film,
it would be one of the greatest films ever made.

JOHN PATTYSON: David invited me to of the first screenings of it.
The cut I saw was well over four hours, and it was deadly long. I said, "So
David, you are going to cut this down?" He looked at me and said, "You
think so?" I go, "Yeah. I do." Who's going to sit through a four-hour film?
I don't care how good it is.

RAFFAELLA DE LAURENTIIS: It was never supposed to be a four-
hour movie. We never set out to make that—we set out to make a regu-

lar-length movie, right? After Ned, it was Bob Rehme that took the lead and wanted to talk about the marketing. I remember very clearly a meeting in his office in which he said, "We cannot release the movie at this length," but I don't think anybody ever wanted to release the movie at that length. It was never the intention.

PENELOPE SHAW SYLVESTER: You put it together, looked at it, and then you start bringing it down and saying, "What's essential? What can we take out?" As with any film, it was way too long. They always are. You always want to show the director everything they shot to start with. Why would he have shot it if he didn't like it?

THOM MOUNT: The notion that a three-hour movie could be a commercial hit was still uncharted territory. It had happened occasionally, meaning *Lawrence of Arabia*, but very rarely. The distribution guys who sell the thing to theaters were terrified, because all that exhibitors would say is, "three-hour movie, we're losing two screenings a day, we're not going to make any money. Don't give us that, give us the smaller version." There was a lot of back and forth.

FRANK PRICE: At that point of distribution, Bill Soady was dealing with exhibitors, so he was handling it, not complaining about it.

THOM MOUNT: Bill Soady was my temporary guy while I found someone to really do this. Bill was a very brief head of distribution but was good.

FRANK PRICE: While I had these pictures coming in, I had to make sure that I could turn this whole thing around, and get good pictures into the pipeline. I managed to get *Out of Africa* away from Columbia. I got *Back to the Future*. I found there were some films in the pipeline that had great potential like *Breakfast Club*.

THOM MOUNT: Frank thinks he inherited *Breakfast Club*? Interesting . . . Ned decided he was leaving the studio. That was fine. I made a deal with Ned to produce some movies for the studio, and those scripts were all John Hughes movies: *Breakfast Club*, *Pretty in Pink*, and *Sixteen Candles*. Those were Ned's babies. Ned said about Frank Price, "The guy wrote one episode of *The Virginian* and thinks he's Faulkner." That defined Frank in my imagination.

FRANK PRICE: I started out as a story editor and writer. I grew up on science fiction, reading in those days *Amazing Stories* and *Fantastic Adventures*, and then *Astounding Science Fiction*. I like science fiction. I can play out my favorite way to get into a story, which is "what if?" . . . In editing, my technique is I go through it and try to write the picture with film. If something doesn't work, cut it out or figure out how to make a sequence work. I couldn't see what I could do with *Dune*. They had done the best job they could with what they had. The production was there. That was certainly a lot of money at the time. Once you spend it, I don't worry about it because if you've got a million-dollar sequence and it doesn't work, you cut it out. You can't say, "Well, we spent a million dollars on that, we've got to have it in the picture." If it doesn't work, it doesn't work.

PENELOPE SHAW SYLVESTER: Maybe Tony wasn't quite as much on David's wavelength. David would go for a long time on shots, whereas Tony knew he had to get it moving. They had different rhythms. It may not have been the best match. They never argued or anything, but Tony was confused sometimes by what he was trying to achieve. David had never done something on this scale. At the beginning, he was given pretty much an open hand until things started not to gel together the way they wanted . . . Probably halfway through shooting. Realizing, you know, "We're halfway through shooting, and we've got a lot to go."

MARY VOGT: It was only because we were in Mexico that the studio wasn't really there. They didn't know what was going on. What do you expect when you hire David Lynch to direct? Do you think you're going to get a commercial film? It's not Steven Spielberg, it's David Lynch!

THOM MOUNT: Sid inserted himself, I think, mostly because he was embarrassed that he had gone way out on a limb for this thing. Now he had this unwieldy, three-hour-plus movie that David and Dino were not showing a lot of enthusiasm for bringing down to a manageable size. Honestly, I saw a longer version of the movie at about just under three hours— which I knew would never get through the system—but that version of the movie I liked a lot better than the final version of the movie.

FRANK PRICE: Sid Sheinberg was trying to do some re-cutting. I just felt he was abusing David Lynch. I didn't like it . . . Lynch is a good director. I thought he'd done a good job on it, the best job he probably could, but it was still muddled. There was no way I could see straightening that out. It was what it was. Sheinberg judged them differently than I do. He tended to feel he could do something by re-cutting with directors, and I wasn't going to do that. It's insulting to the directors.

THOM MOUNT: David's vision was more complete. The idea of people sitting through a three-hour movie on this subject matter wasn't a kosher way to see things at that moment in history. In the company today, with a landmark director like David, if he wanted to make a three-hour movie, a lot of people would support that.

FRANK PRICE: When I was at Columbia, there was a too-long picture that nobody wanted to distribute called *Tess*. I took it on and decided we could make it work. What I did was put in an intermission, and that helped with theater owners because they had a second chance to sell popcorn.

THOM MOUNT: Once Sid took the project over, everybody at Universal—myself, Ned, Rehme—nobody wanted to have a fight with Sid over finishing the movie. Sid took it over—it became his project. He's the one who got us way out on a limb financially, so there's some sense of balance in that, but the flipside is when Sid was left to his own devices to produce movies . . . Sid was a terrific guy in many ways, but he was not a creative animal. He just didn't have the chip that would let him figure out how to make a movie that really touched people. He basically took over the picture as well as the Dino relationship on that picture for obvious reasons. None of the rest of us wanted to be taking the rap for the continuing upgrade of the picture.

RAFFAELLA DE LAURENTIIS: It was just, "How do we get with what we've shot . . . ?" In the end, it was not possible, so that's why David went back into the script and wrote the new scene that bridged things.

> *David Lynch's new "bridging scene" took Paul out of the sietch and into the desert for a hasty Water of Life ceremony where he experiences a powerful (and empowering) epiphany that gives him control over the worms. This replaced six or seven scenes that were cast away and never completed.*

RAFFAELLA DE LAURENTIIS: I remember the first cut was four hours, and then we had to figure out how we take it down to two, and that was the most difficult part. David went into the script and rewrote this whole section.

SEAN YOUNG: When we shot the stuff at the end of the movie, where he takes the Water of Life in the middle of the desert, that was part of a reshoot in El Paso. We were pretty much done with the film, but we knew we had some kind of reshoot. David and Kyle took me to a golfing range one day when we weren't shooting, and that's where I discovered I totally suck at golf. I couldn't hit that ball.

KYLE MACLACHLAN: Having more time to tell the story on the back half would have been helpful, particularly more detail on Paul's build-up to taking the Water of Life, those transitions happening.

THOM MOUNT: There were some reshoots that Sid agreed to pay for. Sid would periodically explain to one or the other of us, "Oh, these are necessary, that picture is going to be great. This is great. We've got to do this."

ERIC SWENSON: There was a pick-up shot starring David where he's working the spice harvester. We did that in Burbank at a local construction yard in some piece of Cat equipment. He got exactly what he wanted! I don't even know why that came up. That could have been a bridge.

This Hitchcockian Lynch cameo as a spice worker communicating with spotter control is indeed concealing something. Van der Veer was unable to execute the storyboarded visuals of spotter craft, which were meant to be flying near the harvester looking for signs of worm activity. Only Duke Leto's ornithopter is shown hovering overhead. Later the spotters were supposed to have landed around the harvester so the spice workers could escape. The spotters are even referred to in dialogue as if they're there:

—*"See the spotters over it? They're watching for wormsign, the telltale sand waves."*
—*"Spotter control, there's no sign of the carryall . . . Spotter control, give me a report by the numbers . . . Report One."*
"No contact."
"Report Two."
"Negative."
"Report Three."
"Negative, sir."
"Report Four."
"No contact. Repeat, no contact."
—*"All spotters are ordered to comply."*
—*"Two men in each of the spotters! You, over here! Run!"*

In essence, Lynch used his cameo to imply the spotters through radio chatter. Kynes' mention of "seismic probes on the surface" may have been an overdub added in post to refer to the land vehicles seen in two shots (actually LJN toys, as explained in the pre-production oral history), perhaps implying that they are spotters also.

BARRY NOLAN: I don't remember that at all. This is when they were flying? That should have been . . . There are so many confusing things.

ERIC SWENSON: I don't remember. That's a great story, though. They refer to something that never shows up! [*laughs*] I also shot David's hand, so he's in the movie more than once. He said, "What can we do that's really different?" I came up with—again—the fish tank, and we shot it. We were looking up at David's hand coming into the water. Another one of those shots was David wanted a closeup of an eyeball during the spice sequence when he's getting all drugged out. I set up the camera with this big long snorkel lens, and Barry shot a 1K into my eye! We brought David down. "What do you think?" He goes, "That looks great." We say, "Okay, who do you want to get?" He says, "We'll use yours." That's my eye in the film. My wife loves telling people, "His eye's in the movie!"

THOM MOUNT: Everybody in the movie business is a cruel mistress. There is no subjective standard for making a film work. I have a lot of sympathy for anybody who thinks they're in charge of a movie. To some degree they are, and to a much greater degree, the movie's in charge of them. It's an interesting dynamic.

PENELOPE SHAW SYLVESTER: David didn't have final cut, so it became Tony's responsibility when they said it was too long. Tony and Raffaella worked together. David was always there, but they'd work on stuff and then show it to him.

FRANK PRICE: David was a very talented guy I liked. I was dealing with David Lynch, and once we were into cutting, I dealt with Raffaella. I don't know specifically how David responded to Sid's re-editing, but I'm sure he was dismayed. Raffaella did a good job on any picture she was on and was an excellent intermediary.

PENELOPE SHAW SYLVESTER: I remember David always being there in the building with us. He may not have been happily there, but he was there. Raffaella was extremely cordial and very down to earth. She mucked in with everybody. She wasn't up in the tower, you know? She was with us all the way. I think she tried to give David as much as she possibly could of what he wanted, but she wasn't in charge of bringing in the money. Dino was. There were certain times when we said, "Okay, well, that's not happening now."

FREDERICK ELMES: You wouldn't be building, lighting, and shooting it if you didn't think it was going to be there in the movie. *Dune* is such a massive piece of writing. I remember David had conversations about, "Well, if we have to cut those scenes, then we'll just cut that character out." If they're so intertwined in the book, it's hard to know what you can do without and then what impact that has on the rest of the story, but it's hard to have it all. You had to be fair to the ones you were going to put in. David enjoyed telling that story, picking the ones that were key to the thrust of the plot but also interesting to him.

PENELOPE SHAW SYLVESTER: At that point, we knew we didn't have an option. There was nothing to fight. They would say it has to be a certain length because they wanted to fit in so many screenings a day. It was just, "Okay, what can we do? What's the least destructive way to bring this down?" That's what you're faced with.

THOM MOUNT: The next thing I saw was the 2-hour-and-20-minute releasable version of the picture, and I frankly thought it was 25% worse than David's version. I really did. I think the cuts didn't help it. I think the bravado, the brio that David had baked into the filmmaking got curtailed in a really deleterious way. There you go. Movies get hurt if you fuck 'em up, you know?

In addition to the hatchet job on Dune, *around this time Sid Sheinberg also took a "creative focus" on re-cutting Terry Gilliam's dystopian satire* Brazil *and Ridley Scott's dark fantasy* Legend. *While Scott was cooperative with the studio in changing his film's soundtrack and cutting the runtime down, Gilliam went nuclear. The Monty Python vet staged a scorched earth campaign where he ran Sheinberg down in* Daily Variety *and on national television, then scored a coup by covertly screening his cut of* Brazil *to the Los Angeles Film Critics Association . . . which handed his cut of the film Best Screenplay, Best Director, and Best Picture.*

FRANK PRICE: I saw no reason to recut Terry's film. It was what it was, with some brilliant sequences. Its problem was it cost $15 million and couldn't earn that back. Sid, perhaps feeling responsible for it getting made, felt there was a commercial film there he would produce by re-cutting. Terry made him look like a fool to the critics. Ridley was always easy to deal with since he wanted the best picture possible. Since I had not greenlit these pictures, I didn't have a creative focus on them. I made my own judgment, but if he felt he could save them, far be it from me to say you can't do that. If he was misguided enough to believe he could save them . . .

THOM MOUNT: The studio didn't do David or Dino or the movie any favors, but Dino wanted Sid to keep writing checks, and Sid did. I would have handled it differently. I would have released it at three hours only if we did a limited Academy consideration release toward the end of the year in New York, Los Angeles, maybe one or two other cities with a real focus on the thing that was exciting about that cut. David's gusto was in the movie, and the final version of the movie fell flat. It wasn't that giant scenes were missing, it was that the juice of the movie had somehow been . . . like letting the air out of a balloon.

PAUL M. SAMMON: Price and Sheinberg had nothing to do with the film's 2:17 runtime. That mandate came from Dino De Laurentiis, who'd imposed the same regulation on John Milius for *Conan the Barbarian*. Both *Dune* [137 minutes] and *Conan* [129 minutes] had roughly the same runtimes during their original theatrical releases. Dino had worked out the maximum number of screenings any film can have in a day at a theater. Three hours would have meant less screen time for exhibitors, hence less revenue. However, I believe 2 hours and 19 minutes was Dino's magic number. Whatever the case, Milius certainly knew about this regulation while he was making his movie. I never asked David directly about the same matter, but gossip flows around a set, and from what I picked up, I'd assumed that Lynch was working under the same mandate.

KENNETH GEORGE GODWIN: David didn't have a final cut. It's never actually existed in a David Lynch cut, because it was just continually pared down until it got to that 137 minutes under the insistence of the studio.

FREDERICK ELMES: That sense of being left adrift broke David's heart because he was counting on this finishing as a great experience. To see it fall and not be what it could have been . . . He had such limited experience. Mel Brooks really stood behind him and made *The Elephant Man* the way David wanted to do it, and *Eraserhead* was David's own film where he could do the things he wanted to do. Here he wasn't able to do that, and the support he had during production wasn't there through the very end. Kind of a crushing experience for him.

PENELOPE SHAW SYLVESTER: Probably toward the end as things were cut down and cut down, I would think it must have been . . . I think he knew at that point, it wasn't his vision anymore. I would say he was sad toward the end. He was in his office, but he wasn't coming in and hanging out with us. What could he do? He couldn't do anything. If you don't have final cut . . . He wanted the film to be released, so he had to work with what he was allowed to do.

BARRY NOLAN: Raffaella said they watched *Eraserhead,* and if Dino had come in while they were watching it, he would've never let them make the movie.

RICHARD MALZAHN: They cut upstairs at Van der Veer in Burbank, Antony Gibbs and Penny. I remember occasionally watching Tony cut on a Moviola and was like, "Oh my God, you're kidding me, right?" Looking back, it's like, "How do people do that?" And yet he was there, just banging it out.

CRAIG CAMPOBASSO: My office was across the hall from Antony Gibbs, the editor. I remember Dino coming in. They're watching the film on the Moviola. Dino is standing there looking at it going, "Good . . . cutta cutta cutta . . ." I would see David's face . . . Like, "Oh my God, he's just chopping my thing to pieces." He'd go, "Boom boom boom" and then "Cutta cutta cutta cutta cutta." So ingrained in my psyche.

PENELOPE SHAW SYLVESTER: That was Dino's favorite phrase. [*laughs*] He said that more than once and not just on this job. I was working on another Dino project and he said to me the same thing, "Just cutta cutta cutta." But remember, nobody ever was in the editing room. They were in screening rooms. It's a different environment. I would be taking the notes.

VIRGINIA MADSEN: I was coming back and forth to Mexico from L.A. recording my voiceover narration, which allowed me to be in the editing room with David and watch him edit on film. He would have me come in, and he showed me things he was cutting, things that are not in the film anymore. I was like, "That's unbelievable!" And he was like, "Well, let me show you this." He would put up another reel, and he would show me more and it was so beautiful. The movie was so big—it was a huge epic. I still feel in awe. I remember stuff with the unborn child in utero that was floating around in spice and things with people taking in the spice, because they had added the blue special effect so I could see the before and after with the blue eyes. There was cool space battle stuff, and there was Kenny flying around looking really disgusting, then somebody popping his boils.

PAUL M. SAMMON: Some of the sequence where the Baron pulls the heart plug from his terrified servant boy was cut down. Mostly shots of the Baron smearing oil or blood over the kid.

ERIC SWENSON: The bathing in blood sequence was obviously one of the longer sequences that got cut. He pulls the plug out of the slave, and he's just rubbing the blood all over him.

MARY VOGT: That is the stuff that nightmares are made of. People thought *The Joker* was so outrageous, but David did that in *Dune* 40 years ago!

There also exist storyboards and shooting descriptions of a gorier death scene for Feyd, with notations like "the floor cracks and Feyd's internal organs explode."

PAUL M. SAMMON: Can't speak to a bloodier Sting death. Never saw any evidence of that, although I'm not 100% certain here either.

BOB RINGWOOD: Freddie Jones was such a lovely man. They cut his death scene out of *Dune*. There's more on the cutting room floor than there is on the screen!

FREDERICK ELMES: My work was mainly little cutaways or abstract things. I did some dreamy stuff, some of it involved smoke. A lot of that part of the storytelling wasn't in the version I saw. Slightly more poetic visual storytelling was the first stuff to go. The cut that I saw is really about dialogue and fight scenes.

BARRY NOLAN: They needed to shorten the movie up. A lot of the intrigue that went on after Paul got captured and is in this underground community had been cut. When they first meet the Fremen and they're down in the caves, there was another girl in there who was one of the Fremen. She had two children. She was an important part—her name was Molly. They completely cut her out of the film. There's only one shot they couldn't cut her out of, when they're in the Great Hall and she's standing with two children beside her.

MOLLY WRYN: There was a great seduction scene with Kyle that I was prepared for. I remember reading it again on the plane, and it was cut before I ever filmed it. I thought, "Dang! That was going to be so fun." It would have really shown me physically and given some emotional insight into what Harah was thinking. He obviously rejects me, but I'm wanting to be his wife, not a servant. I tried to seduce him . . . not get him in the sack but get him interested in looking at me in that way. That would have been the biggest scene I was in.

DANNY CORKILL: In the water ceremony for Jamis, the initial inability to reach was not scripted; it became part of the scene. I couldn't quite get the knife up there. It was something that came up as we did it, and somebody helped out and became part of it. They decided that was a good ad-lib. That was one of the few times where the camera was on me. David spent some time explaining what was going on and what I was doing and why I was doing it. It was weird at that point to be the center of attention, having been an ornament for so much time with no lines.

MOLLY WRYN: I got to ride a worm. They were rockin' that big platform, and you're holding on and shouting and using that weapon.

DANNY CORKILL: There was a scene with Diego and me riding a worm. We were standing on a sheet of plywood with a bunch of tires underneath it, simulating the movement. The shot was all from the waist up. I never saw that anyplace.

VIRGINIA MADSEN: There was some space stuff, and there was stuff with the little girl. Can you believe that she is so famous now?

ALICIA WITT: One of my favorite scenes was cut from the movie. Paul has taken the Water of Life, and we are feeling what's happening with him as it's going on. I'm so glad that it resurfaced on YouTube. You can tell it was cut because none of us have the blue-on-blue eyes in it.

The theatrical cut contained snippets of this scene depicting Lady Jessica and Alia in the sietch with bloody noses while Siân Phillips is shown simultaneously writhing on the floor of the Emperor's throne room on Kaitain, blood also oozing out her nose. A production still indicates that Princess Irulan and The Emperor were also in the throne room for that scene, Irulan leaning against a pillar as if her energies had been sapped.

VIRGINIA MADSEN: Yeah, we were all supposed to be affected by that. I didn't really understand what that was about, but I think it was more explained in David's version of it. It's like everyone's really, really hypnotized and stoned and not in control of their powers. That was the only thing I knew! [*laughs*]

ALICIA WITT: It's also the only scene out there that has my own unadulterated voice on it, because they put an effect on my voice in the movie, obviously, right?

KENNETH GEORGE GODWIN: I saw David in London in 1984, when he was still doing ADR on *Dune*. I spent an afternoon there. He still seemed very upbeat, very enthusiastic. I don't know what he was really feeling inside. They were trying to find an actress who would dub Alia. I don't think the one they found is particularly good. It's always tricky when you're using an adult to voice a child.

MOLLY WRYN: They redid her voice. I guess Francesca actually did her voice later.

ALICIA WITT: I didn't understand why. I can remember at age nine going to the movie theater in Boston—it was the first time I'd ever been to the movies—and being surprised when I heard that. I was like, "What is that?" Unless you're on the creative side, like a producer, you often don't know about those decisions, right? I know actors that went to see something they were in only to find they were cut from it completely. It's awful, but it's not that awful. It goes with the territory.

MOLLY WRYN: A scene that David improvised was that he picked me to name Alia in the naming scene. In later books, I become her caretaker, sort of a sietch nanny.

Another cut scene has Harah tell Jessica the Fremen are scared of her daughter, causing Alia to arrive and psychically attack Harah using the Voice. Wryn provided me with a copy of this until-now lost deleted scene, which Lynch gave her for her reel.

VIRGINIA MADSEN: Yeah, Alicia was very powerful, and I got to see some of that.

ALICIA WITT: I haven't thought about that probably since I filmed it because it's not out there, but I can remember Francesca's reaction. I believe she was quite tearful, or the character's choice was to be tearful as Harah was explaining to her the Fremen are afraid of her daughter, because to her, that's just her little girl. She didn't mean to create a monster by drinking the Water of Life while she was pregnant; it just happened. Alia is not a monster—I never saw her as that.

MOLLY WRYN: It was a very powerful scene, as you saw. I was feeling privileged to sit across from Francesca and Alicia. In that clip, that's her real little girl voice and she was dead on. I know the powers that she has. However, in my thinking, I also love that child. I'm vulnerable to her.

ALICIA WITT: I think it was a lot of fun for me to play that I was getting into someone's mind, and I seem to remember being quite gleeful in my interpretation of it. ESP was not unfamiliar to me at all. I was very connected to the ability that humans have to think of something and put it into someone else's mind, communicate without words. Something my mother and I shared was the ability to have dreams that would foretell the future. To me, that scene made perfect sense.

MOLLY WRYN: David called me "One-Take Molly." He believed in me, which meant everything. He believed I brought what was needed into the scene, so he didn't really direct me. We had to do one more because the sound guy said they were having a hard time picking up my voice. I have a soft voice. The first time when she affects me, I put my hands over my face. David said, "Next time don't put your hands over your face." That was the direction.

ALICIA WITT: I don't believe that was one of the scenes I auditioned with, but I'm certain the Water of Life scene with the bloody noses was one of my audition scenes.

Danny Corkill and Diego Gonzalez rehearsed a scene that was never shot, with the benefit of a unique stunt coordinator.

DANNY CORKILL: They decided they wanted a scene in the end of the big battle with Diego and me knife fighting with people. They outfitted us each with these little bone prop daggers. We had two or three days, half an hour to an hour each day learning knife fighting moves . . . and they had Kyle teaching us. They did not have a stunt director going over things. David brought Kyle over to teach Diego and me how to stage fight with these knives. Even at 9, I'm like, "It just seems weird that we don't have a crew guy doing this." [*laughs*] Kyle doesn't have enough on his plate? The lead in the movie is teaching two kids how to knife fight for a scene which they never filmed, by the way. We put in the time, but we must have been terrible.

Although there is only a brief flash of it in the theatrical version, there was also a whole sequence of Alia on the battlefield at the end.

ALICIA WITT: I had a rubber crysknife in the scene with my hair blowing in the breeze at the end of the battle. It's just a tiny moment in the movie, but there was an all-night shoot where we filmed all kinds of things with me walking through the battlefield and finishing off soldiers who were dead. I had my knife out and that was a wonderful experience, but my dad always loved to tell how I accidentally poked one of the fellows who was lying there, supposed to be dead. I wasn't aware of it because I fake-stabbed him with this rubber crysknife and then kept on walking, but he said it was the funniest thing because I was supposed to stab right next to his body—it wasn't sharp or anything—but I guess I just missed it, and I poked him with the rubber knife and then kept on walking. [*laughs*] He said the guy popped up and everybody was losing it laughing at the monitor! I just kept on walking obliviously while the dead guy behind me popped up after being stabbed!

KYLE MACLACHLAN: Alia is given pretty short shrift in that. We just kind of hustled through the greatest hits of the last part of *Dune*. It's a summation, and it deserved more than that; we just didn't have time. As the movie stands, it's 2 hours and 17 minutes . . . not enough time to tell that story, sadly.

Madsen's narration was used as a Band-Aid to stitch together the "Last week on Dune!"-style recaps in the last act of the movie. One infamous example: To show Paul and Chani falling in love, Princes Irulan simply says in voiceover, "Paul and Chani's love grew," over an image of them kissing.

VIRGINIA MADSEN: Oh, I forgot about that. You're right. That's just awful. Who knows what they would have shown? It got cut to pieces. It makes me think about so many other films that got ripped off, so many other films where they didn't get to explore what they wanted to explore.

FREDERICK ELMES: It's so unfair it's not David's edit. The movie is so distorted by adding narration. I know that was not something David ever had in mind, to abridge something they've cut out and quickly give the audience just enough information to get through and understand it without the boring details like the acting. [*laughs*]

KYLE MACLACHLAN: It wasn't that we shot a lot of stuff that didn't make it in; the throughline of the story just needed more time. The ending gets really shrunk. We kind of say, "and then this happened, and this happened, and then here we are."

VIRGINIA MADSEN: I went four or five times because he wouldn't do all my voiceover at once. He would bring me back to do the next part:

"Okay, I'm ready for the next bit of Virginia's dialogue." Then they would fly me back in, and I would do that little bit. He was doing it in order.

MARY VOGT: That was an afterthought. That narration was put in later. Virginia Madsen turned into a really good actor, but at that time, she was not. She hadn't really grown into being the actor she is now. Maybe if Francesca Annis or someone else had done the narration, it would be more serious, but I think Universal got her because she's the prettiest one. Very disappointing.

VIRGINIA MADSEN: All I had to do was look intense, which I did.

PENELOPE SHAW SYLVESTER: We were worried about how it was going to play, whether people would understand what the vision is. Some of the stuff with the Baron and things is quite grotesque. Are people really going to appreciate the visual that David's trying to create or are they gonna go "ewww"? David is, what I would say, quirky. If you look at some of his other films like *Eraserhead*, some people are fascinated by it, and other people go, "Ohhh." Same thing with *Blue Velvet*.

Even Lynch's storyboarded spiritual ending in which Paul enters a dream state and has a vision of a golden lotus was changed for the more conventional ending where he becomes a benevolent god who can make it rain on Arrakis, as opposed to a flawed leader who sparks a bloody universal jihad in the novel.

KYLE MACLACHLAN: I just was like, "This is how it's done in film. Okay." I knew there were things that were missing. I began to understand there's just not time, there's just not room for that kind of subtlety in this journey. It's kind of balls to the wall. Any moment of quiet and stillness and reflection was . . . they were there, but you just didn't have that many opportunities to have that. I felt like it was a rush to an end that he suddenly becomes this God and seems to be without any kind of . . . In the book, he's got a lot of uncertainty. There's a lot of, "Is this right?" Starting a jihad, resisting it all the way through. He says, "I cannot become this, I cannot become this," and yet he does. So those moments? Yeah, that would have been really great.

FRANK PRICE: I was staying out of trying to recut or chop up the film because I didn't think it was going to change anything. Why not let them have the picture they set out to make? The result would have been about the same either way. It was a waste of time cutting it out. I would have gone with it at that length, three hours. At least you would be seeing the actual work.

RAFFAELLA DE LAURENTIIS: It's a process, though. It's not uncommon. What was more difficult was to come up with something to replace those scenes that would bridge what we had cut out and make it understandable. I don't know if we succeeded in doing that, really.

THOM MOUNT: We finally ended up with a 2-hour-and-20-minute movie and we still got terrible blowback from exhibitors who didn't want to lose a screening a day. "Oh my God!" All this nonsense.

FRANK PRICE: Nobody wanted to take responsibility for any of these films. I could not wring out who greenlit anything. It was a mystery. It didn't seem to be Ned, it didn't seem to be Bob, so I gave up trying to find out. It didn't matter who greenlit them, it was my job to figure out what to do.

THOM MOUNT: The next thing that happened is—and I don't mean to keep pillorying Sid—but Sid then had control over the marketing campaign. Oy vey. As perishable as a movie is, a marketing campaign is even more fragile. If you get off on the wrong foot or you're doing the wrong thing or you're selling the wrong stuff, you can almost never recover from it.

PAUL M. SAMMON: I started working on this film at Universal with a great deal of enthusiasm and in-house support. As months wore on, the studio realized the type of picture they were getting was not a slam-bang *Star Wars* adventure but a dense, dark, occasionally surreal futuristic costume drama/court intrigue/anti-imperialist epic. Universal became confused, anxious, and finally dismissive. My reaction to their reaction was, "Hasn't anyone here read Herbert's novels? Or seen *Eraserhead*? Or, you know, looked at Lynch's script?!?" Apparently, this was not the most diplomatic question to bandy about, since the overwhelming response was, "No!"

FRANK PRICE: We tried to do the best job of marketing possible, but a picture that puzzles people is hard to market.

THOM MOUNT: I thought that marketing campaign was terrible for *Dune*. It was sad. I felt we let David down. I felt, in a weird way, we let Dino down. We gave him financial support at the cost of creative support, which the picture needed.

ERIC SWENSON: At Van der Veer, we had a little 40×40 insert stage for shooting pick-up shots for TV shows and stuff. A couple of models came in, and View-Master did 3D shots of the Heighliner, one of the or- nithopters . . . It was pretty fun because I got to see their 3D camera rig, basically a Nikon on a little sliding piece. Somewhere out there, you could probably find on eBay the *Dune* View-Master slides.

*One key part of the marketing was the film's poster, of which several different ver- sions were created. Drew Struzan (*Star Wars, Back to the Future*) was commis- sioned to do a comp for the US one-sheet emphasizing a phallic sandworm behind an image of Paul and Chani staring into each other's eyes, which was rejected in favor of one by Tom Jung (*Star Wars, Super Fly*) featuring Paul's more heroic desert warrior pose in front of Chani, a Fremen army, and a vast fleet of Atreides ships. (Incidental- ly, Tom Jung also did the original poster for 1957's notorious* Plan 9 From Outer Space.*) The main poster used to sell foreign territories was rendered by Italian artist Renato Casaro, whose extensive work with Dino began in 1960 all the way to 1982's* Conan the Barbarian *US poster and beyond.*

RENATO CASARO: Dino De Laurentiis and I had a kind of father-son-re- lation. He trusted me already when I was still very young. The first impor- tant film was the giant project *The Bible*. I was just 28 when I got the order to work on this movie. Before *Dune* and *Conan the Barbarian*, I worked on important films like *Waterloo* and *Flash Gordon*; both luckily made a perfect box office. When *Dune* came, I was already known for my style and ad- mired by Dino.

Although he made several comp sketches, including a more Rabban- and Sardaukar- heavy villain rendition, Casaro's final international one-sheet featured two opposing factions: Lady Jessica and Paul (pointing a weirding module) on the left, and Baron Harkonnen and Feyd (brandishing a knife) on the right, all floating over a two-moon Arrakis desert landscape. Above the figures was a composite of the wooden stairwell on Caladan and the opening archway of the Great Hall on Arrakis with Fremen warriors emerging. Like much of Casaro's work, the poster is both painterly and highly realistic. It was seen in countries like Italy and the Netherlands.

RENATO CASARO: Dino decided on the image after being presented with the sketches. With *Dune*, I didn't follow up where the poster was used, but definitely around the world. From the first sketches to the final art- work took about one month. The technique was tempera and airbrush on cardboard. Certainly, everybody was very satisfied. It is always interesting to study other artists to the same theme, but—without any vanity—my version was the best composition adapted to the film and tells the potential visitor all and nothing of the movie.

While Sammon attempted to court sci-fi fans around the country, he faced an uphill battle from the marketing unit at Universal.

PAUL M. SAMMON: I screened the "Destination Dune" featurette at numerous cons and some mainstream venues around the United States. David never understood why this featurette was an important marketing tool, aimed right at the core audience, seen by thousands. I was also acting as a producer on a proposed one-hour NBC TV special that was going to prominently feature behind-the-scenes footage of *Dune* and position it as an epic along the lines of *The Ten Commandments*, *Lawrence of Arabia*, and *2001*. Universal had friendly relations with the actor Charlton Heston, and he was talking to the studio about narrating this special. The plug was pulled on the special early on, as soon as *Dune* started looking problematic in terms of the studio's waning interest in it.

THOM MOUNT: They didn't get it, you know . . . they didn't get it. I've personally produced 27 movies, but also supervised 200-plus movies at Universal and the marketing focus is so critical. *Animal House* is a wonderful movie, I love it, but if we had marketed it poorly, we would have suffered and that movie never would have become the iconic hit that it is today. You can see it over *Smokey and the Bandit*, a movie that my distribution people hated. They thought it was designed only for four states, all of them named Alabama. It needs thought, it needs good creative work, and it needs inspiration. We didn't have that. I think we failed *Dune*.

PAUL M. SAMMON: The biggest missed opportunity? To market the film as a sweeping, serious, slightly psychedelic science-fiction epic, not as a pop fantasy shoot-'em-up. The book was there, the core audience was there, the ecological subtext and grandeur and David's peculiar visions were there. The proper advertising wasn't.

FRANK PRICE: Everything in motion pictures is word of mouth. You can do a great trailer and advertising. That gives you a terrific opening week, but once people see the picture, they make their judgment. As they're walking out of the theater, they tell the people standing in line what they think.

BOB RINGWOOD: Did I tell you about the crew showing? The whole crew was there.

MARY VOGT: We went to a screening of it at Disney of all places, in a small screening room. David was there, Raffaella was there. It was just a mess. I wish they could release the four-hour version that we saw in Mexico, the editor's version before anyone else got their hands on it. No music, no effects, but it was beautiful. Shakespearean. Epic. We were expecting a cut-down version of that, this really serious film, instead of this nutty thing with this crazy narration.

BOB RINGWOOD: The film ended, and usually there's applause and cheering, but there was this strange atmosphere of silence and depression. The crew was shocked, and everyone thought the film was complete rubbish.

GILES MASTERS: We saw a cut of the film in Mexico which was over five hours long. It didn't have a lot of the visual effects in it or the final music, but it was good. When it got cut down to 2 hours and 20 minutes, a lot of it became confusing.

MARY VOGT: Bob and I just looked at each other when the movie was over. I was like, "Oh my God." To me, it was like, "Throw this in the garbage." No comparison to what we saw in Mexico.

BOB RINGWOOD: I walked up the central aisle, and there were David and Raffaella standing there, waiting for praise, and nobody was praising.

MARY VOGT: We were walking out, and he goes up to David. I thought, "Oh, here it comes." David goes, "Oh, hi, Bob!"

BOB RINGWOOD: I just looked at them both and said, "Well, you've just fucked this up really regally!" And walked on.

MARY VOGT: Ringwood goes, "Well, you really fucked that up, didn't you?" David was like, "Well, what do you mean? You didn't like it?"

BOB RINGWOOD: I'm amazed they ever spoke to me again after that, because we were all so shocked at how bad the film was. It wasn't good. It was a really bad day.

MARY VOGT: We had seen this version that was so brilliant, and it was so disappointing to see this kind of bizarro thing that they made out of it. It's like taking the Mona Lisa and throwing a bunch of crap at it. Why would you do that?

RAFFAELLA DE LAURENTIIS: You really can't put that book in a two-hour movie. The thing they were smart about on this new one is that they did two movies.

BOB RINGWOOD: Before we went into production, the script was like reading the Bible. I said, "Why don't you cut this into two and do Part One and Part Two? You can't tell this whole story in one." They all laughed at that idea.

FREDERICK ELMES: They were thinking about it as this one unit. "It's not going to be two parts. Don't ever entertain that." [*laughs*]

PENELOPE SHAW SYLVESTER: I was never aware of it being considered as two parts, which—in retrospect—would have been much better. David had all these wonderful ideas, and it's hard to get that compressed down. That story is so vast. No one else has done it in a single film. Either you have the miniseries or the new one that's been broken up. We all know why it's been broken up, because it's impossible to give it the richness that David wanted in one two-hour version. You can't do it.

KYLE MACLACHLAN: One of the things about the new film—the redo—that is going to be very helpful is they stopped in the middle. The book itself is in three parts, there are three sections of *Dune*, so you could break this into three movies if you wanted to. You can do two, end with meeting the Fremen and that transition that happens there, and then you pick up with Paul as he develops his power and starts ascending to where he goes.

BOB RINGWOOD: You can't do the one film, and that's why the film was cut with those terrible voiceovers.

RAFFAELLA DE LAURENTIIS: It was not only the voiceover. It was also in the dialogues, trying to explain some of those things that are so hard to explain. I wonder if we should have.

Molly Wryn did not discover that her major character of Harah—along with her entire storyline—had been almost completely excised from the finished film until she attended the premiere in Los Angeles.

MOLLY WRYN: Imagine? My heart crushed. Broke. It hurt. David had said to me not long before that, "You know, some of your stuff has been cut." Something very gentle. I said, "Okay," but I had no idea I was completely cut. They even shot me for the credits, when they show everybody's face, but didn't use it, which was sad. I remember how shocked I was. And then at the end, not even my face that they filmed. It took a while, they film from all directions and then pick out what they want to use and . . . gosh, I'm getting teary about it.

TERRI HARDIN: People would say, "Oh, that movie was so terrible." What you don't realize is there's like seven hours on the cutting room floor. Frank Herbert at the screening was devastated, so sad that he had to show us this movie. I think he had seen it before, but he was heartbroken by the movie. So many people were disappointed by the results. The De Laurentiises weren't at our screening, mostly the builders and below-the-line people. It was supposed to be two films, and it became one, really short and really not very comprehensible.

FREDERICK ELMES: What's on the screen isn't really David's film. It's a different edit. It's a different version of the film, and that made me very sad.

KENNETH GEORGE GODWIN: I knew there was stuff that would have made a stronger film. You're 45 minutes into it before the Harkonnens attack, and mostly what we've got is just setting up all these royal families. You've got this huge exposition at the beginning, then a pretty rushed midsection. After he's with the Fremen, they start to follow him and attack . . . That's all compressed into a couple of montages. There was way more shot. Then you've got the ending, a big battle scene. A huge chunk of the meat of the story got ditched.

JANE JENKINS: I don't know that I ever understood it any better than when I struggled through the book. I think that the movie was not as successful as David could have made it. He had a vision to do it in black and white. He didn't want to do it in color. I think that it had the potential if David had been left entirely to his own devices to make it a stronger movie. I don't know that I have enough distance from it to give you a really clinical . . . I thought the worms were ridiculous.

GILES MASTERS: The stories of what David went through are well-documented, and it wasn't the film that he wanted. It wasn't the film most of us expected to see when we went to the premiere; everybody was a little like, "Oh, what happened?"

IAN WOOLF: I went to the premiere at the Kennedy Center in Washington with my wife and a friend of ours. After the 2 hours and 20 minutes, you could hear a pin drop in the theater. It's like, "What the fuck was this?" It wasn't good.

VIRGINIA MADSEN: I didn't go to that one. I went to the premiere at the Chinese, or maybe it was Westwood? They handed out this little dictionary. I saw that and I thought, "Oh no, this movie is in trouble . . . you need a dictionary."

ERIC SWENSON: I don't remember everybody being bummed or super-excited. It was like, "Hey, that's pretty cool." Everybody hates their own stuff, and thinks they could do it better. I'm looking at Rambaldi's creatures and the forced perspective miniatures. Some of those sets like the Emperor's palace were still left over when I got there, and to see them up on the big screen was phenomenal.

ALICIA WITT: I loved it! I loved it. I also missed a lot of the scenes that were missing. It was amazing to have that first experience of having watched something being filmed and then seeing it made into a real-life movie. That's always magical, and it never stops being magical. No matter how many times I've done it now, you watch a scene being filmed over and over again from all the different angles and then you see it turned into a story. I also remember being confused by the feedback that I heard after the movie that people didn't understand it, because obviously I knew the story backward and forward and it made perfect sense to me, but I can see now how it might have been confusing to people who hadn't already read the book.

VIRGINIA MADSEN: It was kind of hard for me to recover from the fact that my face was 25 feet tall in the theater. That was the coolest thing I could have ever dreamt of as a little girl. There it was. I might not have been Barbara Stanwyck, but there I was. To me, everything about the movie was perfect because I was so proud to be a part of something that big when I was such a sci-fi/fantasy/horror fan. It was very exciting and very beautiful. I wanted to see it again immediately. [*laughs*]

PENELOPE SHAW SYLVESTER: They were all very complimentary at the Royal premiere in London. We all went out and partied afterward. I remember going into the ladies' room, and Sting's wife's dress had come apart and she was in a panic. I said, "Don't worry!" Being a Girl Scout, I had my safety pins; we pinned her up and back she went.

CRAIG CAMPOBASSO: I was on the movie from beginning to end, all the way to the Royal premiere in London. I think the London premiere was the big one, because there were a lot of British actors. At the after party at Blondies, Duran Duran was there and Grace Jones because she did *Conan the Destroyer*.

LUIGI ROCCHETTI: In addition to the human side of Lynch, I admire his vision of things. The film could have been better. It's a very complicated and difficult story to tell, and surely David's version was better when it was uncut.

KENNETH GEORGE GODWIN: If David had been left alone with the editor, it would have been better, had more coherence. The emphasis was never so much on the story as on creating four different worlds with all their architecture, the sense that these places all have different histories, different societies. That kind of world building appealed to him more than the story of this kid who becomes a god.

Harlan Ellison wrote articles at the time alleging that Price thought Dune *was "a dog" and was deliberately withholding it from the press.*

FRANK PRICE: Not a dog. It was not bad. David Lynch does good work. Harlan Ellison was always around with a chip on his shoulder.

PAUL M. SAMMON: Prior to its release, there was a great deal of journalistic interest in *Dune*. Fan interest was somewhat split prior to the film's opening, though. There was the inevitable skepticism of, "Isn't this the same producer who gave us that mediocre remake of *King Kong*?" That was balanced by Frank Herbert's very vocal enthusiasm about how faithfully David Lynch was "doing" his book. In fact, I included some footage of Frank heartily (and genuinely) endorsing *Dune* in my "Destination Dune" convention featurette, but then the release date kept being pushed back and audience/press interest began waning.

BARRY NOLAN: I would imagine the release delay was because there was a dead zone in there where nothing was being done. The effects were not being put together when they could have because we were regenerating.

ERIC SWENSON: I would agree with that. If you want to get your effects done, what do you do? You throw more money at it? More houses, more people, more equipment? They weren't going to do that.

CRAIG CAMPOBASSO: They didn't do any press screenings. That's where all that anger came from the press. People started writing bad stuff because of that.

FRANK PRICE: Oh yeah. You don't want to give critics time to destroy you. I had a picture at Columbia that is a good example called *Neighbors*. It had John Belushi and Dan Aykroyd. When we test-screened it, audiences hated it. I told the marketing head, "Get every theater you can get, every seat, because we've got to get everything out in a week." We did great business for a week, and then it collapsed. Word of mouth destroyed it. But with *Dune*, you can't get your money back in a week.

CRAIG CAMPOBASSO: They didn't want anybody to knock it down before it was released, but not letting them see it had the opposite effect. Then the movie came out, and it just didn't do well.

KENNETH GEORGE GODWIN: I was hyped up. I had never been involved in anything like this. I went opening day here in Winnipeg, and it washed over me purely as a visual spectacle. "This is amazing!" I saw it again a few days later and could see all the dramatic issues, the clunkiness of the storytelling. On second viewing, I felt disappointed that it could have been so much more. Because I'd been on set, I had this awareness of stuff that is not in the film. "Why did you keep this stuff? You could have had this instead?"

THOM MOUNT: The real problem was people didn't show up. It's hard to know. When we did *The Deer Hunter*, I was told by everybody repeatedly that the picture would be a total failure, that no one wants to see this long exegesis on our painful exit from Vietnam. Six Academy Awards and hundreds of millions of dollars in income later, they were wrong. But on the other hand, you're talking to the guy who gave *Xanadu* the go-ahead. I know what it is to lose every dime.

After the film earned a paltry $30 million in North America, there was very little in the way of awards love. The only Academy Award nomination the film received was Best Sound, for which Steve Maslow was one of the four nominees, having won twice before. They lost to Amadeus. *Alan Splet was not included in the nomination.*

STEVE MASLOW: Alan Splet was not a mixer, so his division of editors would have nominated him if they thought he was worthy, probably for Best Sound Editing. The Oscar promotion generally was print ads, but some of them got much more. They spent based on, "Well this film's not going to make it." Oscars are pretty much all the same in terms of driving up with a limo, going through the red carpet, nobody knows who the hell you are. You sit down and just sweat it out for a half-hour until you lose. I didn't think we had . . . I thought we had some chance, but I thought *2010* was the shoo-in because that was kind of a cool movie. I thought we had a slim chance, but I was pretty much correct. [*laughs*]

Perhaps due to the drubbing they received from critics, Barry Nolan and others involved in the visual effects were mostly overlooked except for a Saturn nomination.

BARRY NOLAN: I presented it for an Academy Award. They hired an editor, and we went in there and spent two days making a demo reel to give the Academy. Edited the sound and added all kinds of things. They did a first-class job. Most people just take the demo reel in with a bunch of effects cut together, but we made a beautiful thing. Of course, I didn't win anything. I lost to the time travel Arnold one, *The Terminator*, which was—in my opinion—a much better film. [*laughs*]

Bob Ringwood's bold and stunning costumes, which proved very influential in years to come, were roundly snubbed except for a lone Saturn Award.

BOB RINGWOOD: I was surprised it didn't get nominated. It was so different from any other science-fiction film, and a lot of the clothes were very nice in it. They were. But I was hated because I flew into Hollywood as a completely unknown person and took over all the big films, and they didn't like it. When they do nominate for Oscars, they get six people on a committee, the costume designers, and then decide the shortlist of people that could be eligible for nomination. One of my friends was on that committee and said they were "never going to let him get an Oscar." That whole thing is so corrupt that it's pointless having an award that is worth nothing, really.

BARRY NOLAN: I was asked to join the Academy as a technical adviser by three or four top members. I went through everything, then they said, "No, you don't have enough screen credits. Sorry." I went to all the meetings, and there was so much good ol' boy stuff. I thought, "There are things going on here that aren't up to par."

MARY VOGT: After we saw the movie, we just wrote it off. I never even went to a premiere or saw it in a big theater. I never saw it again until it came on television. Bob won the Saturn Award from the Science Fiction Academy.

BOB RINGWOOD: I think I won two or three of those. I threw them in the dustbin. They are so ugly. I don't really believe in awards. If you're in it for accolades and awards, then you're in it for the wrong reason, I think.

The fact that Anthony Masters' gorgeous production design work was overlooked for the Best Art Direction award must have stung at the time, especially considering that one of the actual nominees, 2010, *was largely a rehash of Masters' work on* 2001.

GILES MASTERS: When we were working on it, we were very excited about the whole thing. It did look magnificent, and it was huge. The amount of design work that goes into a film like that was extraordinary, the number of sets that were built. The thing is that if a film doesn't do well, it does get overlooked often. It happens. *2001* didn't win the Oscar because when it opened, it didn't do well. When they were making *2010*, they called my father up and said, "Can we please have all your designs?" He said, "You better call Mr. Kubrick." I don't think they got much out of Mr. Kubrick. I'm sure he didn't answer their phone calls. My father never really talked about that. I don't think it upset him or anything. I think it was disappointing for everybody that the film didn't catch on when it came out.

Dune *still carries the reputation for being "the* Heaven's Gate *of sci-fi," but does it deserve that reputation?*

PENELOPE SHAW SYLVESTER: You're talking to somebody that worked previously on *Heaven's Gate*, so this one wasn't so bad, you know? Michael Cimino was so difficult to work with and really nasty to people. David was never, never nasty to anybody. I wouldn't put them in the same boat at all.

RAFFAELLA DE LAURENTIIS: Look, it's not an easy adaptation. If you have not read the book and you're not familiar with the book, you'll get lost easily. One of the mistakes—and I'll take responsibility for that—was David would have probably been a lot more esoteric, but I was concerned about people being able to follow the story. Sometimes I was pushing to explain things, to remain close to the book, to be faithful to the book. I'm not sure that was always the right decision to make.

SEAN YOUNG: Honestly, in my early 20s—I don't mean to sound so blasé—I learned pretty quickly that it's really hard to get this stuff off the ground, make it fly, and then hope it soars. I didn't really think *Dune* was going to soar because there was no special energy. Sometimes you get on a film, and you know it's special. Then you get on a film and you're like,

"Oh, there's no energy here." Everybody's showing up, but . . . it's hard to define. Things have an energy, or sometimes they lack energy and you don't really know why. It lacked energy. Everybody had a great time in Mexico City, but like I said, there was a lot of drinking going on and people lose their focus.

MARY VOGT: Everyone was expecting so much more. Sometimes when filmmakers get too close to their baby, they don't realize they gave the baby two heads.

JANE JENKINS: There was a lot of interference in David's version. He was not a powerful enough director at that point in his career to say, "All right, everybody back off," and have final cut. Very interesting guy. Even though I found *Eraserhead* very odd, to say the least, all his films have been very interesting. *Dune* is probably the least successful because he didn't have enough control to do what he wanted.

THOM MOUNT: The essence of all this is that if we had a better view of the market and a greater loyalty to the creative side of the movie and if our campaign had made sense and all those things, life would have been a lot different. Would it have been a *Star Wars* kind of hit? I don't know.

FRANK PRICE: It wasn't a sacrificial lamb; it was just in this lineup of pictures that nobody owned. Clearly, they weren't mine, but whose were they? Ned didn't claim them. Bob didn't claim them. Sid didn't claim them. Nobody seemed to have greenlit them. Universal wasn't financing it all— Dino was bringing money out of Italy. I think *Stick* was probably a worse hit to the bottom line than *Dune*. *Stick* was made entirely with Universal's money, whereas Dino was in with the Italian money, which made it more attractive.

RAFFAELLA DE LAURENTIIS: This is what I know: The movie at Universal is in the green. Believe it or not, they're in profit, but I know that the perception of the movie is that it didn't make its money back. It did make its money back. I don't know if it was equal parts between here and foreign. I think it did better in Europe because they have more patience, the European moviegoers.

. . .

—IV—
LEGACY

"Mother, they're still not sure it is a baby!"

—*Mary X*, **Eraserhead**

Dune Aftermath

After 1961's Bay of Pigs Invasion disaster, US President John F. Kennedy remarked, "There's an old saying that victory has a hundred fathers and defeat is an orphan . . .." That quote originated from Count Galeazzo Ciano, the Italian fascist and son-in-law of Benito Mussolini.

It took another Italian to do a proper mea culpa for the cinematic disaster that was *Dune*. In the 2001 BBC documentary *Dino De Laurentiis: The Last Movie Mogul*—made in the wake of his receiving the honorary Irving Thalberg lifetime achievement Academy Award—Dino took full responsibility for the film that nearly became his Waterloo . . . not to be confused with his 1970 movie *Waterloo*:

> The problem with *Dune* . . . you know what is the problem with *Dune*? We had a fantastic movie when we did our cut. It was three-hour movie. And Universal said, "Please, Dino. Please, Dino. We don't need three hours, we want two hours. Two hours . . ." And I did the mistake to listen Universal, I cut one hour from the movie. When we cut one hour from the movie, it was not the same movie. It was not the same movie. We destroy in the editing room the movie.

In contrast, Lynch has for the most part attributed the film's downfall to his not obtaining the almighty "final cut privilege" that would have allowed his true vision to take flight, or at the very least grant the filmmaker ownership of its failure.

While in conversation at Brisbane's Gallery of Modern Art in 2015, Lynch remarked:

> It's very important for a filmmaker to have final cut, total creative control. I knew that even before *Dune*. For some reason, I thought everything would be okay, and I signed the contract. Everything wasn't okay. It was a terrible thing, and as I always say, the film was not a success. So, I died the death in that regard, and then I felt I had sold out, so I died twice. I loved Dino. I love Raffaella, his daughter. Dino taught me how to cook rigatoni. Dino was such a great character; I really loved him. We just didn't see eye to eye, and he had the power.

In 1986, Raffaella De Laurentiis was making her next big epic (and future bomb) *Tai-Pan* in China, and she told the *Los Angeles Times*:

> *Dune* was a labor of love. We all thought we were doing the right thing. Then you look at it and you say, "Well, somewhere down the line I made a mistake." David and I still talk about it. I don't think we're over it yet. We were just too faithful to the book. We loved the book and Frank Herbert so much, and we felt the fans could not be betrayed. But we ended up with something that was just too complicated to understand.

Raffaella interestingly described the budget of *Dune* as being $38 million before prints and advertising. This is a far cry from the $45 million figure that her father threw around bombastically in the press, not to mention the fact that the De Laurentiis company apparently earned a great deal of their investment back just by keeping their liquidity in Mexican banks where the exchange rate was favorable.

"*Dune* wasn't $45 million," Lynch confided to Brad Keywell at a Chicago Ideas panel in 2019. "Dino said it was $45 million because he came from a time when big and grandiose was the best, but really in the time he said these things, people were turned off by that amount of money. But Dino was a crafty fellow, and he did it for far less than $45 million."

"At a certain point in the making of *Dune*, I think David got scared and felt like he was on a sinking ship and didn't know whether he would be able to make a great movie," Sean Young narrated in a video she posted to YouTube in 2010. "He was a little spoiled in that he'd only made great movies up until then."

Young was philosophical about the experience after the film's release, telling *The Courier-Journal* in April of 1985, "You do the very best you can each time out, and try not to worry about it. I spent five months filming in Mexico City and ended up with three minutes of screen time. But I had the experience of working on the character, and the benefit of what I learned from it. That'll never be lost."

Francesca Annis commented in 2021 [*Deadline*]:

> My experience of working on *Dune* was that if David Lynch had been able to make his own film, it would have been brilliant, but unfortunately, Dino oversaw every single tiny thing. Dino was already thinking about the video sales. David had wanted to make the scenes very dark, all the underworlds very dark and look very sinister. Dino wouldn't allow it. It had to be lit brightly so that it would transfer well to video, where I think at that time things went down a shade. David and DoP Freddie Francis were constantly being hamstrung, and I don't think David made the film he wanted to make.

"David Lynch is . . . a director who has a real vision," Richard Jordan told *The Press Democrat* in July 1985. "I sat there for two-and-a-quarter hours of *Dune* and I couldn't figure out what was happening, but at least I wasn't bored."

Like many other critical figures from Herbert's book (including Duncan Idaho, Reverend Mother Ramallo, and Shadout Mapes), Liet-Kynes was reduced to minimal screen time in the final film, to the point that it doesn't even register that Max von Sydow is meant to be playing the father of Young's character Chani. In 1993, von Sydow told interviewer Steve Newton:

> I enjoyed that; I was just very sorry that he was not allowed to make a longer film. It was not fair to the project, not fair to the subject, not fair to David Lynch to cut it down to as much as it was. It should have been a long film, or—even better—it should have been a miniseries for television. It's such a fantastic book, I must say, but the film—as far as I can see—failed because it was too short, and all the wonderful structure, all the backgrounds, all the worlds—which I think were very intelligently portrayed in the book—you didn't really understand them in the film. They had to put in a narrator to explain things, etc. It was not fair to David Lynch. David is such an imaginative filmmaker.

"Looking back on *Dune*, there was nothing about the people and their relationships that you cared about, and in the book, you care a great deal about the people, like they have really special bonds, like how you might have with your father, unspoken but very strong," Kyle MacLachlan lamented to the *L.A. Times* in 1990. "In the movie, not much attention was paid to that at all."

MacLachlan was already reassessing his feelings to the *SouthtownStar* in 1994, a decade after the film came out:

> Looking back on *Dune* now, it's not as bad as people were saying at the time. But ultimately it didn't work, and we all sort of destroyed it. I certainly bore some of the responsibility, as did David and the De Laurentiis family. The bright spot is that I got a very good agent out of something that was branded a disaster, but I still had to prove myself all over again. It took about two very long years.

Proving himself as a viable star should have been a hole-in-one with MacLachlan's high-profile debut, but after *Dune* faltered, he had difficulty getting his mojo back. After firing his agent at CAA and hiring a public relations firm, there were many auditions—including for the leads in *Platoon* and *Top Gun*—but nothing clicked. Lynch had already chosen MacLachlan to lead *Blue Velvet*, but production on that was delayed after the *Dune* fallout.

MacLachlan spent a moribund year appearing in regional theater, going to the gym, and hanging out in his apartment. He was so anxious he arrived on the North Carolina set of *Blue Velvet* two weeks early.

As he recalled it in 1998 [*Encore Magazine*]:

> Trying to gain an understanding of the producer's point of view was very hard. It's about money. That's why people put money into a film, so they can make money. And I wasn't a desirable actor because I did not make money. Whether you're good or not, that's sort of an added thing. I don't say that I've accepted that, but it's sort of the nature of the business and it's up to us to fight it.

"When you have a failure, it's real destructive to this idea process," Lynch told *Sunday Democrat* in 1986. "You want to stay home. It shuts down ideas."

Lynch went AWOL for a while from Hollywood, spending time recharging and recovering with his family in Virginia. At one point, after yanking out weeds in his front lawn by hand and pulling a muscle, he just stayed in bed for four days straight.

"I felt, not like giving it all up, but I started to think in strange ways," Lynch said of his feelings after *Dune* to *Twilight Zone* in 1988. "It was seven days a week of shooting for a year, just shooting, and then six days a week of post-production for more than a year. And then when the film fails . . . well, you can easily lose your mind."

While promoting *Blue Velvet* during a 1986 interview with Brian Linehan on the TV talk program *City Lights*, Lynch stated, "The making of *Dune* went wrong because we had a 2-hour and 15-minute limit on the length of the picture, and it was too much to tell in that amount of time. So, it was like a fantastic Porsche car kind of compacted down into . . . it's still a Porsche, but it's hard to drive it and it doesn't look so good anymore."

In the 2013 documentary *Jodorowsky's Dune*, Chilean filmmaker Alejandro Jodorowsky recalled being crestfallen when he heard David Lynch had taken over the project that had once been his. However, when he finally saw the finished *Dune* in cinemas, he had a schadenfreude reaction that put a smile on his face:

> When I heard David Lynch will direct that, I have a pain because I admire David Lynch. He can do it! He is the only one in this moment who can do it, and he will do it! I suffer because was my dream. Another person will do that maybe better than me. Then when they show the picture here, I say I will not go to see that because I will die. My sons say, "No, we are warriors. You need to come to see that." They take me, like an ill person I came to the theat-

er. Even I think I will cry. I start to see the picture, and step by step, step by step, step by step, I became happy because the picture was awful! It's a failure! Well, it's a human reaction, no? It's not beautiful, but I have that reaction. I say, "Is not possible. Is not David Lynch because he is a big artist." Is the producer who did that.

Lynch did blame heavy-handed producers. In 2000, Charlie Rose asked Lynch point blank if *Dune* was his worst mistake. "It wasn't a mistake," Lynch replied. "I learned a lot. It was a little bit, well more than a little bit . . . I sold out. I didn't have final cut, and I knew the way people were and I adjusted. You really can't do that."

TV critic team Siskel and Ebert were still getting their jabs in a year later in 1985 while reviewing another big-budget sci-fi fiasco, *Enemy Mine*, which Gene Siskel inexplicably loved.

"Wild creatures, that thing coming out of the sand . . . remember how much we hated *Dune* with its worms?" Siskel asked to Roger Ebert's agreement. "This has the kind of worms *Dune* should have had!"

MacLachlan discussed his changing take again in 2020 [*IndieWire*]:

My feelings about it evolve over time. I look at it as a flawed gem. It's stunning in so many ways. As a story, and trying to recreate that story, it's almost impossible. It's incredibly dense and a little bit like a house of cards. If you leave out one element of the story or another, the structure tends to wobble, and you don't get the full effect. There's a mysticism about it that is difficult to capture on film. That, combined with a straight-ahead story and characters that are really well-created. They're full people, and you want to spend time with each one of them. And that eats up your film time. It's a real puzzle. It's just so many elements that you have to bring together.

Still holding the story dear, MacLachlan recently tweeted out a concise synopsis of the *Dune* plot entirely with emojis:

On the plus side, the film's failure seemed to have saved Lynch from being lashed to the *Dune* franchise for what could have been the rest of the decade. This big out from a planned trilogy was something he told *Inner Views* in 1992 that he was grateful for, even though he had already been hammering out a draft of the aborted *Dune Messiah* film in late 1984. "Yes, that's a plus," he said. "Though I was really getting into *Dune II*. I wrote about half the script, maybe more, and I was really getting excited about it. It was much tighter, a better story."

Almost two years to the day after his wife, Beverly, had passed away, author Frank Herbert died on February 11, 1986, at age 65 after suffering a pulmonary embolism during recovery from surgery. A week after his death, a small ceremony in the woods was held on the Olympic Peninsula, where a McIntosh apple tree was planted in his honor. His son Brian wrote of realizing that no one had remembered to water the hole where the tree was planted: "At that moment, to our amazement, rain began to fall, not unlike the rain at the end of the David Lynch film version of *Dune* that watered the parched planet."

Dino did give Lynch final cut on his next film, 1986's haunting neo-noir *Blue Velvet.*

"Dino said to me one day, 'You want to make *Blue Velvet?*" Lynch remembers in a November 1986 edition of *Democrat and Chronicle.* "I said, 'Yes.' He said, 'I have a crazy idea: You cut your own salary and cut the budget, and I'll give you total artistic freedom.' To a filmmaker, that's the greatest thing that can happen."

While some, including actors involved in *Dune*, have speculated that Lynch made *Velvet* for Dino as a means to complete his contract and get out from under him, that does not appear to be the case. *Velvet* was always been in the cards as his potential next movie, even while *Dune* was filming. Indeed, an article from October of 1984 in North Carolina's *The News and Observer* confirms Lynch's intention to shoot *Blue Velvet* in North Carolina, even before *Dune* came out. In interviews, Lynch is effusive in his praise for the De Laurentiis family, even telling Brian Linehan in the same 1986 interview that having someone like Dino on a runaway production like Michael Cimino's *Heaven's Gate* would have been beneficial.

> With too much money and too much freedom, sometimes you're just floating out in space, and it becomes something other than film-

making. Maybe somebody like Dino could have made a tighter corral around the whole process, and it could have sparked something and something better could have happened. I don't know. I like a boundary, some sort of restriction. It pushes me. For artistic business, I like freedom there. I think the two things can coexist. You need a real good producer who is totally organized but also keeps you from getting too crazy.

Made in North Carolina under the auspices of Dino's newly formed company De Laurentiis Entertainment Group (DEG), *Blue Velvet* reunited Lynch with MacLachlan as the hero Jeffrey Beaumont, who is transported from his idyllic suburban life into a seedy urban underworld after finding a severed ear in a field. The role nearly went to the man who almost nabbed the part of Paul Atreides, Val Kilmer.

"I was given a copy of that script because at one point I was involved with *Dune*," Kilmer told *Movieline* in 1995. "It would have been my first job for damn near a year. So, Dave gave me the script, and it was straight-out, hard-core pornography before page 30. I never finished it. I said, 'Good luck, but I can't do this.' It isn't what he ended up making. That movie, I would have done."

MacLachlan told the Criterion Collection in 2022:

> *Blue Velvet* was kind of a rebirth for me, because we'd done *Dune* together in '83 and *Dune* didn't turn out that well. After that, I felt like I was a pariah in the business, no work, no nothing. But David, bless his heart, he'd given me the script to *Blue Velvet* when we were filming *Dune* in Mexico City, and I read it and I was like, "whoa, this is very, very intense." I really liked it and really identified with the character of Jeffrey. David and I were planning to go shoot *Blue Velvet* right after *Dune* was released in winter of '84, and because *Dune* didn't do so well, they postponed it, and then finally *Blue Velvet* came to pass in the summer of '85 . . . As traumatic as *Dune* was for him, I know *Blue Velvet* was a whole different reality, and we were in our element. He came back to me—that's the point. We did *Dune* together and he could easily have said, "well, Kyle didn't really help the movie and so I'm going to find somebody else," and he didn't do that. He wanted me, and I'll be forever grateful.

Other *Dune* alums in *Blue Velvet* include Brad Dourif as Raymond, henchman to Dennis Hopper's memorable psychotic Frank Booth, as well as Jack

Nance as Paul and Dean Stockwell as the sexually ambiguous Ben, who memorably lip syncs to Roy Orbison's "In Dreams." Isabella Rossellini brilliantly portrays Dorothy Vallens, the damaged singer under Booth's thumb. Lynch had at one time wanted Francesca Annis to read for the role, but she was barred from doing so by Dino, who may have still been reeling from visions of an incestuous Paul and Jessica from Ridley Scott's version. Baron Harkonnen actor Kenneth McMillan was also considered for a role, most likely the similarly degenerate and over-the-top Frank Booth.

Where *Dune* was an unwieldy epic, *Blue Velvet* was a low-budget, small-scale mystery thriller, a genre that would become Lynch's bread and butter in the ensuing years. It earned close to $9 million in North America alone on a $6 million budget. A return to form in every respect, the film collected an outpouring of accolades, including a Best Director Oscar nomination for Lynch. It is now considered a masterpiece on the level of Alfred Hitchcock's *Vertigo*.

Lynch was scheduled to make his *Blue Velvet* follow-up, *One Saliva Bubble*, for DEG as well. Cowritten with Mark Frost (*Hill Street Blues*), the script centers around a computer glitch caused by the title bit of spittle, which inadvertently leads a satellite to shoot a laser at the small Kansas town of Newtonville, resulting in residents swapping bodies. Steve Martin and Martin Short were set to lead *One Saliva Bubble*, with MacLachlan also anticipated to co-star, telling *The Daily Tar Heel* in September of 1987, "It's supposed to be a much more recognizable comedy." Sets were supposedly being built six weeks out from filming before DEG ultimately went bankrupt, effectively ending the company's partnership with Lynch.

"I was casting it, we went location scouting, and I was going to shoot it," Lynch said in David Hughes' *The Complete Lynch*. "And then Dino's company went bankrupt."

Like other mini-major studios in the '80s, such as Charles Band's Empire Pictures or Menahem Golan and Yoram Globus' Cannon Group, the Beverly Hills–based DEG quickly rose and fell. Announced in 1985, not long after *Dune*, DEG was an ambitious undertaking kicked off by acquiring the distribution arm of Embassy Pictures from Coca-Cola for $17 million plus stock, as well as its 244-movie library, which included *The Graduate* and *This Is Spinal Tap*. There was also a brand new 32-acre movie studio in Wilmington, NC.

Dino explained in 1984 [*The Guardian*]:

> We chose North Carolina because of our good experience there with *Firestarter*. The climate is perfect, it's an hour from New York, and

it's much cheaper. You feel comfortable on a $35 per diem. We aren't building the studio to rent to somebody else. We have so many pictures of our own. We built six sound stages and found we needed more, so we built two more.

He had a second studio under construction along Australia's Gold Coast. $240 million in capital had been raised through a combination of banks and public stock offerings, with Dino himself taking a 70% share of ownership. He jump-started production by buying back projects he had waiting in the wings all over town (*Maximum Overdrive*, *Tai-Pan*, etc.) from studios who were, according to a 1989 *Spy* magazine article, "happy to get rid of them."

Unlike Mario Kassar and Andrew G. Vajna's Carolco Pictures, which kept a roof over its head by making big (eventually unsustainable) bets on winners like *Rambo: First Blood Part II* and *Terminator 2: Judgment Day*, the films that emerged from the DEG years never came close to hitting their target. Of the 19 movies De Laurentiis' studio produced between 1986 and 1988, almost *none* of them grossed more than their budget, bringing in $37.95 million at the box office altogether out of a nearly $200 million collective investment. Even though pre-sales to TV, VHS, and foreign distributors covered the budgets, money was still hemorrhaged on prints and advertising. While they were churning out dreck like *Date with an Angel* or *Million Dollar Mystery*, some hit pictures the company developed but ultimately passed on making included *Platoon*, *Bull Durham*, and *Pet Sematary*.

With the company $16.5 million in debt, Raffaella De Laurentiis (whose $25 million production of *Tai-Pan* only made $2 million) resigned as DEG's president of production in August 1987. After trying and failing to save her father from his own worst instincts, it was time to strike out on her own. According to the *L.A. Times*, this action "deeply pained" her father. By February 1988, Dino himself would resign as chairman. An Australian production of Bruce Beresford's initial version of *Total Recall* starring Patrick Swayze was aborted after $3.4 million worth of sets had been built, only for the project to be resurrected by Carolco in 1990 starring Arnold Schwarzenegger. By the time DEG finally filed for bankruptcy, they had $197 million in assets and $243 million in liabilities, with the stock only worth 37 cents a share.

It wasn't all doom and gloom, though. There were no home runs at the time, but the De Laurentiis Entertainment Group was responsible for several genre pictures that eventually garnered cult followings (and profitability), including *Evil Dead II*, *Near Dark*, and *Manhunter*. Films like *Blue Velvet* and

Beresford's *Crimes of the Heart* earned accolades and Oscar nominations. Some of the company's output released after May 1988—including *Pumpkinhead* and *Bill & Ted's Excellent Adventure*—scored financially after other studios picked them up for domestic distribution. Nelson Entertainment, the company run by ex-DEG execs that spawned out of their home video division, went on to great fortune by joining forces with Rob Reiner's Castle Rock Entertainment on hits like *When Harry Met Sally . . .*, *Misery*, and *City Slickers*. They also had a moderate winner with Raffaella's first film as a solo producer, the holiday movie *Prancer*.

Lynch had taken the *Dune* gig in hopes of getting his long-cherished surreal rock-and-roll fantasy *Ronnie Rocket* made, with Carlo Rambaldi at one point signed on to create the title character and A&M Records interested in a soundtrack.

"It's abstract," Lynch described *Ronnie Rocket* to AP in January 1984. "It's about a little guy, three feet tall with red hair and physical problems . . . It's a cool film."

"*Ronnie Rocket* is the picture I hope to make where I would use things I learned from doing *Dune*," Lynch expressed to *Enterprise Incidents* #25. "There's something about *Dune* that I'll use in *Ronnie Rocket* but not so much in *Blue Velvet*."

It ultimately proved too strange for Dino's sensibilities. Both *Ronnie Rocket* and *One Saliva Bubble* would be held up by legal complications when Carolco bought the rights out from DEG (along with the North Carolina studio complex) in 1989 after the company went bankrupt. Those rights reverted back to Lynch three years later—after he'd had a falling out with Steve Martin—but *One Saliva Bubble* was ultimately abandoned, with elements of it recycled for the Dougie–Dale plotline of *Twin Peaks: The Return*. *Ronnie Rocket* continued to be a potential project for Lynch decades later. He even offered it to French company CIBY 2000 as part of his three-picture deal with them, but they too passed.

Other vehicles Lynch had percolating before his six-year adventure with the De Laurentiises came to an abrupt end included another script with Frost titled *Venus Descending*, a thinly veiled biopic based on Anthony Summers' book *Goddess: The Secret Lives of Marilyn Monroe*. Because the powers that be were not pleased that the duo's script implicated Bobby Kennedy in the death of Monroe, the project died. Another film he was paid to develop while holed up at the DEG offices on Wilshire Boulevard was *Up at the Lake*, a mystery story involving a murder on a lake near the woods set in a "mental city" not unlike Spokane, Washington (but distinct from *Twin Peaks*). He pitched it to Raffaella while making *Dune*, but nothing came of it, and Lynch only wrote down a few story fragments before the company collapsed.

Inspired by their work on *Venus Descending*, Lynch and Frost set about telling a story of another fallen beauty with a secret dark history: Laura Palmer. One part hard-edged noir and one part Lake Wobegon whimsy, the ABC serial drama series *Twin Peaks* debuted on April 8, 1990, becoming an instant cult sensation. The cast was led by Lynch's muse/alter-ego MacLachlan as FBI Special Agent Dale Cooper investigating the death of teen homecoming queen Palmer (Sheryl Lee), along with an assortment of colorful characters who inhabit the fictional Washington State town. Arrakis' Everett McGill and Jack Nance were once again part of the fray.

MacLachlan recalled in 2020 to *The Hollywood Reporter*:

> Early on, when I began working with David, our first film was *Dune*, and I would pepper him with questions. I was really familiar with the book, and I just had all sorts of questions, thoughts, and ideas. He was very gracious, and he would listen to me for like 10 or 15 minutes. Then, he'd say, "Okay, that's enough. No more questions." [*laughs*] Over time, I began to realize that he doesn't really like to answer questions about the work that he's doing, whether he's created it or adapted it. So, by the time I got to *Twin Peaks*, I'd stopped asking questions, and I said, "I'm just going to go the way I want to go." So far, it's worked out pretty well.

Consisting of eight episodes, Season 1 was a runaway success, so a 22-episode second season was rushed into production with Lynch's input largely absent save for the four episodes he directed himself. According to staff writer Harley Peyton, Lynch even had the temerity to turn down an offer from Steven Spielberg to helm the Season 2 premiere, preferring to direct it himself. With the series in creative disarray and ratings declining, the show was canceled in 1991.

Lynch was absent in part to make and promote his next feature, the surreal and violent romantic road movie *Wild at Heart* starring Nicolas Cage and Laura Dern. Based on the novel by Barry Gifford, and also featuring Freddie Jones and Jack Nance, the couple-on-the-run movie won the prestigious Palme d'Or at the Cannes Film Festival, received an Academy Award nomination for Diane Ladd's supporting performance, and made $14.6 million in North America. Lynch also directed the music video for Chris Isaak's single off the soundtrack, "Wicked Game," which shot to #6 on the US *Billboard* Hot 100 after being featured in the film.

Since *Dune*, Lynch has never ventured into full-on sci-fi territory again, but he almost did in the early '90s when Lucasfilm's Nilo Rodis-Jamero (a prominent designer on *The Empire Strikes Back* and *Return of the Jedi*) approached him with the opportunity to write and direct an adaptation of the Japanese manga *Domu: A Child's Dream*. Written and drawn by Katsuhiro Otomo of *Akira* fame, the story follows an old man and a child possessing psychic powers who may be connected to 32 mysterious deaths within an apartment complex. Rodis-Jamero had struck a deal with Otomo and Bandai to produce the live-action film within a 12-month turnaround period. Lynch, who was by then cutting all of his film projects at Lucas' Skywalker Ranch, took to the idea immediately.

Rodis-Jamero recalled in *SlashFilm*:

> I told David the opening scene, and before I could finish the opening scene, he said, "I'm in." David and I took it to Propaganda Films. They were the production company that did *Wild at Heart* for him. Unbeknownst to me, David and Propaganda Films' relationship was beginning to come apart. Propaganda was more interested in my sweetheart, my sweetheart being Bandai. "Why did Bandai give you this?" This being full production, full marketing and prints, and I'm nobody . . . They were more interested in getting that deal from Bandai than in making the movie for David and me. That's really when it started to come apart. Finally, my attorney told me, "You need to walk away from this. They're offering you money to walk away from this. Walk because with the turnaround, they're never going to be able to shoot the movie. You're never going to be able to get this shooting within so many weeks because the turnaround deadline is coming." So yeah, I walked away.

Lynch was also eyeing an adaptation of British poet D. M. Thomas' 1981 novel *The White Hotel*, which chronicles a (fictional) female patient of Sigmund Freud named "Anna G," an opera singer whose erotic fantasies are intermingled with horrifying visions of her future death two decades later during the Holocaust. A famously "cursed" project that continues to float in development hell to this day, over the decades *The White Hotel* has accrued a laundry list of talent who have attached and then de-attached themselves, including stars Barbra Streisand, Meryl Streep, and Nicole Kidman, along with directors such as Bernardo Bertolucci, Terrence Malick, Hector Babenco, Emir Kusturica, and David Cronenberg, the latter of whom wound up making the similarly themed *A Dangerous Method*. Lynch's version for producers John Roberdeau and Robert Michael Geisler (*The Thin Red Line*) would have starred his then-girlfriend, Isabella Rossellini. The screenplay by Dennis Potter (*The Singing Detective*, *Pennies from Heaven*) disposed of the Freud scenes in Vienna and changed the lead from an opera singer to a high-wire artist for a Berlin circus, replacing the classical music with "Potteresque" tunes from the 1930s.

D. M. Thomas later wrote in *The Guardian* in 2004:

> Geisler and Roberdeau explained that Lynch didn't feel he could deal with European high art. He liked the lively Potter screenplay, and so, with reservations, did they. Their dream—though certainly not mine, with that screenplay—was about to be fulfilled; they were to be in Paris on New Year's Eve, 1990, and Lynch was to fly from L.A. to join them and—sign! As they were getting ready to pop the champagne cork at the Ritz, a maître d' handed Bobby Geisler a phone. It was Lynch, still in LA. He and Isabella had parted, and he could not make the film without her. Sorry. Happy New Year.

Despite 1990 being a banner year for Lynch with the success of both *Wild at Heart* and *Twin Peaks*, 1991 was something of a turning point with the latter show's premature demise. 1992 proved even more of a disaster as Frost and Lynch's next ABC series—the 1950s TV station sitcom *On the Air*—was canceled by the network after only airing three of the seven filmed episodes. This effectively ended the partnership between Lynch and Frost for many years after.

Also that year came the feature film spinoff *Twin Peaks: Fire Walk with Me*, a prequel financed by CIBY 2000 that tells the lurid tale of what actually happened to Laura Palmer, including an incest subplot involving the father who eventually murders her (Ray Wise). Although Sheryl Lee got to give a showcase lead performance, Lara Flynn Boyle, Sherilyn Fenn, and Richard Beymer refused to reprise their roles from the show, and MacLachlan—fearing being typecast—asked for a reduced part that was more or less an extended cameo. Jürgen Prochnow made an appearance as an enigmatic Woodsman. *Fire Walk with Me* received disastrous reviews and a mere $4.2 million at the box office, and was considered a depressing follow-up not in keeping with the show's quirkier aspects. Frost's levity was sadly absent. As with *Dune*, two planned follow-up films to *Fire Walk with Me* were abandoned, with Lynch telling *Empire* in 2001 that *Twin Peaks* was "dead as a doornail." Unlike *Dune*, a wealth of deleted material excised to keep the runtime to 2 hours and 15 minutes was later released under the title *Twin Peaks: The Missing Pieces*. The 91-minute compilation included excised parts from series regulars Michael Ontkean, Joan Chen, Wendy Robie, and Everett McGill.

Lynch commented in 2018 [*Deadline*]:

> I love the film. With *Dune*, I sold out on that early on, because I didn't have final cut, and it was a commercial failure, so I died two times with that. With *Fire Walk with Me*, it didn't go over well at the time, but I loved it so I only died once, for the commercial failure and the reviews and things. Over time, it's changed. So now, people have revisited that film, and they feel differently about it. When a thing comes out, the feeling in the world—you could call it the collective consciousness—is a certain way, and so it dictates how the thing's going to go. Then the collective consciousness changes, and people come around.

It would be five years before Lynch got behind the camera again for the 1997 noir nightmare *Lost Highway*. Written by *Wild at Heart* author Barry Gifford, the nonlinear narrative follows a musician played by Bill Pullman who begins receiving videotapes of himself and his wife in their home. The film would serve as Jack Nance's final collaboration with Lynch before his death, and would be a critical and financial disappointment.

Lynch's next film would be an all-around different affair. *The Straight Story* is a G-rated Disney movie based on the true story of Alvin Straight (Richard Farnsworth), an elderly man who decides to drive his John Deere lawn mower across Iowa and Wisconsin. Everett McGill played a small role in the film, which would also serve as the swan song of cinematographer Freddie Francis. Although critically praised and landing Farnsworth an Academy Award nomination for Best Actor, the film only earned a meager $6 million at the box office.

Originally conceived as a 90-minute pilot for an ABC TV show in 1999, *Mulholland Drive* was denied a series pickup by the network but gained new life as a feature film when Lynch reunited the cast for reshoots to turn it into a self-contained story. Following an aspiring actress (Naomi Watts) and an amnesiac woman (Laura Harring), the twisting noir narrative was a box-office success when it arrived in 2001 and something of a comeback film for Lynch, who scored his third Oscar nomination for Best Director. It also helped launch Watts as a bankable leading lady. A 2022 *Sight &*

Sound poll of 1600 critics named *Mulholland Drive* the eighth-greatest movie of all time.

A particular scene features hotshot film director Adam Kesher (Justin Theroux) in a boardroom confrontation with a mafioso named Luigi Castigliane, played by longtime Lynch composer Angelo Badalamenti. Luigi quietly insists that Adam must cast a certain actress in a coveted role, based off a black and white headshot. Adam feels blindsided and defensive, though he later acquiesces. One can't help but be reminded of Dino De Laurentiis, whose gray hair was slicked back like Luigi's and who also had a penchant for espresso and designer suits. This *Mulholland Drive* subplot brings to mind concessions Lynch had to make to Dino during *Dune*. Incidentally, Dino's real-life brother was named Luigi De Laurentiis.

Lynch took another five-year break before unleashing the experimental narrative *Inland Empire*, which was shot digitally (still a rarity in 2006) and featured clips from some of his short films made for the internet. The three-hour, partially self-financed film played mostly to art houses and grossed $4 million worldwide, but earned immense acclaim for Laura Dern's lead performance. Lynch sat in a chair on the corner of Hollywood Boulevard and North La Brea next to a live cow and a "For Your Consideration" sign to promote Dern for possible Oscar nomination. As of this writing, *Inland Empire* stands as the last feature directorial project of David Lynch.

"Things changed a lot," Lynch told *The Sydney Morning Herald* in 2017, confirming that he had no plans to make more theatrical movies. "So many films were not doing well at the box office even though they might have been great films, and the things that were doing well at the box office weren't the things that I would want to do."

Feature films can often take years in development, and for many filmmakers (including visionaries such as Spike Lee, Spike Jonze, Wes Anderson, Terry Gilliam, and Martin Scorsese), one of the ways they sustain themselves financially (and often creatively) is directing commercials. These ads are often developed by the creative departments at various agencies, with an appropriate filmmaker slotted in for a spot that is already fully storyboarded, but the signature style of a chosen filmmaker can sometimes shine through. David Lynch is no exception, and since 1988 he has made commercials for brands like Alka-Seltzer, Barilla pasta, Adidas, Honda, Nissan, Citroën, Sci-Fi Channel, Sony PlayStation, Georgia Coffee, Christian Louboutin nail polish, and even Clear Blue home pregnancy tests. He is also a go-to director for high-end fragrance brands like Yves Saint Laurent, Calvin Klein, Giorgio Armani, Lancôme, Dior, and Gucci.

One of Lynch's oddest team-ups during his time making ads was with the late music superstar Michael Jackson. It clicks that Jackson would want to work with the *Elephant Man* filmmaker, considering the King of Pop once bid $1 million to the London Hospital Medical College in a failed attempt to purchase Joseph Merrick's bones. Jackson personally asked Lynch to do a special 30-second theatrical trailer for his 1991 album *Dangerous*. They conjured up a red room with abstract black trees and a geyser of flames from which Jackson's head emerges inside a glowing crystal ball and shoots toward the camera. The animation and effects work re-teamed the director with John Dykstra after the latter's *Dune* efforts were cut short. Although Lynch is proud of the ad, he was less pleased with Jackson himself, who spent 10 hours in makeup trying on two vans' worth of clothes brought over by Donatella Versace . . . even though he was only being shot from the neck up.

The filmmaker was even able to capitalize on his reputation as a weirdo icon by releasing his own David Lynch Signature Cup Coffee. Lynch directed a four-minute commercial in 2011 where he (off-camera) has a meandering conversation with a Barbie doll he's holding, also voiced by Lynch: "You're going to get me a cup of coffee? . . . Yeah, I'm going to get you a cup of coffee . . . Whoa. Geez, Dave, thanks. It's really beautiful. I just feel dreamy thinking about it . . . Let's go get that cup of coffee, baby."

Lynch's writing off *Dune* as "selling out" to do a big commercial studio film is arguably a little hypocritical, given all the actual commercials he made. However, it makes sense to separate Lynch's filmography proper from his advertising work, just as we keep a healthy distance between Alfred Hitchcock's movies and the many books, magazines, and TV shows which bore his name without the Master of Suspense's actual participation. Similarly, we cherish all the movies Orson Welles directed and not so much the trash he acted in for money like *Necromancy*, *The Legend of Doom House*, or his bleary-eyed Paul Masson wine ads.

"I sometimes do commercials to make money," Lynch told an audience at Livraria Cultura in 2008. "But every time I learn something. Efficiency in saying something and new technologies. But product placement in a film putrefies the environment. It's so absurd, but it's happening more and more. What kind of a world is this?"

Lynch's next big project after *Inland Empire* would be different. In 2005, he became a full-on self-help guru when he founded the David Lynch Foundation for Consciousness-Based Education and World Peace (DLF). A practitioner since 1973 of Transcendental Meditation as taught by Maharishi Mahesh Yogi, his twice-daily practice of 20 minutes of mantra-based meditation had become a cornerstone of his life and creativity. He even took a "Millionaire's Enlightenment Course" with the Maharishi "in-person" (appearing only on a television screen), the fee for which was $1 million. The DLF's purpose was to fund the teaching of TM in schools, with an eventual expanded focus on "at-risk" groups, including military vets, prisoners, and the homeless. The DLF has reportedly sponsored between 70,000 and 150,000 students in 350 schools throughout the US. He even penned a book promoting the topic in 2006 titled *Catching the Big Fish: Meditation, Consciousness, and Creativity.*

As he writes in this book *Catching the Big Fish*:

> For me, *Dune* was a huge failure. I knew I was getting into trouble when I agreed not to have final cut. I was hoping it would work out, but it didn't. The end result is not what I wanted, and that's a sadness. Here's the thing, though: When you meditate and bliss starts coming up inside, it is not as painful. You can ride through things like this and live through it, but it has killed a lot of people. It has made them not want to make a film again.

Mirroring Stanley Kubrick's increasingly long absences during the final decades of his career, it would be another 11 years before Lynch came back with a new project in 2017, the long-awaited third season of *Twin Peaks*. Titled *Twin Peaks: The Return*, the $41 million Showtime production consisted of 18 episodes coming in at a whopping 16-plus hours of television, reuniting Lynch with Mark Frost on the scripts for all episodes, which Lynch directed entirely himself. MacLachlan returned as Agent Cooper and his various doppelgangers, alongside *Dune* cohorts Everett McGill and Alicia Witt as well as Lynch himself as Gordon Cole. A critical and ratings success, *Twin Peaks* helped revive the Lynch brand.

Indie filmmaker Jim Jarmusch (*Down by Law, Mystery Train*) said in 2019 [*Vulture*]:

> The best of American cinema of the last decade, probably, for me, is *Twin Peaks: The Return*, an 18-hour film that is incomprehensible and dreamlike in the most beautiful, adventurous way. That is a masterpiece. Why can't they just give David Lynch whatever money he needs? He needs money to make something; just give it to him! I don't understand.

Although the franchise always included the supernatural, the third season of *Twin Peaks* places the show more firmly in sci-fi territory. There are even some subtle callbacks to *Dune* throughout all three seasons and the film:

—A green signet ring with a symbol (associated with a character called The Arm) in the middle bears a resemblance to the red ducal signet ring in *Dune*.

—The Fireman's fortress on a rocky atoll near a sea strongly evokes Castle Caladan.

—A Season 2 Dale Cooper quote mirrors the Litany against Fear: "All things considered, being shot is not as bad as I always thought it might be, as long as you can keep the fear from your mind. But I guess you could say that about most anything in life: It's not so bad as long as you can keep the fear from your mind."

Author Adi Tantimedh of *Bleeding Cool* noted in 2021:

> Lynch's version of *Dune* was an unintentional rehearsal for *Twin Peaks* . . . The movie opens with Princess Irulan (Virginia Madsen) narrating to the camera like the Log Lady's weekly addresses to the camera recapping the story . . . Lynch's big theme in *Dune* is Paul Atreides trying to make sense of odd, prophetic dreams to solve the mystery of his life. This is parallel to FBI Agent Dale Cooper trying to make sense of odd, prophetic dreams to solve the mystery of both Laura Palmer's murder and Twin Peaks' link to the Red Room itself. Lynch's Paul Atreides and Agent Cooper are practically the same character, both played by Kyle McLachlan.

As of this writing in 2023, the filmmaker is (reportedly) poised for an epic TV project for Netflix under the working titles *Wisteria* and *Unrecorded Night*. It is rumored to consist of 13 episodes with an estimated budget of $85 million.

Despite going into far more detail on the production of *Dune* in his 2018 autobiography *Room to Dream*, Lynch continues to distance himself from the film:

> "*Dune* is a huge, gigantic sadness in my life because I did not have final cut on that film, total creative control I didn't have," Lynch reiterated to a fan during a virtual Q&A at the UK arts hub HOME in 2019. "The film is not a film I would have made had I had that final control, so it's a bit of a sadness. But, I'm still happy that you like it . . . I like many, many parts of *Dune* myself."

Oral History: Legacy

The following individuals were interviewed by the author for this section:

—Kyle MacLachlan (Actor, "Paul Atreides")
—Sean Young (Actor, "Chani")
—Everett McGill (Actor, "Stilgar")
—Alicia Witt (Actor, "Alia")
—Virginia Madsen (Actor, "Princess Irulan")
—Molly Wryn (Actor, "Harah")
—Danny Corkill (Actor, "Orlop")
—Raffaella De Laurentiis (Producer)
—Frank Price (President of Universal Pictures, 1983–86)
—David Paich (Composer, Toto)
—Steve Lukather (Composer, Toto)
—Bob Ringwood (Costume Designer)
—Mary Vogt (Costume Assistant)
—Frederick Elmes (Additional Unit Cinematographer)
—John Dykstra (Visual Effects Supervisor, Apogee, Inc.)
—Barry Nolan (Special Photographic Effects)
—Jane Jenkins (Casting Director)
—Craig Campobasso (Production Office Assistant)
—Ian Woolf (DGA Trainee)
—Kenneth George Godwin (Production Documentarian)
—Giles Masters (Art Department)
—Paul M. Sammon (Universal Pictures Publicity Executive)
—Penelope Shaw Sylvester (Assistant Editor)
—Renato Casaro (Poster Artist)
—Zach Galligan (Actor, *Gremlins*)
—James Cameron (Director, *Avatar*)
—Simon Pegg (Actor, *Shaun of the Dead*)
—Patton Oswalt (Actor, *Ratatouille)*
—Robert Eggers (Director, *The Witch*)
—Naomi Watts (Actor, *Mulholland Drive*)

CRAIG CAMPOBASSO: David was sad. He was sad.

To this day, Lynch does not like to speak of his experience on Dune.

CRAIG CAMPOBASSO: I remember the day I was at his house, and he was cleaning out his office, sweeping stuff in the garage to throw in the trash. He was like, "Craig, just take this . . . take this . . . take this . . ." His *Eraserhead* sign from his AFI door . . . The Bob's Big Boy doll with the *Dune* stillsuit on it . . . He kept giving me all his stuff. He didn't want any remembrances of the movie because he was so sad. It's really hard working on a movie for four years and then not having people like your work. Not being able to say in the press, "I didn't get my final cut, and this really isn't the movie I wanted to release." Now they put that stuff in your contract where you can't speak out against the movie. David didn't do that. He was just sad and stayed silent all these years. Dino was in and out. Raffaella was always running things, having lots of meetings. She doesn't wear her emotions on her sleeve ever. I'm sure she was totally disappointed that it didn't go. Dino never stopped believing in her, and she produced a lot of movies afterward for her father.

KYLE MACLACHLAN: I remember people telling me, "This will change your life, you're going to be a big star." I didn't even know what that meant. Part of what kept me slightly off whatever trajectory could have been was the simple fact that I could not go out and meet, audition, do anything. I didn't even stay in LA; I just came back to Seattle. I said, "Well, I can't do anything in LA." I had no interaction with the business as I was supposedly ascending, and people were excited to see what was going to happen with *Dune* and this new actor, blah, blah, blah. I was off somewhere else. I did get good representation, but there was nothing they could do. Here I am going along, waiting for the movie to come out, and people are telling me it's going to be this and I'm doing tours talking about the movie. The movie comes out and doesn't fare very well, kind of disappears. People are like, "Okay, well . . ." I was like, "Now what?"

Although the film and the possibility of many sequels went down in flames, MacLachlan's enthusiasm for Dune *has never wavered. Unlike Lynch, he even kept a few souvenirs of the experience.*

KYLE MACLACHLAN: I have the *Dune* game. I have an action figure somewhere, but it's lost in storage, and I have the worm, but I didn't think to collect the stuff as it came out. I don't know why. It was kind of weird. I didn't save anything. I have the ring, and I have a version of the crysknife, but it was a dummy version. Wasn't the real thing. Also, for some reason, I have the Emperor's blade, this weird gold thing that Sting used. That's it. No wardrobe. No costumes.

MARY VOGT: Dino had a big studio in Wilmington. I was there helping supervise. We very carefully packed all the clothes up and sent them to North Carolina.

MOLLY WRYN: When we all left, we thought we were coming back for two more films. I would have swiped stuff if I'd known we weren't coming back . . . or asked. [*laughs*] Other people did, and I was like, "We'll be back. We can't take anything." I would have liked to have had a crysknife.

KYLE MACLACHLAN: Would have been fun to have costumes, but they didn't want anything to go out. We were supposed to do another *Dune* picture and they needed to save everything. It's got to be in a warehouse somewhere, unless they dumped it.

BOB RINGWOOD: They all went to North Carolina. Someone told me it burned down, but then I see clothes coming up in auction, so they obviously didn't burn down.

MARY VOGT: I don't know where it ended up, because at the end of the movie, Raffaella gave all the clothes to a local high school or something. Bob told me at that point she was so sick of the film she just wanted to get rid of it, so not much exists.

Dino's son-in-law Alex De Benedetti executive produced Sam Raimi's splatstick sequel Evil Dead II *for DEG in 1987. The North Carolina–lensed film features a cameo from one of Ringwood's black Fremen Waterbearer costumes being worn by a medieval monk during the final scene.*

BOB RINGWOOD: Oh, yes, I've seen that! I've seen stills from that film with them wearing the clothes. Totally, they do. They were based on Russian Orthodox monks because I was doing the Habsburg Empire for all that. The Caladan uniforms had all the *Dune* stuff stripped off, and they've been used in many films since with new badges and things.

KYLE MACLACHLAN: I don't remember David talking about *Dune II* with me. The only thing that happened was there were many *Dune* options. My contract was ridiculous—it was like a book.

MOLLY WRYN: I thought in a second one I would definitely be more involved. I was signed for three *Dune* films. I was to be Everett's wife from then on in the next film, so I was very excited to get to work with him. He was such a good guy.

EVERETT MCGILL: I was signed for as many sequels as the De Laurentiis family decided to produce.

STEVE LUKATHER: Never got that far, for the obvious reason. Had it been a huge success, we may have had another conversation. As a charter member of the "Shoulda Woulda Coulda Club," shit happens.

KYLE MACLACHLAN: I had five *Dune* pictures laid out for me. "You're going to be paid this much, you're going to be working these years." Then they tacked on two and then they added another non-*Dune* picture, so they had three more pictures. I had, like, eight movies. I said, "Well, I guess I'll be working until I'm 70." Then, when *Dune* came out and didn't have the reception they wanted, that all went away. It wasn't until David came back with *Blue Velvet* that things picked back up again.

VIRGINIA MADSEN: I got the feeling that we're going to wait until this movie came out and then we go on to the next one. [Lynch's] focus seemed to be on this movie, and he seemed so excited and passionate about it and working so hard.

FREDERICK ELMES: He mentioned something, he talked about more. More open space. Continuing the story, basically. It wasn't a detailed conversation. We didn't really get that far, but I know he was writing on it—he was working on story and he liked that idea. He liked being able to come back and do it again.

GILES MASTERS: David never described his sequel ideas in any detail. I presume it would have gone back to the books. There were so many books, plenty of room for further movies. If the new one lands and is popular, maybe they'll go on and make some more, because they're great books and they're still relevant to politics today.

RON MILLER: The intention was to follow up by adapting Herbert's own sequel. Sets, models, and costumes were set aside for that . . . but that's as far as it got. I never saw a word of another script.

KYLE MACLACHLAN: I don't remember David talking about sequels. I don't know that we were all thinking this is going to happen, but I never saw anything that he wrote. I liked the book *Dune Messiah*, I don't remember it as well as *Dune*, but I remember liking that one too. *Dune* is still my favorite. *Dune Messiah* was great, and then in *Children of Dune*, Paul becomes The Preacher. Would have been interesting to play that character; I would have enjoyed that.

BARRY NOLAN: There were four books—I read all of them. While we were doing the blue eyes for Kyle, I did one . . . If you've read the other stories, you'll know that Paul Atreides' eyes get burned out looking at an atomic explosion or something like that. I said, "In case we do a second one, here . . . I've made his eyes black." David thought it was so great. "Let's go back and not make them blue. Let's go back and do all of them black!" [*laughs*] "No thanks, David. We'll leave it the way it is."

KYLE MACLACHLAN: It would have been fun, actually, because I love the character of Paul so much. In a strange way, I got to do that with Dale Cooper. Different scale, but I got to be with that character and live with that character for a long period of time. That really is the most fun, to take this character through different journeys.

Although Madsen spent most of the film standing around "looking intense," she conveyed a great deal without words. Specifically, there's the scene toward the end where the Emperor hands Feyd his knife. Irulan is looking down, disgusted at this transaction. It says a lot about Irulan's sympathies for Paul.

VIRGINIA MADSEN: Wow, that's very true, and it was because that was information that was being given to me. That would have gone into the second film. I would have had something to do with all of those Fremen, all the other characters. As I understood it, my character was going to be in love with Paul. That didn't happen, but I had a whole subplot in my mind.

ALICIA WITT: I don't remember ever knowing that he was writing the sequel. That must have really added to his heartbreak at the reception and the fact that they forced him to cut it down as much as they did before it was released.

PAUL M. SAMMON: David was definitely writing a follow-up script, since the initial thought was *Dune* would be enough of a hit to warrant a sequel. I'm not sure he ever completed *Dune Messiah*, though. At one point, David told me he'd not.

RAFFAELLA DE LAURENTIIS: I don't remember any of it. I don't remember reading a script on *Dune II*. Was there even a book for *Dune II* by the time the movie came out? Had Herbert written the second novel? Yes? Maybe I just don't remember.

If Dune *had been successful, the man with the power to trigger sequels would have been Frank Price, who had not been keen on the project to begin with. Nevertheless, he said that he would have greenlit it if things had gone better.*

FRANK PRICE: Sure. Yeah. If you can follow up on anything . . . I mean, I've never been that big on sequels. But if it's possible to do one productively, I certainly do. I was not in favor of the first *Ghostbusters* sequel, because it was a child in jeopardy and I wouldn't have done that. I think that hurt it. It was cliché and threatening. Women's audience gets turned off.

KYLE MACLACHLAN: The whole idea of that franchise . . . This is 1984 and *Star Wars* had run its course. You look at some of the franchises now and you're like . . . I mean, the Marvel franchise is crazy. There is a certain relief that comes with a guarantee that you're going to make this much, your life is going to be like this. You're kind of set, and then it's up to you to exercise the artist in you as you wish. "What kind of things do you want to do? Now you can do anything, it doesn't matter." I don't even know what that journey would have been with all those *Dunes*. It was some kind of weird thing out there, "I guess we'll deal with it when we get there."

FREDERICK ELMES: David could have gotten into it had it turned a little differently.

BOB RINGWOOD: I think he was too young in his film career to take on a film of that scale, an epic like that. I think if he'd taken it on now, he would have made a very different film. He went on to do some wonderful films.

KENNETH GEORGE GODWIN: *Dune* was very important for Lynch's development as a filmmaker. It was actually a good thing that it crashed. He very rapidly went from *Eraserhead* to *Elephant Man* then to *Dune*. That's a steep learning curve. What he got out of *Dune* was the realization that, "No, I don't fit into this industry studio model." When it was a box office failure, Dino gave him *Blue Velvet* as sort of a consolation prize, because originally it was going to be a *Dune* trilogy.

PENELOPE SHAW SYLVESTER: I knew he was working on *Blue Velvet* because he showed me a script. He accepted what *Dune* was and was already making plans.

MARY VOGT: My image of David is him sitting in his director's chair hugging a script of *Blue Velvet*. That's my impression of why he was doing *Dune*, because then you could do *Blue Velvet*. And *Blue Velvet* is, like . . . it's him. It's so him.

After Dune, *Dino and Lynch did not give up on each other. In fact, the two collaborated again on* Blue Velvet, *with Dino's new company DEG ponying up the $6 million budget and giving the director what he'd always wanted but never had: final cut privilege.*

FREDERICK ELMES: Dino believed in David. That went deep, and it worked both ways. They understood each other, and they could trust each other's words.

RAFFAELLA DE LAURENTIIS: Dino was a huge fan of David. Dino loved two directors in his life, that he believed were really, really, really talented: Federico Fellini and David Lynch.

FREDERICK ELMES: That's what a good relationship is, and that's what a producer does for a director, just stand behind. That's how *Blue Velvet* got made.

CRAIG CAMPOBASSO: Kyle did not want to do *Blue Velvet*. He did not want to do it, but they made him. Now—in hindsight—he's glad he did, because it's a great movie.

KYLE MACLACHLAN: He gave me *Blue Velvet* while we were filming *Dune*. Like, "Read this." There was a long fallow period between the finish of filming on *Dune* to filming *Blue Velvet*; it was like two years. It wasn't for lack of trying, because first of all I couldn't do anything, and then when I could, after *Dune*, there was no interest!

CRAIG CAMPOBASSO: I would go around with David when *Blue Velvet* was first going, and we would hit all the Melrose shops buying jewelry for the lead characters. Then it got postponed. When it restarted, I had nothing to do with it.

Although Dino, Kyle, Dean Stockwell, Brad Dourif, Jack Nance, and director of photography Fred Elmes all got pulled back into the fold, some members of the Dune *cast and crew felt left out of the party.*

RAFFAELLA DE LAURENTIIS: We were doing *Blue Velvet*. We started doing it together and then I ended up in China on *Tai-Pan*. He did *Blue Velvet* without me, which I was very sorry about because I had spearheaded that movie for a very long time. I really wanted to do it, but you can't be in two places at once.

SEAN YOUNG: I don't think I would ever have done *Blue Velvet*. I don't recall whether that was a discussion among agents because they don't tend to tell you much. I don't think that was ever something that was discussed. I have no idea why.

VIRGINIA MADSEN: I was not right for *Blue Velvet*, absolutely not right. Any of the movies he's done, there hasn't been anything that's been right for me. I don't think it's because he's somehow forgotten. He hand-picks actors that are perfect for those roles. There's no one else besides Isabella Rossellini.

BOB RINGWOOD: He asked me to do *Blue Velvet*, but I was already engaged on another project. I'd like to have done it because by the time we finished *Dune*, I began to understand him more. I could have worked with him better. Once you've turned someone down, they don't ask you again very much, right? I was sad because I would have liked to work with him again. I grew to be very fond of him.

MOLLY WRYN: Yes, I've been envious of Kyle's connection, because I was going to be one of them. Envious of Laura Dern. It's like, "Why not me?" Laura is magnificent.

Those that did return found Lynch in good spirits even as the material proved darker.

FREDERICK ELMES: *Blue Velvet* was his story, something he had lived with for a while, that he originated. That was an idea he had many years before. He and I used to talk about that during *Eraserhead*, a story about the underside of a small town. He found that intriguing. The idea of secrets, things that people knew but weren't supposed to know. We'd always been throwing around ideas about what the town looked like. When he learned about Dino's interest in the town of Wilmington and what North Carolina was like, it somehow fit into David's view of that small town.

KYLE MACLACHLAN: It wasn't until David came back with *Blue Velvet* and we were making it that David was much happier. It was a film that he wrote and he knew. We had a lovely time.

FREDERICK ELMES: He realized he could do it his way, and that was the saving grace. You don't really need a franchise. You just need the power to get it done the way you want to do it. It's much more satisfying to make a movie on that scale. You had the control, and it didn't take 200 people coming to set every day to make things happen. You could do it much smaller.

IAN WOOLF: David brought me on *Blue Velvet*, where I was key second AD. That was an amazing experience. We had no idea it was going to be what it turned out to be. My wife worked in the accounting department, and she was the lady who would bring the per diem on Fridays, the little manila envelopes of cash, which are long gone now. We don't do that in the business anymore. It's a check. You take taxes out of it. We didn't have computers. Everything was by hand. It was scheduling.

Blue Velvet *was a contemporary movie when it shot in North Carolina from August to November 1985. Many who read it in advance referred to it as "David's 1950s movie."*

KENNETH GEORGE GODWIN: It was more of a mood thing. He liked the cars with fins. He liked the diners with Formica tables, the chrome. Could you actually say when that movie is set?

FREDERICK ELMES: I asked David about that and he said, "Really, there's no time period. No period specifically that we want to tie to, but the '50s sounds pretty comfortable. I just want to put all these cool things into the movie. I like the shape of this car, and I like this and that." I don't even remember that there was much we wanted to avoid. I guess there are no computers in the movie. We were really designing David's world without a date on it.

KENNETH GEORGE GODWIN: The film was very close to what I read. I thought the first half of the script was really strong and kind of petered out, didn't hold together in the second half. What he shot was very close to what I read, but in the shooting of things that didn't work on the page . . . they worked cinematically.

STEVE LUKATHER: I have a copy of the original script of *Blue Velvet*, which has some interesting things not in the film. [*laughs*] So out there that Universal said, "Dude, you can't do this." You know how odd that movie already is! There's some shit in there with Frank Booth doing all this [*breathing amyl nitrate*]. Saying all that crazy shit. In the original script, there's helium mixed in. If you can imagine him saying all that crazy shit with a straight face with helium coming out . . . that's David Lynch.

One strange (filmed) scene in the movie involves Booth's sleazy associate Paul (Jack Nance) telling Jeffrey (Kyle MacLachlan) "I'm Paul, what's your name?" A few minutes and a lot of pacing later, Nance returns and claps in Kyle's face, again repeating "I'm Paul." Was this an in-joke inserted by Lynch between two Dune *alumni regarding MacLachlan's previous role as Paul Atreides?*

KYLE MACLACHLAN: "I'm Paul." You know what? I didn't even think about it relating to Paul Atreides. Maybe. "I'm Paul."

FREDERICK ELMES: You might be right. It could be, it could be. I don't know. It must have happened in Dean Stockwell's place. I guess I didn't pay that much attention to it. It was another odd loose end.

KYLE MACLACHLAN: All I remember is that I didn't have to do a lot of acting in that scene in the car. I was basically trapped with four crazies, Dennis Hopper being—of course—the biggest lunatic, but Brad Dourif, Jack Nance, J. Michael Hunter, Isabella up front. Oh my God. All I had to do was react to the craziness.

Another crazy (possibly apocryphal) story I've heard through the grapevine over the years was that Stephen King was making his directorial debut for DEG's ill-fated production of Maximum Overdrive *and—wanting to give King a crash course in filmmaking 101—Dino brought in another director to shoot the opening scene where a drawbridge opens up while dozens of vehicles are still on it. This causes utter pandemonium as cars flip onto one another while people and cars fall through the opening in the center. The director that was hired for King to shadow? David Lynch, who was prepping* Blue Velvet *at the same time in July 1985.*

IAN WOOLF: I remember Stephen being down there and always walking around with a six-pack of Budweiser in his hand. I don't remember David helping him, not to say that didn't happen. We had other weird things . . . when we were prepping *Blue Velvet*, I was tasked to find a guy without ears in North Carolina. It was like, "Yeah, find somebody who doesn't have any ears." I was calling hospitals. Back then there was no Googling or internet. It was all Yellow Pages and White Pages, phone books from different areas.

I found a guy who was missing one ear from cancer, and so I said, "Dave, I couldn't find anybody that didn't have any ears." From what I understand from the hospitals, if you have no ears, you're weeks from reconstructive surgery. "But I got a guy who's missing one ear." So, we brought this guy [Dick Green] down, and we found somebody who had ears similar to his real ear that he had. We did a mold of that, and that's how we had the earless man.

Dino was so excited about Blue Velvet *that he set up a test screening for an audience going to see* Top Gun *to see if Lynch's film would play to a mass audience. The scores were awful, and the producer made the wise decision to keep the film in its art-house lane. After the modest success of* Blue Velvet, *De Laurentiis still had big hopes for Lynch, reportedly telling him "I know you have a $100 million movie inside you." Sadly, plans for their next film as a team starring Steve Martin, Martin Short, and Kyle MacLachlan were dashed by DEG's bankruptcy and eventual collapse.*

RAFFAELLA DE LAURENTIIS: We were trying to make this other movie called *One Saliva Bubble* together. That never happened. I don't think we went as far as building sets. That was a great concept, but it was hard to sustain for a whole movie.

CRAIG CAMPOBASSO: When *Blue Velvet* finished, I know Kyle still had movies to do for Dino, but that's where the trail ended. Did he get offered other Dino movies that he turned down? I really don't know. David was always trying to get *Ronnie Rocket* off the ground as well, which was really cool.

RON MILLER: I did some concept art for Lynch's yet-to-be-made *Ronnie Rocket*, which I hope he finally makes. I would sell three pints of my soul to work on that!

DEXTER FLETCHER: I have the script for *Ronnie Rocket!* With the personal note in it and drawings. It's at home somewhere—he gave it to me a long time ago. It's an incredible script. I haven't read it for a long time. I'll have to dig it out. I wonder if he'd let me make it? That would be a real full circle, that would be. Let's put it out there! I want to make *Ronnie Rocket!* I do have a script.

RON MILLER: The script was complete. I reread it every few years, the best thing David ever wrote. I didn't talk to David about how *Ronnie* was to be accomplished.

BARRY NOLAN: I did an effects breakdown on the cost and things like that for *Ronnie Rocket*, but nothing ever came of it. I watched *Twin Peaks*, and the weirdness in *Twin Peaks* wasn't bad. It was alluring. Then I went to work with David on *Ronnie Rocket*, and I said, "How's *Twin Peaks* going to end?" He says, "Don't worry. It'll all be resolved in the final show and you'll be happy." It did not resolve, it just stopped.

FREDERICK ELMES: He had other stories, other ideas. In a way, *Dune* was the more down-to-earth one. The others were getting pretty fantastical. Things change as you go along, but certainly *Dune* made a difference to *Blue Velvet*, to his attitude and desire to make it the way he wanted. To stick with the root of his vision.

KENNETH GEORGE GODWIN: With only $6 million and being left alone, he made *Velvet*. Coming out of *Dune* taught him who he was as a film-maker, and definitely who he was not. After that, everything he's done has definitely been David Lynch. Nobody has hired him to do the next *Indiana Jones*, because everybody knows he can't do that. That's not who he is. He's never done a big-budget film since.

ALICIA WITT: *Blue Velvet* is one of the most incredible movies ever made. On my list of Top 10 movies, so I am grateful that he brought that into the world.

Paul Sammon (currently working on his own book about his Dune *experience) regrets that time for personal and professional reasons.*

PAUL M. SAMMON: My greatest regret on *Dune* was not being able to form a more personal relationship with David Lynch, whom I enjoyed interacting with and admired both then and now. If I'd been crewing *Dune* instead of flying back and forth as a studio exec, things would have taken a different turn. The same disappointing situation occurred during my work on *Blue Velvet* for the De Laurentiis Entertainment Group. I was either in Beverly Hills at the DEG offices or traveling the country promoting *Blue Velvet* instead of spending time in Wilmington. I did visit that set for a couple days, wish it could have been more.

IAN WOOLF: I stayed in touch with David over the years. Your paths diverge. You go in different directions, and sometimes you connect back up. Other times, you don't.

For years after Dune, *Lynch told the press he wished to go back and take a second pass to restore the sci-fi epic to its proper length. Although an extended cut was manufactured, it was without Lynch and Raffaella's involvement.*

CRAIG CAMPOBASSO: Universal asked him to do the extended cut while he was working on *Wild at Heart* or whatever. He said, "I would really love to do that. Can you wait for me?" They said, "No. We'll go ahead and do it anyway."

RAFFAELLA DE LAURENTIIS: They contacted me and I spoke to David, and David was willing to do it. He said he would do it, and then they didn't want to pay him. Anything. He said, "Then I'm not going to do it." Then none of us did it. None of us got involved, and they did their own thing.

CRAIG CAMPOBASSO: He said, "Then you take my name off the movie." That's why it says, "Directed by Alan Smithee."

This was in 1988 before the advent of DVD and even before the idea of a director's cut was popularized with the release of Ridley Scott's original cut of Blade Runner. *That failed sci-fi film got a whole new lease on life with its* Director's Cut *and subsequent* Final Cut, *and is now considered a masterpiece far removed from its poor reception in 1982. Would a similar reappraisal have met a David Lynch director's cut of* Dune? *One has to wonder if Universal's shortsightedness left millions of dollars on the table.*

RAFFAELLA DE LAURENTIIS: Imagine today, right? It was very unwise on their part, but that's what they did. I've never seen it. There was a department at Universal that used to do that. They used to take movies and recut them. David was asked, and David said yes. We all said yes, that we would work on it, but then they didn't want to pay David any money and then -rightfully so- David said, "Well, then I don't want to do it." Because it is a lot of work.

RON MILLER: I think David should go back and do it. Or at least someone intimately familiar with his intentions . . . something not done on the "restored" version for TV, which was a total travesty.

FREDERICK ELMES: I hope so. I do. You want to set it right. It so misses the point.

RON MILLER: Sadly, the decision to cut the film came before all of the VFX had been completed, so there would have to be recreations of those, but with CGI, that would be relatively easy now. Another problem would be finding all of the bits and pieces. I have heard they have been scattered far and wide.

MOLLY WRYN: I was reminded by someone that there was a fire at Universal and a lot of film got destroyed. I don't really know the details.

RAFFAELLA DE LAURENTIIS: I don't know about the footage. I never even thought of asking. I can find out.

RON MILLER: David shot a film that was to be about 45 minutes longer than the version released. Most of what got left in was exposition. When storytelling and character development were cut, the movie lost much of its core and continuity. But finding all of those missing pieces would probably entail a monumental search. Again, it might be necessary to resort to CGI to recreate missing scenes based on what is known about them.

BOB RINGWOOD: I love the movie it could have been. If David ever gets around to doing a recut, I think that will possibly be good, but I suspect that a lot of the footage is lost. We shot enough footage to do a six-hour film. I think he's talking about possibly recutting it. It's very painful for David—he doesn't even like talking about it. If the footage survives, he could cut a better film. He's more experienced now. I do wish he would do it.

MOLLY WRYN: That makes me sad: I'm in the one film David hates that he did, because it's not his. That's the one I'm in, but I have no regrets. I loved Harah; I just wish I had more scenes. It was a shock to have been cut. It really was. I wish he'd re-edit it. I love that you told me David's thinking about it. That means everything to me. I would like David to have some pride in it and redo it and put his name back on it. That would mean a lot to me personally. He should do it for posterity, for history. He put his life into that.

MARY VOGT: It's too bad David had a bad experience with the end product of *Dune* because there's a great movie there. He brought a really interesting sensibility to it that you see in German expressionist films, like a UFA film.

DAVID PAICH: I know it's become kind of a cult movie here in the United States.

GILES MASTERS: Now, years later, it's a cult movie, and I love watching it every now and then. I'd love to see it on the big screen again because it was a big movie and it's always best to watch those on the big screen. I saw it on the big screen twice when it came out. It has a place. We'll see how the new one comes out and how that plays.

BOB RINGWOOD: I haven't seen the new one. I've only seen stills and a clip, but from what I can see it looks very good. But people that I know who've seen it said it suffers from the same thing that our one suffered from, which is not a very good script. Frankly, I think the stillsuits were an improvement.

MARY VOGT: I like the artsy weirdo aspect of Lynch's *Dune*, but the other one is more of an adventure movie. I like the first stillsuits better, but I think they did a good job on the second one. They're hard to make. A lot of clothes in that movie.

KYLE MACLAHLAN: It's kind of fun to see the scene in the new movie where they've escaped, they've actually ridden out the storm, they've landed, they get into that weather station somewhere in the south, and they have that moment of pause before they're overrun again. I liked all that, seeing that sequence where Duncan Idaho goes down. More of that.

RAFFAELLA DE LAURENTIIS: I hadn't seen the new one until last week, because I was on location. I came back and it wasn't out in theaters, and I wanted to see it on a big screen. Then I said, "I really have to see it, because I need to vote," and I was surprised. Obviously, it's the same story, so it will be similar, but they made a lot of the same choices. They made a lot of the same mistakes. I was surprised that they're very parallel to each other, in a strange way.

JANE JENKINS: I just saw the new film, and I was so confused. Aside from the effects being entirely different, the story is basically the same, but they use different characters. I kept saying, "Where's Princess Irulan? Where's the little girl?" I was trying to cross-pollinate actors that played that part in my movie. It was half a story.

JOHN DYKSTRA: I think David did an incredible job of making a meal out of a taco truck's worth of kitchen. He's incredibly creative. He knew the story that he wanted to tell. I was impressed he was able to condense that tome into a single movie. Even contemporary filmmakers can't do that.

MOLLY WRYN: I liked it, so beautifully shot, but I love mine better. There wasn't a lot in it. When the second one comes out, will it make a whole? It was just a piece.

RAFFAELLA DE LAURENTIIS: I was watching the new one, and I have to say it made me want to look at the movie we made again because I haven't seen it in 30 years or more. My husband had watched it with me . . . he got lost, he had no idea what was going on. It is a problem, and then they had the advantage of digital effects which we didn't have. I'm very proud of what we were able to do without digital effects. It's so easy today. The thing that amazed me the most looking at the new *Dune* is the shot of the landing. It's the same thing except we had to piece it together.

JANE JENKINS: The effects and technology are a zillion times better than our worms. I never thought they would break. But there was a heart to our story. They were people. I never felt for one second any concern about the new group of people.

FRANK PRICE: As somebody who likes science fiction, I wouldn't have done *Dune*. Enjoyed reading it, it's a good read, but to me not a movie. Maybe somebody has figured out a way to do it. The latest one that's coming out I haven't seen, but maybe with computer graphics they're able to do a better job today?

JOHN DYKSTRA: That was part of the problem: That was a book where you had to read the first 100 pages with blind faith that it would come to make sense, because it didn't. There was no interpretation of the foreign languages that were being spoken. You had to slog through it until you came to understand who these characters were. David did quite a credible job of doing that. There's something that hews to that. In other words, efforts you made to read that first portion of the book from the point of view of blind faith was an investment that you made in the story. David manages to do that with the movie. He introduced these incredibly complex characters, and managed to get most of the story points in there. It was a bit of a cram job, and he wasn't working with the most craftsman-like of tools, but it was there.

FRANK PRICE: I'm a bit of a skeptic, because it's in that category of *Huckleberry Finn* and *What Makes Sammy Run?*: books that I happen to love that just don't make good movies. *Tom Sawyer* makes a good movie. *Huckleberry Finn* and its intellectuality are such that you can't capture them. Or an unappealing leading character. It's hard to follow somebody all through a story that you don't really care for. That's the case with *What Makes Sammy Run?*

JANE JENKINS: Leave it as a book. Some things are better left alone, and they keep trying to climb Mount Everest to do this story. I don't know that it's easily accomplished. David's movie was not very successful in the overall scheme of things. This new one is more successful, but I think that's because people could actually go to a movie theater and just sit there with their masks.

JOHN DYKSTRA: Say what you will, but I'd be happy to see somebody else's two-and-a-half-hour version of that. There are some things that are successful and some things that aren't. David's expressionistic filmmaking technique captured what that book was like, because the book was a series of vistas in these places that you made up in your mind. You had to imagine what Arrakis and all the different places were like, and the stillsuits and all that. It's very difficult to do that in shorthand. It's very difficult to do the *Reader's Digest* version.

KYLE MACLACHLAN: I've always thought *Dune* would be a fantastic multi-episode show for television like a *Game of Thrones* where you just go and go. The banquet scene is a great scene that sets up all of the elements and the political intrigue and you see how the Duke and Jessica relate, how Paul understands the whole political dynamic. That would have been great to see.

FREDERICK ELMES: There are people out there that I bump into that just loved it. Especially after the new *Dune* came out, they love David's even more. [*laughs*]

JANE JENKINS: I left the new movie saying David made a much better movie. In terms of cohesiveness of the story and the impact, and who these people are and what they're trying to do. I have no idea what was going on in the new version. You couldn't tell who was a good guy or who was a bad guy. Then there's Javier Bardem, who I adore. He comes in, and I'm going, "Who is he?" But I have not seen David's *Dune* since 1984. It's a pretty impossible book to capture. Did you ever see the documentary about another crazy person who wanted to make it?

Director Frank Pavich and producer Stephen Scarlata's 2013 documentary Jodorowsky's Dune *brought the earlier attempt to the public consciousness in a big way. There were many departures in Alejandro Jodorowsky's planned version of* Dune, *and many of those ideas branched off into his and Mœbius' famous graphic novel* The Incal *(1980–88). Scarlata explained some of the* Dune *ideas that survived for that comic book and others by Jodorowsky:*

STEPHEN SCARLATA: One of them was the gold planet, the image of a rocket flying toward a gold planet. I actually found more stuff in *The Metabarons*, believe it or not. The spaceships being more aquatic looking . . . there's a spaceship that looks like a shark. The whole blood birth is in *The Metabarons*. There are golden palaces. In our documentary, we have the stuntman that was teaching Brontis all of his martial arts. They put a tribute to that in *The Metabarons* where it looks like a young Paul sitting across from the stuntman, both with shaved heads. I found a few images similar to the Baron in *The Technopriests*. There are so many things from *The Incal* that also branched off into other things like *The Fifth Element* and *Star Trek*. A lot of times, Dan O'Bannon didn't have a lot of stuff to do on *Dune*, so he was hanging out around the office and wrote a story called "The Long Tomorrow" and gave it to Mœbius, who turned it into this comic strip. That comic strip was a huge influence on *Blade Runner*. There is a robot from *Empire Strikes Back* hidden in one of the pictures in that. You can find the Engineer being attacked by that squid thing in *Prometheus* in one of the pictures. It's sparked off so much stuff.

This author visited the set of Ridley Scott's Prometheus *follow-up* Alien: Covenant *in 2016 and can report that production had tons of Mœbius reference art on the wall from books like* The Incal *and* Arzach.

STEPHEN SCARLATA: Also, do we have *Alien* without Jodorowsky's *Dune*? What would have happened with that script without Dan O'Bannon crashed on Ron Shusett's couch? Jodorowsky is the one who introduces Giger to O'Bannon. Then after *Alien*, you get *Galaxy of Terror*, an *Alien* rip-off. Then James Cameron gets discovered off of that movie. It's insane. *The Long Tomorrow* starts cyberpunk and influences *Blade Runner*. All because of this little hive of artists that were there hanging out and getting to know each other.

Even as Lynch continued to work with Dune *alumni on other projects, the same loyalty could be seen in Dino and Raffaella.*

SEAN YOUNG: Dino De Laurentiis is the only producer in my entire career who ever paid me a million dollars for a movie, *Once Upon a Crime*, which I did with Richard Lewis. He took the whole cast to a restaurant where the theme of the restaurant is throwing plates on the floor. It was a big clean-up after you get through eating at this restaurant. After every course, we took the plate and threw it into the fireplace.

EVERETT MCGILL: Dino, Martha, and Raffaella were all very supportive of me. Dino was a popular and successful film producer, and from what I saw, was involved in every aspect of production.

IAN WOOLF: The De Laurentiis family were very good to me. They brought me down there. Raffaella gave me my first opportunity to move up to second assistant director on *Prancer*. I did a show for them in Virginia called *Vanishing Son*. My first feature as a first AD was *Kull the Conqueror* in 1996. She was really good to me over the years. We've stayed very close friends.

BOB RINGWOOD: Dino was obsessed. His record of film production is amazing.

CRAIG CAMPOBASSO: There was nothing that he didn't think that he could do.

IAN WOOLF: When I first started working as a PA in the Dino De Laurentiis Corporation, Dino came into the New York office from his apartment on Central Park South at 6 a.m. every morning. He had business deals in Europe, which was five or six hours ahead. I decided no matter what, I was going to be waiting at the front door of the office when Dino showed up. It was, "Morning, Mr. De Laurentiis," then I would go in the back room and stay busy until people showed up at 8 or 9 a.m. I did that every day when I first started there. That was just my work ethic. He was a force to reckon with, a genius producer. He gave a lot of people their first break in the business. A lot of directors and a lot of actors have him to thank for their careers.

CRAIG CAMPOBASSO: I saw Jessica Lange at a Ryan Murphy thing for *Bette and Joan*. I said, "Jessica, you and I both started our careers with Dino De Laurentiis." You could see her eyes spark. She goes, "Yeah, and we're both still fucking here."

BOB RINGWOOD: He produced some good films, the Fellini films. He was absolutely in love with films, but he wasn't an intellectual, which was a very strange thing.

EVERETT MCGILL: I remember one moment from a *Silver Bullet* meeting between Dino, Dan Attias, and me regarding the transformation from

Reverend Lowe to wolf. Dino came from behind his desk to show us a movement he had conceived whereby the Reverend's foot turns backward like Linda Blair's head. It was a rare moment burned into the back of my eyelids watching Dino twist in agony as he made his point. When his foot would not go that way, he flattered me with my dance and mime background, saying I could, no doubt, get frighteningly close to it. Dan and I had a great laugh on the way back to the set when we imagined the call sheet from a clever first assistant: "Thursday, 2:00 p.m., Soundstage B, Everett puts his best foot backward: Emergency Services standing by." This was before the dancer performing in the werewolf suit with second unit had some issues and was let go. Dino asked me to take over and presented a substantial contract incentive to do so, but it was one of the biggest mistakes of my career agreeing to do it. The werewolf suit was a nightmare, and no pun intended.

FRANK PRICE: I dealt with Martha and Dino later at the USC Cinema School. Martha was a regular supporter. Now I'm chairman emeritus of the board of counselors, but for 30 years, I was chairman of that board. One of the things I was doing was trying to make sure we got endowed chairs for the faculty. When we started the board, we had zero endowed chairs, and I think we have 32 now.

Ron Miller was hired by the De Laurentiis company off of his work on Dune *to concoct some truly stunning designs for David Cronenberg's aborted* Total Recall, *but another major project never really came to fruition after that.*

RON MILLER: Even though I went right back to working for magazines and creating books, I would love to work on another film sometime! I have helped with production design or matte art for a number of small, low-budget, usually direct-to-video sci-fi films. A feature-length documentary was made from one of my books about Chesley Bonestell a few years ago. That was pretty cool.

After working as a casting associate on Spielberg's Amazing Stories, *Craig Campobasso became a full-fledged Hollywood casting director beginning with Raffaella's* Prancer. *Other De Laurentiis movies he's cast include* The Rift, Timebomb, *and* Sky Captain and the World of Tomorrow.

CRAIG CAMPOBASSO: It was Raffaella who catapulted me into my casting career, because after the four years on *Dune*, she said, "Well, what did you like? What department?" And I said, "I like casting." She put me on her next film *Tai-Pan* as a casting assistant, and halfway through that, I got offered a job to be a casting associate on *Amazing Stories*. I left and went there, then went back to Dino and Raffaella and started casting films for them. Dino spoke broken English, but when I cast movies for him, I could decipher what he wanted.

After a decade of working under her father, Raffaella eventually broke ranks with the flailing DEG to strike out on her first film production sans Dino: 1989's holiday hit Prancer, *which—unlike* Dune—*did spawn two sequels:* Prancer Returns *(2001) and* Prancer: A Christmas Tale *(2022).*

RAFFAELLA DE LAURENTIIS: We did many movies together, and then I had to fly off, because I had to see if I could do it on my own.

CRAIG CAMPOBASSO: On *Prancer*, she was on her own, and that was a great experience for all of us. That was the last time I saw Silvana Mangano in the office. There was a double rainbow. Then she passed away. Very sad for all of them.

Ron Howard's 1991 thriller Backdraft *was another win. Her penchant for big, epic popcorn movies continued with a trio of Rob Cohen-directed hits: the biopic* Dragon: The Bruce Lee Story *(1993), Sylvester Stallone vehicle* Daylight, *and fantasy adventure* Dragonheart *(which also had four direct-to-video sequels and counting).*

JANE JENKINS: Raffaella was on *Dragon*, but she was silent for *Backdraft* where I worked with Ron Howard. I don't remember Raffaella being terribly involved. She's one of the producers, but it was Ron's movie. By that time, I'd done a number of Ron's films.

*Charles Edward Pogue's script for a planned third Conan adventure (*Conan the Conqueror*) was transformed into a different Robert E. Howard adaptation in the form of 1997's* Kull the Conqueror *starring Kevin Sorbo. Raffaella was also a producer on the groundbreaking CGI-driven film* Sky Captain and the World of Tomorrow *(2004) and more recently ushered in the successful Netflix sci-fi entry* What Happened to Monday *(2017) starring Noomi Rapace and Glenn Close. Raffaella looks back in stride on the disasters she had to reckon with on* Dune.

RAFFAELLA DE LAURENTIIS: I had a good time; it was a great experience. I learned so much. On sets today I'll go, "On *Dune* this happened, and this is how we dealt with it and I said I would never do this again and here I am doing it again." You learn from every movie. The thing I do constantly is working with young directors. Lately I'm working with a lot of really young directors because they grow up making films on their phones. They don't know how easy it is to make a movie today. Everything is digital; you can pass on information so fast. Sometimes it's too fast—you cut your prep, and you don't do your homework as well as you should. I remember when we didn't have email, we didn't have faxes. Communication was really difficult.

In later years, Raffaella showed her friendship to Lynch in the most Lynchian way possible: She gave the director her uterus . . . sort of.

RAFFAELLA DE LAURENTIIS: That story has been going around so much. I did have a hysterectomy, but Matthew [Feitshans, her stepson] found a uterus of a pig and put it in a jar and we put a bracelet that I had at the hospital. David didn't find out until a couple of years ago that it wasn't real. He was duped for many years!

Jane Jenkins retired in 2017 along with her partner Janet Hirshenson.

JANE JENKINS: It's a different world now. We didn't videotape everybody on *Dune*. You just didn't do that. My partner Janet and I started our career working with Francis Coppola. In 1980, Francis was a big proponent of Betamax, and we did video auditions way before this was a common thing. You had to call the Screen Actors Guild and get permission, but it wasn't a common occurrence. Now not only is everything videotaped, but actors don't even come in person anymore. Everything is a self-tape, and either they're on the nose or they're not because you don't meet them. You can't adjust if you think that they're kind of right. It's a whole other universe, which is one of the reasons I'm no longer casting. We had much more freedom than a lot of people do now with the studio hovering over everything.

Kyle MacLachlan had several years of struggle ahead of him in the aftermath of Dune *before his career momentum picked up steam again.*

KYLE MACLACHLAN: They were like, "Well, you've got to come to LA, and you've got to start auditioning, and you better start reading, and you better start . . ." I'm like, "Okay! Great. Fine, I'm up for it, whatever." I was still at an age when it was like, "We'll do that too. We'll just take that on and it'll be fine," you know?

This period included failed auditions for the leads in such films as Top Gun *and* Platoon, *where MacLachlan found himself going up against many of the same young men he beat out for* Dune. *One of those was Zach Galligan, who dodged a shield-piercing bullet since not getting Paul freed him up for the Spielberg smash* Gremlins.

ZACH GALLIGAN: I met Dino De Laurentiis when I auditioned for Oliver Stone for *Platoon*. There were two rounds of *Platoon* casting, the first one when he did the tit-for-tat deal with De Laurentiis to write *Year of the Dragon* for Michael Cimino and in exchange Dino was going to let him do *Platoon*. In the first round, it was between me and Craig Sheffer. My audition was still the longest of my career, two and a half hours. Stone grilled me for about 90 minutes about my life, personality, and drug usage. Then Oliver and Dino sue each other, and that iteration fell apart. Ten months later, they went back, and Stone had an idea that the movie have echoes of *Apocalypse Now*, so he wanted Emilio Estevez to play the lead in *Platoon*. Emilio decided to direct that vanity project *Wisdom* with his girlfriend Demi Moore, so he declined. Stone was like "Shit. Well, I guess I'll take Charlie. He's the closest thing to Martin Sheen." I didn't get a shot at that iteration.

MacLachlan even had the misfortune of being hired and then fired from a project without shooting a single frame.

KYLE MACLACHLAN: That was a weird experience. It was exciting, because Martha Coolidge was going to direct John Hughes' script for *Some Kind of Wonderful*. I don't think he'd let other directors take on his material; he was usually the writer-director. Martha started to change John's vision a little bit darker. It got more intense, and I was cast as the villain. Eric Stoltz and Mary Stuart Masterson were the two leads, and I was the antagonist, along with Kim Delaney. She went on to do other stuff in New York, *NYPD Blue*. John came in and said, "Nope," and fired everybody. Kept Mary Stuart and Eric, brought in Howie Deutch to direct the movie that he'd written that Martha was changing. They hired Craig Sheffer for my role. I was like, "Oh, yeah, that's too bad . . . Okay, we'll figure out something." I got paid, so that was good. Then *Blue Velvet* came out, and they were like,

"Oh." [*laughs*] Not that the last laugh is important, but you rarely get that in Hollywood.

MacLachlan had another milestone with Lynch's Twin Peaks, *and in the afterglow, Oliver Stone hired him to play keyboardist Ray Manzarek opposite Val Kilmer's Jim Morrison in 1991's big-budget biopic* The Doors. *Since Manzarek and Morrison had resentments in real life, one wonders if Oliver Stone cast MacLachlan knowing that the actor had essentially usurped the* Dune *lead from Kilmer?*

KYLE MACLACHLAN: I don't know—I never asked Oliver. I mean, everybody in Hollywood went in to meet because they thought they could play Jim Morrison, myself included, which is such a laugh. I met Oliver, and we talked through *Platoon* because that hadn't worked out. I don't know why he cast me as Ray Manzarek, don't think I even read for it. Maybe I did. He likes to play with you, psychological manipulation. Maybe he knew that story, or Val shared that story with him. I don't know, but Val and I got along great. I never felt any hard feelings or any strangeness from Val, really enjoyed his company. He and Oliver had moments that were tough, but on that movie, I stayed in the background a little bit, did my stuff, wasn't there that much. I enjoyed Val, we got to know each other, became friends, and I just really care for him. I'm sorry he wasn't nominated for that performance, because he was amazing. I remember hearing that Val Kilmer was the guy for *Dune*. He was a Juilliard grad; I went to U Dub, and we had a similar training program. Juilliard was four years, we were three years, but same kind of thing. We were all trained to do repertory theater, to use acting as an art, and he was great.

After making her debut in Dune, *Alicia Witt's parents prioritized her education and childhood over a burgeoning Hollywood career. That changed after taping the* That's Incredible! *reunion special in 1988.*

ALICIA WITT: I wasn't given permission to go to L.A. at that young age, so I didn't have an agent, wasn't auditioning. If I'd had my druthers after I came home from making *Dune*, I would have gone right into it, but my family didn't want to uproot everyone. Doing the *That's Incredible!* reunion show, as you mentioned, had a lot to do with my family becoming a little more comfortable with the notion of LA. When I was 13, I did a piano competition at UCLA. My mom and I stayed out there for three weeks.

She started to see, "Okay, L.A. isn't the wasteland of violence and depravity we were seeing on the local news." At 14 was the time my mother and I came out and spent about five months there. I had an agent, and I was meeting everybody auditioning and getting that gift of David having written the part of Gersten on *Twin Peaks*. Suddenly being on one of the most talked-about and critically acclaimed shows gave me a big boost in terms of meetings I was able to get and other jobs that came along. I got better auditions. A lot of things I got really close to but didn't get, but all that adds up when you're building your career. David having given me a job again was a really big part of actively getting into the business.

After her initial appearance on Twin Peaks *(which highlighted her piano playing), Witt reunited with Lynch again on an HBO series.*

ALICIA WITT: When he asked me to play Diane in *Hotel Room*, that was my first adult role. I just turned 17, but given the fact that this couple was from the south and we were in the very early 1930s, it wasn't unheard of that a 17-year-old might be a young bride who had just lost a 2-year-old child. It was a beautiful experience, and definitely the most challenging, complex, leap-of-faith role that I've been given so far. I felt very proud to be able to deliver that for him. There was one moment David got very frustrated, but it made so much sense: We did a scene and the props master had forgotten to give Crispin [Glover] and me our wedding bands, and our hands were very visible in the shot. We started filming quickly in the morning, and nobody remembered about the bands. It was a take he really liked and he was furious, because we couldn't use it now. The fact that this moment sticks in my mind is telling of how calm he is. I remember getting my first standout review off of that in *Time* magazine. They put a picture of me from the episode and said it was the pick of the week. I'd never had a role that was significant enough to garner any mention like that. That made a difference in all the things that came after. David's been instrumental throughout my life in that way.

As if chronicling her transformation from child to adult, Lynch had Witt reprise the part of Gersten Hayward on 2017's Twin Peaks: The Return.

ALICIA WITT: The last time working with him it felt like a time capsule, so much like the previous *Twin Peaks*. There was no way it felt like 25 years later, even though so much had changed, but it felt like popping back in time. That's hard to explain, because I never filmed in Washington State when I was on it previously, and that's where my stuff was filmed this time. It was unmistakably the same atmosphere, same show, same character. I had no idea what Gersten was doing, and he wouldn't tell me where it fit into the story or what the story was. There's an absolute faith that all actors put in him because all you want is to deliver exactly what he's talking about. With the scene outside against the tree, he said that I was seeing the answer to my questions up in the sky, that I was seeing the most beautiful light up there and that I knew everything was going to be okay. That's, in a nutshell, what he told me. It was calming. All the anxiety I was feeling melted away when I looked up and saw that most incredible sky. Working on the return of *Twin Peaks* was so unexpected and such a gift. There's a magic about working with him. I hope I get to do it again.

In December 2021, Witt's parents died tragically in their Massachusetts home due to a lack of adequate heat during freezing temperatures. This event happened only two months before I spoke to Witt. The couple had been a fixture on the Dune set and presumably Alicia's memories of the film were intertwined with her parents, but she spoke openly and fondly of them.

ALICIA WITT: Even at such a young age, it wasn't about making my parents proud. To my parents' credit, I never thought much about making them proud because I knew that I always did. One thing I knew even at the time—and I certainly knew it later—was my dad having the experience of being on the set and talking with actors . . . he'd grown up watching José Ferrer, so getting to sit next to him in a director's chair and just shoot the breeze had a profound effect on my father. It was not his being proud of me, he was always the proudest of me no matter what, but in his support of me choosing this as a vocation. When I later begged him to be okay with me moving to L.A. when I was only 17 and needed to get my own place and really focus and not be living with my mother anymore, he said yes. He signed the lease for me. That experience of him getting to talk to veteran actors, and see how well-versed and kind and traveled and empathic most successful actors actually are, helped offset the scandalous stories that tend to rise to the forefront. Again, if you're outside of the business and you watch the evening news, you hear about actors who are a mess. Most actors aren't like that. It's an incredible journey and an amazing life filled with adventures. To make a living out of that you have to be very good with people and you have to really love new experiences. I think my dad got a profound sense of that, and that reassured him that I was choosing the life of an actor for all the right reasons. That those were the kinds of people I would be associating with. I have a memory of looking over and seeing him get to know all the actors, and in later years, whenever he would visit me on set, he loved getting to know the actors and everyone else as well. The people that inhabit other people for a living . . . that's really cool. It's a really cool life.

Lynch's longtime friend Jack Nance died under mysterious circumstances in December 1996. Lynch's 1997 film Lost Highway *was his final screen role. Kenneth George Godwin had first encountered Nance while writing an article about the making of* Eraserhead *in 1981 and watching him film a role in Wim Wenders'* Hammett. *A script Godwin wrote for Nance after* Dune, Café Universal, *was optioned by MacLachlan's agent Jack Leustig, but nothing ever came of it.*

KENNETH GEORGE GODWIN: The few years I knew Jack Nance, I saw him going up and down. He would have long dry stretches where he would get that under control, but then he'd fall off the wagon—things would go bad again. It was really sad because he was such a nice guy. He had this demon that would undermine all that. Maybe he would have had a bigger career? He was a very good actor, but also obviously a character actor because he's such an odd little guy. He did a lot of little bits and pieces, he was in *Ghoulies* and things like that, but the outcome was it definitely held him back from becoming something bigger.

FREDERICK ELMES: Oh God, Jack was just great, such a character to be around. A wonderfully dry sense of humor about things. He was so very different from David, yet they seemed to completely understand each other and what the character would be doing and the way he would be doing it. It seemed like a natural pairing, for some reason, that Jack really was this guy. I remember those times working on *Eraserhead* pretty fondly, working in this little set that we built. It was kind of magical.

Unfortunately, all of the 75 hours of behind-the-scenes material Godwin shot with Anatol Pacanowsky was callously discarded after Dune *flopped. His adventures gathering that material on set are chronicled in the book* Dune, The David Lynch Files: Volume 2. *As for Lynch, Godwin only encountered him once more after* Dune.

KENNETH GEORGE GODWIN: I didn't see him again until 2002 when a friend and I went to a big Transcendental Meditation thing that he was hosting in Iowa. The funny thing about that was on opening night the person introducing him listed all his films, but *Dune* wasn't on the list.

Lynch's longtime DP Elmes worked with him again on Blue Velvet *and* Wild at Heart, *but no features after that. This did not mean they separated completely.*

FREDERICK ELMES: We fell out of sync a little bit. He was into the television series *Twin Peaks*, which I loved but wasn't available to work on. The pilot overlapped the *Wild at Heart* schedule—it was a complicated affair. We remained friends, did some commercials together, some odd short films as well. We're still in touch.

*Elmes went on to become more closely associated with filmmakers like Jim Jarmusch (*Broken Flowers, Paterson*) and Ang Lee (*The Ice Storm, Ride with the Devil*). While* Dune *was a positive experience for Elmes, with the exception of Lee's 2003* Hulk, *he has mostly stayed away from the world of blockbuster filmmaking.*

FREDERICK ELMES: They don't appeal to me that much as movies or stories. There are only a handful of them that I would say I like. I like smaller, intimate stories better where there's more concentration on acting and storytelling. That appeals to me, challenge-wise. I appreciate the challenge of doing a big, complicated film. It's mind boggling how complicated they all get to be when you work on that scale. The things you have to keep track of and oversee because you need control over things . . . but intimacy is a much more satisfying thing in the end for me.

Virginia Madsen is still holding out hope to work with Lynch again someday.

VIRGINIA MADSEN: I never got to be in another movie of his. He'd put me in if there was a role that was right. He would call me himself, but it has to be right. I'm kind of waiting. I would like the opportunity because it would be really incredible to be on a show where I'd be more involved, where we'd be hand in hand. The longer you're in the business, these things come to pass, you just have to hang in there. I remember crying hysterically leaving a show I loved. Still very young, going through the grieving process. There was a much older man on the crew, and he said, "I know you're sad, but you're going to be in this business a long time. I know you are. The longer you're in it, you're going to run into these people. Not very many of them, but you'll run into people again, years down the road, and you'll have a story to tell." That happens. You're like, "Oh my God, we worked together in 1994!" I've told a lot of young actors that story when they're sad they're leaving, because it's like leaving camp. "We'll meet again, and you'll meet somebody on this crew down the road."

There was a time in the early 2000s when Madsen's own career was looking grim, until Alexander Payne chose her for the female lead in his 2004 dramedy Sideways, *earning her an Oscar nomination for Best Supporting Actress. This prompted a career resurgence opposite leading men like Harrison Ford (*Firewall*) and Jim Carrey (*The Number 23*) or in prestige films like Robert Altman's* A Prairie Home Companion.

VIRGINIA MADSEN: If you sprint, you're not going to last. You don't want to be in the fast lane—you want to be on the slow climb. There's going to be a lot of times you don't work, and you've got to take it one project at a time. It's just hard. It's really hard. It's hard to be in it past 35, but you can do it.

Proving how hard it is to build a career in Hollywood, Molly Wryn never managed to parlay her experience on Dune *into any more major roles, not for lack of trying.*

MOLLY WRYN: A lot of my career is missed opportunities. I had an agent at the time who did nothing. He didn't put me up for *Dune*; I wrote David. After *Dune*, David sent me to his agent Rick Nicita. He thought Rick would take me, but he didn't. He said he had turned down Geena Davis. That was a disappointment, because David thought he would take me. Rick said I was too similar to somebody else. He said he might regret turning me down, and I probably said, "Yeah, you will." I lost a couple roles to Kirstie Alley. *North and South*, I wanted to do that. I was cast by Lawrence Schiller in the *Peter the Great* miniseries, but I became involved with one of the Russian actors and the director said he was sending me home. Maximilian Schell also got involved with a Russian, but I was the first. I regret how it ended—it was an Emmy-winning series. If I hadn't been the first, I would have been in the show. As a woman, I went through some MeToo stuff, which was horrific. Those Hollywood producer types can be . . . I remained naive for so long that I wouldn't see that coming, but that's very common. After my daughter Emily was born, I worked with young people in auditions, some of them for school plays or theater. I haven't done any other acting.

Another frustrating missed opportunity for Wryn was to nearly become part of the iconic cast of Lynch's Twin Peaks.

MOLLY WRYN: At one point during filming on *Dune*, David said I would always be in his stable of actors. He tried to find me for *Twin Peaks*, but I had become pregnant and disappeared from my manager at the time. I moved away to a little town to have Emily. When David's secretary finally found me it was right before Christmas. She said, "Oh Molly, we've been looking for you. David wants you for *Twin Peaks*." I have my little Emily in my arms and I'm thinking, "yeah," 'cause I'm a single mom with no child support, struggling, whatever. I knew life would be forever changed. Then she said, "Okay, we'll get back to you after the holidays." And she did. She said, "Molly, I'm so sorry. When I called you, I didn't know that David had given up on finding you and cast somebody else." Later, I saw David when Emily was about four or five. We went to see him in his office. I said, "So which part was it?" He's so sly. He said, "It was good." He never told me who he wanted me for.

The actor who played her son, Danny Corkill, got to co-star in another sci-fi block-buster hopeful the next year as Turtle Fox in 1985's D.A.R.Y.L. *where an android boy (Barret Oliver) befriends a suburban family. It tanked.*

DANNY CORKILL: I came back from the *Dune* shoot after school started in September with my perm, which was great. I saw it at the Norridge Theater in Illinois, near my house. Being nine years old, it just went right over my head. I thought it was cool to see it. I was surprised I wasn't in it. I grew up never taking anything personally. It'd be cool if *Dune* had been this giant sci-fi epic, and I had an action figure somewhere, Orlop with a little perm. Most of what I did didn't make it in . . . Okay, no big deal, move on with your life. I left the day after Christmas to go do *D.A.R.Y.L.* That was Paramount's big kids' adventure movie for the summer, and *Goonies* was somebody else's. There's always a winner, there's always a loser.

When Dawn Steel took over as president of production at Paramount Pictures in 1985, much of that year's slate from the previous regime wound up tanking, including

Explorers, Clue, King David, Rustlers' Rhapsody, That Was Then . . . This
Is Now, *De Laurentiis'* Silver Bullet, *and* D.A.R.Y.L.

DANNY CORKILL: Two years ago, TBS announced that one of four
shows they had under development was a reboot of *D.A.R.Y.L.* with Tony
Hale playing D.A.R.Y.L. as an adult in a half-hour sitcom. The tagline of the
show was "The boy everybody wanted is now the adult nobody needs in
the show that nobody asked for." The core joke at the crux of the show was
as the world became more digital, *D.A.R.Y.L.* became more obsolete as an
adult. I laughed. Who in the world reboots *D.A.R.Y.L.* when it wasn't a success the first time around? It shows up in the weirdest places. There's a *Family
Guy* joke about *D.A.R.Y.L. A.I.* was very similar; I saw that movie and was
like, "I've seen this before." I still brag to people about Season 3 of *Stranger
Things*: They were running out of the theater at the mall, and *D.A.R.Y.L.*
was one of the movies on the marquee. *D.A.R.Y.L.* could have been a big
movie at the time. They were certainly hoping for it to be. I would have
loved it because it was the best production I was ever part of. I would have
done as many sequels as they asked for. They were talking about a sequel,
batting around ideas when we were filming it. I didn't walk off *Dune* feeling like, "I can't wait to go do that again!" On *D.A.R.Y.L.*, I felt that way.

*Corkill made more films but started to prioritize his life over Hollywood work until
he eventually quit acting.*

DANNY CORKILL: I had a spell where I did three movies in the span of
a calendar year: I did *D.A.R.Y.L.*, I did a television movie with Farrah Faw-
cett called *Between Two Women*, and a television movie called *Alex: The Life
a Child*. After that, it's one of those things where you either keep pushing,
keep working, and really make a career, or you take six months off and go
play little league baseball for a while. That's what we did. After that, I worked
one time in two years on *Rocket Gibraltar*, which I got only because the casting agent pushed so hard for me. But that's okay. That was the right decision
for everybody involved. I was away a lot. Your friends have different friends
when you come back. My family and friends always did a remarkable job of
keeping me centered. "You know what, it's been fun. I got to do so much.
Let's call it a day." I never cared about being famous. Look at what happened
to all the child stars who went through that . . . it very rarely worked out well.

Since leaving the business, Corkill has led an epic life of his own.

DANNY CORKILL: I finished high school after that. I went to Arizona State, tried out for the basketball team. I am 5-foot-6 and about 150 pounds, so they made me a manager. Best job I ever had. I got to practice, travel, all kinds of fun stuff. Left there, went to an archaeology program in Chicago, did that for a few years. I worked in Peru on a project for three summers, which was amazing. Met my wife at grad school. We ended up moving to Milwaukee for her job, then to Minnesota. I've been in sales for a number of years. I took about six years off work after our third kid. When you have three kids in daycare, you start doing the math on what you're bringing home versus what it costs to keep them in daycare. I'm incredibly blessed with happy, healthy kids, great house, the dog, good family, good friends. With the exception of the people who would miss me and not seeing my kids, I could keel over dead tomorrow and be like, "Yep, it was fun." Working with high-level sports teams, acting as a professional in movies, digging 5000-year-old pyramids in Peru . . . it's a joke. Nobody should get to have the amount of fun I've had in my life.

Sean Young went on to appear in several more hit films, including No Way Out, Wall Street, *and* Ace Ventura: Pet Detective. *She also became known for all the films she was let go from for various reasons, including* Dick Tracy *and* Batman, *as well as an infamous (tongue-in-cheek) appearance on* The Joan Rivers Show *where she advocated for being cast as Catwoman in* Batman Returns . . . *in costume.*

SEAN YOUNG: Let me say that I perceive that my reputation has been sullied a bit unfairly over the years because I pissed people off for saying things they didn't necessarily want to hear. The actuality of my nature is I'm really practical. I don't travel with a lot of clothes. I can walk up to a fight with a carry-on, always have stretchy pants. I keep it pretty simple. It makes it easier for me, right? I won't have an argument with somebody that's not of any value. There's no point. I always thought my job is to be as helpful as possible. I've never really been opinionated. If I don't like something, I'll say something. It's great to work with people, to have camaraderie. My favorite person on the whole *Dune* shoot was Francesca. She made me laugh, and I made her laugh. We were giggling sisters the whole time, quite fun.

CRAIG CAMPOBASSO: I've since done many, many movies with Sean, and she was great. She was a fun Chani, and she was fun to be around.

Sean Young did not participate in either the press tour or premiere of Dune *due to another big fantasy film she was shooting for Disney.*

SEAN YOUNG: I was never at a screening when that movie came out because I was in Africa doing a movie called *Baby: Secret of the Lost Legend*. It was a long shoot. Africa wasn't as bad as Mexico City, in my opinion, because when I finished *Dune*, I was so glad. I did kiss the ground when I made it back to New York. I never even saw the picture at all until 18 years later when I watched *Dune* on TV one day. I didn't have a whole lot of thought about it, but I do remember the reshoot scene at the end that we shot day for night. I thought that was pretty good.

Young harbors no ill will toward the filmmakers for reducing her role of Chani almost to the point of haiku.

SEAN YOUNG: This is going to sound ridiculous, but I couldn't have cared less. It didn't matter to me. That's show business. That's what I mean about practicality. When you take stuff personally in show business, it makes life harder. How many people put their money in to make this movie? They paid you, right? They don't owe you a storyline unless you put it in your contract: "I must have a storyline that takes up a half-hour of this picture at least." Nobody will do that. If I could do one thing differently, it would be nice to appear in one of the gowns. Francesca got to wear nice gowns and she was also in the stillsuit, so she had both. Chani only had the stillsuit. That was it. Well, I had a little ropey see-through thing for the love scenes. It would have been nice to have a spiffed-up *My Fair Lady* moment. [*laughs*]

In April 2010, Young posted a 6-minute YouTube video of Super 8 footage she shot on the set of Dune, *providing a rare glimpse into the film's making, including footage of Aldo Ray and many of the other performers.*

SEAN YOUNG: It's a bit of historical documentation of the making of it. I don't know if there is a lot of other footage. I didn't know so much behind-the-scenes footage had been thrown out. That was stupid. Who made that call? Most of the people that comment on the little YouTube video are like, "I think the movie is better than people say. It didn't get received well, but it should have." Then some people are like, "Oh, it should have been better. I wish it had been great." Science fiction fans are very dedicated fans.

Denis Villeneuve's legacy sequel Blade Runner 2049 *only featured Young's classic character of Rachel as a short CGI cameo, but it led to a full circle situation for the actress' youngest son, Quinn Lujan:*

SEAN YOUNG: I met Denis Villeneuve in Budapest during *Blade Runner 2049*. It wasn't necessary for me to go to Budapest. They basically called me there to sit next to Denis while other people were working, because I had done all the special effects stuff in Los Angeles. I thought it was shit that I wasn't included in *2049* in a real way, just as a cameo afterthought. I was not pleased about that, but it ended up being fine because I asked him, "Do you have a job for my son?" They said, "Oh, yeah, we think that's fine." I would have put him in the camera department because that's where all the stars are, but I asked my son, who said, "I'd rather go with the visual effects department." That was a smart move. I don't think anybody thought he was going to be an asset, but everybody ended up loving him. Now he's working with Denis Villeneuve on the second *Dune*.

Visual effects man Barry Nolan continued his association with the De Laurentiis clan on many films, including Red Sonja, King Kong Lives, Prancer, *and* Leviathan. *Nolan had a particularly terrible experience working on that last film with director George P. Cosmatos, whom he refers to derogatorily as "Comatose." It was not long afterward that Nolan decided to retire.*

BARRY NOLAN: I left Van der Veer at some point, and we started a company called Perpetual Motion Pictures. Richard Malzahn still has that company. My wife passed away, and I just didn't want to get along with anybody, so I retired. I'm back to enjoying movies more now. I was always standing behind the camera, and when I went to a movie, the whole crew was there with me. That's gone. Now I can enjoy them. My son works for Henson—he's carried on into robotics and various things that I started in before. We are associated with quite a few of the Disney people that are turning out all of the *Star Wars* shows, so I enjoy watching those. Some of them.

The Toto score for Dune *was Wagnerian and powerful, yet the band never composed the soundtrack for another movie.*

DAVID PAICH: Working on that film discouraged me a little bit from working on films. I thought, "If this is the way it's going to be . . ." I wanted it to be a blockbuster like *Jaws*, and it wasn't. It met with mixed reviews. I was starting to write songs again after *Toto IV* for the next album.

STEVE LUKATHER: It was a one-and-done for us, as far as I was concerned. It was a great experience, but it was not something I wanted to do for a living. It's very difficult, tedious work, and I just want to run on stage and play my ass off and get paid and go home. I spent a lot of time in recording studios from 1976 to 1992, doing 20 sessions a week . . . and having a band.

DAVID PAICH: I was involved later on with some film production. A friend of mine named Dick Rudolph—who was married to Minnie Riperton—hired me to do the movie *Shirley Valentine*, which Alan and Marilyn Bergman had written a song for. I got to produce that. At the same time, he was in charge of *Black Rain* with Michael Douglas and Ridley Scott. Hans Zimmer hired me to produce the main title and end title, which I got to play on and use my band, and Gregg Allman sang on it, a really happening thing. I got sparked back into wanting to produce aspects of film music for people, but my heart and my passion have always come back to songwriting.

STEVE LUKATHER: I saw *Dune* a million times when we were doing it. I could move my lips to the dialogue. Oftentimes, some of the phrases from the film we still use to talk to each other—it just comes out of nowhere. That's part of our history.

DAVID PAICH: I didn't get a lot of big-time offers. I got some small offers for, you know, "Little Miss Business 2" or something like that. My friend James Newton Howard, who is a great composer, tried to get me some work, but there are so many great composers and only a limited amount of work. You have to have a reputation, and there are a lot of variables involved with becoming a film composer.

STEVE LUKATHER: There are guys that do it so well. I just want to stay in my lane, if you will. I'm not the right guy to spend the rest of my life doing that.

Released in 1984 by Polydor, the Dune *soundtrack album was, according to the band, not a bestseller despite being released in close proximity to their gold-certified fifth album* Isolation. *The label reissued the soundtrack on CD in 1997 with previously unreleased cues. Although out of print, it is still a popular download on iTunes. In 2020, Jackpot Records reissued it in a limited 2000-copy "Spice-Colored" vinyl run.*

STEVE LUKATHER: It wasn't a blockbuster, I can tell you that, but I really have no idea. It's probably a couple hundred thousand copies or something over the years. It's not like there was a hit single. It's a quirky little weird thing.

DAVID PAICH: I think that's an oddity for Toto. The one guy that came up to me was Billy Idol, who told me, "By the way, I love the *Dune* album. That's my favorite Toto record of all time." Made me feel really good.

STEVE LUKATHER: Billy Idol was a friend of mine and said, "My favorite Toto album is *Dune*." [*laughs*] I said, "I love you for that, Billy!" For our last live video on our 40th-anniversary tour, we put together a medley of the themes of *Dune*, in a Pink Floyd-y sort of way. Our super-fans get it, like, "I can't believe they're playing something from *Dune!*" We didn't play the main theme; that would have been too obvious and kind of silly. We aren't John Williams, but we gave it a go! The irony is the singer in our band, Joseph Williams, his father is John Williams.

DAVID PAICH: I still love all film composing. My one guilty pleasure is I love listening to film soundtracks by John Williams and Jerry Goldsmith, mainly. I love talking about films and film music. Joseph Williams and I talk a lot about this.

You can definitely hear hints of Paich's Dune *theme in the memorable themes for 1988's* Scrooged *and 1989's* Batman *by Danny Elfman, another rocker-turned-composer. Shades of it occur in the* Dune *2021 track "Stillsuits" by Hans Zimmer.*

DAVID PAICH: I can't tell you how many people called me and told me that one right there, the Danny Elfman. There's another one, a *Star Wars*, and they blatantly use that theme in it. I just take it as flattery, you know?

STEVE LUKATHER: I'll tell you the funny story: On the last tour we did with Jeff Porcaro before he sadly passed, we were headlining these big-ass festivals, and we were on one called Rock at the Ring in Germany for 50,000 people. Sting and Toto were the headliners. I had never met Sting before. I was a big fan. We went on before them, and we killed it, had a great show. At the time, I was still boozing it up a little bit and had this cheap fucking bottle of German schnapps. I walked up to Sting with a little bit more bravado than I would have if I'd been completely sober. I put my arm around him, holding the bottle, and I went, "*DUNE*." He looked at me and he goes, "Hey man, at least you didn't have to wear the blue Speedo!"

Although he continued to produce movie posters through the '90s (including the Rambo *trilogy and De Laurentiis'* Army of Darkness*), the phone stopped ringing for Renato Casaro once hand-painted key art fell out of fashion in favor of artless*

Photoshop jobs. He took to painting wildlife compositions. This wasn't the end of the line for the artist behind over 2000 posters, though. In 2018, Quentin Tarantino personally commissioned 86-year-old Casaro to render several new one-sheets for the fictional spaghetti westerns in which Leonardo DiCaprio's Rick Dalton stars in the 2019 hit Once Upon a Time . . . in Hollywood. *This led to a retrospective of the artist's work touring Europe, along with new commissions from Netflix.*

RENATO CASARO: I would say it was like going back to my roots. It was the best possible pleasure to work on Tarantino's movie. Over the years, I had developed a completely different style, so it was a challenge to go back to the '60s . . . but it worked, as confirmed by Tarantino! Now I have regular inquiries. If the right movie would come, I'm ready for it.

John Dykstra is another great craftsman who has worked with Tarantino several times in recent years, providing visual effects on Inglourious Basterds, Django Unchained, The Hateful Eight, *and* Once Upon a Time . . . in Hollywood. *He also took home his third Oscar for 2004's* Spider-Man 2. *Despite the ignominy of being forced off* Dune, *Dykstra is fairly certain it didn't damage his or Apogee's rep in the industry.*

JOHN DYKSTRA: Not that I know of. Who knows? I mean, I'm sure in some camps it did because we ended up backing out of a show. I'm confident, but you've got to remember that other people who negotiated with Dino at the time were facing similar kinds of issues. It wasn't as though we were unique. I think there were other companies working with him facing some of the same problems.

The life preserver Dykstra reached for in the wake of Dune *was an even more infamous sci-fi boondoggle: Tobe Hooper's 1985 apocalyptic nudie cosmic space monster epic* Lifeforce. *Made for the schlockmeisters at Cannon Films, it featured Patrick Stewart's first onscreen kiss . . . with Steve Railsback.*

JOHN DYKSTRA: That was hilarious. It was kind of the same: an indie film trying to do a big production. Tobe Hooper had grandiose ideas and a really limited budget. It was a B movie with a C budget. There was no producer on it, no line producer at the studio during production. Trying to do stuff in England was tough, because I didn't have my team—people that I'm used to working with—and they didn't have the technology. Stepping motors and things that I used as a matter of course here were not as readily available, and the interfaces between those numeric control systems and cameras weren't readily available. It was okay, but it was guerilla visual effects . . . and it showed! [*laughs*] They should have just called it *Space Vampires* the way it was originally supposed to be. That was the name of the book. That was the movie we made! It was a vampire movie.

In 1991, Dykstra reunited with Lynch for a theatrical ad for Michael Jackson's album Dangerous.

JOHN DYKSTRA: It was great! I love David. He's incredibly imaginative and articulate. A nice guy, fun to work with. He can describe what he wants and be very specific about it. I also did *Fire Walk with Me* with David. It was in the transitory period, but it wasn't so much CGI as the ability to composite digitally. That was one of the things that we did was we shot original film elements, but rather than doing the composite in an optical printer, we did it digitally. That was before we were making objects or effects with a computer; we were simply doing combinations.

Universal's Sid Sheinberg and Frank Price were largely shielded from blame for the Dune *fiasco. While Sheinberg had to deal with fallout from a public feud with Terry Gilliam over* Brazil, *Price had an even uglier situation with a noted filmmaker.*

FRANK PRICE: I, the studio, generally had final cut, but I used persuasion rather than an arbitrary assertion. The one notable exception was Peter Bogdanovich on *Mask*. There was conflict from the beginning. He insisted it had to be shot in black and white because it would be too distasteful in color. I said we needed it in color and we'd shoot tests to see how it would look. To make sure he didn't sandbag me, I told the cinematographer and makeup man that if the color tests didn't work, we weren't making the picture. The tests looked fine. Peter had a neurotic obsession with [murdered girlfriend] Dorothy Stratten, keeping a kind of shrine to her in his home. In post-production, Peter insisted he had to have Bruce Springsteen records on the soundtrack. He'd placed Springsteen posters on the set, but hadn't provided for these costs in the budget. When we tried to license these tracks, CBS records—headed by Walter Yetnikoff—demanded outrageous terms, precedent-setting and way out of line. I said, "find another singer."

In screening Peter's cut, much of which was good, the scenes with the motorcycle gang were badly done and phony. I suggested he cut the gang way down, get rid of the embarrassing footage. Peter left for Europe without any further editing. I conferred with Marty Starger, who agreed with me on what needed to be done. I asked Peter to come back and finish the cuts. He didn't respond. Marty and I cut the picture, taking out most of the biker stuff, and substituted Bob Seger for Springsteen. I learned that Springsteen was Dorothy Stratten's favorite singer, and that was the basis of Peter's obsession.

As we completed dubbing and scoring the picture, I got a call from a director friend who was shooting in Norway. He alerted me that Peter was calling fellow directors to add their names to a *Variety* ad condemning me and Marty. A week before the opening, Peter publicly attacked the movie, hurting us with critics. I filed a complaint with the Directors Guild, charging him with unprofessional conduct. The Guild was then required to convene a panel of top directors and studio heads to hear the charges from both sides and adjudicate, censuring either the director or the studio. Marty and I showed up at the hearing. Peter shows up with attorney Gloria Allred representing him. Marty and I told our story. Gloria was in over her head. The final result was a slap on the wrist to Peter. One prestigious holdout—Miloš Forman—prevented serious censure. Miloš said in any dispute between director and studio, he sided with the director regardless of facts. Several of the directors, Arthur Hiller being one, came to me privately and apologized for Peter's unprofessional behavior.

Price delivered a few major wins for Universal such as greenlighting the mega-hit Back to the Future *and Best Picture Winner* Out of Africa, *both 1985. By September 1986, Price wound up resigning as chairman after the embarrassingly costly failures of* Legal Eagles *and George Lucas dud* Howard the Duck. *The headline in* Variety *famously read, "Duck Cooks Price's Goose." There were rumors of a fistfight between Price (age 56) and Sid Sheinberg (age 52) over pre-purchased network ad time for* Howard. *Price denied this to the* Los Angeles Times *in August 1986 (only a month before he resigned), calling it "a rumor started by idiots for the consumption of idiots . . . I haven't had a fistfight since I was 16." According to the* Times' *Jack Mathews, Price and Sheinberg had an icy, arm's length relationship in terms of the films they wanted to make, and that Price's camp within Universal represented "a studio within a studio."*

FRANK PRICE: When I got *Out of Africa* over, I had autonomy because I could greenlight. I gave Sid a copy of the script. He read it and said, "I don't get it. I don't understand it at all." I said, "Well, I understand. Redford understands. Sydney Pollack understands. Why don't you understand? It's a love story set in Africa." He was negative all the way along on that. For the Academy Awards, he was rooting for *The Color Purple*. I dressed him down once because he came into an *Out of Africa* marketing meeting and gave his opinion that *The Color Purple* would sweep the Oscars. After everybody was gone, I said, "Sid you can't do this. I want the marketing team to fully believe we are going to win. That's the only way we're going to win. They have to believe. If you're telling them what I'm making them do is a waste of time, that is not going to help. Do not do that again." But he maintained it. He was shocked the night we swept the Academy Awards.

Bob Ringwood went on to costume major sci-fi films, including A.I. Artificial Intelligence, Star Trek: Nemesis, Demolition Man, *and the third and fourth* Alien *pictures. Mary Vogt became a sought-after costume designer in her own right, including genre fare like the* Men in Black *trilogy and* Kong: Skull Island *as well as lauded work on* Crazy Rich Asians. *Ringwood's* Dune *stillsuits led to groundbreaking designs for the superhero genre in Tim Burton's first two* Batman *films.*

BOB RINGWOOD: Those stillsuits got me *Batman*, basically. I got stuck in what I call "rubber goods." I hated doing all those rubber goods films. I couldn't escape—it was a nightmare.

MARY VOGT: That stillsuit was a whole new thing that wasn't really done before. Bob did something similar on the first *Batman*. The first *Batman* suit was like a continuation of the stillsuit.

BOB RINGWOOD: Definitely, I think that I carried that forward to the batsuit. When we did the first batsuit, no one had really done full-body prosthetics—it was a completely new world. The designer they got rid of on *Dune* is the same designer they got rid of on *Batman*. The designer and Tim Burton didn't get on very well. I was designing a Bond film [*License to Kill*] for Barbara Broccoli and discovered my mother was incredibly ill with cancer and I couldn't leave England, so I resigned. I was walking down the corridor, and Chris Kenny—a producer I'd done *Empire of the Sun* with—was by chance sitting in his office with his head in his hands, almost sobbing. I said, "Oh, Christopher, what's the matter? I see you don't look very happy." He said, "We've just lost the costume designer on this film with this fucking cokehead in the next room directing it. We haven't got a costume designer, and we're supposed to be going into production." I said, "I could help you out here." Chris said, "He's a fucking cokehead, and he's a nightmare. He wants to do Batman as Ratman." I've got drawings by Tim of Ratman. That's why he wanted Michael Keaton, he's a weaselly little creature . . . Tim wanted to do one of his own films.

MARY VOGT: Burton wanted it more like "Rat Boy," which is like a furry costume. Michael Keaton is perfect for "Rat Boy," but the studio was like, "Yeah, forget this Rat Boy, get over it. We're not doing Rat Boy."

BOB RINGWOOD: Chris said, "Go in and persuade him not to do that. If he wants to continue with his Ratman rather than Batman, they're going to fire him and get another director. Tell him he's got to do an American superhero." He took me by the hand and shoved me in an office and said to Tim Burton, who was sitting there doing a lot of this [*sniffs, rubs nose*] . . . there was a lot of drug taking going on . . . Chris said, "Tim, this is your new costume designer." He offered me the job almost immediately; he was so relieved there was anybody. I had to persuade him not to do Ratman. I had to say, "Batman is a superhero that America loves, and you can't do one of your numbers on it because the studio won't accept it." Tim and I had a very odd relationship on the first two films, and I think it's because he always felt that I had slightly stabbed him in the back by stopping him doing his Ratman version. He was going to be fired the next day—he was very close to losing that job.

MARY VOGT: Bob had to come up with something to make Michael look more heroic. The stillsuits were very heroic because they had muscles built in. They didn't look like solid rubber, because there were joints and the actors could actually move in them. When you look at the first *Dune*, the actors are moving. They're not stiff things, and that's because of the way Bob designed it with all the joints open. The rubber was in pieces, so it was a much more organic costume that you could integrate with the actor. It became part of the actor; it wasn't separate. The first *Batman* was a little stiffer than the stillsuits, but not as stiff as things got.

BOB RINGWOOD: I got pulled in, and they'd already designed all the sets. The set designer [Anton Furst] was a genius, but he'd gone so over-budget—already spent $6 million—they only gave me $45,000 to do all the clothes. They wouldn't give us any more money. I begged and borrowed and stole and got everybody I knew to make clothes for free; it was a nightmare. We had to make the batsuits, and so I got Vin Burnham [*Brazil*] and she did it for almost nothing in her little workshop. They could have been a lot better made, which has to do with the timescale, which was only six weeks, and the lack of money.

SEAN YOUNG: I love Bob. He's a lot of fun. I ran across him on *Batman*, but I didn't get to do *Batman*. I almost did that. I fell off a horse and then didn't get to do it. I worked with him a little bit at the beginning.

MARY VOGT: I didn't work on the first *Batman* because that was all done in England. I did the second one with Bob, which was done here in LA. The second Batman wasn't done with carved foam, it was sculpted silicone, and then it was molded. With Don Post on *Dune*, it was sculpted muscles that were glued on, much more permanent but they looked pretty good.

BOB RINGWOOD: Tim asked me to do the second one, which was very nice and we had more money. We could do the suits properly. I brought Vin Burnham over to America and she did the second suit, which a lot of people think is the best suit. *Batman Returns* is the best Batman film to date, really, and I thought Tim's first film was pretty good.

MARY VOGT: Tim Burton got away with it because the first film was successful, so they let him really go for that German expressionist thing. I really love working with actors, even if sometimes they can be horrible, but 90% of the time they're really great. We're there to help them create their character. Even if the costumes are kind of showy, the characters come above it because of their personality. With someone like Bette Midler [*Hocus Pocus*], it's impossible to make something that's too big for her. With Michelle [Pfeiffer], because she moves so beautifully in that, the costume was great for her, but most people would look terrible in that Batman suit.

*While Ringwood's experience with Burton was a little fraught, his time on the next two by Joel Schumacher (*Batman Forever *and* Batman & Robin*) was a misery.*

BOB RINGWOOD: I did go on to do two more, but I took my name off the fourth one. Joel Schumacher was a complete asshole of the first order, the most hideous man I've ever worked with. He beat me up one day, literally. He's a 6-foot-4 man, and he actually beat me up in a screening. I hated him. I could have sued him for millions. Why I was so nice about it, I don't know. A huge display of flowers arrived at my house the next morning with a great letter of apology. "I'm so sorry. I've behaved badly . . ." I should have sued him for every penny he'd ever earned. He was the most horrible man you've ever met, a control freak. About three-quarters of the way through filming on the last one, I had a heart attack and was rushed to hospital . . . the stress of working with Joel Schumacher. The studio wouldn't let me back on the lot because they said if I had a heart attack on the lot, I'd probably sue them. They knew that he'd driven me to it. The production designer and one or two of the other people working on it took over. They've got these horrible silver things painted all over the suits, and they did that without my permission. I was so angry they touched my work that I took my name off it.

CRAIG CAMPOBASSO: Bob was always wrung out. He never had sleep. That *Dune* costume department was crazy. In later years, he had a heart attack, and that's why he simmered down.

After serving as costume designer on Batman Returns *and* Fantastic Four: Rise of the Silver Surfer, *Vogt—like Ringwood—doesn't have a fondness for superheroes, especially now in an era when many of those costumes are applied digitally in post.*

MARY VOGT: I wasn't that crazy about them. [*laughs*] I really believe that the costumes have to become part of the actor to support them and their character. A lot of the superhero stuff is the costume, and you don't see the character. It wasn't like that with Michelle Pfeiffer; hers was very integrated with her character Selena and Catwoman. Bob's stuff is better than most. I didn't want to go into the Marvel thing—it got so rubber costume that you've lost the character. They have great actors in those films, and you see this thing that doesn't move. It's strictly a paycheck movie because they're not really acting at that point.

Despite his distaste for "rubber goods" movies, Bob Ringwood's Dune *stillsuits could actually be seen as the template for the modern superhero movie. That goes doubly when you learn he designed the leathery look for both* Batman *and 2000's* X-Men, *arguably the key catalysts for the superhero subgenre as we know it.*

BOB RINGWOOD: I got stuck in it—that's what I was offered. I did a lot of stuff I'm not credited for. I did the X-Men clothes for the first two films; the girl that was designing it [Louise Mingenbach] had fucked up the leading costumes. The head of Fox rang me up and said, "Can you come over and see me? We're doing this film, *X-Men*, and the costumes are hopeless.

We start shooting next week. Can you possibly design the X-Men costumes for me in a week?" As a favor, I said, "Well, all right," and in a week, we made costumes for Famke [Janssen] and the other four of them. They got shooting, and then I supplied a few more. He said, "Don't worry, I'll see you're okay." Then he paid me two weeks' salary, which was about $4,000 or something. I told him he was an absolute fucking asshole. "I've come in and killed myself, worked 24 hours a day for five days to get your X-Men costumes on your leading actors and you give me two weeks' salary?" Louise got the Costume Designers Guild Award for Science Fiction and Fantasy that year. Then when they did the second one, they rang me up again! I stupidly said I'd do them, and they still didn't pay very much money. I've done that on quite a lot of films, come in as the film doctor. I stopped doing that because I wasn't being credited and I wasn't being paid properly.

Exploitation in the film business is something Ringwood had to reckon with many times before he finally retired after the 2004 epic Troy.

BOB RINGWOOD: It's one of the troubles. When I did *Empire of the Sun* with Steven Spielberg, there was a scene on the Bund [historical district in Shanghai] where we dressed 6000 Chinese people. We made all those peasant clothes that didn't exist to rent. They paid them all a propelling pencil with Steven Spielberg's name and the name of the film. That's what they were paid. If you're paying that sort of stuff out, you get the poorest people. They didn't even pay them. I thought that was appalling. On *A.I.*—the Pinocchio thing—there was a scene which was basically cut with homeless people. They tried to cast it, and I said to Steven, "Listen, downtown Los Angeles is knee-deep in homeless people. They're all starving on the streets. I'll go down there and recruit your 70 homeless people. You can pay them $20 a day, they come for two days, that's $40 each." I interviewed people literally living in cardboard boxes and got them all to come on a certain day to the studio. They were real homeless people. I said, "You're going to get union people and pay them a fortune? You can pay these people less, and it gives them something they wouldn't get." They all told me their stories, why they were homeless. Heartbreaking stories, people that lost everything.

Over four decades after The Elephant Man *and his failed* Dune *audition, Dexter Fletcher is now an A-list director after helming such hits as* Eddie the Eagle *and* Rocketman. *He still holds Lynch in the highest esteem.*

DEXTER FLETCHER: He's always very lovely and generous to me when I do see him again, David. Last time I saw him was at the Academy when they were giving him an honorary award, just around the time of *Rocketman*. I went and said hello. I said, "Dunno if you remember me?" He went, "Dexter, of course I remember you." I mean, he's known me since I was 14, it's 40 years. I'm immensely proud of my connection to that, and I think you couldn't choose a better subject if you're going to write about American film history than David Lynch.

As it stands, Dune *remains (remarkably)* Lynch's highest domestic earner at the box office. In his autobiography, Dino De Laurentiis even claimed it was in the black, saying "it's not completely true that the film was a flop. It wasn't a triumph . . . but the original investment was largely recouped due to excellent worldwide distribution." Whatever the case,* Dune *continues to carry a deep resonance for those who take a shine to it as well as those who made it.*

VIRGINIA MADSEN: My residual check for *Dune* is like 14 cents. I don't get those kinds of residuals from that movie. There's a bar in L.A. called Residuals, and if you have a residual check that's $1 or less, they'll give you a free drink. I haven't quite gotten there yet. I think I get like $1.50 or something, but when I get it, I'm like, "Oh, that's from the Netherlands! *Dune* is playing in the Netherlands. Wow." [*laughs*]

RAFFAELLA DE LAURENTIIS: Universal only had domestic. I think Fox had some of the foreign territories. It was done as an independent film. In England, it's still playing in theaters. I was casting a movie in London two years ago, and in front of the casting office, they were playing *Dune* in a theater.

MOLLY WRYN: For me, it was such a huge part of my existence. That was my big thing. That was the big thing that happened to me.

VIRGINIA MADSEN: I thought it was the greatest thing, and everybody was so good. I really liked it. I still do. It was on the other day. It's so much more complex than people may realize, but there is something about that movie. It has never died. Older fans with kids still gravitate toward that film, enough to bring them to the new one. It means something to people. I don't know whether it's the tone of the movie, because it's a fairy tale.

FREDERICK ELMES: *Dune* has the feeling of a very handcrafted movie. David was the person who drove all those artisans to do their best stuff:

Tony Masters to get that detail into things and to make sure it stayed there and stood out, and Freddie the way it was lit, and Bob Ringwood . . . all those people who helped build the props and doodads and gizmos were on board with what David wanted. He so involved them in the process of doing it. It's the way a movie should work. I think it works best in creating those dramatic moments.

KYLE MACLACHLAN: It was 100% David's signature and his movie, and therefore definitely worthwhile. You look at his body of his work and this is one I know he is not happy with, but I think there are some visuals in there that are just . . .

FREDERICK ELMES: It's really David's hand that guided the film, and that's so evident in the detail of character and mannerism that David could control because everyone listened to him. They weren't making their own movies. He was the one in charge, and they really wanted to honor that vision. That's what we all did, we honored David's vision, and that's baked into the film. That's really there to stay.

VIRGINIA MADSEN: *Dune* never goes away. It's always on somewhere. *Dune*, *Electric Dreams*, and *Candyman* are the #1 movies that I get piles of fan mail for. I'm very proud of that. I'm grateful I got my foot in the door because of those movies, and they were wonderful experiences. It's hard for an actor when you had a bad experience on the movie that won't go away, but fortunately for me, I had really good experiences with people I worked with.

RAFFAELLA DE LAURENTIIS: Definitely a flawed movie, and definitely a movie with issues based on the fact that the best adaptation of *Dune* is *Star Wars*. They took the idea, the planets, the desert, and they did their own thing very, very, very successfully. I think we were being too faithful to the book, and they said, "What a great idea: Have all these planets and all these worlds, these spaceships that can go from . . ." and they just did their own thing.

VIRGINIA MADSEN: It was ahead of its time. The sci-fi that was out was a little more straightforward. This was for grownups. The books are very complex. Who would have thought they could make *The Hobbit* into a movie? I think *Dune* really stands up well after all these years. It's still something people want to watch. The Twitterverse and the online people that really love that film will always love that film. *Dune* is something that's really personal to people. I think it was the character development, the sound, the look of the film. I hadn't seen it for a long time until the other day and I was like, "Wow, this film was really cool. It really is."

CRAIG CAMPOBASSO: Years later, I saw Kyle at Paramount. He looked at me, and he goes, "God, can you believe those times?"

ALICIA WITT: It's hard to forget *Dune*.

―――――――――

Actress Naomi Watts, whom David Lynch elevated to stardom with her award-winning performance in Mulholland Drive *and who later appeared in his* Inland Empire *and* Twin Peaks: The Return, *succinctly explained to me why all of Lynch's films (including* Dune*) matter to her.*

NAOMI WATTS: Any film of his is just getting into a mindset that is so extraordinary. I love his films. I love each and every one of them for different reasons, and they're just pure poetry. I love the surreal aspect of not having to explain everything, trusting that the audience has a way to interpret it and access it in their own personal ways. That's why he's such an important filmmaker.

I had the opportunity to speak with James Cameron, one of the most successful filmmakers of all time. With visually striking sci-fi classics like Aliens, The Abyss, Avatar, *and the first two* Terminator *films under his belt, he seemed like the perfect person to weigh in not only on Lynch's* Dune *but other films that were unsuccessful at the box office but are nonetheless visual marvels.*

JAMES CAMERON: The classic example is *Blade Runner*—that movie didn't make a nickel. But it stunned everybody, and it's remembered like it's this vastly important—and it is, artistically—classic that was resoundingly well-received . . . except not. Nobody went. All of its success was artistic, aesthetic, and downstream. It influenced a generation of filmmakers . . . So your example, Lynch's *Dune*, to me, it's an unsuccessful film. Not just commercially, but artistically . . . I think it came out a week after *Terminator*, because I remember taking great satisfaction that we still beat them in our second weekend at the box office. We cost, I think, one-tenth as much as *Dune* did . . . I just never was able to get into it, but it's got some amazing imagery in that film. I'm sure it was a challenge constantly in the back of

Denis Villeneuve's mind, like, "Shit, I've got to come up with compelling imagery now." With all the technology available here, thirty-some years later, I think he was able to do that. But just the design of Lynch's *Dune*, it was almost like the raw subconscious. It was like being in a dream, like being in a dream state watching that film. And of course, that's what Lynch does, he just taps directly into his own subconscious and then puts it up on the screen without a lot of mediation. He just goes for it. He doesn't question whether anybody will understand it, or get it, or will even like it. He just goes for it, which is great. That's almost reminiscent of the aesthetic of the surrealists back in the turn of the 20th century. We just do the unmediated image, whether it was Dalí or Magritte or whomever. We just see it, we paint it, and we don't question it, and we don't expect anybody to understand it any better than we do. So, I love that about it.

He added more examples of films and filmmakers he admires on the same visual terms.

JAMES CAMERON: There have been a number of films that I think just visually, stylistically, have been powerful. Robert Rodriguez, a friend of mine, came up with what I call the deconstructed style, where he literally translated graphic novels to the screen using a lot of bluescreen and the desaturation of black and white, which he did on *Sin City*. Then Zack Snyder came along after that with *300*, and he incorporated different motion styles in that fast, slow . . . you know what I mean? That sort of thing. You have these films that I think are aesthetic successes, and *300* would also be a commercial success. But I also think you have an audience that craves the different now more so than back then. I knew *300* was a hit weeks before it came out because my kids were obsessed by the trailer. They were in their mid-teens at the time. They were responding to style. Just to style.

I also had the chance to speak with actor-writer Simon Pegg who, besides being of Shaun of the Dead *fame, is also one of the few actors to appear in both the* Star Trek *and* Star Wars *movie franchises. As he's a true-blue science-fiction fanboy, I was sure if anyone had an opinion on Lynch's* Dune, *it would be him.*

SIMON PEGG: It's a strange and wonderful movie. I remember David Lynch being tapped to direct *Return of the Jedi* at one point, I don't think that ever was common knowledge until after the fact, but *Dune* is definitely a David Lynch science-fiction film. I think Denis Villeneuve took as much inspiration from that, perhaps, as he took from Frank Herbert's book for his movie, because there are elements of it. I was slightly beguiled by it, I guess, when I saw it as a youngster. It wasn't *Star Wars* by any means, but then everything was positioned as that, even the Roger Corman *Battle Beyond the Stars*. Obviously, *Star Wars* was kind of unassailable. If people went in expecting more of that, then *Dune* was a real slap in the face, which I'm sure is what David Lynch intended. I love him. I think he's great. Any artist who is so uncompromising and has such a vision, you have to respect them.

Comedian and actor Patton Oswalt has made no bones about what a game-changer Star Wars *was in his childhood, including in a hilarious anti-prequel bit titled, "At Midnight I Will Kill George Lucas with a Shovel."* Dune *did not have the same impact, as he told me.*

PATTON OSWALT: What was weird or surreal for me was amongst my friends—because I was such a precocious film nerd—I knew who David Lynch was. I'd seen *Eraserhead*, I'd seen *The Elephant Man*. My friends weren't really of the mindset to connect the director to a film. In my mind, I thought the novel *Dune* was a slog, so I was like, "What? How is . . . how is David Lynch going to make this movie *watchable*?" And I also remember this very clearly, I was at Toys "R" Us, and they actually made *Dune* action figures. It's all the Fremen in their shit brown suits. So, it's shit brown action figures. Like, no color, no nothing for kids to play with. "Come play with your shit brown action figures!" I just thought that was so funny. I think I saw the movie on videotape; I don't think I watched it in the theater. No, it didn't make much of an impression. Sorry. "Shit brown action figures!" There's my quote for ya.

One of the most promising film talents to emerge in the last decade has to be Robert Eggers, the production designer turned director whose first three films bear a strong resemblance to the career trajectory of David Lynch. Like Lynch's Eraserhead, *Eggers' 2015 debut* The Witch *was a small-scale film filled with hauntingly surreal visuals that made a big splash with audiences and retains a cult following. His second time at bat, 2019's* The Lighthouse, *was a step up into a bigger arena of movie stars (Robert Pattinson and Willem Dafoe) that still retained an art-house flavor, shot in black and white no less, which is all parallel to* The Elephant Man. *Finally, like Lynch's big leap with* Dune, *Eggers' third picture—Viking epic* The Northman (2022)— *plays out on a large-scale canvas filled with lavish sets, an international cast (Alexander*

Skarsgård, Nicole Kidman, Anya Taylor-Joy, Ethan Hawke, Björk), and a $90 million budget with extensive visual effects. I spoke to Eggers about those Lynch parallels and what he thinks of Dune *as a whole.*

ROBERT EGGERS: I mean, it looks so beautiful. The costumes and the sets are truly so beautiful and inspiring and inspired. For all of its flaws, I love *Dune,* and when things got tricky on *The Northman* in post, I was reading *Lynch on Lynch* and reading his experiences with *Dune* to kind of help me cope with what I was going through. But I will say that, unlike Lynch, in the end I'm really happy with this movie, and I ended up with a director's cut. I think Lynch understood where Dino was coming from, and I understood where the studio was coming from, but grateful. Thankfully, my collaborators and I were able to find a way to interpret the studio notes in a way that we were really proud of, and I think that's partially because we didn't have the canvas of *Dune.* But I definitely have probably said, like, more than once, "I'm not going to be Duned!" You know? With all respect to the master.

. . .

Dune in Pop Culture

W hile Lynch's *Dune* did not saturate popular culture at anywhere close to the level *Star Wars* did, it still managed to have—and continues to have—a lasting impact on several films (and filmmakers), TV shows, video games, and even the music world.

Movies

The look and feel of director Kenneth Branagh's 2011 Marvel Studios blockbuster *Thor* were specifically inspired by the look of *Dune*. Branagh also elaborated on his *Dune* audition experience in a behind-the-scenes DVD featurette for *Sleuth*, his 2007 adaptation of the 1970 play:

> We find ourselves toward the end of the morning of what we think is the last day . . . It's certainly the last scheduled day. When I was a very, very young actor, I met David Lynch to try out for the young man's role in *Dune*, which Kyle MacLachlan eventually played. A very, very wise piece of casting on David Lynch's part. I did not get the part, but he was very, very kind in the interview, very chatty. I asked him what were the best and worst parts about filming. He said he loved shooting and he hated finishing the shoot, because then he realized that's all he's got. You go into editing, and it seems to be a sort of unwritten rule that there'll be something you missed.

Of course, *Thor* wasn't the last time Arrakis and Asgard would meet. In 2021's Disney+ behind-the-scenes documentary *Marvel Studios: Assembled: The Making of Loki*, visual effects supervisor Luke McDonald remarked on how Lynch influenced a hallmark of the *Loki* series that Tom Hiddleston and company travel through:

> The technology that they're using needs to feel like it's not futuristic, but it's not archaic. It needs to be this ethereal place in time. The way that it was written and described in the script from the writers as a "glassy time door," it instantly started to all click into place. One of the things that really inspired us for the time doors was David Lynch's *Dune*, when they're practicing fighting and they have these shields over them.

In director Ron Underwood's sleeper 1989 hit *Tremors*, a cluster of strange underground creatures known as "graboids" are killing residents of an isolated Nevada desert town. There is a 1998 home video featurette for the film titled "The Making of *Tremors*" where Amalgamated Dynamics effects designer Alec Gillis describes the process of creating the creatures (which as of now have featured in seven movies and a TV series) whose mouths in the script were described as opening "like a grotesque flower":

> So, we started thinking that implies almost a bending kind of muscular action. What we did not want to do was repeat what had been done in *Dune* because in *Dune*, the sandworms were like earthworms, more muscular, and they seem like a long muscular tube rather than anything with a skeletal structure or armor plating. So, we decided that the tack we would take would be from as realistic a standpoint as possible. If a creature were to be swimming through sand or dirt. it would need a pointed armored head so that it could push that matter away. The rest of the body then would have some sort of muscular action, but the idea was that they would speed through the dirt like killer whales.

Another sci-fi franchise that's taken a page or twelve from Herbert are the Riddick movies of writer-director David Twohy: 2000's *Pitch Black*, 2004's *The Chronicles of Riddick*, and 2013's *Riddick*. All three of them have shades of *Dune*, with desert settings, Islamic-inspired peoples (Imam/Fremen) obsessed with water, the glowing blue eyes of Richard B. Riddick (Vin Diesel), Riddick becoming something of a Muad'Dib-like leader at the end of *Chronicles*, the Bene Gesserit-esque Elementals represented by Judi Dench, and the Necromonger culture's fighting style, which is similar to Herbert's weirding way. Besides the parallel story elements, *The Chronicles of Riddick* has been noted for years as having a strong aesthetic cohesion with Lynch's *Dune*, from the baroque sets to the overall styling.

In his 2004 review of *Chronicles*, Vic Holtreman of *Screen Rant* states, "This movie had the most amazing production design I've seen in a sci-fi flick since *Dune*." Likewise, *Empire*'s Ian Nathan wrote upon the film's release, "Twohy's universe is a scattershot of cod-mythology refracted from Tolkien, *2000 AD*, Frank Herbert, and the upper echelons of L. Ron Hubbard's featherbrained cyber-cult, Scientology . . . It's no *Battlefield Earth*, but it's no *Dune* either."

In the 2008 animated film *Space Chimps*, there is a scene where the chimp astronauts land on the alien planet and are greeted by a bed of purple flowers that turn out to be giant worms that have the same three triangular lobes containing rows of teeth as the sandworms in *Dune*.

———————

In the 2011 comedy *Our Idiot Brother*, Adam Scott's Jeremy enters the apartment of Miranda (Elizabeth Banks), his neighbor who has a crush on him. As he enters, he deadpans, "Hey. *Dune* is on Showtime. Director's cut. You wanna—" Jeremy is cut short when he sees Ned (Paul Rudd) standing in the kitchen. Jeremy thinks he might be Miranda's boyfriend, but she corrects him by introducing Ned as her brother.

NED
I'll watch *Dune* with ya.

JEREMY
Oh yeah?

NED
I love that movie.

JEREMY
Oh yeah, me too.

Ned then puts a toothbrush to his nose to mimic the stillsuit breathing tubes and quotes, "Father, the sleeper has awakened."

———————

On the January 18, 2022, episode of the podcast *The Movies That Made Me* hosted by screenwriter Josh Olson and director Joe Dante, filmmaker Adam McKay (*Anchorman, Don't Look Up*) sang the praises of 1984's *Dune*:

> People forget that Lynch had a window where he was a big Hollywood director, which is hard to imagine, but the movie—of course—is *Dune*. By the way, I still love the Lynch *Dune*; I'm one of, like, nine people on planet Earth. I think the new one is terrific and Denis is amazing, but I still love that one. I just think the art design, the look, the bold choices . . . Is it flawed? Of course it is, but I could drink in every frame of that. I love the whisper thing that he does for the internal thoughts—I thought it totally worked. I'm surprised more people haven't stolen that.

In McKay's Oscar-winning 2015 film *The Big Short*, which explores the housing market collapse of 2008, there is a scene where stock trader Mark Baum (Steve Carell) is having lunch with specialist Mr. Chau (Byron Mann) to discuss the mechanics of CDOs. Baum becomes more and more visibly agitated, causing Ryan Gosling's Jared Vennett to exclaim as he looks on, "Oh boy, your boss is about to explode . . . his face is starting to boil, he looks like the bad guy from *Dune*."

Steven Spielberg's 2018 pop culture explosion *Ready Player One* named-rops *Dune* during a scene where Parzival (Tye Sheridan) is showing off some spaceship builds to Art3mis (Olivia Cooke). These include the *Galactica* from *Battlestar Galactica*, the *Sulaco* from *Aliens*, and the *Valley Forge* from *Silent Running*. He then asks:

PARZIVAL
Oh, where's the Harkonnen
dropship? That thing is sick!
Folds space like a boss. I mean,
you can get from Incipio to
Arrakis in under three seconds . . .

This confirms that Arrakis is a destination within the virtual world of the Oasis, something that could be potentially explored in a sequel now that Warner Bros. (who made *Ready Player One*) also owns the rights to *Dune*. Incipio is the main player hub planet within the Oasis. As to the "Harkonnen dropship," Parzival is referring to the Harkonnen hammer-ship/frigate, the long black ship which the Harkonnens used to travel to Arrakis with the Sardaukar. In his novel *Armada*, *Ready Player One* author Ernest Cline mentions both the Litany against Fear as well as the weirding modules from Lynch's movie and how they were not in the books.

Cline and co-screenwriter Zak Penn told *GameSpot* in 2018 about that particular Lynchian prop, which they wanted one of the characters to fire but could not secure the rights for: "[Co-screenwriter Zak Penn] and I are both big fans of the David Lynch adaptation of *Dune*, and we wanted to have one of the characters, i-R0k (TJ Miller), fire a weirding module at one point, and we couldn't get that."

In 2022, Rian Johnson's *Glass Onion: A Knives Out Mystery* used a brief sample of the opening strings note from *Dune* as Princess Irulan appears in the stars. You can hear it at 1 hour and 47 minutes in, shortly after Daniel Craig's Benoit Blanc says, "I keep returning, in my mind, to the glass onion."

Television

In the 14th episode of the first season of NBC's *Punky Brewster*, "Play It Again, Punky" (airdate January 20, 1985), there's a relatively timely reference to *Dune*, which was still playing in theaters. A ditzy secretary Heather (Wendel Meldrum) is at her desk polishing her nails and listening to headphones, when Punky's foster dad Henry (George Gaynes) barges into the office, startling her:

HENRY
Young lady! Have you seen a little
girl and her music teacher?

HEATHER
No, but I can't wait to see *Dune*!

The fourth episode of NBC's *The Facts of Life* Season 7, "Men for All Seasons" (airdate October 19, 1985), showed George Clooney's recurring character George Burnett being handed a newspaper by Tootie (Kim Fields) when he enters the store.

TOOTIE
Hey George, here's your paper.
What's the news from Kuwait?

GEORGE
Kuwait's having a cold spell.
It's down to 124. They had their own
Academy Awards. *Dune* won for
Best Use of Sand.

Clooney would win a Best Supporting Actor Oscar for the 2005 movie *Syriana*, playing a veteran CIA officer trying to stop arms trafficking in the Middle East.

America's animated sitcom institution *The Simpsons* has paid tribute to *Dune* a few times. In the 1994 episode "Homer and Apu," Lisa eats some food prepared by Apu that is so "spicy" she exclaims, "I can see through time." In the 2019 episode "The Clown Stays in the Picture," Krusty the Clown goes to Juárez, Mexico, to shoot an adaptation of the sci-fi book *The Sands of Space*, whose prophecy narrative, desert setting, and undernourished production all resemble Lynch's film.

The 2013 episode "The Fabulous Faker Boy" probably features the most elaborate Herbert parody on the show, where Bart goes to several potential music instructors, including Comic Book Guy (Hank Azaria), who plays a baliset like the one Patrick Stewart plays in the *Extended Cut* of *Dune*.

Behind him on a shelf in his comic book shop are *Dune* books, including *Dune*; *Dune Messiah*; *Dune and Out in Beverly Hills*; *And Then There Were Dune*; *Accountants of Dune*; *Dune, Where's My Car?*; and *Out of Ideas*. Paul's likeness on these covers comes specifically from Lynch's movie. As if that weren't enough of a tribute, Gurney actor Patrick Stewart also voices an unrelated character in the episode.

Matt Groening's other popular animated series *Futurama* paid tribute to Bob Ringwood's stillsuits in the 2012 episode "Viva Mars Vegas" during a very quick montage where the Planet Express crew tries on the outfits.

In a 2007 episode of the spy comedy *Chuck*, "Chuck Versus the Sandworm," lead character Chuck (Zachary Levi) has a one-sheet for Lynch's *Dune* in his bedroom. At the end of the episode, Chuck and Morgan (Joshua Gomez) share a large sandworm costume when they attend a Halloween party. Since the show *Chuck* was produced by NBCUniversal, the reference was probably easy to clear since *Dune* was a Universal picture.

The *Dune* poster would pop up in several other episodes, as would the quote "Fear is the mind-killer." In the 2010 episode, "Chuck Versus the Nacho Sampler," John Casey (Adam Baldwin) and Chuck are going through files on a computer engineer named Manoosh (Fahim Anwar). Casey says that Chuck and Manoosh are, "Oddly similar . . . *Battlestar Galactica, Dune*, nacho sampler . . . sounds like your dream date."

The UK's Channel 4 sitcom *Peep Show* referred to *Dune* in its 2003 debut episode "Warring Factions." In the scene, Mark (David Mitchell) has been caught making fun of a song recorded by his roommate Jeremy (Robert Webb). Feeling guilty, Mark prepares an elaborate apology dinner, including a Region B DVD copy of *Dune*.

> **MARK**
> I'm making chicken tikka.
> Plus, I've bought us loads of great stuff.
> *Dune* on DVD, Bakewell slices, gin, and . . .
> Sara Lee. Plus, I was thinking—you know that
> 30 quid you owe me? Let's call it quits,
> yeah? I mean, not quits but, you know . . .
> I'm just really, really, really,
> really sorry, Jeremy.

In the cold opening of *The Big Bang Theory* Season 3, Episode 8, "The Adhesive Duck Deficiency" (airdate November 16, 2009), Leonard (Johnny Galecki), Howard (Simon Helberg), and Raj (Kunal Nayyar) are on a camping trip where they've set up a satellite feed so they can still get cable in the great outdoors.

> **HOWARD**
> All right, let's see what's on
> the east coast feed.
> **LEONARD**
> Oh, hey. *Dune*.
> **RAJ**
> Not a great movie, but look at
> that beautiful desert.

Adult Swim's stop-motion animated parody show *Robot Chicken* has featured two skits revolving around Lynch's *Dune*, the first appearing in the Season 6 episode "Disemboweled by an Orphan" (airdate October 21, 2012). This skit has the distinction of featuring the original LJN action figures from 1984, as well as Patrick Stewart doing a voice reprisal of his character Gurney Halleck as he wheels around Paul Atreides (Seth Green) in a dune buggy.

PAUL

We have learned the weirding way,
and with this knowledge,
we will force—

GURNEY

Whoo-hoo! Forget about the
weirding ways, have you seen
these things? They call it
a "dune buggy." Can you believe
we've been walking all over these
dunes? Well, fuck that from now on.
Why didn't anyone think of this
before? We've all been drinking
our own piss while we could have
been bitch-slapping these dunes?

The next skit appeared two years later in the Season 7 episode "Stone Cold Steve Cold Stone," where Paul (Seth Green) and a squad of three other Fremen warriors have crashed a Harkonnen ornithopter in the middle of Arrakis' southern desert and have to escape to the safety of rock. One of them remarks that if they walk without rhythm, they won't attract the worm, and then looks questioningly at the only black member of their party, Jamal (Keegan-Michael Key), asking him to hang back. Jamal insists that he can, in fact, walk without rhythm, but after a few seconds of trying, he goes into an involuntarily "groovy" rhythmic walk and a sandworm eats him.

In the opening of the final episode of Cartoon Network's *Scooby-Doo! Mystery Incorporated*, "Come Undone" (airdate April 5, 2013), Scooby's girlfriend—the Cocker Spaniel named Nova—gives an opening narration that parodies Princess Irulan's narration in Lynch's *Dune*. The parody even uses the same sound effects and music as the Anunnaki-possessed Nova—her head illuminated in front of a starfield—reveals the history of the Evil Entity.

NOVA

A beginning is a very delicate
time, much more so an ending.
Know that this is the year 10,191.

We, the Anunnaki, travel between
layers of the many universes.
We came to help you grow, evolve.
But not all of us are good. Some
are evil, wanting to feed
on your energies . . .

In the 15th episode of the CW's *Supergirl* Season 2, "Exodus" (airdate March 6, 2017), Winn Schott (Jeremy Jordan) and the alien refugee Lyra Strayd (Tamzin Merchant) talk about a date they had watching *Dune* while chatting at a bar with Jimmy Olsen (Mehcad Brooks).

WINN

And Lyra loved the movie version
of *Dune*, as I expected,
except for . . .

LYRA

The Sandworms. I mean, the Fremen
just peel apart their scales with
hooks and suddenly worm-riding is
a viable mode of transportation?
I don't think so. So unrealistic.

In Season 23, Episode 8 of Comedy Central's animated satire *South Park*, "Turd Burglars" (airdate November 27, 2019), Kyle's mom Sheila needs a fecal transplant to replace her microbiome. Kyle becomes obsessed with acquiring the stool of NFL hero Tom Brady, which a doctor refers to as "the spice melange" in a whispered inner monologue *à la Dune*.

Later Kyle has a dream which includes closeups of water droplets, an open hand, and a microbiome, from which he wakes up with glowing blue eyes. Even Toto's soundtrack is playing during the sequence.

Later in the episode, a glowing-eyed Kyle breaks into Tom Brady's house and finds a cache of bottled turds inside a secret room behind a bookcase, with Toto's music once again playing, finding enough "spice" for everyone.

In the ninth episode of the sixth season of NBC's *Superstore*, "Conspiracy" (airdate February 11, 2021), an employee beef reminds Jonah Simms (Ben Feldman) of the time he was mad at Garrett McNeil (Colton Dunn).

JONAH

Man, those two are pissed at each
other. This is bigger than our *Dune* fight.

GARRETT

What's a *Dune* fight?

JONAH

When we were roommates, remember?
I came home, and you and Randy were
watching the director's cut
of *Dune* without me, even though
I specifically said that I wanted to.

There have been innumerable references to *Dune* made over the years on the movie-riffing institution *Mystery Science Theater 3000*, the most prominent being the February 2, 1991 episode "Godzilla vs. the Sea Monster" where Crow T. Robot (Trace Beaulieu) states: "In the movie *Dune*, Sting did appear in tiny leather underpants, a little thong thing, and delivered the line, 'I *will* kill him!'"

Video Games

Dune (1992)

With visuals clearly inspired by Lynch's film, including likenesses of actors such as Kyle MacLachlan, Sting, and Francesca Annis, this adventure strategy game was developed by the French company Cryo Interactive. It allows the player to act as Paul Atreides to destroy the Harkonnens while also dealing with spice extraction and other concerns. After six months of work, Martin Alper of Virgin Games USA did not like what he saw of the French team's work, shifting the job over to Westwood Studios. But the European branch of publisher Virgin Interactive still had faith in the Cryo team and kept funding them even though the rights were uncertain. Once they saw further work, Alper approved the game and released it, with Westwood's far different real-time strategy game *Dune II: The Building of a Dynasty* being released separately the same year. Aside from using the movie font for its box art, *Dune II* contains nothing influenced by the Lynch film.

"From the introduction, one can see that a lot more work has gone into the presentation of this game," Dorian Black wrote of the CD-ROM version of the game in an August, 1993 edition of Australia's *The Age*. "Princess Irulan's introductory speech from the David Lynch movie *Dune* is shown in full-screen video-quality motion complete with stereo speech."

Dune 2000 (1998)

Released by Westwood Studios as a CD-ROM for PC play and then for Sony's PlayStation, this game is essentially a remake of the strategy portion of *Dune II* with more window dressing resembling Lynch's film, especially in the over 30 minutes of cinematics. Familiar sights in the live-action portion include the Emperor's gold throne/palace ship and movie costume, the Harkonnen flagships, spice harvesters, the bald look of the Bene Gesserit, the visual schemes of filmbooks, the big-eyebrowed appearance of the Mentats along with their "juice of sapho" mantra, and even the boils on the skin of the Baron. At one point, explosive footage from the '84 film is shown on an in-world screen. The ornithopters are made to resemble their dragonfly-like descriptions from the books as opposed to the ones from the movie. The Fremen stillsuit costumes are similar but not identical to Bob Ringwood's.

The cast of the cinematics is headlined by John Rhys-Davies of the *Lord of the Rings* and *Indiana Jones* films as Atreides Mentat Noree Moneo. Richard Marcus (*Tremors*) plays Edric O of House Ordos, smugglers of Ixian technology who first appeared in 1984's *The Dune Encyclopedia* but are never mentioned in the books. Musetta Vander (*O Brother, Where Art Thou?*) features as the Bene Gesserit Lady Elara, the Emperor's bound concubine and truthsayer. Noted voice actress Vanessa Marshall (*Star Wars: Rebels*) narrated the game in her debut video game performance.

Emperor: Battle for Dune (2002)

Informally known as *Dune III*, this Westwood game continues the trends from the previous game. Taking place after the first great spice war on Arrakis, it depicts the great houses of Arrakis, Harkonnen and Ordos, once again vying for territory on the desert planet. More footage from the 1984 movie is used in the cinematics along with designs like the sandworms or Guild representatives, although the set pieces resemble the various *Star Wars* movies more than Lynch's films, including an opening political meeting straight out of *The Phantom Menace*. The Fremen even carry weirding modules for gameplay.

Familiar faces included Patrick Stewart's *Enterprise* shipmate Michael Dorn (*Star Trek: The Next Generation*) as Duke Achillus Atreides, Michael McShane (*Office Space*) as Baron Rakan Harkonnen, character actor Vincent Schiavelli (*Batman Returns*) as Yanich Kobal, Nicholas Worth (*Darkman*) as Kolinar Koltrass, and Musetta Vander reprising her previous role as Lady Elara.

Music

Perhaps the most famous *Dune* reference in a song is 2001's "Weapon of Choice" off of the third studio album by English recording artist and DJ Fatboy Slim (né Norman Quentin Cook), *Halfway Between the Gutter and the Stars*. The song peaked at #33 on *Billboard*'s Modern Rock charts and #3 for Dance/Club in the US, but is most recognized for director Spike Jonze's award-winning music video featuring actor Christopher Walken—trained in musical theater—dancing through a hotel lobby.

The lyrics sung by Parliament-Funkadelic's Bootsy Collins include the line "Walk without rhythm and it won't attract the worm." The song also mentions the "tone of my voice" being the "Weapon of Choice," i.e. Paul Atreides using his voice to kill.

Canadian singer Grimes, whose favorite novel is *Dune*, released her debut album *Geidi Primes* in 2010, the title of which refers to the home world of the Harkonnens. Every track of the concept album features an allusion to *Dune*, including "Caladan," "Sardaukar Levenbrech," "Feyd Rautha Dark Heart," "Shadout Mapes," and "Beast Infection." The latter refers to Glossu "The Beast" Rabban.

For the 2021 Met Gala, Grimes wore a custom "Bene Gesserit" gown created by Iris van Herpen along with a look by stylist Turner that was specifically inspired by *Dune*. The outfit included a silver prop sword. She even recalled a previous gala where she fangirled out on Sting.

"I think I annoyed Sting because I was trying to tell him how his per-formance in *Dune* was so great," Grimes told *Vogue*. "He didn't know what I was talking about at first, and I was like, *Dune*, like the movie? He was like, 'Wait, what?' Maybe people don't remember he's in *Dune* or some-thing? He's Feyd Rautha, who's my favorite character in *Dune*."

An unreleased original version of rap group The Beastie Boys' "Inter-galactic" opened with, "The worm is the spice, and the spice is the worm." This alternate version of the song is from 1993, well before making it onto their fifth studio album *Hello Nasty* in 1998. "Intergalactic" was the first sin-gle off that album, reaching #28 on the US *Billboard* Hot 100 and earning the group a Grammy Award.

British electronic music producer Dev Pandya, a.k.a. Paradox, released the single "A Certain Sound" in 1997. The drum and bass dance track heav-ily sampled Kyle MacLachlan's lines about the weirding modules: "Through sound and motion . . . We will teach you that some thoughts have a certain sound."

Satirical musician Tom Smith has been performing his song "Crystal Gayle Killed Frank Herbert" at conventions since 1986. A parody of Gay-le's 1977 hit "Don't It Make My Brown Eyes Blue," here is a sample lyric . . .

> Dad got control over all that spice,
> But Baron Harkonnen had him iced—
> Tried to kill me, too,
> And don't it make my brown eyes,
> Don't it make my brown eyes,
> Don't it make my brown eyes blue.

Dune Reunions

While there were reunions of *Dune* cast and crew in Lynch's subsequent films, there were many other cinematic instances where the desert thespi-ans found themselves once again sharing the screen together, or at least appearing in the same production.

Stranger in Town (1984) – Brad Dourif and Toto

Code Name: Emerald (1985) – Max von Sydow and Patrick Stewart

The Doctor and the Devils (1985) – Patrick Stewart and Siân Phillips (directed by Freddie Francis)

Blood & Orchids (1986) – José Ferrer and Sean Young

Vanity Fair (1987) – Siân Phillips and Freddie Jones (3 of 16 episodes: "Arcadian Simplicity," "Who Played on the Piano?", and "Widow and Mother")

Sonny Boy (1989) – Paul L. Smith and Brad Dourif

License to Kill (1989) – Everett McGill and Honorato Magaloni (cast by Jane Jenkins)

Dark River (1990) – Siân Phillips and Freddie Jones

The Hot Spot (1990) – Virginia Madsen and Jack Nance

A Kiss Before Dying (1991) – Sean Young and Max von Sydow

Maverick (1994) – Paul L. Smith and Linda Hunt (her scenes were deleted)

Nicholas and Alexandra (1994) – Siân Phillips and Francesca Annis (voices only)

Air Force One (1997) – Jürgen Prochnow and Dean Stockwell (cast by Jane Jenkins)

Urban Legend (1998) – Alicia Witt and Brad Dourif

The Rainmaker (1997) – Dean Stockwell and Virginia Madsen

The Libertine (2004) – Francesca Annis and Freddie Jones

Mysterious Island (2005) – Kyle MacLachlan and Patrick Stewart

Gingerclown (2013) – Brad Dourif and Sean Young

Spare Room (2018) – Virginia Madsen and Alicia Witt

In 2005, Stewart reunited onscreen with MacLachlan for the Hallmark Channel TV movie based on Jules Verne's *Mysterious Island*, directed by Russell Mulcahy.

MacLachlan said in a cast featurette:

> The chance to work with Patrick Stewart, who is a good friend of mine . . . We've done a few things together. We first worked togeth-

er in a film called *Dune* over 20 years ago. We remind ourselves it was over 20 years ago, and both look at each other and can't believe it's been that long. We just recently did a play in New York together about this time last year. So, when Nemo was mentioned as Patrick, I was very excited about that opportunity.

Stewart said in his own featurette:

> One of the principal attractions of being in *Mysterious Island* is that it reunites me with Kyle MacLachlan. Not as some might think— who only go to the movies—after 22 years since *Dune*. In fact, Kyle and I did a play on Broadway. We worked on Harold Pinter's *The Caretaker* together for five months, which was a thrilling experience. Kyle was wonderful in that. Prior to that, we came together on David Lynch's *Dune* in Mexico City, another phenomenal location. Another amazing city to shoot in, like being here in Thailand. Kyle and I became quite unlikely good friends. We both had a background in classical theater, and have remained close over the decades.

Pyrrhic Victory: Fan Tributes

In addition to cast and crew, I also spoke to several fans—some in the entertainment industry, some not—who have each paid tribute to Lynch's *Dune* in their own way.

"Chuck Versus the Sandworm" (2007)

Phil Klemmer began his career as an assistant to director Michel Gondry before earning a story editor position on the CW's teen sleuth series *Veronica Mars*. He eventually graduated to producer and writer status on the NBC spy comedy *Chuck* in 2007. His other TV credits include *Undercovers*, *The Tomorrow People*, and showrunner for *Legends of Tomorrow*.

Growing up, Klemmer found the *Dune* books too intimidating, preferring the high fantasy of Terry Brooks' *Shannara* series. A mere fourth grader when Lynch's film came to theaters, his first encounter came when it premiered on HBO:

> I'm imagining it would have been a sleepover, a bunch of young guys checking something out. Everybody was *Star Wars* crazy, and sci-fi for us was just pop culture. We probably watched *Dune* expecting a *Star Wars* experience. I remember these moments of being unsettled and confused. It's so grotesque. I haven't seen it in years, but some things are indelible. It's the opposite of *Star Wars*, which is so wholesome, glossy, and sexy. You can plug into Luke if you're that age, you can plug into Han. *Dune* didn't invite anybody. The Lynch fans hated it. Herbert fans hated it.

Two decades later, Klemmer was on staff for *Chuck*. He penned the sixth episode, "Chuck Versus the Sandworm" (airdate October 29, 2007). Although there were many references to *Dune* throughout the show's five seasons, he was the first writer to introduce the idea that the title electronics store employee-turned-spy played by Zachary Levi was a huge *Dune* geek.

Klemmer revealed:

> That was something I figured out on the page. We'd already broken the episode, and I was off writing the script when I came up with that. I did receive support from Chris Fedak, the creator. He was

captivated by it. We were all guys in our 30s writing a character who was supposed to be 25, so we imbued Chuck with our own backstories. We could relate to this guy who doesn't fit in. He's the opposite of Captain Awesome, and Ellie or Sarah are all alphas. They're all good looking and confident, know their place in the world. The whole premise of *Chuck* was a guy having a quarter-life crisis that he could have gone somewhere with his life and chose not to. The whole series was a guy struggling with, "What is keeping you tethered to your past? Why can't you grow up?" Morgan Grimes is really the heartbreaking story of a guy's best friend who's actually holding him back, a little like *Good Will Hunting* with Ben Affleck. Morgan's the townie who loves the Buy More. Chuck was doing his fancy-pants college thing and dropped out. Your childhood obsessions become those anchors in your life . . .

In the episode, Morgan (Joshua Gomez) fears he might be losing his best friend when Chuck chews him out for unprofessional behavior at the Buy More. Eventually, the two reconcile and put on the two-man sandworm costume that is their Halloween party mainstay.

Klemmer commented:

I love a good dick joke as much as the next guy. I don't know what was so funny about a sandworm because when I saw that movie there's nothing funny about that. It was terrifying. I imagine Chuck and Morgan were like me, they discovered that movie, it freaked them out but fascinated them. When they were in fifth grade, they decided this is the cool costume. "We're going to blow people's minds." Time moves on, all of a sudden you're 25. If you show up to a party wearing the same costume you did in fifth grade maybe it's charming, but it's a little bit pathetic. It's also really super-sweet that everybody at the Halloween party is sexy, like Adam and Eve. Sarah is dressed as Leia, the quintessential fetish for any teenager. You don't even have to be into *Star Wars* to put on a Leia bikini. It doesn't have to mean anything other than, "Whoa!" They went the opposite of sexy, they went hardcore sci-fi deep-dive nerds wearing a giant phallic costume that you have to share with another person. You're not going to hook up at the party if you're sharing the sandworm costume. I like the idea that Chuck would be like, "I'm all in, Morgan. That's our thing. I'll never outgrow it even though it has become this preposterous relic of our childhood."

The sandworm is more than a throwaway reference, baked into the episode plot, not to mention the title. Although *Dune* may have been esoteric for mainstream television in 2007, other sci-fi properties were never considered.

Klemmer admitted:

> It was *Dune* from the get-go. I was worried at the time because it was obscure. You're there on set and they show up with the costume and you're like, "Oh, I don't know." At the time, you have no idea, like, "Two guys dressed up as a sandworm at a Halloween party on network TV?" It's outlandish, and if it doesn't land it fails pretty spectacularly. Credit to those guys for selling it. The fact that *Dune* kept popping up in later episodes must have been the room running with it. It's funny how a one-time joke can become canon.

In an interesting twist, the episode's director of photography was Buzz Feitshans IV, whose father, producer Buzz Feitshans, is actually married to *Dune* producer Raffaella De Laurentiis.

Klemmer added:

> I knew who Buzz's dad was, but I did not realize that he was married to her. I knew that he was Hollywood royalty, but I didn't realize he had a connection to *Dune*. This is very geeky, but I think we were the last show in network television to shoot on Super 16. Buzz was super-talented, but it was also the end of an era because that was the last show that used that format.

"Chuck Versus the Sandworm" helped cement the tone of the show, with IGN's Eric Goldman writing in his 2007 review: "Chuck running in slow motion to get to Morgan at the Halloween party was funny no matter what, because it so clearly evoked the end of a romantic comedy-drama. Of course, here, rather than a big 'I love you' moment, it was two friends whose reconciliation came by wearing a *Dune* sandworm costume together."

The episode became a personal favorite for Klemmer as well:

> It was the first one I ever wrote for the show. There is this terror because you're writing these characters for the first time for a creator you just met with a group of writers you're still getting to know. In the early part of a series, the tone is up for grabs. Everybody's inadvertently—or on purpose—trying to put their stamp on what that

show is. The pilot was fantastic, but those early episodes were an exploration. When you go back and watch shows, it's eerie because you're like, "Oh my God, it's finding itself." It's wandering around in the dark fumbling upon things that work and don't work. As things work, it gives you permission to take other chances. *Chuck* became one of those "you can try anything" shows. That's part of the magic. If it made everybody laugh in the room as all eight of us are sitting around, all of a sudden it's, "All right, that's good enough for America." There are not a lot of shows that are allowed to be that willfully odd or stridently weird at times. That's what I love about *Chuck*. It became a little more consistent, but those early episodes represent the aesthetic of the individual writer who was doing it. When I watch those early episodes like "Chuck Versus the Wookie," you're like, "Oh, that's Ali!" "Sandworm" felt like my thing.

When I spoke to Klemmer in November 2021, he had yet to see the Villeneuve *Dune*. Despite its availability via HBO—the venue he'd seen the original on—he didn't want to experience this update the same way. Mentioning COVID-19, he said:

I have not seen the new one because I haven't seen a movie in the theater yet. I was being fussy to the point of shooting myself in the foot. I wanted to go see the super IMAX, and get, you know, in the proper mind state to watch it. Just couldn't bring myself to watch it on HBO Max. Sorry. I'm technically an employee of Warner Bros., but I can't do that, man. It can't be just any theater, and not just any IMAX. You've got to go to Universal City. I can't, I'm not out in the world like that. I don't know . . . Fuck it, I'll go today. What time is it? Yeah, I can probably make it there. I've got 3 hours and 35 minutes to kill. Hit the dispensary, go to Universal City, and *boom*, there goes my day.

Planet Dune (2021)

One week after Denis Villeneuve's *Dune* hit theaters in October 2021, mockbuster kings The Asylum—the studio known for direct-to-video fare like *Transmorphers*, *Avengers Grimm*, and the *Sharknado* franchise—put out the low-budget sci-fi flick *Planet Dune*.

Ostensibly made for gullible audiences thinking they're seeing the Villeneuve picture or snarky hipsters looking for B-movie fun to drink a six-pack to, *Planet Dune* tells the tale of a space crew sent on a rescue mission to a barren sandy planet. Of course, it turns out to be not-so-barren thanks to a handful of nasty giant sandworms! The female-heavy cast includes Emily Killian, Anna Telfer, Cherish Michael, and, most notably, a 1984 *Dune* alumnus in the form of one Sean Young.

"I showed up for *Planet Dune*, which I knew was going to be a low-budget sort of thing," Young said during her interview for this book. "But I walked onto the set there and I recognized it from the Star Trek fan movie *Renegades* that I did. That was the exact same set being used for *Planet Dune*. I was kind of laughing, like, 'Getting the most out of this set?' It was very funny."

The film was codirected by real-life couple Glenn Campbell and Tammy Klein, who both have extensive visual effects experience. I spoke to Campbell only to learn that he was an industry veteran whose work included *Star Trek: The Motion Picture* and *Lifeforce* with John Dykstra's Apogee, who *almost* provided effects for Lynch's *Dune*.

"*Dune* is one of my all-time favorite books, so sadly I didn't get to work on Lynch's version," Campbell told me. "People at Apogee indicated that the complete chaos of the production was the cause for their departure, but I have no actual details. Apogee has never been less than professional in the approach and execution of their work, so I tend to believe that they were not the cause of the problems."

He also had a hand in doing effects for the Sci-Fi Channel productions of *Frank Herbert's Dune* and *Children of Dune*:

> I was ecstatic to learn I'd be getting a shot at *Dune* for Sci-Fi, particularly because I felt that Lynch had gotten so many things right but equally so many things wrong. The pus-covered Baron, the 'thopter, and the lame hazmat suits on the Sardaukar come to mind. I was not on set for the Sci-Fi version, and only the live-action edit after we'd started the CG. I was disappointed that our Sardaukar were only a marginal improvement. Great suits, lame chef hats. The very conscious decision to treat the production like a stage play was a bad one, motivated by a desire to be budget conscious. *Children of Dune* had a different director, and he shot bluescreen for his exteriors, which made a huge difference. We shot two desert movies back-to-back and never shot one frame outdoors. I'm very proud of the work we did on both TV movies. We designed Arrakeen, all the spaceships

and aircraft, and we're especially proud of the worm capture sequence, which we designed in its entirety. The worm was built as an actual model for the first TV movie but was deemed unusable after a week of miniature photography. We built our CG worm to match the miniature version, so it was no big deal to take over.

Produced from a screenplay by improv comedians Lauren Pritchard (*MADtv*) and Joe Roche (*InAPPropriate Comedy*), *Planet Dune* wound up being only the second directorial outing for Campbell after his 2019 debut on The Asylum's *Adventures of Aladdin* (released not coincidentally the same month as Disney's live-action *Aladdin*), as well as the feature directorial debut of Tammy Klein.

Campbell said:

> The new *Dune* was very much on the Asylum radar, and as always, they were ready to do a "mockbuster." The writers focused solely on the worms and wrote something far more akin to *Tremors* in space, as opposed to a sprawling saga of political intrigue and sociology set against an ecological backdrop. We just had worms chase people and eat 'em. The writers did intentionally pay tribute to Frank Herbert's book by having two guys ride a worm briefly, which we were unable to pull off successfully.

While Sean Young was game to take part in another *Dune* movie nearly four decades after the original, she did not spend much time spinning tales of the Lynch version.

"She was wonderful to work with," Campbell said of Young. "She was only on set for two days. We spent more time talking about her kids and her art than anything else. The original *Dune* never came up in conversation."

Young added:

> You know what you're walking into, you're walking into a low-budget situation that doesn't really matter in the long run. Believe me, if I got a really great show, I'd know. I've been doing this for like . . . shit. It would be great to get hired and offered a really great role and I would do my very best, but the truth is I do my very best for *Planet Dune* just like I would for *Out of Africa*, if I ever got offered a role that good.

"Our producers like to have a name actor in many of their productions, and they thought it would be awesome if she was available," Campbell added. "There was a rumor that her people reached out suggesting a cameo in the new *Dune* and been rebuffed, so I think it tickled her to be in this one. I don't know if that rumor is true."

"I had met Denis on *Blade Runner 2049*," Young explained. "I had emailed him and said, 'Could you please include me in the next *Dune*? That makes perfect sense. Give me something, a little part in it,' but he never did. I stopped asking after that. Obviously, he's got his vision, and I'm not in it. That's show business."

As a *Dune* aficionado himself, Campbell understands that some fans may have been upset by the transparent cash grab of *Planet Dune*, but knows there are some out there who appreciate what he and Klein were trying to do with it:

> *Dune* and *Lord of the Rings* fans fall into two categories: Smart people who enjoy literate writing with brilliantly interwoven threads of science, religion, politics, race, and sociology, or people who think they're smart because they read a book that contains all those things. They wrap their lives around the book like a Bible. Smart people looked at *Planet Dune*, smiled, and nodded knowingly. Most never bothered to watch it, and if they did they chuckled and went about their day. The other group wrote angry "reviews" based on just the trailer, speculating on how much we'd desecrated their raison d'être. Then they really went to town after they saw it, complaining how its mere existence diminished and even tarnished the great work it's shamelessly ripping off. We just chuckle and go about our day.

Dune Art Prints

Within the world of collectible pop culture art prints, the names Chris Thornley (Raid71), Matt Griffin, and Karl Fitzgerald are synonymous with bold, striking images that capture fan-favorite properties in ways no studio-sanctioned one-sheet could. Rather than Photoshopped floating head pieces that typically front a big movie release, these men craft images in the spirit of hand-painted posters of yore.

Another thing all three have in common: They love Lynch's *Dune*, having created wildly different but equally impressive art prints of the movie to prove it.

MATT GRIFFIN: I got my passion for movies from my dad. He grew up in the era of the epic: *Quo Vadis, Ben-Hur, Lawrence of Arabia*, etc. Film was a big part of our family life, and *Dune* was one of the favorites. I was five when it came out, so a year or two after we had the VHS and would watch it at least twice a year. I was mesmerized. I came to the books later, around age 14, so Lynch's film was my intro to Arrakis and I still love it. The reason I love films and books is simple: escapism. It's about going to new worlds and forgetting about the mundane. The Lynch film has its flaws, and while it may not be the *Dune* people know from the book, it is a portal to a new world. The production design, the sets, the cinematography, the score by Toto . . . it's epic in every sense. Even Sting's winged underpants are epic.

CHRIS THORNLEY: I remember seeing the film reviewed on a TV show—I think it was Barry Norman, the British reviewer. They showed a clip of fighting with shields. I love everything sci-fi, so I wanted to see it. This film was my first introduction to the world of *Dune*. Without it, I wouldn't have picked up the books. Yes, the ending feels rushed, but everything else works: the production design, baroque spaceships, red-stained deserts, industrial worlds, and some of the best casting around. The effects are dated and the music is a little cheesy, but everything feels like some spice-induced dream with a sense of adventure.

KARL FITZGERALD: At art college, I wasn't aware of David Lynch nor had I read *Dune*, so I found it a difficult watch. It was confusing trying to follow the messy space politics through its awkward, over-explanatory inner monologues. The art design was incredible, though. I enjoyed watching the different warring factions with their unique identities and ambitions. After reading the book and watching *Twin Peaks*, the second viewing was a more fluid experience. I better understood the film's narrative and Lynch's dreamlike style. The uncanniness I felt about the actors on my first watch made more sense. Even the soap opera–like inner monologues of *Dune* became fun rather than irksome.

All three art prints were commissioned by London's Vice Press and New York's Bottleneck Gallery, which typically specialize in authorized images geared toward high-end collectors who seek these pieces out for their beauty and limited print runs. Of the three, Griffin's feels like it most captures the scale and surreal majesty of Lynch's movie, focusing on imagery specific to the folding space sequence.

MATT GRIFFIN: What I wanted to achieve was epic-ness. Not just in scale and composition, but in terms of storytelling. It was important to get that balance of setting (space, ships, desert) and the spiritual, spectral side to the story. My favorite piece of set design in any film ever is that vast gate into the Guild Heighliner and the line of Atreides ships going into it. The ornate design is like something you'd find in a church, a nod to the "more-than."

Unlike some other fan pieces, Fitzgerald's image is not from the film directly, but rather evokes the power of Shai-Hulud.

KARL FITZGERALD: It's interesting to paint a scene that's not a shot from the film. I don't want to paint actors' likenesses. I try and focus on the atmosphere of the film and overall theme with a handful of symbolic elements that work together to create a dynamic composition that will read from a distance. The sandworm works as an iconic symbol for *Dune*. Focusing on this creates a massive sense of scale and forms a useful diagonal composition. The tiny figure of Paul in the center is there to give scale to Shai-Hulud and also adds a vague narrative to the piece.

Thornley's minimalist piece also hones in on the overwhelming power of the sandworm in relation to Paul's destiny, amplified by an overlay of abstract lines and symbols.

CHRIS THORNLEY: David Lynch is so good a pulling together those surreal moments, so I played around with the awakening theme, space and time coming together. There's no one quite like David Lynch; it's hard to really define his qualities, and that's what makes him interesting. I don't think he's really a commercial filmmaker, more experimental. His *Dune* feels both familiar and truly alien, as if there's some bigger picture underneath the surface. Given full creative control, I often think of the *Dune* that could have been.

While much has been lifted from Herbert's books over the years, the novels continue to endure. Griffin has been able to illustrate new covers for Herbert's books as well as new volumes in the series by Brian Herbert and Kevin J. Anderson.

MATT GRIFFIN: I've been very lucky to have a property I'm passionate about become such a huge part of my professional life. Most recently, I've also done the art for the deluxe editions of *Messiah* and *Children*. Working on the new generation of books by Brian and Kevin is a huge privilege. It's an affirmation that I'm not doing the property a disservice, that I get to make art that's part of its legacy. A nod of approval from the Herbert estate is very valuable to me. I've heard Brian say that I "get it." I can't ask for a higher compliment. I guess I get it because I love it so much.

Super7 *Dune* ReAction Figures

Nowadays, LJN's original *Dune* action figures and accessories from 1984 can go for hundreds, sometimes thousands of dollars on eBay in their original packaging (often with a Toys "R" Us remainder bin sticker on 'em). For '80s kids, these were an oddity you would spot on shelves while hunting for *Star Wars* toys, or maybe amid a box of clutter at a yard sale. Those who only know David Lynch's film as a cult oddity find it hilarious Universal thought the film would warrant a merchandizing juggernaut.

For years, many fans of the movie have found it cost-prohibitive to pick up that original lineup of figures, but not anymore. San Francisco–based boutique collectible company Super7 has issued new, officially licensed *Dune* figures modeled after the original LJN series, with the first wave in their 3.75"-inch ReAction line consisting of Paul Atreides in regal uniform, Paul-Muad'Dib in his desert stillsuit, Stilgar, Baron Harkonnen, and a Sardaukar warrior. Some of them even come with accessories like a dagger, maker hook, or weirding module. Each retails for a mere $20 apiece.

The mastermind behind the *Dune* ReAction figures is Super7's Vice President of Design Josh Herbolsheimer, who told me how the line came to be:

> I oversaw *Dune* with this old Kenner sculptor who worked on *Star Wars* stuff. Our sculptures were pulling from the LJN figures, then were produced, cast, scanned digitally, and some clean-up for joint articulation. We carried it through to factory, sampling, test shots, paint samples, all that jazz.

Herbolsheimer came across *Dune* in a Lynch retrospective a decade after its release:

> I watched it for the first time in high school, probably 1995. There was this arthouse movie theater in my hometown that had a midnight Lynch series. Some friends and I started going to all of them. I saw *Dune* and it was like, "Whoa, that's pretty cool." I had always been aware of it as a thing, but had never watched it. I knew the toys existed but hadn't really paid much attention to them at that point. That was my entry point to anything *Dune*.

Like many, Herbolsheimer was a little flabbergasted at the avalanche of tie-in merch produced for Lynch's weirdo sci-fi epic:

> They produced a lot of stuff expecting it to take off, like View-Master slides, bedsheets, and coloring books. Did the toys end up in landfills? Were they quietly tucked away in people's collections? I don't know. The toys are more interesting as this esoteric object unconnected to a story. There's this guy in military dress uniform, this great big guy, and this dude with a weird cat. What is this? They thought, "Oh, it's going to be another space movie with creatures and stuff. It'll be awesome for kids." As toy objects, they recreate—in a toyetic way—what was on screen, but the story doesn't connect with a six-year-old. There is a huge disconnect there, that's what makes them cool.

Working with their team of artists, Super7 went to great lengths to recapture the look and feel of LJN's primitive but charming toys. Herbolsheimer explained:

> The scale's a little different. The LJN ones are five and a half inches, but we went back and forth: "Should we make three-and-three-quarter action figures more literal to the film, or reference the toys?" For me, the toys were the stronger connection. We licensed *Dune* from Universal, but LJN got absorbed by Acclaim in the '90s, who's now owned by somebody else two or three times over. There wasn't an entity to seek clearance from in that way . . . not that anybody cared. The styling is pretty close to the format, in terms articulation. Some of the costumes are simplified a bit where they have the breaks at the shoulders or hips. At a glance, they look similar, but if you hold the two of them together, it's pretty apparent. The old ones have that Battle-Matic arm motion that ours do not.

Simplistic as these ReAction figures may seem to modern toy collectors (used to Hasbro or McFarlane creating toy likenesses based on digital scans of actors' faces), "simplistic" is precisely the level of nostalgia that Super7 has been so good at mining for properties like *Alien*, *Planet of the Apes*, or *Masters of the Universe*.

According to Herbolsheimer:

> If we had given a film-literal look to the figures, we probably would have gone further down that road. If you're going retro, do them the way you remember them. Do it all the way. It has to be the right type of shitty.

For hardcore *Dune* action figure–collector Frank Turner, who owns many of the original LJN prototypes, Super7's new series is exactly the right type of shitty.

"It's the revival of the LJN toy," enthused Turner. "I was so pleased with how well they did it because they're *Star Wars* size, which is the size we all know and love, the perfect size for an action figure."

As for the future of the *Dune* ReAction line, things look as bright as the Canopus sun of Arrakis. Herbolsheimer assured us:

> It's been a good middle ground: not a runaway smash, but successful enough. The people that found it are very into it, because there's been so little around this version of *Dune*. It's a placeholder for those original figures. I'd love to do a glow-in-the-dark Paul Atreides. Get to the unproduced LJN things like Jessica and Gurney. A second series is warranted. As long as people stay interested and they sell enough to justify themselves. I would love to make every character in the film. The sandworm, that'd be awesome, where they go up and ride on it, like a sandworm chariot.

Turner added:

> Because of the absence of Feyd and Rabban, I'm hoping they're going to carry on, because they can easily do Gurney and Jessica. It was so good to see the last *Dune* film cause a revival in the Lynch *Dune* so we've had new lunchboxes come out, these Super7 figures, the Arrow Blu-ray, and now you're writing the book. I love David Lynch, but I would disagree with him when he talks about *Dune* being his greatest failure. It's a thing of wonder and beauty.

"David Lynch's *Dune* Sweded" (2014)

Michel Gondry's 2008 movie *Be Kind Rewind* told the story of two wacky dudes (played by Jack Black and Yasiin Bey) who accidentally erase all the VHS tapes in the local video store. To replace them, they create their own no-budget versions of the movies like *Ghostbusters* or *RoboCop* with cheap costumes and cardboard sets. While *Be Kind Rewind* itself didn't set the world on fire, the process the movie's two heroes refer to as "sweding" became something of a lo-fi phenomenon, leading to YouTubers posting their own swedes of famous movies on the internet.

Enter Twin Cities Sweding, a Minnesota-based comedy troupe consisting of Jerry Belich, Melissa Kaercher, and Brian Quarfoth . . . and their many friends. They began in 2012 with a parody of the trailer for Peter Jackson's *The Hobbit: An Unexpected Journey*, followed by a *Die Hard* Swede filmed at the 2012 CONvergence convention in Minneapolis featuring the group's pal (and *Doctor Strange* screenwriter) C. Robert Cargill. The latter used a burning stack of playing cards as Nakatomi Plaza. The ambitious group decided to tackle David Lynch's *Dune* for their third outing.

Group leader Jerry Belich recalled:

> I had a lot of feelings about *Dune*. On the one hand, this is unlike anything I've ever seen, which is very David Lynch. He's bursting with imagination and fearless, for better or worse. When you're college age, you want to feel smart, so if you don't understand something you're like, "it must be me." Later, I realized this is legit bonkers. When it comes to sweding films, we didn't select Lynch's *Dune* because we love it more than anything, right? It's about finding that movie that's iconic for good and bad reasons. The bad reasons give you a lot of leverage in poking fun at it and having fun with it. The good reasons you can mimic and bring back things that people enjoy about it.

The *Dune* Swede started as all "shits and giggles," but quickly spiraled into something so large it necessitated an Extended Edition, ala the '84 film:

> We did the Extended Cut because we're like, "This doesn't quite flow and it gets harder to watch, but we made so many scenes we need to have them visible." Other things started inflating it, like friends of mine, The Dregs, did the song over the credits that's a spoof of "Africa." The lead singer Tim Wick forced himself not to down-pitch it at all. He's barely hitting the notes, which makes me laugh. We had to perfectly emulate the credits, so all the characters fading in and out over the water broke some Swede rules we set for ourselves, which is making decisions as quickly and cheaply as possible.

The end Toto song parody by The Dregs is wonderful: "It's gonna take a lot to take me away from Dune/There's nothing that a hundred Fremen or more could ever do/I bless the worms here on Arrakis/And in time I'll be the Kwisatz Haderach."

The shoot for "David Lynch's *Dune* Sweded" presented a few hairy situations in and of itself, including the cardboard box shields. Belich admitted:

Filming all of the shield practice stuff in my attic during a hot summer was nearly 100 degrees. Man, we're running around with garbage bags on, suffering for these stupid shots. We went over the border to Wisconsin to buy Everclear 190, because it's illegal in Minnesota. We poured it on sand and started these low-burning fires, which was fun. The scenes in the garage with the Baron Harkonnen—that's Melissa's husband Fes and he pulled that shit off. We put very sloppy latex makeup on his face, then put him on a piece of wood so he could kind of float. We ended up having a really frank discussion about the scene where he spits on Jessica: "Oh my God, this looks like a really bad spoof of a porn." We asked the actress Eryn if it was okay.

While the two cuts of the *Dune* sweding together garnered over 40,000 views on YouTube, the group's dream was to see Lynch's reaction. Belich recalled:

I was visiting a friend in LA while we were making it, and my friend's roommate was friends with Lynch's personal assistant. I was like, "Oh my God, it's so close." Unfortunately, it took so long to finish the connection withered away. I do sometimes think, "Is there some way that I could get him to see this and get a reaction?" I admittedly haven't put real effort into that.

Belich admits a kinship with Lynch and what he went through making *Dune*:

I understand what it is to have worked on something that has not gone the way you want. Even just looking in its direction makes you feel physically ill or pain. It can be hard when you've invested so much of yourself into something and it falls to pieces. It's iconic for a reason, and not because it's the greatest film ever or it's a perfect *Dune* adaptation. It does have something unique and special about it. Lynch was able to leave a print on it and not in a negative way. I do love that it is in the world.

While their parody of Lynch's film got some press, Belich's career trajectory spelled the group's end. Boasting an MFA in Experience Design, he raised $75,000 on Kickstarter for the award-winning interactive fiction game console called The Choosatron. This led to a run of jobs as a narrative designer, including a position at Squanch Games. The dream of Twin Cities Sweding has more or less faded away:

The thing I loved about it is it's a process where loving the journey of the making is the goal. That is the core of it. Having done so much creative work over the years, and having gone through burnout multiple times, it's one of the things I've realized is so hard to achieve in your work . . . yet it is the thing that makes a difference in whether you're happy.

An Annual Tradition

Whitney Matheson is a veteran journalist and author, perhaps best known for creating and curating *USA Today*'s *Pop Candy* blog for over 15 years. Below Matheson shares a fascinating interview with her father, who has made Lynch's *Dune* something of an annual tradition:

> *Quick facts about my dad: Barry Matheson (age 73, retired science teacher in Fredericksburg, VA) has been watching Dune on his birthday (May 29) every year for the last 20-plus years. He's not really a David Lynch fan or a cinephile . . . he just really loves this movie!*

WHITNEY MATHESON: Tell me about when *Dune* first came into your life.

DAD: I may have just gotten a rental VHS tape, but it wasn't long after it came out. I had read the books back when I was in college in '67 or '68. When I saw the movie, I understood everything that was going on, but evidently, that wasn't the case with a lot of people. I remember one coworker had seen it and was just totally in the dark and didn't understand the backstory.

MATHESON: Is the film faithful to the book?

DAD: Pretty much! The book goes into a lot more explanation about the people and the environment and the science, and they had to cut out a lot of that. But the plot held up really well in the movie. You don't just have a superhero-type guy, you have a superbeing. And fifty years down the road, you can still relate to things about the drugs, the spice, the physics of folding space, and things like that give it substance and depth. The movie depends a lot on the story and the people, and it's not overwhelming as far as special effects. Even though the movie came out after *Star Wars*—and *Star Wars* was all about special effects and things that had never been seen or done before—they didn't do that in *Dune*. I think maybe the strongest feature of the whole movie was the depth of the cast and the impression that they made. They had people like Kyle MacLachlan and Francesca Annis, but you had others like Patrick Stewart, Sting, Sean Young, Max von Sydow, José Ferrer . . . I mean, even Linda Hunt was in there! The Harkonnens were really vile. They were over-the-top mean and the ultimate villains. The uniforms and the costumes, it's almost like the European 19th-century. They're not trying to look futuristic; they're a throwback to an earlier time. The more I think about it, I think it's the right tone. It sets an archaic feeling into the future. The more advanced and farther into the future, there are still some basic things from the past.

MATHESON: Do you remember how the tradition of watching *Dune* on your birthday started?

DAD: I think one time on my birthday I wanted to watch a good movie, something where I could sit back and relax, have a bottle of wine. A year's interval is about right to watch it again. It's not a cult thing or anything like that—it's just that it seems a good, appropriate time, and I enjoy it. It's a tradition I drifted into.

Lynch *Dune* Fandom

When I was interviewing talent for this book, actress Virginia Madsen put the question back toward me: "What is it about this movie that sticks with you? You're a young man, why are you so attached to this movie?"

It's a good question: What makes a person a fan of Lynch's *Dune*? Does it stem from a love of Herbert's books? Of wanting to see a beautifully realized sci-fi world akin to *Star Wars*? Could it be the weird energy, or the cult cache that Lynch brings from his other successes like *Twin Peaks*? Why does a big-budget sci-fi bomb from the '80s endure to this day among certain circles?

Frank Turner, who has one of the largest collections of *Dune* merchandise in the world, told me:

> It's the novelty of being one of the very few *Dune* collectors. You couldn't fill a telephone box with the people who are into *Dune* in the same way that people are into *Star Wars*. They can fill convention centers with people who are into the Kenner toy line, and yet people who are into *Dune* . . . there's me, there's Mark Bennett, there's another guy who's also called Mark who has a prototype collection of *Dune* stuff. There's a Polish guy who collects nothing but the books that Mark knows, and that's pretty much it.

Matt Caron is a fan of the collector variety. He owns the '84 *Dune* on VHS, LaserDisc, and CED. He has the original Fleer cards, the LJN sandworm toy, the Marvel Comics adaptation, the pop-up book, and even a 35 mm copy of the original theatrical trailer.

"I don't know how preserved the inside frames of the trailer are, but FotoKem is pretty close by," Caron explained. "I'm just waiting for a good time to scan this and do a little dust and scratch removal, get it scanned in at 4K. It also has the stereo optical track on the side. I'm going to geek out and try to do my own restoration project."

A director of post-production at Legendary Digital Networks (the company also making the current *Dune* movies), Caron has made a few video tributes for *Nerdist* dedicated to Lynch's film, including an '80s-style trailer that matches the sound of the Lynch movie with the visuals of the Denis Villeneuve film, even adding in Lynch touches like the blocky shields.

"As a kid, I enjoyed it because it was different than *Star Wars*," Caron explained of his fandom. "Knowing what Lynch was forced to put together, and that he doesn't really like that movie . . . It's fascinating comparing it to the rest of his work. I will always associate his visuals anytime I'm reading the original story."

Sean Crespo is a two-time Emmy nominee and two-time WGA Award-winning writer (*Full Frontal with Samantha Bee*) and actor (*Gotham*, *Blue Bloods*). In 2017, he and Janelle James (*Abbott Elementary*) co-starred in a sitcom pilot Crespo created titled *Alternate Side Parking*, where they play two struggling New Yorkers who live in their car. The episode began with Ilana Becker (*Them*) delivering the Princess Irulan space monologue, but differently:

> A beginning is a very delicate time. Know then that it is the year two thousand one seven. In this time, the most precious substance in the New York universe is a friend. A friend extends the time you can survive here. A friend gets all your stupid movie references.

Despite the pilot not being picked up, Crespo still considers *Dune*—which he saw in '84 with his mother and future stepfather—a personal favorite:

> It's a bit of a hot mess, but it's a beautiful hot mess, and it was my hot mess. Part of why I loved it is it spoke to anybody with father issues. Paul's a bastard, basically. His mom's the concubine, it's not an official relationship. That remove from Leto being his legit royal

line father, but still being loved like his one and only son the way a father should be, is very touching. Then he loses him, and we don't get to find out what kind of relationship they would have had, which is very sad, right? I don't have much of a relationship with my parents, so that's clearly a movie about my life!

WGA winner and three-time Emmy nominee Andrés du Bouchet, who worked on Conan O'Brien's shows for over a decade, also exorcised "daddy issues" via *Dune*, and even has a tattoo of the desert kangaroo mouse (a.k.a. Muad'Dib) from the book:

> That movie resonated with me because it's about a kid who is essentially pushed around by his parents and his family and expectations of society and yada yada yada. Then he kind of loses his marbles and kills everybody and takes over the planet, and it's the ultimate young male fantasy: "You can't fucking tell me what to do, and check it out, I'm the fuckin' Messiah now . . . fuck off." There definitely were major daddy issues with me, with a father who was not very loving or supportive or whatever. Kyle MacLachlan's performance is fuckin' awesome in that movie, and as a 13-year-old seeing that, it made me feel like, "Okay, I can stand up to some stuff and maybe forge my own path." It was hardwired into me to be very resentful of how I was being raised. That moment where the Reverend Mother yells at him and he goes, "SILENCE!" was empowering to a nerd always getting bullied in school.

Mark Bennet first saw Lynch's *Dune* on UK television in 1992. In 1994, he discovered Ed Naha's book *The Making of Dune* at a secondhand bookshop and proceeded to scan some of the photos and post them online. This gave birth to the website *DuneInfo*, which has been going strong for 27 years and covers everything from the Jodorowsky version all the way through to the new Warner Bros. films. Like his compatriots Matt Caron and Frank Turner, he has many rare *Dune* collectibles, but he leads with a true love for what Lynch did with the property:

> I always compare it to the Venus de Milo, the statue with the missing arms. What we've got is beautiful, but it's clearly not the whole film. Someone online said, "Love Lynch's *Dune* for what it is, not hate it for what it's not." There are cut scenes; there's information in *The Making of Dune* book and in the various sci-fi magazines. I've been

gradually piecing together the scripts and trying to get an understanding of what Lynch was going for and what it could have been. For me, that's almost more interesting than the film itself. It's almost an unmade film like Jodorowsky's. We've got part of it there, but it's not what the true Lynch's *Dune* would have been.

I'm still trying to figure out the answer to Virginia Madsen's question, but Bennett's philosophy rings true for this author. There is something more tantalizing about a movie that is a flawed masterpiece as opposed to a straight-up masterpiece. With a masterpiece, you're inclined to say, "Okay, that's a great movie . . . what's to complain about? It is what it is." There have even been movies with extremely chaotic productions that turned out brilliantly, such as *Casablanca*. A "missed opportunity," an "also ran," or an "almost" where you see flashes of brilliance tend to be—to me—more fascinating to reckon with.

Gholas: The Remakes

L ynch was the first filmmaker to bring Arrakis to the screen, but he was not the last.

Frank Herbert's Dune (2000)

In 1996, the film rights to *Dune* were acquired by producer Richard P. Rubinstein, best known for his long association with director George Romero (*Dawn of the Dead, Creepshow*) as well as several Stephen King adaptations, including *Pet Sematary* and the 1994 TV miniseries of *The Stand*. His company New Amsterdam developed a television miniseries for the Sci-Fi Channel eventually titled *Frank Herbert's Dune* to signify its fidelity to the material.

Academy Award–winner William Hurt (*Kiss of the Spider Woman*), who stated he'd wanted to be in the 1984 film, got top billing as Duke Leto, with Alec Newman as Paul Atreides and Giancarlo Giannini as the Emperor. Produced on a budget of $20 million, *Frank Herbert's Dune* was written and directed by John Harrison (*Tales from the Darkside: The Movie*) in a decidedly theatrical style, and shot by Vittorio Storaro (*Apocalypse Now*), who had been eyed to shoot Ridley Scott's version years earlier.

"Earning high ratings but mixed reviews, the six-hour version ironically reopened discussion about Lynch's version, and even led to a cautious reappraisal of the theatrical *Dune*," writes David Hughes in *The Complete Lynch*. "Asked about the show a few weeks after its widely publicized broadcast, Lynch responded, 'What miniseries?'"

It was followed by *Frank Herbert's Children of Dune* (2003), which featured an early lead role for James McAvoy. Interestingly, he later took over the Professor X part in the *X-Men* series from Patrick Stewart; being in *Dune* is clearly a prerequisite for playing Charles Xavier. Alec Newman reprises his role as Paul Atreides and also portrays The Preacher that Paul transforms himself into. Alice Krige is Lady Jessica, while Susan Sarandon is Princess Wensicia, the Emperor's daughter. The story is a melding of the novels *Dune Messiah* and *Children of Dune*.

Peter Berg Version (2007–09)

In December 2007, actor-turned-filmmaker Peter Berg (*Friday Night Lights, The Kingdom*) told MTV that he was signed to direct a new big-screen

Dune for Paramount Pictures. He referred to his vision as "big, big, big." This news was later confirmed by *Variety* in March of 2008, who claimed that Kevin Misher would produce, having worked with Berg on 2003's action comedy *The Rundown*. Richard Rubinstein of the two miniseries would also produce alongside Sarah Aubrey of Berg's Film 44 production banner, with John Harrison and Michael D. Messina executive producing.

In October 2021, author-humorist John Hodgman told the newsletter *The Reveal* about meeting Berg on a plane ride around 2007 and noticing that he was reading a copy of *Dune*. When Hodgman inquired, Berg told him he was thinking of making a new movie of it. Hodgman recalled:

> He was saying, "Look, this is a classic hero's journey about a chosen child who must heed a call to adventure and all this Joseph Campbell-ian stuff. Then Peter Berg, being the artist that he is, takes out a spreadsheet and points out the top-grossing movies of all time and he's like, "Chosen one narrative, chosen one narrative, chosen one narrative, chosen one narrative." I'm like, "Yeah, I get it, Peter Berg. White guys love to see movies about white guys who are the chosen special ones." Basically, Peter Berg's take on *Dune* was that he was going to focus on the adventure and the warfare and a little bit less of the psychosexual stuff. He was like, "David Lynch made his version." I don't want to put words in Peter Berg's mouth, but he was like, "I'm going to make this a guy's movie, not a weird guy's movie."

Not long after, Hodgman's manager asked if he would be interested in pitching to write the screenplay for Berg's *Dune*. He swiftly declined, citing a likely irreconcilable difference in his "nerd" sensibility and Berg's "jock" leanings, having been a fan of the weirder aspects of Lynch's movie such as the heart plugs.

For screenwriter, Berg instead hired Joshua Zetumer, who later penned the 2014 *RoboCop* remake and Berg's 2016 Boston Marathon bombing drama *Patriots Day*. Concept artwork done by Scottish comic book artist Mark "Jock" Simpson depicted frenetic, Giger-like, asymmetrical sandworms as well as a shaved-head bruiser look for Paul Atreides straight out of Zack Snyder's *300*. Robert Pattinson, then hot off of *Twilight*, was rumored to have been Berg's first choice to play Paul, and the two met in May 2009 to discuss the role.

Berg said in 2009 [*Sci-Fi Wire*]:

> I had a much more different experience, I think, with the book than David Lynch did. To me, I think my interpretation will feel signifi-

cantly different from that and the miniseries that aired. I have a different experience than both of those filmmakers did. [The book] was much more muscular and adventurous, more violent, and possibly even a little bit more fun. I think those are all elements of my experience of the book that can be brought in without offending the diehard fans of the Bene Gesserit and Kwisatz Haderach. There's a more dynamic film to be made.

During my talk with Stephen Scarlata, he discussed the Zetumer–Chase Palmer script for Berg's *Dune*, which he read:

The one thing I'll say about Peter Berg's version is they do have the banquet scene in it. That's the weirdest thing about that one. The treatment starts off with the banquet scene, and that's how you get familiar with all the characters. It's reminiscent of the opening scene of *The Godfather*. The one thing about the Berg version people would have had a hard time with is he was going to merge Duncan and Gurney into one character. I liked the way his worms would look and everything, but what the writers were doing . . . the script is exactly 120 pages. It's an action movie. I think that's what they were probably forcing him to do, and he probably had the right mind to step away from it.

Ultimately Paramount wound up passing on Berg's vision in October 2009 after an initial budget came in approaching $175 million. The director instead got his science-fiction rocks off by inexplicably adding alien invaders to his $200 million Milton Bradley game adaptation *Battleship* in 2012, which was an enormous flop that lost Universal roughly $150 million.

Berg spoke that year to *Film School Rejects* about his shelved plans for *Dune*:

My feeling was, I wanted to make a grittier, rougher film than the Lynch movie. My experience with *Dune* was just a really great adventure story, and it was muscular, violent, and intense. Obviously, there was a very cerebral, mystical, almost-supernatural component to it, and mind communication, and the Bene Gesserits were kind of a bunch of badass witches. At its core, I wanted to make something that felt more like *Star Wars*, where it just had more grit to it.

Pierre Morel Version (2009-2011)

In October 2009, *Pajiba* reported that Paramount was looking for a new director to take over the *Dune* remake project who had a "pre-existing passion for the novel." While they initially looked at two "Neils," Neill Blomkamp (*District 9*) and Neil Marshall (*The Descent*), they eventually went with French helmer Pierre Morel of *Unleashed* and *Taken* fame, who was confirmed to take over in January 2010 ahead of the release of his John Travolta action flick *From Paris with Love*.

Morel, a fan of the book since he was a teenager, told MTV in February 2010:

> We're starting from scratch. Peter had an approach which was not mine at all, and we're starting over again. I don't think we're going to keep any elements of the Peter Berg script. Everything that is in Paul's head, we'll have to show it on screen and find the right approach to make it visually interesting, but I think the technology we have now allows us much more than we could do before, so we'll see.

Morel also planned a push to shoot the film in 3D, after the phenomenal success of *Avatar* the previous year made that viable: "Will they do it in 3D? I'd push for that, but I don't know. As a viewer, I've just been watching *Avatar* with my kids twice in the theater already and had a blast. It's an amazing experience."

As far as his feelings toward the book and the Lynch movie, Morel falls right in line with the man who would ultimately land the job, Denis Villeneuve, saying to MTV:

> As a David Lynch movie, I loved it. As a *Dune* fan, I was not such a big fan. I've been a fan of that book since I was a teenager. I read that when I was 15. I've been reading it over and over again—well, I'm 45 now, so for 30 years. There were six books in that first series that Frank Herbert wrote. Every time I was going to buy a new one, I was reading the previous ones so I would not forget anything. By the time I bought the sixth book, I had already read the first one six times! My movie is all about the first book. I'm trying to be very respectful to the original novel, but it's a challenge. There's a lot of expectation; all the readers will be waiting for me with their shotguns. All the nonreaders will also be waiting for us, because it's such a complex, rich novel, and you have to make it accessible to those who have not read the book. It's a tough challenge, but I'm very excited about that.

However, Morel's tenure on the project would not last long. By November 2010, word on the street was that Morel had stepped away from the project (remaining as an executive producer) as the clock ticked on Paramount's stake in the rights. He had developed a new draft with writer Chase Palmer, who later went on to co-pen the hugely successful 2017 adaptation of Stephen King's *It*. Rubinstein, who favored Morel's take, was confident that Palmer's script had cracked the code on how to turn *Dune* into a viable epic, and did not want Paramount dragging its feet to greenlight the film.

"We don't want to extend an option and watch the studio take seven years," Rubinstein told *Deadline*. "This is on a short tether. It's a major book franchise; you can't walk into a store and not see a shelf full of *Dune* books."

In March 2011, Paramount officially opted out of the *Dune* property, ending four years of development. Rubinstein and producer Kevin Misher hoped to re-approach Morel and Palmer once interest from a new studio could be found to pony up the roughly $100 million budget they required. Rubinstein said that month to *Deadline*:

> Paramount's option has expired, and we couldn't reach an agreement. I'm going to look at my options, and whether I wind up taking the script we developed in turnaround, or start over, I'm not sure yet. Sure, it's frustrating, how long this has taken, but most of what I've done that worked out well over the years, like the miniseries *The Stand*, took a long time. Since I know what I want, eventually, I'll find someone who'll agree with me.

Dune (2021)

In 2016, *Variety* reported that Legendary Entertainment (*Jurassic World*, *Godzilla*, and *The Dark Knight* trilogy) had acquired the film and TV rights to *Dune* from the Frank Herbert estate. One month later, *The Hollywood Reporter* announced that French Canadian filmmaker Denis Villeneuve (hot off of his sci-fi hit *Arrival*, but before his sequel *Blade Runner 2049* came out) was in early talks to direct a new version of *Dune* for Legendary. Brian Herbert confirmed the news on Twitter.

The new film would be written by Jon Spaihts (*Passengers*), Villeneuve, and Eric Roth (*Munich*), and produced by Villeneuve, Mary Parent, and Cale Boyter.

During a Facebook Live interview to promote *Blade Runner 2049* in November of 2017 with Yahoo's Kevin Polowy, Villeneuve (still on the first draft of the screenplay) confirmed that his film would have nothing to do with Lynch's:

> David Lynch did an adaptation in the '80s that has some very strong qualities. Lynch is one of the best filmmakers alive; I have massive respect for him. But when I saw his adaptation, I was impressed, but it was not what I had dreamed of, so I'm trying to make the adaptation of my dreams. It will not have any link with the David Lynch movie. I'm going back to the book, and going to the images that came out when I read it.

With an estimated budget of $165 million, the movie that would later be promoted as *Dune* but carried the in-film title of *Dune: Part One* began filming on March 18, 2019, at Origo Film Studios in Budapest, Hungary, as well as the Wadi Rum valley in Jordan and the Liwa Oasis in the United Arab Emirates. It wrapped in July 2019, but production went back to Budapest in August 2020 for additional reshoots. However, due to the COVID-19 pandemic the original theatrical release date of December 18, 2020, was pushed to October 22, 2021, for a hybrid simultaneous release in theaters and on the streaming service HBO Max. This decision led to some discontent between Legendary (who funded 75% of the film) and distributor Warner Bros. over the damage it might do to the film's box office and audience appreciation.

However, by the time *Dune: Part One* hit theaters a year later, Villeneuve was fully on board promoting it, even taking time out to speak of Lynch's version.

"I'm a big David Lynch fan, he's the master," Villeneuve told *Empire* in August of 2021. "When I saw [Lynch's] *Dune*, I remember being excited, but his take . . . there are parts that I love and other elements that I am less comfortable with. I remember being half-satisfied. That's why I was thinking to myself, 'There's still a movie that needs to be made about that book, just a different sensibility.'"

"I have zero interest in *Dune*, because it was a heartache for me," Lynch told *The Hollywood Reporter* in April 2020 when asked about the forthcoming remake. When queried again about seeing another filmmaker's interpretation, he bluntly reiterated, "I said I've got zero interest."

Piter actor David Dastmalchian said [*Screen Rant*]:

> I loved David Lynch's *Dune* when I saw it as a kid, I thought that it was visually so spectacular. There are so many incredible performanc-

es in it. Tonally, it's so fantastic . . . The order I would recommend: read the book, then go see Denis' film, and then in November you could do Lynch's, the Syfy version, and the documentary *Jodorowsky's Dune*. Then we'll all be authorities on *Dune*, and we'll get online together to have long discussions and debates. I can't wait to hear everybody's reactions to what Denis has created. It's nothing short of a masterpiece.

Ultimately the new *Dune* film's $400 million worldwide box office take, impressive streaming numbers, and critical praise paved the way for *Dune: Part Two*, which was greenlit by Warner Bros. on October 26, 2021, with a projected November 3, 2023 release date. This will be made concurrently alongside an HBO Max event series about the Bene Gesserit order titled *Dune: The Sisterhood*, in development with Spaihts penning the scripts and Alison Schapker as showrunner. The second *Dune* features Léa Seydoux (*No Time to Die*) as Lady Fenring. In an interesting connection, Seydoux's grand-uncle, Michel Seydoux, was slated to produce Jodorowsky's failed attempt in the '70s and was featured in the documentary *Jodorowsky's Dune*.

A third film based on Herbert's second *Dune* book, *Dune Messiah*, is also in the wings to potentially close out the trilogy.

"The thing I envision, the adaptation of two books, *Dune* and *Dune Messiah*," Villeneuve told *Screen Rant* in September of 2021, giving fans hope that Third-Stage Guild Navigators have a future in his movies. "We decided to split the first novel in two, so now we are at three movies. Those movies are very long to make. For my mental sanity, I decided to just dream about three movies."

Dune was nominated for 10 Oscars, including Best Picture. During the 94th Academy Awards on March 27, 2022 (infamous for being "the night Will Smith slapped Chris Rock onstage"), *Dune* won 6 of the 10 Oscars it was nominated for: Best Cinematography, Best Editing, Best Visual Effects, Best Original Score, Best Production Design, and Best Sound. While these wins were well-earned and certainly not a slap in the face to Lynch's picture, it shows just how close to greatness the '84 film might have come adapting the same material with some tweaks on the creative end . . . or the studio's.

Modern Impressions of *Dune*

The following individuals were interviewed by the author for this section:

- John DeVore, *Medium*
- Jordan Hoffman, *Vanity Fair*
- Roxana Hadadi, *Vulture*
- Zaki Hasan, *San Francisco Chronicle*
- Scott Collura, *IGN*
- Rosie Knight, *Nerdist*
- Drew Taylor, *TheWrap*
- Jenna Busch, */Film*
- David Crow, *Den of Geek*
- Rick Marshall, *Digital Trends*
- Michael Gingold, *Rue Morgue*
- Edward Douglas, *Below the Line*
- Scooter McCrae, *Fangoria*

Looking at critical reviews from December 1984 gives valuable insight into how Dune *was initially received, but I also wanted to talk to contemporary film critics who grew up on Lynch's movie about the lasting impressions it had.*

JOHN DEVORE: I have a very childlike memory of it, being overwhelmed by *Dune* because it was marketed as a *Star Wars* movie.

ZAKI HASAN: I was about five years old when *Dune* came out, so I was fascinated by that *Star Wars*-esque marketing campaign with the toys and coloring books.

JOHN DEVORE: I will forever love my mom for seeing this disgusting "ribbed for your pleasure" worm toy and being like, "Yes, my son, you can have a toy that Freud would advise against buying." Also, I'm a little kid, and the Baron Harkonnen action figure had painted black toenails? What the fuck is that? Versus my He-Man dolls that didn't have nipples, right? It was kinky.

MICHAEL GINGOLD: I went to see *The Last Starfighter* which had that amazing *Dune* trailer attached, a whole couple of seasons beforehand, which was not done as much back then. I remember being blown away by it.

JORDAN HOFFMAN: It was a thing and it was in the theater, and any kind of sci-fi movie I would have wanted to see in the theater. I remember when *Krull* came out, and I did get to see that, and *Last Starfighter* and all the other classics of that era, but I didn't see *Dune* in the theater, so it was a big deal to me when it was finally available to watch on HBO.

SCOTT COLLURA: In 1984, I was actively seeking out genre movies like *Star Trek III: The Search for Spock* and *2010: The Year We Make Contact.* Yet I have no memory of the first time I saw *Dune*. It didn't leave an impression. That sums up my take on it, in a way.

EDWARD DOUGLAS: When I was in my teens, I lived in Westport, Connecticut. Had already read Frank Herbert's *Dune* and had my own idea of what a movie might look like. My brother was also a sci-fi fan, and when David Lynch's *Dune* opened in December 1984, we were both pretty excited.

SCOOTER MCCRAE: Towards the end of first semester of freshman year at college on December 13, a cry echoed through the common area of the dorm: "Come now if you want to see *Dune!*" I jumped off the couch and ran barefoot towards the stranger's voice. Someone's friend of a friend was a projectionist at the local theater and the film print of *Dune* had arrived. Now that the venue was closed, they were going to unspool it for the first time for whoever wanted to come… for free, no less!

EDWARD DOUGLAS: It was playing one town over in Norwalk. Not sure how long *Dune* had been playing before we ventured out to see it, but I have a feeling it was close to the end of its run. Neither my brother nor I heard about negative reviews or the movie bombing.

SCOOTER MCCRAE: I did not own a car, so I ran towards everyone else and hopped into a stranger's vehicle with as many other people as could fit, and off we went. To be clear, I was still barefoot and without a jacket in mid-December, on my way with a group of unknown fellow students to a movie theater for an unofficial secret screening of *Dune*. This is precisely the thing one does when they are 18 years old.

EDWARD DOUGLAS: We decided on a 9 p.m. screening in Norwalk, but when we got to this theater, we were told we were the only people there for the movie and they wouldn't run it unless at least five people showed up. Something like that would be unheard of in this day and age where theaters are obligated to play movies at the times scheduled, but this was long before digital, so putting wear on a film print may have been a concern.

But my brother and I waited. One other person showed up and was told the same thing. Then we waited some more. Alas, it was just the three of us, and therefore, no *Dune*.

SCOOTER MCCRAE: Arriving at the theater, I headed directly to the front row, concerned about stepping on sticky spots and leftover candy crap in the other rows. Grabbed the center seat and curled up into it to keep myself and my feet warm as *Dune* was projected on the tremendous (and quite close) movie screen, pummeling me into submission for the next 137 minutes… I loved every single one of those minutes. I ended up seeing *Dune* four more times during its theatrical release. And yes, I wore shoes at all future screenings.

MICHAEL GINGOLD: When I saw it in 1984, I found *Dune* hard to follow. I loved seeing a movie this big and expensive with so much bizarre stuff in it, all the strange characters. Baron Harkonnen floating around, waiting for that moment in the trailer where he says, "He who controls the spice controls the universe!" and spits something out when he says "spice." That always got a laugh when I saw that trailer.

JOHN DEVORE: I didn't understand it except on the level of bad guys and monsters. I remember being upset when Leto's tooth was taken out and put back in. Also by the way Dr. Yueh tells him what's happening and what is going to happen. I was very upset by the heart plug thing.

RICK MARSHALL: I was born in '77, and watched *Dune* '84 around '86 or '87. I remember being very confused; memories of climbing the sandworm and the pain box, Kyle MacLachlan and Sting fighting, being terrified by Baron Harkonnen.

JENNA BUSCH: I remember seeing it when it came out on VHS and laughing at it. I did this time as well. Not to sound disparaging—I laughed because it was fun. The costumes were silly. There was a Princess (Irulan) I wanted to know more about in the book. No one other than Sting seemed to be taking it very seriously. At the time, that was what I wanted.

JORDAN HOFFMAN: When the new cable guide came out, *Dune* was one of the big movies on HBO that month. The first night it was on, 8 p.m., big movie, we only had one TV in the living room. This was the '80s, so my sister's language was like, "This movie is retarded, I'm not going to watch this." I'm like, "No, I really want to see it." She's like, "No." So I bribed her. I said, "Hey, look, Sting is in this movie." And she's like, "Okay, then I'll watch it." I was able to convince my eldest sister to let me leave it on the TV because Sting was half-naked in it.

ZAKI HASAN: I didn't end up renting the film until the late '80s, couldn't make heads or tails of it. It stayed with me enough that I revisited it in the '90s. Conventional wisdom was this is not a good movie. I thought, "there's something here."

JORDAN HOFFMAN: It never struck me as odd. I liked it as much as *Krull* or . . . maybe not *Last Starfighter*, that really snaps together well . . . or *Flash Gordon*, any of that crap. It didn't strike me as weird or unusual. It wasn't until years later I was informed, "Oh, that's a bad movie," or "That movie is crazy." "It is? It's no crazier than *Krull*. It's awesome."

ROXANA HADADI: I think I was in middle school. I watched it on TV, one of those Saturday afternoon reruns on UPN or WB or maybe even Syfy. I hadn't yet read the book, so I remember thinking the movie was weird and interesting but also noticing certain things that puzzled me, like the use of Arabic or Farsi words pronounced in a very incorrect way.

Many of these critics also happen to be appreciators of Herbert's book.

ROXANA HADADI: The experience of watching that movie, butchered with commercials, is what inspired me to read the book, and that made me even more frustrated with the very white way that '80s *Dune* was imagined.

JOHN DEVORE: Herbert was writing about colonialism. People accuse *Dune* of having a white savior complex, but in later books, he very plainly gives his thoughts on messiahs. Paul doesn't save the universe; he just makes it more complicated.

ROSIE KNIGHT: The crux of the story of *Dune*—the big twist or story arc—comes so late in the novels that every adaptation—the TV one, the movie, the new movie—still fit into that notion of a white savior story . . . but that's not what the story is.

JOHN DEVORE: Paul's story in the later books is more interesting than anything in the second half, what he becomes. Herbert's book is written so dully, but he's a guy in the '60s looking at American imperialism in a way we're still wrestling with.

ZAKI HASAN: My fascination with the Lynch movie made me read the book. The 2000 Sci-Fi Channel miniseries is a truer representation of the totality of that story, but I watched the miniseries being like, "I wish it

IV. LEGACY. Modern Impressions of *Dune* | **491**

looked like the David Lynch movie." The Lynch movie got the stillsuits right, and the Villeneuve movie carried that forward, very similar to what Bob Ringwood designed. Lynch is like, "I don't want to talk about it," and I respect that but there's so much that movie did right that you have to admire the hustle.

DAVID CROW: I've only seen the David Lynch cut two or three times, first in high school before I read the novel. I had no idea what was going on. It did not leave a strong impression other than I did not like it. As an adult, I finally got around to reading the novel, and when I rewatched the Lynch movie it made sense to me, but that didn't make it good.

ROSIE KNIGHT: It suffers from the ultimate unfair struggle: the book established these tropes, but by the time the movie came out, those tropes had been in some of the biggest movies, like *Star Wars*. It ended up feeling derivative or not as accessible, even though *Dune* was deeply archetypal to the sci-fi that came afterward.

DREW TAYLOR: Something I got out of the new one was how much everything is taken from *Dune*. Like the *John Carter* scenario where they finally get around to making the movie, yet it feels old hat because so many things were borrowed from Edgar Rice Burroughs in the previous 100 years. There's so much of that in *Dune*. It's weird they didn't change it. We'd just seen dragonfly helicopters in *Black Panther*, do something else.

SCOTT COLLURA: I don't think that much of Lynch's, actually. It was so derided back in 1984 and then gained cult classic status—this thing that happens to older movies, right? I went back to rewatch it because the new one was coming out, and I was like, "God." I can enjoy a little, then, "Oh my God, I've got to stop this and pick it up tomorrow." It's such an odd movie. You cast Max von Sydow to explain how a stillsuit works. I don't think he does much else in the movie—just gets killed.

RICK MARSHALL: I'm shocked how much I enjoyed the rewatch because we've had decades and decades of criticism directed at it, that the 1984 *Dune* was the reason we haven't had a *Dune* movie since then. "It was that bad, it was a franchise killer."

DAVID CROW: Watching the Siskel and Ebert review from the '80s, they're overly harsh calling it the worst movie of 1984. It is not the worst movie of that year. They call it ugly. They say it's impenetrable, or impossible to follow. I honestly think if you haven't read the book, that is very true, specifically the second half of the movie.

JENNA BUSCH: Science-fiction books tended to be self-serious back then. A lot of writers felt they were defending the genre as legit in a time when people thought it wasn't. I used to do a show with Stan Lee, and he told me he would downplay what he wrote at parties in the beginning because no one thought comics were "real" writing. I actually brought up *Dune* and books like that. We talked about how many people laughed at the fantasy and science element. That laughing at sci-fi ended up being how many early sci-fi films were done. In a way, I think that helped things. It lightened up the writers, the readers, and the viewers, reminding them that imagination could be fun.

ZAKI HASAN: The first two-thirds is a pretty good adaptation of book one in the first book. Then they're like, "Oh, crap, we have to finish it," and suddenly they hit fast forward on the rest of it. It hits all the bases. The voiceover stuff I'm not crazy about.

SCOTT COLLURA: I guess you'd call it "narration," but the actors thinking to themselves? You get why they go for it, but it obviously doesn't work. Then when you see the Denis version, I don't think they needed to do that. You're able to convey enough without those.

JOHN DEVORE: If *Dune* had been an enormous hit, hushed inner monologue narration would have become more popular. We'd have Marvel movies where Steve Rogers doesn't say anything, just stares and thinks, "Iron Man, Tony Stark. He's a friend."

Lynch's work since 1984 has often led fans to debate Dune's *place in his filmography.*

RICK MARSHALL: I have more awareness of David Lynch, what he does and what to expect from him. Looking back, I'm like, "Oh, this actually did a bunch of things pretty well." It really leaned into the mutated human guild navigators that excrete energies from their orifices to fold time and space. That's a bold strategy.

ZAKI HASAN: Making guild navigators look like vagina face people. . . that was a choice.

RICK MARSHALL: In the Denis Villeneuve one, navigators are not present. Lynch leaned into a lot of the weirdest parts of the story in ways that the more recent film didn't, and that's a very David Lynch thing to do.

JORDAN HOFFMAN: I had a slight awareness of David Lynch from a VHS of *Elephant Man*, and that was terrifying and strange and uncomfortable. Why my parents let me see *Elephant Man* at age seven, I have no idea. I did not put together that it was the same guy, but you can see it. With the exception of *The Straight Story*, which is a whole other universe, *Dune* is the least David Lynch–style David Lynch movie, but you can still very much see sequences, shots, moments that are just as weird as anything in *Twin Peaks*.

DAVID CROW: Is it really David Lynch's *Dune*? I'm not entirely certain. He has definitely disowned it, plus the whole Alan Smithee thing where they made an Extended Cut for television and he did not let his name be used.

MICHAEL GINGOLD: They had the Alan Smithee cut on TV and I could immediately see why he took his name off.

DREW TAYLOR: It's not a David Lynch movie I've returned to frequently. On television, I might watch it for a little while, but it doesn't have that Lynchian essence that I return to again and again. It kept me at a distance, and isn't as coherent for a *Dune* world newbie.

JORDAN HOFFMAN: The part when Brad Dourif drinks the little juice and has the poem he repeats. If you're not accustomed to Lynch's style, you might think, "Man, this is weird. What the hell's going on here?" But if you like Lynch, you're going to like that part. You almost hear Lynch telling Dourif, "No, faster with less emotion."

SCOTT COLLURA: As idiosyncratic as this is, as much of a Lynch fan as I am, as much as I love the cast—half the cast of *Twin Peaks* is in this thing!—it always feels like such a slog. There's weird stuff that's interesting and funny, intentional or not. Brad Dourif does this weird thing where he's flicking his chin or something when he's interacting with the Baron.

ZAKI HASAN: The marriage of David Lynch with this subject matter. . . I don't know what the De Laurentiis people were expecting, but it's fairly certain they weren't expecting this. What did you think you were going to get letting the *Eraserhead* guy do a big sci-fi movie? They wanted their *Star Wars*, but the subject matter is not really a *Star Wars* thing. Then you give somebody as idiosyncratic as Lynch that big a budget and say, "Go nuts." We're never going to see something like that again.

EDWARD DOUGLAS: I did eventually see Lynch's *Dune* when you could rent the videotape. It was very much a product of the '80s, a decade where there was so much overspending and so many fingers in the filmmaking process. Maybe *Dune* was the trial by fire Lynch needed to know to stay away from studio fare.

JENNA BUSCH: Years later, we take sci-fi seriously again, but not in the same way. We understand as viewers and as writers and filmmakers that a lot of it is a way of expressing things that would seem too obvious in a straightforward story. All of that—the 1984 film, the way the books and authors were treated, the movement forward into fun versions, then the serious ones—paved the way for Villeneuve's vision. Now we're looking at something serious that still allows for fun. We can appreciate what it's saying on more than one level.

ROXANA HADADI: I think of it as very much a product of its time, which is to say that it's very excessive in its world-building: The bordering-on-campy performances, the costume and production design (those CGI blue eyes), Kyle MacLachlan's magnificent hair.

ROSIE KNIGHT: I am a diehard practical effects person, so you can be in this space feeling like you're really in a world that's textured, physical, and weird. I love how just absolutely weird *Dune* is. It blows my mind how ambitious and committed it is. In comparison to the new one, the old one is so grotesque and scary and textured.

2021's Dune *is still fresh; comparing it with Lynch's has become a sport unto itself.*

MICHAEL GINGOLD: The great thing about Lynch's movie is that, as you would expect, he leaned into the bizarre. He really went for strange visuals and a non-linear approach. I think Villeneuve's version wears its reverence like a shroud. Some of Lynch's *Dune* does not make sense, but it is over the top and crazy and fun. The new one had all the fun bleached out of it. I was not engaged with the characters.

ROSIE KNIGHT: I thought Timothée Chalamet was really good and had this flitting between the reluctant hero but with echoes of what would come later. There's this tyrant, this person who ends up in a situation that they can exploit, and they do.

DAVID CROW: Villeneuve made it very accessible in a way that keeps the intelligence of Herbert's world. Paul Atreides is so easy to make into the boy hero. That is what the Lynch movie did with its ridiculous ending. While Chalamet's Paul is the handsome millennial version, our idea of youthful exuberance, he's also incredibly brooding. That's turned some people off because they expect more of a traditional Chosen One protagonist.

DREW TAYLOR: I was very taken by Denis Villeneuve's version. I found it more understandable. The emphasis on palace intrigue of the different sects trying to take over this planet and what they want was all a little bit clearer.

RICK MARSHALL: The modern one grounded a lot of the story, and that's where they both differ a lot. I love the new one that Villeneuve did. It has beautiful visuals, it's epic in scope, and really well executed. But yes, it's very grounded, and it didn't feel as crazy mystical. It was missing that "I'm just going to read to the end and hope things make sense" feeling.

JORDAN HOFFMAN: Villeneuve's version was fine, not as creative visually as Lynch's, quite frankly. The color palette in the new *Dune* is just rust and dust, and that's it. In Lynch's Emperor's palace, you have a lot cooler stuff happening with color and weirdo clothing. The costumes in Lynch's *Dune* destroy Villeneuve's version, but I do think this version has a lot of cool shit. It does feel a bit like Jason Momoa is in a totally different movie, and his movie is the one I want to see more of.

SCOTT COLLURA: *Dune: Part One* is obviously more polished, certainly a better movie. I liked the new one. I didn't love it the way some people seem to. Part of that is the inherent issue of *Dune* being such a big chunk of story to adapt, but Denis decided to cut it into two. The Lynch one feels so rushed. The Denis one seems to drag things out at times.

DREW TAYLOR: The Villeneuve one is a pretty spectacular big-budget movie of a different variety, but one that you can totally get lost in. There's an almost fetishistic quality to the different machines and races and planets, a tactile quality. I was completely immersed in this new one, whereas the original I was always trying to decode as it went along.

DAVID CROW: You can argue that Villeneuve's version is an incomplete film because it doesn't have an end, it's all first and second act and there is no third act. But the movie is so well-crafted I don't mind. It is a much better film than Lynch's and benefitted from watching the mistakes of the 1984 film which proves you cannot fit this into two hours. I don't think you could have fit it into three hours.

RICK MARSHALL: Sometimes it's the overall vibe that matters, more than the actual story structure. The 1984 one established a weird, surreal, unpredictable atmosphere, where the more recent one focused on telling a very clear story with tangible themes along the way.

Cultural touchstones of Herbert's story have made every adaptation problematic.

JOHN DEVORE: There is some problematic stuff in the books. Baron Harkonnen being this gay predator character is a homophobic trope. Lynch finds an elegant solution by making him not explicitly gay but just a guy that likes to kill twinks.

ROXANA HADADI: It is a little narrow in its interpretation of Herbert's original text. I haven't read enough about Lynch's approach to adaptation to know why he cut or dampened the book's incorporation of Muslim and MENA influences. I have to assume that the post-Iranian-hostage-crisis 1980s did not particularly welcome that kind of content.

ZAKI HASAN: The Lynch movie dispenses with a lot of the Islamic terminology, they don't say "Lisan al Gaib." It broad brushes things that have specific cultural context. They were trying to do their own hero's journey/Luke Skywalker thing. The Fremen are a bunch of white guys in the desert. In the newer film they've very deliberately cast all black and brown people as the Fremen, and that makes a huge difference. Everett McGill as Stilgar is not who I picture when I read the book, but I think he works within the world they've created in that film. Now we would expect more of a spectrum on display.

JOHN DEVORE: In terms of seeing the Fremen as space Mexicans, that's my projection. There's a part of me that likes that Lynch's Fremen are all white, versus Denis' version where it's like they're all at Burning Man.

ROXANA HADADI: Villeneuve's version of *Dune*, compared with Lynch's, is pretty lateral in terms of its incorporation of Islamic concepts and languages like Arabic and Farsi or MENA cultural elements. You could argue post–9/11 Hollywood is even more uncomfortable now than it was in the '80s with integrating these ideas into a major blockbuster film. I find it disheartening that the way this film barely acknowledges Herbert's original intentions are still erasure. I'm thinking of Hans Zimmer's score, how it clearly mimicked the ululation sound found in Arabic, but then Zimmer made up a language for the choir to sing rather than use Arabic. Or how we see a group of Fremen seemingly praying in a Muslim pose outside the Arrakeen compound, but there are no MENA actors playing Fremen.

ZAKI HASAN: The story only works as an interrogation of colonialism and white savior myths. The arc of the first several books is not singing the praises of white savior stories, it's critiquing them. Paul Atreides buys his own hype, that's his downfall. Something as simple as casting actors of color as the Fremen is a big part of acknowledging what Herbert was really doing with these stories.

JOHN DEVORE: Denis' solution—really a half-solution—is to basically say they are a multicultural group. As a boy, I felt being biracial in this country is to be acutely aware of who you are within the context of the races that your parents are. Walking around with a mother who's a different color than you, and to have people look at you and not see that you are the child of another person. Even as a young kid visiting Texas with my mother's side of the family, you got a sense that Texas is very segregated, but it has a bifurcated culture. There is a white Texas and a Mexican American Texas. Texas has occupied Mexico. That occupation is not about resources, just white manifest destiny. I did see that in Herbert's allegory, that these were people who had a place, who had a land, and other people have come in and taken that land. I used to lie to friends about my mom. "Is that your mom?" "No, no, that's my maid." There was a lot of shame I had about being different. No kid wants to be different, so the feelings that *Dune* stirred up in me made it a magic bullet movie. It stirred up so much shit.

ZAKI HASAN: There was a critique on social media about the lack of MENA actors in the new one, and I'm not at all diminishing that. Personally, as a Muslim person, it didn't bother me at all because Javier Bardem is an amazing actor, and this is not the Middle East. It's Arrakis. It'd be nice, but I feel like that's getting lost in the weeds. Granted, I'm a fan of this book for more than 20 years, so maybe I'm coming at it from, "Hey, don't say a bad thing about my thing." I reflexively blanch at the, "Oh, it's just propagating white savior myths and saying colonialism is good." How can you claim *Dune* is saying colonialism is good? It's the exact opposite.

ROXANA HADADI: Neither film does a good job, but I will say that watching the conversation about this more recent *Dune* play out with nearly universal praise—and barely any mention from the filmmakers or critics about the flattening of Herbert's deliberate integration of Muslim and MENA culture—is pretty demoralizing, given how much lip service we now pay to "diversity and inclusion."

JENNA BUSCH: I do hope that Villeneuve will take out a lot of the more sexist elements in the way Herbert portrayed his female characters in *Part Two*. Herbert built them up beautifully, then just dropped them back into "female roles" at the end of the book.

SCOTT COLLURA: I feel like they haven't quite cracked the code on adapting *Dune*.

JORDAN HOFFMAN: Not every book should be a movie. *Dune* is a better book because so much of it is interior monologue. So much of what makes *Dune* interesting is every chapter has that epigram from the sacred scrolls or whatever as blocks of text. You can't get that. I don't know that *Dune* was meant to be made into a movie. Even though this newer one makes it more understandable, the big swing of the first one is far more interesting.

A Lynch re-cut of Dune *is still a pipe dream, but some have not given up hope . . .*

ROSIE KNIGHT: I would love to see *Dune* '84 on the big screen. I watch a lot of old movies at the cinema, but that is not one I've seen yet. It'll be really interesting to see Lynch go back and create a version of the film that he's happy with. If you recut it, *Dune* could have a really interesting life in rep houses, or even as a small platform release. Universal could throw a few million at it and put the new version on Peacock. There are ways this can be profitable. I think it's ripe. We are living in unprecedented remaster times, so the fact that nobody has spoken to Lynch and been like, "How do we do this in a way that makes you happy? That expands the vision of what this film can be, and also, we can make a ton of money selling it on Blu-ray?" Seems easy.

ZAKI HASAN: As an admirer of what Lynch was attempting to do, I want to know what his unfiltered vision is. I may or may not end up liking that, but if given that opportunity. . . it doesn't rain at the end of the book. The ending of the book is much darker. Given what we know about Lynch's output, I think his preference would have been something dark. He was locked into this would-be franchise machine. I don't know that there are enough pieces available to fix what's there, but if there's the ability to see more of the movie in a form that Lynch approves of, bring it. *Dune* is not necessarily a movie in my personal canon, yet I've owned it on VHS, twice on DVD, on Blu-ray, and on 4K. That tells you something.

DAVID CROW: I'm of two minds on giving artists space to create something like the Zack Snyder cut of *Justice League*. If Lynch got that kind of treatment as an experiment or an exercise in artful filmmaking, I think that'd be very interesting. From a business or commercial point of view, when the original is bad, I don't think it's worth throwing more money, necessarily. I don't think the original Frankensteined *Justice League* by Joss Whedon is a good movie, but *Zack Snyder's Justice League* is simply a more interesting failure. That would be my prediction of a longer David Lynch-produced Extended Cut.

JORDAN HOFFMAN: I know he hates the movie, but he had a terrible time making it, so he has personal bad vibes. If you're miserable during a time in your life—bad relationship, bad working experience—and you create something during that period, you probably don't want to look back at it. Somebody on Twitter was mocking Lynch boosters by saying, "even Lynch hated that effing movie, so shut up." You know, Franz Kafka ordered all his work thrown in the fire. He hated his work too, and that's borne some fruit in the decades since. Just because a creator doesn't like their own piece, that's not a valid reason to dismiss it.

SCOOTER MCCRAE: Lynch's *Dune* is a thoughtful rumination on the cultural desire towards a messianic impulse conditioned into human existence by external forces. Yeah, there are some explosions here and there, but also a cat/rat poison antidote milking machine, so I think Lynch got a good opportunity to explore his other interests in the midst of all the science-fictional trappings. It's a legitimate masterpiece, not without flaws, and the kind of visually daring genre movie rarely conceived of anymore by studios more concerned with constricting minds of paying viewers instead of trying to expand them.

JOHN DEVORE: It's a movie filled with whispers and hands opening and all of these weird juxtapositions. It's a very feverish movie that, clearly, I don't talk enough about in therapy.

Mysteries of Love: *Dune* Symbols

"I think about symbols, mood, repetition of shapes, connecting threads—all intuitive stuff. That's what makes it magic for me."

—*David Lynch, Prevue magazine February 1984*

While this book is not centered on analysis, Lynch's use of symbols—both abstract and tangible—plays such a pronounced part in his *Dune* that it would be foolish not to at least touch on a few of these loaded motifs:

Pug

The pug dogs are likely meant as a symbol of power. You can see a horde of pugs being led on leashes at the beginning that are property of the Emperor. The Atreides have a pug that is seen next to the Duke in his study as he seals his declaration to continue his conflict with House Harkonnen. You see the pug again in Paul's lap as they make their space journey to claim Arrakis. A pug shuffles through a crumbling hallway when the Harkonnens attack. The last time you see an Atreides with the pug is in Gurney's arms as he is going into the army's final battle after that attack, shouting "Long live Duke Leto!" That is the last point where the Atreides have power. You don't see the animal again until the end, when Harah's children are holding a pug in the Great Hall, symbolizing that the Fremen now hold the power. It's certainly more than a cute and quirky touch added to the film for no reason.

Writer John DeVore (James Beard Award-winner, creator of Medium's Humungus blog, and cohost of *The Dune Conversations* podcast with Jordan Hoffman) agreed with my theory of the pug's symbology, while also taking it one step further during our conversation for this book. He told me:

> I love that it's become a meme. I believe Herbert mentions in the book that Judaism survives 20,000 years in the future, but Lynch is saying also the pug—and only the pug—survives. I desperately love that the shot of Patrick Stewart holding a pug while shooting a laser rifle has become iconic. That's something that the new *Dune* film

misses. House Atreides, House Harkonnen, and the Emperor all have this decaying 19th-century tsar royal vibe, and those royals loved lap dogs. Those kinds of dogs that had no utility were an immense sign that you had money. You had food to give a dog that does nothing but just sit on your lap. The pug is also an example of intense genetic breeding. A pug is not natural; it is the result of humans manipulating bloodlines over hundreds of years. So, in a way, the pugs are the Kwisatz Haderach of domesticated canines, the result of Bene Gesserit–style breeding. Why wouldn't it be a symbol of power?

Hands

Hand imagery is rampant in *Dune*. It begins with Duncan Idaho placing his hand on Paul's chest and imploring, "May the hand of God be with you," with Paul replying, "May the hand of God be with us all, Duncan." Hands become even more critical during the test with "the box," where his hand is psychically taken apart and put back together again, a tenet of spiritual progress. When Stilgar introduces Paul to his guard, the Fedaykin, he holds up a hand smeared with red. The image of a hand is imprinted on Arrakis' first moon of Krelln, which Paul looks to and sees destroyed in his dreams. During Paul's second address at the Hall of Rites, after he has taken the Water of Life, he prominently holds up his hand with purpose. One of Paul's most prominent visions is of an opening hand, which is—in the context of filming in post-production—David Lynch's own hand.

Voice

The Bene Gesserit gift of the Voice ultimately saves Paul and Jessica from death at the hands of the Harkonnens. Forceful command of other people is exemplified by use of the Voice, but is also noted in the shift of Paul's actual tone of voice to something more mature after he drinks the Water of Life.

The weirding way, which he passes on to the other Fremen, involves a module that emits, essentially, a sonic bullet using the Voice. By the end of the film, Paul's confidence and power have grown so great he no longer needs the module, able to "kill with a word." Paul's final line in the film, "One cannot go against the word of God," equates his voice in messianic terms. The Fremen term for messiah, "Lisan al-Gaib," literally translates as "the voice from the outer world."

The power of voice also extends to mouths, specifically with the Duke's deadly exhalation after the memory of Yueh's lips exclaiming, "The tooth! The tooth!" The Mentats' mouths are stained, a side effect of the amphetamine-esque sapho juice while also emphasizing the information that comes out of them. Even the worms, with their endless vortex of inner teeth, have a roar so crippling it forces Jessica to yell, "It's deafening!" Members of the guild speak in a discordant, alien drone that has to be muffled and translated through a special microphone.

It's fitting that Lynch would be fascinated with elements of voice, as his and Alan Splet's sound work on their early films was an integral part of the filmmaking process. Lynch has said that Splet worked out the soundscapes of *Eraserhead* for nine hours a day for 63 days.

Starfields

Even though Lynch has stated he is not a science-fiction fan per se, the image of a starfield has been present in many of his films, including *Eraserhead*, *The Elephant Man*, and *The Straight Story*.

Water

The scarcity of water is of utmost strategic importance in the film. Paul has visions of water droplets, emphasizing the importance of H_2O over spice. There are visual allusions to sand waves that move like water waves. The sand waves relate to storms and the desert power that both Leto and Paul see as their greatest ally. Finally, the crashing waves of Caladan are brought forth to Arrakis as Paul unleashes a torrent of water on a planet where not a drop has ever fallen.

Dreams

This is an especially important motif for both the book itself and in Lynch's overall filmography. Notably, Denis Villeneuve's version opens over a black screen—before we even get a studio logo—with the intonation (possibly by Leto II far into the future), "Dreams are messages from the deep."

"Paul's future-vision is a form of dream," Lynch told *The Kansas City Star* in December 1984. "There were dreams in *The Elephant Man*, and *Eraserhead* was one long dream, so you can see that I love to treat dreams cinematically."

TM

"Dune is a story of a quest for enlightenment,
and that's part of why I did it."

—*David Lynch, Room to Dream*

"It is a story of political, economic, and social commentary . . .
carried along with the drama of the Messiah. It originated as a study of
the Messianic impulse in humankind—why do we follow the leader?"

—*Frank Herbert, Starlog #66*

In researching *Dune*, I've realized Lynch either found or added many elements that relate to Transcendental Meditation (TM) in the story. Concepts like the Litany against Fear and awakening a reservoir of power inside you are part of Herbert's book, but things like weirding modules were invented by Lynch. They're sources of power activated by a single word, very similar to the precepts of mantra meditation.

When I broached this idea to MacLachlan, he replied:

> Oh, that's cool. That's the first I've ever heard of that. I liked hearing that. Traveling through space, that whole sequence of circular things coming at you, is one of the most brilliant interpretations of what that might look like. "Traveling without moving." It was glossed over in the recent movie, and I missed the feeling of "What does that mean?" It's definitely a spiritual, transcendent process. Very good point. I always thought, "Oh, the weirding way and using the sound . . . it's kind of a cool idea, but it's not Frank's idea."

Being the *Dune* scholar that he is, MacLachlan had his own vision for how the weirding way should have been depicted instead of the modules:

> The weirding way, that manner of fighting . . . It might have been too acrobatic or balletic, but remember *Crouching Tiger, Hidden Dragon?* Remember how they use the cabling on that? It was a lot of martial arts in that movement. It got very balletic, but if you toned that down, that kind of body control . . . When I saw that, it felt like what he was describing as the weirding way, this kind of circular movement where you could do things that were out of the ordinary. Of course, that was just in my head!

"Yeah, I think you're probably right," Lynch's DP Frederick Elmes said about my theory. "There's something very pure about it, but there is a line for that character in his growing up and evolving. That's very strong in the way it's written in the script, but also in the way David directed Kyle to act. It's certainly an evolution. His personal evolution is part of it, and I know that's very important to David."

When I spoke to Alia actress Alicia Witt, she agreed some subtext might be found:

> OH! I never thought of that. I have practiced TM. I know how, and use it still. I also use other methods, but I do make it a practice to meditate every single day and that has changed my life. Based on what you just said, the weirding modules were unlocked with a word, and that's literally how TM works. You access that world of peace and power through a mantra that is given to you. I think you're onto something. I don't believe I have seen *Dune* since I got into TM about eight years ago. I'm very curious to watch it again with this in mind. I did ayahuasca four or five years ago and came out of that experience thinking that was also very similar to some worlds that David has described. I reached out to him and asked if he had ever done it, and I don't think I heard back, so he probably hasn't done ayahuasca. All of those practices and the sacred plant medicine connect us to that in-between place. I would say an ayahuasca journey is also very reminiscent of some of David's visions.

Molly Wryn was startled at this theory. "You're right," she told me. "What you observed, it's . . . I don't know why I didn't see it. A light bulb went on over my head."

Wryn became involved in TM during the filming of *Dune*, at Lynch's suggestion:

> He got me into it. It was in the break between my two stints in Mexico that I took the class. I got to come back and tell him about it. I'd never been in anything like that before. It felt meaningful, it helped me. I should go back to it . . . not that TM is the only way to meditate. There are many ways to meditate. The process of doing it is being able to go deeper. I wouldn't pay $1,000 for it. It didn't cost that years ago. I'm supposed to go back and re-up or something, but I know the deal and use it. He got a lot of people into it.

Steve Lukather responded:

> I've never heard that TM theory before. I find it interesting, and it would make me look at it completely differently. I didn't get into it

until '92, George Harrison brought me down to the TM center and introduced me. I got a mantra. I use it all the time. It's very calming. Lynch is way into it. He's a very calm guy. I never saw him completely lose his shit. I see him all the time with Ringo. I've been in Ringo's band for 12 years, and they're tight because of their TM thing, which I do myself.

In addition, I had the chance to speak to actor Ben Foster (*Hell or High Water, 3:10 to Yuma*), a longtime practitioner who studied at the Maharishi University of Management in Iowa known for its "consciousness-based education" system.

"Practicing TM allows me to get quiet inside," he told me. "It allows me to hear my own voice. David's work certainly deals with the dream state, and I suppose when work is at its best, I'm not outsmarting it. It's almost that I can hear it, I can feel it. I'm not thinking about it, and perhaps that's the drug we're chasing is to get lost in the moment. I think meditation is a great way to exercise that place inside."

By the filming of *Dune*, Lynch had been practicing TM for 11 years, and his storyboarded ending for the movie involved an abstract effects sequence in which Paul transcends to another plane of consciousness and power, symbolized by a drop of water transforming into a golden lotus. The lotus pose is commonly used in the practice of meditation.

Lynch explained in 1985 [*Enterprise Incidents*]:

> When you meditate, you go to a beautiful place inside yourself, but it's hard to say what it does for you because it's a slow process. Your outlook on the world gets better, and slowly but surely, it does make things get better. You're able to capture ideas at a deeper level. You can really sit and think and get down there inside yourself where the big ideas are swimming and capture more space for ideas. Plus, there's a real interesting, fantastic feeling that comes along too . . . a physical feeling of happiness and floating. What I think a lot of people are looking for with drugs and other things is that you get a powerful experience right away. Meditation is a slow process.

Frank Herbert sought to tell the story of how a decent boy transforms— against his own best intentions—into a dangerous, problematic leader of men. Lynch's film turns Paul into a benevolent god who makes it rain and brings "peace" (according to Irulan's tacked-on voiceover), changing the nature of the story. It was so anathema to Herbert's vision that the producer herself forgot that's how the film ends.

"We never say that it was going to rain on Arrakis, do we?" Raffaella De Laurentiis asked me. "See, there you go. I don't even remember this. Interesting, isn't it? It must have been something that I don't remember, frankly. That's why I want to see the movie again. I don't remember it raining at the end of the movie. I must have canceled it from my brain."

"The rain ending was done at the last moment to give the movie a 'happy' ending," Ron Miller clarified. "The decision was made when someone somewhere—probably Dino—decided that there would be no sequels, so the film needed a definite finale."

This resolution of Paul's story can be seen as less a violation of the book and more a reflection of two fundamentally different men: Herbert was a journalist who worked in politics and had a strong distrust of charismatic leaders, whereas Lynch is an artist who practices Transcendental Meditation and is devoted to a charismatic leader, Maharishi Mahesh Yogi.

"If you were to ask me what *Dune* is about, I'd say it is, at base, terribly simple," explained Lynch to *The Guardian* in 1984. "It's about a messiah who was born and trained to free his people. It is a film about control and power, about private thoughts and public action. You might call that political but I'm not that kind of filmmaker, so it's not."

There are many areas of overlap between the book and the 1984 movie, but to understand and accept this as "A David Lynch Film," it's critical to understand that Lynch brought his own philosophy to the piece.

MacLachlan told me:

> I know that was one of Frank's major themes of the book: Power corrupts, absolute power corrupts absolutely. In another way, there are things about *Dune* that David just wasn't interested in exploring or talking about or going into. He had other things that were driving him, and he followed those impulses. He made *Dune* his own. It really is an amalgam of both Frank and David, and David is a great artist. Of course, you're going to let him run with that, and who knows what you'll get? But it's certainly going to be something amazing, as we know, because that *Dune* is here and it still has resonance and it still is really interesting to watch for many, many reasons.

Interview: David Lynch

I n the years after the failure of *Dune* (and as he came into his own artistic brand of surreal neo-noir), David Lynch became less and less open to discussing it. On those rare instances when it is brought up, he is vocal about his displeasure with how the film turned out and the experience of making it. Knowing this, it was an honor to get a bit of time with the master filmmaker to ask some nagging questions, as well as an opportunity for him to clear the air about his feelings toward *Dune*. It was incredibly gracious of Lynch to engage on a subject he rarely speaks of.

You've said many times that Dune *was a great sadness since it was a failure and you didn't have final cut and it felt like you sold out, so you essentially died twice.*

DAVID LYNCH: Well, here's the deal. I didn't really want to . . . I don't like to talk about *Dune* for those reasons, that it's a failure, and I didn't want to do this interview because it's talking about *Dune*, to rehash the whole thing. But what I wanted to say today is a little bit set the record straight. For me personally, *Dune* is a failure. The reason is—I've said it a thousand times—I didn't have final cut. I didn't have creative freedom. But I want to say today that I was so fortunate to work with the greatest bunch of actors and the greatest crew! So, none of this failure is their fault. They were fantastic! Every one of 'em. And you know, I feel so bad that they might have been hurt by this failure, because they did such great jobs, all of 'em. They all did such great work. So, I want people to know that, how much I appreciated them and how much I appreciated working with them, and it even goes to Dino De Laurentiis. I love Dino, and I got along with him great. It's just that obviously, he and I didn't think alike and he had the final say. So that's my fault for signing that contract, but I did sign it and so I have to live with it. And Raffaella De Laurentiis, I love her so much. I love working with her, and she is a great, great, great producer, great person. I want people to know that. She's fantastic. I have great memories of the cast and crew, and I had a great, great time living in Mexico City and being in that vibe. The most romantic, incredible, magical mystery city in the world, and I just loved it. So that's what I wanted to tell you today.

That brings up something I wanted to ask you, which is a lot of times when a director has a big failure, they tend to separate themselves from the actors and producers and others afterward, to distance themselves from everyone involved. But in the work you made later, you doubled down on Kyle, on Dino, and so many of the other cast and crew who worked on this film. Is it an important thing for you in the course of your career to not throw the baby out with the bathwater, so to speak?

DAVID LYNCH: Sure! You know, it's like, common sense, really. I always say casting is where you try to get the right person for the part. You may love somebody, love working with them, but they're not right for the part. But when they are right for the part, and you've worked with them before and you have a relationship, then that's beautiful and you work with them again and again. But sometimes it doesn't work out because they just don't jive with their part. Same way with the crew in a way. I work with lots and lots of great people, and I like working with the same crew. You know what it's going to be, and you're friends. When it works that way, it's fine.

Rob Reiner once told me that a movie production is like a fish: It stinks from the head down. So, if the director is happy, the cast is happy, and vice versa. Everyone I spoke to from Dune *said you were always pleasant, and never hinted that making this film was a nightmare for you, as you admitted later. By 1983 to '84, you'd been doing TM for about a decade, so how did your practice help you navigate this three-year trial by fire on* Dune?

DAVID LYNCH: Toward the end of *Dune*, I probably would have . . . eh, I might have committed suicide if it weren't for Transcendental Meditation. It is so powerful because TM allows a human being to transcend experience in the treasury within, and that level of life which is eternal and always been there. The big treasury, the unified field, the kingdom of heaven, the Dao, home of total knowledge. It's one field with all these different names, always been there. It's the self of all of us, and there's a line, "Know thyself." If you can transcend every day and experience that, you start to infuse that and grow in that. Expand whatever consciousness you had, and say goodbye to negativity. It'll get you through some very, very tough times, and you'll enjoy the good times even more. It's money in the bank for the human being. Don't ever forget it! If you hear this message, go out and get Transcendental Meditation right away. You'll never be sorry.

Were there aspects of Frank Herbert's book—the idea of traveling without moving, defying fear, or awakening a reservoir of power within—that you were drawn to from your own spirituality?

DAVID LYNCH: I think so. And I don't even know, some of the things . . . You said "traveling without moving"? I'm not sure if that was in the book or if I made that up. It would be interesting if you found out because I made up a bunch of stuff, but it was always inspired by Frank Herbert's book. Things like, "my own name is a killing word." Those kinds of things. I don't know if that was in the book, or the weirding modules dealing with sound? Yeah, I'm not sure if that was in the book. But anyway, Frank Herbert's book was filled with many different kinds of things. Some contradicted themselves to each other, but there was a spiritual thing that I related to in it, certain things. But I did not make the movie I should have made and that's why it's just not so much fun to talk about it.

Funny you mention the weirding modules. That's arguably your biggest original contribution to the Dune *universe, and they are essentially sources of power activated by a single word. That sounds a lot like mantra meditation, no?*

DAVID LYNCH: Yeah, yeah! Exactly.

You originally wanted to do Dune *in black and white, but it wound up being your first color movie.*

DAVID LYNCH: I don't think I ever wanted to make *Dune* in black and white. I don't think that's true. Some films are meant to be made in color. Like the film *Blue Velvet!* It's got the word "blue" in there. Very strange to make it in black and white. *Black Velvet*, maybe. But *Dune* was a color film, there's no question about it. So anyway, I wanted to tell you those things today, that I love the cast and the crew. They all did great, great, great work, and I just loved working with all of them. So that's the message today.

Well, I just want to say thank you for making this movie. I know it's a great sadness in your life, but you should know it's brought a lot of people a lot of joy in the years since it came out, including myself.

DAVID LYNCH: Fantastic, man. I appreciate your talking to me and have a great day. Take it easy, pal. Cheers!

FINAL THOUGHTS

After 18 years as a professional movie journalist, this was my first book. There were many challenges putting it together, yet there was always a certain level of assurance knowing fans of Lynch's *Dune* would be interested in the same obsessive details and little cul-de-sacs I was . . . mainly because I was also a fan of the film.

Although there had been fantastic books written about the making of *Dune* by both Ed Naha and Kenneth George Godwin, both of those are very much rooted in '83 and '84. Hence, I wanted to create a book that recounted the making (and unmaking) of the film as well as the fallout of its failure and its continuing impact. Whether or not it made a dime, Lynch's film left reverberations in many who have seen it, including filmmakers, critics, and fans of unusual cinema everywhere.

Being able to speak to Lynch personally made the entire experience of this book worthwhile. Not only did he live up to his reputation as a genial, infectiously polite man with a charm of his own, but also helped solidify my "thesis" that *Dune* is, essentially, his big Transcendental Meditation movie. While I don't seek to endorse the practice of TM or the organization behind it, it remains a huge facet of the director's life for five decades. Ignoring TM subtext in *Dune* would be tantamount to acting like Alfred Hitchcock didn't have a thing for blondes, Steven Spielberg doesn't have daddy issues, or Christopher Nolan isn't obsessed with dead wives.

The fact that Lynch—infamous for not discussing the symbolism behind his own work—confirmed that some of his additions to Herbert's universe were influenced by his own spiritual practice is an important revelation. Hopefully, this will help audiences see *Dune* in a new light. Whatever you think of it, you cannot deny the film is an expression of a singular individual making a huge commercial enterprise personal. Those who consider *Dune* the least Lynchian entry in the man's filmography should now be able to accept that it is exactly what it advertises in the opening credits: "A David Lynch Film" (except for the Alan Smithee version).

In a way, Lynch's career mirrored the journey of Paul Atreides, in the sense that he experienced this personal tragedy with *Dune*, but from the rubble, he self-actualized who he was as a filmmaker, came back and conquered with *Blue Velvet*, then stayed mostly in that smaller-scale neo-noir lane for the rest of his directing life. The experience jarred something deep inside Lynch, and the sleeper awakened.

As I wind down this two-year journey, there's a feeling that even though this book rolled past the 500-page mark (original target length was 150 pages, ha!), I'm leaving a lot on the table. So many mysteries remain about this movie, many of which I uncovered in my last days of writing. Just as I hope Lynch will someday create a definitive edit of *Dune*, I also hope to revise this book with more findings and new interviews. I sincerely hope that nobody involved was hurt by anything stated by me, or any of the interviewees. My biggest wish is that David Lynch may chat with me again someday to clear up some dangling threads. The man does love a mystery, though, so perhaps it is best some *Dune* tales remain untold.

Toward the end of writing this book, I thought back on the question Virginia Madsen asked me: "What is it about this movie that sticks with you? You're a young man, why are you so attached to this movie?"

It honestly didn't occur to me until close to the end why *Dune* and its backstory have such a hold on my psyche. Like many other movie journalists, my original ambition was to make movies. My sci-fi student film *Eskimo Hill* won several festival awards in 2003–04 and was shown on PBS, hosted by rocker Joan Jett! Myself and the friends I made that movie with all rallied together to create an even more ambitious follow-up short titled "Blue Lollipop," with years spent creating detailed production designs, sets, 150 CGI shots, and even a desert monster not dissimilar to *Dune*'s sandworm. By the time it was done, four years had elapsed and the technology used in making it was already dated as 2K and 4K cameras and photoreal CG became the norm. It was devastating to not see it met with the same enthusiasm as my student film, even seeing its colorful, irreverent aesthetic in hits like *Guardians of the Galaxy*. The hope of making it into a feature gradually faded.

So yes, I too know what it's like to struggle for four years to make an elaborate sci-fi film only to have it die on the vine. It is a great sadness for me, though I still hope to keep trying to one day make a feature. Seeing how David Lynch pulled himself up from the rubble, learned from his mistakes, and ultimately moved forward with gusto should be inspiring to anyone with a creative bone in their body. Everyone at one point in their life has a *Dune*, a crucible they have to walk through to get someplace better. If you're one of those people reading this book, I encourage you, with all my heart . . . go out there and make it rain.

ACKNOWLEDGMENTS

First and foremost, I want to thank my wife Nicole Evry for allowing me to indulge myself for two years on a project that had no guaranteed payoff. Thank you for believing in me.

A huge thank you to all the supremely talented cast and crew who spoke to me about their time working on *Dune*. Those interviews not only form the spine of this book, but will stand as a document for future generations of film fans who want to know how this movie was made. Also, much gratitude to all my friends in the film community who took the time to talk to me about their personal memories and impressions of *Dune*. If you read any of their insightful comments and wondered why they weren't writing this book instead of me, I don't blame you.

Extending a loud shout-out to all those who went above and beyond over the long-haul jigsaw puzzle of putting this book together, including Sabrina S. Sutherland, Michael T. Barile, Matthew Feitshans, Seth Rosen, Clint Morris, Heather Buckley, Nick Holmes, Natasha Lance Rogoff, James Grixoni, Bryan Cairns, Nikki Calderon, Wilson Morales, James Faccinto, Clint Weiler, Genevieve Maxwell, Louise Hilton, Steve Karas, Bryan Reesman, Cass McCune, Emma Liegler, Justin Cook, Susan Karlin, Katrina Weidknecht, Patrick Read Johnson, Gaby Casaro, Ted Geoghegan, Jenn Wexler, Larry Fessenden, and an extra big, big thank you to Craig Campobasso.

Enormous appreciation to my old Videology movie trivia buddy Joel Arnold for being a trustworthy Los Angeles connection, uncovering the Ark of the Covenant of *Dune* casting secrets.

Next, a special thanks to publisher Matthew Chojnacki, editor extraordinaire David Yost, cover artist Chris Thornley and everyone at 1984 Publishing for getting behind this book and allowing me extra time to complete it, especially after my second child was born. Another big thank you to my friend Michael Gingold for putting in the good word and having long discussions about *Dune* with me for years.

Thank you to my father, Ron Evry, for being a fan of the *Dune* novels and urging me to read the first one as a kid.

Finally, an acknowledgment of all those who worked on *Dune* that are no longer with us, particularly makeup artist Christopher Tucker who—

underlying how important it was for me to interview as many of those involved as possible—passed away before we had a chance to talk for this book.

"Hello Max. Yes, that should be OK—Bit busy at the moment and have rather a lot on my plate. Maybe in a week or so? Sounds interesting. Phone would probably be best. If you are in contact with Raffaella please send her my regards." —Christopher Tucker, email from November 2022. Died December 14, 2022 (age 81).

Other members of the cast and crew who have passed on include Silvana Mangano, Kenneth McMillan, Dean Stockwell, Freddie Jones, Paul Smith, José Ferrer, Max von Sydow, Richard Jordan, Jack Nance, Leonardo Cimino, Federico De Laurentiis, Dino De Laurentiis, Martha De Laurentiis, Freddie Francis, Anthony Masters, Antony Gibbs, James Devis, Ned Tanen, and, of course, Frank Herbert.

Oh, and thank you, David Lynch. How's the weather today? Let's grab coffee sometime.

IMAGE CREDITS

Photo plate 28 (*top*) – Frank Turner
Photo plate 28 (*bottom*) – Max Evry

Photo plate 29 and **30** – Craig Campobasso

Photo plate 31 (*top*) – Max Evry
Photo plate 31 (*bottom*) – Jim Turner/Sean Crespo

Photo plate 32 (*top*) – Max Evry
Photo plate 32 (*middle*) – Andre Du Bouchet
Photo plate 32 (*bottom*) – Twin Cities Sweding

Additional photos are courtesy of the following individuals, from their private collections. Pages: **115** (Penelope Shaw Sylvester), **116** (Craig Campobasso), **118** (Ron Miller w/a cartoon by Mentor Huebner), **123** (Ron Miller), **195** (Barry Nolan), **261** and **264** (Mark Bennett), **284** (Michael Gingold), and **379** (Kyle MacLachlan).

ABOUT THE AUTHOR

Max Evry has been a film journalist since 2005, serving at various times as a writer, interviewer, graphic designer, podcaster, video creator, features editor and managing editor. Past media outlets have included *MTV*, */Film*, *IGN*, and *Fangoria*. For home video companies Arrow and Kino Lorber he has provided audio commentaries for classic and contemporary films including *Flatliners*, *Blackhat*, and best picture Oscar winner *Marty*.

Currently he resides in Brooklyn, New York with his wife, two daughters, and a pile of truly marvelous unsold screenplays. This is his first book.

Author photo: **Brent Eysler**